THE ROUTLEDGE COMPANION
TO EUROPEAN HISTORY SINCE 1763

The Routledge Companion to European History since 1763 is a compact and highly accessible work of reference. It covers a broad sweep of events since 1763, from the last days of the *ancien régime* to the ending of the Cold War, from the reshaping of Eastern Europe to the radical expansion of the European Union in 2004.

Within the broad coverage of this outstanding volume, particular attention is given to subjects such as:

- the era of the Enlightened Despots
- the Revolutionary and Napoleonic era in France, and the revolutions of 1848
- nationalism and imperialism, and the retreat from Empire
- the First World War, the rise of the European dictators, the coming of the Second World War, the Holocaust, and the post-war development of Europe
- the Cold War, the Soviet Union and its break-up
- the protest and upheavals of the 1960s, as well as social issues such as the rise of the welfare state, and the changing place of women in society throughout the period

With a fully comprehensive glossary, a biographical section, a thorough bibliography and informative maps, this volume is the indispensable companion for all those who study modern European history.

Chris Cook is former Head of the Modern Archives Unit at the London School of Economics, and co-author (with John Stevenson) of *Britain in the Depression*. He is author of the forthcoming *British Political Archives since the Second World War*. **John Stevenson** is Reader in Modern History at Worcester College, Oxford. He is the editor of *English Historical Documents, 1914–1957*.

Routledge Companions to History
Series Advisors: Chris Cook and John Stevenson

Routledge Companions to History offer perfect reference guides to key historical events and eras, providing everything that the student or general reader needs to know. These comprehensive guides include essential apparatus for navigating through specific topics in a clear and straightforward manner – including introductory articles, biographies and chronologies – to provide accessible and indispensable surveys crammed with vital information valuable for beginner and expert alike.

The Routledge Companion to Britain in the Nineteenth Century, 1815–1914
Chris Cook

The Routledge Companion to World History since 1914
Chris Cook and John Stevenson

The Routledge Companion to European History since 1763
Chris Cook and John Stevenson

The Routledge Companion to the Crusades
Peter Lock

The Routledge Companion to Decolonization
Dietmar Rothermund

The Routledge Companion to Medieval Warfare
Jim Bradbury

The Routledge Companion to Fascism and the Far Right
Peter Davies and Derek Lynch

THE ROUTLEDGE COMPANION TO EUROPEAN HISTORY SINCE 1763

Chris Cook and John Stevenson

LONDON AND NEW YORK

First published 2005
by Routledge
2 Park Square, Milton Park, Abingdon, Oxon OX14 4RN

Simultaneously published in the USA and Canada
by Routledge
270 Madison Ave, New York, NY 10016

Previously published 1987 by Addison Wesley Longman

Second edition 1992

Third edition 1998

Routledge is an imprint of the Taylor & Francis Group

© 2005 Chris Cook and John Stevenson

Typeset in Times by Keyword Publishing Services Ltd
Printed and bound in Great Britain by St Edmundsbury Press,
Bury St Edmunds, Suffolk.

British Library Cataloguing in Publication Data
A catalogue record for this book is available from the British Library

Library of Congress Cataloging in Publication Data
has been applied for

ISBN 0-415-34582-0 (hbk)
ISBN 0-415-34583-9 (pbk)

CONTENTS

LIST OF MAPS

PREFACE AND ACKNOWLEDGEMENTS

This new Routledge Companion (the successor to the former *Longman Handbook of Modern European History*) attempts to provide a convenient reference work for both teachers and students of modern European history from 1763 until the present day. It is a highly condensed work, bringing together chronological, statistical and tabular information which is not to be found elsewhere within a single volume. The Companion covers not only political and diplomatic events, but also the broader fields of social and economic history. It includes biographies of important individuals, a useful glossary of commonly used historical terms and a wide-ranging topic bibliography. No book of this type can be entirely comprehensive, nor is it intended as a substitute for textbooks and more specialist reading, but we have attempted to include those key facts and figures which we believe are most useful for understanding courses in later modern European history. The coverage of the volume is European-wide in its broadest sense, including events in the former Soviet Union, the Balkans, Scandinavia and the Baltic where they are of importance. The Companion also covers very recent events, from developments in post-Communist Europe to the historic expansion of the European Union in May 2004. As courses in European history continue to change, and as new research puts events in European history in a different perspective, both authors would welcome suggestions for additional material to be included in future editions of this Routledge Companion.

Chris Cook, London School of Economics
John Stevenson, Worcester College, Oxford
January 2005

I
PRINCIPAL RULERS AND MINISTERS

ALBANIA

Albania achieved independence from Ottoman rule in 1912, but Italian forces occupied the country from 1914 to 1920. Albania became a republic in 1925 and a monarchy in 1928. The ruler from 1928 to 1939 was King Zog I (Ahmed Zogu). During the Second World War Albania was under Italian and German rule. A republic was proclaimed on 12 January 1946. The effective ruler until 1985 was Enver Hoxha.

Presidents

O. Nishani	1946–53
H. Lleshi	1953–82
R. Alia	1982–92

Following the collapse of communism, Sali Berisha became president from 1992 to 1997. He was succeeded by R. Mejdani in July 1997. Alfred Moisiu became president in July 2002.

AUSTRIA

Maria Theresa	1740–65 (sole ruler)
Maria Theresa and Joseph II	1765–80 (co-rulers)
Joseph II*	1780–90 (sole ruler)
Leopold II	1790–92
Francis II	1792–1804 (when he became Francis I, Emperor of Austria)

*Joseph II was also Holy Roman Emperor (*see* Holy Roman Empire p. 18).

On 11 August 1804, the Habsburg rulers took the title Emperor of Austria. Francis II renounced the title of Holy Roman Emperor (*see* Holy Roman Empire, p. 18) on 6 August 1806.

Emperors of Austria

Francis I	1804–35
Ferdinand I	1835–48
Francis Joseph	1848–1916 (after 1867 Emperor of Austria–Hungary)
Charles	1916–18 (abdicated)

3

Principal ministers, 1804–1918

The following individuals (extracted from a long list) wielded effective power in the last days of the Empire:

Prince C. Metternich	1809–48
F. von Kalowrat	1848
Prince F. von Schwarzenberg	1848–52
A. Bach	1852–59
A. von Schmerling	1861–65
Count F. Beust	1867–70
Count E. von Taaffe	1870–71
Prince C. von Auersperg	1871–78
Count Taaffe	1879–93
Field Marshal A. Windischgrätz	1893–95
Count C. Badeni	1895–97
M.W. von Beck	1906–08
Count R. von Biernerth	1908–11
Count C. von Sturgkh	1912–16

Presidents (after the proclamation of the Republic on 12 November 1918):

Presidents

Dr X. Seits	1918–20 (stood in for head of state)
Dr M. Hainisch	1920–28
Dr W. Miklas	1928–38

From 1938 to 1945, Austria was part of the German Reich.

Prime ministers/Chancellors (prior to the Anschluss)

E. Dollfuss	1932–34
K. Schuschnigg	1934–38
A. Seyss-Inquart	1938–45

Presidents after 1945

K. Renner	1945–50
T. Körner	1951–57
A. Schárf	1957–65
F. Jonas	1965–74
B. Kreisky	1974 (Apr.–July)
R. Kirchschláger	1974–86
K. Waldheim	1986–92
T. Klestil	1992–2004
H. Fischer	2004–

BAVARIA

Electors

Maximilian III	1745–77
Charles Theodore I	1777–99
Maximilian IV	1799–1825
(King Maximilian 1 after 1806)	

Kings

Maximilian I	1806–25
Ludwig I	1825–48
Maximilian II	1848–64
Ludwig II	1864–86 (became insane)
Otto I	1886–1913 (insane; regents in charge)
Ludwig III	1913–18

In 1918 a republic was proclaimed.

BELARUS

Belarus adopted a declaration of independence from the Soviet Union on 25 August 1991. It adopted the name Republic of Belarus in September. A new constitution was only adopted in 1994.

Presidents

S. Shuskevich	1991–94
M. Hryb	1994 (Jan.–July)
A. Lukashenka	1994–*

*Re-elected 2001.

BELGIUM

Independence from Holland was proclaimed on 18 November 1830.

Kings

Leopold I	1831–65
Leopold II	1865–1909
Albert I	1909–34
Leopold III	1934–51*
Prince Charles (Regent)	1944–50

Leopold III	1950 (20 July–10 Aug.)
Baudouin, Prince Royal	(after 11 Aug. 1950)
Baudouin I	1951–93
Albert II	1993–

*Leopold III was a prisoner of war, May 1940–45. There was a Regency (1944–50) after which Leopold briefly resumed his duties (1950), Baudouin then took over, and Leopold formally abdicated in July 1951.

BOSNIA–HERZEGOVINA

Formerly part of the Ottoman Empire, it became a protectorate of the Austro–Hungarian Empire in 1878 (and was annexed to Austria–Hungary in 1908). Became a part of newly-formed Yugoslavia after the First World War. Following the disintegration of Yugoslavia, and after a referendum within Bosnia–Herzegovina, a declaration of independence was promulgated in March 1992.

Presidents

A. Izetbegovič	1990–98
Z. Radisič	1998–99
A. Jelavič	1999–

BULGARIA

Bulgaria remained under Turkish rule until 1878. It gained full independence (as the Kingdom of Bulgaria) in 1908. An ally of Germany, it was occupied by the Soviet Union in 1944 and a Socialist People's Republic was founded in 1946. A new constitution was adopted in 1991.

Kings

Ferdinand I	1908–18
Boris III	1918–43
Simeon II	1943–46

On 8 September 1946 a plebiscite ended the monarchy and established a republic, but there was no head of state until the new constitution came into force in December 1947. During communist rule after 1946 the head of state was the Chairman of the Praesidium. The most important figure was T. Zhivkov who was in power from 1971 to 1989.

Heads of state (since fall of communism)

Z. Zhelev	1990–97
P. Stoyanov	1997–2002
G. Parvanov	2002–

CROATIA

Prior to 1918, Croatia was part of the Austro–Hungarian Empire. It subsequently formed part of Yugoslavia. An independent Fascist puppet state existed in the Second World War. Following a declaration of disassociation from Yugoslavia in June 1991, a formal declaration of independence was promulgated on 8 October 1991.

President

| F. Tudjman* | 1990–99 |
| S. Mesic | 2000– |

*Elected by the *Sabor,* May 1990; re-elected by popular vote, August 1992. Died in office, 1999.

CZECHOSLOVAKIA

Founded as an independent state on 14 November 1918. The state was dissolved and the Czech Republic and Slovakia became independent states on 1 January 1993.

Presidents

T. Masaryk	1918–35
E. Beneš*	1935–38
E. Hácha	1938–45

*Beneš was President of the Czech government-in-exile after the proclamation of a German Protectorate in March 1939. Beneš returned to Czechoslovakia in 1945.

E. Beneš	1945–48
K. Gottwald	1948–53
A. Zápotecký	1953–57
A. Novotný	1957–68
L. Svoboda	1968–75
G. Husák	1975–89
V. Havel*	1989–92

*Havel became President of the new Czech Republic.

CZECH REPUBLIC

The Czech Republic was formed on 1 January 1993 when Czechoslovakia ceased to exist, having split into the separate Czech and Slovak Republics.

Presidents

V. Havel	1993–2003
V. Klaus	2003–

DENMARK

Sovereigns (Norway as well as Denmark until 1814)

Frederick V	1746–66
Christian VII	1766–1808
Frederick (Crown Prince Regent)	1784–1808
Frederick VI	1808–39 (not King of Norway after 1814)
Christian VIII	1839–48
Frederick VII	1848–63
Christian IX	1863–1906
Frederick VIII	1906–12
Christian X	1912–47
Frederick IX	1947–72
Margaret II	1972–

ESTONIA

Prior to 1918, part of Tsarist Russia. An independent republic, 1918–40. Forcibly incorporated into Soviet Union, 1940. Following the collapse of communism, Estonia declared independence on 20 August 1991.

Presidents

L. Meri	1992–2001
A. Ruutel	2001–

FINLAND

Finland proclaimed independence on 6 December 1917 (having previously been part of Tsarist Russia).

Presidents

Prof. K.J. Ståhlberg	1919–25
Dr L. Relander	1925–31
Dr P.E. Svinhufvud	1931–37
K. Kallio	1937–40
Dr R. Ryti	1940–44
Field-Marshal C. Mannerheim	1944–45

J. Paasikivi	1945–56
Dr U. Kekkonen	1956–81
Dr M. Koivisto	1981–94
M. Ahtisaari	1994–2000
T. Halonen	2000–

FRANCE

Kings

Louis XV	1715–74
Louis XVI	1774–93 (deposed, Sept. 1792; executed Jan. 1793).

First Republic, 1792–95

Maximilien Robespierre was the dominant figure from July 1793 to July 1794.

The Directory, 1795–99

The Directory: the following filled the five Directorships, 1795–99: Paul, Count de Barras; Jean François Rewbell; Louis-Marc de Larevellière-Lépeaux; Charles Le Tourneur; Lazare Carnot; François de Barthélemy; Nicolas François; Philippe de Douai; Jean Baptiste Treilhard; Louis Gohier; Jean François Moulin; Roger Ducos; Emmanuel Sieyès.

The Consulate, 1799–1802

The Directory was overthrown by Napoleon on 9 November 1799. Napoleon set up the Consulate, in which he filled the post of First Consul from 9 November 1799 until 18 May 1804 (alone from 4 August 1802). His fellow-consuls from 9 November 1799 until 27 December 1799 were Emmanuel Sieyès and Roger Ducos; from 27 December 1799 until 4 August 1802 Jean Jacques de Cambacérès and Charles Lebrun.

The Empire, 1804–14, 1815 (Mar. –June)

Napoleon became Emperor on 18 May 1804, abdicating on 6 April 1814. He returned briefly as Emperor, 10 March 1815 until his second abdication on 22 June 1815.

Kings, 1814–48

Louis XVIII	1814–24 (but see above)
Charles X	1824–30 (abdicated)
Louis Philippe	1830–48 (Feb.) (abdicated)

Prime ministers, 1815–48

Duc de Talleyrand	1815 (July–Sept.)
Duc de Richelieu	1815–18
Marquis Dessolles	1818–19
Comte de Décazes	1819–20
Duc de Richelieu	1820–21
Duc de Villèle	1821–28
Vicomte de Martignac	1828–29
Prince de Polignac	1829–30
Duc de Mortemart	1830 (July)
Marquis de Lafayette	1830 (July)
Duc de Broglie	1830 (Aug.)
Jacques Lafitte	1830–31
J. Casimir Périer	1831–32
Duc de Dalmatie	1832–34
Admiral de Rigny	1834 (Mar.–July)
Comte Gérard	1834 (July–Oct.)
Duc de Broglie	1834 (Oct.–Nov.)
H.B. Maret	1834 (Nov.)
Duc de Trevise	1834–35
Duc de Broglie	1835–36
Adolphe Thiers	1836 (Feb.–Sept.)
Comte Molé	1836–39
Duc de Dalmatie	1839–40
Adolphe Thiers	1840 (Mar.–Oct.)
Duc de Dalmatie	1840–47
François Guizot	1847–48

Second Republic

Louis Bonaparte (President)	1848–52

Second Empire

Napoleon III (the title adopted by Louis Bonaparte on the proclamation of the Second Empire)	1852–70 (abdicated)

Third Republic

Presidents

A. Thiers	1871–73
Marshal MacMahon	1873–79

J. Grévy	1879–87
S. Carnot	1887–94 (assassinated)
J. Casimir-Pèrier	1894–95
F.F. Faure	1895–99
E. Loubet	1899–1906
A. Fallières	1906–13
R. Poincaré	1913–20
P. Deschanel	1920 (Jan.–Sept.)
A. Millerand	1920–24
G. Doumergue	1924–31
P. Doumer	1931–32
A. Lebrun	1932–40

On 11 July 1940 Marshal Pétain took over the powers of president and added them to his own as prime minister. He then appointed a chief of state.

Chief of state

| Adm. Darlan | 1941–42 |
| P. Laval | 1942–44 |

The provisional government of de Gaulle was recognized in October 1944. A new constitution came into force on 24 December 1946 (Fourth Republic).

Prime ministers: Interwar France

G. Clemenceau	1917–20
A. Millerand	1920 (Jan.–Oct.)
M. Leygues	1920–21
A. Briand	1921–22
R. Poincaré	1922–24
F. Marsal	1924 (June only)
E. Herriot	1924–25
M. Painlevé	1925 (May–Nov.)
A. Briand	1925–26
R. Poincaré	1926–29
A. Briand	1929 (July–Nov.)
A. Tardieu	1929–30
M. Steeg	1930–31
P. Laval	1931–32
A. Tardieu	1932 (Feb.–June)
E. Herriot	1932 (June–Dec.)
J. Paul-Boncour	1932–33
E. Daladier	1933 (Jan.–Oct.)

A. Sarraut	1933 (Oct.–Nov.)
C. Chautemps	1933–34
E. Daladier	1934 (Jan.–Feb.)
G. Doumergue	1934 (Feb.–Nov.)
P.-E. Flandin	1934–35
F. Bouisson	1935 (June only)
P. Laval	1935–36
A. Sarraut	1936 (Jan.–June)
L. Blum	1936–37 (June–June)
C. Chautemps	1937–38 (June–Mar.)
L. Blum	1938 (Mar.–Apr.)
E. Daladier	1938–40
P. Reynaud	1940 (Mar.–June)
Marshal P. Pétain	1940–42

Fourth Republic

President of the Republic

V. Auriol	1947–53
R. Coty	1953–58

A new constitution came into force on 5 October 1958 (Fifth Republic).

Fifth Republic

President of the Republic

Gen. C. de Gaulle	1958–69
G. Pompidou	1969–74
A. Poher	1974 (Apr.–May, interim)
V. Giscard d'Estaing	1974–81
F. Mitterrand	1981–95
J. Chirac*	1995–

*Re-elected, May 2002.

Prime ministers (after 1946)

F. Gouin	1946 (Jan.–June)
G. Bidault	1946 (June–Dec.)
L. Blum	1946–47 (Jan.)
P. Ramadier	1947 (Jan.–Nov.)
R. Schuman	1947–48 (July)

A. Marie	1948 (July–Sept.)
R. Schuman	1948 (Sept.)
H. Queuille	1948–49
G. Bidault	1949–50
H. Queuille	1950 (July)
R. Pleven	1950–51
H. Queuille	1951 (Mar.–Aug.)
R. Pleven	1951–52
E. Fauré	1952 (Jan.–Mar.)
A. Pinay	1952–53
R. Mayer	1953 (Jan.–June)
J. Laniel	1953–54
P. Mendès-France	1954–55
E. Fauré	1955–56
G. Mollet	1956–57
F. Gaillard	1957–59
M. Debré	1959–62
G. Pompidou	1962–68
M. Couve de Murville	1968–69
J. Chaban-Delmas	1969–72
P. Messmer	1972–72
J. Chirac	1974–76
R. Barre	1976–81
P. Mauroy	1981–84
L. Fabius	1984–86
J. Chirac	1986–88
M. Rocard	1988–91
Mme E. Cresson	1991–92
P. Bérégovoy	1992–93
E. Balladur	1993–95
A. Juppé	1995–97
L. Jospin	1997–2002
J.-P. Raffarin	2002–

GERMANY

The German Empire was established on 18 January 1871. Henceforth, until 1918, the Kings of Prussia were Emperors of Germany.

Emperors

William I	1871–88
Frederick III	1888
William II	1888–1918 (abdicated)

Chancellors

O. von Bismarck-Schönhausen	1871–90
L. von Caprivi	1890–94
Prince von Hohenlohe-Schillingsfürst	1894–1900
Baron von Bülow	1900–09
T. Bethmann-Hollweg	1909–17
G. Michaelis	1917
G. von Herling	1917–18
Prince Max of Baden	1918
Friedrich Ebert	1918

The Republic was proclaimed on the abdication of Kaiser William II, on 9 November 1918.

Presidents

Friedrich Ebert	Feb. 1919–Feb. 1925
P. von Hindenburg	Apr. 1925–Aug. 1934

Reich Chancellors, 1919–33

P. Scheidemann	1919 (Feb.–June)
G. Bauer	1919–20
H. Müller	1920 (Mar.–June)
C. Fehrenbach	1920–21
J. Wirth	1921–22
W. Cuno	1922–23
G. Stresemann	1923 (Aug.–Nov.)
W. Marx	1923–24
H. Luther	1925–26
W. Marx	1926–28
H. Müller	1928–30
H. Brüning	1930–32
F. von Papen	1932 (May–Nov.)
K. von Schleicher	1932–33 (Jan.)

Chancellors and Führer

Adolf Hitler	Aug. 1934–Apr. 1945
Adm. C. Dönitz	Apr. 1945–June 1945

After the Allied administration of Germany after 1945, the Federal Republic of Germany (i.e. West Germany) came into being in September 1949. In October 1990, the two halves of Germany were reunited and Kohl became first chancellor of a reunited Germany.

(1) Heads of state (presidents)

T. Heuss	1949–59
H. Lübke	1959–69
G. Heinemann	1969–74
W. Scheel	1974–79
K. Carstens	1979–84
R. von Weizsächer	1984–94
R. Herzog	1994–99
J. Rau	1999–2004
H. Koehler	2004–

(2) Chancellors

K. Adenauer	1949–63
L. Erhard	1963–66
K. Kiesinger	1966–69
W. Brandt	1969–74
H. Schmidt	1974–82
H. Kohl	1982–98
G. Schröder	1998–

In the German Democratic Republic (East Germany), the position was:

Heads of state (President until 1960, Chairman of the Council of State thereafter)

W. Pieck	1949–60
W. Ulbricht	1960–73
W. Stoph	1973–76
E. Honecker	1976–89*

*After the collapse of communist rule, Manfred Gerlach became interim head of state. East Germany was united with West Germany in October 1990.

GREAT BRITAIN

Sovereigns

George III	1760–1820
George IV	1820–30 (Prince Regent since 1811)
William IV	1830–37
Victoria	1837–1901
Edward VII	1901–10
George V	1910–36

Edward VIII	1936 (abdicated, never crowned)
George VI	1936–52
Elizabeth II	1952–

Prime ministers

George Grenville	1763–65
Marquess of Rockingham	1765–66
Earl of Chatham	1766–68
Duke of Grafton	1768–70
Lord North	1770–82
Marquess of Rockingham	1782 (Mar.–July)
Earl of Shelburne	1782–83
Duke of Portland	1783 (Apr.–Dec.)
William Pitt	1783–1801
Henry Addington	1801–04
William Pitt	1804–06
Lord Grenville	1806–07
Duke of Portland	1807–09
Spencer Perceval	1809–12
Earl of Liverpool	1812–27
George Canning	1827 (Apr.–Aug.)
Viscount Goderich	1827–28
Duke of Wellington	1828–30
Earl Grey	1830–34
Viscount Melbourne	1834 (July–Nov.)
Duke of Wellington	1834 (Nov.–Dec.)
Sir Robert Peel	1834–35
Viscount Melbourne	1835–41
Sir Robert Peel	1841–46
Lord John Russell (Earl Russell)	1846–52
Earl of Derby	1852 (Feb.–Dec.)
Earl of Aberdeen	1852–55
Viscount Palmerston	1855–58
Earl of Derby	1858–59
Viscount Palmerston	1859–65
Earl Russell	1865–66
Earl of Derby	1866–68
Benjamin Disraeli	1868 (Feb.–Dec.)
W.E. Gladstone	1868–74
Benjamin Disraeli	1874–80
W.E. Gladstone	1880–85
Marquess of Salisbury	1885–86
W.E. Gladstone	1886 (Feb.–July)

Marquess of Salisbury	1886–92
W.E. Gladstone	1892–94
Earl of Rosebery	1894–95
Marquess of Salisbury	1895–1902
A.J. Balfour	1902–05
Sir Henry Campbell-Bannerman	1905–08
H.H. Asquith	1908–16
David Lloyd George	1916–22
A. Bonar Law	1922–23
Stanley Baldwin	1923–24 (Jan.)
J. Ramsay MacDonald	1924 (Jan.–Nov.)
Stanley Baldwin	1924–29
J. Ramsay MacDonald	1929–35
Stanley Baldwin	1935–37
Neville Chamberlain	1937–40
Winston Churchill	1940–45
Clement Attlee	1945–51
Winston Churchill	1951–55
Anthony Eden	1955–57
Harold Macmillan	1957–63
Sir Alec Douglas-Home	1963–64
Harold Wilson	1964–70
Edward Heath	1970–74
Harold Wilson	1974–76
James Callaghan	1976–79
Margaret Thatcher	1979–90
John Major	1990–97
Tony Blair	1997–

GREECE

Greece proclaimed independence from the Ottoman Empire, which recognized her independence on 14 September 1829.

Kings

Otto (of Bavaria)	1833–62
George I	1863–1913
Constantine I	1913–17
Alexander	1917–20
Constantine I (again)	1920–22
George II	1922–23
A Republic was in existence	1924–35
George II (again)	1935–44

Regency	1944–46
George II (again)	1946–47
Paul I	1947–64
Constantine II	1964–74*

*When the monarchy was formally voted out.

Presidents (after 1973)

G. Papadopoulos	1973 (June–Nov., Provisional President)
P. Ghizikis	1973–74
M. Stassinopoulos	1974–75
K. Tsatsos	1975–80
K. Karamanlis	1980–85
C. Sartzetakis	1985–90
K. Karamanlis	1990–95
C. Stephanopoulos*	1995–

*Re-elected February 2000.

HOLY ROMAN EMPIRE*

Francis I (of Lorraine)	1745–65
Joseph II	1765–90
Leopold II	1790–92
Francis II	1792–1806

*Until 1806, when the Holy Roman Empire was dissolved.

HUNGARY

Hungary became an independent republic on 16 November 1918.

Count Karolyi   Nov. 1918–Mar. 1919 (Provisional President)

In January 1920, Hungary was proclaimed a monarchy, but Admiral M. von Horthy was Regent, 1920–45. The absent Charles (*see* Austria) never assumed the throne. A republic was proclaimed in 1945 and a republican constitution came into effect in 1946.

Presidents (Chairman of Praesidium after 1952, Chairman of the Presiding Council after 1967)

Z. Tildy	1946–48
A. Szakasits	1948–50
S. Rónai	1950–52

I.M. Dobi	1952–67
P. Losonczi	1967–88
B.F. Straub	1988–89
I. Pozsgay	1989 (Jun.–Oct.)

The People's Republic was abolished on 23 October 1989. Presidents since the fall of communism have been:

A. Göncz	1990–2000*
F. Mádl	2000–

*Re-elected 1995.

IRELAND

Heads of state

After 1922, although Ireland was a self-governing Dominion, the British sovereign was still recognized as head of state. After December 1937, when the constitution of the Irish Free State as an independent sovereign state came into force, the following have been presidents:

Presidents

Douglas Hyde	1938–45
Sean T. O'Kelly	1945–59
Eamon de Valera	1959–73
Erskine Childers	1973–74
Cearbhall O. Dalaigh	1974–76
Patrick Hillery	1976–90
Mary Robinson	1990–97
Mary McAleese	1997–

Prime ministers (Taoiseachs) (after 1922)

Michael Collins	1922
(Finance and General Minister in the Provisional Government)	
W. Cosgrave	1922–32
E. de Valera	1932–48
J.A. Costello	1948–51
E. de Valera	1951–54
J.A. Costello	1954–57
E. de Valera	1957–59
S. Lemass	1959–66
J. Lynch	1966–73

L. Cosgrave	1973–77
J. Lynch	1977–79
C. Haughey	1979–81
G. FitzGerald	1981–82
C. Haughey	1982 (Mar.–Dec.)
G. FitzGerald	1982–87
C. Haughey	1987–92
A. Reynolds	1992–94
J. Bruton	1994–97
B. Aherne	1997–

ITALY

For Italy prior to unification, see under Sardinia, the Two Sicilies and the Papacy.
The Kingdom of Italy was formed on 17 March 1861.

Kings

Victor Emmanuel	1861–78
Umberto I	1878–1900
Victor Emmanuel III	1900–46 (abdicated)
Umberto II	1946 (abdicated)

A republic was proclaimed on 18 June 1946.

Presidents

L. Einaudi	1948–55
G. Gronchi	1955–62
A. Segni	1962–64
G. Saragat	1964–71
G. Leone	1971–78
A. Fanfani	1978 (June–July)
A. Pertini	1979–85
F. Cossiga	1985–92
O. Scalfaro	1992–99
C.A. Ciampi	1999–

LATVIA

Prior to 1918, Latvia was part of Tsarist Russia. It was an independent republic from
1918 to 1940 when it was forcibly incorporated in the Soviet Union. Independence
was restored in 1991.

Presidents

| G. Ulmanis | 1993–99 |
| V. Vike-Freiberga | 1999– |

LITHUANIA

Prior to the 1917 Revolution, Lithuania was part of Tsarist Russia. It was an independent republic from February 1918 to June 1940. It regained its full independence in 1991.

Heads of state

V. Landsbergis (Chairman of the Supreme Council)	1990–93
A. Brazauskas* (President)	1993–98
V. Adamkus	1998–

*Elected by popular vote, 14 February 1993.

MACEDONIA

Prior to 1992, Macedonia was part of former Yugoslavia. It declared independence on 20 November 1992 and was admitted to the United Nations as the 'Former Yugoslav Republic of Macedonia' in deference to Greek unease.

Presidents

| K. Gligorov | 1991–99 |
| B. Trajkovski | 1999– |

MOLDOVA

With the collapse of the Soviet Union, Moldova declared its independence in August 1991.

Presidents

M. Snegur	1991–96
P. Lucinschi	1996–2001
V. Voronin	2001–

THE NETHERLANDS

Known as the United Provinces until 1795, it was ruled by William V of Orange-Nassau, hereditary Stadtholder from 1751 to 1795. Under French occupation after 1795, the

Southern Provinces were annexed to France, the Northern Provinces becoming the Batavian Republic. Louis Bonaparte ruled as King of Holland, 1806–10. From 1810 to 1813, Holland was annexed to France. Independence was confirmed in 1815, when Belgium was added to Holland to form the Netherlands.

Sovereigns

William I	1813–40
William II	1840–49
William III	1849–90
Wilhelmina	1890–1948 (abdicated)
Juliana	1948–80 (abdicated)
Beatrix	1980–

NORWAY

For the period up to 1814, see under Denmark. For the period 1814–1905 see under Sweden.

Kings (of independent Norway after 1905)

Haakon VII	1905–57
Olaf V	1957–91
Harald V	1991–

OTTOMAN EMPIRE (SEE TURKEY)

THE PAPACY

Popes (since 1763)

Pope	Family name	
Clement XIII	Carlo della Torre Rezzonico	1758–69
Clement XIV	Giovanni Vicenzo Antonio Ganganelli	1769–74
Pius VI	Giovanni Angelo Braschi	1775–99
Pius VII	Luigi Barnabo Chiaramonti	1800–23
Leo XII	Annibale della Genga	1823–29
Pius VIII	Francesco Xaverio Castiglione	1829–30
Gregory XVI	Bartolommeo Capellare	1831–46
Pius IX	Count Giovanni Maria Mastai-Ferreti	1846–78
Leo XIII	Gioacchino Vincenzo Rafaele Luigi Pecci	1878–1903
Pius X	Giuseppe Sarto	1903–14
Benedict XV	Giacomo della Chiesa	1914–22
Pius XI	Achille Ratti	1922–39
Pius XII	Eugenio Pacelli	1939–58

John XXIII	Angelo Giuseppe Roncalli	1958–63
Paul VI	Giovanni Battista Montini	1963–78
John Paul I	Albino Luciani	1978
John Paul II	Karol Wojtyla	1978–

POLAND

Kings (until 1795)

| Augustus III | 1733–63 |
| Stanislaw Poniatowski | 1764–94 |

In 1795, the Third Partition of Poland took place. From 1806 to 1815, a Grand Duchy of Warsaw existed, the creation of Napoleon. The Congress of Vienna created a Kingdom of Poland (under the Russian Crown). After the 1830 Rising this was suppressed. Not until 1918 did Poland regain independence, when an independent state was proclaimed on 5 November 1918.

Presidents

J. Pilsudski	1918–22
Gabriel Narutowicz	1922 (assassinated)
S. Wojciechowski	1922–26
I. Mościcki	1926–39

On 29 September 1939 the German occupation of Poland began. The Polish government was in exile until the end of the war.

Prime ministers of the government-in-exile

| General Wladyslaw Sikorski | 1939–43 |
| Stanislaw Mikolajczyk | 1943–45 |

In July 1945 a Provisional Government of National Unity was set up, composed of the London government-in-exile and the Russian-backed Committee of National Liberation. Its task was to run Poland until free elections could take place. The elections were held in 1947, resulting in an overwhelming victory for the Communist-Socialist candidates.

President

Boleslaw Bierut   1945–52

On 22 July 1952 a new constitution replaced the office of President with a Council of State.

President of the Council of State

A. Zawadski	1952–64
E. Ochab	1964–68
Marshal M. Spychalski	1968–70
J. Cyrankiewicz	1970–72
H. Jabłoński	1972–85
W. Jaruzelski	1985–89*

From 1956 to 1970, Gomulka was the most powerful figure in Poland, when he was succeeded by Gierek. From 1981 until the collapse of communist rule, General Jaruzelski was Poland's strong-man.

*President 1989–90, but not elected.

President (by popular election)

| L. Walesa | 1990–95 |
| A. Kwaśniewski* | 1995– |

*Re-elected, October 2000.

PORTUGAL

Monarchs (Braganza dynasty) (to 1910)

Joseph	1750–77
Pedro III	1777–86
Maria I	1777–1816
John VI	1816–26
Pedro IV	1826
Maria II	1826–28
Miguel	1828–34
Maria II (again)	1834–53
Pedro V	1853–61
Luiz I	1861–89
Carlos I	1889–1908
Manuel II	1908–10

A republic was proclaimed in 1910.

Presidents

| A. Carmona | 1926–51 |
| A. Salazar[1] | 1951 (Apr.–July) |

Marshal F. Lopes	1951–58
A. Tomás	1958–74
A. de Spinola	1974 (Apr.–Sept.)[2]
F. Gomes	1974–76
A. Eanes	1976–86
M. Soares	1986–96
J. Sampãio	1996[3]–

[1]Salazar ruled Portugal as a dictator. See p. 320.
[2]A military junta seized power on 25 April, ending the dictatorship.
[3]Re-elected, January 2001.

PRUSSIA

Kings

Frederick II (the Great)	1740–86
Frederick William II	1786–97
Frederick William III	1797–1840
Frederick William IV	1840–58 (insane)
Regency	1858–61
William I	1861–88
Frederick III	1888
William II	1888–1918 (abdicated)

N.B. The creation of the German Empire was in 1871, after which the Kings of Prussia became German Emperors.

ROMANIA

Kings, 1881–1947

Carol I	1881–1914
Ferdinand	1914–27
Michael I	1927–30
Carol II	1930–40 (abdicated)
Michael I*	1940–47 (abdicated)

*Michael I resumed the throne in 1940. However, in 1947, as a result of a plebiscite a republic was established and the king abdicated.

Presidents

C. Parhon	1948–52
P. Groza	1952–58

I. Maurer	1958–61
G. Gheorghiu-Dej	1961–65
C. Stoica	1965–67
N. Ceausescu	1967–89
I. Iliescu	1989–96*
E. Constantinescu	1997–2000
I. Iliescu	2000–

*A new constitution was adopted by referendum on 8 December 1991. Iliescu was elected president in May 1990 and re-elected 11 October 1992. The reformist Traian Basescu won the 2004 presidential election.

RUSSIA (USSR, 1922–91)

Tsars

Catherine II (the Great)	1762–96
Paul I	1796–1801
Alexander I	1801–25
Nicholas I	1825–55
Alexander II	1855–81
Alexander III	1881–94
Nicholas II	1894–1917 (abdicated)

Prime ministers

Under Nicholas II,	*1894–1917*
J.N. Durnovo	1895–1903
S.J. Witte	1903–06
I.L. Goremykin	1906 (May–July)
P.A. Stolypin	1906–11
W.N. Kokovtsov	1911–14
I.L. Goremykin	1914–16
B.W. Stürmer	1916 (Feb.–Nov.)
A.F. Trepov	1916 (Nov.)–1917 (Jan.)
N.D. Golitsin	1917 (Jan.–Mar.)

Under the provisional government	
G.J. Lvov	1917 (Mar.–July)
A.F. Kerensky	1917 (July–Nov.)

A constitution for the Federal Republic was adopted on 10 July 1918, by a government which had taken office on 8 November 1917.

President of the Council of People's Commissars

V.I. Lenin   1917–22

A new constitution of 30 December 1922 replaced this office by a Central Executive Committee with four chairmen. A new constitution came into force on 5 December 1936 establishing the office of Chairman of the Presidium of the Supreme Soviet of the USSR, as head of state.

Chairmen

M.I. Kalinin	1936–46
N.M. Shvernik	1946–53
Marshal K.E. Voroshilov	1953–60
L.I. Brezhnev	1960–64
A.I. Mikoyan	1964–65
N.V. Podgorny	1965–77
L.I. Brezhnev	1977–82
Y.V. Andropov	1983–84
K.V. Chernenko	1984–85
M. Gorbachev*	1985–91

Effective rulers (1917–91)

V.I. Lenin	1917–22
J. Stalin	1927–53
N. Khrushchev	1953–64 (deposed)
L.I. Brezhnev	1964–82
Y.V. Andropov	1982–84
K.V. Chernenko	1984–85
M. Gorbachev*	1985–91

*Gorbachev became President of the USSR in 1988 then (1990) Executive President until the collapse of the USSR. He resigned, 25 December 1991. Following the collapse of the Soviet Union in December 1991, the Russian Federation became a founder member of the Commonwealth of Independent States (see p. 337). Boris Yeltsin was directly elected President of the Russian Federation in 1991.

Presidents

B. Yeltsin	1991 (June)–99*
V. Putin	1999**–

*Re-elected in 1996, resigned 31 December 1999.
**At first Acting President.

Prime ministers

The first prime minister of the Russian Federation after the fall of the USSR was Yeltsin, who was succeeded by Gaidar (June–Dec. 1992). Apart from Chernomyrdin (1992–98), the 1990s saw a succession of short-lived appointments. In May 2000, Kasyanov became Prime Minister under Putin.

SARDINIA

(Sardinia–Piedmont–Savoy)

Kings

Victor Amadeus III	1773–96
Charles Emmanuel IV	1796–1802

Sardinia was annexed to France, December 1798; subsequently occupied by Russian and Austrian forces, June 1799–June 1800; French rule was then restored; Charles Emmanuel abdicated in 1802, in favour of his brother.

Victor Emmanuel I   1802–21 (abdicated)

Charles Felix ruled as Regent; returned to Sardinia, 1821.

Charles Felix I	1821–24
Charles Albert I	1824–49
Victor Emmanuel II	1849–78 (after 1861, King of Italy q.v.)

SERBIA

An independent kingdom after 1878.

Kings

Milan Obrenovitch	1882–89 (abdicated)
Alexander Obrenovitch	1889–1903
Peter	1903–21*

*See also reference to Yugoslavia in this section.

TWO SICILIES

(Naples and Sicily)

Kings

Ferdinand I	1759–1825*
Francis I	1825–30
Ferdinand II	1830–59
Francis II	1859–60

*Joseph Bonaparte was declared king, 1806. He renounced the throne in 1808. Joachim Murat was declared king, 1808, and deposed in 1815.

SLOVAKIA

Part of Czechoslovakia from 1918 to 14 March 1939 when it was declared an independent country with Dr J. Tiso as president (Oct. 1939–Apr. 1945). Slovakia, which had been a Nazi-puppet state, was reincorporated into Czechoslovakia in April 1945. Slovakia split from Czechoslovakia to become an independent republic on 1 January 1993 (the so-called 'Velvet Divorce').

Presidents

M. Kovac	1993–98
R. Schuster	1999–

SLOVENIA

Slovenia declared its independence from former Yugoslavia on 8 October 1991, the culmination of a series of moves towards separation which began in October 1989.

President

M. Kučan	1992–2002
J. Drnovšek	2002–

SPAIN

Kings

Charles III	1759–88
Charles IV	1788–1808 (abdicated)
Ferdinand VII	1808

From 1808 to 1812, when he abdicated, Spain was ruled by Joseph Bonaparte.

Ferdinand VII (again)   1813–33
Isabella II   1833–68 (fled)

Interregnum from 1868 to 1874.

Alfonso XII   1874–85
Alfonso XIII   1886–1931 (abdicated)

A republic was proclaimed on 14 April 1931.

Presidents

N.A. Zamora y Torres   1931–36
M. Azaña   1936–39

Chief of the state

Gen. Francisco Franco   1939–75

King

Juan Carlos I   1975–

Prime ministers

F. Franco Bahamonde   1939–73
L. Carrero Blanco   1973 (June–Dec.)
T. Fernández Miranda (acting)   1973–74
C. Arias Navarro   1974–76
A. Suarez Gonzalez   1976–81
L. Calvo-Sotelo Bustelo   1981–82
F. González Márquez   1982–96
J.M. Aznar López   1996–2004
J.L. Rodríguez Zapatero   2004–

SWEDEN

Kings

Adolphus Frederick   1751–71
Gustavus III   1771–92
Gustavus IV Adolphus   1792–1809
Charles XIII   1809–18 (also King of Norway after 1814)
Charles XIV John (Bernadotte)   1818–44
Oscar I   1844–59

Charles XV	1859–72
Oscar II	1872–1907 (renounced Norwegian throne, 1905)
Gustavus V	1907–50
Gustavus VI, Adolphus	1950–73
Charles XVI, Gustavus	1973–

TURKEY

Sultans

Mustafa III	1757–74
Abdul Hamid I	1774–89
Selim III	1789–1807
Mustafa IV	1807–08
Mahmud II	1808–39
Abdul Mejid I	1839–61
Abdul Aziz	1861–76
Murad V	1876
Abdul Hamid II	1876–1909
Mohammed V	1909–18
Mohammed VI	1918–22

The office of Sultan was abolished in November 1922. Prince Abdul Mejid was Caliph from 1922 to 1924. A republic was proclaimed on 29 October 1923. Its first President, from 1923 to 38, was Kemal Atatürk.

Presidents

M. Kemal Atatürk	1923–38
I. Inönü	1938–50
C. Bayar	1950–60
C. Gursel	1961–66
C. Sunay	1966–73
F. Korutürk	1973–80
I.S. Caglayangil	1980 (Apr.–Sept.)
K. Evren	1980–89
T. Özal	1989–93
S. Demirel	1993–2000
A.N. Sezer	2000–

UKRAINE

Ukraine, formerly part of the Russian Empire, was briefly independent between 1919 and 1922, when it became a constituent republic of the Soviet Union. The independence of Ukraine was declared on 5 December 1991.

Presidents

| L. Kravchuk | 1991–94 |
| L. Kuchma | 1994–* |

*The disputed presidential election of 2004 was eventually won by the opposition candidate, Viktor Yushchenko. He took office in January 2005.

UNITED KINGDOM (SEE GREAT BRITAIN)

UNITED PROVINCES (SEE NETHERLANDS)

USSR (SEE RUSSIA)

YUGOSLAVIA

The independent Serb, Croat and Slovene State was formed in December 1918. The name was changed in October 1929 to Yugoslavia.

Kings

Peter I	1903–21 (formerly King of Serbia)
Alexander I	1921–34
Peter II	1934–45 (abdicated)

A republic was proclaimed in 1945.

President of the Praesidium

Dr I. Ribar   1945–53

President of the Republic

Marshal I. Broz-Tito   1953–80

After 1980, a 'Collective Presidency' was established, with the Presidency rotating on an annual basis. After a civil war in 1991, Yugoslavia officially ceased to exist in January 1992. Slovenia and Croatia were recognized as independent states by the international community in January 1992. The independence of Bosnia–Herzegovina (declared in 1992) was delayed by the civil war (see p. 214). Meanwhile, a reconstituted 'rump' Yugoslavia (consisting of Serbia and Montenegro) was declared in April 1992. The effective ruler of this rump Yugoslavia was Slobodan Milosevic from 1992 to 2000. After the revolution of October 2000 the president was Vojislav Kostunica. In 2003 a new union of Serbia and Montenegro was born with Svetozar Marovic as the first head of state from 7 March 2003.

The Bonaparte family

(† = died.)

Charles de Bonaparte, † 1785, m. Maria Lætitia Ramolini, † at Rome, 1836

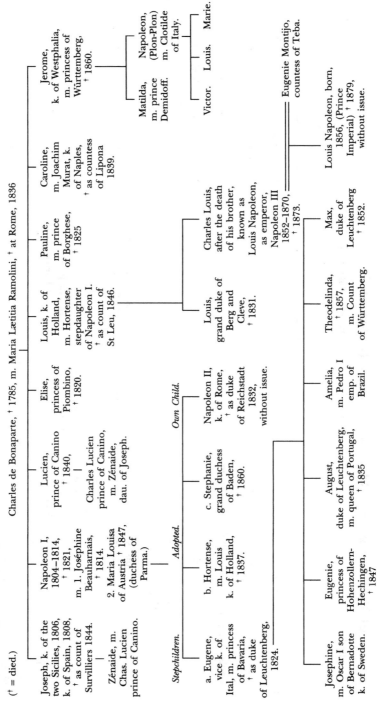

33

House of Bourbon in the older and younger (Orléans) line

(† = died.)

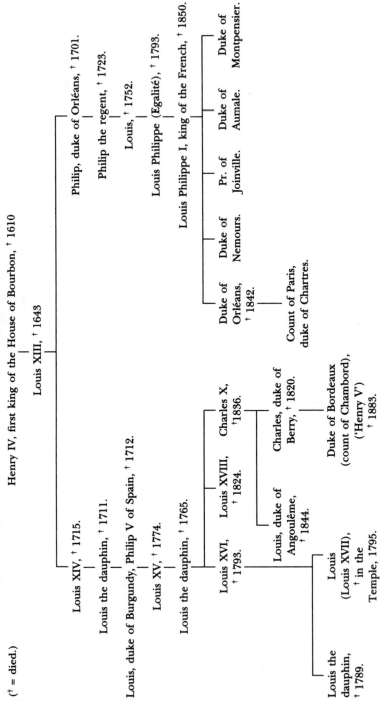

Henry IV, first king of the House of Bourbon, † 1610

Louis XIII, † 1643

Louis XIV, † 1715.

Louis the dauphin, † 1711.

Louis, duke of Burgundy, Philip V of Spain, † 1712.

Louis XV, † 1774.

Louis the dauphin, † 1765.

Louis XVI, † 1793.

Louis XVIII, † 1824.

Charles X, † 1836.

Louis, duke of Angoulême, † 1844.

Charles, duke of Berry, † 1820.

Duke of Bordeaux (count of Chambord), ('Henry V') † 1883.

Louis (Louis XVII), † in the Temple, 1795.

Louis the dauphin, † 1789.

Philip, duke of Orléans, † 1701.

Philip the regent, † 1723.

Louis, † 1752.

Louis Philippe (Egalité), † 1793.

Louis Philippe I, king of the French, † 1850.

Duke of Orléans, † 1842.

Duke of Nemours.

Pr. of Joinville.

Duke of Aumale.

Duke of Montpensier.

Count of Paris, duke of Chartres.

II
POLITICAL CHRONOLOGIES

EUROPE AT THE END OF THE ANCIEN RÉGIME

1762

Catherine the Great becomes Tsarina of Russia. Publication of Rousseau's *Social Contract* and *Emile*.

1763

Peace of Paris ends Seven Years War; Britain makes extensive colonial gains in North America and India from France. Peace of Hubertusburg between Prussia and Austria; Prussia retains Silesia but evacuates Saxony.

1764

Stanislaw Poniatowski, protégé of Catherine the Great and Frederick the Great, becomes King of Poland.

1765

Beginning of Stamp Act crisis between Britain and her American colonies. Joseph II becomes Emperor of Austria and joint-ruler with Maria Theresa, his mother, of the Austrian states.

1766

Russian influence in Poland forces Polish Diet to agree to equal rights for non-Catholics and administrative reform.

1767

Catherine appoints reforming Great Commission. Alliance of Russia and Prussia to protect Polish non-Catholics.

1768

Polish Confederation of Bar wages war against King Stanislaw who is supported by Russia.

1771

Conflict between French Chancellor Maupeou and Parlement of Paris; it is abolished and replaced by the Conseil du Roi.

1772

First Partition of Poland between Russia, Prussia and Austria. Gustavus III of Sweden, by a bloodless *coup d'état,* becomes absolute ruler and introduces enlightened reforms.

1773

Pugachev Revolt begins in Russia.

1774

Treaty of Kutchuk-Kainardji between Turkey and Russia. Accession of Louis XVI; Parlement of Paris restored. Turgot becomes Comptroller General.

1775

First armed conflict between American colonists and British at Lexington. Conciliation attempts fail and open warfare develops.

1776

American Declaration of Independence. Adam Smith's *Wealth of Nations* published.

Turgot begins overhaul of French finances, but is dismissed. Necker becomes Comptroller.

1778

France allies with the American colonists; war declared between Britain and France.

1779

Spain declares war on Britain, Franco–Spanish fleet besieges Gibraltar. Congress of Teschen terminates war of Bavarian Succession.

THE FRENCH REVOLUTION

1783

(Dec.) The Queen's favourite, Calonne, appointed as Minister of Finance.

1786

(Aug.) Calonne proposes a land tax and a stamp tax. These would be assessed by Provincial Estates. He persuades the King to summon an Assembly of Notables as he knows parliament will resist his proposals.

1787

(22 Feb.) The Assembly of Notables meets and declares against Calonne.

(17 Apr.) Calonne driven from office.

(May) Lorriene de Brienne, Archbishop of Toulouse, becomes Chief of the Council of Finance. The Assembly of Notables grants his request for a new loan of 60,000,000 livres.

(25 May) Dissolution of the Assembly of Notables which has refused to agree to new taxes. There is conflict with the Parlement of Paris which refuses to accept the proposed land and stamp taxes. It asserts the States-General has the sole right to levy taxes.

(6 Aug.) The decrees on taxation are passed by a '*lit de justice*'.

(7 Aug.) The Parlement gains great popularity by challenging the validity of a '*lit de justice*'.

(14 Aug.) Parlement exiled to Troyes by the King.

(24 Sept.) The King and Brienne agree to drop their demand for new taxes and the Parlement returns to Paris.

1788

(8 May) The May Edicts. Louis persuaded to hold a '*lit de justice*' suppressing the Parlements and establishing new Courts of Appeal.

(June/July) The Revolt of the Nobility.

(21 July) At a meeting of the Estates of Dauphiné the nobility condemn the May Edicts and demand a convocation of the States-General and Provincial Estates. They also speak in support of the Third Estate.

(16 Aug.) Brienne announces a national bankruptcy.

(25 Aug.) Brienne dismissed by the King. The States-General summoned to meet on 1 May 1789.

(27 Aug.) Necker recalled as Minister of Finance.

(Sept.) Recall of the Paris Parlement which recommends the States-General be held as in 1614.

(6 Nov.) Meeting of the second Assembly of Notables.

(27 Dec.) Decision by the Royal Council on the doubling of the Third Estate.

1789

(Feb.–Apr.) Election of States-General. *Cahiers* drafted.

(27–28 Apr.) The Reveillon Riots in Paris.

(5 May) Meeting of the States-General opened by the King at Versailles.

(17 June) The Third Estate assumes the title of National Assembly, ignoring the existence of the other Estates and securing the leadership of the nation.

(19 June) By a majority of one the clergy vote to join the Third Estate.

(20 June) The Tennis Court Oath taken by the Third Estate. They swear not to disband until a constitution is established and confirmed on solid foundations.

(23 June) At a Royal Séance the King makes important concessions, but declares the edicts of 17 June illegal, insisting that the Estates should meet separately and that the Assembly should be dissolved.

(27 June) The clergy and nobility join the Third Estate for fear that opposition could endanger the King's life.

(6 July) A Committee is appointed to frame a new constitution.

(11 July) The electors of the Third Estate of Paris form a Civic Guard to maintain order in Paris. Under the influence of Court extremists Louis dismisses Necker.

(12 July) The Parisian mob seizes arms, fearing the dismissal of Necker was the signal for a royal *coup d'état*. The electors refuse to sanction the mob's action.

(14 July) The fall of the Bastille. Louis is told by a close adviser 'it is not a revolt, it is a revolution'. Troops withdrawn from Paris.

(15 July) The adoption of the Tricoleur; Bailly appointed Mayor of Paris; Lafayette appointed Commander of the Civic Guard which becomes the National Guard. The King recalls Necker.

(16 July) Necker returns; flight of Artois, Condé and Broglie, first of the émigrés.

(17 July) Louis visits Paris where he accepts the Tricoleur and confirms Bailly and Lafayette in their posts.

(20 July) The beginning of the worst stage of the '*Grand Peur*' (Great Fear) in the countryside.

(22 July) The murder of Fouillon and Berthier in Paris.

(4 Aug.) The abolition of tithes worth 120,000,000 francs.

(4–11 Aug.) Decrees of the National Assembly abolishing feudal rights and many privileges in French society. Representatives of the Nobles make a voluntary surrender of all feudal rights and privileges.

(26 Aug.) Declaration of the Rights of Man and Citizens: makes all equal before the law.

(10 Sept.) The Assembly rejects the proposal of a second chamber nominated by the King as contrary to democratic sentiment.

(11 Sept.) The Assembly accepts a suspensory veto for the King.

(1 Oct.) The Queen and Dauphin attend a banquet at Versailles where loyal toasts are made and anti-Republican sentiments expressed.

(5 Oct.) The March of the Women to Versailles. Lafayette prevents the violence getting out of hand.

(6 Oct.) The Royal Family return to Paris at Lafayette's insistence.

(10 Oct.) Talleyrand proposes the confiscation of church lands to pay state debts. Louis XVI decreed 'King of the French'.

(12 Oct.) The National Assembly follows the King to Paris.

THE REMAKING OF FRANCE, 1789–91

(19 Oct.) The National Assembly meets in Paris.

(21 Oct.) A decree on Public Order provides for the use of martial law.

(29 Oct.) Decree on electoral regulations distinguishes 'active' and 'passive' citizens. Only certain taxpayers are entitled to vote.

(31 Oct.) Decree passed providing for a uniform tariff covering all France.

(2 Nov.) Nationalization of ecclesiastical estates to relieve financial difficulties.

(6 Nov.) Mirabeau defeated over the question of whether the King's ministers should be allowed to sit in the Assembly.

(7 Nov.) Decree excluding Deputies from ministerial posts.

(9 Nov.) The National Assembly moves into the Manége.

(10 Nov.) Church property confiscated and the state makes provision for the clergy.

(12 Dec.) The first issue of *assignats* – government notes backed by public lands, the value of which is not to be exceeded by the issue of notes.

(12–14 Dec.) Decrees passed to reorganize local government.

(22 Dec.) Local administration reorganized; 83 new Departments and 374 Cantons created.

1790

(28 Jan.) The removal of civic disabilities for Jews.

(13 Feb.) The suppression of religious orders except for those involved in teaching or charitable work. Monastic vows abolished; monks and nuns were to receive state pensions.

(15 Mar.) Decree passed concerned with the terms of the redemption of seigneurial dues.

(Apr.) Assignats declared legal tender.

(13 Apr.) The Assembly passes a decree giving absolute toleration to every form of religion.

(21 May) Paris reorganized into sections.

(22 May) Wars of conquest renounced. The King given sole right to decide whether France should go to war or stay at peace.

(11 June) The inhabitants of Avignon (a papal enclave) declare their wish to become part of France.

(19 June) The Nobility's status and titles abolished.

(12 July) The Civil Constitution of the Clergy suppresses all cathedral chapters, and intervenes in other church questions. The Pope is not consulted and foreign bishops are forbidden to interfere in the French church.

(14 July) First *Fête de la Fédération*. The King accepts the Constitution.

(16 Aug.) The reorganization of the judiciary. Debate on the mutiny at Nancy.

(27 Aug.) Louis XVI reluctantly agrees to the Civil Constitution of the Clergy.

(4 Sept.) Necker resigns.

(26 Oct.) For the first time Louis authorizes overtures to foreign courts concerning possible intervention in France.

(29 Oct.) Rebellion in San Domingo.

(27 Nov.) Decree to enforce the Civic Oath on the clergy passed.

(26 Dec.) The King compelled to sign the decree on the Civil Constitution of the Clergy.

1791

(4 Jan.) Large-scale refusal to take the oath leads to division in France and the King more willing to gain foreign aid.

(9 Feb.) The first Bishops of the Constitutional Church elected.

(2 Mar.) Abolition of guilds and monopolies.

(10 Mar.) The Pope's pastoral letter condemns the Civil Constitution and the Declaration of the Rights of Man.

(2 Apr.) The death of Mirabeau; the breach between King and Assembly widens.

(13 Apr.) The Civil Constitution is condemned by the Papal Bull *Charitas*.

(18 Apr.) The mob prevents Louis from spending a day hunting at St Cloud.

(15 May) Blacks living in the French colonies and of free parentage are declared equal with whites in civic rights.

(16 May) The 'Self-Denying Ordinance' excludes Deputies of the National Assembly from membership of the Legislative Assembly.

(14 June) The '*Loi Chapelier*' – The Combination Law.

(20 June) The flight to Varennes; the King and Royal Family are prevented from escaping from France.

(25 June) The King is suspended and forced to return under duress to Paris. Louis remains under suspension until he accepts the Constitution (14 September).

(14 July) Second *Fête de la Fédération*.

(16 July) A Decree provides for the reinstatement of the King on completion of the Constitution.

(17 July) The Massacre of the Champ de Mars.

(27 Aug.) The Declaration of Pilnitz. The King of Prussia and the Emperor of Austria threaten intervention in France.

(Sept.) France annexes Avignon.

(3 Sept.) The new Constitution becomes law; the National Assembly becomes known as the Constituent Assembly.

(14 Sept.) Louis accepts the Constitution.

(30 Sept.) Dissolution of the National Assembly.

(1 Oct.) Meeting of the Legislative Assembly.

(20 Oct.) Brissot calls for military action to disperse the émigrés.

(9 Nov.) Decree made against émigrés suspected of conspiracy ordering their return on pain of death.

(12 Nov.) The King vetoes the decree against the émigrés.

(29 Nov.) The decree against non-juring priests forbids them to officiate in public and deprives them of their pensions.

(12 Dec.) Brissot threatens the King with insurrection.

(14 Dec.) Louis tells the Assembly that an army of 150,000 men has been sent to the frontiers.

(19 Dec.) Louis vetoes decree against non-juring priests.

(30 Dec.) Robespierre opposes Brissot at the Jacobin Club.

1792

(2 Jan.) The declaration that 1 January 1789 should be the first day of the 'Era of Liberty'.

(25 Jan.) The Assembly demands Leopold II should renounce his recent treaty with Russia and ensure the dispersal of the émigré army.

(2 Feb.) The property of the émigrés was declared forfeit to the nation.

(10 Mar.) Formation of Dumouriez's 'Patriot Ministry'.

(5–6 Apr.) Decree suppressing the Sorbonne and all religious congregations.

(20 Apr.) Declaration of war on Austria.

(May) The King's bodyguard of 12,000 men disbanded.

(27 May) Decree against non-juring priests (vetoed on 19 June).

(8 June) Decree providing for a military camp at Paris (vetoed on 19 June).

(13 June) Dismissal of the 'Patriot Ministry' by the King.

(20 June) The first invasion of the Tuileries by Parisians. Louis XVI crowned with the 'Cap of Liberty'.

(28 June) Brissot returns to the Jacobins.

(29 June) Lafayette attempts to close the Jacobin Club.

(1 July) Petition of 20,000 signatures against the events of 20 June.

(11 July) Decree provides for the proclamation of '*La Patrie en danger*'.

(14 July) Third *Fête de la Fédération*.

(22 July) Permanence of the Sections recognized. Proclamation of '*La Patrie en danger*'.

(28 July) The Brunswick Manifesto (threatening the destruction of Paris should any harm come to the Royal Family) reaches Paris.

(30 July) The Théâtre Français Section admits 'passive' citizens. The Marseilles Battalion arrives in Paris.

(31 July) The Maunconseil Section of Paris repudiates its allegiance to the throne and invites other sections to join in its demonstration demanding the deposition of the King.

(1 Aug.) Passive as well as active citizens admitted to the National Guard.

(3 Aug.) Petition of the Sections demands that the King be deposed.

(4 Aug.) Vergniand condemns the Maunconseil Section for its republicanism.

(8 Aug.) The Assembly exculpates Lafayette, rejecting Robespierre's demand that he should be impeached for supporting the King in June.

(9 Aug.) The Assembly postpones consideration of any republican petitions.

(10 Aug.) The Revolution of 10 August. The Tuileries is stormed by Parisian sansculottes and Marseilles Federals. The Monarchy is suspended. The Patriot Ministers are reinstated.

(11 Aug.) The Commune terrorizes the Assembly into authorizing the arrest of people suspected of 'crimes against the state'.

(17 Aug.) The Commune forces the Assembly to create the extra-ordinary tribunal of 17 August elected by the Sections and possessing final powers to try prisoners arrested under the proviso of 11 August.

(19 Aug.) Defection of Lafayette to the Austrians and a Prussian army crosses the frontier.

(20 Aug.) Fall of the fortress of Longwy.

(21 Aug.) The guillotine claims its first political victim. A noble is executed for raising irregular troops for royal service.

(25 Aug.) Redemption charges for seigneurial dues abolished.

(30 Aug.) The Assembly tries to dissolve the Commune.

(Sept.) The French attack Nice and Savoy.

(2 Sept.) Fall of the fortress of Verdun to the Prussians.

(2–6 Sept.) The 'September Massacres': prisoners murdered in Paris prisons.

(18 Sept.) The Assembly attempts to provide an armed guard for the Convention.

(20 Sept.) France defeats Prussia at Valmy. The Prussian retreat begins.

(21 Sept.) First Session of the Convention. The Monarchy is abolished. Year I of the Republic begins.

(24–25 Sept.) The Brissotins lead an attack on the power of Paris.

(29 Sept.) The French occupy the Sardinian territory of Nice.

(10 Oct.) Brissot expelled from the Jacobin Club.

(11 Oct.) The Constitutional Committee created.

(19 Oct.) The Sections protest against the attacks on Paris.

(29 Oct.) The Brissotins' second attack on the power of Paris.

(5 Nov.) Robespierre defends Paris and the Montagnards.

(6 Nov.) Battle of Jemappes. Commencement of the French invasion of Belgium.

(19 Nov.) Declaration of Fraternity: the French offer aid to all peoples striving to recover their freedom. The strategically sensitive Scheldt declared an open river.

(20 Nov.) Discovery of the secret cupboard in the Tuileries.

(28 Nov.) Savoy, formally Sardinian territory, is declared the eighty-fourth French Department.

(3 Dec.) The Convention makes the decision to try the King.

(11 Dec.) Louis interrogated by the Convention.

(15 Dec.) Decree on the treatment and government of occupied territories.

(27 Dec.) Buzot and Salle call for a referendum on the King's fate.

1793

(Jan.) Trial of Louis XVI.

(14–17 Jan.) The Convention votes to decide Louis' fate.

(21 Jan.) Execution of the King on the Place de la Révolution.

(24 Jan.) The British government orders the French ambassador to leave.

(1 Feb.) Declaration of war upon Great Britain and Holland.

(14 Feb.) The Principality of Monaco annexed.

(15 Feb.) Condorcet's constitutional proposals.

(23 Feb.) Ballot for the army extended to include all of France.

(24 Feb.) Levy of 300,000 men decreed.

(25 Feb.) Food rioting in Paris.

(1–7 Mar.) Belgian revolt.

(7 Mar.) France declares war on Spain.

(9 Mar.) First authorization of missions by Convention members to the provinces and armies.

(9–10 Mar.) Further rioting in Paris – supposed plot against the Convention.

(10 Mar.) Revolutionary Tribunal set up by decree.

(16 Mar.) Beginning of rising in the Vendée.

(18 Mar.) The French suffer defeat at Neerwinden resulting in Dumouriez's evacuation of The Netherlands. Austria fails to follow up this victory and destroy the French army.

(21 Mar.) The creation of local revolutionary committees.

(5 Apr.) Defection of Dumouriez to the Austrians.

(6 Apr.) First Committee of Public Safety (set up on 26 March) reduced to nine members.

(13 Apr.) The impeachment of Marat.

(15 Apr.) The Sections demand a purge of the Convention.

(4 May) The first 'maximum' on grain prices is decreed. Previously only Paris was covered by the 'Maximum' (since 12 Sept. 1792).

(10 May) The Convention moves to the Tuileries.

(12 May) The Commune forces the Convention to establish a *sansculotte* army to guard Paris.

(20 May) The Commission of Twelve is appointed to investigate plots against the Convention of Paris.

(30 May) Conservative *coup d'état* in Lyons.

(31 May) Unsuccessful rising in Paris. The Tuileries are surrounded by a mob who compel the Convention to abolish the Commission of Twelve. However it refuses to proscribe its own members.

(2 June) The Revolution of June the Second. The Convention is purged by the Montagnards and the Sections of Paris. Brissot and others are arrested.

(6 June) Federalist movement against the Convention at Bordeaux and Marseilles.

(6–19 June) The Protest of the 75.

(9 June) The Vendéans take Sanmur.

(24 June) The Convention accepts the Radical Constitution of 1793 which is to be brought in at the end of the war. Under the constitution all adult males are given the vote.

(10 July) Fall of the fortress of Condé.

(13 July) Marat murdered. The end of the Normandy rising.

(17 July) The final abolition of all feudal rights without compensation.

(23 July) Fall of the fortress of Mayence.

(26 July) Decree against hoarding, making it a capital crime.

(27 July) Robespierre becomes a member of the Committee of Public Safety.

(28 July) The fortress of Valenciennes falls. The outlawing of eighteen 'Brissotin' Deputies.

(1 Aug.) France adopts the metric system. The order for the arrest of all nationals of countries with which the Republic is at war, unless they were resident in France prior to 14 July 1789.

(10 Aug.) Festival of Unity in honour of 1793 Constitution.

(23 Aug.) The decree of *levée en masse*.

(27 Aug.) Toulon surrenders to the British and Sardinians.

(3 Sept.) A compulsory loan of 1,000 francs enforced. The Law of the Maximum enforces prices on pain of death. Hébertist rising in Paris. Terror becomes the order of the day as the Convention makes the war effort increasingly radical.

(6 Sept.) A Revolutionary Army is established to support the Committee of Public Safety.

(8 Sept.) French defeat allied army threatening Dunkirk.

(11 Sept.) The fortress of Lequesnoy falls.

(17 Sept.) Decree of the Law of Suspects orders the arrest of all those who have shown themselves to be enemies of liberty.

(22 Sept.) The first day of Year II.

(25 Sept.) The Committee of Public Safety survives attack in the Convention.

(29 Sept.) A new law on the general Maximum in restraint of prices and wages.

(3 Oct.) Brissot and 44 other Deputies are impeached.

(5 Oct.) Revolutionary Calendar established (as from 22 Sept.).

(9 Oct.) Lyons recaptured by Convention forces.

(10 Oct.) 'Revolutionary Government' decreed (sanctioned for the duration of the war).

(16 Oct.) Battle of Wattignies, Austria defeated and Maubeuge relieved. Marie Antoinette executed.

(17 Oct.) Vendéans defeated at Chollet.

(22 Oct.) Creation of a Central Food Commission.

(24–31 Oct.) Trial of Brissot and 20 other 'Girondin' Deputies.

(31 Oct.) Execution of the Brissotins.

(10 Nov.) Festival of Reason in Notre Dame.

(21 Nov.) Robespierre denounces atheism as aristocratic.

(22 Nov.) Closure of churches in Paris by the Commune.

(4 Dec.) The Law of Revolutionary Government (14 Frimaire).

(5 Dec.) The first issue of the *Vieux Cordelier* which initiates a campaign against the Hébertists.

(15 Dec.) The third issue of the *Vieux Cordelier* attacks 'the Terror'.

(19 Dec.) The British pull out of Toulon.

(23 Dec.) Vendéans defeated at Savenay.

(25 Dec.) Robespierre's speech on the principles of revolutionary government.

(26 Dec.) The French recapture Landau. The Prussian army routed at Weissenburg.

(30 Dec.) The Festival of Victory.

1794

(12 Jan.) Arrest of Fabre d'Eglantine.

(27 Jan.) The Convention decrees the appointment of teachers of the French language in regions where French is not the native language.

(4 Feb.) Slavery abolished in the French colonies.

(5 Feb.) Robespierre speaks on the principle of political morality.

(21 Feb.) Revision of the Maximum price control policy.

(26 Feb.–3 Mar.) The Laws of the Ventôse allowing for the division and distribution of suspects' property among poor and needy patriots.

(4 Mar.) Insurrection attempt at the Cordeliers Club.

(14 Mar.) Hébertist extremists attempt to organize a *sansculotte* rising against the Convention but are prevented.

(24 Mar.) Hébertists arrested and executed.

(30 Mar.) Danton arrested.

(5 Apr.) Dantonists executed.

(27 Apr.) The Police Law of 27 Germinal.

(7 May) Robespierre introduces the worship of the Supreme Being.

(18 May) Battle of Tourcoing. The Allies routed in Belgium.

(23–24 May) Attempts to assassinate Robespierre.

(1 June) 'The Glorious First of June'. Howe defeats the French fleet off Ushant.

(8 June) Festival of the Supreme Being.

(10 June) The Law of 22 Prairial speeds up the work of the Revolutionary Tribunal by removing prisoners' safeguards.

(26 June) Battle of Fleurus. The French invade Belgium, Coburg is routed and the British withdraw.

(23 July) The Commune imposes a new scale of wage regulations.

(26 July) In his last speech Robespierre calls for a purge.

(27 July) The '9th Thermidor'. Robespierre and his followers denounced. The Convention abolishes the Commune of Paris.

(28 July) Robespierre and 115 others executed.

(30–31 July) Reorganization of the Committee of Public Safety.

(13 Aug.) The Revolutionary Tribunal is reorganized and most people are acquitted. Repeal of the Law of 22 Prairial.

(18 Sept.) The State withdraws financial support of all forms of religious worship.

(Oct.–Jan. 1795) Holland retaken; gains made against both Austria and Prussia.

(12 Nov.) Closing of the Jacobin Club ordered by the Convention.

(21 Dec.) The sale of the property of the friends of émigrés ceases.

(24 Dec.) Abolition of the Maximum.

1795

(21 Feb.) Decree providing for freedom of worship and the separation of church and state.

(1 Apr.) Day of 12 Germinal. Parisian sansculottes invade the Convention demanding 'bread and the Constitution of 1793'. Nothing concrete is achieved due to a lack of leadership.

(5 Apr.) Peace Treaty with Prussia made at Basle.

(10 Apr.) The National Guard reorganized as a middle-class force.

(16 May) Peace with Holland. France recognizes the 'Batavian Republic'.

(20 May) The Rising of 1 Prairial. The Paris sansculottes invade the Convention, again repeating the demands of 12 Germinal.

(23 May) The army disarms the Paris sections.

(May–June) 'White Terror' in the South during which Royalists murder many former Jacobins.

(8 June) The captive Louis XVII dies; the Count of France becomes Louis XVIII.

(21 July) Hoche destroys the émigré force at Quiberon.

(22 July) Peace made with Spain, by which France gives up conquests and Spain cedes half of San Domingo to France.

(22 Aug.) The Constitution of Year III marks a return to a restricted electorate based on the payment of taxes.

(31 Aug.) The decree of 13 Fructidor empowers the Convention to fill any unfilled seats in the Legislative Assembly (as a result of Deputies being elected for more than one constituency).

(5 Oct.) The Rising of 13 Vendémiaire. The army is used to stop the insurgents as they march on the Tuileries.

THE DIRECTORY

(26 Oct.) The Convention dissolved and replaced by the Directory.

1796

(11 Mar.) Napoleon leaves Paris to take control of the Army of Italy.

(11 Apr.) Mandats issued in place of assignats, but soon fall to 1 per cent of their face value.

(11–14 Apr.) Napoleon breaks through Austrian front in Italy.

(28 Apr.) Armistice of Cherasco with Sardinia.

(May) Conspiracy of Babeuf.

(10 May) French victory at Lodi. Napoleon crosses River Adda.

(15–17 Nov.) French victory at Arcola, near Mantua.

1797

(14 Jan.) French under Napoleon win victory at Rivoli.

(30 Jan.) Conspiracy of the Royalist Abbé Brottier suppressed.

(12 Apr.) Napoleon renews offensive in Italy.

(18 Apr.) Napoleon agrees preliminaries of peace at Loeben with Austria.

(4 Sept.) *Coup d'état* of 18 Fructidor; Legislative Assembly is purged.

(30 Sept.) The 'bankruptcy of the two thirds'. This leads to two-thirds of the public debt being cancelled and bonds, which are soon to be of no value, are issued instead.

(17 Oct.) Treaty of Campo Formio concluded with Austria.

1798

(15 Feb.) Proclamation of the Roman Republic.

(12 Apr.) Proclamation of the Helvetic Republic. The Directory decides to authorize an expedition to Egypt rather than England.

(11 May) *Coup d'état* of 22 Floréal; results in a purge of the Legislature.

(21 July) Napoleon's victory at the Battle of the Pyramids.

(1 Aug.) Nelson destroys the French fleet at the battle of the Nile (Aboukir Bay).

(5 Sept.) Law on Conscription passed.

1799

(26 Jan.) Proclamation of a satellite republic at Naples.

(12 Mar.) France declares war on Austria.

(29 Apr.) Russians enter Milan; during the summer successive Austrian and Russian victories all but end French influence in Italy except for a besieged garrison at Genoa.

(18 June) *Coup d'état* of 30 Prairial.

(25–27 Sept.) Russians defeated and retreat in Switzerland.

(9–10 Nov.) *Coup d'état* of Brumaire.

THE REVOLUTIONARY CALENDAR

After the fall of the Bastille, the year 1789 was known as the 1st Year of Liberty. When royalty was abolished in France on 21 September 1792, the 4th Year of

Liberty became the 1st Year of the Republic, the two terms sometimes being used concurrently. When the Revolutionary Calendar was adopted in October 1793, its effect was retrospective to the first anniversary of the abolition of royalty, so that 22 September 1793 became the 1st day of the month of Vendémiaire of the Year II of the Republic. Thereafter the months of the Year II ran as follows:

Vendémiaire	1–30 the month of vintage	= 22 Sept.–21 Oct.
Brumaire	1–30 the month of fog	= 22 Oct.–20 Nov.
Frimaire	1–30 the month of frost	= 21 Nov.–20 Dec.
Nivôse	1–30 the month of snow	= 21 Dec.–19 Jan.
Pluviôse	1–30 the month of rain	= 20 Jan.–18 Feb.
Ventôse	1–30 the month of wind	= 19 Feb.–20 Mar.
Germinal	1–30 the month of budding	= 21 Mar.–19 Apr.
Floréal	1–30 the month of flowers	= 20 Apr.–19 May
Prairial	1–30 the month of meadows	= 20 May–18 June
Messidor	1–30 the month of harvest	= 19 June–18 July
Thermidor	1–30 the month of heat	= 19 July–17 Aug.
Fructidor	1–30 the month of fruit	= 18 Aug.–16 Sept.

17–21 September inclusive: Sansculottides – days of Festival. The Calendar was discarded on 1 January 1806.

NAPOLEON AND FRANCE

1799

(9–10 Nov.) *Coup d'état* of Brumaire. Bonaparte gains power.
(24 Dec.) Constitution of Year VIII proclaimed, vesting power in Bonaparte as First Consul.

1800

(Jan.) Constitution approved by plebiscite (3,011,007 for, 1,562 against, 4 million abstained).
(13 Feb.) Bank of France founded; from the outset it was linked with the management of government loans and taxation.
(17 Feb.) Local government reorganized in a way which marked a return to centralized government not dissimilar to the *ancien régime.*
(15 June) Victory at Marengo re-established French command of North Italy.
(12 Aug.) Commission appointed to begin work on a uniform Civil Code for France. 84 sessions, 36 of which Bonaparte presided over in person, were held to discuss various drafts of the Code.
(3 Dec.) Moreau defeats the Austrians at Hohenlinden.
(24 Dec.) Chouan plot fails to kill Napoleon and Josephine as they drive to the Opera. Bonaparte uses the plot to suppress former revolutionaries and Jacobins, despite the fact that the plot is the work of Royalists who are duly punished.

1801

(9 Feb.) Peace Treaty of Lunéville concluded with Austria.

(21 Mar.) Deflationary liquidation of public debt.
(June–Sept.) French army in Egypt surrenders to the British.
(15 July) Religious Concordat concluded with Pope Pius VII. Bonaparte sees the value of religion as a tool to strengthen his position in France. The Concordat in conjunction with Bonaparte's Organic Ordinances places the Church under strict state control, but recognizes its position (see p. 265).
(Aug.) Press censorship increased.

1802

(Jan.) Napoleon becomes President of the Cisalpine Republic.
(25 Mar.) Peace of Amiens with Britain.
(18 Apr.) Legislature approves the Concordat.
(26 Apr.) Amnesty for émigrés.
(1 May) Beginning of education reforms with the establishment of 'lycées'.
(19 May) Bonaparte creates the Legion of Honour, establishing a new aristocracy.
(16 Aug.) Bonaparte confirmed as Consul for life by plebiscite.
(24 Aug.) Constitution of Year XII promulgated which strengthens Bonaparte's position.

1803

(Apr.) Loi le Chapelier strengthened.
(14 Apr.) Reorganization of the Bank of France gives it a monopoly of note issue.
(16–18 May) Britain declares war on France; all British subjects in France are jailed.
(2 Dec.) 'The Army of England' concentrates 150,000 men in the Boulogne area for a cross-channel invasion.

1804

(25 Feb.) Establishment of the Excise Bureau.

(21 Mar.) Promulgation of the Civil Code.

(18 May) Napoleon proclaimed Emperor of the French by the Senate. A Plebiscite approves the Constitution of Year XII.

(2 Dec.) Pius VII officiates at crowning of Napoleon as Emperor of the French in Notre Dame.

(21 Dec.) Schoolteachers to be appointed by the State.

1805

(1 Jan.) Press censorship increased.

(26 May) Napoleon becomes King of Italy.

(24 Aug.) 'Army of England' broken up and Imperial forces march into Germany.

(20 Oct.) Austrian surrender at Ulm.

(21 Oct.) Battle of Trafalgar.

(13 Nov.) Napoleon enters Vienna.

(2 Dec.) Austro–Russian defeat at Austerlitz. Austria sues for peace.

(26 Dec.) Peace of Pressburg with Austria gives Napoleon influence over the whole of Italy.

1806

(1 Jan.) Abolition of the Revolutionary Calendar.

(22 Apr.) Bank of France put under State control.

(May) Imperial University proposed.

(12 July) Confederation of the Rhine established.

(Aug.) Senatus-consultum allows Napoleon to grant hereditary fiefs. Code of Civil Procedure, largely a re-enactment of earlier Ordinances, maintained the principle that conciliation must be attempted before recourse to law courts.

(15 Sept.) Britain and Russia joined by Prussia against France.

(14 Oct.) Prussia defeated at Jena-Auerstadt.

(27 Oct.) Napoleon enters Berlin.

(21 Nov.) Establishment of the Continental System by the Berlin Decrees.

1807

(July) Theatres severely censored.

(7–9 July) Treaty of Tilsit between France, Russia and Prussia.

(17 Dec.) The Milan Decrees strengthen the Continental System.

1808

(17 Mar.) Formal establishment of new Imperial University.

(2 May) Rising against the French in Madrid.

(Aug.) British forces land in Portugal.

(Sept.) Decrees of the Imperial University enforced. The Code of Criminal Procedure passed.

1809

(Spring) Austria joins Britain against France.

(13 May) The French occupy Vienna.

(17 May) Breach in relations between Pius VII and Bonaparte when Papal States annexed (see p. 265).

(11 June) Napoleon excommunicated.

(6 July) Austrians defeated at Wagram. Orders issued for the Pope's arrest: Pius VII imprisoned at Savona.

(14 Oct.) Austria signs the Peace of Vienna by which Illyria (i.e. Carinthia, Trieste) was ceded to France.

(13 Dec.) Napoleon seeks the Tsar's sister's hand in marriage.

(16 Dec.) Napoleon divorces Josephine as they have no son.

1810

(9–18 Feb.) Napoleon asks for the hand of Archduchess Marie Louise of Austria.

(Apr.) Penal Code decreed.

(2 Apr.) Marriage of Napoleon and Marie Louise.

(9 July) Holland annexed by France.

(31 Dec.) Russia breaks the Continental System by authorizing trade with Britain. Press censorship increased.

1811

(Spring) French driven out of Portugal.

(Autumn) Preparations made for Russian campaign.

(Sept.) Austro–Prussian promise to aid Napoleon against Russia.

(17 Sept.) The press severely suppressed and the three remaining Paris newspapers confiscated.

1812

(24 June) Napoleon approves the Russian campaign.

(Summer) French defeats in Peninsular battles.

(Aug.–Sept.) Indecisive French victories at Smolensk and Borodino.

(14 Sept.) Napoleon enters Moscow.

(19 Oct.) The French retreat begins.

(14 Dec.) The French campaign in Russia ends as last troops cross the Niemen.

(18 Dec.) Napoleon returns to France to deal with abortive *coup d'état.*

1813

(10 Jan.) Napoleon promised 350,000 more conscripts by the Senate.

(25 Jan.) Pius VII forced into signing a new Concordat.

(24 Mar.) The Pope withdraws his signature, though Napoleon does not recognize this action.

(25 Apr.) Napoleon takes command of the French army at Erfurt.

(2 May) Napoleon victorious at Lutzen.

(21 May) French victory at Bautzen.

(21 June) Wellington's victory at Vittoria, causing Joseph to flee to France.

(16–19 Oct.) 'Battle of the Nations' (Leipzig) results in French defeat and withdrawal.

(17 Nov.) Dutch rising against Napoleon under the Prince of Orange.

(Winter) The Allies enter France.

1814

(Jan.) The Pope freed and restored.

(30–31 Mar.) Fall of Paris.

(3 Apr.) Napoleon deposed by the Senate.

(6 Apr.) Napoleon abdicates in favour of his son.

(3 May) Napoleon lands in Elba.

(1 Nov.) First meeting at Vienna.

1815

(1 Mar.) Napoleon begins 'The Hundred Days' when he returns to France.

(20 Mar.) Napoleon reoccupies the Tuileries. He secures the support of most of his former ministers, including Davout as Minister of War, Carnot as Minister of the Interior, and Fouché as Minister of Police.

(23 Apr.) 'L'Acte Additionel' re-enacts the Charter established under Louis XVIII,* but makes Chamber of Peers hereditary and abolishes press censorship. Lafayette, the Liberal leader, demands a meeting of the Chambers in early June.

(1 June) Napoleon takes oath of fidelity to the Constitution at the Champs de Mars.

(12 June) Napoleon takes command of the French army seeking separate swift victories against Britain and Prussia in Belgium.

(16 June) Napoleon defeats the Prussians at Ligny; British held at Quatre Bras.

(18 June) Waterloo. Napoleon defeated.

(21 June) The Chambers refuse to co-operate with Napoleon on his return to Paris.

(22 June) Napoleon abdicates.

(17 July) Napoleon surrenders to the British.

(17 Oct.) Napoleon arrives at St Helena.

1821

(21 May) Napoleon dies.

*Note: Louis's Constitutional Charter was issued on 4 June 1814, establishing an elected Chamber of Deputies and a Chamber of Peers nominated by the King. Liberty of worship and the press granted, 'careers open to talent', and land sales since 1792 recognized.

THE FRENCH REVOLUTION
AND EUROPE

1789

(14 July) Storming of the Bastille.

1790

(Feb.) Archbishop of Alsace and local princes appeal for the protection of the Imperial Diet against loss of feudal privileges by French decree of 4 August 1789. The Electors of Cologne, Treves, and Mainz give shelter to the French émigrés.

(Oct.) France refuses to support Spain in war against Britain over the Nootka Sound incident in accordance with the Family Compact of 1761. The Assembly replaces the dynastic Family Compact by a national treaty for mutual defence.

1791

(6 July) Leopold II of Austria issues circular inviting rulers of Europe to demand release of Louis XVI and to intervene if Royal Family harmed.

(27 Aug.) Leopold II and Frederick William II issue Declaration of Pilnitz, promising armed intervention in France if other powers will co-operate.

(Sept.) The French Assembly votes for the incorporation in France of Avignon and the Venaissin. In November French troops take control of the area.

(9 Nov.) The Assembly votes that all émigrés must return to France on pain of death.

(14 Dec.) French send an army of 150,000 men to the frontier.

1792

(25 Jan.) French Assembly demands that Leopold renounce the treaty with Prussia and disperse the émigré army.

(7 Feb.) Leopold II and Frederick William II sign Treaty of Berlin, each guaranteeing the other's territories and agreeing mutual support in the event of French declaration of war.

(20 Apr.) France declares war on Austria.

(24 July) Prussia declares war on France.

(23 Aug.) Prussians take Longwy and then Verdun (2 Sept.).

(20 Sept.) At battle of Valmy, French revolutionary armies halt Prussian advance on Paris. French seize Nice and Savoy.

(6 Nov.) Austrians defeated at Jemappes, French enter Brussels (14th).

(19 Nov.) Declaration of Fraternity. The French Convention offers its support to assist any people against their rulers. They also proclaim the Scheldt an open river in defiance of existing treaties. Widespread alarm expressed in Britain, Austria and Russia.

1793

(21 Jan.) Execution of Louis XVI.

(23 Jan.) Second Partition of Poland by Russia and Prussia.

(26 Jan.) Belgian army incorporated into that of France.

(1 Feb.) France declares war on Britain and Holland.

(7 Mar.) France declares war on Spain. First Coalition (see note on p. 62) formed, including

Great Britain, Prussia, Austria, Spain and Holland.

(18 Mar.) Austrians defeat the French at Neerwinden in The Netherlands. The French commander, Dumouriez, goes over to the Austrians (5 Apr.).

(23 July) Prussians take Mainz.

(27 Aug.) Admiral Hood lands forces to support counter-revolutionaries in Toulon. French open siege of Toulon (7 Sept.).

(8 Sept.) French defeat allied army threatening Dunkirk at Hoondschoote. Sardinian army driven out of Savoy.

(15–16 Oct.) Jourdan defeats Austrian army at Wattignies, relieving immediate threat to Paris.

(18 Dec.) British evacuate Toulon which falls to the French (19th).

(26 Dec.) Hoche defeats the Prussians at Weissenburg.

1794

(18 May) Austrians and British defeated at Tourcoing, rendering renewed advance on Paris impossible.

(1 June) Admiral Howe defeats French off Brest in engagement known as 'the Glorious First of June', but important grain convoy safely arrives at Brest.

(25 June) Jourdan routs the Austrians at Fleurus, forcing the British to withdraw into Holland and the Austrians to the Rhine.

(Sept.) French defeated at Clairfait, near Mainz.

(Oct.) French overrun Brabant and invade Holland. Jourdan takes Cologne, Andernach and Coblenz.

(31 Dec.) Armistice signed with Austrians.

1795

(Jan.) French enter Amsterdam.

(5 Apr.) Treaty of Basle signed between France and Prussia. Prussia agrees to become neutral and the French agree to regard the states of northern Germany as neutral.

(16 May) Treaty of Basle signed between Holland and France. The Dutch agree to abolish the Stadtholderate and set up the Batavian Republic under French domination.

(21 June) Allies and émigrés land at Quiberon.

(22 July) Treaty of Basle with Spain. France gives up her Spanish conquests but is ceded half of San Domingo.

(24 Oct.) Third Partition of Poland by Prussia, Austria and Russia shares out last independent areas of Poland.

1796

(27 Mar.) Bonaparte appointed to command of army of Italy.

(12–13 Apr.) Bonaparte defeats the Sardinian army at the battles of Montenotte, Dego and Millesimo, and advances on Turin.

(28 Apr.) By Armistice of Cherasco, Victor Amadeus III of Sardinia agrees to its neutrality and surrenders fortresses commanding the Alpine passes. By a subsequent treaty Nice and Savoy are given up.

(10 May) Bonaparte, after crossing the River Po, defeats the Austrians at Lodi and enters Milan (15th).

(6 June) King of Naples makes an armistice with Napoleon.

(23 June) Napoleon signs an armistice with Pius VI, in return for 20,000,000 francs and many works of art.

(2 Aug.) Napoleon defeats Austrians at Lonato and at Castiglione (5th).

(5 Aug.) Secret treaty of Prussia and France agrees to extension of French frontier to the Rhine in return for the Bishopric of Munster.

(19 Aug.) France signs Treaty of Ildefonso with Spain.

(19 Sept.) Archduke Charles of Austria defeats Jourdan at Altenkirchen on the Rhine.

(8 Oct.) Spain declares war on Britain.

(15–17 Nov.) Bonaparte defeats Austrians at Arcola.

(16 Nov.) Pro-French Tsar Paul becomes Tsar.

(Dec.) Peace negotiations between Britain and France collapse.

(16 Dec.) General Hoche sails with expeditionary force to Ireland, but landing at Bantry Bay fails (21–27 Dec.).

1797

(14 Jan.) Napoleon defeats Austrian army at Rivoli, and defeats a relieving force sent to Mantua (16th).

(2 Feb.) Mantua surrendered to Napoleon, giving France control of Lombardy.

(14 Feb.) At Battle of Cape St Vincent, British under Admiral Jervis defeat a Spanish fleet.

(19 Feb.) At Treaty of Tolentino Pius VI agrees to cede Bologna, Ferrara and the Romagna to France and to pay 30,000,000 francs to the Directory immediately and a total of 300,000,000.

(22–24 Feb.) French landing force at Fishguard in Pembrokeshire is quickly forced to surrender.

(16 Apr.) British fleet at Spithead mutiny. (Ends 5 May)

(17 Apr.) Napoleon signs preliminaries of peace with Archduke Charles at Leoben by which Austria accepts the Rhine as the boundary of France, including Belgium as French. Austria gives up Milan in return for Venice. A congress to be held at Rastadt to make peace.

(12 May) Beginning of mutiny among British fleet at the Nore; suppressed by 13 June and leaders executed.

(16 May) Napoleon occupies Venice. By Treaty of Milan the Grand Council is abolished and a new democratic council established; Venice to pay 6,000,000 francs as well as surrender works of art and manuscripts.

(15 June) Ligurian Republic established in Genoa and neighbourhood.

(28 June) French occupy the Ionian Isles.

(9 July) Cisalpine Republic established in Lombardy.

(11 Oct.) Dutch fleet carrying aid and 15,000 troops to the Irish defeated by Admiral Duncan off Texel.

(16 Oct.) Napoleon appointed to command the 'Army of England'.

(17 Oct.) Treaty of Campo Formio between France and Austria. The treaty follows from the preliminaries signed at Leoben. The Rhine frontier of France is recognized and the independence of the Cisalpine Republic, including Milan. Austria receives Venice and Venetian territory in Istria and Dalmatia. The Stadtholder of Holland and the Duke of Modena receive territory in Germany. Secret clauses provide for Austria to evacuate Mainz and Rhine fortresses and for France to support the claim of Austria to Bavaria and the Archbishopric of Salzburg.

(29 Dec.) The French enter Mainz.

1798

(15 Feb.) Roman Republic proclaimed and acknowledged by France.

(20 Feb.) Pius VI deported to France.

(Mar.) French seize Berne and exact 23,000,000 francs indemnity from Switzerland.

(5 Mar.) Directory abandons plans for invasion of England.

(12 Apr.) Napoleon appointed to command the 'Army of the Orient'. Annexation of Geneva and creation of Helvetic Republic.

(May–July) Irish rebellion. Main Irish force defeated in Wexford (June) and rebellion suppressed.

(19 May) Napoleon sails from Toulon for Egypt.

(12 June) Surrender of Malta to Napoleon.

(1–2 July) Army of Orient lands in Egypt and takes Alexandria.

(3 July) French occupy Turin.

(21 July) Napoleon defeats Mamelukes at the Battle of the Pyramids and enters Cairo (25th).

(1–2 Aug.) Nelson destroys French fleet at the Battle of the Nile in Aboukir Bay.

(23 Aug.) French force under Humbert lands in north-west Ireland. Surrenders on 8 Sept.

(29 Nov.) Ferdinand of Naples takes Rome with Neapolitan troops commanded by Austrian General Mack.

(4 Dec.) France declares war on Kingdom of Naples.

(6–13 Dec.) Mack defeated by French troops and Ferdinand flees from Rome.

(21 Dec.) Royal Family flee from Naples.

(29 Dec.) Second Coalition formed of Great Britain, Austria, Russia, Naples and Portugal.

1799

(23 Jan.) French enter Naples and proclaim the Parthenopean Republic.

(1 Mar.) War breaks out between the Second Coalition and France.

(25 Mar.) Austrian Archduke defeats Jourdan's invasion of Germany at Stockach.

(5 Apr.) Austrians defeat the French at Magnano in Northern Italy.

(27 Apr.) Russian army under Suvorov defeats the French under Moreau at Cassano in Northern Italy and enters Milan (29th).

(17–19 June) Suvorov defeats French army from Naples at Trebbia.

(30 July) Mantua surrendered by the French.

(Aug.) British force under Abercromby lands in Holland and seizes the Dutch fleet in the Texel.

(15 Aug.) Suvorov defeats Joubert at Novi.

(23 Aug.) Napoleon sails for France.

(19 Sept.) Allied force of British and Russians under the Duke of York wins minor victory at Alkmaar.

(26 Sept.) Masséna defeats a Russian army near Zurich but Suvorov, the commander, withdraws his troops in good order from Switzerland.

(18 Oct.) Duke of York and British forces evacuate Holland after the Convention of Alkmaar.

(4 Nov.) Austrians defeat the French at Cenola and drive them back into France. Collapse of the Italian Republics.

(9–10 Nov.) *Coup d'état* of Brumaire in Paris.

(14 Dec.) Napoleon becomes First Consul.

1800

(Apr.) Moreau leads French army across the Rhine and after a series of victories drives the Austrians back to Ulm.

(15 Apr.) Napoleon begins crossing of the Alps by the St Bernard Pass.

(20 Apr.) Genoa besieged by the Austrians.

(4 June) Fall of Genoa to the Austrians.

(14 June) Napoleon defeats the Austrians at Marengo.

(19 June) Following their defeat at Marengo the Austrians sign the Convention of Alessandria, giving Genoa, Piedmont and Milan to France.

(20 June) Austria makes a treaty with Britain to continue the war with the assistance of subsidies and the promise of part of Piedmont.

(15 July) Armistice between Austria and France.

(5 Sept.) The British take Malta.

(5 Nov.) Austro–French hostilities resume. French under Brune take Verona and Treviso. (Dec.) French army under Macdonald invades the Tyrol. Brune and Macdonald march on Vienna.

(3 Dec.) Moreau defeats Austrians at Hohenlinden and marches on Vienna.

(18 Dec.) Formation of Second Armed Neutrality by the Baltic powers (Russia, Sweden and Denmark and, later, Prussia) to resist British interference with their trade.

1801

(15 Jan.) Franco–Austrian Armistice at Treviso. France and Austria sign Peace of Lunéville. Austria cedes to France all territory west of the Rhine, including Belgium and Luxembourg, and recognizes the independence of the Cisalpine, Ligurian, Batavian and Helvetic Republics. The Adige is to be the boundary between French and Austrian possessions in Northern Italy. The Duke of Parma is to rule Tuscany, now known as the Kingdom of Etruria. The ex-Duke of Tuscany and dispossessed German Princes are to receive compensation in Germany at France's discretion.

(23 Mar.) Assassination of Tsar Paul I; accession of Alexander I.

(2 Apr.) At Battle of Copenhagen the British fleet attacks the Danish fleet anchored off Copenhagen in an attempt to force them out of the League of Armed Neutrality.

(2 Aug.) Duke of Parma proclaimed King of Etruria.

(Sept.) Batavian Republic given a new constitution, making it virtually a puppet state of France.

(1 Oct.) Preliminaries of peace between Britain and France signed at Amiens.

1802

(Jan.) Napoleon becomes President of the Cisalpine Republic.

(25 Mar.) Peace of Amiens: (i) Great Britain to keep Ceylon and Trinidad, but restore other colonies to France, Spain and Holland; (ii) France agrees to evacuate Naples and the Papal States and restore all its territory to Portugal; (iii) Malta is to be restored to the Knights of St John; (iv) The Ionian Isles are recognized as a republic; (v) Egypt is to revert to the Ottoman Empire.

(29 June) New Genoese constitution makes city subservient to Napoleon.

(26 Aug.) France annexes Elba.

(21 Sept.) Napoleon incorporates Piedmont into the French Republic.

(15 Oct.) Napoleon intervenes in Switzerland in civil war between the towns and the forest cantons as 'Mediator of the Helvetic League'.

1803

(19 Feb.) French Act of Mediation in Switzerland sets up a new constitution, weakening the federal government and giving greater authority to the individual cantons.

(18 May) Britain declares war on France. Imminence of invasion leads to the enrolment of over a quarter of a million volunteers.

(1 June) French occupy Hanover.

(15 June) Camp at Boulogne established for 'Army of England'.

(July) Emmett's rebellion in Ireland suppressed.

(23 Aug) Further camps for the invasion of England formed at St Omer and Bruges and invasion flotillas assembled to await command of the Channel.

(9 Oct.) Franco–Spanish alliance formed.

1804

(21 Mar.) Duc d'Enghien kidnapped by French soldiers from the neutral state of Baden and executed.

(10 May) Pitt returns as Prime Minister of Britain.

(18 May) Napoleon assumes the title of Emperor.

(Sept.) Alexander I breaks off negotiations with France in protest at occupation of Hanover and execution of the Duc d'Enghien.

(6 Nov.) Francis II of Austria makes a secret treaty with Russia to resist further French aggression in Italy.

1805

(Mar.) 'Army of England' waits in readiness to invade, pending Villeneuve's arrival.

(11 Apr.) Anglo–Russian alliance signed in St Petersburg aiming to: (i) expel the French from Hanover, northern Germany and Italy; (ii) protect the independence of Holland, Switzerland and Naples; (iii) restore Piedmont to the Kingdom of Sardinia; (iv) raise an army of half a million men against France. Britain to provide subsidies for other members of the anti-French coalition.

(26 May) Napoleon crowns himself King of Italy.

(4 June) France annexes Genoa.

(July) Naples forced to sign new treaty with France.

(9 Aug.) Third Coalition. Austria joins the Third Coalition with Britain, Russia and Sweden in return for a subsidy of £3,000,000.

(24 Aug.) Bavaria signs treaty with Napoleon.

(25 Aug.) Major units of the French army begin to leave the camp at Boulogne for a continental campaign against the Third Coalition.

(3 Sept.) Napoleon and last elements of the 'Army of England' leave Boulogne.

(8 Sept.) Austrian army under Mack invades Bavaria and takes up position near Ulm.

(26 Sept.) Napoleon's *Grande Armée* crosses the Rhine.

(7 Oct.) French forces cross the Danube cutting Mack off from Vienna.

(14 Oct.) Marshal Ney defeats Mack's attempt to escape encirclement at Elchingen.

(20 Oct.) Surrender of Mack at Ulm with 25,000 troops.

(21 Oct.) Nelson defeats the Franco–Spanish fleet under Villeneuve at Trafalgar, inflicting a decisive blow to French sea-power and virtually eliminating any realistic hope of invading Britain, although the theoretical possibility remains.

(29 Oct.) Archduke Charles defeats Masséna at Caldiero in Northern Italy.

(3 Nov.) Treaty of Potsdam between Russia and Prussia, agreeing that unless Napoleon will make terms on the basis of the Treaty of Lunéville Prussia will join the Third Coalition. Prussia's action is forestalled by the Battle of Austerlitz (2 Dec.).

(14 Nov.) Napoleon enters Vienna.

(2 Dec.) At Battle of Austerlitz Napoleon crushingly defeats combined Austro–Russian army, shattering the Third Coalition.

(4 Dec.) Austria makes an armistice with the French. Russians withdraw to their frontier. Prussia, on news of Austerlitz, refuses to join the war against Napoleon. Russian, British and Swedish forces withdraw from Pomerania. British and Russian forces leave Naples.

(15 Dec.) Prussia signs Treaty of Schoenbrunn with France. Prussia receives Hanover, but cedes Cleves and Neuchâtel to France and Ansbach to Bavaria.

(26 Dec.) Peace of Pressburg signed: (i) Austria cedes Venetia to the Napoleonic Kingdom of Italy; (ii) Austria recognizes the Electors of Württemberg and Bavaria as independent Kings and the Elector of Baden as Grand Duke; (iii) Austria cedes the Tyrol to Bavaria and its Swabian territory is divided between Baden and Württemberg.

(27 Dec.) Napoleon deposes Ferdinand of Naples who flees to Sicily.

1806

(23 Jan.) Death of William Pitt.

(30 Mar.) Joseph Bonaparte created King of Naples.

(1 Apr.) Murat made Grand Duke of Berg and Cleves.

(16 May) British blockade of French ports begins.

(5 June) Napoleon makes his brother Louis, King of Holland.

(July) Negotiations between Britain and France reveal to Prussia that France is prepared to return Hanover to Britain.

(4 July) General Stuart leads a British army to victory over the French at Maida in Calabria, but then withdraws. The French conquer southern Italy.

(12 July) Napoleon creates the Confederation of the Rhine with himself as 'Protector'. The leading figures are the Kings of Bavaria and Württemberg, the Grand Duke of Baden and the Landgrave of Hesse. Other smaller rulers are 'mediatized', passing under the authority of the Princes in whose states their lands are situated. The Confederation declares itself separated from the Empire, makes an alliance with France and agrees to supply 63,000 men to serve in the French armies.

(18 July) Masséna captures Gaeta in Italy.

(20 July) Franco–Russian peace treaty.

(6 Aug.) Abolition of the Holy Roman Empire.

(9 Aug.) The Prussian army mobilizes.

(24 Aug.) Tsar Alexander refuses to ratify peace with France.

(26 Sept.) Prussia sends an ultimatum to France demanding the immediate withdrawal of French armies across the Rhine and Napoleon's assent to a North German Confederacy under Prussian control.

(7 Oct.) French troops invade Saxony.

(8 Oct.) Prussia declares war.

(14 Oct.) Battles of Jena and Auerstadt. In separate engagements Marshal Davout defeats a Prussian army under Brunswick at Auerstadt, while Napoleon routs an army under Hohenlohe at Jena.

(27 Oct.) Napoleon enters Berlin.

(7 Nov.) Lübeck stormed by the French and Blücher surrenders. By the 11th, all major Prussian fortresses, including Spandau, Stettin, Kustrin and Magdeburg are in French hands.

(21 Nov.) Promulgation of the Berlin Decrees inaugurates the Continental System. They declare the British Isles to be in a state of blockade, order the confiscation of British goods in French territory and the imprisonment of British subjects, and close all ports in French or Allied territory to ships coming from Britain or British colonies.

(27 Nov.) Napoleon enters the city of Poznan.

(28 Nov.) Marshal Murat enters Warsaw, abandoned by the Prussians.

(10 Dec.) Saxony signs the Treaty of Posen with France; its Elector becomes King of Saxony and joins the Confederation of the Rhine.

(18 Dec.) Napoleon enters Warsaw.

(23 Dec.) Napoleon goes from Warsaw towards Golymin and Pultusk, where he waged an indecisive, bloody battle against a Russian army headed by General Bennigsen.

1807

(3 Jan.) Napoleon returns to Warsaw where he transfers his headquarters.

(7 Jan.) British promulgate an Order in Council in retaliation for the Berlin Decrees, making neutrals liable to confiscation of ships and cargo if they trade between ports from which British ships are excluded.

(25 Jan.) By the Warsaw Decree Napoleon orders the seizure of all British and colonial goods in the Hanse towns. In retaliation, Britain tightens its blockade of north German ports.

(8 Feb.) Battle of Eylau between Napoleon and Russian army under Bennigsen forces the Russians to retire.

(18 Mar.) Danzig besieged by French.

(1 Apr.) Napoleon compels Prussia to close its ports and those of Hanover to British ships.

(26 Apr.) Convention of Bartenstein signed between Russia and Prussia, and later joined by Sweden and Great Britain, to continue the war against Napoleon.

(27 May) Fall of Danzig to French.

(14 June) Napoleon defeats Russians at Friedland and forces them back across the Nieman.

(25 June) Napoleon and Alexander meet at the River Nieman.

(27 June) Britain and Sweden conclude an alliance.

(7–9 July) Treaty of Tilsit signed between Russia and France: (i) Prussia loses her territory west of the Elbe which is to be included in a Kingdom of Westphalia, with Napoleon's brother Jerome as King; (ii) Prussia's Polish territories are given to the King of Saxony, along with the southern part of the West Prussian duchy of Warsaw; (iii) Russia cedes to France the Ionian Isles and the district of Cattaro in Dalmatia, but receives Bialystock; (iv) Alexander promises to mediate between France and Great Britain and recognizes the French puppet states in Italy, Holland and Germany; (v) Danzig is to remain a free port but Prussian ports are to be closed to British commerce; (vi) Napoleon promises not to restore the independence of Poland. By a secret treaty: (i) Napoleon agrees to support Alexander taking Finland from Sweden and Moldavia and Wallachia from Turkey; French help is promised for Russia's claim to the Danubian Principalities; (ii) if Britain refuses to come to terms, Alexander agrees to support Napoleon against her and force Denmark, Sweden and Portugal to make war on her.

(7–9 July) Treaty of Tilsit between France and Prussia: (i) Prussia cedes to Napoleon for disposal all lands between the Rhine and the Elbe; (ii) cedes to Saxony the circle of Cottbus; (iii) cedes for the creation of a Duchy of Warsaw all lands taken from Poland since 1772; (iv) Prussia recognizes the sovereignty of the three brothers of Napoleon; (v) all Prussian ports and territories are closed to British ships and trade; (vi) Prussia agrees to limit her army to 42,000 men. Prussia has lost half her territory.

(12 July) By the Treaty of Königsberg it is agreed that Prussia's fortresses will only be evacuated and restored when Prussia has paid her arrears of war indemnities: these are set at 120 million francs by the French (raised to 140 million in 1808). Until that time, the

reduced state of Prussia has to support 150,000 French troops.

(19 July) Grand Duchy of Warsaw set up.

(16 Aug.–7 Sept.) To forestall Denmark's entry into the war, the British send a fleet and 18,000 troops to Copenhagen, bombard the city (2–5 Sept.) and force the surrender of the Danish fleet (7 Sept.) into British hands.

(20 Aug.) French take Stralsund from the Swedes.

(4 Oct.) Baron von Stein becomes Minister of Home Affairs in Prussia and helps to superintend an era of civil and military reform.

(9 Oct.) Edict of Emancipation in Prussia. Serfdom and feudal dues abolished, although lords retain their judicial rights over tenants. Legal class distinctions are abolished and all occupations opened.

(27 Oct.) Secret Treaty of Fontainebleau between France and Spain, allowing French troops to pass through Spain on their way to Portugal and agreeing the division of Portugal.

(11 and 25 Nov.) Further British Order in Council declares that any port from which British goods are excluded is in a state of blockade and declares unlawful all trade in articles produced by excluding countries; requires neutrals sailing to Europe to call at a British port; encourages neutral vessels to land goods in England and to re-export on favourable terms.

(30 Nov.) French occupy Lisbon.

(Dec.) French invade Spain.

(17 Dec.) Second Milan Decree by the French declares that any neutral ship diverting its course from a French to a British port should be liable to capture.

1808

(Feb.) Austria accepts the Continental System.

(20 Feb.) Marshal Murat appointed Napoleon's 'Lieutenant' in Spain.

(29 Feb.) French seize Barcelona.

(19 Mar.) Rising in Aranjuez in Spain. Charles IV resigns in favour of his son Ferdinand who betrays popular hopes by returning to Madrid and awaiting the arrival of the French.

(2 May) Rising in Madrid against the French suppressed.

(6 May) Ferdinand surrenders the throne to Charles IV who abdicates.

(6 June) Napoleon proclaims Joseph Bonaparte King of Spain.

(8 June) Cordoba taken by French troops.

(9 June) Prussia creates national *Landwehr* of all citizens.

(15 June) Spanish government accepts Joseph Bonaparte as King of Spain.

(16 June) Siege of Saragossa.

(13 July) Spanish defeat at Medina del Rio Seco.

(20 July) French army under Dupont forced to surrender by Castaños at Baylen. This reverse causes Joseph to flee Madrid (1 Aug.) and the French army to withdraw to the Ebro.

(1–8 Aug.) Arthur Wellesley (the future Duke of Wellington) lands with 9,000 men in Portugal.

(21 Aug.) Wellesley defeats French force under Junot at Vimiero.

(30 Aug.) By Convention of Cintra, Junot allowed to evacuate Portugal with all arms and equipment. Widespread criticism of the Convention in Britain leads to recall of commanders and appointment of Sir John Moore.

(27 Sept.) Congress and Convention of Erfurt between France and Russia. Napoleon is forced to accede to Russian possession of Moldavia and Wallachia and also of Finland. Alexander agrees to make common cause with France if Austria declares war but refuses to support its dismemberment. A joint appeal is sent to George III to reopen peace negotiations but this comes to nothing.

(5 Nov.) Napoleon takes command of the Army of Spain.

(10 Nov.) Soult routs Spanish army at Burgos.

(11 Nov.) Army of Galicia defeated at Espinosa.

(23 Nov.) Armies of Andalusia and Aragon defeated at Tudela.

(4 Dec.) Napoleon recaptures Madrid for Joseph.

(24 Dec.) Moore begins retreat to Corunna.

1809

(16 Jan.) Moore defeats Soult outside Corunna, but is killed. British troops successfully embark.

(24 Jan.) Napoleon leaves Spain for Paris.

(20 Feb.) Saragossa surrenders to the French.

(29 Mar.) Soult captures Oporto.

(9 Apr.) Austria attacks Bavaria.

(10 Apr.) Tyrolese rise against Bavaria under Hofer and take Innsbruck (14th).

(20 Apr.) Napoleon defeats part of Archduke Charles's army at Abensberg and the main body at Eckmuhl.

(26 Apr.) Wellesley lands at Lisbon to command British and Portuguese forces.

(12 May) Wellesley crosses the Douro river and drives Soult out of northern Portugal.

(13 May) Napoleon enters Vienna.

(21–22 May) Austrians worst the French at the Battle of Aspern-Essling.

(3 June) Archduke Ferdinand forced out of Warsaw.

(2 July) Napoleon's forces joined by army of Italy under Beauharnais.

(6 July) Napoleon defeats the Archduke Charles at Wagram, although the Austrians retreat in good order.

(12 July) Armistice of Znaim ends fighting between French and Austrians.

(27–28 July) Wellesley and Cuesta defeat French at Talavera in Spain, but because of failure of Spanish allies retreat into Portugal.

(29 July–30 Sept.) British land 40,000 troops at Walcheren in Holland with aim of capturing Antwerp. Flushing taken (16 Aug.), but advance bogs down and the British evacuate after losing 4,000 men from disease.

(14 Oct.) Treaty of Vienna or Schoenbrunn between France and Austria: (i) Austria gives up the 'Illyrian Provinces' (Trieste, Carniola, Carinthia, Croatia and Dalmatia) to France, cedes Salzburg and much of Upper Austria to Bavaria, and gives most of Western Galicia to the Grand Duchy of Warsaw; (ii) Austria recognizes French authority in Italy, Portugal and Spain; (iii) Austria pays an indemnity to France.

(1 Nov.) Tyrolese under Hofer defeated at Iselberg.

(19 Nov.) Spanish defeated at Ocana and Andalusia overrun.

(11 Dec.) Gerona surrenders to the French.

(13 Dec.) Napoleon unsuccessfully seeks marriage with the Tsar's sister.

(16 Dec.) Napoleon divorces Josephine.

1810

(9 Feb.) Napoleon asks for the hand of Archduchess Marie Louise of Austria.

(11 Feb.) French blockade Spanish fortress of Ciudad Rodrigo.

(21 Feb.) Tyrolese leader Hofer shot by French at Mantua.

(16 Mar.) Louis Napoleon cedes part of Holland to Napoleon.

(2 Apr.) Napoleon marries Marie Louise.

(17 Apr.) Napoleon appoints Masséna to command in Portugal.

(9 July) Napoleon annexes Holland; King Louis resigns.

(10 July) Fall of Ciudad Rodrigo opens way to French invasion of Portugal.

(5 Aug.) Trianon Tariff allows importation of British colonial produce at a tariff of 50 per cent.

(21 Aug.) Bernadotte elected Crown Prince of Sweden.

(15 Sept.) Masséna invades Portugal after taking Almeida.

(27 Sept.) Wellesley (now Wellington) defeats the French at Busaco and retreats behind the defence lines of Torres Vedras (11 Oct.).

(18 and 25 Oct.) Fontainebleau Decrees order that all British manufactured goods found in French territory should be burnt and special tribunals established to try those in breach of the decrees.

(10 Dec.) Napoleon annexes the north-west coast of Germany, including the free city of Lübeck and the Grand Duchy of Oldenburg, territory of the brother-in-law of Alexander I.

(31 Dec.) Tsar Alexander authorizes trade with Britain, thus breaking the Continental blockade.

1811

(5 Mar.) Masséna retreats from lines of Torres Vedras to Ciudad Rodrigo

(4 Apr.) losing 25,000 men in the process.

(11 Mar.) Badajoz falls to Soult.

(20 Mar.) Birth of son to Marie Louise; made King of Rome.

(3–5 May) Wellington defeats Masséna at Fuentes d'Onoro and captures Almeida (11th).

(7 May) Beresford besieges Badajoz, but has to raise siege to defeat relieving force under Soult at Albuera (16th).

(24 May) Siege of Badajoz resumed by Wellington.

(19 June) Wellington forced to abandon siege of Badajoz by advance of superior French army.

(Aug.) Wellington besieges Ciudad Rodrigo but forced to retire by pressure of French army.

(23 Dec.) Napoleon begins military preparations for war with Russia.

(31 Dec.) Tsar Alexander issues decree against French trade.

1812

(8 Jan.) Start of Wellington's second siege of Ciudad Rodrigo.

(10 Jan.) France occupies Swedish Pomerania.

(19 Jan.) Fall of Ciudad Rodrigo to Wellington.

(24 Feb.) Alliance between France and Prussia. Prussia undertakes to supply French armies marching to Russia and to provide 20,000 men.

(10 Mar.) Alliance between France and Austria. France promises to restore the Illyrian Provinces.

(16 Mar.) Wellington besieges Badajoz.

(6 Apr.) Badajoz stormed and taken by Wellington.

(9 Apr.) Russo–Swedish alliance at Treaty of Abo. Sweden agrees to cede Finland to Russia and to supply 30,000 men to co-operate with Russia; Russia agrees to help Sweden to secure Norway.

(8 May) Spanish Cortes at Cadiz proclaims liberal constitution.

(28 May) Russia makes peace with the Ottoman Empire at the Treaty of Bucharest, receiving Bessarabia.

(18 June) Britain and USA go to war over British interference with American shipping and press-ganging.

(24 June) Napoleon crosses the Nieman and begins invasion of Russia.

(28 June) Napoleon enters Vilna, capital of Russian Poland.

(18 July) Britain makes peace with Russia and Sweden and by the Treaty of Orebro Britain promises to subsidize Russia.

(22 July) Wellington defeats French at Salamanca, allowing Wellington to occupy Madrid (12 Aug.) and forcing Soult to evacuate southern Spain.

(18 Aug.) Napoleon enters Smolensk.

(7 Sept.) French and Russians fight indecisive battle of Borodino, but the Russian army is forced to retreat, leaving the road to Moscow open.

(14 Sept.) Napoleon enters Moscow, but Alexander fails to come to terms.

(19 Sept.) Start of the siege of Burgos.

(18 Oct.) Murat defeated by the Russians at Vinkovo. Napoleon leaves Moscow.

(23 Oct.) Conspiracy of General Malet in Paris against Napoleon.

(24 Oct.) Russians defeated at Malo-Yaruslavetz, but Napoleon is forced to retreat along a more northerly route than intended.

(2 Nov.) French reoccupy Madrid.

(27–29 Nov.) French fight their way across the River Beresina.

(5 Dec.) Napoleon leaves the *Grande Armée* on news of the Malet conspiracy.

(13 Dec.) Last French troops cross the Nieman.

(18 Dec.) Napoleon reaches Paris.

(30 Dec.) Commander of Prussian contingent in *Grande Armée,* York, concludes Convention of Tauroggen with Russians by which he agrees to remain neutral and to take no steps to prevent the Russian pursuit of the French.

1813

(Jan.) Stein, on behalf of Alexander I, summons the Estates of East Prussia, who make a general levy of the population against the French.

(10 Jan.) Senate promises Napoleon 350,000 more conscripts.

(25 Jan.) Napoleon and Pope sign a second Concordat.

(3 Feb.) King of Prussia issues an edict calling all Prussians to arms.

(28 Feb.) Treaty of Kalisch between Prussia and Russia, making an alliance against the French. Alexander promises that Prussia will receive back all the territory lost since 1806. An invitation is extended to Austria and Britain to join the alliance. Fourth Coalition begins to form.

(3 Mar.) Treaty between Britain and Sweden. Britain agrees to pay a subsidy to Sweden to enable her to put an army of 30,000 men in the field under Prince Bernadotte. Britain promises not to oppose the union of Norway with Sweden.

(4 Mar.) French abandon Berlin and Russians enter.

(17 Mar.) Prussia declares war on France.

(24 Mar.) Pope withholds his signature from new Concordat.

(27 Mar.) Russians occupy Dresden; flight of the King of Saxony.

(25 Apr.) Napoleon takes command of his army at Erfurt.

(2 May) Napoleon defeats a Russian and Prussian army at Lutzen.

(l8 May) Swedish troops land in Pomerania.

(20 May) Napoleon defeats the Allies at Bautzen.

(4 June) The Allies offer Napoleon an armistice, the Armistice of Pleischwitz, to last until 28 July but renewed until 10 August.

(12 June) The French evacuate Madrid.

(15 June) Britain concludes a subsidy treaty with Prussia and Russia at Reichenbach.

(21 June) Wellington defeats the French at Vittoria; Joseph flees to France.

(27 June) Treaty of Reichenbach. Russia, Prussia and Austria agree that the Grand Duchy of Warsaw and the Confederation of the Rhine should be abolished; that Austria will receive back the Illyrian Provinces; that Prussia will receive the territory she has lost since 1806 and France restore the north German territory taken

in 1810. If France refuses to accept these terms, Austria will declare war.

(15 July–10 Aug.) Congress of Prague: the French representative, Culaincourt, and representatives of the Allies, Metternich and von Humbold, fail to agree terms for peace.

(12 Aug.) Austria declares war on France.

(23 Aug.) Bernadotte defeats the French at Grossberen, saving Berlin from capture.

(25 Aug.) Blücher defeats the French at Katzbach and drives them out of Silesia.

(26–27 Aug.) Napoleon defeats main allied army under Schwarzenberg at Dresden.

(30 Aug.) French defeated by Russians at Kulm, saving Schwarzenberg from pursuit.

(6 Sept.) Ney's thrust at Berlin is defeated at Dennewitz.

(9 Sept.) Austria, Prussia and Russia form an alliance at Teplitz. It agrees: (i) on a firm union and mutual guarantee for their respective territories; (ii) each party to assist each other with at least 60,000 men; (iii) and not to make a separate peace or armistice. Secret articles provide for the restoration of Austria and Prussia to their situation in 1805, including the dissolution of the Confederation of the Rhine and the recognition of the independence of the states of southern and western Germany.

(7 Oct.) British army crosses from Spain into southern France.

(8 Oct.) Treaty of Ried between the Allies and the King of Bavaria who withdraws from the Confederation of the Rhine and agrees to give up the Tyrol to Austria and send a contingent to fight against Napoleon in return for recognition of his sovereign rights.

(16–19 Oct.) The Battle of Leipzig (or 'The Battle of the Nations'). Napoleon, outnumbered and virtually surrounded by four allied armies is defeated and forced to retreat from Leipzig which is stormed on the 19th. Prince Jerome is forced to flee Westphalia and the King of Saxony is captured. Death of Marshal Poniatowski.

(30 Oct.) Napoleon defeats Bavarian army at Hanau which has been attempting to block his retreat to France.

(2 Nov.) Napoleon crosses Rhine into France at Mainz.

(9 Nov.) Allies offer peace terms to Napoleon at Frankfurt, involving the surrender of all French territory beyond the Rhine, Alps and Pyrenees, but keeping Belgium, Nice and Savoy. Napoleon refuses.

(15 Nov.) Dutch rise against French, expelling French officials.

(Nov.–Dec.) Rest of German states of the Confederation of the Rhine join the Allies. A few German cities remain in French control, notably Hamburg.

(21–25 Dec.) Schwarzenberg enters Switzerland.

(31 Dec.) Castlereagh, British foreign secretary, sent to Germany with full powers to give assistance to the Allies. Blücher crosses the Rhine, beginning the invasion of France by the main Allied armies.

1814

(14 Jan.) Peace of Kiel. Following a short winter campaign by Prince Bernadotte against Denmark, Denmark renounces the possession of Norway in favour of Sweden in return for Pomerania and Rugen. Britain restores all Danish possessions except Heligoland.

(29 Jan.) Napoleon defeats Blücher at Brienne.

(1 Feb.) Napoleon defeated at La Rothière, but wins engagements at Champaubert, Montmirail and Vauchamps.

(5 Feb.–19 Mar.) Congress of Chatillon-sur-Seine. The Allies offer Napoleon the possessions of France at her frontiers of 1791. Conference suspended on 10 Feb. – resumes on 17 Feb. Owing to his victory at Montereau (18 Feb.) Napoleon refuses to come to terms.

(1 Mar.) Allies sign Treaty of Chaumont: (i) Great Britain, Austria, Prussia and Russia each agree to provide 150,000 men to defeat Napoleon; (ii) Britain provides a subsidy of £5,000,000 to the Allies; (iii) the Allies each agree not to make a separate peace with Napoleon and continue the war until France is reduced to her boundaries of 1791.

(9 Mar.) Napoleon defeated at Laon.

(12 Mar.) Wellington occupies Bordeaux and raises Bourbon flag.

(20–21 Mar.) Napoleon defeated at Arcis-sur-Aube.

(30 Mar.) Defeat of French forces in suburbs of Paris. Marie Louise flees.

(31 Mar.) Alexander I and Frederick William of Prussia enter Paris. The Senate declares the throne forfeited and sets up a provisional government.

(6 Apr.) Napoleon abdicates in favour of his son (this is rejected on 11 Apr.).

(11 Apr.) At Treaty of Fontainebleau Napoleon renounces for himself and for his son all claims to the French, Italian and Austrian crowns, though retains Imperial title. He receives the Principality of Elba and a pension of 2,000,000 francs. Marie Louise receives the duchies of Parma, Piacenza and Guastalla with sovereign power.

(3 May) Louis XVIII enters Paris. Napoleon lands at Elba.

Note: The Coalitions against Revolutionary and Napoleonic France are variously enumerated by historians, as common action against France was not always marked by formal agreements. The four major coalitions between the great powers are numbered here, but some add those of 1806, at the opening of the war with Prussia – the Jena campaign, and of 1809, when Austria re-entered the war – the Wagram campaign, and renumber those following accordingly.

THE PEACE SETTLEMENT OF 1814–15

THE FIRST TREATY OF PARIS, 30 MAY 1814

The Treaty of Paris was made between representatives of the Allies and France following the restoration of Louis XVIII. The terms towards France were relatively lenient, to assist the Bourbon restoration, although provisions were made for a strengthening of the states bordering France. The main provisions were:

1. France retained her boundaries of 1792, representing 3,280 square miles more than those of 1790, including Avignon and the Venaissin, but surrendering the left bank of the Rhine, Belgium, and territory annexed or controlled in Italy, Germany, Holland and Switzerland.
2. France was allowed to retain the art treasures plundered by Napoleon and the revolutionary armies.
3. France was to be returned most of the colonies she had lost with the exception of Malta, Tobago, St Lucia and the Isle of France.
4. Switzerland was to be independent.
5. Holland and Belgium were to be united under the House of Orange as an independent state.
6. Germany was to become a federation of independent states.
7. Italy was to consist of several independent states apart from territory ceded to Austria.
8. France promised Britain to abolish the slave trade.
9. It was agreed that the final settlement of Europe was to be made at a Congress to be held shortly at Vienna.
10. *Secret clauses.* Without reference to France, the Allies agreed that Austria should receive the territory of Venetia and the Kingdom of Sardinia would receive Genoa.

THE SECOND TREATY OF PARIS, 20 NOVEMBER 1815

Following the 'Hundred Days' and the final defeat of Napoleon at Waterloo, the Allies felt it necessary to enforce more rigorous terms on France because of the widespread support given to Napoleon. But although some of the Allies, notably Prussia, demanded that France cede major parts of her territory, rivalry between the powers and the continuing desire to secure the Bourbon restoration made the peace settlement less onerous than it might have been. The main provisions were:

1. France was reduced to her frontiers of 1789. While retaining Avignon and the Venaissin, she ceded Chambéry and part of Savoy to Sardinia and some territory to Switzerland.
2. France had to pay an indemnity of 700 million francs and maintain an Allied army of occupation in 17 border fortresses for up to five years at a cost of 250 million francs a year.
3. France was to restore the art treasures plundered from Europe.

THE CONGRESS OF VIENNA, 1 NOVEMBER 1814–18 JUNE 1815

As agreed at the first Treaty of Paris (see p. 63), a congress met at Vienna to settle the future boundaries of Europe. Almost every state in Europe was represented. The Emperors of Austria and Russia, the Kings of Prussia, Denmark, Bavaria and Württemberg and many German Princes, including the Elector of Hesse, the Grand Duke of Baden and the Dukes of Saxe-Weimar, Brunswick and Coburg, attended in person. The principal negotiators were: Austria, Metternich; Prussia, Hardenberg and von Humbolt; Russia, Nesselrode and Rasoumoffski; Great Britain, Castlereagh, and later, Wellington; France, Talleyrand and Dalberg. Although interrupted by the 'Hundred Days' and beset by rivalries, the Congress achieved a settlement which, while altered in the next century, remained in force in much of Central and Eastern Europe until the First World War. The main provisions were:

Prussia

1. In Germany, Prussia received half of Saxony, the Grand Duchy of Berg, part of the Duchy of Westphalia, and territory on the left bank of the Rhine between Elken and Coblenz, including Cologne, Trèves, and Aix-la-Chapelle. Prussia also received Swedish Pomerania and the King of Prussia was recognized as Prince of Neuchâtel.
2. In Poland, Prussia retained the territory gained in the previous partitions, the province of Posen, and the cities of Danzig and Thorn.

Austria

1. In Italy, Austria received Venetia, Lombardy and Milan (now called the Lombardo-Venetian Kingdom), the Illyrian Provinces (Carinthia, Carniola and Trieste), Dalmatia, and the seaport of Cattaro (now the kingdoms Illyria and Dalmatia).
2. In Poland, Austria kept eastern Galicia, with Cracow made a free city.
3. In Germany, Austria received the Tyrol and Salzburg.

The German states

1. By the Act of Confederation, signed 8 June 1815, and supplemented by the final Act of Vienna, 15 May 1820, a German Confederacy was set up to

replace the old Holy Roman Empire. The number of German states was reduced from over 300 to 39. A Diet was established under the Presidency of Austria, to which states were to send delegates. The Diet consisted of the Ordinary Assembly sitting permanently at Frankfurt and a General Assembly. Each state was to be independent in internal affairs, but war between the individual states was forbidden and the consent of the Confederacy was necessary for foreign war.

2. Bavaria received Rhenish Bavaria, extending from the Prussian territory on the Rhine to Alsace, including the city of Mainz.
3. Hanover became a kingdom and received East Frisia and Hildesheim.

Russia

1. In Poland, Russia received the greater part of the Grand Duchy of Warsaw which was to be made into a separate Kingdom of Poland. Cracow became a free city state under the protection of Russia, Austria and Prussia.
2. Russia retained Finland, conquered from Sweden in 1808.
3. Russia retained Bessarabia, taken from Turkey in 1812.

Italy

1. Ferdinand I was recognized as King of the Two Sicilies.
2. The Pope received the Legation of Bologna and most of Ferrara, but was refused the restoration of Avignon.
3. Tuscany was assigned to the Grand Duke Ferdinand, uncle of the Emperor Francis; Modena to the Archduke François d'Este, another Habsburg prince.
4. Parma, Piacenza and Guastella were granted to the Empress Marie Louise for life.
5. Genoa was given to the Kingdom of Sardinia.

Low Countries

The formation of the Kingdom of The Netherlands was ratified, comprising the former Republic of Holland and Austrian Belgium, under the former hereditary Stadtholder as King William I. The sovereignty of The Netherlands was given to the House of Orange, and the King of The Netherlands was made Grand Duke of Luxembourg, making him a member of the German Confederation.

Switzerland

The 19 existing cantons were increased to 22 by the addition of Geneva, Wallis, and Neuchâtel. Switzerland became a confederation of independent cantons with its neutrality guaranteed by the Great Powers.

Sweden and Denmark

Sweden retained Norway which had been ceded to her by Denmark at the Peace of Kiel (14 Jan. 1814). The Norwegians were guaranteed the possession of their liberties and rights.

Denmark was indemnified with Lauenburg.

Spain and Portugal

Spain lost Trinidad. Portugal lost Guiana to France.

France

Apart from the provisions of the Second Treaty of Paris, France received French Guiana from Portugal, Guadeloupe from Sweden, and Martinique and the Isle of Bourbon from Great Britain.

Great Britain

Great Britain retained Malta, Heligoland and the protectorate of the Ionian Isles (the latter by a treaty signed 5 Nov. 1815), as well as Mauritius, Tobago and Santa Lucia from France, Ceylon and the Cape of Good Hope from Holland, and Trinidad from Spain.

The slave trade

In February 1815, the Congress condemned the slave trade as inconsistent with civilization and human rights.

THE HOLY ALLIANCE, 26 SEPTEMBER 1815

On the initiative of Alexander I, Russia, Austria and Prussia signed the Holy Alliance, declaring that Christianity was the basis of good government and bound the three sovereigns to act with Christian brotherhood towards each other. It was eventually signed by most European rulers with the exception of the Prince Regent, the Pope and the Turkish Sultan. The Holy Alliance had little practical effect, but came to represent the interests of the absolute powers.

THE QUADRUPLE ALLIANCE, 20 NOVEMBER 1815

In order to secure the settlement of Vienna, the Allies agreed to a Quadruple Alliance to guarantee each other's possessions. The principal provisions were:

1. Austria, Prussia, Russia and Britain agreed to maintain by armed force the exclusion of the Bonaparte dynasty from France for 20 years.
2. The Allies agreed to hold meetings at fixed periods to discuss their 'great common interests' and to take such action as was necessary 'for the maintenance of the peace of Europe', giving rise to the 'Congress system', or 'Concert of Europe'.

THE CONGRESS SYSTEM

In accordance with the Quadruple Alliance (see p. 66), the Allies met on a number of occasions after 1815 to consider major issues. The principal conferences were:

AIX-LA-CHAPELLE, SEPT.–NOV. 1818

The Allies agreed to a conference (met 27 Sept.) to consider French issues, notably the withdrawal of the army of occupation. It was agreed that the troops should be withdrawn by 30 November 1818 and France was invited to join the councils of the Great Powers (15 Nov.). Having paid her war indemnity promptly, there was a final adjustment of French debts.

Alexander I also proposed that all governments should agree to maintain the territorial settlements concluded at Vienna and guarantee the position of all legitimate rulers against revolutionary movements. At a time when the Spanish colonists were in revolt against Spain, both Britain and Austria opposed the use of the Quadruple Alliance to interfere with the internal affairs of another state.

On 15 November the Quadruple Alliance between Russia, Austria, Prussia and Britain was renewed in secret to safeguard against another possible revolution in France. Although the powers declared their intention to maintain their close union, Britain refused to make a formal alliance with her allies and with France.

VIENNA, NOV. 1819–MAY 1820

Following a meeting of ministers in September at Carlsbad, where repressive legislation was passed to suppress revolutionary movements in the German Confederation, further sittings at Vienna passed the Final Act of the Conference of Vienna authorizing the German Confederation to interfere in the affairs of those states unable to maintain public order and the principles of despotic government.

TROPPAU, OCT.–DEC. 1820; LAIBACH, JAN.–MAY 1821

Against the background of revolts in Spain, Naples and Portugal, and continuing unrest in Germany, Tsar Alexander I demanded another meeting of the major powers. The Conference met on 23 October 1820 and was attended by Austria, Russia and Prussia, and by observers from France and Britain. The Conference was adjourned on 17 December 1820 and reconvened at Laibach on 12 January 1821, concluding on 12 May.

On 19 November 1820, Russia, Austria and Prussia agreed a Preliminary Protocol that if developments in any state threatened any other state then the powers bound themselves to expel those nations undergoing revolutions from the Concert of Europe and allowed other states to intervene to crush revolts by force if necessary. This agreement was repudiated by Britain on 16 December 1820.

After moving to Laibach, the Congress heard an appeal from King Ferdinand of Naples who had been forced to grant a constitution. Ferdinand denounced the rebels and appealed for aid. Because of Austria's special interests in Italy she agreed (13 Feb.) that she would send an army to suppress the revolt (after suppressing the revolt and abolishing the constitution, an Austrian army garrisoned Naples until 1828).

No action was taken in respect of Spain and Portugal.

VERONA, OCT.–DEC. 1822

Against the background of unrest in Spain and revolt in Greece another congress was held at Verona on 20 October, attended by representatives of Austria, Prussia, France, Russia and Britain.

Britain advocated non-intervention in Spain, and, with the support of Metternich, prevented the sending of a European army to crush the rebels. On 19 November a French plan for intervention was approved if Spain was attacked or Ferdinand VII was deposed. (In 1823 a French army of 100,000 men crossed the Pyrenees and restored Ferdinand to absolute power.)

THE END OF THE CONGRESS SYSTEM

Growing divisions between the Great Powers and the increasing isolation of Great Britain broke down the principle of regular conferences as envisaged by the Quadruple Alliance. Although *ad hoc* conferences were held, Britain soon ceased to send full representatives and refused to allow herself to be represented at conferences on Spain (1823–24) and the Eastern Question (1824). Increasingly, individual Powers or groups of Powers acted selectively to further their own interests.

TSARIST RUSSIA, 1762–1914

1762

Peter III becomes Tsar. In May the gentry are emancipated from state service. Peter deposed and murdered; Catherine II (the Great) ascends the throne.

1764

Final secularization of church lands.

1766

Catherine encourages the development of self-government for towns. The Great Commission elected from all classes and nationalities is summoned to Moscow; sitting for 18 months it debates subjects such as serfdom and local government.

1768

War with the Ottoman Empire causes the Commission to be prorogued, though various sub-committees sit until 1774.

1768–72

The Confederation of Bar puts up armed resistance to Russian demands in Poland.

1772

First Partition of Poland.

1773–75

Widespread discontent comes to a head in Pugachev's revolt.

1774

Peace with the Ottoman Empire concluded at Kutchuk-Kainardji.

1775

Pugachev executed in Moscow. Town justice reorganized; establishment of courts to protect orphans and widows.

1780

Further rationalization of provincial administration.

1783

The Crimea is incorporated into Russia.

1785

Issue of the charter for towns. The Charter of the Nobility confirms their position in society and their hereditary character.

1787–92

War with the Ottoman Empire.

1788–90

War with Sweden.

1792

Russia and the Ottoman Empire sign the Treaty of Jassy. Russians invade Poland.

1793–95

Second Partition of Poland. Polish insurrection under Kosciusko suppressed (Mar.–Nov. 1794). Third Partition of Poland (1795).

1796

Catherine succeeded by Tsar Paul; at his coronation, he proclaims law of succession which defines the succession to the throne on the basis of primogeniture. Tsar Paul repeals the Charter of the Nobility. Limitations on the labour a serf has to carry out.

1799

Second anti-French coalition; Suvorov campaigns in Northern Italy and Switzerland.

1800

Franco–Russian alliance.

1801

Paul's increasing tyranny results in his murder by the Palace Guard. Alexander I becomes Tsar.

1803

Landowners are given the power to free their serfs though few actually do so. However, serfdom is abolished in Estonia and a few other non-Russian provinces. The sale of serfs as a substitute for army recruits is abolished.

1806

War with the Ottoman Empire.

1807

Speransky appointed to draw up a comprehensive system of constitutional government. Setting up of the Grand Duchy of Warsaw and Treaty of Tilsit (see p. 57).

1808

War with Sweden.

1809

Russo–Swedish conflict ends with the treaty of Frederiksham.

1810

The setting up of a Council of State, composed of ministers appointed by the Tsar to draft new laws and preside over the legality of the administration, proves to be the only proposal put forward by Speransky to survive noble opposition.

1812

Russo–Turkish War ends with the Treaty of Bucharest. Napoleon's Russian campaign (see p. 60).

1813–15

Grand Alliance against France.

1815

Formation of 'The Kingdom of Poland' under Russian control.

1817

Secret societies begin to form.

1820

News of mutiny in the Semenovsky regiment helps prompt Alexander to sign a treaty with Prussia and Austria renouncing liberal ideas. Increased control of Kazan university and press censorship.

1821

Outbreak of the Greek revolt.

1822

Return to high protective tariffs begins.

1825

Death of Alexander I causes confusion over the succession. In 1822 Constantine secretly renounced the throne in favour of his brother

Nicholas. On Alexander's death the brothers proclaim each other Tsar and in the ensuing confusion the Decembrists (see p. 339) lead a revolt, but this is easily suppressed once Nicholas establishes himself as Tsar.

1826–28

Russo–Persian War.

1826

Nicholas re-establishes the Third Section, Russia's secret police which have been abolished by Alexander. Rigid censorship introduced on all kinds of writing. The first of six commissions to study the peasantry is set up.

1827

Destruction of the Ottoman fleet at Navarino Bay.

1828–29

Russo–Turkish War.

1829

Treaty of Adrianople (see p. 218).

1830–31

Polish revolt suppressed.

1832

The question of Greek independence is settled.

1833

Treaty of Unkiar Skelessi (see p. 218). Russia, together with Austria and Prussia, sign the reactionary Munchengratz agreement. Speransky instructed to tabulate the Russian law code.

1841

Auction of serfs forbidden; conditions for state serfs improved. Convention of London leads to Straits Act (see p. 219).

1849

Intervention in Hungary.

1853–56

The Crimean War (see p. 208).

1855

Alexander II succeeds to the throne.

1856

Alexander advocates the abolition of serfdom; few nobles support him (Mar.). Alexander issues a manifesto pardoning political prisoners; recruitment into the army is suspended for a period of three years (Sept.). The collection of unpaid taxes is also suspended for three years. The Congress of Paris (see p. 219).

1857

Introduction of moderate protective tariffs.

1858

A department is set up to deal with the emancipation question (Apr.). Acquisition of Amur and the maritime provinces from China.

1859

Two committees, later dovetailed into one, begin to draft the laws necessary for emancipation of the serfs.

1860s

Emergence of populism, a form of socialism which advocates solving the land question to the satisfaction of the peasants.

1860

Reform of the State Bank; the growth of financial institutions is actively encouraged.

1860–73

First railway boom.

1861

Emancipation of the serfs; seen as a landmark in the history of Russia, opening the door to western-style modernization. The serfs gain legal, but not economic, freedom. As subjects of the government they pay redemption money for the land they receive; this land is held as shares in the collective or *Mir* (village). The Mir replaces the gentry; it is responsible for collecting the redemption money. In real terms, emancipation abolishes personal servitude and substitutes communal responsibility. Army reforms; the army ceases to be used as punishment for criminals; the most brutal forms of punishment are abolished as are military colonies.

1863

Polish revolt suppressed.

1863–64

Educational reform: academic freedom is restored to universities which are expanded and governed by councils elected from the various faculties. Secondary education becomes available to all who pass the necessary examinations; special local authorities are established to promote education. Censorship of books decreases and grants allow students to travel abroad.

1864

Local government reorganization: new district and provincial assemblies *(zemstvos)* are established; despite the electoral system favouring landowning nobles, townsmen and peasants are also represented in the zemstvos. The zemstvos are primarily concerned with public health, public works, welfare and primary education; but they have no control over the police and they can be overruled by government officials. (Nov.) Legal reform: a new legal system based on western practices is introduced. The changes include making judicial proceedings public, the introduction of equality before the law, the use of juries in serious cases and the declaration that judges of the higher courts are to be independent and irremovable except by the decision of a court of law.

1865

Changes in press censorship laws: preliminary censorship replaced by a punitive system, punishment is placed in the hands of the law courts who are invested with wide-ranging powers.

1866

Karakosov's attempt to assassinate the Tsar causes Alexander to move towards more reactionary policies over education and the press. He fears the spread of socialism and atheism.

1868

Introduction of a law restricting the sale of certain publications to regular subscribers. Reduction in the control zemstvos have over taxation.

1870

Municipal reforms introduced; these are along similar lines to those of local government. Self-government under councils elected by the propertied classes is set up.

1871

In an atmosphere of increasing repression, magazines have to be submitted to a preliminary censor four days before publication and preliminary enquiries into state offences are transferred to the gendarmes. Convention of London (see p. 220).

1873

The Minister of the Interior is given the power to forbid the discussion of sensitive questions for up to three months.
(Apr.) Another attempt on the Tsar's life.

1874

The populists fail in an attempt to convert the peasantry to their ideals. Ordinary courts are no longer to try political cases. Milyutin, the Minister of War, introduces universal military service: conscripts are to be drawn from all classes, the period of active service is reduced from 15 to six years. Conditions in the service are improved and some basic education is introduced; this is of importance as it increases literacy among the lower classes.

1876

Bakunin, Lavrov and Chernyshevsky organize the 'Land and Liberty' secret society out of the failed populist movement. 'Land and Liberty' is soon suppressed by the government which fears any signs of revolution. Plekhanov speaks at a demonstration in Kazan Cathedral Square.

1877

Russo–Turkish War, ended by the 1878 Treaty of San Stefano (see p. 220).

1878

After the acquittal by jury of a woman who spat at the Prefect of Police in St Petersburg, political cases to be dealt with by courts martial. Congress of Berlin (see p. 220).

1878–79

Mass strikes in St Petersburg.

1879

Bakunin's ideas inspire the growth of nihilism, rejecting traditional values and institutions, and encouraging the growth of terrorism. The 'Will of the People' organization is formed; its plans include the use of assassination to coerce the government into reform.

1880

Khalturin attempts to assassinate the Tsar. Alexander appoints the popular General Melikov in an attempt to reduce domestic unrest; becoming Minister of the Interior in August, Melikov goes on to release hundreds of political prisoners.

1881

Melikov believes that allowing the people a greater share in government will extinguish extremism and may also produce liberal support for the government.
(31 Mar.) Alexander agrees to a committee to discuss change; however, the same day he falls victim to a terrorist bomb. He is succeeded by Alexander III.

1882

The reactionary Delyanov is appointed Minister of Education; further changes in press censorship laws. Introduction of legislation limiting the use of child labour.

1883–86

Bunge, the Minister of Finance, abolishes the poll taxes and appoints tax inspectors in an effort to improve the taxation system.

1883–84

Plekhanov and others set up small groups to study the work of Marx.

1884

Further legislation to protect minors in industry, including some provision for their education. A new university statute removes all autonomy granted by Alexander II. Student clubs banned. During this period there is much student unrest; only one new university is founded though technical schools of all types are encouraged.

1885

Restrictions placed on night work by women and children in textile factories.

1886

Decrees provide for the enforcement of new factory legislation; factory inspectors have wide-ranging powers. Production of pig iron increases greatly as the result of the discovery of vast resources of coal and iron in southern Russia.

1887

Bunge driven from office by a charge of 'socialism'. France grants Russia the first of several large loans. Ul'yanov (Lenin) and Shevynev involved in attempt to assassinate the Tsar.

1890

Employers' pressure results in provisions to grant licences for children to work at night. French and Russian Chiefs of Staff discuss defence measures.

1891

Construction of the Trans-Siberian railway begins. Thousands of Jews evicted from Moscow and forced into ghettos; under Alexander III the Jews lose rights they have gained under Alexander II.
(July) Alexander fosters Franco–Russian relations by welcoming French warships at Kronstadt.

1891–93

Severe famine in Russia for which the administration is ill-prepared.

1892

Sergei de Witte appointed Minister of Finance and Commerce; he insists on the adoption of the Gold Standard, the nationalization of the liquor trade and is involved in the implementation of improved factory legislation.

1893

Lenin participates in the formation of a Marxist circle in Samara.
(June) France and Russia sign a commercial treaty; at the end of the year the two powers sign a secret alliance. Factory rules altered in the interests of employers. This is to result in large-scale strikes in 1897 and limits are again placed on hours; however, these limits are undermined by a circular issued in the following year by the Minister of Finance which allows the addition of unlimited extra hours.

1894

(1 Nov.) Alexander III dies; succeeded by Nicholas II.

1895

Lenin organizes the St Petersburg 'League of Struggle for the Emancipation of the Working Class'. He is arrested later that year.

1896

Russo–Chinese treaty; concessions granted for Trans-Siberian railway through Manchuria.

1896–1902

Several commissions investigate the condition of the peasants.

1897

Lenin exiled to Siberia; Russia adopts Gold Standard.

1898

China leases Port Arthur to Russia. The Social Democratic Labour Party, the forerunner of the Communist Party, is founded by

Plekhanov and nine other representatives of Marxist groups. First national students' strike.

1900

Leninist newspaper *Iskra* (the 'Spark') founded. Russian troops move into southern Manchuria.

1901

Foundation of the Social Revolutionary Party, mainly concerned with peasant problems and advocating the nationalization of land.

1902

Further strikes and student disturbances. Publication of Lenin's *What Is To Be Done?*

1903

In London, the Social Democratic Party splits into two groups, the Bolsheviks led by Lenin and the Mensheviks. The Bolsheviks advocate a small disciplined party which could lead a revolution.

(July) General strike in Baku; strikes and peasant disturbances throughout Russia.

1904

Murder of Plehve, Minister of the Interior.

(10 Feb.) The Russo-Japanese War breaks out (see p. 209).

(May) Lenin publishes *One Step Forward, Two Steps Back*. Japanese victory at the Yalu; Port Arthur besieged.

(Nov.) The Zemstvo Conference requests a wider range of liberal reforms.

(Dec.) The Baku oil workers strike. The Bolshevik paper *Forward*, edited by Lenin, is published in Geneva.

1905

(1 Jan.) Russians surrender Port Arthur.

(22 Jan.) 'Bloody Sunday'. Father Gapon leads a peaceful protest of thousands of people to the Winter Palace with a Petition for the Tsar: troops open fire, killing many protestors. The incident triggers a series of strikes and increased unrest in Russia. Russian defeats at the hands of the Japanese add to the crisis.

(Apr.–May) The Third Congress of the Russian Social Democratic Labour Party meets in London.

(May–July) Strike at Ivanovo–Vosnesenk; one of the first Soviets of Workers' Deputies is formed.

(May) The first edition of the *Proletarian*, edited by Lenin, published in Geneva.

(June) Mutiny on the battleship *Potemkin*. Armed rising at Lodz.

(July) Publication of Lenin's book, *Two Tactics of Social Democracy in the Democratic Revolution*.

(6 Aug.) The draft law on the establishment of the Consultative State Duma published.

(5 Sept) The Treaty of Portsmouth ends the Russo–Japanese conflict.

(Oct.) The Constitutional Democratic Party (the Cadets) is formed.

(7 Oct.) Nationwide political strikes begin.

(13 Oct.) The St Petersburg Soviet of Workers' Deputies holds its first session.

(17 Oct.) Tsar issues 'October Manifesto' promising a constitution and an elected parliament with genuine legislative power. The Tsar also grants freedom of the press, free speech and religious toleration.

(20 Oct.) Political demonstrations in Moscow.

(24–28 Oct.) Armed forces revolt at Kronstadt.

(Oct.–Dec.) Formation of Workers' Soviets in major Russian cities and towns.

(Nov.) Rise of the moderate Octobrist Party.

(11–15 Nov.) Rising in Sevastopol.

(21 Nov.) First sitting of the Moscow Soviet.

(Nov.–Dec.) The Bolshevik daily newspaper *New Life*, edited by Lenin, is published in St Petersburg.

(Dec.) Moscow Soviet stages uprising (23 Dec.); widespread armed risings in Russia.

(Dec. 1905–Jan. 1906) Moscow rising crushed. Punitive expeditions by Tsarist forces near Moscow, in the Baltic and Siberia.

1906

(Apr.) Elections boycotted by Social Democrats and Social Revolutionaries; Constitutional Democrats ('Cadets') win largest number of seats.

(6 May) Tsar issues Fundamental Law of the Empire by which the Tsar retains most of his autocratic power. Legislative power is to be divided between the Duma and the Upper House, half the members of which are to be appointed by the Tsar. When the Duma is not in session the government may legislate by decree.

(10 May) First Duma assembles; votes no confidence in the government.

(June) Stolypin becomes Prime Minister.

(July) Soldiers and sailors rise in Skeaborg and Kronstadt. The Russian economy is bolstered by a series of enormous loans negotiated by Witte.

(21 July) Deadlock over the constitutional issue leads to the dissolution of the Duma. Cadet leaders issue Vyborg Manifesto calling for a refusal to pay taxes and enter military service, but no response.

(25 Aug.) Stolypin makes large tracts of land available to the peasants.

(1 Sept.) In an attempt to suppress the revolutionary movement, the government introduces Field Courts Martial; as a result over six hundred people are executed.

(Oct.) Peasants are allowed to leave their village communes or to join others. Stolypin also removes the restrictions on the election of peasants to the zemstvos. Peasants also become eligible for any rank in government service.

(22 Nov) Stolypin's Agrarian Reform Act ends communal system of land-holding. Peasants are allowed to leave the commune at will and claim their share of land in private property.

1907

(5 Mar.) The Second Duma meets, dominated by opposition to the autocracy.

(16 June) Stolypin dissolves Duma and introduces a new electoral law, legalizing arbitrary restrictions which had preceded the second election and also greatly increasing propertied representation.

(Nov.) Election of the Third Duma.

1908

(June) During public discussion of the budget, Guchkov blames the government for the military failures in the Russo–Japanese conflict.

1911

(Sept.) Stolypin assassinated in a Kiev theatre.

1913

Election of Fourth Duma.

1914

(Summer) General Strike in St Petersburg.

(1 Aug.) Germany declares war on Russia.

THE EVOLUTION OF NATIONALISM IN EUROPE, 1815–48

1815

(31 May) Holland and Belgium united under House of Orange.

(9 June) Congress of Vienna ends. Poland divided between Russia and Prussia. Cracow made an independent City Republic.

(7 Nov.) Russia grants the Poles a constitution.

1816

First signs of Decembrist organization in Russia.

(Nov.) Diet of German Confederation meets.

1817

Festival of Wartburg to celebrate 300th anniversary of the Reformation. Absolutist texts and military effigies burnt.

(23 June) In Italy the rising at Macerata collapses.

(5 Nov.) The Ottoman Empire grants Serbia partial autonomy.

1818

(27 Sept.) Congress of Aix-la-Chapelle.

1819

In Russia military settlers rise at Chuguev.

(23 Mar.) Kotzebue, a Russian dramatist, reactionary and secret agent murdered by German students.

(Sept.) 'Carlsbad Decrees' suppressing revolutionary activity promulgated.

(Oct.) Prussian trade treaty with Schwarzburg–Sonderhausen lays foundation of the Zollverein.

1820

Disturbances among Semenov guards in St Petersburg.

(Jan.) Disturbances among troops at Cadiz force a return to the 1812 constitution.

(13 Feb.) Duc de Berry assassinated. In France repressive action is taken against the press and freedom of elections.

(May) Final Act of Vienna signed.

(2 July) Rebellion in Naples.

(6 July) Naples promised a constitution.

(Aug.) Lombardy and Venetia declare membership of the Carbonari high treason. Portuguese garrisons in Oporto and Lisbon revolt against British influences. A Cortes is called which produces a liberal constitution.

(23 Oct.) Congress of Troppau.

1821

Rise of the Northern and Southern Societies of Decembrists.

(12 Jan.) Congress of Laibach.

(Feb.) Austria sends aid to Ferdinand of Naples.

(6 Mar.) Revolt in Moldavia and Wallachia. Rebels appeal to the Tsar for aid against the Ottoman Empire.

(13 Mar.) Constitutionalist rising in Piedmont. Victor Emmanuel abdicates, leaving Charles Felix as Regent; he proclaims the Spanish Constitution of 1812. Charles Felix of Modena calls on Austrian military aid.

(23 Mar.) Austrian troops enter Naples; rebels defeated and punished.

(8 Apr.) Austrian victory at Novara. Austrian forces enter Turin and Alessandria unopposed.

(22 Apr.) Greeks massacre Turks in the Morea (the Peloponnese). Turkish repression begins.

(19 June) Turks defeat Greeks at Dragashan.

(5 Oct.) Greek rebels capture Tripolitza.

1822

(13 Jan.) Greeks declare Independence.

(22 Apr.) Turks capture Chios and massacre Greeks.

(15 July) Turkish invasion of Greece.

(20 Oct.) Congress of Verona.

1823

Formation of the Society of United Slavs – the Decembrists. French forces intervene in Spain freeing Ferdinand VII who instigates a harsh reaction.

(Sept.) The newly elected Pope Leo XII continues the reactionary misrule of the Papal States.

(15 Oct.) Britain refuses to aid John VI of Portugal against the forces of reaction.

(2 Dec.) Establishment of Provincial Diets in Prussia.

1824

(Feb.) John VI issues a decree for the recall of the Cortes. However, a coup by his brother Dom Miguel causes John to flee. He is able to regain his throne by enlisting British aid.

(24 Apr.) Byron dies at Missolonghi while supporting the Greeks.

(13 June) Accession of Grand Duke Leopold II in Tuscany.

(16 Sept.) Charles X becomes King of France.

1825

(4 Jan.) In the Kingdom of the Two Sicilies Ferdinand I is succeeded by the weak Francis I.

(Dec.) Decembrists take advantage of confusion over the succession to Alexander I to rise in St Petersburg.

(6 Dec.–Jan.) Chernigov Regiment rises in the Ukraine under Decembrist leadership. Risings suppressed.

1826

John VI is succeeded in Portugal by Dom Pedro's daughter Maria, ruling by a charter providing for parliamentary government.

(4 Apr.) By the St Petersburg Protocol, Britain and Russia agree on Greek autonomy.

(5 Apr.) Russia sends the Ottoman Empire an ultimatum over Serbia and the Danubian provinces.

(27 Oct.) By the Ackerman Convention, Russia gains influence over Serbia and the Danubian lands.

1827

Student revolutionaries in Moscow.

(30 Apr.) National Guard disbanded in France.

(5 June) Turkish forces enter Athens.

(6 July) By the Treaty of London, Britain, Russia and France recognize Greek autonomy.

(6 Aug.) The Ottoman Empire rejects the powers' terms.

(20 Oct.) Turkish fleet annihilated at Navarino Bay.

(5 Nov.) Creation of 76 new peers in France. During election riots, barricades appear in the streets and there are some deaths.

(8 Dec.) Allied ambassadors leave Constantinople.

1828

(4 Jan.) Martignac's ministry replaces Villèle's in France. Dom Miguel puts an end to liberalism in Portugal.

(19 July) London Protocol signed.

(6 Aug.) Turks under Mehemet Ali agree to leave Greece.

(11 Oct.) Russian forces occupy Varna.

(16 Nov.) Recognition of Greece as an independent state.

(10 Dec.) In France, Beranger jailed for political songs.

1829

The reactionary Baron Wenklein becomes effective ruler of Parma.

(8 Aug.) Polignac forms an administration in France.

(14 Sept.) Treaty of Adrianople ends the Russo–Turkish conflict.

1830

(3 Feb.) Greek independence guaranteed by Britain, France and Russia at the London Conference.

(16 May) Dissolution of the Chamber of Deputies in France.

(26 July) Ordinances of St Cloud promulgated in France.

(27 July) Revolution in France. In Paris there is fighting in the streets.

(31 July) Charles X abdicates.

(7 Aug.) The Duke of Orléans, Louis Philippe, is persuaded to become King.

(14 Aug.) Constitutional Charter of July published.

(17 Aug.) Charles X retires to Britain.

(25 Aug.) The Belgians revolt against union with Holland.

(22 Sept.) Revolts in Hesse, Brunswick and Saxony dethrone the rulers and result in new constitutions.

(18 Nov.) In Belgium a National Congress declares Independence.

(22–24 Nov.) Belgium votes for a monarchy, but the House of Orange is vetoed.

(29 Nov.) The Polish revolt against Russia.

(21 Dec.) Polignac and other ministers jailed indefinitely.

(30 Dec.) Belgian Independence agreed on by the Powers at a London Conference. Rising in Sevastapol.

1830–31

Cholera riots in Russia.

1831

(5 Jan.) Hesse-Cassel granted a constitution.

(22–27 Jan.) Powers' protocol for the separation of Belgium accepted by the Belgians but rejected by the Dutch.

(25 Jan.) Declaration of Independence by the Polish Diet.

(2 Feb.) Election of Pope Gregory XVI. Rising in Modena against Francis IV, rebellion in the Papal States. Wenklein flees from Parma.

(3 Feb.) To placate Britain, Louis Phillipe rejects the election of the Duke of Nemours as King of Belgium. Eventually Leopold I of Saxe Coburg becomes King, ruling by a liberal constitution.

(7 Feb.) Proclamation of the Belgian constitution.

(4 Mar.) In response to the Pope's appeal Austrian troops invade Italy.

(21 Mar.) Austrian forces enter Bologna.

(10 May) The ambassadors of the Great Powers produce a memorandum on the reform of the Papal States which is largely ignored.

(26 May) Polish forces suffer defeat at Ostrolenke.

(26 June) The '18 Articles' proposed by the London Conference rejected by the Dutch.

(2 Aug.) The Dutch invade Belgium.

(20 Aug.) Facing a French army in Belgium, the Dutch retreat.

(4 Sept.) Constitution granted in Saxony.

(8 Sept.) The Polish revolt collapses when the Russians capture Warsaw.

(21 Oct.) The '21 Articles' of the London Conference rejected by the Dutch.

(15 Nov.) The Powers accept a treaty incorporating 24 Articles.

(27 Dec.) In France the hereditary peerage abolished after the creation of 36 new peers.

1831–32

Military settlers in the Novgorod province of Russia rise.

1832

(Jan.) Austrian forces put down risings in Romagna. Louis Philippe sends troops to occupy Ancona. 'Young Italy' founded by Mazzini.

(26 Feb.) Abolition of the Polish constitution.

(10 Apr.) The Ottoman Empire declares war on Mehemet Ali.

(27 Apr.) Mehemet Ali takes Acre.

(27 May) In Germany the Hambach festival advocates revolt against Austrian rule.

(5–6 June) Republican insurrection in Paris put down.

(28 June) Metternich's Six Articles.

(21 Dec.) Turks defeated at Konieh.

(23 Dec.) The capture of Antwerp by French forces compels the Dutch to recognize Belgian independence.

1832–35

Ukrainian peasants' movement at its height.

1833

Donna Maria restored to the Portuguese throne.

(18 Mar.) Acquittal of Bergeron and Benot on a charge of trying to assassinate Louis Philippe.

(23 Mar.) Establishment of the Zollverein, from which Austria is excluded.

(May) Belgium and Holland conclude an indefinite armistice.

(3 May) Egypt granted independence from the Ottoman Empire.

(June) Treaty of Unkiar Skelessi between Russia and the Ottoman Empire.

(Sept.) Congress of Munchengratz.

(Oct.) Russia, Austria and Prussia agree to maintain the integrity of the Ottoman Empire.

1835

(May) Baden joins the Zollverein.

1837

(June) Ernest Augustus suppresses the Hanover Constitution.

1838

(Oct.) Austria evacuates the Papal States apart from Ferrara.

1839

In Italy the Scientific Congress discusses the problem of unity.

(Apr.) By the Treaty of London final agreement is reached on Belgian–Dutch borders. Luxembourg is created a Grand Duchy. The Turks invade Syria.

(24 June) The Ottoman Empire defeated at Nezib.

(1 July) Sultan Mahmud dies and is succeeded by Abdul Mejid. Turkish fleet surrenders at Alexandria.

(3 Nov.) Decree of Reform throughout the Ottoman Empire.

1840

The Magyar Diet succeeds in having Magyar substituted for Latin as the official Hungarian language.

(7 June) Frederick William IV crowned King of Prussia.

(15 June) The Quadruple Alliance of Britain, France, Austria and Russia supports the Ottoman Empire against Mehemet Ali.

(11 Sept.) The Royal Navy bombards Beirut.

(3 Nov.) The British take Acre. Mehemet Ali leaves Syria.

(5 Nov.) By the Convention of Alexandria, Mehemet Ali agrees to the Treaty of London.

1841

Russian peasants rise in Guria.

(13 July) The Great Powers guarantee the Ottoman Empire. The Straits are closed to all warships.

1843

In *The Moral and Civil Supremacy of Italy*, Gioberti advocates a united Italy under papal rule.

1844

(25 July) Bondiero brothers shot for attempted revolt in Calabria.

1846

(15 June) Pius IX becomes Pope and makes several liberal concessions, including reduced press censorship and the establishment of a Council of State.

1847

(3 Feb.) Frederick William summons a united Diet.

THE 1848 REVOLUTION IN FRANCE

1845–46

Widespread agricultural distress as a result of poor harvests.

1846

International financial crisis contributes to a high level of unemployment – about one-third of the working population of Paris starve or are living on charity.

1847

Reform banquets calling for measures such as universal suffrage and parliamentary reform are held throughout France.

1848

(14 Jan.) Guizot bans the holding of the 71st banquet in Paris scheduled for 22 February. The opposition politicians plan a compromise to save face but events overtake them.

(21 Feb.) *Le National* publishes a detailed plan for a demonstration and calls on the people of Paris to support a procession prior to the banquet. That evening the Deputies meet at Thiers's house and cancel the banquet.

(22 Feb.) Only a handful of the opposition, including Lamartine, wish to go ahead and *Le National* calls for calm behaviour. However, unaware the banquet has been cancelled, a crowd gathers in the Place de la Madeleine, though this is dispersed by the Municipal Guard.

(23 Feb.) Guizot is replaced. Thiers joins the new ministry. Though tension in Paris relaxes, the barricades and crowds remain. The flash point comes when demonstrators reach the Ministry of Foreign Affairs. A shot is fired and soldiers discharge a volley into the crowd, leaving 52 dead. The parading of the dead around Paris results in the erection of many barricades and up to 100,000 Parisians take to the streets. At first Louis Philippe determines to crush the rising; however, under Thiers's influence the troops are withdrawn.

(24 Feb.) Louis Philippe abdicates in favour of his grandson. Lamartine sets up a provisional government in the Hôtel de Ville, a rival workers' government is abandoned when Louis Blanc and two socialist colleagues join Lamartine. The government passes a number of liberal proclamations, including the abolition of slavery, universal suffrage and freedom of the press. A Republic is proclaimed.

(27 Feb.) Inauguration of Louis Blanc's plan for public relief.

(28 Feb.) Institution of National Workshops to provide 'a permanent commission for the workers'.

(5 Mar.) Elections decreed for 9 April, later postponed to 23 April.

(16 Mar.) Demonstration of *bonnets à poil.*

(17 Mar.) Left-wing counter demonstration.

(23 Apr.) Elections for the Constituent Assembly.

(4 May) The first meeting of the National Assembly where elections based on universal suffrage return a moderate republican majority.

(15 May) Demonstration of the Clubs. Fresh risings in Paris. A mob enters the Assembly and declares it dissolved, but is dispersed by the National Guard.

(June) Four Departments and Paris elect Louis Napoleon to the Assembly.

(22 June) Start of the 'June Days' (22–26 June). The Assembly decrees that all unmarried workers in the 'National Workshops' should join the army and that married men must go to the provinces to do public works. Barricades go up and fighting breaks out.

(22–26 June) Bloody fighting in Paris as General Cavaignac suppresses the revolt.

(26 Sept.) Louis Napoleon takes his seat in the Assembly.

(4 Nov.) Constitution of the Second Republic.

(10 Dec.) Louis Napoleon elected President by a massive majority.

1849

(Jan.) The republican society 'Solidarité Républicaine' is banned. Under pressure the Assembly votes for its dissolution.

(Apr.) Expedition to Rome.

(26 Apr.) French forces land in the Papal States.

(May) Elections to the Legislative Assembly.

(13 June) Attempted rising in Paris comes to nothing. Only in Lyons is there violence as demonstrations are dispersed. The government passes further repressive measures.

(4 July) French troops enter Rome; Pius IX restored.

(Oct.) Louis Napoleon dismisses the Barrot Ministry.

1850

(Mar.) Loi Falloux on education gains Louis Napoleon Roman Catholic support. Left-wing victories in by-elections.

(May) As a result of left-wing victories, a new law restricting the franchise to those who can prove three years' residence in the same canton is passed. The new law will also disfranchise anyone who has been found guilty in court. The overall effect is to reduce the electorate by one-third.

1851

(10 Jan.) Louis Napoleon dismisses General Changarnier, commander of the Paris garrison and National Guard.

(July) Louis Napoleon fails to gain the necessary two-thirds majority required to change the constitution and extend his tenure of presidency.

(2 Dec.) Louis Napoleon carries out a successful *coup d'état*.

(4 Dec.) Little opposition in Paris; risings in the provinces crushed.

(14 Dec.) A plebiscite shows that 92% of the poll ratifies Louis Napoleon's action.

AUSTRIA–HUNGARY IN 1848

1848

(3 Mar.) Kossuth demands total change in the government of Hungary.

(11 Mar.) Moderate Czechs and Germans meet in Prague to urge liberal reforms, but achieve little due to internal division caused by extremists.

(12 Mar.) Revolution in Vienna heralded by student demonstrations.

(13 Mar.) Following demonstrations in Vienna, Metternich resigns; the middle class gains the right to form a national guard.

(15 Mar.) The liberal and constitutional reforms advocated in March 1847 are accepted by the Hungarian Diet.

(11 Apr.) Hungary confirmed as a separate state. Kossuth abolishes feudalism and divides land among the peasants. However, his demands for Magyarization cause dissension among other races and create willing allies for Austria.

(25 Apr.) Austria granted a constitution which includes a provision for responsible government.

(15 May) Second rising in Vienna. The National Guard refuses to intervene.

(17 May) The Emperor flees from Vienna to Innsbruck, afraid to trust his troops.

(June) Austria supplies secret aid to Croatia for future use against Hungary.

(2 June) Meeting of the Pan-Slav Congress in Prague.

(13 June) Czech rising in Prague.

(17 June) Windischgratz crushes the Czech rising.

(July) Meeting of the Constituent Assembly of the western provinces in Vienna with the aim of drawing up a constitution based on universal suffrage.

(12 Aug.) Emperor Ferdinand returns to Vienna.

(7 Sept.) Abolition of serfdom and the 'robot' (forced labour) in Austria.

(11 Sept.) Jellacic invades Hungary.

(24 Sept.) Kossuth proclaimed President of the Committee for the National Defence of Hungary.

(Oct.) Jellacic driven from Hungary.

(3 Oct.) Austria declares war on Hungary.

(6 Oct.)Third rising in Vienna.

(7 Oct.) Viennese court flees to Olmuk.

(22 Oct.) The Assembly adjourns to Kremsier in Moravia.

(31 Oct.) Windischgratz, aided by Jellacic and his forces, bombards Vienna into surrender.

(Nov.) New ministry formed under Schwarzenberg.

(2 Dec.) Ferdinand abdicates to be succeeded by Francis Joseph.

1849

(1 Mar.) The Austrian Reichstag completes the Kremsier constitution which provides for a decentralized federal type of government.

(4 Mar.) Proclamation of an Austrian constitution designed to rally German and Czech support.

(7 Mar.) Dissolution of the Austrian Assembly.

(6 Apr.) Hungarian forces under Gorgei defeat Windischgratz at Isaszeg.

(14 Apr.) Declaration of Independence by the Hungarian Diet under the leadership of Kossuth.

(21 Apr.) Austria appeals to the Tsar for aid. (May) Gorgei retakes Budapest, but the Hungarians fail to take decisive action.

(13 Aug.) Austria supported by Russia defeats the Hungarians at Vilagos. Kossuth flees to the Ottoman Empire.

1851

(31 Dec.) Austrian constitution abolished.

THE 1848 REVOLUTIONS IN ITALY

1848

(Jan.) 'Tobacco Riots' against Austrian influence in Lombardy.

(12 Jan.) Revolt and proclamation of a provisional independent government in Sicily. The King accepts the 1812 constitution which is also extended to Naples.

(10 Feb.) Ferdinand II proclaims a constitution in Naples.

(11 Feb.) In Tuscany the Grand Duke allows representative government and a constitution to be declared.

(14 Mar.) Pius IX reluctantly grants a constitution in Rome.

(17 Mar.) Daniele Manin leads a revolt in Venice.

(18 Mar.) Uprising in Milan causes Radetzky to evacuate the city.

(20 Mar.) Revolt in Parma.

(22 Mar.) Manin proclaims the Venetian Republic.

(23 Mar.) Charles Albert issues a proclamation sympathizing with Lombardy and Venetia. Piedmontese troops attack Austrian forces in Lombardy.

(8 Apr.) Austrians defeated by Piedmontese forces at Gioto.

(13 Apr.) Sicily declares itself independent of Naples.

(28 Apr.) The Papacy joins the war against Austria.

(29 Apr.) Pius IX ceases to support the nationalist movement.

(30 Apr.) Austrians defeated at Pastrengo.

(15 May) Collapse of revolt in Naples.

(29 May) Austria defeats Tuscany at Curtatone.

(22 July) Radetzky wins a major victory at Custozza. Sardinian troops forced out of Milan and Lombardy.

(9 Aug.) Sardinia and Austria sign the Armistice of Vigevano.

(11 Aug.) Venice expels Sardinian troops.

(15 Nov.) Count Rossi, premier of Papal States, assassinated.

(24 Nov.) Pius IX flees from Rome to Gaeta.

1849

(7 Feb.) The Grand Duke of Tuscany also flees to Gaeta.

(9 Feb.) Mazzini's proclamation of a Roman Republic.

(12 Mar.) Sardinia terminates truce with Austria.

(23 Mar.) The Austrians win a major victory at Novara. Charles Albert abdicates; succeeded by Victor Emmanuel II.

(28 Apr.) The French land troops in the Papal States.

(15 May) Neapolitan troops occupy Palermo.

(4 July) French troops enter Rome. Pius IX restored.

(6 Aug.) End of the Austria–Sardinian conflict called by the Peace of Milan.

(28 Aug.) Surrender of Venice to the Austrians.

ITALIAN UNIFICATION, 1850–70

1850

(11 Oct.) Cavour appointed Minister of Agriculture, Commerce and Marine in Piedmont.

1852

(6 May) Leopold II abolishes the Tuscan Constitution.
(4 Nov.) Cavour becomes Prime Minister.

1855

(26 Jan.) Piedmont enters the Crimean War on the Allied side. (May) General La Marmora joins the Allies in the Crimea.

1857

(15 Aug.) Garibaldi forms the Italian National Association for Unification of Italy under Piedmontese leadership.

1858

(14 Jan.) Orsini bomb plot, an abortive attempt to assassinate Napoleon III.
(20 July) Cavour and Napoleon sign the Pact of Plombières.
(Sept.) Victor Emmanuel's daughter Clotilde marries Napoleon III's cousin Jerome.

1859

(Jan.) Formalization of the Franco–Piedmontese agreement made at Plombières.
(Jan.) Victor Emmanuel uses provocative language aimed at Austria. Finance Minister La Marmora makes war loans.
(19 Jan.) Franco–Sardinian alliance signed.

(19 Apr.) Austrian ultimatum issued, demanding unconditional demobilization within three days.
(26 Apr.) Austria's ultimatum is rejected.
(29 Apr.) Austrian troops enter Sardinia.
(3 May) France declares war on Austria.
(4 June) Austria heavily defeated at Magenta.
(24 June) Austria defeated at Solferino. Both armies suffer heavy losses.
(11 July) Napoleon III concludes the Peace of Villafranca, the terms of which cause Cavour to resign.
(Aug.) Constituent Assemblies meet in Parma, Modena, Tuscany and Romagna forming a military alliance and demanding Victor Emmanuel as King.

1860

(20 Jan.) Cavour regains power.
(Mar.) Almost unanimous vote by plebiscite in the central Italian states for union with Piedmont.
(24 Mar.) Sardinia cedes Nice and Savoy to France.
(2 Apr.) Meeting of the first 'Italian' Parliament in Turin.
(5 May) Garibaldi's expedition sets sail for Sicily.
(11 May) Garibaldi lands in Sicily.
(27 May) Garibaldi's forces take Palermo.
(22 Aug.) Garibaldi lands on the Italian mainland.
(7 Sept.) Fall of Naples; Francis II flees.
(11 Sept.) Sardinian troops enter the Papal States.
(18 Sept.) Garibaldi defeats papal forces at Castelfidardo.
(21 Oct.) Sicily and Naples decide to unite with Sardinia.

(26 Oct.) Garibaldi proclaims Victor Emmanuel King of Italy.
(4 Nov.) Umbria votes to unite with Sardinia.

1861

(13 Feb.) Francis II of Naples formally surrenders to Garibaldi at Gaeta.
(18 Feb.) Italian Parliament proclaims Victor Emmanuel King of Italy.
(17 Mar.) Formal proclamation of the Kingdom of Italy.
(6 June) Cavour dies.

1862

(Mar.) Ratazzi Ministry in Turin encourages Garibaldi to mount a campaign from Sicily to overthrow the Pope.
(29 Aug.) Garibaldi, having made a triumphal progress through Sicily, crosses to the mainland, but is defeated and captured by Italian royal troops at Aspromonte and imprisoned at Spezzia.

1864

(Sept.) By the September Convention, Napoleon III consents to the withdrawal of French troops from Rome, in return for the Italians showing their renunciation of Rome as the national capital by removing the seat of government to Florence from Turin. Proposal causes serious disorder in Turin.

1865

(26 Apr.) Florence proclaimed capital of Italy. French troops gradually withdraw from Rome and Italian kingdom bound by the Convention not to attack papal territory.

1866

(Jan.) Military influence at the Austrian court causes the rejection of an Italian offer to buy Venetia.

(8 Apr.) Secret offensive and defensive alliance between Italy and Prussia. La Marmora Cabinet borrows three million francs and places army and fleet on a war footing.
(24 June) Italian forces under La Marmora's command defeated at Custozza. All Italian forces forced to retreat and Garibaldi defeated and wounded in skirmish at Monte Suello. Italian secret convention with France.
(5 July) Following the defeat by the Prussians at Königgrätz (Sadowa) on 3 July, Francis Joseph of Austria cedes Venetia to the Emperor Napoleon and through him to the Italians in return for the mediation of France in the Austro–Prussian War.
(20 July) Italian fleet under Persano defeated by the Austrians at Lissa in the Adriatic.
(21 Oct.) Venetia formally votes to unite with Italy. Italy entirely free of foreign troops.

1867

(Oct.) Garibaldi raises volunteers for a march on Rome.
(27 Oct.) Napoleon III sends troops back to Rome to protect the Pope.
(3 Nov.) French troops defeat Garibaldi's army at Mentana. The Italian government arrests Garibaldi, while French troops remain to protect Rome. French minister Rouher declares that the Italians will 'never' enter Rome.

1870

(Sept.) Defeat of France at Sedan and collapse of Napoleon III's government leads to removal of French troops from Rome. New French Foreign Minister, Jules Favre, indicates that France will not prevent the fall of Rome. King Victor Emmanuel marches on Rome.
(20 Sept.) Italian forces enter Rome near the Porta Pia after resistance by papal troops. Papal troops marched out of Rome and sent away by sea.

(2 Oct.) Plebiscite in the Papal States approves union with Italy and National Assembly votes to remove capital from Florence to Rome. The Pope is allowed to retain authority over the Vatican.

1871

(2 July) King Victor Emmanuel takes up residence at the Quirinal Palace as the first ruler of a fully united Italy.

THE UNIFICATION OF GERMANY

1848

(17 Mar.) Uprising in Berlin: Frederick William IV grants a constitution.

(31 Mar.) The *Vorparlement* meets at Frankfurt.

(2 May) Prussia invades Denmark over Schleswig-Holstein question.

(18 May) German National Assembly meets in Frankfurt.

(22 May) Berlin meeting of Prussian National Assembly.

(26 Aug.) Denmark and Prussia make peace at the Treaty of Malmo.

(5 Dec.) Dissolution of the Prussian National Assembly.

1849

(23 Jan.) Prussia advocates a United Germany, excluding Austria.

(27 Mar.) The German National Assembly offers Frederick William IV the title 'Emperor of the Germans'.

(3 May) Prussian forces suppress revolt in Dresden.

(6 June) German National Assembly moves to Stuttgart.

(18 June) Troops carry out the dissolution of the National Assembly.

(23 June) Rebels in Baden surrender to Prussian forces.

1850

(31 Jan.) Prussia grants a liberal constitution.

(20 Mar.) Frederick William IV summons a German Parliament to Erfurt.

(29 Apr.) The Erfurt Parliament opens.

(May) Schwarzenberg revives the old Diet of Frankfurt and invites the German states to discuss the revision of the old Confederation and the establishment of an authority for Germany. Prussia does not attend.

(2 July) Under Russian pressure Prussia and Denmark sign the Peace of Berlin, a treaty which favoured the Danes.

(Oct.) The Tsar promises moral support to Austria if Prussia opposes federal execution in Hesse-Cassel. Resignation of the Prussian Foreign Minister, Radowitz.

(20 Nov.) Prussia humiliated by the Convention of Olmutz imposed by Austria. Prussia agrees to abandon the Erfurt Union and to restore the Confederation. The Convention also includes demobilization on terms unfavourable to Prussia.

(Dec.) The Dresden Conference; Schwarzenberg has to abandon his plan to include the Habsburg Empire in the Confederation. The only consolation for Austria was a three-year defensive alliance with Prussia.

1853

German customs union renewed for a further 12 years; Austria only gained a commercial treaty with Prussia, not the Austro–German customs union desired by Bruck, Austrian Minister for Commerce.

1855

(Jan.) Bismarck, as Prussian Minister at Frankfurt, persuades the Diet that Germany should keep out of the Crimean War, to the annoyance of Austria.

1859

(11 Dec.) Albert von Roon becomes Prussian Minister of War.

1860

(Feb.) Von Roon places his proposals for military reform before the Prussian Landtag.

1861

(2 Jan.) Accession of William I to the Prussian throne on the death of Frederick William IV.

(Oct.) Saxony proposes a scheme for a tripartite reorganization of the Confederation.

(Dec.) Prussia rejects the scheme on the grounds that the Confederation could not be reformed and declares further that unification could only come under Prussian leadership.

1862

(Feb.) Austria puts forward a modified version of the Saxon scheme; though it wins the support of several states, Prussia rejects it.

(22 Sept.) Bismarck becomes Minister President of Prussia.

(30 Sept.) Bismarck makes his 'Blood and Iron' speech on the question of German unification.

(7 Oct.) The Prussian Diet rejects the military budget.

(Dec.) Bismarck warns Austria of the dangers of not recognizing Prussia as an equal in Germany. Bismarck fails to gain a promise of French neutrality in the event of war.

1863

(Jan.) Austrian proposals for the Confederation finally defeated in the Diet after Prussia threatens to walk out.

(8 Feb.)The Polish revolt provides the opportunity for Bismarck to sign an alliance with Russia.

(30 Mar.) Schleswig incorporated into Denmark.

(Aug.) Bismarck convinces William not to attend the Austrian-organized meeting of the princes.

(1 Oct.) The German Diet votes for action against Denmark.

(13 Nov.) Danish Council of State approves the Constitution for Schleswig.

(15 Nov.) Frederick VII of Denmark dies. Succeeded by Christian IX.

(24 Dec.) Hanoverian and Saxon forces move into Holstein.

1864

(16 Jan.) Austro–Prussian alliance committing them to joint military action against Denmark and to deciding the future of the Duchies by joint agreement.

(1 Feb.) Austro–Prussian invasion of Schleswig.

(18 Apr.) Danish forces defeated at Duppel.

(25 June) London Conference fails to solve the Danish problem.

(July) Danes defeated.

(30 Oct.) The Peace of Vienna. Denmark cedes Schleswig-Holstein to Austria and Prussia who are to make a private agreement over their control.

(Nov.) Bismarck bullies the Diet into leaving Austro–Prussian forces in sole control of the government.

1865

(14 Aug.) Convention of Gastein: Austria received Holstein. Prussia gained Schleswig and purchased Lauenberg.

(4–11 Oct.) Bismarck and Napoleon meet at Biarritz.

1866

(Jan.) Austro–Prussian friction over the Duchies.

(28 Feb.) Prussian Crown Council takes up Austria's challenge even at the risk of war.

(8 Apr.) Secret military alliance between Prussia and Italy.

(21 Apr.) On hearing rumours of Italian troop movements, Austria mobilizes her southern forces. Prussian mobilization ordered.

(7 June) Prussian invasion of Holstein which is subsequently annexed.

(10 June) Bismarck outlines plans for a new state excluding Austria from Germany.

(12 June) Austria and Prussia break off diplomatic relations.

(14 June) The German Diet takes a vote to mobilize against Prussia.

(15 June) Prussian ultimatum to Saxony, Hanover and Hesse-Cassel.

(16 June) Prussian invasion of Saxony, Hanover and Hesse-Cassel.

(20 June) Italy declares war on Austria.

(29 June) Hanoverian victory over Prussia at Langensaza, but by the end of June Hanover capitulates.

(3 July) Major Prussian victory over Austria at Sadowa-Königgrätz.

(5 July) Austria attempts to preserve her supremacy in Germany by seeking the mediation of France, agreeing to cede Venetia to the Emperor Napoleon, and through him to the Italians, freeing 100,000 Austrian troops in Italy for the defence of Vienna. French claims to the Rhine boundary are rejected by Prussia, but France is unable to go to war because of her involvement in Mexico.

(26 July) After a rapid Prussian advance on Vienna, Prussia and Austria sign preliminaries of peace at Nikolsburg, near Vienna.

(13–22 Aug.) Prussia signs peace treaty with Württemberg, Baden and Bavaria.

(23 Aug.) Treaty of Prague signed on the basis of the preliminaries of Nikolsburg. Austria is excluded from German affairs and the German Confederation of 1815 is dissolved. Schleswig-Holstein, Hanover, the whole of Hesse-Cassel, Nassau and the free city of Frankfurt are annexed by Prussia, adding five million subjects. Austria is to pay a war indemnity of 40,000 thalers and to cede Venetia to Italy. The North German Confederation is formed, comprising Prussia, Saxony, the grand duchies of Oldenburg, the two Mecklenburgs, Brunswick, part of Hesse Darmstadt, the Thuringian States and the free cities of Hamburg, Bremen and Lübeck. Elections for a North German diet prescribed on the basis of direct manhood suffrage. Secret understanding reached between Prussia and the South German states in the form of an offensive and defensive alliance based upon a reciprocal guarantee of territorial integrity. The southern states place their entire military force under the command of the King of Prussia in the event of war.

(3 Sept.) Peace signed between Prussia and Hesse.

(21 Oct.) Peace signed between Prussia and Saxony.

1867

(24 Feb.) First Diet of the North German Confederation agrees a constitution with the states. Presidency of the league is united with the Crown of Prussia, which represents the confederation in international relations, diplomacy and matters of war and peace. The governments are represented in the Council of the Confederation (Bundesrath), in which Prussia has 17 votes and the other 21 members 26 votes. An Imperial Diet (Reichstag), elected by universal manhood suffrage, is to meet in Berlin and make laws for the states which, however, retain their local laws and customs. The federal forces are to be reorganized under the command of the King of Prussia and introduce compulsory military service. Customs, postal and telegraph services are united. Count Bismarck becomes Chancellor of the Confederation.

(7–11 May) London Conference on the Luxembourg question. Napoleon III's attempt to purchase Luxembourg from the King of Holland prevented by the opposition of Prussia, who reveals her military agreement with the South German states. Napoleon demands that the Prussian garrison should evacuate the fortress of Luxembourg. The Conference agrees that the neutrality of Luxembourg be guaranteed by the Great Powers in common and that the Prussian garrison be removed and the fortifications demolished.

1870

(2 Jan.) Baden joins North German Confederation.

(May) North German Confederation votes subsidies to support the St Gothard tunnel through the Swiss Alps, with the aim of increasing trade with Italy. Criticized by the French for diverting trade from their Mont Cenis route.

(2 July) News of acceptance of Spanish throne by Leopold, Prince of Hohenzollern, becomes general, greatly increasing Franco–Prussian tension.

(12 July) Leopold's candidature withdrawn.

(13 July) The French ambassador seeks assurance from the King of Prussia at Ems that the Spanish candidature will not be renewed. The King refuses to discuss the matter and refers the ambassador to the regular method of communication through the foreign embassy in Berlin. The King's report of the conversations to Bismarck is doctored by him and released to the press (the 'Ems Telegram') in order to inflame Franco–Prussian relations. War fever in France.

(15 July) William I enthusiastically received in Berlin on his return from Ems.

(16 July) South Germans rally to Prussia after Ludwig II of Bavaria mobilizes his army in opposition to the French threat.

(19 July) Delivery of French declaration of war.

(23 July) Unanimous vote of war credits by the Reichstag.

(2 Aug.) King William of Prussia takes command of united German armies at Mainz.

(19 Aug.) After a series of defeats, a large portion of the French army is besieged in and about Metz.

(2 Sept.) Major Prussian victory at Sedan; surrender of Napoleon III to William I and the surrender of Sedan.

(19 Sept.) German armies begin siege of Paris.

(27 Oct.) French forces at Metz capitulate.

(15 Nov.) Württemburg, followed by Bavaria (23rd), ally with North German Confederation.

(10 Dec.) Following meetings in Berlin and in the South German states calling for German unity, a deputation of the North German Parliament offers William I the crown of the new German Empire, which he accepts.

1871

(18 Jan.) Proclamation of William I as German Emperor (Kaiser).

(28 Jan.) Capitulation of Paris.

(26 Feb.) Preliminaries of peace at Versailles.

(21 Mar.) First Imperial Parliament meets.

(14 Apr.) Imperial constitution adopted: the King of Prussia to bear the title German Emperor (Kaiser) and represent the empire in international relations and command the armed forces. The representatives of the 25 governments form a federal council (Bundesrath) under the Presidency of the Chancellor of the Empire (Bismarck). An Imperial Parliament of 382 members (Reichstag) is to be chosen by direct manhood suffrage. Centralized military system set up based on universal compulsory service of three years, plus four in reserve. Uniform postal and telegraph service set up and uniform coinage and weights and measures.

(10 May) Peace Treaty of Frankfurt am Main with France. France cedes Alsace (except Belfort) and German Lorraine, including the fortresses of Metz and Strasburg. France required to pay a war indemnity of 5,000 million francs, 1,000 million in 1871.

GERMANY, 1871–1929

1871

(18 Jan.) William I of Prussia proclaimed German Emperor (Kaiser) at Versailles.

(28 Jan.) Paris capitulates and armistice with France signed.

(10 Apr.) German Empire receives Constitution remodelled from that of North German Confederation (see p. 93).

(10 May) Peace of Frankfurt between Germany and France (see p. 93).

(July) *Kulturkampf* (cultural struggle) with Catholic Church begins with suppression of Roman Catholic Department for Spiritual Affairs. The Bishops of Breslau and Ermeland and the Archbishop of Cologne request that the Prussian government dismiss Old Catholics (those who have resisted the doctrine of papal infallibility) from schools and Catholic theological faculties at universities. The government refuses on the grounds of religious toleration. The bishops persist in their demands, as a result of which their state subsidies are suspended.

1872

In a series of measures Bismarck seeks to subordinate the Church to the State. Jesuits are forbidden to set up establishments in Germany and provision is made for the expulsion of individual Jesuits. Germany severs diplomatic relations with the Vatican.

1873

(11–14 May) The first of the May Laws are passed in Prussia. They govern the education and appointment of the clergy. Bismarck relinquishes the post of Minister-President of Prussia for a short time, rapidly reassuming it when it becomes apparent that it provides the real basis of his power.

1874

(Jan.) Centre Party vote doubles.

(May) Civil Marriage introduced in Prussia; all births, deaths and marriages have to be notified to the registrar, not the Church authorities. States gain the power to restrict the freedom of movement of the clergy and expel offending priests.

1875

Formation of the German Social Democratic Party. The *Kulturkampf* reaches a peak with laws empowering Prussia to suspend subsidies to the Church in dioceses or parishes where the clergy resist the new legislation. All religious orders in Prussia, apart from those involved in nursing, dissolved. Pope Pius condemns this legislation and resistance is widespread. Creation of the Reichsbank. Standardization and modernization of the legal system.

1876

Rigid enforcement of the *Kulturkampf* results in exile or arrest of all but two Prussian bishops. However, in the face of increasing opposition, the Chancellor, fearing for the unity of the Empire, realizes it is time to cut his losses and reconcile the Church and State. Formation of the Central Association of German Industrialization as a result of the clamour for a protective tariff from landowners and industrialists.

1878

Bismarck breaks openly with the National Liberals over the question of taxing tobacco. (7 Feb.) Death of Pope Pius IX; his successor Leo XIII wishes to settle the dispute, expressed in a letter of 20 February to the Emperor. During the summer Bismarck meets a papal envoy at Bad Kissingen in an effort to end the deadlock.

(May–Oct.) Two assassination attempts on the Emperor provide Bismarck with the excuse to draft an anti-socialist bill; his first effort is heavily defeated. However, the second attempt on the Emperor's life is more serious: Bismarck dissolves the Reichstag and in the election which follows the National Liberals lose 29 seats and a new anti-socialist law is passed. Though the bill places many restrictions on socialism and includes a ban on trade union activity, it does not interfere with elections.

(Autumn) The campaign for tariff reform reaches a new intensity.

1879

(12 July) Introduction of a general tariff bill, the passage of which produces a new 'alliance of steel and rye' as landowners and industrialists turn to conservatism on the common ground of protection. Bismarck's political support now becomes solidly conservative. Imperial Court of Appeal is established. The Exceptional Law, aimed at the Social Democratic Party, prohibits society meetings and publications concerned with spreading socialist principles. The police are authorized to deport suspects and trade unions are declared illegal. Agreement is reached with the Church by which the government is to be notified of all impending papal appointments and the German clergy is to cease to resist the government. In return, Bismarck begins to repeal anti-clerical legislation.

1881

Bismarck informs the Reichstag that the welfare of the working classes must be actively promoted; this will be put into practice by the introduction of a comprehensive welfare system during the next decade. The rejection of the tobacco monopoly and of a proposed increase in indirect taxation by the Reichstag ruins Bismarck's plans for financial reform.

1883

(1 May) Passage of an Act providing medical treatment for three million workers and their families; the cost is shared between workers and employers.

1884

Passage of an Accident Insurance Act financed by employers; benefits and burial grants are provided for incapacitated workers.

1886

Accident and sickness insurance extended to seven million agricultural workers.

(Nov.–Dec.) Bismarck asks the Reichstag to agree to an increase in military finance in the light of the changing international situation. Liberals demand greater control over military budget.

1887

(Jan.) In the face of Reichstag opposition over military expenditure, Bismarck dissolves the House. In the ensuing elections Bismarck exploits nationalism to gain a Reichstag favourable to his policies.

1888

(9 Mar.) Crown Prince Frederick succeeds Emperor on his death.

(15 June) Frederick dies and is succeeded by Crown Prince William who has the intention of removing Bismarck from office given a suitable opportunity. To this end he appoints General Waldersee as Chief of the General Staff on the retirement of Moltke; Waldersee

is one of a group of conservatives who seek to remove Bismarck.

1889

Bismarck and the Emperor clash over social policy.

1890

(Jan.–Feb.) The Reichstag rejects Bismarck's anti-socialist bill. During the Reichstag elections in February Bismarck refuses to countersign William's proclamation promising social legislation and announcing an international conference on the subject of social questions. A massive rise in the socialist vote, together with large gains by the Radicals, show Bismarck's position is weakening. In a last-ditch attempt to maintain office, Bismarck revives a Prussian cabinet order of 1852 which maintains that all Prussian ministers have to go through their Minister President, in this instance Bismarck, before communicating with the Emperor. The Kaiser demands the repeal of the order, while Bismarck fails in his attempt to create a new power base in the Reichstag.

(Mar.) William and Bismarck clash, William demanding repeal of the 1852 order or his Chancellor's resignation. Bismarck is saved the humiliation of resigning over a domestic dispute when William accuses him of dereliction of duty over foreign policy (in this instance it is over his failure to warn Austria of 'ominous' Russian troop movements in the Balkans). Bismarck resigns on 17 March, ostensibly over the Emperor's anti-Russian stance. Bismarck is succeeded as Chancellor by a middle-aged soldier, General Leo von Caprivi. In his first speech to the Prussian Landtag he states that he is embarking on 'a new course'.

(1 Oct.) Expiry of anti-socialist legislation of 1878. Industrial courts established to arbitrate in wage disputes.

(21 Oct.) The German Socialist Party, now organizing openly, commits itself to a Marxist policy at the Erfurt Congress. Factory inspection improved. The Reichstag passes an Act regulating working conditions; workers gain the right to form committees to negotiate with employers as to their conditions of employment.

1891–94

Caprivi signs a series of commercial treaties with Austria, Hungary, Italy, Switzerland, Spain, Romania and Russia; this stimulates the formation of the protectionist Agrarian League in 1893.

1891

Count Schlieffen succeeds Waldersee as Chief of the General Staff.

1892

The Schlieffen plan is devised (see p. 355). German strategy becomes based on the principle of dealing a swift knock-out blow in the West against France.

(Nov.) Caprivi introduces an army bill which will facilitate the carrying out of the Schlieffen plan. It aims to increase the army by 84,000 men, though the period of service is reduced from three to two years. While the Reichstag is to be allowed to review the army grant every two instead of seven years, the bill is rejected.

1893

(July) With the defeat of the army bill Caprivi dissolves the Reichstag and elections are held in a nationalistic atmosphere, producing a House more amenable to the army reforms, though Caprivi's bill only gains a very narrow majority. Formation of the Agrarian League. Pan-German League founded.

1894

(Oct.) Caprivi stands firm against the Emperor's demands for more anti-socialist legislation. The Chancellor resigns, to be succeeded by Prince Hohenlohe. The Reichstag is asked to pass a Subversion Bill making it a punishable offence to incite citizens to class hatred, to make public attacks on the family, marriage or property, or to denigrate the State.

1895

The Subversion Bill is defeated.

1896

(3 Jan.) William sends 'Kruger Telegram', congratulating Transvaal on failure of Jameson raid. Saxony introduces a three-class system, effectively eliminating socialists from the Landtag.

1897

(20 Oct.) Bülow becomes Foreign Minister. The Prussian Landtag is asked to give the police the power to dissolve all societies threatening law, order or the security of the State. However, the move is opposed and defeated.

(Nov.) Bülow sums up Germany's growing desire for power when he states 'we do not wish to put anyone in the shade but we do demand our place in the sun'. Admiral von Tirpitz appointed Secretary of State for the Navy (June) with the aim of getting a new navy bill through the Reichstag. The bill, introduced in November, proposes to create 17 ships of the line during the next seven years.

1898

Tirpitz helps found the Navy League (*Flotterverein*) which campaigns vigorously for naval expansion. The League receives financial assistance from industrialists, such as Krupp and Stumm. The bill is greeted with enthusiasm by the middle classes and it is carried in March by 212 votes to 139.

1898–1901

Germany rejects Chamberlain's overtures for an alliance.

1899

William asks the Reichstag to pass a law to penalize workers who compel others to form trade unions or to go on strike; the defeat of the bill and the middle-class opposition mark the end of the policy of repression. Tariff changes reduce duties to the 1892 levels, on the demands of the Agrarian League.

1900

Introduction and passage of the second naval bill. The second bill, which proposes increasing the number of ships of the line to 36, is passed by a large majority. Count von Posadowsky-Wemer, Secretary of State since 1897, introduces the first of a series of social reforms when he extends the scope of accident insurance. He sees no future in a repressive anti-socialist policy and actually gains socialist support for his new measures.

1901

A new law makes industrial courts compulsory in all towns with a population of more than 20,000.

1903

The period covered by sickness insurance is increased, while the prohibition of the use of child labour is extended. Opposition to increased tariffs manifested in the gain of 26 seats by the socialists.

1904–05

The government and the Centre Party clash over the question of colonial affairs. Centre opposition to his policies in colonial Africa causes Bülow to dissolve the Reichstag and allows Bülow to manipulate a 'bloc' of Conservatives and National Liberals against the Centre, holding it together by proposing some mildly liberal measures and retaining ministers such as Posadowsky, whom the liberals and socialists regard as too conservative. This 'bloc' is never particularly strong and collapses in summer 1909.

1905

The Tangier Incident (see p. 119).

1907

Britain, France and Russia sign the Triple Entente.

1908

(Oct.) 'The *Daily Telegraph* Affair' – the Emperor's article in the *Daily Telegraph* published in Britain increases Anglo–German tension. The Bosnian Crisis (see p. 120).

1909

(14 July) Defeat of Bülow's finance bill; in order to cover an increasing deficit Bülow intends to raise indirect taxation and extend the scope of death duties. Various parties in the Reichstag oppose Bülow and, on the defeat of his finance bill, he resigns. His successor, Bethmann-Hollweg, is appointed by William who accepts Bülow's resignation as merely tactical.

1910

Amalgamation of the previously split radical groups into the *Fontsckmitte Vereinigung* which supports the socialists, entering into an electoral pact with them. Increasing demand for electoral reform in Prussia prompts Bethmann-Hollweg to introduce a bill to the Landtag which is to increase the middle-class vote at the expense of the landowners and workers. Bitter Conservative and Centre Party opposition leads to the withdrawal of this proposal.

1911

(July) The Agadir incident (see p. 120).

1912

(Jan.) Public dissatisfaction with the Right results in 110 seats for the socialists in the Reichstag, making them the largest party. An Anglo–German conference on naval strength fails to halt the naval race. Passing of another naval bill and large increase in the army approved.

(Oct.) War in the Balkans (see p. 210).

1913

(Jan.) A new army bill further increases the peacetime strength of Germany's land forces. (Nov.) The Zabern 'Incident' shows continued ability of the army to operate with little formal constitutional restraint.

1914

(4 Aug.) With the outbreak of war, the Emperor, in a speech to the Reichstag, declares 'I know no parties any more, only Germans'; the party leaders respond with a political truce for the duration of hostilities, the *'Burgfriede'*. Bethmann-Hollweg speaks of Germany as the victim of unprovoked aggression; the war credits are passed unanimously before the Reichstag adjourns.

(8 Aug.) Rathenau, director of the giant industrial combine AEG, persuades the War Minister Falkenhayn to establish the War Raw Materials Department.

(25–30 Aug.) Hindenburg and Ludendorff smash one of two invading Russian armies at the battle of Tannenberg.

(5–14 Sept.) The battle of the Marne; the German advance into France is halted; Moltke breaks down and is replaced by Falkenhayn. The conflict now develops into static trench warfare.

1915

(Feb.) The waters around the British Isles are declared a war zone; enemy warships become liable to be sunk without warning. The Russians are defeated decisively at the battle of the Masurian Lakes.

(May) The sinking of the liner *Lusitania* with great loss of life outrages Allied public opinion and that of the United States.

(Sept.) Unrestricted submarine warfare ceases in British waters.

(Oct.) Austro–German forces defeat Serbia.

(Dec.) Spahn of the Centre Party on behalf of all non-socialist parties presents a declaration in which are demanded territorial acquisitions to safeguard Germany's military, economic and political interests.

1916

(Jan.) In a bid to retain socialist support, Bethmann-Hollweg persuades the Emperor to promise reform of the Prussian constitution.

(Feb.–June) Battle of Verdun; Germany and France both suffer massive losses as Falkenhayn attempts to 'bleed France white'.

(Feb.) German submarines ordered to sink any merchant ships in the war zone without warning.

(Apr.) The sinking of the liner *The Sussex* causes the United States to threaten to break off diplomatic relations; to avert this, Bethmann-Hollweg, to the annoyance of the Conservatives, places restrictions on submarine warfare.

(July–Oct.) Battle of the Somme; Germany and Britain suffer huge losses. The Conservatives demand the replacement of Falkenhayn by Hindenburg. Bethmann-Hollweg joins the campaign to replace Falkenhayn; he holds the misguided view that a strong, popular figure like Hindenburg can achieve a negotiated peace without alienating the Right.

(29 Aug.) Falkenhayn replaced as Chief of General Staff by Hindenburg. Ludendorff appointed Chief Quarter-Master-General. Auxiliary Service Act passed by the Reichstag; Ludendorff has demanded the immediate mobilization of the whole population, including compulsory labour for women and restrictions on the workers' freedom to change jobs. The aim is to establish an equality of sacrifice between soldiers and civilians. However, the Act itself is less far reaching; it introduces direction of labour for all males between 17 and 60, but safeguards the right of the working population to change jobs. Though women and children are excluded, an intensive campaign is launched to mobilize them for the war effort. The Majority Socialists and the Labour Fellowship vote against the budget.

(Oct. 1916–Mar. 1917) The 'turnip winter'. Severe cold destroys the potato crop, causing widespread hardship; the hardship is increased by a lack of transport. Bethmann-Hollweg realizes constitutional changes will be necessary to avoid serious disturbances.

(Dec.) Hindenburg and Ludendorff demand unrestricted submarine warfare.

1917

(9 Jan.) Bethmann-Hollweg agrees to unrestricted submarine warfare.

(31 Jan.) America informed of German decision to renew unrestricted submarine warfare on 1 February.

(1 Feb.) Unrestricted submarine warfare begins.

(25 Feb.) Three Americans killed when Germans sink *Laconia*.

(1 Mar.) Telegram from German Foreign Minister, Zimmermann, to German Minister in Mexico, calling for German–Mexican alliance and Mexican invasion of USA in the event of an American declaration of war, published in the American press after interception by British naval intelligence.

(17 Mar.) Bethmann-Hollweg hints at the need for change during a speech to the Prussian Landtag; however, news of the Russian revolution stirs the Reichstag into life, the Radicals demand universal suffrage in all states, the Independent Socialists demand parliamentary government and peace without annexations. The Majority Socialists, supported by the National Liberals, manage to establish a committee to consider constitutional reform.

(Apr.) The Chancellor persuades William to issue an Easter message promising reform of the Prussian upper chamber after the war and the introduction of the secret ballot and direct election for the Lower House. The Emperor's message arouses little enthusiasm and produces consternation among the conservatives.

(6 Apr.) USA enters the war.

(6 July) Matthias Erzberger, a rising figure on the left of the Centre Party, declares unrestricted submarine warfare a failure and urges Germany to commit itself to a policy of peace and reconciliation.

(12 July) Bethmann-Hollweg falls from power.

(14 July) Michaelis is appointed Chancellor.

(19 July) In the Reichstag a peace resolution is carried by 212 votes to 126. Ludendorff and Hindenburg threaten to resign if it is accepted.

(11 Sept.) Michaelis demands that Germany give up its claim to Belgium.

(1 Nov.) Count Hertling replaces Michaelis as Chancellor and promises to base his foreign policy on the peace resolution and to reform the Prussian franchise.

(5 Dec.) German and Russian delegates sign armistice at Brest-Litovsk.

1918

(8 Jan.) President Wilson outlines his 'Fourteen Points'.

(3 Mar.) Treaty of Brest-Litovsk with Russia. Only Independent Socialists in the Reichstag vote against it.

(21 Mar.) Ludendorff begins 'St Michael' offensive on the Western Front.

(26 Mar.) After initial success, the first German offensive comes to a halt within 75 miles of Paris.

(9 Apr.) Renewed German offensive in Flanders.

(27 May) Germans reach the Marne.

(18 July) Allied counter-attack begins.

(8 Aug.) 'The Black Day of the German Army' (Ludendorff) as German forces break under fresh Allied offensive.

(11 Sept.) Allies break through the Hindenburg Line.

(28 Sept.) Ludendorff concedes that military victory is impossible.

(30 Sept.) Hertling resigns in the face of proposals to transform Germany into a democracy.

(1 Oct.) Ludendorff asks parliament to make peace.

(3 Oct.) Prince Max of Baden appointed Chancellor and asks the USA for an armistice on the basis of the 'Fourteen Points' (see also p. 342).

(12 Oct.) Germany and Austria–Hungary agree to Wilson's terms that they withdraw from occupied territory, but hesitate over demands for a democratic, civilian government.

(20 Oct.) Germany suspends submarine warfare.

(21 Oct.) German sailors at Wilhelmshaven mutiny.

(23 Oct.) Wilson refuses to make peace with an autocratic regime in Germany.

(26 Oct.) Ludendorff is forced to resign. The Reichstag makes the Chancellor dependent on parliament and military appointments to be countersigned by the Minister of War.

(29 Oct.) The Emperor leaves Berlin for army headquarters at Spa.

(2 Nov.) Scheidemann, one of the Majority Socialist leaders, writes to Prince Max requesting William's abdication.

(3 Nov.) German Grand Fleet mutinies at Kiel. Sailors set up their own workers' and sailors' councils, mainly for redress of grievances.

(7 Nov.) Bavaria is proclaimed a republic and a Socialist government is set up in Munich. In Berlin the Majority Socialist Party executive threatens to withdraw support from the government unless the Emperor abdicates.

(9 Nov.) General Strike in Berlin. The Emperor flees to Holland. Prince Max resigns and hands over office to Ebert. Scheidemann proclaims a republic from the Reichstag building and Ebert forms a Socialist-dominated government. Ebert makes pact with Groener, with the army

assuring support in return for suppression of Bolshevism.

(11 Nov.) German representatives sign armistice with Allies at Compiègne.

(22 Nov.) Agreement reached for transitional government until National Constituent Assembly meets.

(20 Dec.) Workers' and soldiers' delegates in Berlin demand nationalization of major industries.

(30 Dec.) German Communist Party (KPD) founded by Spartacists and other groups. They decide to boycott the elections for the National Constituent Assembly and stage a rising in Berlin.

1919

(5–11 Jan.) Spartacist revolt in Berlin put down by Ebert-Noske government using 'Free Corps' (*Freikorps*) of ex-soldiers.

(15 Jan.) Rosa Luxemburg and Karl Liebknecht, leaders of the Spartacists, are arrested and murdered by the *Freikorps.*

(19 Jan.) National Constituent Assembly elected on basis of proportional representation but fails to give any party an outright majority.

(8 Feb.) National Constituent Assembly meets at Weimar.

(11 Feb.) Ebert becomes President of Weimar Republic, following formation of coalition of Majority Socialists and the Centre and Democratic parties under Scheidemann.

(13 Feb.) Scheidemann forms a Cabinet.

(21 Feb.) Assassination of the premier of the Bavarian Republic, Kurt Eisner, by right wingers.

(Apr.) Socialist Bavarian Republic overthrown by Federal German forces.

(29 June) Treaty of Versailles signed (see p. 130).

1920

(13–17 Mar.) Kapp Putsch; *Freikorps* officers attempt to make Wolfgang Kapp chancellor of the Reich in pro-monarchist *coup d'état* in

Berlin. Although troops refuse to fire on the *Freikorps,* and the government is forced to flee Berlin, a general strike frustrates the putsch.

(Apr.) Hitler's German Workers' Party changes its name to the National Socialist German Workers' Party (Nazis).

1921

(29 Aug.) Assassination of Matthias Erzberger, the leader of Centre Party, by right-wing officers.

1922

(16 Apr.) Treaty of Rapallo provides for economic and military co-operation between Germany and Russia.

(24 June) Assassination of Walter Rathenau, foreign secretary, by right-wing nationalists.

1923

(11 Jan.) Non-payment of reparations leads to French and Belgian troops occupying the Ruhr. Germany adopts passive resistance to the occupation.

(12 Aug.) Stresemann becomes Chancellor.

(Sept.–Nov.) Massive inflation in Germany. Interest rates raised to 90% (15 Sept.) but by October German mark trading at rate of 10,000 million to the pound.

(26 Sept.) Passive resistance in Ruhr ends. A state of military emergency is declared.

(22 Oct.) Bavarian troops take an oath of allegiance to right-wing regime in Bavaria. Communist revolt in Hamburg is put down and left-wing governments are deposed in Saxony and Thuringia.

(8–9 Nov.) Unsuccessful 'Beer Hall' putsch in Munich led by Hitler and Ludendorff. Hitler captured.

(20 Nov.) German currency stabilized by establishment of the *Rentenmark,* valued at one billion old marks.

(23 Nov.) Stresemann becomes Foreign Minister.

1924

(1 Apr.) Hitler sentenced to five years' imprisonment for part in Munich putsch (but released in Dec.).

(9 Apr.) Dawes Plan provides a modified settlement of the reparations issue.

(4 May) In Reichstag elections, Nationalists and Communists gain many seats from the moderate parties.

(7 Dec.) In further elections, Nationalists and Communists lose seats to Socialists.

(15 Dec.) Beginning of Cabinet crisis in Germany.

1925

(15 Jan.) Hans Luther, an independent, succeeds Wilhelm Marx of the Centre as Chancellor with Stresemann as Foreign Minister.

(28 Feb.) Death of President Ebert.

(26 Apr.) Hindenburg elected President.

(7 July) French troops begin to leave Rhineland.

(16 Oct.) Locarno Pact guarantees Franco–German and Belgian–German frontiers and the demilitarization of the Rhineland. (Signed, 1 Dec.)

1926

(17 May) Marx takes over from Luther as Chancellor.

(8 Sept.) Germany admitted to the League of Nations.

1927

(29 Jan.) Marx takes over from Luther as Chancellor again.

(13 May) 'Black Friday' with collapse of economic system.

(16 Sept.) Hindenburg, while dedicating the Tannenberg memorial, repudiates Article 231 of the Versailles Treaty, the 'War Guilt' clause.

1928

(20 May) Social Democrats win victory at elections, mainly at the expense of the Nationalists.

(28 June) Hermann Müller, a Socialist, is appointed Chancellor, following resignation of Marx's ministry on 13 June.

1929

(6 Feb.) Germany accepts Kellogg–Briand Pact, outlawing war and providing for the pacific settlement of disputes.

(7 June) Young Committee provides for a rescheduling of German reparation payments in the form of annuities, on the security of the German railways, for the next 60 years.

(6–13 Aug.) At Reparations Conference in The Hague, Germany accepts the Young Plan and the Allies agree to evacuate the Rhineland by June 1930.

(3 Oct.) Stresemann dies.

(29 Oct.) Wall Street Crash leads to the cessation of American loans to Europe.

(22 Dec.) German referendum upholds the Young Plan.

FRANCE, 1851–1945

1851

(2 Dec.) *Coup d'état* of Louis Napoleon: leaders of Orléanists and Republicans seized and imprisoned, National Assembly dissolved, and constitution annulled.

(3–4 Dec.) Protests in Paris against the coup are crushed.

(14 Dec.) Plebiscite ratifies Louis Napoleon as President for ten years and empowers him to frame a constitution by 7,430,000 votes to 640,000.

1852

(9 Jan.) Opponents of regime banished by decree of the President.

(l4 Jan.) Louis Napoleon establishes a constitution with a Senate, Council of State and Legislative Assembly.

(22 Jan.) Orléans family banished from France by decree of the President.

(17 Feb.) Press censorship introduced.

(7 Nov.) Senate proposes creation of Empire.

(21 Nov.) Plebiscite ratifies revival of French Empire by 7,824,189 votes to 253,145.

(2 Dec.) Second Empire proclaimed and Louis Napoleon takes title of Emperor Napoleon III.

1853

(29 Jan.) Marriage of Napoleon III to Eugénie de Montijo.

(14 June) French squadron joins British fleet at the Dardanelles.

1854

(12 Mar.) Britain and France conclude alliance with the Ottoman Empire against Russia.

(27 Mar.) France declares war on Russia and enters Crimean War.

(26 May) Franco–British forces occupy Piraeus in Greece to enforce Greek neutrality.

(June) French forces land at Varna on the Black Sea.

(14 Sept.) French, British and Turkish troops land in the Crimea.

(20 Sept.) Franco–British forces defeat Russians at Alma.

(17 Oct.) Siege of Sevastapol begins.

(5 Nov.) Franco–British forces defeat Russians at Inkerman.

1855

(11 Sept.) French and British occupy Sevastapol.

1856

(25 Feb.) Peace Conference at Paris ends Crimean War.

(16 Mar.) Birth of the Prince Imperial.

(2 Dec.) Franco–Spanish frontier defined.

1857

(14 June) Commercial Treaty between Russia and France.

(Dec.) Occupation of Canton by French and British forces.

1858

(14 Jan.) Orsini plot to assassinate Napoleon III fails.

(19 Feb.) *Loi de sûreté générale* permits the government to arrest and exile without trial in certain cases.

(20 July) Napoleon and Cavour begin meetings at Plombières to plan unification of Italy.

1859

(19 Jan.) Treaty of alliance between France and Sardinia.

(17 Apr.) Louis Napoleon grants an amnesty for political prisoners.

(3 May) France declares war on Austria, following Austrian invasion of Sardinian territory.

(4 June) French defeat the Austrians at Magenta.

(14 June) French and Sardinians defeat the Austrians at Solferino.

(8 July) Franco–Austrian armistice.

(11 July) Peace of Villafranca. Austria cedes Parma and Lombardy to France for subsequent transfer to Sardinia.

1860

(23 Jan.) Free trade treaty (Cobden–Chevalier Treaty) signed between Britain and France.

(24 Mar.) Sardinia cedes Nice and Savoy to France.

(24 Nov.) Decree extends power of the French legislature by allowing an address to the throne. Senate and Assembly allowed to discuss policy once a year and Ministers 'without Portfolio' appointed to the Assembly to explain government policy. Full publication of debates permitted in *Journal Officiel*.

1861

(31 Oct.) France, Britain and Spain sign London Convention to protect their interests, after Mexico suspends repayment of debts, by sending a joint expedition to enforce payment.

(11 Nov.) Financial powers of French legislature extended.

1862

(19 Feb.) Joint expedition to Mexico forces Treaty of La Soledad on Juarez, who promises to pay an indemnity and arrears of debt. England and Spain withdraw from the expedition but Napoleon III decides to maintain forces there with a view to setting up a new monarchy.

(28 Mar.) French acquire six provinces of Cochin China.

(May) After repulse of French troops from Puebla, 25,000 French troops are sent as reinforcements to Mexico.

(2 Aug.) Prusso–French commercial treaty.

1863

(1 May) French elections show increase in opposition from five to 35, supported by two million voters. Paris elects nine opposition deputies, including Thiers.

(23 Nov.) Thiers forms opposition Third Party.

1864

(10 Apr.) Archduke Maximilian of Austria becomes Emperor of Mexico with the support of French troops.

1865

(4–11 Oct.) Biarritz meetings between Napoleon III and Bismarck. Napoleon sanctions Prussian supremacy in Germany.

1866

(12 June) Secret treaty between Austria and France. Napoleon III promises French neutrality in return for Venetia which France will hand over to Italy.

(4 July) Napoleon III announces Austria's cession of Venetia.

1867

(12 Mar.) French troops withdrawn from Mexico. Maximilian refuses to leave.

(11 May) London Conference guaranteeing the neutrality of Luxembourg forestalls Napoleon III's attempt to purchase it.

(19 June) Execution of Maximilian in Mexico.

(28 Oct.) French troops sent to assist the Pope whose territories have come under attack from Italian volunteers. Napoleon III declares former treaty with Italians broken.

(3 Nov.) Italian forces defeated by French and papal forces at Mentana and Garibaldi captured. Rome receives a French garrison.

1868

(11 June) Freedom of press and limited right of public meeting granted in France.

1869

(May) Although the government receives a large majority at the elections, there is the first evidence under the Empire of active participation by opposition parties. Radicals win victories in Paris and Lyons.

(12 July) Parliamentary system adopted by Napoleon III.

1870

(2 Jan.) Ollivier becomes French Premier. Repeal of the *loi de sûreté* and dismissal of the prefect of the Seine, Hausmann.

(20 Apr.) A new liberal constitution introduced by a decree of the Senate, making the Senate an upper house sharing legislative powers with the Assembly.

(23 Apr.) Imperial decree calls on French nation to accept or reject by plebiscite the 'liberal empire' and the alteration of the constitution.

(24 Apr.) Imperial proclamation circulated in support of the plebiscite.

(8 May) Plebiscite gives positive vote of 7,336,000 against 1,560,000.

(2 July) News of acceptance of Spanish throne by Leopold, Prince of Hohenzollern, reaches France.

(12 July) Leopold's candidature withdrawn.

(13 July) French ambassador seeks assurances from the King of Prussia at Ems that the Spanish candidature will not be renewed. The

King's report of the conversation to Bismarck is doctored by him and released to the press (the 'Ems Telegram') to inflame Franco–Prussian relations. As anticipated, the result is 'war fever' in France.

(19 July) France declares war on Prussia.

(4 Aug.) French under MacMahon defeated at Weissenberg.

(6 Aug.) French defeats at Worth and Spicheren.

(10 Aug.) Fall of Ollivier ministry and formation of new ministry under Montauban-Palikao, the Bonapartist Minister of War.

(14 Aug.) French defeated at Colombey-Nouilly.

(16 Aug.) French worsted at Vionville.

(18 Aug.) French defeated at Gravelotte and St Privat.

(19 Aug.) French army in Metz besieged.

(1 Sept.) French defeated at Sedan.

(2 Sept.) Napoleon III capitulates with his army at Sedan and is taken to Wilhelmshohe.

(4 Sept.) Republic proclaimed in Paris. Formation of Government of National Defence. Flight of Empress Eugénie to England.

(19 Sept.) Siege of Paris begun by Prussians following failure of negotiations.

(27 Oct.) Capitulation of French troops at Metz.

1871

(8 Jan.) Prussians begin bombardment of Paris.

(19 Jan.) Last sortie from Paris repulsed.

(28 Jan.) Capitulation of Paris by the convention of Versailles and three weeks' truce.

(8 Feb.) Elections held for a National Assembly.

(12 Feb.) National Assembly meets at Bordeaux.

(23 Feb.) Thiers ministry formed.

(26 Feb.) Preliminary Peace of Versailles between France and Germany:

(i) France cedes Alsace (except for Belfort and its surrounding territory) and Lorraine, including Metz, a total of 4,700 square miles and 1.5 million inhabitants; (ii) France agrees to pay 5,000,000 francs indemnity in three years.

(1 Mar.) German troops enter Paris. The National Assembly ratifies the peace treaty.

(18 Mar.) Rising of the Paris Commune. Hôtel de Ville taken over by Central Committee of National Guard. Thiers leaves Paris for Versailles.

(19 Mar.) National Guard announces elections in Paris for a Commune.

(22 Mar.) Commune proclaimed at Lyons, but soon collapses.

(23 Mar.) Marseilles Commune declared.

(28 Mar.) Proclamation of the Paris Commune and first decrees issued the next day.

(4 Apr.) Communard forces retreat from Versailles. Collapse of Marseilles Commune.

(6 Apr.) Paris communards besieged by troops of the National Assembly.

(19 Apr.) Commune's 'Declaration to the French People'.

(1 May) Communards set up a Committee of Public Safety. Versailles troops begin bombardment of Paris.

(10 May) Definitive Treaty of Frankfurt signed by France and Germany.

(21–28 May) Versailles troops enter Paris and begin a week of fighting to subdue the Commune's strongholds. Hostages taken by the communards, including the Archbishop of Paris, are shot. Widespread summary executions of communard prisoners.

(28 May) Last communard barricades captured.

(31 Aug.) Thiers elected President of France.

1872

(25 Jan.) Henry, Count of Chambord, legitimist claimant to the throne of France, makes Antwerp Declaration, calling for a 'Revolutionary Monarchy' in France.

(28 July) France adopts conscription.

(5 Nov.) Anglo–French commercial treaty signed.

(22 Nov.) Count of Paris, head of Orléanist line, accepts compensation for confiscation of his French estates. Execution of leading communards.

1873

(9 Jan.) Death of Napoleon III at Chislehurst, England.

(24 May) Thiers forced to resign by coalition of monarchist parties. Marshal MacMahon elected president of the National Assembly.

(27 Oct.) Count of Chambord, after reconciliation with the Count of Paris, virtually ends hope of monarchical restoration by refusing to accept the tricolour.

(20 Nov.) French monarchists confer presidential powers on MacMahon for seven years.

1875

(30 Jan.) Republican Constitution in France passed by one vote. Legislative power exercised by two chambers: the Chamber of Deputies, elected by direct elections and manhood suffrage for four years; and the Senate, partly elected by the Senate itself, and the majority by electoral colleges composed of deputies, councils of departments and districts, and delegates from the communes. Executive power is entrusted to a president who, after the expiry of MacMahon's term (after 1878), is to be elected by the Senate and Chamber of Deputies united as a national assembly, for a period of seven years. The President may be impeached by the Chamber.

(16 July) French Constitution finalized.

(Dec.) Adoption of new electoral law, *scrutins d'arrondissement*, and separation of the National Assembly into its two components, the Chamber and Senate.

1876

(Jan.–Feb.) New elections result in a Senate balanced between republicans and monarchical parties, with republicans in a majority in the Chamber.

1877

(16 May) 'Seize Mai' crisis. Ministry headed by Simon is replaced by act of the President.

De Broglie forms a pro-monarchist government. 363 members of the Chamber vote against the action of the President.

(4 Sept.) Death of Thiers.

(Oct.) Republican majority returned at the elections.

(19 Nov.–13 Dec.) De Broglie resigns, but MacMahon forms a royalist ministry under Rochebouet (23 Nov.). Continuing refusal of the Chamber to work with the ministry results in formation of republican ministry under Dufaure.

1879

(16 Jan.) Pardon of 2,000 communards.

(30 Jan.) MacMahon resigns and is succeeded by Grévy.

(25 June) Anti-Jesuit legislation passed.

(1 July) Death of Prince Louis Napoleon in South Africa.

(4 Aug.) Alsace–Lorraine declared integral part of the German Reich.

(27 Nov.) French Chamber moves from Versailles to Paris.

1880

(30 Mar.) Proclamation dispersing the Jesuits. Non-authorized religious associations have to regularize their positions or leave.

(30 June) Jesuits forcibly removed from religious houses.

(11 July) General amnesty for communards.

(19 Sept.) Ferry ministry.

(16 Oct.) Unauthorized congregations expelled from their religious houses.

1881

(30 Apr.) French troops invade Tunis from Algeria.

(12 May) Tunisia becomes a French protectorate.

(14 Nov.) Ferry resigns after attacks on his Tunisian policy and Gambetta forms ministry.

1882

(27 Jan.) Gambetta falls on a motion to adopt *scrutin de liste*. Freycinet forms ministry.

(29 Mar.) Free, compulsory primary education introduced. Religious teaching in schools abolished.

(9 Nov.) Franco–British dual control of Egypt established.

1883

(1 June) French war with Madagascar.

(24 Aug.) Death of Count of Chambord without an heir effectively ends legitimist line.

(25 Aug.) French establish protectorate in Indo-China.

1884

(21 Mar.) Legislation on trade unions.

(5 Aug.) The 75 life senatorships set up in 1875 are abolished. Members of former dynasties are excluded from the Presidency.

1885

(19 Sept.) Grévy re-elected President.

1886

(7 Jan.) General Boulanger becomes Minister of War in Freycinet ministry.

(23 June) Orléanist and Bonaparte families banned from France.

1887

(20 Apr.) Schnaebele incident. A French officer and spy is illegally arrested by the Germans. Grévy is criticized for taking the issue too lightly and Boulanger makes himself the spokesman for nationalist feeling over the incident.

(18 May) Boulanger excluded from the Rouvier ministry.

(1 Oct.) Boulanger attempts *coup d'état* amidst the growing scandals associated with Grévy's Presidency.

(2 Dec.) Grévy resigns as President as a result of scandal surrounding the sale of honours. Carnot becomes President.

1888

(27 Mar.) Boulanger retires from the French army, making him eligible for election.
(15 May) Boulanger elected to the Chamber, standing for several constituencies. He advocates a revision of the Constitution through 'a specially elected constituent assembly'.
(30 Oct.) France makes a large loan to Russia.

1889

(10 Jan.) French establish protectorate over the Ivory Coast.
(27 Jan.) Boulanger's attempt to provoke a 'crisis' in Paris fails.
(8 Apr.) Flight of Boulanger, fearing arrest. Republicans remain entrenched as the major party in the elections, securing over 54 per cent of the vote.
(17 July) New law forbids multiple candidature in elections.

1890

(5 Aug.) Anglo–French agreement on spheres of influence in Africa.

1891

(23 July) Visit of French squadron to Kronstadt and further French loan to Russia.
(27 Aug.) Franco–Russian entente.
(30 Sept.) Boulanger commits suicide in Brussels.

1892

(17 Aug.) Franco–Russian military convention.
(18 Aug.) Leo XIII orders French Catholics to accept the Republic.
(10 Nov.) 'Panama Canal Scandal'. De Lesseps and others committed for trial for alleged corruption.

1893

(17 Jan.) Russo–French alliance.
(8–21 Mar.) Panama Trial in Paris; De Lesseps fined.
(10 June) Franco–Russian commercial treaty.
(15–31 July) Franco–British crisis over Siam. Agreement reached that it should be kept as a buffer state.
(13–29 Oct.) Russian squadron visits Toulon.
(17 Nov.) France makes Dahomey a protectorate.
(27 Dec.) Franco–Russian military convention comes into force.

1894

(15 Mar.) Franco–German agreement over African spheres of influence.
(24 June) President Carnot assassinated in Lyons; succeeded by Casimir-Périer.
(15 Oct.) Dreyfus arrested on charge of spying for Germany.
(10 Nov.) French begin invasion of Madagascar.
(22 Dec.) Dreyfus convicted by court martial and sentenced to imprisonment on Devil's Island.

1895

(12 Jan.) French trade unions declare in favour of General Strike.
(13 Jan.) President Casimir-Périer resigns; succeeded by Faure (17 Jan.).
(23 Apr.) France, Germany and Russia intervene against Japan's invasion of China.

1896

(5 Jan.) Anglo–French agreement over Siam.
(18 Aug.) France annexes Madagascar.
(30 Sept.) Franco–Italian convention over Tunisia.

1897

(18 Sept.) Anglo–French agreement about Tunisia.

(15 Nov.) Discovery that the document on which Dreyfus had been convicted was produced by Major Esterhazy. Government enquiry into Dreyfus case.

1898

(11 Jan.) Acquittal of Esterhazy for forgery in the Dreyfus case prompts Zola's *J'accuse* letter to the President.
(23 Feb.) Zola imprisoned for *J'accuse* letter.
(14 June) Anglo–French agreement over Nigeria and Gold Coast.
(10 July) French occupy Fashoda in Sudan, confronting British forces under Kitchener.
(30 Aug.) Forgery admitted by Colonel Henry in the Dreyfus case.
(4 Nov.) After period of tension the 'Fashoda incident' is settled by Marchand marching away from Fashoda.
(26 Nov.) Franco–Italian commercial agreement ends tariff war.

1899

(19 Jan.) Anglo–French Convention on the Sudan.
(18 Feb.) Loubet becomes President of France.
(21 Mar.) Anglo–French Convention on North Africa ends period of tension between the two countries.
(3 June) Dreyfus trial verdict annulled and retrial ordered.
(9 Aug.) French Foreign Minister Delcassé visits St Petersburg and strengthens Franco–Russian alliance.
(9 Sept.) Dreyfus retried and condemned but 'with extenuating circumstances'.
(19 Sept.) Dreyfus pardoned by presidential decree.

1900

(30 Apr.) Republicans form bloc to defend Republic against anti-Dreyfusards.
(14 Dec.) Secret Franco–Italian agreement to support each other's interests in Morocco and Tunisia respectively.

1901

(1 July) Association Law promulgated for compulsory regulation of all religious congregations and associations and the dissolution of those not authorized by the State.

1902

(2 June) Waldeck–Rousseau ministry resigns and succeeded by the more vigorously anti-clerical Combes ministry.
(1 Nov.) Franco–Italian Entente. Italy agrees to remain neutral in the event of war between France and Germany.

1903

(18 Mar.) Dissolution of religious orders in France.
(Apr.) Britain and France oppose construction of Baghdad Railway.
(1 May) Edward VII's visit to Paris marks beginning of improved Anglo–French relations.
(6 July) Diplomatic conversations begin in London on the *Entente Cordiale*.

1904

(8 Apr.) *Entente Cordiale* settles Anglo–French colonial disputes in North Africa.
(17 May) French ambassador withdrawn from the Vatican.
(3 Oct.) Franco–Spanish treaty on Morocco.
(18 Nov.) Combes introduces legislation to separate Church and State in France.

1905

(30 Apr.) Anglo–French military conversations following the first Moroccan crisis.
(8 July) France agrees to a conference on Morocco.
(6 Dec.) Church and State separated in France.

1906

(10 Jan.) Further Anglo–French military and naval conversations.

(16 Jan.) Opening of Algeçiras conference on Morocco.

(8 Apr.) Algeçiras Act signed, giving France and Spain major control in Morocco.

(12 July) Dreyfus completely exonerated by French government.

1907

(8 Apr.) Anglo–French Convention confirms independence of Siam.

(10 June) Franco–Japanese agreement on 'open-door' policy in China.

(4 Aug.) French fleet bombards Casablanca.

1909

(9 Feb.) France's dominant position in Morocco recognized by Germany in return for economic concessions.

1910

(15 Jan.) Reorganization of French Congo as French Equatorial Africa.

(10 Oct.) Troops called out during railway strike and general strike averted.

1911

(17 Jan.) Assassination attempt on French Premier Briand in Chamber of Deputies.

(23 Feb.) French Chamber votes for building two battleships.

(11 Apr.) Jean Jaurès produces scheme for socialist organization of France.

(1 July) 'Agadir incident' increases tension between France and Germany.

(10 July) Russia confirms her support for France as a result of the Moroccan crisis.

(31 Aug.) Franco–Russian military conversations.

(4 Nov.) France and Germany sign convention giving France a free hand in Morocco in return for concessions of territory in the Congo.

1912

(6 Feb.) French Senate ratifies Moroccan agreement.

(30 Mar.) Morocco becomes a French protectorate.

(Sept.) Anglo–French naval convention apportions responsibilities in the event of war.

(22–30 Nov.) Grey–Cambon correspondence strengthens *Entente.*

1913

(17 Jan.) Poincaré elected President of France.

(7 Aug.) French army bill imposes three years' military service.

(20 Nov.) Zabern incident, in which a German officer insults recruits in Alsace–Lorraine, inflames Franco–German relations.

1914

(8 Jan.) *Le Figaro* makes charges against Caillaux, French Finance Minister.

(15 Feb.) Franco–German agreement on Baghdad Railway.

(16 Mar.) Editor of *Le Figaro*, Calmette, assassinated by Mme Caillaux for publishing private letters.

(20 July) President Poincaré visits Russia.

(30 July) Jean Jaurès murdered in Paris.

(1 Aug.) Germany declares war on Russia; France mobilizes.

(3 Aug.) Germany declares war on France.

(4 Aug.) Britain declares war on Germany.

(8 Aug.) First British troops land in France. Britain and France occupy German Togoland.

(12 Aug.) France declares war on Austria.

(14 Aug.) Beginning of 'Battle of the Frontiers'; French receive crushing defeats in Lorraine, the Ardennes, and on the Somme. (For full military chronology, see pp. 122–124).

(24 Aug.) Allies retreat in northern France in face of German advance.

(26 Aug.) Germans cross the Meuse and occupy Lille. French Cabinet reconstructed.

(30 Aug.) Germans take Amiens.

(3 Sept.) French government moves to Bordeaux. Germans cross the Marne and occupy Rheims.

(4 Sept.) France, Russia and Britain agree by Pact of London not to make a separate peace.

(5–9 Sept.) Battle of the Marne. Paris saved from capture and Germans retreat.

(15–18 Sept.) Battle of the Aisne in which German forces withstand Allied attacks establishes trench line on Western Front.

(5 Nov.) France and Britain declare war on the Ottoman Empire.

(10 Dec.) French government returns to Paris.

1915

(22 Apr.) Anglo–French forces land at Gallipoli.

(29 Sept.) US loan to France and Britain.

(29 Oct.) Briand forms a new ministry in France.

(3 Dec.) Joffre becomes French Commander-in-Chief.

1916

(29 Jan.) First air attack on Paris by zeppelin.

(21 Feb.) Battle of Verdun opens.

(1 June) French and British troops join Somme offensive.

(24 Oct.) French move onto the offensive east of Verdun.

(3 Dec.) Nivelle succeeds Joffre as French Commander-in-Chief.

(12 Dec.) French War Ministry formed.

(16 Dec.) Germans end Verdun offensive.

1917

(23 Feb.) Germany begins withdrawal to Hindenburg Line.

(19 Mar.) Ribot Cabinet formed in France.

(16 Apr.) French offensive on the Aisne begins; halted (20 Apr.) with heavy loss. Further offensive in Champagne costs 200,000 men.

(29 Apr.) Pétain becomes French Chief of Staff.

(3 May) Mutinies in several French corps.

(15 May) Pétain succeeds Nivelle as French Commander-in-Chief with Foch as Chief of Staff.

(20 May) Mutinies begin in French army in Champagne.

(26 June) First US troops arrive in France.

(3 Sept.) Painlevé forms Cabinet in France.

(16 Nov.) Clemenceau forms Cabinet on Painlevé's fall.

1918

(14 Jan.) Cailloux, former Premier, arrested for treason.

(21 Mar.) German offensive brings them within 75 miles of Paris. Paris bombarded by long-range guns.

(26 Mar.) Foch assumes united command of armies on Western Front.

(27 Apr.) Renewed German offensive captures Rheims.

(15 July–4 Aug.) Second battle of the Marne halts German offensive.

(22 July) Allies cross the Marne.

(4 Sept.) Germans retreat to Siegfried Line.

(30 Oct.) Allies sign armistice with the Ottoman Empire.

(1 Nov.) Anglo–French forces occupy Constantinople.

(3 Nov.) Allies sign armistice with Austria–Hungary.

(11 Nov.) Allies sign armistice with Germany at Compiègne.

1919

(28 June) Versailles Treaty signed.

(Nov.) Victory of right-wing 'Bloc National' in elections to the Assembly.

1920

(17 Jan.) Deschanel elected President of France. Resignation of Clemenceau; Millerand forms ministry.

(16 May) Joan of Arc canonized.

(7 Sept.) Franco–Belgian military convention.

(23 Dec.) Millerand becomes French President.

(29 Dec.) French socialists at Tours agree to join Moscow International; formation of French Communist Party.

1921

(16 Jan.) Briand becomes Prime Minister.
(24–29 Jan.) Paris Conference agrees reparations for France.
(19 Feb.) Franco–Polish alliance.

1922

(15 Jan.) Poincaré becomes Prime Minister and Foreign Minister.
(9–11 Dec.) International conference in London considers Germany's request for a reparations moratorium.

1923

(11 Jan.) Franco–Belgian occupation of the Ruhr in retaliation for non-payment of reparations; passive resistance by German workers.

1924

(9 Apr.) Germany accepts Dawes Plan on reparations and agreement reached that France should withdraw from the Ruhr.
(May) *Cartel des Gauches* wins victory at the elections.
(10 June) Millerand resigns as President. Doumergue elected President (13th); Herriot becomes Prime Minister (15th).

1925

(10 Apr.) Painlevé becomes French Prime Minister.
(27 July) French begin evacuation of Ruhr.
(1 Dec.) Locarno Treaties guaranteeing Franco–German and Belgo–German frontiers signed.

1926

(31 Jan.) First part of the Rhineland evacuated.
(26 May) Rebel Abd-El-Krim submits to France.
(15 July) Briand resigns over financial crisis; Poincaré becomes premier of French National Union Ministry. Measures taken to stabilize the franc.

1927

(11 Nov.) Treaty of friendship between France and Yugoslavia.

1928

(22–29 Apr.) Left parties win victory at elections.
(24 June) Devaluation of the franc. Decision to build Maginot Line; Military Service cut to one year.
(27 Aug.) France and 64 other states sign the Kellogg–Briand Pact, outlawing war and providing for peaceful settlement of international disputes.

1929

(27 July) Poincaré resigns as Prime Minister and is succeeded by Briand.
(5 Sept.) Briand proposes a European federal union.

1930

(17 May) Young Plan of reduced German reparations comes into force. Briand produces memorandum on united states of Europe.
(30 June) Last portion of Rhineland evacuated.

1931

(27 Jan.) Laval becomes French premier.
(13 May) Doumer elected French President.
(20 June) Hoover Plan of moratorium of one year on reparations and war debts in view of world economic crisis.

1932

(21 Feb.) Tardieu ministry formed.
(1 May) *Cartel des Gauches* successful in elections.
(6 May) President Doumer assassinated; succeeded by Lebrun (10th).
(4 June) Herriot ministry formed.
(18 Dec.) Paul–Boncour ministry formed.

1933

(31 Jan.) Daladier ministry formed.

(Dec.) Flight of Stavisky brings about scandal of financial corruption among politicians.

1934

(30 Jan.) Daladier second ministry formed.

(6–7 Feb.) Rioting in Paris. Police kill 14 right-wing demonstrators.

(7 Feb.) Daladier resigns and Doumergue forms National Union ministry of centre and moderate parties (8th).

(12 Feb.) French *Confédération Generale du Travail* (CGT) calls General Strike. Demonstrations in defence of the Republic.

(16 May) French complete suppression of rebel Berber tribes in Morocco.

(9 Oct.) Barthou, foreign minister, and King Alexander of Yugoslavia assassinated at Marseilles.

1935

(7 Mar.) Saar district restored to Germany following plebiscite (13 Jan.).

(11–14 Apr.) Stresa Conference of Britain, France and Italy.

(2 May) Franco–Russian treaty of mutual assistance.

(14 July) Mass demonstrations throughout France demanding democracy and the dissolution of right-wing Leagues.

(27 July) French government granted emergency financial powers.

(3 Nov.) Socialist groups merge as Socialist and Republican Union under Léon Blum; later forming with Radical Socialists and Communists a Popular Front.

1936

(Jan.) Popular Front agrees common programme.

(3 May) Popular Front wins major success in elections with 387 seats to 231 of the Right.

(4 June) Blum forms Popular Front government.

(7 June) 40-hour week decreed, collective labour agreements, and paid holidays.

(Sept.) Widespread strike in French industry.

(2 Oct.) Franc devalued.

(18 Nov.) In spite of protests from the left, Blum proposes non-intervention in the Spanish Civil War.

1937

(Jan.) Blum slows down social reform programme.

(27 Feb.) French Chamber passes defence plan; Schneider-Creusot factory nationalized and Maginot Line extended.

(21 June) Chamber rejects Blum's programme of financial reforms. Blum resigns and replaced by the radical Chautemps.

1938

(13 Mar.) Blum forms second Popular Front government, but Senate rejects financial reforms.

(10 Apr.) Blum resigns and replaced by Daladier.

(29 Sept.) France signs Munich Agreement.

(9 Nov.) France recognizes Italian conquest of Abyssinia.

1939

(27 Feb.) France recognizes Franco's government in Spain; Pétain sent as first ambassador.

(17 Mar.) Daladier granted powers to speed rearmament.

(31 Mar.) France and Britain guarantee support for Poland.

(13 Apr.) France and Britain guarantee independence of Romania and Greece.

(26–31 Aug.) Negotiations by Daladier and Chamberlain with Hitler fail.

(3 Sept.) Britain and France declare war on Germany.

(4 Sept.) Franco–Polish agreement.

(26 Sept.) Daladier dissolves French Communist Party.

(30 Sept.) British Expeditionary Force sent to France.

(3 Nov.) Roosevelt allows France to purchase US arms on 'cash and carry' basis, amending Neutrality Act of May 1937.

1940

(21 Mar.) Reynaud succeeds Daladier as premier.

(10 May) German attack on Holland, Belgium and Luxembourg.

(12 May) German panzer forces cross into France.

(14 May) German forces cross the Meuse.

(19 May) General Weygand takes command of the French army from General Gamelin.

(20 May) German forces reach Channel, cutting off Allied armies in the north.

(29 May) British begin evacuation from Dunkirk.

(10 June) Italy declares war on France.

(14 June) Germans enter Paris.

(16 June) Reynaud resigns and replaced by Pétain.

(18 June) De Gaulle, from London, calls for continued resistance.

(22 June) French sign armistice with Germany at Compiègne.

(23 June) British government supports London-based French National Committee, 'Free French', headed by de Gaulle and breaks off relations with Pétain government.

(24 June) Armistice signed with Italy.

(1 July) French government moves to Vichy.

(3 July) British attack on French fleet at Mers-el-Kebir.

(5 July) Vichy regime breaks off relations with Britain.

(10 July) National Assembly votes full powers to Pétain as 'Head of the French State', ending Third Republic.

(22–24 Oct.) Laval, followed by Pétain, holds discussions with Hitler at Montoire.

(13 Dec.) Laval dismissed. Replaced by Darlan.

1941

(18 Apr.) Vichy government withdraws from League of Nations.

(May) Darlan offers French air bases in Syria to the Germans.

(8 June) Allied invasion of Syria.

(30 June) Vichy government breaks off relations with Russia.

1942

(18 Apr.) Laval returns to head government.

(11 Nov.) German troops occupy Vichy France.

(27 Nov.) French fleet scuttled at Toulon.

1944

(6 June) Allied landings in Normandy.

(25 Aug.) Paris is liberated.

(23 Oct.) De Gaulle's provisional government recognized by Allies.

THE EASTERN QUESTION

1768–74

The Ottoman Empire at war with Russia.

1774

Treaty of Kutchuk-Kainardji: Russia receives mouth of Dnieper and Crimea, and gains right to intervene on behalf of Christians in Moldavia and Wallachia.

1775

Austria annexes Bukovina from the Ottoman Empire.

1787–92

The Ottoman Empire at war with Russia and Austria.

1789

Austrians take Belgrade.

1791

The Ottoman Empire cedes Orsova to Austria by Peace of Sistova.

1792

By Peace of Jassy between Russia and the Ottoman Empire, Russia obtains Black Sea coast.

1798

French expedition to Egypt; the Ottoman Empire declares war on France.

1800

Turks and Mamelukes defeated by Kleber at Heliopolis.

1801

France returns Egypt to the Ottoman Empire.

1804

Revolt of Serbs.

1806–12

The Ottoman Empire at war with Russia.

1807

British ships force a passage up the Dardanelles.

1811

Russians take Belgrade.

1812

Under Treaty of Bucharest, Russia receives Bessarabia from the Ottoman Empire.

1815

Revolt of Serbs.

1817

The Ottoman Empire grants autonomy to Serbs.

1821–30

Greek War of Independence (see p. 206).

1826

Convention of Ackermann between Russia and the Ottoman Empire.

1827

Battle of Navarino: Turkish fleet destroyed by British and French.

1828

Russia intervenes on behalf of Greeks and takes Varna.

1829

Under Treaty of Adrianople, Russia obtains territory south of Caucasus; Russia occupies Moldavia and Wallachia.

1830

Greece is declared independent under protection of Britain, Russia and France.

1832

The Ottoman Empire declares war on Egypt.

1833

Treaty of Unkiar Skelessi: Dardanelles are closed to all but Russian ships. The Ottoman Empire recognizes independence of Egypt.

1839

War between the Ottoman Empire and Egypt.

1840

Britain, Russia, Austria and Prussia establish Quadruple Alliance for protection of the Ottoman Empire.

1841

Straits Convention: Dardanelles are closed to all foreign warships while the Ottoman Empire was at peace. Egypt loses Syria to the Ottoman Empire.

1848

Russia suppresses nationalist revolt in Wallachia.

1849

Convention of Balta Liman provides for joint Russo–Turkish supervision of Danubian Principalities.

1853

Russia reoccupies Danubian Principalities and claims protectorate over Christians in the Ottoman Empire.

1854

Outbreak of Crimean War: Britain and France declare war on Russia in support of the Ottoman Empire.

1856

Treaty of Paris: Black Sea is declared neutral and the Ottoman Empire's integrity is guaranteed. Proclamation of Reform Edict.

1858

Separate administrations are established in Danubian Principalities; war between the Ottoman Empire and Montenegro. Land Code enacted.

1859

Ottoman ambassador sent to United States.

1860

Massacre of Christians in Syria.

1862

Danubian Principalities become autonomous principality of 'Romania'.

1871

London Conference abrogates Black Sea neutrality clauses of 1856.

1875

Bulgarian revolt; revolt in Bosnia–Herzegovina.

1876

Bulgarian massacres by Turks. First constitutional period proclamed.

1877

London Protocol: Great Powers demand that the Ottoman Empire undertakes internal reforms. First Turkish parliament meets.

1877–78

Russo–Turkish War.

1878

Treaty of San Stefano creates Bulgaria. Romanian independence confirmed. Congress of Berlin. Austria occupies Bosnia–Herzegovina, though the Ottoman Empire retains sovereignty. Parliament prorogued undefinitely.

1885

The Ottoman Empire refuses Britain passage up the Straits.

1886

Bulgaria is recognized as an autonomous united principality.

1894–97

Christian risings in Crete against the Ottoman Empire.

1895

The Ottoman Empire refuses Britain passage up the Straits. Lord Salisbury suggests the partition of the Ottoman Empire.

1897

Greece declares war on the Ottoman Empire.

1898

William II visits Constantinople.

1908

'Young Turks' rising. Bulgarian independence is formally recognized. Austrian annexation of Bosnia–Herzegovina leads to 'Bosnian Crisis'.

1909

Russia accepts Austrian annexation of Bosnia–Herzegovina; Young Turks depose Sultan Abdul Hamid; succeeded by Mohammed V.

1911

Freedom and Accord Party founded.

1912

First Balkan War: the Ottoman Empire attacked by Bulgaria, Serbia, Greece and Montenegro.

1913

The Ottoman Empire cedes most of her European territory. Second and Third Balkan Wars. Treaty of Bucharest. German–Turkish military convention.

1914

The Ottoman Empire becomes Germany's ally and declares war on Britain, France and Russia.

1915

Secret Constantinople Agreements on fate of Ottoman territory after war.

1918

The Ottoman Empire surrenders unconditionally.

INTERNATIONAL BACKGROUND TO THE FIRST WORLD WAR, 1882–1914

1882

(May) Germany, Austria–Hungary and Italy form the Triple Alliance.

1890

(June) Germany allows Reinsurance Treaty with Russia to lapse.

1894

(Jan.) France and Russia sign defensive alliance.

1896

(Jan.) 'Kruger telegram' incident. William II sends a telegram of congratulation to President Kruger of the Boer Republic on the failure of the Jameson raid on the Transvaal. Widely interpreted in Britain as an antagonistic act.

1898

(Mar.–Apr.) Anglo–German negotiations for agreement to resist Russian expansion in the Far East break down.

(Sept.) British forces under Kitchener and French expeditionary force under Marchand confront each other at Fashoda in the Sudan. After a period of great tension between the two countries, a compromise is reached allowing the French to withdraw.

1899

(Mar.) Anglo–French agreement over their spheres of influence in Africa. France is excluded from the Nile Valley but is allowed to consolidate its position in north, west and Saharan Africa. First German Naval Law passed, greatly expanding the German navy.

(May–July) The Hague Peace Conference fails to achieve agreement on disarmament. Oct. Outbreak of Boer War increases British diplomatic isolation.

1900

(June) Second German Naval Law, further expanding the German navy.

1901

(Mar.–May) Franco–German negotiations for an alliance break down.

1902

(Jan.) Great Britain and Japan sign defensive alliance.

1904

(Apr.) *Entente Cordiale*. Great Britain and France sign agreement on colonial disputes.

1905

(Feb.–July) First Morocco crisis (Tangier incident). William II intervenes in Moroccan affairs, a French area of influence. Germany fails to obtain international support but France agrees to an international conference.

1906

(Jan.–Apr.) Algeçiras conference provides peaceful settlement of the Moroccan crisis, but increases German isolation. During the crisis France and Britain hold military talks, including a commitment for a British expeditionary force to be sent to the continent.

(Feb.) Great Britain launches the *Dreadnought,* the first all big-gun battleship, rendering existing naval vessels obsolete and intensifying the naval race with Germany.

1907

(June–Oct.) Germany rejects any scheme for disarmament at the second Hague Peace Conference.

(July) Triple Alliance renewed for six years.

(Aug.) Britain and Russia sign a convention; Britain, France and Russia are known as the Triple Entente.

1908

(Oct.) Austria–Hungary annexes Bosnia–Herzegovina: Russia backs down from intervention. William II's comments in an interview in the *Daily Telegraph* increase Anglo–German antagonism.

1909

(Jan.) Agreement made for international exploitation of Moroccan mines.

(Feb.) France and Germany sign an agreement recognizing France's political rights in Morocco in return for economic equality.

1911

(1 July) Second Morocco crisis. German gunboat, the *Panther,* arrives in Agadir.

(4 July) Germany warned of Great Britain's concern for Moroccan question.

(July–Nov.) Talks between France and Germany result in end of crisis. Germany recognizes the French protectorate in Morocco (11 Oct.), while France signs agreement to pay compensation to Germany (4 Nov.).

(28 Sept.) Italy sends ultimatum to the Ottoman Empire not to resist troops sent to Tripoli in Libya.

(29 Sept.) Italy declares war on the Ottoman Empire; Italian forces bombard Tripoli and make landings.

(5 Nov.) Italian Prime Minister declares Tripoli annexed.

1912

(Feb.) Haldane mission to Germany fails to end naval race.

(Mar.) Germany publishes Third Naval Law.

(18 Apr.) Italian fleet bombards Turkish forts in the Dardanelles.

(Sept.) Serbia, Montenegro, Greece and Bulgaria form Balkan League against the Ottoman Empire.

(6 Oct.) Great Powers back French proposals to avert Balkan War.

(8 Oct.) Montenegro declares war on the Ottoman Empire.

(12 Oct.) The Ottoman Empire refuses to undertake reforms in its Balkan territories proposed by Great Powers.

(17 Oct.) The Ottoman Empire declares war on Bulgaria and Serbia.

(18 Oct.) Italy and the Ottoman Empire sign peace treaty at Lausanne, leaving Tripoli and Cyrenaica under Italian suzerainty.

(24 Oct.) Turks suffer defeats by Bulgarians at Kirk-Kilisse and by the Serbs at Kumanovo.

(9 Nov.) Greeks take Salonica.

(3 Dec.) Armistice between the Ottoman Empire, Bulgaria, Serbia and Montenegro. Russia and Austria–Hungary mobilize.

1913

(6 Jan.) Peace conference between the Ottoman Empire and Balkan states suspended.

(Mar.) Greeks take Janina; Adrianople surrenders to Bulgarians.

(15 Apr.) Turks and Bulgarians cease fighting.

(22 Apr.) Austria–Hungary moves forces to near Montenegrin border.

(30 May) Preliminaries of peace signed between Balkan states and the Ottoman Empire.

(31 May) Serbs and Greeks sign secret military convention against Bulgaria.

(June) Germany makes fiscal provisions to double the strength of her army.

(30 June) Fighting breaks out between Bulgaria and her former allies.

(10 Aug.) Balkan states sign Treaty of Bucharest.

(30 Sep.) Treaty of Constantinople between the Ottoman Empire and Bulgaria ends Second Balkan War.

1914

(15 June) Anglo–German agreement on Baghdad Railway and Mesopotamia.

(28 June) Archduke Francis Ferdinand assassinated by Slav extremists at Sarajevo.

(23 July) Austria–Hungary sends Serbian government a ten-point ultimatum demanding firm steps to suppress anti-Austrian activities by Slav extremists and (clause 6) participation of Austrian delegates in official enquiry into the assassination,

(24 July) Russian government declares it will defend Serbia against Austro–Hungarian attack.

(25 July) Serbia makes conciliatory reply to Austrian ultimatum, but will not accept clause 6 as contrary to the constitution. Austria–Hungary finds the reply unsatisfactory and mobilizes against Serbia.

(26 July) Grey's proposal of an international conference to settle the Austro–Serbian dispute is rejected by Austria–Hungary and Germany. Austrian forces mobilize on Russian frontier.

(28 July) Austria–Hungary declares war on Serbia.

(30 July) Russia begins general mobilization.

(31 July) Germany demands that Russia cease mobilization.

(1 Aug.) Germany declares war on Russia; France mobilizes. Italy declares her neutrality. German–Turkish treaty signed.

(2 Aug.) Germany occupies Luxembourg and sends ultimatum to Belgium demanding passage for her troops. Russians invade East Prussia.

(3 Aug.) Germany declares war on France and begins invasion of Belgium. British ultimatum to Germany.

(4 Aug.) Germany declares war on Belgium; Britain declares war on Germany.

(5 Aug.) Austria–Hungary declares war on Russia.

(10 Aug.) France declares war on Austria–Hungary.

(12 Aug.) Britain declares war on Austria–Hungary.

THE FIRST WORLD WAR

1914

(28 June) Francis Ferdinand assassinated in Sarajevo.

(28 July) Austria–Hungary declares war on Serbia.

(1 Aug.) Germany declares war on Russia.

(2 Aug.) Germany invades Luxembourg; British fleet mobilized.

(3 Aug.) Germany declares war on France.

(4 Aug.) Germany invades Belgium; Britain and Belgium declare war on Germany.

(5 Aug.) The Ottoman Empire closes the Dardanelles.

(5–12 Aug.) Germans seize Liège.

(6 Aug.) Austria declares war on Russia.

(7 Aug.) British troops arrive in France.

(10 Aug.) Austrians invade Russian Poland.

(10–20 Aug.) Austrian advance on Serbia halted at battle of the Jadar.

(12 Aug.) Britain and France declare war on Austria.

(14–24 Aug.) French suffer defeats in Lorraine, the Ardennes and on the Sambre; British retreat from Mons.

(17–20 Aug.) Russians invade East Prussia and Galicia.

(20 Aug.) Germans occupy Brussels.

(22 Aug.) Hindenburg becomes German Commander in East Prussia.

(26–28 Aug.) Germans cross the Meuse.

(26–29 Aug.) Russians defeated at Tannenberg.

(5–9 Sept.) Battle of the Marne.

(5–11 Sept.) Austrians defeated in the battle of Rawa Ruska.

(8–16 Sept.) Serbs halt second Austrian invasion.

(10–14 Sept.) Russians forced to retreat from East Prussia following battle of the Masurian Lakes.

(14 Sept.) Falkenhayn replaces Moltke as German Commander-in-Chief.

(14–18 Sept.) Allied offensive fails at first battle of the Aisne.

(27 Sept.) Russians invade Hungary.

(28 Sept.–1 Nov.) Austro–German offensive in east checked, leading to withdrawal from Poland.

(Sept.–Oct.) 'Race for the Sea': series of out-flanking manoeuvres towards the Channel fails.

(9 Oct.) Germans take Antwerp.

(12 Oct.–11 Nov.) First battle of Ypres: Germans fail to reach Channel ports; Allied counter-attack fails.

(16 Oct.) 'Race for the Sea' concluded by battle of the Yser.

(1 Nov.) Hindenburg becomes German Commander-in-Chief on Eastern Front.

(2 Nov.) Russians renew advance on East Prussia. Britain declares North Sea a war zone and begins blockade of Germany.

(5 Nov.–15 Dec.) Serbs repel third Austrian invasion.

(11 Nov.–24 Nov.) Russians retreat after battle of Lódz.

(14 Nov.) The Ottoman Empire proclaims Holy War.

(2 Dec.) Austrians take Belgrade.

1915

(8–15 Jan.) French attack halted by Germans at battle of Soissons.

(23 Jan.) German and Austrian armies launch offensive in Carpathians.

(7–21 Feb.) Germans encircle Russian Tenth Army at battle of Masurian Lakes; Austrian attack in Carpathians collapses.

(11 Feb.) British air raid on Ostend and Zeebrugge.

(18 Feb.) Germany commences submarine warfare against merchant vessels.

(19 Feb.–18 Mar.) British Navy fails to force the Dardanelles Straits.

(10–13 Mar.) British advance checked at battle of Neuve-Chapelle.

(14–15 Mar.) Battle of Saint-Eloi.

(19–20 Mar.) Germans mount raid on Yarmouth and King's Lynn.

(31 Mar.) Zeppelin raids on southern English counties begin.

(22 Apr.–25 May) Second battle of Ypres: Germans employ poison gas for the first time.

(25 Apr.) Allied forces land on Gallipoli Peninsula.

(2–4 May) Russian line between Gorlice and Tarnow broken by German–Austrian offensive, forcing Russians to retreat.

(4 May) Italy leaves the Triple Alliance.

(7 May) *Lusitania* sunk.

(9 May–18 June) Second battle of Artois.

(15–25 May) Battle of Festubert.

(23 May) Italy enters war on Allied side and declares war on Germany and Austria.

(1 June) German air raid on London.

(20 June–14 July) German offensive in the Argonne fails.

(16–18 July) Russians defeated in battle of Krasnotav.

(4–5 Aug) Germans enter Warsaw.

(6–21 Aug.) Allied attacks in Dardanelles fail.

(18 Sept.) Germany limits submarine attacks.

(25 Sept.–6 Nov.) Allied offensives at Loos and in Champagne.

(28 Sept.) British enter Kut el Amara after defeating Turks.

(5 Oct.) Allied forces land in Salonika.

(7 Oct.) Serbian army collapses in face of joint German–Austrian–Bulgarian offensive, and is evacuated to Corfu.

(3 Dec.) Joffre becomes French Commander-in-Chief.

(7 Dec.) Turkish forces lay siege to British at Kut el Amara.

(19 Dec.) Haig replaces French as British Commander-in-Chief.

(20 Dec.) Allied forces evacuated from Anzac and Suvla Bay in Dardanelles (completed 9 Jan. 1916).

1916

(21 Feb.–18 Dec.) Battle of Verdun results in 550,000 French and 450,000 German casualties.

(15 Mar.) Admiral von Tirpitz resigns.

(29 Apr.) British surrender at Kut el Amara.

(15 May–17 June) Austrians defeat Italians at Asiago but withdraw to strengthen Eastern Front.

(24 May) Britain introduces conscription.

(31 May–1 June) Battle of Jutland.

(4 June–20 Sept.) Massive Russian offensive south of Pripet Marshes results in heavy casualties on both sides.

(5 June) Arab revolt against Turkish rule begins.

(6 June) *HMS Hampshire* sunk: Lord Kitchener drowns.

(10 June) Russians cross Dniester.

(21 June) Turks begin offensive against Persia.

(1 July–18 Nov.) Allied offensive at battle of the Somme fails to achieve major breakthrough.

(26 Aug.) Italy declares war on Germany.

(27 Aug.) Romania enters war and commences invasion of Transylvania.

(29 Aug.) Hindenburg becomes German Chief of General Staff.

(10 Sept.–19 Nov.) Allied forces launch offensive in Salonika.

(15 Sept.) British use tanks for first time during battle of the Somme.

(24 Oct.–18 Dec.) French launch successful counter-attacks at Verdun.

(3 Dec.) Nivelle succeeds Joffre as French Commander-in-Chief.

(6 Dec.) Bucharest captured; Russians and Romanians forced to retreat.

(7 Dec.) Lloyd George forms Coalition government in Britain.

(12 Dec.) Central Powers make peace offer.

(13 Dec.) British begin offensive in Mesopotamia.

(30 Dec.) Allies reject peace offer made by Central Powers.

1917

(31 Jan.) Germans announce resumption of unrestricted submarine warfare.

(23 Feb.–5 Apr.) Expecting an Allied offensive, Germans withdraw to Hindenburg Line.

(25 Feb.) British recapture Kut el Amara.

(11 Mar.) British enter Baghdad.

(12 Mar.) Revolution in Russia leads to abdication of Tsar Nicholas II.

(16–19 Mar.) Germans make stand along Siegfried Line.

(26–27 Mar.) British fail to capture Gaza.

(4 Apr.) British launch offensive in Artois.

(6 Apr.) USA declares war on Germany.

(9 Apr.) French begin offensive in Champagne.

(9 Apr.–3 May) Canadians take Vimy Ridge during battle of Arras.

(16 Apr.–9 May) French offensive fails at second battle of the Aisne.

(17–19 Apr.) British attack fails in second battle of Gaza.

(3–20 May) Outbreak of mutinies in French army.

(15 May) Pétain becomes French Commander-in-Chief.

(7–8 June) British capture Messines Ridge.

(25 June) US troops land in France.

(31 July–6 Nov.) Third battle of Ypres results in capture of Passchendaele.

(20 Sept.) British resume offensive near Ypres.

(24 Oct.–12 Nov.) Italians forced to retreat after battle of Caporetto.

(31 Oct.–7 Nov.) Turks forced to withdraw following third battle of Gaza.

(2 Nov.) Germans retreat behind Aisne–Oise and Ailette Canals.

(4 Nov.) British forces reach Italian front.

(6 Nov.) British take Passchendaele.

(7 Nov.) Bolshevik Revolution in Russia.

(17 Nov.) Clemenceau becomes French premier.

(20 Nov.–3 Dec.) First mass use of tanks at battle of Cambrai leads to temporary breach of Hindenburg Line.

(2 Dec.) Fighting ceases on Russian front.

(3 Dec.) Austro–German campaign in Italy suspended.

(7 Dec.) USA declares war on Austria–Hungary.

(9 Dec.) Romania signs armistice. Allenby enters Jerusalem.

1918

(8 Jan.) President Wilson issues Fourteen Points.

(18 Feb.) Fighting resumes between Russia and Germany.

(3 Mar.) Bolsheviks accept German peace terms at Brest–Litovsk.

(21 Mar.–4 Apr.) Germans launch offensive on the Somme.

(9–29 Apr.) Germans launch offensive on the Lys.

(14 Apr.) Foch becomes supreme commander of Allied forces in France.

(22–23 Apr.) British raid on Zeebrugge.

(7 May) Romania concludes Treaty of Bucharest with Central Powers.

(27 May–6 June) Germans launch offensive on the Aisne.

(9–13 June) Germans launch Noyon–Montidier offensive.

(15–24 June) Italians repulse Austrian attack across the Piave.

(13 July) Final Turkish offensive in Palestine.

(15–17 July) Germans launch final (Champagne–Marne) offensive.

(18 July–6 Aug.) Allied forces launch Aisne–Marne offensive, leading to reduction of Marne salient.

(8 Aug.–3 Sept.) Amiens salient is reduced.

(3 Sept.) German armies commence retreat to Hindenburg Line.

(14 Sept.) Allied armies begin offensive against Bulgarians.

(19 Sept.) Turkish army defeated in battle of Megiddo.

(25 Sept.) Bulgaria requests armistice.

(26 Sept.) Foch launches final offensive, breaching Hindenburg Line on 27 Sept.

(29 Sept.) Bulgaria concludes armistice.

(1 Oct.) French forces take St Quentin. British forces enter Damascus.

(3 Oct.) Prince Max of Baden becomes German Chancellor.

(9–10 Oct.) British take Cambrai and Le Cateau.

(14 Oct.) USA demands cessation of submarine warfare.

(17 Oct.) British reach Ostend.

(20 Oct.) Submarine warfare abandoned by Germany.

(24 Oct.–4 Nov.) Italians defeat Austrians at Vittoria Veneto.

(31 Oct.) Armistice with the Ottoman Empire comes into force.

(3 Nov.) Austria agrees to Allied peace terms. Mutiny in German High Seas fleet.

(4 Nov.) Armistice concluded on Italian front. Germans withdraw to Antwerp–Meuse Line.

(9 Nov.) Revolution in Berlin leads to proclamation of Republic.

(10 Nov.) William II flees to Holland; Emperor Charles of Austria abdicates.

(11 Nov.) Armistice concluded on Western Front.

(21 Nov.) German High Seas fleet surrenders to British.

Manpower and casualties of major European Powers, 1914–18

	Standing armies and trained reserves	Total mobilized	Killed or died of wounds	Total military casualties
Austria-Hungary	3,000,000	7,800,000	1,200,000	7,020,000
British Empire	975,000	8,904,000	908,000	3,190,235
France	4,017,000	8,410,000	1,363,000	6,160,800
Germany	4,500,000	11,000,000	1,774,000	7,142,558
Italy	1,251,000	5,615,000	460,000	2,197,000
Russia	5,971,000	12,000,000	1,700,000	9,150,000
The Ottoman Empire	210,000	2,850,000	325,000	975,000

Naval strength of major European Powers in 1914

	Britain	Germany	France	Italy	Russia	Austria–Hungary	Turkey
Dreadnoughts	24	13	14	1	4	3	1
Pre-Dreadnoughts	38	30	9	17	7	12	3
Battle cruisers	10	6	0	0	1	0	0
Cruisers	47	14	19	5	8	3	0
Light cruisers	61	35	6	6	5	4	2
Destroyers	228	152	81	33	106	18	8
Submarines	24	30	67	20	36	14	0

Naval losses of major European Powers, 1914–18

	Britain	Germany	France	Italy	Russia	Austria–Hungary	Turkey
Dreadnoughts	2	0 (18)*	0	1	2	2	0
Pre-Dreadnoughts	11	1 (0)	4	3	2	1	1
Battle cruisers	3	1 (6)	0	0	0	0	0
Cruisers	13	6 (0)	5	1	2	0	0
Light cruisers	12	17 (23)	0	2	0	3	1
Destroyers	67	66 (92)	12	8	20	6	3
Submarines	54	199 (all)	14	8	20	14	0

*Figures in brackets indicate vessels surrendered.

VERSAILLES AND INTER-WAR DIPLOMATIC AGREEMENTS

1918

(8 Jan.) Wilson issues Fourteen Points (see pp. 342–343) as a basis for peace.

(3 Mar.) Germany signs the Treaty of Brest-Litovsk with the Russian Bolshevik government, making huge territorial gains in the East and releasing fresh troops for an offensive in the West.

(21 Mar.) Germany launches final offensive in the West, but fails to achieve a decisive breakthrough.

(9 Apr.) Renewed German offensive in Flanders against the British also fails to achieve a knock-out blow.

(18 June) Assisted by recently arrived American reinforcements, the Allies begin a counter-attack.

(8 Aug.) With German armies in retreat, Ludendorff refers to this as the 'Black Day' of the German army.

(11 Aug.) Ludendorff offers his resignation to the Kaiser but is refused, but he calls for an end to the war.

(26 Sept.) Foch launches massive offensive against the German lines with 126 divisions.

(28 Sept.) Hindenburg and Ludendorff say that Germany must seek an armistice as military victory is impossible.

(30 Sept.) Bulgarians sign armistice with Western Allies.

(3–4 Oct.) The new German Chancellor, Prince Max of Baden, appeals to President Wilson for an armistice based on the 'Fourteen Points'.

(9 Oct.) Wilson's First Note. Without consulting his allies, Wilson asks if Germany accepts the Fourteen Points unconditionally, and is prepared to evacuate all occupied territory.

(12 Oct.) Prince Max sends a noncommittal but favourable reply to Wilson, but simultaneously a U-boat sinks the liner *Leinster* with the loss of 200 lives, outraging Allied politicians and public.

(14 Oct.) Wilson's Second Note demands an immediate end to submarine warfare, and immediate evacuation of occupied territory. It also calls for guarantees of 'constitutional change' implying that peace depends on the removal of the Kaiser. The High Command and the Kaiser reject this and suggest that Germany can fight on, but Prince Max replies to Wilson promising to stop attacks on civilian vessels and assures him that Germany now has a parliamentary government.

(15 Oct.) Czech Republic proclaimed as Austro–Hungarian Empire begins to disintegrate.

(17 Oct.) Hungary declares independence from the Austro–Hungarian Empire.

(23 Oct.) Wilson's Third Note demands a promise not to resume hostilities after the armistice and says that Wilson will deal only with 'representatives of the German people'.

(27 Oct.) Emperor Karl of Austria tells the Kaiser he intends to sue for peace.

(30 Oct.) Turks sign armistice.

(31 Oct.) War in the Middle East officially ends.

(3 Nov.) Austria–Hungary requests an armistice. Mutiny breaks out in Kiel where the sailors refuse to put to sea, elect a soviet and take over the port.

(7 Nov.) Revolution breaks out in Munich with organization of soldiers' and workers' councils who proclaim a Bavarian Socialist

Republic. In Berlin, the majority Socialist Party calls for the Kaiser's abdication. Unrest spreads throughout Germany.

(9 Nov.) Kaiser Wilhelm II flees to Holland. Prince Max of Baden declares his own abdication and that of the Kaiser, handing over government to the Socialist leader Ebert.

(11 Nov.) Crippled by the collapse of her allies, the dire military situation in the West, and unrest at home, Germany accepts the armistice.

(28 Nov.) Vienna government says it will try those responsible for the war.

(13 Dec.) President Wilson arrives in France for Peace Conference to be held in Paris.

(28 Dec.) Election results in Britain bring victory for Lloyd George coalition after vehemently anti-German election campaign.

1919

(18 Jan.) First formal session of Peace Conference with French Premier Clemenceau in the chair.

(14 Feb.) Delegates to Paris Peace Conference vote to accept creation of the League of Nations.

(17 Feb.) German government formally signs armistice.

(25 Feb.) France proposes extension of French frontier to the Rhine.

(4 Apr.) Allies and Germany sign agreement to make Danzig a free city.

(30 Apr.) German peace delegates arrive at Versailles.

(7 May) German delegates presented with the Peace Treaty.

(20 May) German delegates given more time to consider the Peace Treaty.

(16 June) Allied ultimatum to Germany to sign the Treaty.

(21 June) German sailors scuttle the surrendered German fleet at Scapa Flow.

(28 June) Treaty of Versailles between Germany and the Allies. (For fuller details of Versailles and the other Paris peace treaties, see pp. 130–132). Germany ceded territory and all her colonies to the Allies, returned Alsace–Lorraine to France, promised to pay large reparations and had her armed forces restricted. The Rhineland was demilitarized and occupied, and the League of Nations was created. Germany admitted 'war guilt.

(10 Sept.) Treaty of St Germain between Austria and the Allies, reduced Austria to a rump state following concessions to Czechoslovakia, Poland, Yugoslavia, Hungary, Italy and Romania, from the old Austria–Hungary.

(27 Nov.) Treaty of Neuilly between Bulgaria and the Allies reduced Bulgaria and provided for reparations payments.

1920

(4 June) Treaty of the Trianon between Hungary and the Allies, reduced Hungary to a rump state and provided for reparations payments.

(10 Aug.) Treaty of Sèvres between the Ottoman Empire and the Allies, reduced the Ottoman Empire in size but not accepted by Turks.

1921

(19 Feb.) Alliance between France and Poland.

(18 Mar.) Treaty of Riga between Russia and Poland, ended war between them and defined their mutual border.

1922

(6 Feb.) Washington Naval Agreement between Britain, France, the United States, Japan, Italy and others restricted the size of navies.

(16 Apr.) Treaty of Rapallo formed an alliance between Russia and Germany.

(31 Aug.) The 'Little Entente' formed between Czechoslovakia, Yugoslavia and Romania under French auspices.

1923

(24 July) Treaty of Lausanne between the Ottoman Empire and the Allies replaced the Treaty of Sèvres. Confined the Ottoman Empire to Asia Minor and the area around Constantinople.

1925

Locarno Pact between Britain, France, Germany, Italy and Belgium guaranteed the current West European borders.

1928

(27 Aug.) Kellogg–Briand Pact between Britain, France, the United States, Germany, Italy and Japan renounced war as a means to settle disputes. Later adhered to by other states.

1930

(22 Apr.) London Naval Agreement between Britain, France, the United States, Japan and Italy expanded the 1922 Washington agreements.

1934

(26 Jan.) Non-aggression pact between Germany and Poland.

(6 Jan.) Franco–Italian agreement concerning colonies and Austria.

(2 May) Alliance between France and Russia providing for mutual aid against aggression.

(18 June) Anglo–German Naval Agreement.

1936

(7 Aug.) Non-intervention agreement between Britain, France, Germany, Italy, Russia and others, regarding the Spanish Civil War.

(25 Nov.) Anti–Comintern Pact between Germany and Japan.

1937

(6 Nov) Italy joined the Anti-Comintern Pact.

1938

(29 Sept.) Munich Agreement between Britain, France, Germany and Italy forced Czechoslovakia to cede territory to Germany, Hungary and Poland.

1939

(31 Mar.) France and Britain guaranteed Polish integrity.

(22 May) 'Pact of Steel' between Germany and Italy formalized the Rome–Berlin 'Axis'.

(23 Aug.) German–Soviet Pact promised Russian neutrality in war involving Germany.

PEACE TREATIES AFTER THE FIRST WORLD WAR I

The Treaty of Versailles, 28 June 1919

1. Germany surrendered territory:
   (a) Alsace–Lorraine to France.
   (b) Eupen–Malmédy to Belgium (following plebiscite in 1920).
   (c) Northern Schleswig to Denmark (following plebiscite in 1920).
   (d) Pozania and West Prussia to Poland, Upper Silesia to Poland (following plebiscite in 1921).
   (e) Saar put under League of Nations control for 15 years and mining interests under French control (returned to Germany following 1935 plebiscite).
   (f) Danzig (Gdansk) put under League of Nations control.
   (g) Memel placed under Allied control, then transferred to Lithuania.
   (h) German colonies become mandated territories of the League of Nations: German East Africa (to Britain); German South-West Africa (to South Africa); Cameroons and Togoland (to Britain and France); German Samoa (to New Zealand); German New Guinea (to Australia); Marshall Islands and Pacific Islands north of the Equator (to Japan).
2. Germany lost concessions and trading rights in China, Egypt and Middle East.
3. Demilitarization of the Rhineland and Heligoland.
4. German army limited to 100,000 men, denied U-boats and airforce.
5. Army of occupation on west bank of the Rhine and bridgeheads at Cologne, Coblenz and Mainz from January 1920.
6. Germany accepts 'war guilt' clause.
7. Germany agreed to pay reparations and accepted responsibility for war damage.
8. The Treaty of Brest-Litovsk declared void; Germany required to evacuate Baltic States and other occupied territory.
9. The Covenant of the League of Nations written into the Treaty.

The Treaty of St Germain, 10 September 1919

1. The Austro–Hungarian Empire was effectively dissolved:
   (a) Austria and Hungary to become separate states with total loss of control over other former parts of the Austro–Hungarian Empire.
   (b) New state of Czechoslovakia created.
   (c) New state of Yugoslavia set up.
   (d) Galicia ceded to Poland.
   (e) Transylvania ceded to Romania.
   (f) South Tyrol, Trentino and Istria ceded to Italy.
   (g) Plebiscite to define boundary with Austria in southern Carinthia.
2. Austria forbidden to unite with Germany without League of Nations approval.

3. Austrian army limited to 30,000 men.
4. Reparations required for war damage.
5. Covenant of League of Nations written into the Treaty.

The Treaty of the Trianon, 4 June 1920

1. Hungary accepted break-up of Austro–Hungarian Empire and surrender of territory to Romania, Czechoslovakia, Yugoslavia, Poland, Italy and the new Austrian republic.
2. Hungarian army limited to 35,000 men.
3. Hungary required to pay reparations.
4. Covenant of the League of Nations written into the Treaty.

The Treaty of Sèvres, 10 August 1920 (never ratified by Turkey)

1. Turkish Empire lost territory:
   (a) Cyprus to Britain.
   (b) Rhodes, the Dodecanese, and Adalia ceded to Italy.
   (c) Part of European Turkey to Bulgaria.
   (d) Eastern Thrace to Greece; Greek claims to Chios and other islands recognized; Greece allowed to occupy Smyrna for five years until a plebiscite held.
   (e) Hejaz and Arabia become independent.
   (f) League of Nations mandates over Syria (to France); Palestine, Iraq and Transjordan (to Britain).
2. The Straits placed under international control.
3. Turkey occupied by British, French and Italian troops.
4. The Covenant of the League of Nations was written into the Treaty.

The Treaty of Neuilly, 27 November 1919

1. Bulgaria lost territory:
   (a) Territory along Bulgaria's western boundary ceded to Yugoslavia.
   (b) Part of western Thrace ceded to Greece.
2. Bulgaria gained territory from European Turkey.
3. Bulgarian army limited to 20,000 men.
4. Bulgaria made liable for reparations.
5. The Covenant of the League of Nations written into the Treaty.

Treaty of Lausanne, 24 July 1923

1. Turkey surrendered its claims to territories of the Ottoman Empire occupied by non-Turks, effectively surrendering the Arab lands.

2. The Turks retained Constantinople and Eastern Thrace in Europe; both sides of Greek–Turkish border demilitarized.
3. Turkey takes Smyrna from Greece but surrenders all the Aegean Islands except Imbros and Tenedos which return to Turkey.
4. Turkey recognizes the annexation of Cyprus by Britain and of the Dodecanese by Italy.
5. Turkey left free of foreign troops.
6. The Straits were declared to be demilitarized (in July 1936 by the Montreux Convention Turkey was allowed to refortify the Straits).
7. No restrictions were placed on Turkey's armed forces and no reparations required.

THE LEAGUE OF NATIONS

1919

(28 Apr.) Draft Covenant of the League approved by a plenary session of the Paris Peace Conference. Headquarters of the League to be in Geneva.

(19 Nov.) Vote in the US Senate prevents American membership of the League.

1920

(10 Jan.) League of Nations formally comes into existence. Joined by almost all European states as well as more than twenty extra-European states.

(Feb.) First meeting of its Council held in London and appoints High Commissioner to administer Danzig, now a 'free city' under League of Nations authority.

(14 Mar.) Vote by US Senate against United States joining the League.

(Apr.–Oct.) Vilna seized from Lithuania by Poland in contravention of the League's wishes. Russo–Polish War decides the eastern boundary of Poland without reference to the League and confirmed in the Treaty of Riga (Mar. 1921).

(Nov.) First meeting of the Assembly of the League.

1921

League settles Aaland Islands dispute between Finland and Sweden. Permanent Court of International Justice set up at The Hague.

1922

Mussolini defies the League with his absorption of Fiume into Italy. Hungary joins the League. League sanctions Polish possession of Vilna.

1923

French occupy the Ruhr without reference to League and the League is unable to prevent the Italian occupation of Corfu.

Disarmament Commission of the League proposes a Treaty of Mutual Assistance in which countries would offer mutual protection to each other. Accepted by France and Czechoslovakia, it was rejected by other states as too binding.

1925

League resolves border dispute between Bulgaria and Greece.

1926

Germany joins the League.

League successfully arbitrates between Britain and Turkey over Mosul. International Disarmament Conference meets and prepares a report for future discussion.

1930

Disarmament Commission agrees a draft convention but is opposed by Germany and the Soviet Union.

1931

Japanese invade and overrun Manchuria; China appeals to the League of Nations for support. League sends fact-finding mission under Lord Lytton.

1932

(Feb.) Sixty nations meet in Disarmament Conference chaired by Arthur Henderson, British Foreign Secretary. Fails to reach mutually acceptable conclusions. Lytton Report on Manchuria condemns Japanese aggression but no action taken.

1933

Following the accession of Hitler, Germany withdraws from the disarmament conference and also from the League.
Japan leaves the League.

1934

Soviet Union joins the League.
Last session of League's Disarmament Conference meets without conclusion. Haile Selassie, Emperor of Ethiopia, appeals to League of Nations in dispute with Italy. League recommends negotiation.

1935

(Oct.) Italian attack on Ethiopia. Council and Assembly of League declare Italy the aggressor and apply economic sanctions, but excluding oil, coal and steel. Several countries decline to apply even limited sanctions.

1936

League abandons sanctions following Italian conquest of Ethiopia.

1937

Italy withdraws from the League.
League of Nations building completed in Geneva.

1938

Austria, now incorporated into Germany by the *Anschluss*, leaves the League.
Munich agreement over Czechoslovakia reached without reference to the League.

1939

Soviet Union expelled from the League. Last meeting of the League.

1943

Principle of a new international organisation for the maintenance of peace and international security agreed by Britain, China, the United States and the Soviet Union.

1945

At the San Francisco Conference, fifty nations at war with Germany agree to form the United Nations.

1946

League of Nations dissolved but with many of its welfare functions absorbed by the UN and its judicial bodies (such as the International Court of Justice) maintained.

ITALY, 1896–1945

1896

(1 Mar.) Defeat of Italian forces at battle of Adowa (Abyssinia) inflicts national humiliation.
(5 Mar.) Fall of the final Crispi administration.

1898

(May) Repression of widespread disturbances and food riots.

1899

Beginning of ten-year period of economic growth symbolized by foundation of Fiat.

1900

General elections. Resignation of Pelloux.
(29 June) Assassination of Umbert I; succeeded by Victor Emmanuel III.

1901

(Feb.) Start of the Giolitti era with formation of the Zanardelli–Giolitti administration.

1902

(June) Beginning of the Franco–Italian entente.

1903

Giovanni Giolitti Prime Minister for first time.
(Aug.) Election of Pius X as Pope following death of Leo XIII.

1904

(Sept.) Failure of general strike across Italy. Followed by election (Nov.).

1906

Foundation of *Confederazione Generale del Lavor.*
(Feb.) First Sonnino ministry (entry of Radicals and Republicans into government.)

1907

(Sept.) Papal encyclical attacks Modernism.

1909

(Oct.) Russo–Italian Accord (the Racconigi Agreement).

1910

(Dec.) Italian Nationalist Association founded.

1911

(Sept.) Beginning of the war in Tripolitania (the Libyan War) after declaration of war on Ottoman Empire.

1912

(June) New electoral law gives near-complete manhood suffrage.
(July) Mussolini rises to prominence at Reggio Emilia Conference of Socialist Party.
(Oct.) Libyan War ended by Treaty of Ouchy.
(Dec.) Final renewal of Triple Alliance.

1913

(Oct–Nov.) General elections.

1914

(Mar.) Fall of Giolitti's fourth ministry. Antonio Salandra becomes Prime Minister.

(June) General strike and widespread agitation during 'Red Week.'

(3 Aug.) Italy declares itself neutral in First World War.

(20 Aug.) Death of Pius X (election of Benedict XV on 3 Sept.).

(Oct.) 'Active neutrality' advocated by Mussolini. Formation of *Fascio Rivoluzionario d'Azione Internazionalista.*

(25 Nov.) Mussolini founds *il Popolo d'Italia* and is expelled from Socialist Party.

(Dec.) Foundation of *Fascio d'Azione Rivoluzionaria.*

1915

(26 Apr.) Italy signs Pact of London, joining the Entente powers.

(24 May) War declared on Austria–Hungary.

1916

(June) Paolo Boselli replaces Salandra as Prime Minister, forming a National Union Government.

(28 Aug.) War declared on Germany.

1917

(24 Oct.) Opening of Battle of Caporetto. Retreat of Italian forces to River Piave. Vittorio Orlando becomes Prime Minister (until June 1919).

1918

(Apr.) Signing of Pact of Rome of oppressed nationalities.

(June) Battle of the Piave.

(Oct.) Battle of Vittorio Veneto.

(Nov.) Italy signs armistice.

1919

(Jan.) Formation of Italian Catholic Party (*Partito Popolare Italiano*)

(23 Mar.) Foundation of the first *Fasci di Combattimento* by Mussolini in Milan.

(Apr.) Italian delegation clashes with Woodrow Wilson over Treaty of Versailles.

(25 Aug.) Italian forces evacuate Fiume.

(2 Sept.) Universal suffrage and proportional representation introduced.

(12 Sept.) D'Annunzio seizes Fiume.

(11 Nov.) The Pope lifts the prohibition against Catholics participating in political life.

(16 Nov.) Socialists (PSI) and Catholics receive strong support in the elections; Fascists gain only a fraction of the vote. PSI largest party in parliament.

1920

(9 June) Giolitti takes over as Prime Minister from Nitti.

(31 Aug.–Sept.) Widespread strikes and lockouts in engineering, metal and steel industries. Industrialists form *Confindustria.*

(12 Nov.) Treaty of Rapallo settles disputes between Italy and Yugoslavia. Fiume to be an independent state.

(21 Nov.) Fascists fire on crowd in Bologna during inauguration of mayor.

(1 Dec.) D'Annunzio declares war on Italy.

(24–25 Dec.) Clashes between Italian troops and Fiuman troops. *Andrea Doria* shells the royal palace.

(31 Dec.) D'Annunzio makes peace with Italy.

1921

(5 Jan.) D'Annunzio leaves Fiume. Foundation of Italian Communist Party (PCI).

(27 Feb.) Communists and Fascists clash in Florence.

(15 May) Liberals and Democrats successful at the elections. Fascist alliance with Giolitti secures them 35 seats. Mussolini elected to parliament.

(26 June) Giolitti Cabinet falls, replaced by Bonomi. End of last Giolitti ministry.

1922

(9 Feb.) Bonomi government resigns.

(25 Feb.) Facta heads new government. Pius XI elected Pope.

(May) Fascist takeover in Bologna.

(3–4 Aug.) Fascist takeover in Milan. Socialist general strike fails.

(24 Oct.) Mussolini calls on Facta to resign and for the formation of a Fascist Cabinet. Facta refuses.

(28 Oct.) Fascist 'March on Rome'.

(30 Oct.) Mussolini arrives in Rome and organizes victory march.

(31 Oct.) Mussolini forms Cabinet.

(25 Nov.) Mussolini is granted temporary dictatorial powers to institute reforms.

(Dec.) Creation of Fascist Grand Council.

1923

(14 Jan.) King Victor Emmanuel authorizes voluntary Fascist Militia (MVSN).

(Apr.) Popular Party (a left-wing parry) leaves Mussolini's cabinet.

(21 July) Electoral law proposed, guaranteeing two-thirds of the seats in the Chamber to the majority party.

(Aug.) Corfu incident.

(Oct.) Francesco Giunta becomes PNF secretary.

(Nov.) New electoral law passed (the Acerbo Law).

(Dec.) Fusion of Nationalists with PNF. New press laws enacted. Palazzo Chigi Pact between *Confindustria* and Fascist labour syndicates.

1924

(27 Jan.) Treaty with Yugoslavia recognises Fiume as Italian, but cedes surrounding area to Yugoslavia.

(6 Apr.) Fascists obtain almost two-thirds of votes in election amidst widespread use of violence and intimidation. Fascists take 374 seats.

(30 May) Matteotti launches attack on the Fascist government.

(21 June) Matteotti is abducted and murdered. Non-Fascists resign from Chambers and condemn violence (the Aventine secession).

(July) Press censorship introduced.

1925

(3 Jan.) Mussolini's speech to parliament effectively begins the dictatorship.

(12 Feb.) Farinacci becomes secretary of PNF.

(Apr.) Congress of Fascist Intellectuals meets.

(1 May) *Dopolavoro* created (Fascist leisure-time organization).

(2 Oct.) Palazzo Vidoni Pact between industrialists' association (*Confindustria*) and the Fascist syndicates. Launch of 'Battle for Grain'.

(24 Dec.) Mussolini's dictatorial powers increased. Press censorship tightened, secret non-Fascist organisations banned, and widespread arrests. Banning of opposition parties.

1926

(31 Jan.) Government decrees given the power of law.

(3 Apr.) Right to strike abolished; collective contracts reserved to the Fascist syndicate. Fascist Youth Movement formed (ONB, or *Ballila*).

(7 Apr.) Mussolini wounded in assassination attempt.

(July) Creation of Ministry of Corporations – effective birth of the corporate state.

(25 Nov.) Law for defence of the state; creation of a special tribunal for political crimes; death penalty introduced for plotting against Royal Family or head of state.

1927

(21 Dec.) Exchange rate fixed at 'quota 90' (*Quota Novanta*) (92.45 lire to £1) in a revaluation of the currency.

1929

(11 Feb.) Lateran treaties with Papacy creating the Vatican City as a sovereign independent state.

1932

(30 Oct.) *Decennale* celebrations–Fascists celebrate tenth year of power in Italy.

1934

(17 Mar.) Mussolini signs the Rome Protocols with Austria and Hungary.
(14 June) Meeting of Hitler and Mussolini at Venice.
(July) Mussolini sends troops to the Austrian frontier following Hitler's attempted coup.
(10 Nov.) Council of Corporations inaugurated at Rome.

1935

(Mar.) Stresa Front (see p. 158).
(3 Oct.) Italy begins invasion of Abyssinia (Ethiopia) (see p. 211) following increased drive for economic autarchy.

1936

(5 May) Italian forces occupy Addis Ababa.
(24 Oct.) Rome–Berlin Axis formed.

1938

(l4 July) Publication of *Manifesto della Razza* –first anti-Semitic measures.

1939

(19 Jan.) Creation of the *Camera del Fascie delle Corporazioni*, replacing parliament.
(7 Apr.) Italy invades Albania.
(22 May) Pact of Steel signed between Hitler and Mussolini.

1940

(10 June) Mussolini declares war and invades France. First air attacks on Malta.
(3 Aug.) Italy invades British Somaliland.
(13 Sept.) Italian forces invade Egypt.

(28 Oct.) Italy invades Greece.
(11–12 Nov.) Destruction of large part of Italian fleet at Taranto by British aircraft.
(9 Dec.) British offensive in North Africa routs the army of Graziani.

1941

(24 Mar.) Italians defeated in British Somaliland.
(27–28 Mar.) Italian fleet defeated at Cape Matapan.
(6 Apr.) British enter Addis Ababa.
(16 May) Capitulation of Italian forces under the Duke of Aosta.
(11 Dec.) Italy declares war on USA.

1942

June Allied convoys resupply Malta.
(4 Nov.) British break through Axis line at El Alamein.

1943

(May) Surrender of Axis forces in North Africa.
(10 July) Allied invasion of Sicily.
(25 July) Grand Council of Fascism votes Mussolini out of power. Badoglio takes over the Italian government.
(17 Aug.) Sicily finally conquered by the Allies.
(8 Sept.) Italian surrender announced. Nazis take over power in Italy.
(9 Sept.) Salerno landing by US 5th Army.
(12 Sept.) Skorzeny rescues Mussolini.
(23 Sept.) Mussolini announces creation of Fascist social republic of Salo.

1944

(22 Jan.) Anzio landing by US 5th Army; German counter-attack stalls advance.
(15 Mar.) Allies bomb Monte Cassino.
(17 Mar.) Monte Cassino falls.
(4 June) Rome falls.

1945

(28 Apr.) Mussolini executed by partisans at Dongo.

GERMANY, 1929–45

1929

(Feb.–June) Nazis combine with Hugenberg and German Nationalists to oppose the Young Plan.

(7 June) Publication of Young Plan for rescheduling German reparation payments in the form of annuities over 59 years, amounting to a quarter of the sum demanded in 1921.

(9 July) Nationalists and Nazis form a National Committee to fight the Young Plan with Hugenberg as chairman and Hitler a leading member.

(3 Oct.) Death of Stresemann.

(29 Oct.) Wall Street Crash and cessation of American loans to Europe.

(29 Dec.) National referendum accepts Young Plan, frustrating Nationalist hopes.

1930

(Mar.) Young Plan approved by Reichstag and signed by Hindenburg.

(17 Mar.) Muller's Socialist Cabinet resigns in Germany.

(30 Mar.) Heinrich Brüning, of the Centre, forms a minority coalition of the Right.

(17 May) Young Plan reparations come into force.

(30 June) Last Allied troops leave Rhineland.

(16 July) Hindenburg authorizes German budget by decree on failure of Reichstag to pass it.

(14 Sept.) In Reichstag elections, Hitler and the Nazi Party emerge as a major force with 107 seats, second only to the Socialists with 143 seats.

(Oct.) Röhm becomes leader of SA or 'Brownshirts'.

1931

(July) Worsening economic crisis in Germany. Unemployment reaches over 4.25 million. Bankruptcy of German Danatbank

(13 July) leads to closure of all banks until 5 August.

(11 Oct.) Hitler forms an alliance with the Nationalists led by Hugenberg at Hartzburg – the Hartzburg Front.

1932

(7 Jan.) Brüning declares that Germany cannot and will not resume reparations' payments.

(13 Mar.) In presidential elections Hindenburg receives 18 million votes against Hitler's 11 million, and the communists' 5 million. With failure to achieve an overall majority, a new election is called for 10 April.

(10 Apr.) Hindenburg re-elected President with an absolute majority of 19 million against Hitler's 13 million and the communists' 3 million.

(14 Apr.) Brüning attempts to disband the SA and SS.

(24 Apr.) Nazis achieve successes in local elections.

(30 May) At Hindenburg's withdrawal of support for disbanding the SA and SS, Brüning resigns.

(1 June) Franz von Papen forms a ministry with von Schleicher as Minister of Defence and von Neurath as Foreign Minister.

(16 June) Ban on SA and SS in operation since April is lifted.

(31 July) In Reichstag elections Nazis win 230 seats and become largest party, producing a stalemate since neither they nor the Socialists (133 seats) will enter a coalition.

(13 Aug.) Hitler refuses Hindenburg's request to serve as Vice-Chancellor under von Papen.

(12 Sept.) Von Papen dissolves the Reichstag.

(14 Sept.) Germany leaves disarmament conference.

(6 Nov.) New elections fail to resolve the stalemate, with the communists only gaining a few seats from the Nazis.

(17 Nov.) Von Papen forced to resign by Schleicher; Hitler rejects Chancellorship.

(2–4 Dec.) Schleicher becomes Chancellor and forms a ministry, attempting to conciliate the Centre and Left.

1933

(28 Jan.) Schleicher's ministry is unable to secure a majority in the Reichstag and resigns.

(30 Jan.) Hindenburg accepts a Cabinet with Hitler as Chancellor, von Papen as Vice-Chancellor and nationalists in other posts.

(27 Feb.) Reichstag fire blamed on communists and made pretext for suspension of civil liberties and freedom of press.

(5 Mar.) In elections, the Nazis make gains, winning 288 seats, but fail to secure overall majority.

(13 Mar.) Goebbels becomes Minister of Propaganda and 'Enlightenment'. Pius XI praises Hitler's anti-communism.

(17 Mar.) Schacht becomes President of the Reichsbank.

(23 Mar.) Hitler obtains Enabling Law with the support of the Centre Party, granting him dictatorial powers for four years.

(30 Mar.) German bishops withdraw opposition to Nazis.

(1 Apr.) National boycott of all Jewish businesses and professions.

(7 Apr.) Civil Service law permits removal of Jews and other opponents.

(5 July) Centre Party disbands.

(8 July) Concordat signed between Nazi Germany and Holy See.

(14 July) All parties, other than the Nazis, suppressed. The Nazi Party is formally declared the only political party in Germany.

(20 July) Concordat ratified.

(Sept.) Ludwig Müller, leader of minority 'German Christians', becomes 'Bishop of the Reich'.

1934

(21 Mar.) 'Battle for Work' begins.

(May) German Protestants at Barmen synod express disapproval of Müller and 'German Christians' and their close complicity with Nazis.

(14 June) Hitler visits Mussolini in Italy.

(20 June) Hindenburg demands dissolution of SA.

(30 June) 'Night of the Long Knives'. Nazis liquidate thousands of opponents within and without the Party. Over 70 leading Nazis lose their lives, including Röhm, leader of the SA, and Gregor Strasser, leader of Berlin Nazis. General von Schleicher also a victim.

(2 Aug.) Death of President Hindenburg. Hitler assumes Presidency, but retains title *Der Führer*. Army swears oath of allegiance. Schacht becomes Minister of Economics.

(24 Oct.) German Labour Front founded, Nazi organization to replace trade unions.

1935

(13 Jan.) Saar plebiscite favours reabsorption into Germany.

(16 Mar.) Germany repudiates disarmament clauses in Treaty of Versailles, restores conscription and announces expansion of the peacetime army to over half a million men.

(18 June) By Anglo–German Naval Agreement, Germany agrees that her naval tonnage shall not exceed one-third of that of the Royal Navy.

(15 Sept.) Nuremberg Laws prohibit marriage and sexual intercourse between Jews and German nationals.

1936

(7 Mar.) German troops reoccupy the demilitarized Rhineland in violation of the Treaty of Versailles.

(Aug.) Olympic Games in Berlin turned into an advertisement for Nazi Germany.

(24 Aug.) Germany adopts two-year compulsory military service.

(19 Oct.) Hitler announces four-year plan under Goering as Economics Minister.

(1 Nov.) Rome–Berlin Axis proclaimed.

(18 Nov.) Germany and Italy recognize the Franco government.

1937

(Dec.) Schacht resigns as Minister of Economics. Leading members of the Protestant opposition arrested, including Pastor Niemöller.

1938

(4 Feb.) Hitler appoints Joachim von Ribbentrop Foreign Minister. Fritsch is relieved of his duties as Commander-in-Chief of the army. Hitler takes over personal control of the armed forces. The War Ministry is abolished and OKW (High Command of the Armed Forces) is set up.

(11 Mar.) German troops enter Austria (the *Anschluss)* which is declared part of the Reich (13 Mar.).

(23 Apr.) Sudeten Germans living within boundary of Czechoslovakia demand autonomy.

(12 Aug.) Germany mobilizes over Czech crisis.

(18 Aug.) Beck resigns as Chief of the Army General Staff.

(30 Sept.) Munich Agreement gives Sudetenland to Germany.

(9–10 Nov.) Anti-Jewish pogrom, the *Kristallnacht.*

1939

(21 Jan.) Schacht dismissed as President of Reichsbank.

(15 Mar.) German troops occupy remaining part of Czechoslovakia.

(23 Aug.) Nazi–Soviet Pact signed.

(1 Sept.) Germany invades Poland.

(3 Sept.) Great Britain and France declare war on Germany.

(21 Sept.) Polish Jews ordered into ghettos.

(27 Sept.) Warsaw surrenders; end of Polish campaign.

(7 Oct.) Himmler appointed Reich Commissioner.

(8 Oct.) Western Poland incorporated in Reich.

(12 Oct.) Austrian Jews deported to Poland; October sees first Jewish ghetto established in occupied Poland.

(23 Nov.) Polish Jews ordered to wear the yellow Star of David.

1940

(7 Apr.) Germany invades Norway and Denmark.

(10 May) Germany invades Holland, France and Belgium.

(14 May) Dutch army surrenders.

(28 May) Belgium capitulates.

(29 May–3 June) British and Allied forces evacuate from Dunkirk.

(14 June) Germans enter Paris.

(22 June) France concludes armistice with Germany.

(July–Sept.) Battle of Britain fails to destroy the Royal Air Force.

(23 Aug.) Beginning of 'Blitz' on Britain by *Luftwaffe.*

(14 Sept.) Postponement of 'Operation Sealion', the invasion of Britain.

(18 Dec.) Hitler issues secret plan for invasion of Russia – Operation Barbarossa.

1941

(9 Feb.) German troops under Rommel sent to assist Italians in North Africa.

(6 Apr.) German ultimatum to Greece and Yugoslavia.

(18 Apr.) Yugoslav opposition collapses.

(10 May) Rudolf Hess lands in Scotland on mysterious mission and is captured.

(13 May) Bormann succeeds Hess as Head of Party Chancellery.

(22 June) German forces launch invasion of Russia.

(16 July) Germans take Smolensk.

(31 July) Goering gives Heydrich a written order to achieve a 'general solution to the

Jewish problem in areas of Jewish influence in Europe'.

(3 Sept.) Germans lay siege to Leningrad.

(25 Oct.) German offensive against Moscow fails, followed by Russian counter-offensive (5 Dec.).

(11 Dec.) Hitler declares war on America.

1942

(20 Jan.) Heydrich puts forward 'final solution' to the 'Jewish Problem'.

(Feb.) Speer becomes Reich Minister of Armaments and Production.

(Mar.) Sauckel made plenipotentiary general for allocation of labour.

(30 May) First '1,000 bomber' raid against Cologne by RAF.

(28 June) German offensive begins in southern Russia.

(July) Beginning of liquidation of Jewish ghetto in Warsaw.

(Aug.–Sept.) German advance in North Africa halted at El Alamein.

(23 Oct.–4 Nov.) British forces defeat and pursue Axis forces at El Alamein.

(8 Nov.) Anglo–American landings in North Africa – Operation Torch.

1943

(27 Jan.) US Air Force makes first raid on Germany.

(2 Feb.) German army at Stalingrad surrenders.

(18 Feb.) Goebbels declares mobilization for total war at mass demonstration in Berlin Sportspalast. Under direction of Speer, arms production rises threefold.

(13 Mar.) Attempt to kill Hitler on a flight between Smolensk and Rastenburg fails.

(5–12 July) Mass air-raids on Hamburg kill many thousands and destroy large parts of the city.

(3 Sept.) Italy forced out of the war.

(Oct.) American air-raids on Schweinfurt ball-bearing factories cause extensive damage but at insupportable cost to attackers.

(Nov.) Series of mass air-raids on German capital known as the 'Battle of Berlin'.

1944

(May) Americans begin air attacks on German synthetic oil production.

(6 June) D-Day. Opening of second front with Anglo–American landings in Normandy.

(23 June) Russian offensive begins on central front.

(20 July) 'July Plot'. Hitler wounded in bomb attack at headquarters in East Prussia. Attempted *coup d'état* is put down by loyal troops and leading conspirators and thousands of suspects are arrested and executed.

(26 July) Russians reach the Vistula.

(31 July) Allied break-out in Normandy.

(17 Aug.) Russians reach East Prussian border.

(16 Dec.) Germans begin counter-offensive in the Ardennes.

1945

(12 Jan.) Red Army begins final campaign against Germany.

(1 Feb.) American forces reach Siegfried Line.

(13 Feb.) Allied bombing of Dresden.

(22 Mar.) Allies cross Rhine.

(11 Apr.) Western Allies halt on the Elbe.

(16 Apr.) Russian offensive against Berlin begins.

(21 Apr.) Russians reach outskirts of Berlin.

(30 Apr.) Hitler commits suicide with his wife Eva Braun in the Berlin bunker, along with Goebbels and his family. Admiral Dönitz is named Hitler's successor.

(2 May) Fall of Berlin to Russian forces.

(7 May) General Jodl makes final capitulation of Germany to General Eisenhower.

(8 May) Von Keitel surrenders to Zhukov near Berlin. Official end of the war in Europe.

(5 June) Admiral Dönitz surrenders his powers to the Allied occupation forces.

THE RUSSIAN REVOLUTION, 1914–24

1914

(1 Aug.) Germany declares war on Russia.

(26 Aug.) Russia defeated at battle of Tannenberg.

(3–12 Sept.) Russians force Austrians from Galicia.

(5 Sept.) Russia suffers severe losses at battle of the Masurian Lakes.

1915

(May) Austro–German offensive in Galicia defeats Russians.

(July) Further Austro–German offensive leads, by the autumn, to over a million Russian casualties.

(1 Aug.) Duma meets to consider the way the war is being conducted.

(22 Aug.) Six parties in the Duma form the Progressive Bloc and demand a responsible ministry.

(6 Sept.) Tsar assumes supreme command of the armed forces.

(8 Sept.) Reform programme put before Council of Ministers by Progressive Bloc.

15 Sept.) Tsar rejects offer of resignation by his ministers to make way for a more popular administration.

(16 Sept.) Tsar prorogues Duma.

1916

(15 Feb.) Duma meets. Goremykin replaced as Prime Minister by Sturmer.

(June–Oct.) Brusilov offensive gains territory but fails to achieve decisive victory and costs over a million casualties.

(Sept.–Oct.) Wave of strikes in Russia; sporadic mutinies of soldiers at the front.

(Oct.) Survey of manpower resources reveals that after February 1917 the Russian army will begin to decline in numbers.

1917

(27 Feb.) Duma meets.

(7 Mar.) Tsar leaves Petrograd for army GHQ; beginnings of large-scale demonstrations in the capital.

(8 Mar.) Queues at bakers' shops and crowds continue to demonstrate against the regime.

(9 Mar.) Police fire on crowds.

(10 Mar.) Strikes break out and soldiers join with the people; the Tsar orders suppression of the trouble.

(11 Mar.) Police fire at demonstrators, but more soldiers join the protesters. Tsar prorogues Duma.

(12 Mar.) Formation of Committee of State Duma to replace Tsarist government. Formation of Petrograd Soviet of Workers' and Soldiers' Deputies.

(13 Mar.) Soviet news sheet *Izvestia* calls on people to take affairs into their own hands.

(14 Mar.) Appointment of ministers of the provisional government. 'Army Order No. 1' issued by Petrograd Soviet puts armed forces under its authority and urges rank and file to elect representatives to the Soviet.

(15 Mar.) Tsar abdicates in favour of his brother, Grand Duke Michael, at the same time confirming the new ministry and asking the country to support it. Grand Duke Michael chooses not to accept the throne unless he is bid to do so by the Assembly. The provisional government forbids the use of force against rioting peasants.

(16 Mar.) Constituent assembly meets; abdication of Grand Duke Michael.

(11 Apr.) All-Russian Conference of Soviets overwhelmingly votes to continue war in spite of Bolshevik opposition.

(16 Apr.) Lenin arrives back in Petrograd.

(3–5 May) Bolshevik-organized demonstrations by garrison in Petrograd against the Ministers Guchkov and Milyukov. Kornilov resigns command of forces in Petrograd, and Milyukov and Guchkov resign from the government.

(18 May) Kerensky helps to reorganize provisional government.

(18 June) Start of renewed offensive on southern front.

(26 June) Soldiers at front refuse to obey orders. Kornilov insists on offensive being called off and is appointed Commander-in-Chief.

(2 July) Start of northern offensive backed by Kerensky, Minister of War. Germans and Austrians drive Russians back after early successes.

(12 July) Provisional government restores capital punishment and courts martial.

(16–18 July) Bolsheviks organize demonstrations by sailors and Red Guards but the unrest is put down by loyal troops.

(18 July) Fearing arrest, Lenin flees to Finland.

(20 July) Lvov and Kadet ministers resign.

(21 July) Formation of new government with Kerensky as Prime Minister.

(1 Aug.) Kornilov appointed Commander-in-Chief.

(3 Aug.) Kerensky resigns. Party leaders give him a free hand to form new government.

(25–28 Aug.) Kerensky holds Moscow State Conference to settle differences with Kornilov, but fails to reach agreement.

(3 Sept.) Riga falls to Germans.

(8 Sept.) Troops begin to move against Petrograd, and Kerensky denounces Kornilov 'plot' against the government. Collapse of movement followed by arrest of Kornilov and fellow generals.

(19 Sept.) Bolshevik majority in Moscow Soviet.

(6 Oct.) Trotsky becomes Chairman of Petrograd Soviet.

(23 Oct.) Decision by Bolshevik Central Committee to organize an armed rising.

(25 Oct.) Formation of Military Revolutionary Committee by Bolsheviks.

(1 Nov.) Provisional government tries to remove units from the Petrograd garrison, but Bolsheviks prevent this.

(2 Nov.) Parliament refuses to give Kerensky powers to suppress the Bolsheviks.

(6 Nov.) Bolsheviks organize headquarters in Peter and Paul fortress and move on strategic points. Lenin takes command.

(7 Nov.) Bolsheviks seize power in Petrograd, taking key installations and services. The Winter Palace cut off and ministers of provisional government arrested. Kerensky flees. Lenin announces the transfer of power to the Military Revolutionary Committee and the victory of the socialist revolution.

(8 Nov.) Lenin makes the Decree on Peace, an appeal for a just peace without annexations and indemnities, and the Decree on Land, affirming that all land is the property of the people. A Bolshevik government is formed.

(13 Nov.) Counter-offensive by Kerensky against Petrograd fails.

(15 Nov.) Bolsheviks establish power in Moscow.

(1 Dec.) Left-wing social revolutionaries enter government after agreement with Bolsheviks.

(2 Dec.) Escape of Kornilov and fellow generals from prison in Bykhov.

(3 Dec.) Bolsheviks occupy Supreme Headquarters at Mogilev.

(17 Dec.) Russia and Germany agree a ceasefire and start negotiations for a peace treaty in Brest-Litovsk (22nd).

(20 Dec.) Establishment of the *Cheka* (secret police).

1918

(18 Jan.) Opening of Constituent Assembly.

(19 Jan.) Constituent Assembly dispersed.

(1–14 Feb.) Introduction of the Gregorian calendar.

(9 Feb.) Central Council of the Ukraine concludes separate peace with Central Powers, having declared its independence.

(10 Feb.) Brest-Litovsk negotiations broken off after German ultimatum.

(18 Feb.) Germany resumes hostilities in the Ukraine.

(24 Feb.) Soviet government decides to accept German peace ultimatum.

(2 Mar.) Germans occupy Kiev.

(3 Mar.) Russians sign Treaty of Brest-Litovsk, giving up large areas of pre-Revolutionary Russia (see p. 222). German troops continue to advance into central Russia and the Crimea.

(12 Mar.) Soviet government moves from Petrograd to Moscow.

(13 Mar.) Trotsky appointed People's Commissar of War.

(5 Apr.) Allied ships and troops arrive in Murmansk.

(13 Apr.) Kornilov killed fighting with anti-Bolshevik 'Volunteer army'. Bolsheviks mount drive against anarchists and other deviant elements. Germans take Odessa.

(14 Apr.) Germans and Finns occupy Helsinki.

(29 Apr.) Germans set up puppet Ukrainian government.

(May) Georgia, Armenia and Azerbaijan declare independence.

(8 May) Germans occupy Rostov.

(14 May) Czech Legion (ex-prisoners recruited into service against the Central Powers) clash with Soviets at Chelyabinsk on their way to Vladivostock.

(25 May) Revolt of Czech Legion who seize eastern part of Trans-Siberian railway.

(29 May) Partial conscription introduced for Red Army.

(23 June) Allied reinforcements arrive in Murmansk.

(16 July) Execution of Imperial Family at Ekaterinburg.

(2 Aug.) Establishment of anti-Bolshevik government at Archangel, followed by landing of more troops.

(6 Aug.) White forces take Kazan.

(14 Aug.) Allied forces land at Baku. British, Japanese and American forces land at Vladivostok.

(10 Sept.) Bolsheviks take Kazan.

(13 Sept.) Allied forces leave Baku.

(23 Sept.) 'White' forces set up Directorate as All Russian provisional government.

(9 Oct.) Directorate fixes capital at Omsk.

(13 Nov.) Following armistice between Allies and Germany, the Soviet government denounces the Brest-Litovsk Treaty.

(18 Nov.) Directorate suppressed at Omsk. Kolchak assumes supreme power.

(14 Dec.) Collapse of Skoropadsky regime in the Ukraine.

(17 Dec.) French land in Odessa.

1919

(3 Jan.) Red Army takes Riga and Kharkov.

(6 Feb.) Red Army occupies Kiev.

(5 Feb.) Denikin assumes supreme command of White forces in south-east Russia.

(2–7 May) First Congress of Communist International in Moscow. Creation of Politburo and Communist International.

(13 Mar.) Spring offensive by Kolchak.

(21 Mar.) Allies decide to withdraw forces from Russia.

(5 Apr.) British and Indian troops leave Transcaspia.

(8 Apr.) French evacuate Odessa.

(10 Apr.) Soviet troops enter Crimea.

(19 May) Denikin begins offensive against Bolsheviks.

(4 June) Kolchak defeated in centre and south, but Denikin continues advance, capturing Kharkov by end of month.

(15 July) Red Army takes Chelyabinsk.

(23 Aug.) Denikin takes Odessa.

(31 Aug.) Denikin occupies Kiev.

(19 Sept.) Allies evacuate Archangel.

(28 Sept.) Yudenich reaches suburbs of Petrograd.

(14–20 Oct.) Denikin takes Orel, but is forced to retreat; general retreat of White armies.

(14 Nov.) Defeat of Yudenich by Red Army and occupation of Omsk.

(12 Dec.) Red Army occupies Kharkov.

(16 Dec.) Red Army occupies Kiev.

1920

(4 Jan.) Abdication of Kolchak as Supreme Ruler.

(8 Jan.) Red Army takes Rostov.

(15 Jan.) Czechs hand Kolchak over to revolutionaries in control of Irkutsk.

(7 Feb.) Execution of Kolchak.

(19 Feb.) Northern government at Archangel collapses.

(4 Apr.) Denikin succeeded by Wrangel.

(24 Apr.) Outbreak of Russo–Polish War. Poles invade the Ukraine.

(6 May) Polish forces take Kiev.

(12 June) Red Army retakes Kiev.

(11 July) Russian counter-attack takes Minsk and Vilna (14th).

(20 July) Second Congress of Communist International.

(16 Aug.) Russian forces almost reach Warsaw; beaten back by Polish counter-offensive culminating in Polish victory on the Nieman.

(21 Sept.) Start of Russo–Polish peace negotiations.

(12 Oct.) Russo–Polish provisional peace treaty.

(25 Oct.) Red Army offensive against Wrangel.

(2 Nov.) Wrangel forced to retreat to the Crimea.

(11–14 Nov.) Defeat and evacuation of Wrangel's forces in the Crimea.

1921

(Feb.) Strikes in Petrograd. Red Army invades Georgia.

(1 Mar.) Beginnings of revolt of Kronstadt sailors.

(5 Mar.) Trotsky delivers ultimatum to sailors.

(16–17 Mar.) Bombardment and assault on Kronstadt.

(18 Mar.) Kronstadt Rising crushed. Treaty of Riga defines Russo–Polish frontier. 10th Party Congress; Lenin introduces New Economic Policy (NEP), allowing peasants to keep their surplus grain for disposal on the open market.

(Apr.) Beginnings of famine in the Volga regions.

(Aug.) Famine relief agreements signed with America and the Red Cross.

1922

(Mar.–Apr.) 11th Party Congress. Stalin becomes General Secretary. Lenin forced to convalesce after operation to remove two bullets, the result of Kaplan's attempted assassination in 1918.

(16 Apr.) Treaty of Rapallo with Germany establishes close economic and military co-operation.

(26 May) Lenin has stroke.

(2 Oct.) Lenin returns to Moscow.

(Dec.) Lenin's second stroke.

(23–26 Dec.) Lenin dictates the *Letter to the Congress.*

(30 Dec.) Formation of Union of Soviet Socialist Republics, federating Russia, the Ukraine, White Russia and Transcaucasia.

1923

(4 Jan.) Lenin adds codicil to the *Letter,* warning of Stalin's ambitions.

(Mar.) Lenin's third stroke.

(Apr.) 12th Party Congress.

(July) Constitution of USSR published.

1924

(21 Jan.) Death of Lenin (after suffering fourth stroke).

RUSSIA, 1924–53

1924

(21 Jan.) Death of Lenin.
(1 Feb.) Great Britain recognizes Soviet Union.
(3 Feb.) Rykov elected Prime Minister.
(23 May) 13th Party Conference opens. Zinoviev demands Trotsky's recantation of belief in 'Permanent Revolution'.

1925

(16 Jan.) Trotsky dismissed as War Commissar.
(21 Jan.) Japan recognizes Soviet Union.
(Apr.) 14th Party Conference adopts 'socialism in one country'.

1926

(19 Oct.) Trotsky and Kamenev expelled from Politburo.

1927

(26 May) Britain temporarily severs relations with Soviet Union because of continued Bolshevik propaganda.
(Nov.) Trotskyists organize political demonstrations and Trotsky expelled from Party.
(Dec.) 15th Party Conference condemns all deviations from party line and resolves upon the collectivization of agriculture. Stalin emerges as dominant voice.

1928

(Jan.) Trotsky banished to provinces.
(Spring) Serious grain procurement crisis.
(Sept.) Bukharin publishes opposition articles in *Pravda* in support of peasants.
(1 Oct.) Beginning of First Five-Year Plan aiming to develop heavy industries.

(Nov.) Bukharin and Tomsky exiled to Turkey.

1929

(Jan.) Trotsky exiled to Turkey.
(Autumn) Start of forced collectivization and dekulakization.
(17 Nov.) Bukharin and other 'rightists' expelled from Party.

1930

(Jan.) Quickening of tempo of collectivization; resistance harshly dealt with by force and deportation. Widespread disorder and destruction in rural areas.
(Mar.) Stalin publishes *Dizzy with Success* calling for slowing down of collectivization.
(Nov.–Dec.) Trial of so-called 'Industrial Party' for alleged conspiracy within the State Planning Commission (Gosplan).

1931

(Mar.–July) Trial of Mensheviks. Harvest failure as a result of chaos of collectivization.

1932

(Apr.) Central Committee resolves reform of literary and arts organizations. Beginnings of famine in Ukraine and other parts of Russia.
(Dec.) Introduction of internal passport.

1933

(Nov.) Second Five-Year Plan inaugurated. USA recognizes the Soviet government.

1934

(Jan.) 17th Party Conference.

(July) GPU (former *Cheka*) reorganized as NKVD.

(Sept.) USSR joins League of Nations.

(Dec.) Assassination of Kirov by Nikolayev leads Central Executive Committee to issue a directive ordering summary trial and execution of 'terrorists' without appeal.

(28–29 Dec.) Nikolayev and 13 'accomplices' tried in secret and executed.

1935

(Jan.) Zinoviev, Kamenev and 17 others tried in secret for 'moral responsibility' for Kirov's assassination and sentenced to imprisonment. Widespread arrests of 'oppositionists'.

(Feb.) Statute regulating collective farms promulgated. Commission appointed to draw up a new constitution.

(June) Draft constitution presented to Central Committee for approval.

(Aug.) 'Stakhanovite' programme launched to encourage industrial production.

(Sept.) Reintroduction of ranks in Red Army.

(Dec.) Central Committee declares that the purge is complete.

1936

(Jan.) Renewed purge of party members.

(19–24 Aug.) Trial and execution of Zinoviev, Kamenev and other members of the 'Trotskyite–Zinovievite Counter-Revolutionary Bloc' for alleged plotting against the leadership. Tomsky commits suicide following accusations made at their trial.

(25 Sept.) Yagoda dismissed as head of NKVD and replaced by Yezhov.

(5 Dec.) Eighth Congress of Soviets approves the new constitution.

1937

(Jan.) Trial of Radek, Pyatakov and 15 others for alleged conspiracy with Trotsky and foreign powers to overthrow the Soviet system. Four are imprisoned, the rest shot.

(Mar.) Bukharin, Rykov and Yagoda expelled from the Party.

(June) Tukachevsky, Chief of the General Staff, and other senior officers tried in secret for plotting with Germany and executed. Widespread purge of the armed forces begins, removing over 400 senior officers.

1938

(2–13 Mar.) Third Five-Year Plan inaugurated. Trial of Bukharin, Rykov, Krestinsky, Rakovsky, Yagoda, and other leading party and NKVD members for terrorism, sabotage, treason and espionage.

(28 Mar.) Stalin offers support to Czechoslovakia if attacked.

(9 May) Russia offers to assist Czechoslovakia if Romania and Poland will allow the passage of Russian troops across their territory; both refuse.

(Dec.) Beria succeeds Yezhov as head of NKVD.

1939

(Mar.) 18th Party Congress.

(18 Apr.) USSR proposes defence alliance with Great Britain and France. Offer not taken up by the western allies.

(3 May) Molotov replaces Litvinov as Commissar of Foreign Affairs in the USSR.

(12 Aug.) Anglo–French mission to USSR begins talks in Moscow.

(18 Aug.) Germany makes commercial agreement with USSR.

(22 Aug.) Ribbentrop, German Foreign Minister, arrives in Moscow.

(23 Aug.) Nazi–Soviet Pact signed. A non-aggression pact, it also contains secret clauses on the partition of Poland and allocation of Finland, Latvia, Estonia and Bessarabia to Soviet sphere of influence.

(31 Aug.) Supreme Soviet ratifies German non-aggression pact.

(17 Sept.) Red Army invades eastern Poland.

(22 Sept.) Red Army occupies Lvov.

(28 Sept.) Secret accord with Germany agrees partition of Poland and also transfers Lithuania to Soviet sphere of influence.

(29 Sept.–10 Oct.) Estonia, Latvia and Lithuania conclude treaties with USSR, allowing Soviet military bases in their territory.

(12 Oct.) Talks in Moscow between Finland and USSR. Stalin presents his territorial demands.

(9 Nov.) Finns reject Soviet demands.

(29 Nov.) USSR breaks off diplomatic relations with Finland.

(30 Nov.) Russians bomb Helsinki and Red Army crosses Finnish frontier.

(Dec.) Finnish forces inflict heavy defeats on Russia in the south and east.

1940

(1–12 Feb.) Major Russian offensive on Karelian Isthmus.

(12 Mar.) Treaty of Moscow concludes war. Finns cede 10 per cent of their territory including the Karelian Isthmus and territory in the north-east.

(15–17 June) Soviet troops occupy Lithuania, Latvia and Estonia.

(28 June) Soviet troops occupy Bessarabia and north-eastern Bukovina.

(21 July) Lithuania, Latvia and Estonia 'request' incorporation into USSR.

(17 Nov.) USSR demands control of Bulgaria and withdrawal of German troops from Finland before joining Tripartite Pact of Germany, Italy and Japan.

(18 Dec.) Hitler issues directive for Operation Barbarossa, the invasion of Russia.

1941

(13 Apr.) Non-aggression pact signed with Japan.

(22 June) Germany invades USSR.

(29 June) State Defence Committee formed.

(3 July) Stalin broadcasts to the people.

(12 July) Anglo–Soviet mutual assistance agreement signed.

(15 July) Fall of Smolensk.

(7 Aug.) Stalin becomes Supreme Commander of the Soviet Armed Forces.

(8 Sept.) Kiev captured.

(2 Oct.) German offensive against Moscow opens.

(19 Oct.) Declaration of state of siege in Moscow. Stalin remains in city, though thousands are evacuated or flee in panic.

(27 Nov.) German forces come within 20 miles of Moscow.

(5 Dec.) Russian counter-offensive in Moscow sector. Hitler abandons Moscow offensive for winter.

1942

(Mar.) Soviet winter offensive ends.

(28 June) German offensive in the south.

(9 Aug.) German Army Group A reaches Caucasus.

(Sept.) Army Group B reaches Stalingrad.

(23 Nov.) Army Group B surrounded by Russian offensive.

1943

(2 Feb.) Last German forces surrender at Stalingrad.

(May) Comintern dissolved as a gesture of reassurance towards western allies.

(5 July) Beginning of Operation Citadel, the German attack on the Kursk Salient. Counter-attack by Red Army (from 12 July) begins fresh Soviet advance.

(23 Aug.) Kharkov captured by the Red Army. End of the battle of Kursk.

(Sept.) Re-establishment of Patriarchate and Church administration in Russia. Seminaries and many churches reopened.

(25 Sept.) Smolensk recaptured.

(6 Nov.) Red Army recaptures Kiev.

(28 Nov.–1 Dec.) Roosevelt, Churchill and Stalin meet at Tehran.

1944

(27 Jan.) Siege of Leningrad lifted.

(Mar.) Red Army enters Poland.

(26 Mar.) Red Army enters Romania.

(1 Aug.) Home Army rises in Warsaw but receives no support from Russian forces. Rising quelled by October.

(24 Aug.) Romania accepts armistice terms.

(8 Sept.) Russians enter Bulgaria.

(26 Sept.) Estonia occupied by the Russians.

(6 Oct.) Russians enter Hungary and Czechoslovakia.

(15 Oct.) Russo–Bulgarian armistice.

1945

(12 Jan.) Final Red Army offensive begins.

(4–11 Feb.) 'Big Three', Churchill, Roosevelt and Stalin meet at Yalta.

(13 Apr.) Russian forces reach Vienna.

(16 Apr.) Russians begin final drive on Berlin.

(9 May) Surrender of Germany. Victory day in the Soviet Union.

(17 July–1 Aug.) Potsdam meeting of Stalin, Truman and Churchill (Attlee after 27 July).

1946

Fourth Five-Year Plan inaugurated.

(Aug.) Central Committee establishes party high schools.

(Sept.) Decree that all land being privately cultivated to be returned to the collectives.

1947

(Sept.) Cominform established.

(Dec.) Currency reform.

1948

Beginnings of collectivization in Baltic provinces.

(Jan.) Solomon Milhoels, Chairman of the Jewish State Theatre in Moscow, murdered.

(June) Yugoslavia expelled from Cominform.

(Autumn) Purge of Leningrad party following death of Zhdonov.

(Nov.) Dissolution of Jewish Anti-Fascist Committee.

1949

Closure of Jewish State Theatre in Moscow and arrest of leading Yiddish cultural figures.

1951

Fifth Five-Year Plan inaugurated.

1953

(Jan.) 'Doctors' Plot' announced, alleged to have planned 'to wipe out the leading cadres of the USSR' by medical means.

(5 Mar.) Death of Stalin: Malenkov becomes Prime Minister.

(July) Arrest and execution of Beria.

(Sept.) Khrushchev confirmed as First Secretary.

SPAIN, 1909–39

1909

(26 July) *Semana Tragica.* Committee of anarchists and socialists calls a general strike in Barcelona. The strike is accompanied by the burning of ecclesiastical property, especially convents.
(31 July) Strike suppressed with over 100 deaths.

1912

(12 Dec.) Canalejas, Spanish premier, murdered by anarchists in Madrid.

1917

(13 Aug.) General strike in Spain, calling for Catalan independence.

1921

(8 Mar.) Dato, Spanish premier, murdered by anarchists in reprisal for police actions against anarcho-syndicalists in Catalonia, following widespread campaign of terror and assassination.

1923

(14 Dec.) Primo de Rivera assumes Spanish dictatorship, supported by military and middle classes and with acquiescence of King Alfonso XIII.

1930

(28 Dec.) The King accepts the resignation of Primo de Rivera, following Spain's deteriorating economic condition and failure to achieve progress towards constitutional government.

1931

(14 Apr.) King Alfonso XIII abdicates. Spain becomes a constitutional republic.
(10 May) Left-wing Republican, Azaña, becomes premier.
(20 Oct.) 'Protection of the Republic' Law passed in Spain.
(9 Dec.) Spanish Republican Constitution introduced; Zamora elected President.

1933

(2–12 Jan.) Rising of anarchists and syndicalists in Barcelona.
(19 Nov.) Spanish Right wins elections to the Cortes. Foundation *of Falango Espanola* by José Antonio Primo de Rivera (son of the dictator, Primo de Rivera).

1934

(14 Jan.) Catalan elections won by the Left.
(4 Oct.) Right forms a ministry; followed by Socialist rising in Asturias and Catalan separatist revolt in Barcelona. Moroccan troops used to suppress risings with great ferocity.

1936

(16 Feb.) Popular Front wins elections: Azaña elected President and re-establishes 1931 constitution. Amnesty granted to rebels of 1934; growing clashes between Left and Right with assassinations and attacks on church property.
(20 Apr.) Cortes dismiss President Zamora.

(10 May) Azaña elected Spanish President, although large numbers of voters boycott the elections.

(17–18 July) Outbreak of Spanish Civil War with rising of the army in Morocco under General Franco; revolt spreads to mainland led by General Mola.

(19 July) Rebels reject offer of a ceasefire and the formation of an all-party national government. Republican Giral government formed and orders arming of revolutionary organizations.

(20–31 July) Republican forces seize the Montana barracks in Madrid and secure Catalonia, the Basque country and much of the south. The rebels, or Nationalists, over-run Morocco, parts of southern Spain and much of the north.

(26 July) Léon Blum declares that France cannot intervene on behalf of the Republic. Communist Comintern decides to raise international force of volunteers – the International Brigades – for service in Spain. Hitler offers aircraft and supplies to the Nationalists, as does Mussolini.

(6 Aug.) France and Britain submit draft 'non-intervention' agreement to the European powers.

(19 Aug.) Britain imposes embargo on arms to Spain.

(21 Aug.) Italy accepts non-intervention, but makes exceptions for 'Volunteers' and financial support.

(23 Aug.) Germany accepts non-intervention, as does the Soviet Union, although both continue to supply advisers and other support.

(4 Sept.) Formation of Largo Caballero government in Madrid, composed of republicans, socialists and communists.

(27 Sept.) Nationalists capture Toledo.

(1 Oct.) Nationalists appoint Franco Generalissimo and head of state.

(22 Oct.) Most of Spanish gold reserves shipped to the Soviet Union. Russian advisers supervise reorganization of Republican army and appoint political commissars.

(Nov.) Nationalist forces advance on Madrid. Air-raids on Madrid and Republican forces by German Condor Legion. First International Brigades go into action and assist in repelling Nationalist advance. Republican government moves to Valencia.

(18 Nov.) Germany and Italy recognize Franco government.

(16 Dec.) Protocol signed in London by major powers agreeing non-intervention in Spain.

1937

(8 Feb.) Malaga falls to Nationalists.

(3–12 Mar.) Republican government orders disarming of workers' and anarchist militias in Catalonia following clashes between them and the communists.

(20–23 Mar.) Battle of Guadalajara. Republicans defeat Italian forces advancing on Madrid.

(19 Apr.) Franco orders unification of the Nationalist movement, fusing the Falange and other political bodies into a single political body, and paramilitary groups into a militia responsible to the army.

(26 Apr.) German Condor Legion destroys town of Guernica in Basque country.

(30 Apr.–6 May) Street fighting in Barcelona between workers' militias and republican–communists.

(15 May) Largo Caballero resigns in opposition to communist call for greater control and suppression of rival groups.

(17 May) Negrin government formed with backing of Comintern to pursue victory by means of communist control of the Republican forces.

(18 June) Anarchist militia (POUM) dissolved and leaders arrested; anti-Stalinist leader, Nin, executed.

(19 June) Nationalists capture Basque capital of Bilbao.

(5–28 July) Failure of Republican offensive at Brunete to restore position in north.

(10–14 Sept.) Following attacks on shipping by Italian submarines and aircraft, Nyon Conference of nine European powers agrees to patrol the Mediterranean and sink submarines attacking non-Spanish ships. Italy and Germany do not attend, but sinkings cease.

(17 Oct.) Largo Caballero denounces repressive policies of Negrin government.

(20–22 Oct.) Franco's forces complete reduction of north-west with capture of Gijon and Oviedo.

(31 Oct.) Republican government moves to Barcelona.

(15–26 Dec.) Republican forces go over to the offensive at Teruel to avert threat to Madrid.

1938

(5–22 Feb.) Nationalists launch counteroffensive at Teruel; recaptured (23rd). Nationalist offensive in Aragon.

(Mar.) Nationalists begin advance from Aragon to the Mediterranean with aim of cutting Republican territory in half and achieve rapid early success.

(5 Apr.) Nationalist forces reach Mediterranean at Vinaroz, cutting off Catalonia from the rest of Republican Spain.

(Apr.–May) Opening of French frontier permits some resupply of Republican forces. 200,000 new conscripts called up and organized on flanks of the Nationalist corridor.

(July–Aug.) Last Republican offensive on the Ebro forces Franco to suspend attack on Valencia.

(Aug.) Basque and Catalan separatist ministers resign from Negrin ministry.

(15 Nov.) Last Republican forces driven out of Ebro bridgehead.

(Dec.) Nationalists begin offensive against Catalonia.

1939

(26 Jan.) Fall of Barcelona to Nationalist forces.

(7 Feb.) President Azaña goes into exile in France (resigns on 24th).

(9 Feb.) End of resistance in Catalonia by Republican forces; over 200,000 cross French frontier and are disarmed. Negrin makes last attempt to obtain a negotiated peace without reprisals.

(26 Feb.) Negrin tries to organize last stand of Republic at Cartagena naval base.

(4 Mar.) Negrin appoints communist military leaders to key defence positions.

(5–12 Mar.) Military commander in Madrid, Casado, leads rebellion against Negrin government on account of its communist domination and sets up a National Defence Council. On Comintern instructions, communists attempt to defeat the rebellion, but are themselves defeated by non-communist elements. Negrin flees to France.

(23 Mar.) Casado sends emissaries to Nationalist capital in Burgos to negotiate peace terms. Franco demands surrender of Republican Air Force by 25 March and rest of armed forces by 27 March.

(25 Mar.) Franco breaks off negotiations because his terms not met.

(27 Mar.) Last meeting of National Defence Council.

(28 Mar.) Nationalist forces enter Madrid.

(1 Apr.) General Franco announces end to the Civil War.

EUROPE IN DEPRESSION, 1919–39

1919

Versailles settlement imposes large reparations burden on Germany. Various commentators, most notably J.M. Keynes, in *The Economic Consequences of the Peace*, predict they will cause economic dislocation.

1919–20

Short-lived economic boom in Britain and France as 'return to normalcy' widely predicted.

1921

Post-war trade fails to recover in the UK as a result of widespread political upheaval in central and eastern Europe and the Bolshevik government's renunciation of its foreign debts.

1922

(Jan.–Feb.) British unemployment approaches 2 million, mainly concentrated in the pre-war staple industries, coal, textiles, shipbuilding, and iron and steel. Following Geddes Report, government forced to cut social expenditure on housing and education, leading to widespread disillusionment.
(Sept.) America introduces highest ever protective tariffs, further depressing world trade.
(26 Dec.) Germany declared in default on its reparations. German inflation begins to take off (US $1 is now worth 7,500 marks compared with 550 in August).

1923

Bulgarian currency (the ley) falls to a seventh of its 1919 value.

(Jan.) France reoccupies the Ruhr in compensation for default on German reparations payments.
(May) Hyperinflation seizes hold in Germany; US $1worth 54,000 marks.
(Sept.) German currency virtually worthless with a tram ticket costing 400,000 marks (compared to 600 in June).
(Nov.) US $1 worth 4,200 billion marks. Introduction of *Rentenmark* ends currency chaos with currency based on property values; one new mark equals a billion old ones.
(Dec.) League of Nations launches scheme of economic reconstruction in Hungary after currency crisis drastically reduces value of the crown.

1924

(Apr.) Dawes Plan recommends French withdrawal from Ruhr and German reflation to aid the economy. Plan accepted by Germany (16th).
(Sept.) Dawes Plan implemented.

1925

(28 Apr.) Britain returns to the Gold Standard in an attempt to re-establish pre-war trading conditions. In retrospect, this overvalues British goods by *ca.* 10% and contributes to long-term depression of Britain's staple export industries.

1926

(May) Continuing problems of over-capacity in the British coal industry lead to nine-day General Strike in which Baldwin government faces down the Trades Union Congress, though the miners remain on strike until the autumn when forced back to work on humiliating terms.

(15 July) Briand resigns as French premier over financial crisis. Measures taken to stabilize the franc.

(18 Aug.) Following fall in the value of the lira, Mussolini announces plan to stabilize the currency, but is unwilling to set it as low as his Finance Minister and industrialists want.

1927

(Jan.) Russian agricultural production still below 1913 levels in spite of higher arable acreage and increases in other economic indicators. Beginning of discussion of need to collectivize holdings and liquidate the rich peasants ('*kulaks*') in order to procure sufficient grain for industrial development.

(Dec.) Mussolini revalues Italian currency at 92.45 lire to the £ – the '*Quota Novanta*' (Quota 90), about 25% higher than some had recommended. The resulting 'stabilization crisis', accompanied by higher tariffs and reduced wages, leads to lower imports, reduced economic activity and higher unemployment.

1928

(16 May) Heaviest ever day's trading on Wall Street following panic selling of aero and electrical stocks, demonstrating volatility of the US stock market.

(June) France devalues the franc.

(Oct.) Introduction of First Five Year Plan in the Soviet Union, running until 1932. Retrospectively approved by 16th Party Congress in April 1929.

(Nov.) New records set for trading on Wall Street as shares boom. Stock Exchange closes for a day to clear backlog of trading.

1929

(Jan.) *New York Times* Stock Exchange index stands at 338.

(June) After fall in spring, American stocks begin further upward climb.

(3 Sept.) American stocks reach new index high of 452.

(Oct.) Heavy selling of stocks begins with panic selling after 24th and heaviest fall ever recorded on 29th – 'the Wall Street Crash'. Thousands of investors ruined and millions of dollars wiped off values of shares. The stock market closes on the 30th but business confidence is shattered and the stock market does not recover until 1932. Meanwhile, credit dries up, business activity dwindles and hundreds of thousands are laid off work.

(Dec.) Politburo Commission on collectivization agrees to liquidate the '*kulaks*' and collectivize agriculture rapidly.

1930

(Jan.) Second Reparations Conference at The Hague. Young Plan agreed by German government fixing revised reparations to be paid off by 1988. Central Committee in the Soviet Union passes decree aiming to complete collectivization by 1931–32. Process of crash collectivization begins and leads to 65% of peasant households being collectivized by 1 Mar.

(May) Bank for International Settlements established at Basle. Young Plan becomes operational. British government rejects sweeping reform proposals from Mosley to deal with spiralling unemployment. Mosley resigns from government.

(June) America further raises tariff barriers.

(July) German government issues first emergency decrees to protect the economy. Unemployment in Britain reaches 2.5 million.

(Dec.) Deteriorating economic situation in Spain precipitates resignation of dictator, Primo de Rivera.

1931

(Jan.) Unemployment in Germany reaches 5 million.

(Mar.) Failure of Tariff Truce Convention means that cycle of defensive introduction of protection and further reductions in trading activity continue.

(May) Failure of the largest commercial bank in Austria, the Creditanstalt, provokes banking crisis in Europe with run on German banks and run on sterling.

(June) Collapse of German Nordwolle textile company increases pressure on German banks. President Hoover in America proposes one-year moratorium on reparations and war debts in view of the crisis. New government formed in Austria in attempt to avert financial crisis.

(July) President Roosevelt promises a 'New Deal' for the American people and initiates programmes to assist revival of the American economy. Bankruptcy of German Danatbank (13th) forces closure of German banks until early August. Danatbank taken under government control. In Britain, May Committee reports advocating large cuts in public expenditure to stabilize sterling and restore financial and business confidence and precipitating crisis in Labour government of Ramsay MacDonald.

(Aug.) Labour government in Britain collapses over splits in Cabinet over proposed economy measures. Emergency National Government formed with former premier in charge and support from other parties.

(21 Sept.) Britain abandons the Gold Standard; twelve other countries follow by 1932. 'Stand-still' agreement with creditors of Germany.

(Nov.) Following landslide victory for National Government at the General Election in Britain, massive cuts in public expenditure are made including public service and armed forces pay, as well as cuts in dole payments via the 'means test'.

(Dec.) Dutch government increases tariffs and sets import quotas to protect farmers.

1932

(Jan.) Unemployment reaches 6 million in Germany.

(Feb.) Britain introduces Import Duties Act erecting tariff barriers and ending historic commitment to free trade. French government offers assistance programme to agriculture. Collapse of Swedish match company, I Kreuger.

(Mar.) France sets up National Bank for Commerce and Industry.

(June) Britain reduces Bank Rate to 2% providing the basis for development of consumer industries and boom in house construction financed by cheap mortgages.

(July) At World Trade Conference in Ottawa, Britain grants concessionary tariff status to the Empire – 'Imperial Preference'. Lausanne Conference effectively ends reparations.

(Aug.) In Germany, von Papen announces works creation programme, but unemployment climbs to 7.5 million by October.

1933

(Jan.) Hitler becomes Chancellor in Germany. British unemployment figures peak at just under 3 million, one in four of the insured working population. Second Five-Year Plan launched in Soviet Union. Unemployment in Italy passes one million.

(Mar.) Japan devalues the yen and America abandons the Gold Standard.

(June) German government begins sharp deflationary policy.

(June–July) International Economic Conference in London attempts to reach agreement on stabilizing the currency, but fails.

(Dec.) Polish production estimated to have fallen by 46% of its 1913 level between 1931 and end of December 1933.

1934

Widespread devaluations across Europe by Belgium, Czechoslovakia, Italy and Switzerland.

(Feb.) General Strike called in France.

(Mar.) End of Polish–German tariff war.

(Apr.) Germany extends import controls to all industrial goods.

1935

(Jan.) UK government reacts to crisis of over-capacity in cotton industry by promoting reduction of factories by the industry. A similar policy is pursued with shipbuilding and steel, devastating a number of communities which become high-profile examples of industrial dereliction, such as Dowlais in South Wales and Jarrow in the North-East.

(June) Italy reduces import quotas.

(July) German unemployment falls under Nazis from 2,900,000 in Jan. to 1,754,000.

(Aug.) Emergency Acts in France to stimulate recovery.

(Nov.) French mining industry nationalized in response to economic crisis.

1936

Further devaluations of Swiss franc and Italian lira.

(3 Feb.) Publication by J.M. Keynes of *General Theory of Employment, Interest and Money* offering an intellectual rationale for more liberal economic policies and higher state spending.

(Mar.) Reorganization of Italian economy into corporations demanded by Mussolini.

(Apr.) German–Soviet trade agreement signed, typical of bilateral agreements forged by governments in response to the economic crisis.

(June) French armament industry and military aircraft companies nationalized.

(Sept.) Germany announces Four-Year Plan, an expression of autarkic economic policy, aimed at making her industrially independent, with increased production and development of synthetic rubber and fuel. Placed under Goering's overall control, it continued into the war years.

(2 Oct.) French franc devalued.

1937

(Jan.) Japanese yen devalued again.

(July) Further devaluation of French franc.

1938

(Mar.) Austrian banks taken over by German Reichsbank following the *Anschluss*.

(May) National Economic Plan put forward in France by Daladier. Further devaluation of franc.

(June) Belgian Prime Minister Van Zeeland puts forward plan to enlarge world trade and halt protectionism.

(July) Franco–German trade agreements.

(Dec.) New foreign exchange controls introduced in Germany.

1939

(Jan.) French government plan to reduce public debt and stimulate the economy.

(Mar.) Germany and Romania agree long-term economic co-operation.

(Apr.) Establishment of 'Great German' tariff area.

(Sept.) German–Soviet trade agreement signed following Nazi–Soviet Pact.

INTERNATIONAL BACKGROUND TO THE SECOND WORLD WAR

1933

(30 Jan.) Hitler becomes Chancellor of Germany.

(16 Mar.) Britain's plan for disarmament fails as Germany insists on exclusion of the SA.

(19 Mar.) Mussolini proposes pact between Britain, France, Italy and Germany, signed as the Rome Pact.

(15 July) Rome Pact binds Britain, France, Germany and Italy to the League Covenant, the Locarno Treaties, and the Kellogg–Briand Pact.

(14 Oct.) Germany leaves disarmament conference and League of Nations.

1934

(26 Jan.) Polish–German non-aggression pact.

(14–15 June) Hitler meets Mussolini for the first time in Venice.

(25 July) Austrian Chancellor Dollfuss murdered in Nazi coup.

(30 July) Dr Kurt Schuschnigg becomes new Austrian Chancellor.

(5 Dec.) Italian and Ethiopian troops clash at Walwal inside Ethiopia.

1935

(1 Feb.) Anglo–German conference on German rearmament; Italy sends troops to East Africa.

(15 Mar.) Hitler repudiates the military restrictions on Germany imposed by the Treaty of Versailles, restores conscription and announces that the peacetime army strength is to be raised to half a million men. Germany announces the existence of the *Luftwaffe*.

(11–14 Apr.) Britain, France and Italy confer at Stresa to establish a common front against Germany.

(2 May) France and the Soviet Union sign a treaty of mutual assistance for five years.

(16 May) Czechoslovakia and Soviet Union sign mutual assistance pact.

(19 May) Pro-Nazi Sudeten Party makes gains in Czechoslovak elections.

(18 June) Anglo–German Naval Agreement. Germany undertakes that her navy shall not exceed one-third of the tonnage of the Royal Navy.

(27 June) League of Nations Union 'Peace Ballot' in Britain shows strong support for the League.

(3 Sept.) League of Nations attempts to defuse the Walwal Oasis incident by stating that neither country was to blame as possession was unclear.

(2 Oct.) Italian forces invade Ethiopia.

(7 Oct.) League of Nations declares Italy the aggressor in Ethiopia and votes sanctions (11th).

(19 Oct.) League of Nations sanctions on Italy come into force.

(9 Dec.) Hoare–Laval Pact, lenient to Italy, is met by hostile public reaction in Britain and France.

(13 Dec.) Beneš succeeds Masaryk as President of Czechoslovakia.

1936

(16 Feb.) Popular Front wins a majority in the Spanish elections.

(3 Mar.) Britain increases defence expenditure, principally on the air force.

(8 Mar.) German troops reoccupy the demilitarized Rhineland in violation of the Treaty of Versailles.

(5 May) Italians take Addis Ababa; Emperor Haile Selassie flees. Italy annexes Ethiopia (9th).

(11 July) Austro–German Convention acknowledges Austrian independence.

(18 July) Army revolt under Emilio Mola and Francisco Franco begins Spanish Civil War.

(24 Aug.) Germany introduces compulsory conscription.

(9 Sept.) Conference held in London on non-intervention in Spanish Civil War.

(1 Oct.) Franco appointed 'Chief of the Spanish State' by the Nationalist rebels.

(14 Oct.) Belgium renounces its military pact with France in order to ensure its liberty of action in the face of German reoccupation of Rhineland.

(19 Oct.) Germany begins four-year economic plan to develop its economic base for war.

(1 Nov.) Mussolini proclaims Rome–Berlin Axis.

(18 Nov.) Germany and Italy recognize Franco's government.

(24 Nov.) Germany and Japan sign Anti-Comintern Pact.

(16 Dec.) Protocol signed in London for non-intervention in Spain.

1937

(2 Jan.) Mussolini signs agreement with Britain ensuring the safety of shipping in the Mediterranean.

(15 Jan.) Amnesty granted to Austrian Nazis.

(27 Feb.) France extends Maginot Line.

(18 Mar.) Defeat of Italian push on Madrid.

(27 Apr.) Basque town of Guernica destroyed by German Condor Legion.

(19 June) Spanish Nationalist forces take Bilbao.

(23 June) Germany and Italy withdraw from non-intervention committee.

(17 July) Naval agreements between Britain and Germany and Britain and Soviet Union.

(10–14 Sept.) At Nyon Conference, nine nations adopt system of patrol in Mediterranean to protect shipping.

(13 Oct.) Germany guarantees inviolability of Belgium.

(17 Oct.) Riots in Sudeten area of Czechoslovakia.

(21 Oct.) Franco's forces complete conquest of Basque country.

(5 Nov.) Hitler informs his generals in the Hossbach memorandum that Austria and Czechoslovakia will be annexed as the first stage in *Lebensraum* for Germany.

(6 Nov.) Italy joins Anti-Comintern Pact.

(17–21 Nov.) Lord Halifax (Lord President of the Council) accepts unofficial invitation to visit Germany where he has inconclusive discussions with Hitler on a European settlement.

(29 Nov.) Sudeten Germans secede from Czech Parliament following a ban on their meetings.

(11 Dec.) Italy leaves the League of Nations.

1938

(4 Feb.) Von Ribbentrop becomes German Foreign Minister.

(12 Feb.) At Berchtesgaden Hitler forces the Austrian Chancellor Schuschnigg to accept a Protocol promising the release of Nazis in Austria, accepting a pro-Nazi (Seyss-Inquart) as Minister of the Interior and virtually attaching the Austrian army to that of Germany, subject to the consent of Austrian President Miklas.

(16 Feb.) Amnesty for Nazis proclaimed in Austria; Seyss-Inquart becomes Minister of the Interior.

(20 Feb.) In a speech to the Reichstag, Hitler proclaims the need to protect the 10 million Germans on the frontiers of the Reich.

(6 Mar.) President Miklas of Austria accepts Schuschnigg's proposal of a plebiscite on the future independence of Austria. Announced on 9 March, voting was to take place on the 13th.

(10 Mar.) Hitler mobilizes for immediate invasion of Austria.

(11 Mar.) Schuschnigg accepts Hitler's ultimatum demanding that the plebiscite not be held.

(12 Mar.) German army marches into Austria.

(13 Mar.) Austria is declared part of Hitler's Reich.

(28 Mar.) Hitler encourages German minority in Czechoslovakia to make such demands as will break up the state.

(16 Apr.) In Anglo–Italian pact, Britain recognizes Italian sovereignty in Ethiopia in return for withdrawal of Italian troops from Spain.

(24 Apr.) Germans in Sudetenland demand full autonomy.

(29 Apr.) Britain reluctantly joins France in diplomatic action on behalf of the Czech government.

(9 May) Russia promises to assist Czechoslovakia in the event of a German attack if Poland and Romania will permit the passage of Russian troops. Both, however, refuse.

(18–21 May) German troop movements reported on Czech border; Czech government calls up reservists (20th); and partial mobilization (21st).

(22 May) Britain warns Germany of dangers of military action, but makes it clear to France that she is not in favour of military action herself.

(3 Aug.) Walter Runciman visits Prague on mediation mission between Czechs and Sudeten Germans.

(11 Aug.) Under British and French pressure, the Czech Prime Minister Beneš opens negotiations with the Sudeten Germans.

(12 Aug.) Germany begins to mobilize.

(4 Sept.) Henlein, leader of the Sudeten Germans, rejects Beneš's offer of full autonomy and breaks off relations with the Czech government (7th).

(7 Sept.) France calls up reservists.

(11 Sept.) Poland and Romania again refuse to allow the passage of Russian troops to assist Czechoslovakia.

(12 Sept.) Hitler demands that Czechs accept German claims.

(13 Sept.) Unrest in Sudetenland put down by Czech troops.

(15 Sept.) Chamberlain visits Hitler at Berchtesgaden. Hitler states his determination to annex the Sudetenland on the principle of self-determination.

(18 Sept.) Britain and France decide to persuade the Czechs to hand over territory in areas where over half of the population is German.

(20–21 Sept.) Germany completes invasion plans. The Czech government initially rejects the Anglo–French proposals, but accepts them on the 21st.

(22 Sept.) Chamberlain meets Hitler at Godesberg. Hitler demands immediate occupation of the Sudetenland and announces 28 September for the invasion. The Czech Cabinet resigns.

(23 Sept.) Czechoslovakia mobilizes; Russia promises to support France in the event of her aiding the Czechs.

(25 Sept.) France and Britain threaten Hitler with force unless he negotiates,

(26 Sept.) Partial mobilization in France.

(27 Sept.) The Royal Navy is mobilized.

(28 Sept.) Hitler delays invasion for 24 hours pending a four-power conference at Munich.

(29 Sept.) At the Munich conference Chamberlain, Daladier, Hitler and Mussolini agree to transfer the Sudetenland to Germany, while guaranteeing the remaining Czech frontiers.

(30 Sept.) Hitler and Chamberlain sign 'peace in our time' communiqué.

(1 Oct.) Czechs cede Teschen to Poland. Germany begins occupation of the Sudetenland.

(5 Oct.) Beneš resigns.

(6–8 Oct.) Slovakia and Ruthenia are granted autonomy.

(25 Oct.) Libya is declared to be part of Italy.

(1 Dec.) British prepare for conscription.

(6 Dec.) Franco–German pact on inviolability of existing frontiers.

(17 Dec.) Italy denounces 1935 agreement with France.

(23 Dec.) Franco begins final offensive against last Republican stronghold in Catalonia.

1939

(10 Jan.) Chamberlain and Halifax visit Rome for discussions with Mussolini.

(26 Jan.) Franco's forces take Barcelona.

(27 Feb.) Britain and France recognize Franco's government.

(14 Mar.) Under Hitler's prompting, the Slovak leader Tiso proclaims a breakaway 'Slovak Free State'.

(15 Mar.) German troops march into Prague and occupy Bohemia and Moravia.

(28 Mar.) Hitler denounces 1934 non-aggression pact with Poland. Spanish Civil War ends with surrender of Madrid.

(31 Mar.) Britain and France promise aid to Poland in the event of a threat to Polish independence.

(7 Apr.) Italy invades Albania. Spain joins the Anti-Comintern Pact.

(13 Apr.) Britain and France guarantee the independence of Greece and Romania.

(15 Apr.) The USA requests assurances from Hitler and Mussolini that they will not attack 31 named states.

(16–18 Apr.) The Soviet Union proposes a defensive alliance with Britain and France, but the offer is not accepted.

(27 Apr.) Britain introduces conscription. Hitler denounces the 1935 Anglo–German naval agreement.

(28 Apr.) Hitler rejects Roosevelt's peace proposals and denounces the German–Polish non-aggression pact.

(22 May) Hitler and Mussolini sign a ten-year political and military alliance – the 'Pact of Steel'.

(11 Aug.) Anglo–French mission to the Soviet Union begins talks in Moscow.

(18 Aug.) Germany and the Soviet Union sign a commercial agreement.

(23 Aug.) Germany and the Soviet Union sign non-aggression pact, with secret clauses on the partition of Poland. Chamberlain warns Hitler that Britain will stand by Poland, but accepts the need for a settlement of the Danzig question. Hitler states that Germany's interest in Danzig and the Corridor must be satisfied. The Poles refuse to enter negotiations with the Germans. Hitler brings forward his preparations to invade Poland to the 26th (from 1 Sept.).

(25 Aug.) Anglo–Polish mutual assistance pact signed in London. Hitler makes a 'last offer' on Poland and postpones his attack until 1 Sept.

(28–31 Aug.) Britain and France urge direct negotiations between Germans and Poles, but the Poles refuse.

(31 Aug.) Hitler orders attack on Poland.

(1 Sept.) German forces invade Poland and annex Danzig. Britain and France demand withdrawal of German troops.

(2 Sept.) Britain decides on ultimatum to Germany.

(3 Sept.) Britain and France declare war on Germany.

THE SECOND WORLD WAR

1939

(1 Sept.) Germany invades Poland and annexes Danzig.

(2 Sept.) Great Britain introduces National Service Bill calling up men aged 18 and 41.

(3 Sept.) Britain and France declare war on Germany.

(7 Sept.) Germans overrun western Poland.

(17 Sept.) Soviet Union invades eastern Poland.

(19 Sept.) Polish government leaves Warsaw.

(28 Sept.) Fall of Warsaw. Germany and Soviet Union settle partition of Poland.

(30 Sept.) Last of British Expeditionary Force (BEF) arrives in France.

(6 Oct.) Peace moves by Hitler rejected by Britain and France.

(8 Oct.) Western Poland incorporated into the Reich.

(3 Nov.) United States allows Britain and France to purchase arms in US on a 'cash and carry' basis.

(30 Nov.) Soviet Union invades Finland.

(13 Dec.) German battleship *Graf Spee* forced to scuttle itself off Montevideo after battle of the River Plate.

1940

(12 Mar.) Finland signs peace treaty with Soviet Union ceding territory on the Karelian Isthmus and in north-eastern Finland.

(9 Apr.) Germany invades Norway and Denmark.

(14 Apr.) British forces land in Norway.

(2 May) Evacuation of British forces from Norway.

(10 May) Resignation of Chamberlain as premier, replaced by Winston Churchill. Germany invades Holland, France and Belgium.

(14 May) Dutch army surrenders after bombing of Rotterdam.

(28 May) Belgium capitulates.

(29 May–3 June) Over 300,000 British and Allied troops evacuated from Dunkirk.

(June–Sept.) Battle of Britain.

(10 June) Italy declares war on Britain and France.

(14 June) Germans enter Paris. French government moves to Bordeaux.

(16 June) France declines offer of union with Britain. Marshal Pétain replaces Paul Reynaud as head of French administration.

(17–23 June) Russians occupy Baltic states.

(22 June) France concludes armistice with Germany.

(24 June) France signs armistice with Italy.

(27 June) Russia invades Romania.

(3 July) Britain sinks French fleet at Oran.

(5 Aug.) Britain signs agreement with Polish government-in-exile in London and (on 7 Aug.) with Free French under de Gaulle.

(23 Aug.) Beginning of 'Blitz' on Britain.

(7 Oct.) Germany seizes Romanian oilfields.

(12 Oct.) Hitler cancels Operation Sealion for the invasion of Britain.

(28 Oct.) Italy invades Greece. Britain offers help.

(11 Nov.) Major elements of Italian fleet sunk at Taranto.

(9–15 Dec.) Italian forces defeated at Sidi Barrani in North Africa.

1941

(Jan.–Feb.) Further Italian reverses in North Africa.

(6 Jan.) F.D. Roosevelt sends Lend-Lease Bill to Congress.

(6 Feb.) German troops under Rommel sent to assist Italians in North Africa.

(6 Apr.) German ultimatum to Greece and Yugoslavia. Britain diverts troops from North Africa to Greece.

(7 Apr.) Rommel takes offensive in North Africa.

(11 Apr.) Blitz on Coventry.

(13 Apr.) Stalin signs neutrality pact with Japan.

(17 Apr.) Yugoslavia signs capitulation after Italian and German attack.

(22–28 Apr.) British forces evacuated from Greece.

(10 May) Rudolf Hess flies to Scotland and is imprisoned.

(27 May) *Bismarck* sunk by Royal Navy.

(20–31 May) German capture of Crete.

(22 June) Germans launch invasion of Russia, Operation Barbarossa. Finnish forces attack on Karelian Isthmus.

(6 July) Russians abandon eastern Poland and Baltic states.

(12 July) Britain and Russia sign agreement for mutual assistance in Moscow.

(16 July) Germans take Smolensk.

(11 Aug.) Churchill and Roosevelt sign the Atlantic Charter.

(8 Sept.) Germans lay siege to Leningrad.

(19 Sept.) Germans take Kiev.

(30 Sept.–2 Oct.) Germans begin drive on Moscow.

(16 Oct.) Russian government leaves Moscow but Stalin stays.

(30 Oct.) German attacks reach within 60 miles of Moscow.

(15 Nov.) Renewed German offensive takes advance elements within 20 miles of Moscow.

(20–28 Nov.) German forces take, but retreat from, Rostov.

(5 Dec.) Germans go on to defensive on Moscow front as Russians launch counter-offensive.

(7 Dec.) Japanese bomb Pearl Harbor, Hawaii and British Malaya.

(8 Dec.) Britain and the USA declare war on Japan.

(11 Dec.) Germany and Italy declare war on USA.

1942

(2 Jan.) Britain, United States, Soviet Union and 23 other nations sign Washington Pact not to make separate peace treaties with their enemies.

(1 Feb.) Pro-Nazi Quisling becomes premier of Norway.

(6 Feb.) Roosevelt and Churchill appoint Combined Chiefs of Staff.

(11 Feb.) German battleships make Channel 'dash' from Brest to Germany.

(15 Feb.) Surrender of Singapore to Japanese.

(10 Mar.) Rangoon falls to Japanese.

(28 Mar.) RAF destroys much of Lübeck, first major demonstration of area bombing.

(12–17 May) Russian offensive on Kharkov front defeated.

(26 May) Anglo–Soviet Treaty signed for closer co-operation.

(29 May) Soviet Union and United States extend Lend-Lease Agreement.

(30 May) First 1,000 bomber raid on Cologne.

(6 June) Germans wipe out village of Lidice in Czechoslovakia in retaliation for assassination of Gestapo leader Heydrich.

(10 June) German offensive in the Ukraine.

(21 June) Fall of Tobruk after Rommel's advance in North Africa. Eighth Army retreats to El Alamein.

(25 June) Dwight Eisenhower appointed Commander-in-Chief of US forces in Europe.

(2 July) Fall of Sevastapol.

(28 July) Germans take Rostov and northern Caucasus in drive to take Baku oilfields. Zhukov takes over command of southern armies.

(14 Aug.) Raid on Dieppe ends in failure.

(23 Oct.–4 Nov.) Defeat and pursuit of Axis forces at El Alamein.

(11–12 Nov.) Vichy France occupied by Germans.

(19–20 Nov.) Russians began counter-attack at Stalingrad, cutting off Von Paulus's troops.
(27 Nov.) French Navy scuttled in Toulon.
(29 Dec.) Final failure of effort by German forces to relieve Von Paulus.

1943

(2 Jan.) German withdrawal from Caucasus begins.
(14–24 Jan.) Churchill and Roosevelt meet at Casablanca Conference and declare 'Unconditional Surrender' required of Germany.
(31 Jan.) Von Paulus surrenders at Stalingrad.
(2 Feb.) Last German forces surrender at Stalingrad.
(8 Feb.) Russian offensive takes Kursk.
(14 Feb.) Russians capture Rostov.
(16 Feb.) Russians take Kharkov.
(15 Mar.) Russians forced out of Kharkov.
(20 Apr.) Massacre of Jews in Warsaw ghetto.
(26 Apr.) Discovery of the Katyn massacre and demand by Polish government in London for investigation by the Red Cross. Stalin breaks off diplomatic relations with London Poles.
(12 May) Axis armies in Tunisia surrender.
(17 May) RAF bombs Ruhr dams, causing widespread destruction.
(4 June) French Committee of National Liberation formed under General Charles de Gaulle.
(4 July) General Sikorski killed in an air crash.
(5 July) Germans launch an offensive on Kursk Salient, Operation Citadel.
(10 July) Allied landings in Sicily.
(12 July) Russian counter-offensive against Orel Salient causes Germans to halt Kursk offensive.
(26 July) Mussolini forced to resign. King Victor Emmanuel asks Marshal Badoglio to form a government. Secret armistice signed with Allies.
(4 Aug.) Russians take Orel.
(23 Aug.) Russians retake Kharkov.

(3 Sept.) Allied landings in Italy; Italy surrenders unconditionally.
(25 Sept.) Russians take Smolensk.
(2 Nov.) Moscow Declaration of Allied foreign ministers on international security.
(6 Nov.) Russians take Kiev.
(28 Nov.–1 Dec.) Churchill, Roosevelt and Stalin meet at Tehran.
(20 Dec.) Britain and USA agree to support Tito's partisans.
(26 Dec.) *Scharnhorst* sunk in Barents Sea by British ships.

1944

(22 Jan.) Allied landing at Anzio in attempt to by-pass German forces blocking the road to Rome.
(27 Jan.) Relief of Leningrad.
(15 Feb.) Bombing of Monte Cassino by Allies fails to dislodge German defenders.
(2 Apr.) Russians enter Romania.
(18 May) Fall of Monte Cassino to Allied forces.
(4 June) Fall of Rome to Americans.
(6 June) 'D-Day' landings in Normandy.
(13 June) V-1, 'Flying Bomb', campaign opened on Britain.
(1 July) Monetary and financial conference at Bretton Woods, New Hampshire lays foundation for postwar economic settlement.
(9 July) Fall of Caen to Allied troops.
(20 July) Failure of 'July Plot' to assassinate Hitler.
(26 July) Soviet Union recognizes the Lublin Committee of Polish Liberation in Moscow as the legitimate authority for liberated Poland.
(1 Aug.) Rising of Home Army in Warsaw. American armies begin breakout from Normandy bridgehead at Avranches.
(11 Aug.) Allied landings in southern France.
(13–20 Aug.) German forces destroyed in Falaise Pocket in France.
(25 Aug.) De Gaulle and Allied troops enter Paris.
(30 Aug.) Russians enter Bucharest.
(4 Sept.) Ceasefire between Soviet Union and Finland. Armistice signed on 19th.

(5 Sept.) Brussels liberated by Allied troops.

(8 Sept.) V-2 rockets begin landing in Britain.

(17 Sept.) Arnhem airborne landings in Allied attempt to seize vital river crossings for advance into northern Germany.

(3 Oct.) Final suppression of Warsaw rising by German forces.

(14 Oct.) British troops liberate Athens.

(20 Oct.) Belgrade liberated by Russians and Yugoslav partisans.

(23 Oct.) De Gaulle's administration recognized by the Allies as provisional government of France.

(3 Dec.) Rioting in Athens and British police action sparks off communist insurrection.

(16 Dec.) Germans begin Ardennes offensive, the 'Battle of the Bulge'.

(31 Dec.) Regency installed in Greece by British.

1945

(3 Jan.) Allied counter-attack begins in Ardennes.

(11 Jan.) Truce declared in Greek Civil War.

(7 Jan.) Russians take Warsaw.

(4–11 Feb.) Yalta Conference. Churchill, Roosevelt and Stalin plan for Germany's unconditional surrender, the settlement of Poland, and the United Nations Conference at San Francisco.

(12 Feb.) Amnesty granted to Greek communists.

(13 Feb.) Fall of Budapest to Russians.

(23 Mar.) American armies cross Rhine at Remagen.

(28 Mar.) End of V-Rocket offensive against Britain.

(3 Apr.) Beneš appoints a National Front government in Czechoslovakia.

(20 Apr.) Russians reach Berlin.

(25 Apr.) Renner becomes Chancellor of provisional Austrian government.

(26 Apr.) Russian and American forces link up at Torgau.

(28 Apr.) Mussolini killed by partisans.

(30 Apr.) Hitler commits suicide in Berlin. Dönitz is appointed successor.

(1 May) German army in Italy surrenders.

(2 May) Berlin surrenders to Russians.

(7 May) General Jodl makes unconditional surrender of all German forces to Eisenhower.

(8 May) Victory in Europe, 'VE' day. Von Keitel surrenders to Zhukov near Berlin.

(9 May) Russians take Prague.

(14 May) Democratic Republic of Austria established.

(5 June) Allied Control Commission assumes control in Germany, which is divided into four occupation zones.

(6–9 Aug.) Atomic bombs dropped on Hiroshima and Nagasaki.

(14 Aug.) Surrender of Japan ('VJ' day).

Manpower and casualties of major European Powers, 1939–45

	Total mobilized	Killed or died of wounds	Civilians killed[1]
Belgium	625,000	8,000	101,000
Britain	5,896,000	265,000[2]	91,000[3]
Bulgaria	450,000	10,000	NA
Czechoslovakia	150,000	10,000	490,000
Denmark	25,000	4,000	NA
Finland	500,000	79,000	NA
France	5,000,000	202,000	108,000

(Continued)

(Continued)

	Total mobilized	Killed or died of wounds	Civilians killed[1]
Germany	10,200,000	3,250,000	500,000
Greece	414,000	73,000	400,000
Hungary	350,000	147,000	NA
Italy	3,100,000	149,000	783,000
Netherlands	410,000	7,000	242,000
Norway	75,000	2,000	2,000
Poland	1,000,000	64,000	2,000,000
Romania	1,136,000	520,000	NA
Soviet Union[4]	22,000,000	7,500,000	6–8,000,000
Yugoslavia	3,741,000	410,000	1,275,000

[1]Includes deaths of Jews in the Holocaust.
[2]Includes overseas troops serving in British forces.
[3]Includes 30,000 merchant seamen.
[4]Approximate figures.
NA Not available.

THE HOLOCAUST: NAZI GERMANY AND THE JEWS

1933

(30 Jan.) Hitler becomes Chancellor.

(5 Mar.) Nazi supporters go on anti-Semitic rampage following the elections which confirm the Nazis as the largest party in the Reichstag.

(1 Apr.) National one-day boycott of all Jewish businesses and professions; only partially observed.

(Apr.–Dec.) Legislation dismisses Jews from Civil Service, though pressure from Hindenburg allows many exemptions. Law against the 'overcrowding of German schools and universities' limits the proportion of Jewish pupils and students to 1.5%. Jews excluded from journalism and 'Reich entailed farm law' requires proof of Aryan identity dating back to 1800 for ownership of land.

1934

(5 Mar.) Jewish actors banned from performing on stage and screen.

(July–Dec.) Jewish students systematically excluded from taking examinations in law, medicine, dentistry and pharmacy.

1935

(21 May) Army Law excludes Jews from military service.

(May–Aug.) Increase in propaganda for the boycott of Jewish businesses.

(16 July) Reich Interior Minister Frick instructs registrars not to solemnize any more 'mixed marriages'.

(25 July) Jews definitively excluded from all armed forces.

(15 Sept.) Nuremberg Laws, announced by Hitler at the Nuremberg party conference, defining 'Jew' and systematizing and regulating discrimination and persecution: 'Reich Citizenship Law' deprives all Jews of their civil rights; 'Law for the Protection of German Blood and German Honour' makes marriages and extra-marital sexual relationships between Jews and Germans (*Deutschblütige*) crimes punishable by imprisonment.

(14 Nov.) First Supplementary Decree to the 'Reich Citizenship Law'; Jews dismissed from the public service and from all other public offices.

(26 Nov.) 'Gypsies' and 'Negroes' included in prohibition of racially mixed marriages.

1936

(24 Mar.) Benefit payments are withdrawn from large Jewish families.

(26 Mar.) Jews no longer permitted to run or lease a pharmacy.

(3 Apr.) Jews forbidden to practise as vets.

(26 May) Reich Chamber of Fine Arts demands proof of 'Aryan' ancestry from its members.

(28 May) 'Whitsuntide Memorandum' of the Confessing Church condemns Nazi racial policy.

(July) First Sinti and Roma (gypsies) sent to Dachau.

(15 Oct.) Jewish teachers forbidden to give private tuition to 'Aryans'.

(4 Nov.) Jews are forbidden to use the 'German greeting' (*Heil Hitler*).

1937

(13 Feb.) Jews forbidden to practise as notaries.

(15 Apr.) Jews no longer to be awarded doctoral degrees.

(12 June) Heydrich orders that after serving their prison sentences Jews guilty of 'racial disgrace' (miscegenation) are to be sent to a concentration camp, as are female Jewish partners involved in such relationships.

1938

(Mar.) Anti-Jewish persecution in Austria following the *Anschluss*, including compulsory 'Aryanization' of many Jewish firms and expulsion of Jews into neighbouring states.

(26 Apr.) All Jewish assets over 5,000 RM to be registered. 'Commissioner for the Four Year Plan' (Goering) is empowered to use such assets 'in the interests of the German economy'.

(9 June) Destruction of the synagogues in Munich.

(15 June) Some 1,500 Jews arrested and taken to concentration camps: so-called June Operation against 'asocials'.

(6 July) Conference on problem of Jewish refugees from Germany and Austria (Evian, France) fails to resolve problem.

(23 July) Jews issued with separate identity cards.

(25 July) Jewish doctors forbidden to practise. They are restricted to treating only other Jews.

(10 Aug.) Destruction of Nuremberg synagogues.

(17 Aug.) Jews must take the additional names of Sara and Israel.

(27 Sept.) Jewish lawyers restricted to working for Jewish clients, and must refer to themselves as 'consultants'.

(5 Oct.) Jewish passports to be stamped with 'J'.

(26–28 Oct.) 17,000 Jews with Polish citizenship are expelled from the German Reich, and transported to the Polish border.

(7 Nov.) Herschel Grynszpan assassinates legation secretary Ernst vom Rath in the German embassy in Paris.

(9 Nov.) *Reichskristallnacht*, the 'night of broken glass': a nationwide pogrom. 91 murders; 191 synagogues destroyed. Almost all Jewish cemeteries desecrated. Material damage amounting to many thousands of marks, including cost of ransacking of 7,500 Jewish businesses.

(10 Nov.) Mass arrests of Jewish men.

(12 Nov.) A compensation fee of a thousand million RM is imposed on German Jews. Jews are forbidden to participate in cultural events.

(15 Nov.) Jewish children expelled from German schools.

(3 Dec.) Start of compulsory 'Aryanization' of Jewish businesses.

(Dec.) All 'gypsies' to register with the police.

1939

(24 Jan.) Goering instructs Frick to establish a Reich Central Office for Jewish Emigration; Heydrich appointed Director.

(30 Jan.) In the Reichstag Hitler threatens that another war will mean the 'extermination of the Jewish race in Europe'.

(21 Feb.) Jews required to surrender precious metals and jewellery.

(30 Apr.) Jews evicted from their homes and forced into designated Jewish accommodation.

(21 July) Adolf Eichmann appointed head of Jewish emigration office in Prague.

(1 Sept.) Official date for beginning of Euthanasia Programme (authorized retroactively).

(20 Sept.) Jews required to surrender radios.

(21 Sept.) Decree from Heydrich initiates ghettoization of Polish Jews; it contains references to a 'final objective' which will require 'a much greater time scale' and must be kept 'strictly secret'. Decision taken to move 30,000 'gypsies' to Poland.

(Sept.–Nov.) *Einsatzgruppen der Sicherheitspolizei* ('Special units of the Security Police') and other Nazi formations murder large numbers of Jews. Some incidents amount to large-scale massacres. 4,000 Polish mental patients killed.

(Oct.) Hitler authorizes reintroduction of adult euthanasia of mental patients in Germany.

(12 Oct.) Jews deported from Austria and Bohemia–Moravia to Poland.

(24 Oct.) German occupation authorities in Wloclawec introduce a Jewish identification badge – first such measure in twentieth century.

(23 Nov.) General introduction of the 'Yellow Star' for Jews living in the 'Government-General'.

(25 Nov.) Sexual relations between foreign workers and Germans forbidden.

(Dec.) 87,000 Poles and Jews deported from the new *Reichsgau* Wartheland to the 'Government-General'.

1940

(Jan.) First gassing of mentally handicapped ('Euthanasia Programme', or 'Operation T4').

(23 Jan.) Jews are not issued with ration cards for clothing.

(2–13 Feb.) First deportations of Jews from Vienna, Mährisch-Ostrau and Teschen to Poland; first deportations from Germany (Stettin, Stralsund, Schneidemühl).

(Mar.–Apr.) Ghettoes 'closed' in Cracow, Lublin and Lodź

(27 Apr.) *Reichsführer* SS Heinrich Himmler orders establishment of a concentration camp at Auschwitz.

(30 Apr.) First enclosed Jewish ghetto (Lodź).

(Apr.–May) 2,500 Sinti and Roma deported from Reich to Poland.

(June–Aug.) Plans formulated for the mass deportation of European Jews to Madagascar.

(29 June) Jewish telephones are disconnected.

(Oct.) Jewish ghetto in Warsaw 'closed'.

(22 Oct.) 7,500 Jews deported from Saarland, Baden and Alsace-Lorraine to unoccupied France and interned.

1941

(1 Mar.) Himmler orders building of extensions to concentration camp at Auschwitz, which is to be ready to receive about 100,000 Soviet prisoners of war.

(From Mar.) Jews deployed as forced labour.

(Spring) Four *Einsatzgruppen* ('special units') of Security Police and the SD created for attack on Soviet Union.

(14 May) 3,600 Parisian Jews arrested by French police.

(31 July) Goering gives Heydrich the task of the 'comprehensive solution (*Gesamtlösung*) of the Jewish question'.

(Summer) Himmler instructs commandant of Auschwitz to prepare the camp to play a central part in the 'final solution' ordered by Hitler; Heydrich orders Eichmann to prepare deportation of European Jews for the 'final solution to the Jewish question in Europe'.

Special commission from Himmler for the SS and police leader in Lublin, Globocnik, to murder the Polish Jews ('Operation Reinhard'); the 'Fuhrer chancellery' provides staff from the 'Euthanasia Operation', which has been wound up, though killing continues.

(1 Sept.) All Jews in the Reich from the age of six must now wear the 'Yellow Star'.

(3 Sept.) First trial gassing with Zyklon B at Auschwitz; around 900 Soviet prisoners of war are victims of further experiments in September and October.

(18 Sept.) Jews required to seek permission to use public transport.

(Sept.–Nov.) Planning, siting and beginning of construction of death camps at Chelmno, Belzec, Majdanek and Auschwitz-Birkenau in the winter of 1941–42.

(14 Oct.) Start of the mass deportation of Jews from the Reich to ghettoes in Kovno, Lodź, Minsk and Riga.

(23 Oct.) All Jewish emigration from German-controlled territory is forbidden.

(30 Nov.) Around 10,000 deported German and indigenous Jews shot near Riga.

(12 Dec.) Jews are prohibited from using public telephones.

(Dec.) Use of gas vans for murder of Jews in Chelmno.

1942

(20 Jan.) Wannsee Conference in Berlin under Heydrich, for all government departments participating in 'final solution' and administration of Government-General.

(Feb.) 'Evacuation' of the Polish ghettoes begins; continuous deportations to the death camps.

(15 Feb.) Jews are prohibited from keeping pets.

(Spring) Camps built at Sobibor and Treblinka for 'Operation Reinhard'.

(13 Mar.) Jews are compelled to identify their homes.

(24 Mar.) First deportations of south German Jews to Belzec.

(26–27 Mar.) First transports of Jewish emigrants from western Europe arrive at Auschwitz.

(May–June) Introduction of 'Yellow Star' in occupied western Europe.

(12 May) Jews are prohibited from patronising 'Aryan' hairdressers.

(11 June) Jews excluded from egg rations.

(12 June) Jews must surrender all electrical goods, optical equipment, bicycles and typewriters.

(22 June) Jews excluded from tobacco rations.

(23 June) Systematic gassing of Jews begins in Auschwitz.

(1 July) End of teaching for all Jewish pupils.

(15–16 July) First transports of Dutch Jews to Auschwitz.

(16–18 July) French police arrest 13,000 'stateless' Jews in Paris, 9,000 (including 4,000 children) deported to Auschwitz.

(19 July) Himmler insists Poland must be 'free of Jews' by end of 1942.

(22 July) Mass transports from Warsaw ghetto to Treblinka, where 67,000 Jews are gassed immediately after arrival.

(July–Sept.) Mass deportations from western Europe to Auschwitz.

(Aug.) More than 200,000 Jews gassed at Chelmno, Treblinka and Belzec during last two weeks of the month.

(26–28 Aug.) Jews arrested in Vichy France.

(9 Oct.) Jews banned from 'Aryan' bookshops.

(Nov.) Himmler orders all concentration camps in the Reich to become 'free of Jews'.

(19 Nov.) Jews excluded from meat and milk rations.

(25–26 Nov.) Beginning of deportations from Norway.

1943

(Feb.) Arrest of 'gypsies' remaining in Germany.

(27 Feb.) Jewish munitions workers deported from Berlin to Auschwitz.

(Mar.) Himmler orders deportation of Dutch gypsies.

(Apr.) Beginning of medical experiments in Auschwitz.

(7 Apr.) End of mass murder in Chelmno; gas chambers destroyed by SS.

(19 Apr.) Beginning of Jewish uprising in the Warsaw ghetto.

(30 Apr.) Jews lose German citizenship.

(16 May) *SS-Obergruppenführer* Stroop announces destruction of Jewish ghetto in Warsaw.

(11 June) Himmler orders liquidation of all Polish ghettoes.

(19 June) Goebbels declares Berlin 'free of Jews'.

(21 June) Order to liquidate remaining ghettoes on Soviet territory.

(1 July) German Jews lose protection of law.

(Aug.–Dec.) Liquidation of Russian ghettoes; inhabitants taken to death camps.

(2 Aug.) Prisoners' uprising in Treblinka; destruction of gas chambers.

(16–23 Aug.) Deportation of about 8,000 Jews from Bialystok and destruction of the ghetto following resistance.

(Sept.–Oct.) Around 7,000 Danish Jews smuggled to Sweden.

(Oct.–Nov.) Around 8,360 Jews deported from northern Italy to Auschwitz.

(14 Oct.) Prisoners' uprising in Sobibor; end of gassing.

(19 Oct.) End of 'Operation Reinhard'.

1944

(Mar.–Apr.) More than 6,000 Greek Jews deported to Auschwitz. 1,500 escape to Turkey.

(Apr.–July) Hungarian Jews ghettoized; 437,000 deported to Auschwitz by July; 280,000 gassed.

(May–Aug.) Resumption of mass gassing at Chelmno in connection with the final liquidation of the Łodz ghetto.

(24 July) Soviet troops occupy Majdanek.

(7 Oct.) Revolt of Jewish 'special unit' in Auschwitz.

(27 Nov.) Himmler orders cessation of gassing at Auschwitz.

1945

(27 Jan.) Soviet troops reach Auschwitz.

(21–28 Apr.) Last gassing of mainly sick concentration camp inmates at Ravensbrück and Mauthausen.

(29 Apr.) American troops occupy Dachau.

(7–9 May) Unconditional surrender of armed forces of Nazi Germany.

Estimated number of Jews killed under Nazi rule

	Original Jewish population	Number killed	%
Baltic States (Estonia, Latvia, and Lithuania)	253,000	228,000	10
Belgium	65,000	40,000	40
Bulgaria	65,000	14,000	78
Czech Protectorate (Bohemia and Moravia)	90,000	80,000	11
France	350,000	90,000	74
Germany/Austria	240,000	210,000	10
Greece	70,000	54,000	23
Hungary	650,000	450,000	30
Italy	40,000	8,000	80
Luxembourg	5,000	1,000	80
Netherlands	140,000	105,000	25
Norway	1,800	900	50
Poland	3,300,000	3,000,000	10
Romania	600,000	300,000	50
Slovakia	90,000	75,000	17
Soviet Union (areas under German control)	2,850,000	1,252,000	56
Yugoslavia	43,000	26,000	40
Total	8,851,800	5,933,900	33

(*Source*: Lucy S. Dawidowicz, *The War Against the Jews, 1933–1945*).

Source: derived from T. Kirk, *The Longman Companion to Nazi Germany*, London, 1995, pp. 159–166.

THE COLD WAR AND EASTERN EUROPE, 1942–85

1942

(26 May) Twenty-year Anglo–Soviet Treaty signed but without any territorial agreement for postwar Europe.

(June–Aug.) Stalin steps up demands for opening of 'second front' to relieve pressure on Russia.

(July) British suspension of convoys to Russia because of losses causes Stalin to accuse Allies of lack of genuine support.

1943

(14–24 Jan.) Churchill and Roosevelt agree to insist on the 'unconditional surrender' of Germany. The decision to mount an invasion of Italy, agreed by the Allied commanders, leads to bitter recriminations from Stalin who sees it as bad faith on the part of the Western Powers.

(Aug.) Stalin objects to not being consulted about the surrender of Italy and demands a say in the Italian settlement.

(Oct.) Three-power foreign ministers' conference in Moscow agrees upon an advisory council for Italy and makes broad plans for a world security organization.

(28 Nov.–1 Dec.) Meeting of Big Three (Churchill, Roosevelt and Stalin) at Tehran, the first conference attended by Stalin. As well as discussing arrangements for the Allied landings in Europe and a renewed Soviet offensive against Germany, the main lines of a territorial settlement in Eastern Europe are agreed, including the Polish frontiers. No agreement is reached about the future of Germany, although there is discussion of the dismemberment of Germany.

1944

(21 Aug.–9 Oct.) Dumbarton Oaks Conference draws up broad framework of the United Nations.

(11–17 Sept.) Churchill and Roosevelt meet at Quebec and move towards acceptance of Morgenthau Plan for the destruction of German industry and the conversion of Germany into a pastoralized state.

(9–10 Oct.) Churchill and Stalin meet in Moscow and decide on 'spheres of influence'. Romania and Bulgaria are ceded predominantly to Russian influence, Greece to Britain, and Yugoslavia and Hungary equally between Russia and Great Britain.

(3 Dec.) Attempted communist insurrection in Athens.

1945

(11 Jan.) Communists in Greece seek truce.

(4–11 Feb.) Meeting at Yalta between Churchill, Roosevelt and Stalin decides upon four occupation zones in Germany, the prosecution of war criminals, and prepares Allied Control Council to run Germany on the basis of 'complete disarmament, demilitarization and dismemberment'. Removals of national wealth from Germany are to be permitted within two years of the end of the war and reparations are tentatively agreed. Agreement reached that the provisional government already functioning in Poland, i.e. the communist Lublin-based group, with the addition of other groups including the London Poles, act as the government. A three-power commission based in Moscow would supervise the setting up of the new regime. The provisional government was pledged to hold free and unfettered elections as soon as possible. Declaration on Liberated Europe signed by the major powers to allow European states to 'create democratic conditions of their own choice'.

(12 Feb.) Greek communists granted amnesty and lay down arms.

(Apr.) Members of non-communist delegation to the three-power commission in Moscow arrested. Russians conclude a treaty of alliance with the Lublin administration of Poland.

(5 July) Great Britain and United States recognize provisional government of National Unity in Poland.

(17 July–1 Aug.) Stalin, Truman, Churchill (after 25 July Attlee) meet at Potsdam and finalize four-power agreement on administration of Germany and the territorial adjustments in Eastern Europe. The Oder–Neisse Line is to mark the new boundary between Germany and Poland. Although Germany is to be divided into zones, it is to be treated as a single economic unit. Germans living in Poland, Hungary and Czechoslovakia are to be sent to Germany.

(28 Oct.) Provisional Czech National Assembly meets, representing communist and non-communist parties.

(Nov.) Tito elected President of Yugoslavia.

1946

(6 Mar.) Churchill makes 'Iron Curtain' speech at Fulton, Missouri: 'From Stettin in the Baltic to Trieste in the Adriatic, an Iron Curtain has descended upon the Continent.'

(26 May) At Czech elections communists win 38 per cent of the vote and set up a single party 'National Front' government.

(May) Fighting breaks out in northern Greece, marking renewal of civil war between monarchist forces assisted by Britain and communist guerrillas, backed by Albania, Bulgaria and Yugoslavia.

1947

(21 Feb.) The British inform the Americans that they cannot afford to keep troops in Greece because of their domestic economic difficulties and intend to withdraw them by the end of March.

(27 Feb.) Dean Acheson privately expounds the 'Truman Doctrine' of economic and military aid to nations in danger of communist takeover.

(12 Mar.) In message to Congress President Truman outlines the Truman Doctrine 'to support free peoples who are resisting attempted subjugation by armed minorities or by outside pressures', effectively committing the United States to intervene against communist or communist-backed movements in Europe and elsewhere.

(22 Apr.) Truman Doctrine passed by Congress.

(24 Apr.) Council of Foreign Ministers in Moscow ends without formal peace treaties for Germany and Austria.

(22 May) Congress passes bill for $250 million of aid for Greece and Turkey.

(5 June) George Marshall, American Secretary of State, calls for a European recovery programme supported by American aid.

(12–15 June) Non-communist nations of Europe set up Committee of European Economic Co-operation to draft European Recovery Programme.

(Aug.) First American aid arrives in Greece, followed by military 'advisers' to assist in the civil war against the communists.

1948

(25 Feb.) Czech President Beneš accepts a communist-dominated government.

(10 Mar.) Czech Foreign Minister, Jan Masaryk, found dead in suspicious circumstances.

(14–31 Mar.) Congress passes the Foreign Assistance Act, the Marshall Plan. $5,300 million of 'Marshall Aid' is initially allocated for European recovery.

(17 Mar.) Belgium, France, Luxembourg, The Netherlands and Great Britain sign a treaty

setting up the Brussels Treaty Organization for mutual military assistance.

(20 Mar.) Russian representative walks out of Allied Control Council.

(30 Mar.) Russians impose restrictions on traffic between Western zones and Berlin.

(Apr.) Paris Treaty sets up Organization for European Economic Co-operation to receive Marshall Aid.

(30 May) At Czech elections no opposition parties are allowed to stand and electors called on to vote for a single list of National Front candidates.

(June) Yugoslavia expelled from Comintern, effectively putting it outside direct Soviet control.

(7 June) Beneš resigns as President of Czechoslovakia; succeeded by Gottwald.

(24 June) Russians impose a complete blockade of traffic into Berlin. Berlin airlift begins (25th).

(5 Sept.) Head of Polish Communist Party, Gomulka, forced to resign.

(30 Nov.) Russians set up separate municipal government for East Berlin.

1949

(Jan.) Comecon, communist economic co-operation organization, set up.

(4 Apr.) Creation of NATO. North Atlantic Treaty signed by members of Brussels Treaty Organization, with Canada, Denmark, Iceland, Italy, Norway, Portugal and the United States, It pledges mutual military assistance.

(May) Federal Republic of Germany (West Germany) comes into existence.

(4 May) Representatives of four occupation powers in Germany come to an agreement for ending of Berlin blockade.

(12 May) Berlin blockade lifted.

(15 May) Communists take power in Hungary on the basis of a single-list election for the 'People's Front', replacing the communist-dominated coalition which had been elected in 1947.

(June) Purge of Albanian Communist Party.

(30 Sept.) End of Berlin airlift.

(Oct.) German Democratic Republic (East Germany) comes into existence.

(16 Oct.) Greek communists cease fighting.

(Nov.) Russian Marshal takes command of Polish army.

(Dec. 1949–Jan. 1950) Purge of Bulgarian Communist Party; 92,000 expelled.

1950

(May–June) Last non-Communists expelled from Hungarian government.

(28 May) Pro-Stalinist Hoxha confirmed in power in single-list elections in Albania.

(July) Romanian Communist Party admits to expulsion of almost 200,000 members in past two years.

(Sept.) United States proposes German rearmament.

1951

(Sept.) First Soviet atomic bomb exploded.

1952

(18 Feb.) Greece and Turkey join NATO.

(27 May) Belgium, France, Italy, Luxembourg, The Netherlands, and West Germany sign mutual defence treaty for proposed creation of a European Defence Community.

1953

(5 Mar.) Death of Stalin. Khrushchev confirmed as First Secretary of the Communist Party (September).

(June) Risings in East Germany suppressed.

1954

(5 May) Italy and West Germany enter Brussels Treaty Organisation.

1954–56

Khrushchev launches 'virgin land' campaign to increase grain output in marginal land.

1955

(May) Warsaw Pact formed.
(9 May) West Germany admitted to NATO.

1956

(Feb.) At Russian Twentieth Party Congress Khrushchev attacks abuses of Stalin era.
(June) Workers' riots in Poznan, Poland, suppressed; Gomulka becomes First Secretary of Polish United Workers' Party (Oct.).
(Oct.–Nov.) General strike and street demonstrations in Budapest. Russians intervene and depose Nagy and crush the rising. Kadar becomes the First Secretary of the Hungarian Communist Party and premier. Thousands of Hungarian refugees flee to the West.

1958

(Feb.) Khrushchev replaces Bulganin as Prime Minister.

1961

(Apr.) First manned Soviet space flight. Arrests of dissident writers.
(July) Anti-clerical legislation in Russia, restricting role of the clergy in parish councils.
(Aug.) Berlin Wall constructed to prevent flight from East to West Berlin.
(Oct.) Twenty-Second Party Congress; new Party programme and further 'de-Stalinization', including the removal of Stalin's body from Red Square mausoleum.

1962

(Oct.) Cuban missile crisis after Soviet Union attempts to set up ballistic missile bases in Cuba. Imposition of naval 'quarantine' by the United States forces the Soviet Union to back down in the face of the threat of nuclear war.
(Nov.) Publication of Solzhenitsyn's *A Day in the Life of Ivan Denisovitch* marks first public recognition of the conditions in Soviet labour camps.

1963

(Mar.) Khrushchev warns Writers' Union of 'bourgeois influences'.
(5 Aug.) Partial Test Ban Treaty signed in Moscow, banning nuclear weapon tests in the atmosphere, outer space, and under water (in force from Oct.).

1964

(Oct.) Brezhnev replaces Khrushchev as First Secretary.

1965

(Mar.) Central Committee of the Soviet Union makes a number of agricultural reforms.
(Sept.) Central Committee approves further set of economic reforms.

1966

(Feb.) Trial of leading 'dissidents', Sinyavsky and Daniel, who are given periods of imprisonment.

1967

(June) Arab–Israeli 'Six-Day' War leads to acute tension between United States and Soviet Union.

1968

(Jan.) Dissidents Ginsburg and Galanskov tried and imprisoned. Dubček becomes First Secretary of Czechoslovak Communist Party and process of liberalization begins – 'Socialism with a human face' – including decentralization of economic planning and more open contacts with the West.
(1 July) Non-proliferation treaty signed in London, Moscow and Washington.
(Aug.) The Soviet Union and other Warsaw Pact forces invade Czechoslovakia and end the 'Prague Spring'. The Czech leaders are forced to agree in Moscow to the reimposition of censorship, return to centralized

planning, and abandon closer links with the West. Husák takes over Party Secretaryship from Dubček.

1969

(Mar.) Dubček demoted and sent as ambassador to Turkey; he is eventually expelled from the Party and given menial work.

(Oct.) Czechoslovakia repudiates its condemnation of the Warsaw Pact invasion and consents to the stationing of Russian troops.

1970

(Dec.) Widespread rioting in Poland over food prices and economic conditions; Gierek replaces Gomulka as First Secretary of Polish United Workers' Party.

1971

(Feb.) Mass Jewish demonstration at Supreme Soviet building. Jewish emigration to Israel grows.

1972

(Jan.) Seizure of documents and leading intellectuals in the Ukraine.

(May) Disturbances in Lithuania.

(26 May) Visit of President Nixon to Moscow. Strategic Arms Limitation Treaty (SALT 1) signed between United States and Soviet Union on limitation of anti-ballistic missile systems (in force from Oct.) and interim agreement on limitation of strategic offensive arms.

1973

(Apr.) Andropov and Gromyko join Politburo.

1974

(Feb.) Solzhenitsyn deported from Soviet Union.

1975

(Aug.) Helsinki Agreement on European Security and Co-operation provides for 'Human Rights'.

(Oct.) Soviet physicist and dissident Andre Sakharov awarded Nobel peace prize.

1976

(June) Strikes and sabotage in Poland in opposition to attempted price rises which are temporarily withdrawn, although unrest is severely put down.

1977

(Jan.) Dissident civil rights group 'Charter 77' formed in Prague.

(June) Brezhnev replaces Podgorny as President of the Soviet Union.

1978

(July) Trial of Soviet Jewish dissident and civil rights activist Shcharansky.

1979

(June) Visit of Pope John Paul II to Poland helps to arouse strong national feeling.

(Dec.) Soviet invasion of Afghanistan. The United States imposes a grain embargo on Russia. Large commemorative services held in Poland for those killed in the disturbances of 1970.

1980

(Jan.) Sakharov sentenced to internal exile in Gorky.

(Mar.–Apr.) Dissident groups in Poland advocate boycott of official parliamentary elections on 23 March and mass commemorative service for Polish officers killed at Katyn in April 1940 leads to arrests.

(July) Olympic Games in Moscow boycotted by the United States.

(July–Sept.) Widespread strikes among Polish workers at Gdansk (Danzig) and elsewhere as a result of rise in meat prices. In August, Gdansk workers publish demands calling for free trade unions. Soviet Union begins jamming of Western broadcasts. Resignation of Babinch as Prime Minister (24 Aug.) and of Gierek as First Secretary of the Polish United Workers Party (6 Sept.); replaced by Pinkowski and Kania. Gierek's departure followed by the signing of the 'Gdansk agreement' with Lech Walesa, the leader of the Gdansk 'inter-factory committee'. This recognizes the new Solidarity unions, grants a wage agreement and promises a 40-hour week, permits the broadcast of church services on Sunday, relaxes the censorship laws, promises to re-examine the new meat scales and review the cases of imprisoned dissidents. National Confederation of Independent Trade Unions, 'Solidarity', formed under leadership of Lech Walesa (8 Sept.), attracts an estimated 10 million members. 'Rural Solidarity' claims an estimated half million farmers.

(Dec.) Death of Russian Prime Minister Kosygin.

1981

(Jan.) Walesa visits Pope in Rome.

(Feb.) General Jaruzelski replaces Pinkowski as Prime Minister.

(Dec.) After visiting Moscow, General Jaruzelski declares martial law in Poland. The leading members of Solidarity are arrested and the organization banned.

1982

(Nov.) Death of Brezhnev. Andropov becomes First Secretary of the Communist Party of the Soviet Union.

1984

(Feb.) Death of Andropov. Chernenko becomes First Secretary of the Communist Party of the Soviet Union.

1985

(June) Death of Chernenko. Gorbachev becomes First Secretary of the Communist Party of the Soviet Union.

THE NEW EASTERN EUROPE

1985

(June) Death of Chernenko. Gorbachev becomes First Secretary of the Communist Party of the Soviet Union. Programme of *glasnost* and *perestroika* launched.

(July) Gorbachev replaces four members of Politburo with his own supporters; veteran Foreign Minister, Gromyko, moved to Presidency and replaced by Gorbachev supporter Shevardnadze.

1986

(Jan.) Gorbachev continues process of removing the personnel of the Brezhnev era from central and regional government.

(26 Apr.) Chernobyl nuclear disaster tests new *glasnost*: attempted coverup by Moscow.

(Sept.) Solidarity announces intention of working within the existing system.

1987

(June) Karoly Grosz, an economic liberal, becomes Prime Minister in Hungary.

(July) Protests by Crimean Tartars in Moscow permitted to take place.

(Aug.) Protests in the Baltic states demanding greater autonomy and an end to 'Russification'.

(Nov.) Polish government holds referendum for programme of radical reform; Solidarity calls for boycott and the proposals are rejected. Radical Boris Yeltsin dismissed as head of Moscow Party for outspoken criticisms of conservatives.

(Dec.) President Reagan and General Secretary Gorbachev sign Intermediate Nuclear Forces Treaty in Washington; a major breakthrough in East–West arms negotiations.

(17 Dec.) Gustav Husák resigns party leadership in Czechoslovakia; succeeded by another conservative, Milos Jakes.

1988

(Jan.) Gorbachev calls for acceleration of drive to democratization; calls special party Congress in the summer. Major reform of Soviet Constitution sets up a Supreme Soviet consisting of two chambers to meet in almost continuous session, the members selected by a Congress of People's Deputies representing national areas, social organizations and constituencies. Hungarian government announces end of price controls.

(Feb.) Serious ethnic riots in Nagorno-Karabakh region of Azerbaijan.

(Mar.–Aug.) Wave of strikes and unrest in Poland; Solidarity demands talks with government.

(May) Russian agreement to withdraw all troops from Afghanistan by February 1989. In Hungary, Kadar relegated to post of Party President; Grosz becomes Party Secretary and Prime Minister; purge of conservatives in Central Committee and Politburo.

(Dec.) Polish government accepts 'round table' talks with Solidarity. Gorbachev announces unilateral force reductions of 500,000 troops and 10,000 tanks.

1989

(Jan.) Law on Association in Hungary allows political parties to be formed; new draft constitution (Mar.) drops reference to leading role for Communist Party.

(6 Feb.) Solidarity and Polish government open talks on future of Poland.

(Mar.–Apr.) Solidarity accepts terms for participation in elections; government agrees to admit opposition to the lower house of parliament (*Sejm*), a freely elected Senate, and create office of President. Solidarity legalized.

(June) First free parliamentary elections in Poland since Second World War; Solidarity obtains landslide victory in seats it is allowed to contest. Hungarian government recognizes Imre Nagy, leader of 1956 rising, and permits his reburial with full honours.

(July) General Jaruzelski elected President of Poland by one-vote margin. General Kiszczak appointed Prime Minister but fails to form a government and resigns; Solidarity activist, Tadeuz Mazowiecki, becomes Prime Minister, heading first non-communist government.

(Sept.) Hungary opens border with Austria allowing flight of thousands of East Germans to the West.

(Oct.) Erich Honecker replaced as President by Egon Krenz in East Germany (18th) following flight of East Germans to the West and mass demonstrations in East German cities organized by New Forum opposition group. Krenz meets opposition group (26th); travel restrictions discussed.

(Nov.) East German Council of Ministers resigns *en masse* following huge demonstrations in East Berlin and other cities. New Forum opposition legalized and Politburo resigns (7th–8th). Berlin Wall opened and travel restrictions lifted on East German citizens (9th). Reformer, Hans Modrow, President (13th). President Todor Zhivkov of Bulgaria resigns (10th). Entire Czech Politburo resigns (24th) following mass demonstrations in Prague by Civic Forum opposition group.

(Dec.) Malta Summit between President Bush and President Gorbachev; declares the Cold War 'at an end' (4th). Resignation of Czech Prime Minister, Adamec, forced by further mass demonstrations and General Strike. Communist monopoly of power ended and joint interim government formed with members of Civic Forum (7th–9th).

Resignation of Egon Krenz as communist leader in East Germany (8th). Preparations for free elections begin. Hundreds reported killed in anti-Ceausescu demonstrations in Romanian city of Timisoara (17th). Bulgaria declares it will hold free elections (19th). Brandenburg Gate opened between East and West Berlin as symbolic act of reconciliation between the two Germanies (22nd). Mass demonstrations in Bucharest and other Romanian cities. After initial attempts to disperse them, the army joins the crowds and Ceausescu and his wife flee (22nd). Heavy fighting between pro-Ceausescu forces and the army leaves several hundred killed and wounded in Bucharest and other Romanian cities; Ceausescu and his wife arrested and executed by Military Tribunal (25th). Free elections announced for April 1990; Ion Iliescu becomes President (26th). Václav Havel, former dissident and political prisoner, unanimously elected President of Czechoslovakia (29th); Alexander Dubček earlier elected Chairman (Speaker) of Czech Parliament (28th).

1990

(Feb.) Unanimous vote of the Central Committee of the Communist Party of the Soviet Union to end the leading role of the Communist Party. Lithuanian Communist Party secedes from the CPSU to fight elections in March.

(Mar.) Soviet Congress of People's Deputies votes to abolish Articles 6 and 7 of the Soviet Constitution and end the leading role of the Communist Party. Congress approves the election of Gorbachev to the new post of Executive President with sweeping powers; subsequent elections to be by popular vote. Nationalist movements win victories in multi-party elections in Baltic Republics. Sweeping victory for Lithuanian *Sajudis* movement is followed by declaration of independence and election of non-communist Vytautas Landsbergis as the Republic's first President. Soviet government begins economic blockade of Lithuania. East German elections lead to victory (18th) of pro-unification Alliance for Germany, consisting of the Christian Democratic Union and allies, with over 48 per cent of the vote; coalition government under CDU leader Lothar de Mazière prepares for economic unification in July and all-German elections in December. Hungarian elections result in victory for Democratic Forum with 43 per cent of the vote; coalition government formed with Christian Democrat and Smallholder parties, seeking access to the EEC and rapid adoption of Western economic models.

(Apr.) First multi-party elections in Yugoslavian Republics lead to victories for anti-communist parties in Slovenia and Croatia, increasing pressure of independence movements and the effective dissolution of the Yugoslav Communist Party.

(May) Romanian elections lead to overwhelming victory of National Salvation Front under former communist minister, Ion Iliescu. The Bulgarian Socialist Party, formerly the Communist Party, obtains a clear majority in the first free elections since the overthrow of the communist regime.

(June) Protests in Bucharest at domination of former communists in government lead to serious rioting; police attack demonstrators and National Salvation Front calls on miners to restore order. Czech elections lead to victory for Civic Forum/Public Against Violence with 169 of 300 seats, with backing of President Václav Havel.

(July) East and West German economic unification on the basis of the West German currency. President Gorbachev obtains mandate from Communist Party Congress for further reform, but breakaway group declares it will form a separate party. German–Soviet agreement between Chancellor Kohl and President Gorbachev (16th) that a united Germany will have full sovereignty, including the right to join NATO; Soviet Union agrees to withdraw its 350,000 troops from East Germany within three to four years. Paris meeting (17th) of 'Two plus Four' talks,

consisting of representatives from East and West Germany and the four former Allied powers, the United States, the United Kingdom, the Soviet Union and France, with participants from the Polish government, agrees to guarantee the existing Polish–German border along the Oder–Neisse River with a definitive treaty to be signed following German unification. Agreement to negotiate a second treaty on Polish–German relations, including reparations and protection for the rights of German minorities living in Poland. Ukraine declares its intention to become a sovereign state with its own army and foreign policy.

(Aug.) Lech Walesa declares he will be a candidate for President in forthcoming elections. Growing evidence of splits within Solidarity ranks. Boris Yeltsin asserts the sovereignty of the Russian Republic and offers economic assistance to Lithuania.

(Sept.) Treaty signed (12th) following 'Two plus Four' talks, agreeing to ending of special powers by the wartime Allies over Germany and for the unification with full sovereignty of East and West Germany.

(3 Oct.) Reunification of Germany.

(Dec.) Gorbachev granted sweeping new powers. Widespread anti-communist riots in Albania after first legal opposition party formed.

(2 Dec.) First all-German elections elect conservative Kohl's CDU/CSU government; ex-communist PDS reduced to 17 seats.

(9 Dec.) Lech Walesa elected President of Poland.

(20 Dec.) Soviet Foreign Minister Shevardnadze resigns because of 'reactionary elements'.

1991

(13 Jan.) Soviet special forces kill 14 Lithuanian demonstrators in Vilnius.

(20 Jan.) Special force assault on key buildings in Latvian capital, Riga, kills five.

(Mar.) Huge majorities in Latvia and Estonia for independence. Anti-Gorbachev rally in

Moscow; pro-Union majority for his referendum on maintaining the Union, but many abstentions. Albania opens diplomatic relations with West.

(Apr.) Soviet Georgia declares independence. Miners' strikes in the Soviet coalfields.

(May) First serious casualties in fighting between Serbs and Croats in Yugoslavia.

(25 June) Croatia declares independence from Yugoslavia. Widespread fighting begins as Yugoslav army seizes Slovenian border posts. Fighting between Croatian militias and Serbian irregulars and Federal army.

(Aug.) Gorbachev prepares new all-Union treaty to preserve the Soviet Union. Attempted hard-line coup in Moscow while Gorbachev on holiday in Crimea. Russian premier Boris Yeltsin defies coup and prepares to defend Russian parliament building with aid of loyal troops and populace. Coup collapses in face of popular resistance and declarations of independence by Republics. The leading plotters are arrested. Gorbachev returns to Moscow. Under pressure from Yeltsin, adopts sweeping reforms. Baltic states become independent states of Latvia, Estonia and Lithuania; Communist Party of Soviet Union dissolved, ending 74-year rule; Gorbachev resigns as General Secretary, retaining office of executive President of rapidly dissolving Soviet Union. Negotiates an association with ten Republics for a looser union with a common foreign and defence policy.

(Sept.) Armenia becomes 12th Soviet Republic to declare independence.

(Oct.) First completely free election in Poland produces inconclusive result, proliferation of parties and turnout below 50 per cent.

(4 Nov.) Formation of independent National Guard in the Ukraine.

(18 Nov.) European Community imposes sanctions on Yugoslavia.

(1 Dec.) Ukraine votes overwhelmingly for independence.

(8 Dec.) Leaders of Belorussia, Russian Federation and Ukraine declare that the Soviet Union is dead; in the Declaration of Minsk they proclaim new 'Commonwealth of Independent States' (CIS) with headquarters at Minsk in Belorussia.

(10 Dec.) Ukrainian Parliament ratifies new Commonwealth.

(12 Dec.) Russian Parliament votes 188 to six to approve new Commonwealth. Gorbachev declares 'My life's work is done'.

(13 Dec.) Five Central Asian Republics, meeting in Ashkhabad, vote to join new Commonwealth as founding members: Gorbachev accepts existence and legitimacy of Commonwealth but does not yet resign.

(22 Dec.) Leaders of 11 former Soviet Republics sign Treaty of Alma Ata, establishing new Commonwealth of Independent States. The 11 Republics comprise: Armenia, Azerbaijan, Belarus (formerly Belorussia), Kazakhstan, Kyrgyzstan (formerly Kirghizia), Moldova (formerly Moldavia), the Russian Federation, Tajikistan, Turkmenistan (formerly Turkmenia), Uzbekistan and Ukraine. Only Georgia (where bitter fighting erupts in Tbilisi) does not join new CIS.

(25 Dec.) Formal resignation of Mikhail Gorbachev as President of the now defunct Soviet Union; the Russian flag replaces the Hammer and Sickle above the Kremlin; key EC states (and America) recognize independence of Russian Federation.

(30 Dec.) Minsk Summit of Commonwealth of Independent States agrees future of strategic nuclear forces; no agreement on conventional forces (Ukraine, Azerbaijan and Moldova insist on separate armies) or economic policy.

1992

(Jan.) EU recognizes Croatia and Slovenia.

(21 Feb.) UN Security Council agrees to send a 14,000 strong force to Bosnia. Bosnia–Herzegovina declares independence; Bosnian Serbs proclaim separate state.

(3 Apr.) The leader of Albanian Democratic Party, Sali Berisha, elected President by People's Assembly.

(6 Apr.) Bosnia recognized as independent by EU and US; Serbs begin campaign of 'ethnic cleansing' in north and east Bosnia,

expelling Muslim population to create a pure Serb corridor linking Serb areas of western Bosnia with Serbia. Serbian forces begin artillery bombardment of Sarajevo.

(May) 'Cleansing' of Muslims and Croats from Brcko begins and systematic killing at Banja Luka and elsewhere, resulting in some 3,000 dead. UN trade embargo placed on Serbia.

(June) Yegor Gaidar becomes premier of Russia. Vote of no confidence in Polish government of Prime Minister Jan Olszewski. Czechoslovakian general elections held, dominated by issue of dissolution of the state. Klaus becomes Czech premier, Meciar becomes premier of Slovakia; talks on split proceed in earnest.

(July) Airlift of relief supplies into Sarajevo begins. Slovak National Council approves declaration of sovereignty; resignation of Václav Havel as Federal President.

(Aug.) Existence of Serb-run concentration camps disclosed. President Franco Tudjman and Croatian Democratic Union win victory in first Croatian elections. London Conference sets up Geneva peace talks for former Yugoslavia. Agreement reached on split of Czechoslovakia into two independent states on 1 January 1993.

(Sept.) Lithuania signs agreement with Russia for withdrawal of former Soviet troops.

(15 Sept.) Federal Republic of Yugoslavia excluded from UN General Assembly.

(Oct.) In Georgia, Chairman of State Council, Eduard Shevardnadze, elected parliamentary Speaker and de facto head of state. President Iliescu wins further four-year term in Romania.

(Nov.) Lithuanian ex-communist Democratic Labour Party defeats nationalist Sajudis Party in first post-Soviet parliamentary elections. Czechoslovak Federal Parliament approves split into Czech and Slovak states. UN Security Council enforces naval blockade on Serbia and Montenegro.

(Dec.) Ex-communist President Milan Kučan and ruling Liberal Democrat Party win elections in Slovenia; UN peacekeeping forces deployed in Macedonia to prevent spread of unrest. Russian Congress blocks President Yeltsin's plans for a referendum on the powers of the President; also removes Yegor Gaidar as premier and replaces him with Viktor Chernomyrdin (14th).

(21 Dec.) Slobodan Milesović wins presidential elections in Serbia.

1993

(Jan.) Formal separation of Czech and Slovak states; Havel reappointed President of Czech Republic. Geneva Peace conference on Bosnia opens; Bosnian Serbs provisionally agree to end the war, but fighting continues.

(Feb.) UN Security Council votes to create war crimes tribunal for Yugoslavia. Bosnian town of Cerska falls to Serbs.

(21 Mar.) President Yeltsin announces rule by decree and plan to hold a national referendum on 25 April.

(28 Mar.) Move to impeach the President by Congress defeated.

(1 Apr.) Athens peace talks on former Yugoslavia open.

(3 Apr.) Serbs reject UN peace plan; Bosnian Serbs also reject UN peace plan (25th). Former Yugoslav Republic of Macedonia admitted to UN. Russian referendum gives vote of confidence to President Yeltsin and his socio-economic policy.

(May) War crimes tribunal for former Yugoslavia established at The Hague.

(6 May) UN Security Council declares Sarajevo and other Muslim enclaves UN monitored safe areas.

(June) Provisional agreement at Geneva on three-way partition of Bosnia–Herzegovina into Muslim, Serb and Croat areas.

(July) Guntis Alamanis of Farmers' Union elected President of Latvia.

(Aug.) Last Russian troops leave Lithuania.

(21 Sept.) President Yeltsin suspends parliament and calls for elections.

(3–4 Oct.) Suppression of rising against President Yeltsin's suspension of parliament.

(26 Oct.) Coalition government formed under Polish Peasant Party leader Waldemar Pawlak.

1994

(Jan.) Reformers Gaidar and Fedorov leave Yeltsin government.

(9 Feb.) Serb mortar attack on Sarajevo market, killing over 60 people, leads to UN ultimatum on removal of Serb artillery from 20 km exclusion zone.

(28 Feb.) NATO fighters shoot down Serbian aircraft.

(Apr.) UN safe area of Gorazde comes under Serb attack; NATO aircraft bomb Serb positions; Serbs retaliate by taking UN observers hostage.

(29 May) Former communists, now Hungarian Socialist Party, come to power after two rounds of voting.

(July) Contact Group of diplomats from Russia, USA, France, Britain and Germany propose division of Bosnia, but rejected by Serbs. New constitution adopted in Moldova, establishing a presidential parliamentary republic.

(Aug.) Serbian government imposes sanctions on the Bosnian Serbs.

(Nov.) USA announces unilateral suspension of international arms embargo following renewal of fighting in Bosnia.

(Dec.) Former communists win outright majority in Bulgaria. Four-month truce agreed in Bosnia.

(1 Dec.) Russia gives ultimatum to breakaway Chechen Republic to disband army and free all prisoners; failure to reach agreement leads to major military assault on Chechen Republic (27th). (See p. 214 for the Chechnya conflict.)

1995

(1 Mar.) In Poland, former communist Jozef Oleksy elected Prime Minister following resignation of Waldemar Pawlak.

(May) Croatian forces open fighting against Serbs. NATO planes attack Serb positions and Bosnian Serbs again take UN hostages.

(June) Russia and Ukraine finally settle dispute over Black Sea fleet. Western nations send 'rapid reaction' force to Bosnia.

(July) Serb forces overrun UN safe areas of Srebrenica and Zepa; by the end of the month photographic evidence of mass graves leads to the indictment of Bosnian Serb leader, Radovan Karadzic, and military chief, Ratko Mladic, for crimes against humanity.

(Aug.) Further Serb mortar attacks on Sarajevo lead to NATO air strikes against Bosnian Serb military positions.

(12 Oct.) New ceasefire comes into effect in Bosnia.

(Nov.) Polish President Lech Walesa defeated by former communist Aleksander Kwaśniewski in presidential election. Shevardnadze wins new term as President of Georgia.

(1 Nov.) Yugoslav peace talks open in Dayton, Ohio; peace plan agreed (21st).

(3 Nov.) President Yeltsin forced to relinquish control of four key ministries after second heart attack (resumes powers, 26th Dec.).

(14 Dec.) Yugoslav peace agreement signed in Paris (14th).

1996

(Jan.) Resignation of Polish Prime Minister Oleksy over allegations of once spying for Russia.

(5 Jan.) Resignation of liberal Russian foreign minister Andrei Kozrev.

(29 Feb.) Siege of Sarajevo officially ends.

(Apr.) Presidents of Belarus and Russia sign a treaty providing for political, economic and military integration.

(May) Ruling Albanian Democratic Party claims to have won 100 of 140 seats in general election; widespread protests by opposition.

(June) Ruling Civic Democratic Party wins Czech elections.

(4 July) Yeltsin wins presidential election in second round run-off.

(Sept.) First elections in Bosnia.

(Nov.) Constitutional referendum in Belarus gives greater powers to President.

(Dec.) Romanian general election won by reform candidate. Persistent street demonstrations in Serbia against government's refusal to accept opposition successes in municipal elections.

1997

(Jan.) Serbian government concedes opposition victories after international inspection. Growing attacks on Serbian leaders in Kosovo by separatist Kosovo Liberation Army (KLA). Massive street demonstrations in Bulgaria against Socialist (ex-communist) government. Serious rioting in major towns in Albania. Russian withdrawal of troops from Chechnya completed.

(Mar.) Reorganization of Russian government favours reformists.

(June) Internationally supervised elections held in Albania.

(July) Federal Parliament elects Milosević Yugoslav President.

(8 July) Hungary, Poland and the Czech Republic are invited to join NATO.

(Nov.) Russian agreement with Japan aims at ending dispute over Kurile Islands and formally ends Second World War.

1998

(Jan.) Havel re-elected President in Czech Republic. National Assembly in Poland ratifies Concordat with Roman Catholic Church.

(Feb.–Mar.) Serbian police kill dozens of ethnic Albanians in operations against separatists. Massive anti-Serb demonstrations in Pristina, capital of Kosovo.

(Mar.) Dismissal of Russian Prime Minister Chernomyrdin by Yeltsin.

(Apr.) Sergei Kiriyenko confirmed as prime minister in Russia. Serbs vote 95% against international intervention in a referendum.

(May) Shuttle diplomacy by US envoy Richard Holbrooke.

(June) Viktor Orban becomes Prime Minister in Hungary.

(July) Zeman becomes Prime Minister in Czech Republic.

(July–Aug.) KLA expands control to 40–50% of Kosovo. Massive Serbian offensive weakens KLA. Continued heavy fighting.

(Aug.) Kiriyenko dismissed; Yeltsin reappoints Chernomyrdin.

(Sept.) Yevgenii Primakov approved by Duma as compromise candidate after Duma continues to reject the reappointment of Chernomyrdin. US demands cease-fire in Kosovo. UN Security Council endorses call.

(Oct.) NATO allies authorize air strikes; Milosević agrees to withdraw troops (27th). Observers from Organization for Security and Cooperation in Europe (OSCE) to enter Kosovo.

(Nov.) Constitutional Court confirms Yeltsin cannot stand for a further term in presidency.

(Dec.) Renewed clashes of KLA with Serb border guards. Mediation attempts by US envoy Christopher Hill.

1999

(15 Jan.) Discovery of 45 bodies (presumed ethnic Albanians) in village of Racak. Expulsion of OSCE chief (18th).

(6–23 Feb.) Peace talks at Rambouillet fail to achieve breakthrough over Kosovo.

(Mar.) Czech Republic, Hungary and Poland become full members of NATO.

(18–19 Mar.) Peace deal signed by Kosovo Albanians in Paris. Rejected by Yugoslavia. Massing of Yugoslav troops around Kosovo.

(20 Mar.) Yugoslav armed units begin ethnic cleansing of Kosovo.

(24 Mar.) NATO aircraft begin air strikes against Yugoslav targets. Start of the NATO war on Yugoslavia over Kosovo (see p. 214).

(Apr.) NATO missiles hit Belgrade Ministry of Interior, Socialist Party of Serbia HQ, etc. Yeltsin warns NATO. Sacking of Serb Deputy Prime Minister Vuk Drasković.

(27 May) Confirmation by UN War Crimes Tribunal that Milosević has been indicted as a war criminal. NATO war missions continue.

(10 June) Suspension of NATO bombing campaign after withdrawal of Serb troops from Kosovo. Subsequent stationing of NATO troops in Kosovo (KFOR), which becomes an international protectorate.

(Dec.) Solidarity announces its withdrawal from Polish politics to become an 'organization of employees'.

(31 Dec.) Resignation of Yeltsin in Russia: Putin Acting President.

2000

(Feb.) Moldova becomes first former Soviet republic to vote Communist Party back into power.

(26 Mar.) Putin elected as President of Russian Federation.

(June) Ferenc Mádl elected President of Hungary. Andrej Bajuk's government takes office in Slovenia. Arrest of Russian media tycoon Vladimir Gusinsky.

(Sept.) Election called for 24 Sept. (after amendment to Yugoslav constitution allows Milosević to serve two more terms). Bitterly disputed and rigged election. Federal Elections Commission calls for second round of voting. Growing discontent and protests in Serbia.

(Oct.) Kwaśniewski re-elected President of Poland.

(3 Oct.) Milosević threatens growing number of protesters with crackdown.

(4 Oct.) Protests gather momentum in southern Serbian town of Nis; despatch of thousands of riot police to fight striking miners south of Belgrade.

(5 Oct.) Storming of Serbian parliament in Belgrade. Workers and sympathizers break through barriers, setting fire to parliament.

(6 Oct.) Milosević (now ousted from power) has meeting with Russian Foreign Minister.

(7 Oct.) Kostunica sworn in as president.

(10 Oct.) Belgrade renews diplomatic ties with UK and other NATO countries.

(Dec.) Ion Illiescu re-elected President in Romania.

2001

(30 Mar.) Arrest of Milosević after long police surveillance.

(5 Apr.) Moldovan parliament elects Communist Party leader Vladimir Voronin as President – first ex-Soviet republic to elect a communist to be head of state.

(26 Apr.) Dismissal of Ukraine's pro-Western and reformist Prime Minister, Viktor Yushchenko.

(17 June) National Movement for Simeon II wins Bulgarian election (with 120 seats and 43% of the vote), defeating ruling UDF (Union of Democratic Forces). Bulgaria becomes first eastern European country where a former monarch has made a political comeback.

(July) Former King Simeon II (Simeon Saxe-Coburgotski) formally returns to power as prime minister in Bulgaria. Milosević taken to The Hague to face War Crimes Tribunal. President Kostunica appoints Dragisa Pesić (of Montenegrin Socialist People's Party) as Prime Minister (17th). Russia and China sign Treaty of Friendship, cementing the post-Soviet relations of their countries. Land Bill passes Duma (257–130), reversing nationalization of land carried out in Soviet era.

(13 Aug.) Ohrid peace deal agreed in Macedonia.

(Sept.) Arms embargo on Yugoslavia (imposed in March 1998) lifted by UN Security Council (marks end of last international sanctions against Belgrade). Polish general election gives electoral humiliation to Solidarity, the movement that had destroyed communism.

(Nov.) Bulgarian presidential election won by former communist Georgi Parvanov (now Socialist Party leader).

2002

(Feb.) Trial of Milosević at The Hague begins.
(Mar.) Serbia and Montenegro announce agreement in principle to reconstitute their country as the 'Union of Serbia and Montenegro'.
(2 Sept.) Slovakia returns pro-Western coalition in key elections.
(Oct.) Swing to Nationalists in Bosnia and Herzegovina. Moscow theatre terrorist siege leaves 129 dead.

2003

(Mar.) Putin signs decree giving extended powers to FSB (the successor to the KGB).
(Mar.) Assassination of President Djindic of Serbia.
(Oct.) Arrest in Russia of billionaire oil magnate Mikhail Khodorkovsky.
(Nov.) Swing to Nationalists in Croatian elections. Massive protests in Ukraine call for resignation of the Prime Minister and rejection of cutbacks in public services. Vote rigging in Georgian elections precipitates 'Rose Revolution' to oust Shevadnardze.
(2 Dec.) Russian parliamentary elections result in easy victory for United Russia, the pro-Putin party. Communists a distant second.
(Dec.) Ultra-nationalists (the Radical Party of Vojislav Seselj) win Serbian general election, but fail to obtain a majority.

2004

(Feb.) Latvian politician Indulis Emsis nominated to become Europe's first Green Prime Minister (20th). Death of President Trajkovski of Macedonia in air crash (26th). Impeachment proceedings loom against Lithuanian president. Abrupt dismissal of Russian Prime Minister by President Putin. Replaced by Mikhail Fradkov (in March).
(Apr.) Landslide presidential election victory for Putin. Lithuanian President Paksas became first European leader to face impeachment. Autocratic Slovak politician Vladimir Meciar heads presidential election race. Seven former communist countries, including the Baltic States, Bulgaria and Romania, admitted to NATO.
(1 May) Expansion of EU embraces former communist countries.
(9 May) Assassination of Chechen's pro-Putin President Akhmad Kadyrov.
(21 Nov.) Political crisis in Ukraine after pro-western opposition candidate Viktor Yushchenko denied victory in presidential election. Beginning of widespread protests – the 'Orange Revolution'. Supreme Court orders poll re-run (for 26 December).
(28 Nov.) Romanian presidential election won by reformist Traian Basescu.
(26 Dec.) Yushchenko victorious in re-run of Ukraine presidential election. Defeated candidate, Viktor Yanukovych, resigns as prime minister (31 December).

WESTERN EUROPE SINCE 1945

1945

(5 June) Allied Control Commission set up to administer Germany.

(July) Churchill voted out as Prime Minister in Britain; Labour Party under Attlee takes power, pledges to introduce a 'welfare state'.

(Dec.) De Gasperi becomes Prime Minister of Italy as head of Christian Democrat Party.

1946

(Jan.) De Gaulle resigns as President of French provisional government after his draft constitution is rejected; he tries to rally right-wing opinion in his non-party *Rassemblement du Peuple Français* (RPF).

(Mar.) Churchill makes 'Iron Curtain' speech at Fulton, Missouri.

(May) King Victor Emmanuel of Italy abdicates; a referendum votes Italy a republic.

(July) Bread rationing introduced in Britain; more severe rationing than the war because of economic crisis.

(Oct.) Fourth Republic established in France.

(Dec.) Britain and USA agree economic merger of their zones in Germany.

1947

(Mar.) Anglo–French Treaty of Alliance.

(June) General Marshall proposes economic aid to rebuild Europe; Paris Conference (July) meets to discuss the 'Marshall Plan'.

1948

(Apr.) Organization for European Economic Co-operation (OEEC) set up to receive 17,000 million dollars of Marshall Aid from the United States. Member states: Austria, Belgium, Denmark, France, West Germany, Greece, Iceland, Ireland, Italy, Luxembourg, The Netherlands, Norway, Portugal, Spain, Sweden, Switzerland, Turkey and the United Kingdom. Customs Union set up between Belgium, The Netherlands and Luxembourg – 'Benelux'.

1949

(23 May) German Federal Republic comes into existence on basis of constitution drafted the previous year with Konrad Adenauer as first Federal Chancellor. Council of Europe set up for 'political co-operation', consisting of the OEEC states apart from Spain and Portugal. Strasbourg becomes headquarters for a Consultative Assembly.

(24 Aug.) North Atlantic Treaty Organization (NATO) formed, including United States, Canada, United Kingdom, Norway, Denmark, The Netherlands, Belgium, France, Italy, Greece and Turkey.

1950

Britain rejects idea of joining a European coal and steel community.

1951

(18 Apr.) Paris Treaty between Benelux countries (Belgium, The Netherlands and Luxembourg), France, Italy and West Germany – 'the Six' – sets up a 'Common Market' in coal and steel. A European Commission is set up as the supreme authority.

(Oct.) Fall of Labour government in Britain; Churchill returns to office. De Gaulle retires from politics.

1952

(Oct.) Britain explodes an atomic bomb in Monte Bello islands, off N.W. Australia.

1953

European Court of Human Rights set up in Strasbourg.

1954

Western European Union proposed by the British as a substitute for a single European army.

(May) Defeat for French forces at Dien Bien Phu.

(Aug.) Death of De Gasperi, Christian Democrat Prime Minister of Italy, 1945–53.

1955

(Jan.) West Germany joins NATO.

(5 Apr.) Resignation of Churchill as British Prime Minister. Anthony Eden takes over. Messina Conference of 'the Six' discusses a full customs union. Britain expresses preference for a larger free trade area of the OEEC countries.

1956

(Oct.–Nov.) Anglo–French intervention at Suez.

1957

(9 Jan.) Fall of Eden as a consequence of Suez crisis; Harold Macmillan takes over (10th) as Prime Minister.

(25 Mar.) Rome Treaties between 'the Six' set up the European Economic Community (EEC) and Euratom.

1958

(May) Rioting by French settlers in Algeria leads to French army taking over (13th); De Gaulle voted into power in France after period of chronic political instability (29th) and given power to produce a new constitution.

(9–28 Oct.) Death of Pope Pius XII; election of John XXIII.

(21 Dec.) De Gaulle elected President of Fifth French Republic.

1959

(Nov.) European Free Trade Association (EFTA) set up as a counterweight to the EEC, comprising Austria, Denmark, Norway, Portugal, Sweden, Switzerland and the United Kingdom.

1960

(Feb.) France explodes her first atomic device.

1961

(21 Apr.) French army revolt begins in Algeria against de Gaulle's plans for Algerian independence.

(10 Aug.) United Kingdom, Ireland and Denmark apply for membership of EEC; also Norway (1962).

(17–18 Aug.) Berlin Wall erected to halt flood of refugees to West.

1962

EEC agrees Common Agricultural Policy to come into operation in 1964; a system of high guaranteed prices to be paid for out of a common fund; beginning of period of agricultural prosperity in rural Europe and huge food surpluses.

(Dec.) Britain arranges with USA to adopt Polaris missile system as its nuclear deterrent.

1963

(Jan.) De Gaulle vetoes British entry into EEC; Irish, Danish and Norwegian applications suspended.

(3–21 June) Death of John XXIII; election of Pope Paul VI.

(5 Aug.) France refuses to sign Test Ban Treaty, signalling intention to build up *force de frappe*.

(Oct.) Adenauer retires as Chancellor of West Germany; succeeded by Dr Ludwig Erhard.

1964

(Oct.) Labour, under Harold Wilson, returns to power in Britain after 13 years of Conservative rule.

1966

(Mar.) France withdraws from Military Committee of NATO. Labour government re-elected in Britain.

(30 Nov.) Dr Kurt-Georg Kiesinger becomes Chancellor of West Germany.

1967

(27 Nov.) Further British, Irish, Danish and Norwegian applications to join EEC vetoed by de Gaulle.

1968

(May) Violent student unrest in Paris and mass strikes against de Gaulle's government. (Sept.) Dr Salazar of Portugal, Western Europe's longest surviving dictator, succeeded by Dr Marcello Caetano.

1969

(28 Apr.) De Gaulle resigns as President after unfavourable vote in referendum on the constitution; Gaullist Georges Pompidou becomes President.

(Aug.) First British troops sent to Northern Ireland (see p. 212).

(Oct.) German Social Democrats take power under Willy Brandt; begins policy of *Ostpolitik*, seeking friendly relations with Eastern Europe, and encourages enlargement of EEC.

1970

(Mar.) Heads of East and West Germany meet for first time.

(18 June) Defeat of Labour government in Britain. Edward Heath, a committed European, leads Conservative government.

(9 Nov.) Death of de Gaulle.

1971

(28 Oct.) British Parliament votes in favour of application to join the Common Market.

1972

(24 Mar.) Britain imposes direct rule in Northern Ireland.

(Apr.) Defection from German coalition leads to early election in November.

(5 Sept.) Arab terrorists kill Israeli athletes at Munich Olympics.

(Nov.) Brandt's government returned to power with SPD as largest party in Bundestag.

1973

(Jan.) Britain, Denmark and Ireland join EEC; Norway does not, following unfavourable referendum vote.

(May) Britain in dispute with Iceland over fishing rights – 'Cod War'.

(22 June) West and East Germany join the United Nations.

(Dec.) Conservative Prime Minister Heath declares state of emergency as a result of miners' strike.

1974

(28 Feb.) Heath defeated in general election; Labour government in Britain under Wilson.

(2 Apr.) Death of Georges Pompidou; Giscard d'Estaing becomes President (May).

(25 Apr.) Military junta deposes Portuguese government, ending dictatorship and colonial wars.

(May) Willy Brandt resigns following security scandal; Helmut Schmidt takes over as Chancellor.

(30 Sept.) General Spinola resigns and replaced by Costa Gomes in Portugal.

(10 Oct.) Labour Party in Britain obtains small majority at general election.

1975

(Jan.) British government announces referendum on EEC membership.

(28 Feb.) German opposition leader, Peter Lorenz, kidnapped by terrorists.

(25 Apr.) Portugal holds first free elections for 50 years.

(June) Britain votes by two to one in referendum to remain in EEC. Greece, Spain and Portugal apply for membership.

(20 Nov.) Death of Franco; King Juan Carlos I succeeds to the throne (27th).

(Dec.) Terrorist attacks by Indonesian immigrants in The Netherlands.

1976

(5 Apr.) James Callaghan becomes Prime Minister of Britain following resignation of Harold Wilson.

(19 Sept.) Social Democratic Party in Sweden defeated for first time in 44 years.

1977

(15 June) First general election in Spain for 40 years. Señor Suarez's Democratic Centre Party wins power.

(5 Sept.) German terrorists kill Dr Hans-Martin Schleyer, head of West German Employers' Federation.

1978

(16 Mar.) Aldo Moro, former Prime Minister of Italy, kidnapped in Rome by Italian terrorists; found dead (9 May).

(6–26 Aug.) Death of Pope Paul VI; election of John Paul I.

(28 Sept.–16 Oct.) Death of Pope John Paul I; election of John Paul II, former Cardinal Karol Wojtyla, first non-Italian Pope for 400 years.

(27 Dec.) First democratic government in postwar Spain.

(Dec.–Apr.) 'Winter of Discontent' in Britain with widespread strikes against Labour government's wages policy.

1979

(3 May) Conservatives under Margaret Thatcher take power following general election in Britain. European Monetary System (EMS) introduced with common European Currency Unit (ECU) linking the exchange rates of the individual countries.

(June) First direct elections to the European Parliament.

1980

(30 Apr.–5 May) Iranian embassy in London seized by terrorists and stormed by British specialist anti-terrorist forces, the SAS.

(2 Aug.) Terrorist bomb explodes at Bologna railway station, killing 76 people.

(5 Oct.) German coalition of SPD and Free Democrats retains power in elections.

(4 Dec.) Prime Minister of Portugal, Dr da Carneiro, killed in air crash.

1981

(1 Jan.) Greece becomes member of EEC.

(23 Feb.) Attempted coup in Spain led by Lt-Col. Trejero Milina; leaders arrested.

(26 Mar.) Social Democratic Party formed in Britain by breakaway of four senior figures from Labour Party.

(10 May) François Mitterrand, leader of Socialists, becomes President of France in place of Giscard d'Estaing.

(13 May) Pope John Paul II shot and injured by Turkish terrorist.

(July) Rioting in several inner city areas of Britain.

(Nov.) Sensational by-election successes of British SDP/Liberal Alliance lead to predictions of Alliance victory if an election called.

1982

(Apr.) Britain sends Task Force to recapture Falkland Islands from Argentina (see p. 242).

(30 May) Spain joins NATO.

(15 June) Argentine forces on Falklands surrender.

(19 Sept.) Social Democrats return to power in Sweden.

(Oct.) Felipe Gonzales leads Socialists to victory in Spanish elections. Helmut Kohl of Christian Democrats becomes Chancellor of Germany following breakup of governing coalition.

1983

(Mar.) Crisis economic package in France and Cabinet re-shuffle.

(6 Mar.) Helmut Kohl wins a substantial electoral victory; Green Party passes 5 per cent threshhold for seats in the Bundestag.

(9 June) Mrs Thatcher returned for second term of office in Britain. Labour Party and Alliance split the opposition vote.

1984

(9 Mar.) Beginning of 12-month miners' strike in Britain.

(20 Apr.) Britain confirms intention to leave Hong Kong in 1997 when the lease from China expires.

(19 July) French communists withdraw support from Mitterrand.

(4 Sept.) Herr Honecker, East German premier, cancels trip to West Germany because of Soviet opposition.

(Oct.) IRA bomb explosion at Grand Hotel, Brighton, narrowly misses killing Mrs Thatcher.

(18 Nov.) Demonstrations in Madrid against state control of education.

1985

(Nov.) Anglo–Irish Agreement signed between Mrs Thatcher and Dr FitzGerald, the Irish premier, giving Irish government a consultative role in Northern Irish affairs.

1986

(Jan.) Two Cabinet ministers resign in Britain over 'Westland Affair'.

(1 Jan.) Spain and Portugal join the Common Market.

(Mar.) General election in France gives socialists largest number of seats, but neo-Gaullist Jacques Chirac forms government; beginning of period of 'cohabitation' between socialist President Mitterrand and conservative Chirac.

(12 Mar.) Referendum in Spain favours continued membership of NATO.

(22 June) Gonzales and socialists returned to power in Spanish elections.

1987

(25 Jan.) Helmut Kohl's government confirmed in office at elections.

(June) Mrs Thatcher wins an unprecedented third term as Prime Minister of Britain.

1988

(Apr.–May) Mitterrand defeats Chirac in French presidential elections.

(5–12 June) Mitterrand calls elections for National Assembly but fails to achieve the expected overall majority.

(20 Sept.) Mrs Thatcher's 'Bruges Speech' attacks EEC attempts to introduce socialism by the back door.

1989

(June) European elections witness rise in Green votes throughout Europe. Socialist bloc increases substantially in European Parliament.

(June–July) Victory of Polish Solidarity movement in elections (June) and formation of first non-communist government in Poland signals beginning of breakdown of East European Communist regimes (see p. 179).

(Sept.) Hungary opens borders with Austria, allowing flight of thousands of East Germans to West.

(Nov.) Collapse of East German regime; opening of Berlin Wall (9 Nov.); freedom of travel to West granted. Chancellor Kohl calls for united Germany. Reformer, Hans Modrow, becomes East German premier.

(Dec.) First Four-Power Conference since 1971 to discuss future of Berlin and East Europe. Cold War declared ended at Malta Summit. Brandenburg Gate opened and Kohl visits East Germany to wide acclaim. Preparations for free elections in East Germany.

1990

(Jan.) East German elections brought forward to March.

(Feb.) East German proposal for their neutrality rejected by West Germany. West German Cabinet agrees to currency union between East and West Germany.

(Mar.) Pro-unification Alliance for Germany wins East German elections and prepares for economic union in July and all-German elections in December.

(July) Economic unification of East and West Germany on the basis of the West German currency. West German–Soviet agreement that a united Germany will have full sovereignty, including the right to join NATO. The Soviet Union agrees to withdraw its troops from East Germany within three to four years.

(3 Oct.) Political unification of East and West Germany.

(Nov.) Mrs Thatcher replaced as Conservative leader by Mr John Major following leadership contest.

(Dec.) First all-German elections since 1932 result in victory for Chancellor Kohl's conservative coalition.

1991

(Jan.) Italian Communist Party changes name to 'Democratic Party of the Left' (PDS) and adopts sweeping changes in policy.

(Jan.–Feb.) British and French forces participate in Gulf War against Iraq.

(Mar.) British government abandons Poll Tax.

(Apr.) German Chancellor Kohl suffers humiliating defeat in Rhineland–Palatinate local elections.

(May) Resignation of French premier Rocard; Mme Cresson becomes France's first woman Prime Minister.

(July–Oct.) European Community makes failed attempts to obtain ceasefire agreement in Yugoslavian conflict.

(Oct.) Luxembourg draft plan on European Monetary Union of European Community fails to win agreement.

(Dec.) Maastricht Summit on economic and political union. Britain wins opt-out clauses on monetary union and Social Charter.

1992

(Apr.) Pierre Bérégovoy appointed Prime Minister in France (2nd); President Francesco Cossiga resigns in Italy. John Major leads Conservatives to fourth election victory in Britain (9th).

(May) France's President Mitterrand and Germany's Chancellor Helmut Kohl announce creation of a Franco–German 'Eurocorps'.

(June) Socialist Unity Party leader Giuliano Amato becomes Italian Prime Minister, leading Italy's 51st administration since the war.

(Aug.) Demonstrations and acts of violence against foreign workers in Germany lead to call for restrictions on asylum provisions.

(Sept.) Constitutional changes in Belgium devolve more power to regions.

(23 Nov.) Neo-Nazi fire bombing in Möln kills three Turkish women.

1993

(Jan.) Social Democrat coalition government takes office in Denmark.

(Feb.) Belgium takes first steps towards a federal state.

(Apr.) Italian referendum approves modification of proportional representation system for elections to Senate; Carlo Ciampi forms new government after resignation of Amato.

(June) Spanish Workers' Socialist Party wins general election with reduced majority.

(Aug.) Italian Senate and Chamber of Deputies approve of electoral reform for the Chamber.

(Nov.) General Strike in Belgium against economic austerity package.

1994

(28 Mar.) Right-wing and nationalist Freedom Alliance coalition wins overwhelming victory in elections to reformed parliament in Italy.

(Apr.) Silvio Berlusconi appointed Italian Prime Minister.

(June) Resignation of French Socialist Party leader, Michel Rocard, after defeat in European elections.

(Aug.) Labour Party leader Wim Kok leads coalition government in The Netherlands. IRA announce a ceasefire in Northern Ireland.

(16 Oct.) Chancellor Helmut Kohl's ruling Christian Democrat coalition remains in power following general election.

(16 Nov.) Fall of Irish government led by Albert Reynolds.

(22 Dec.) Resignation of Prime Minister Berlusconi after Northern League abandons coalition government.

1995

(13 Jan.) Former Italian Treasury Minister, Lamberto Dini, appointed new Prime Minister.

(23 Apr.) Lionel Jospin, the French socialist candidate, wins most votes in first round of presidential elections.

(7 May) Jacques Chirac wins French presidential election.

(12 Oct.) Socialist Party takes power in Portugal as minority government, ending ten years of Social Democratic rule.

(15 Nov.) French Prime Minister Alain Juppé introduces reforms to cut health and social security expenditure.

1996

(8 Jan.) Death of former President François Mitterrand. Resignation of Greek Prime Minister, Andreas Papandreou, due to ill-health; replaced by Costas Simitis.

(3 Mar.) In Spain, Conservative Popular Party, led by José Maria Anzar, defeats ruling socialists in general election.

(21 Apr.) Olive Tree Alliance wins Italian general election; former Italian Prime Minister, Bettino Craxi, fined £15 million and sentenced to eight years' imprisonment for corruption.

(May) Strikes in Germany against austerity measures.

(July) Following end of conscription, announced in May, France announces the disbandment of a quarter of regiments to create a purely professional army by 2002.

(8 July) NATO offers membership to Hungary, Poland and the Czech Republic.

1997

(Jan.) Spain refuses to recognize Gibraltar-issued passports.

(Feb.) Widespread protests in France against new law to control illegal immigration.

(Mar.) Kohl declares willingness to stand for re-election as Chancellor in 1998. Flood of refugees from Albania leads to declaration of state of emergency in Italy.

(May–June) General election in France, Centre-right heavily defeated by Socialists and Communists. Resignation of Alain Juppé. Lionel Jospin becomes prime minister.

(July) Kidnap and murder of Basque town councillor by ETA leads to 6 million strong protests in Spain.

(Sept.) Catholic church accepts responsibility for its part in wartime deportation of Jews in France.

(Oct.) Romano Prodi survives in office in Italy despite split with his Communist partners.

1998

(Feb.) French parliament approves reduction in working week to 35 hours by 2000.

(Mar.) Advances by National Front in regional elections in France secure it the balance of power in several areas. Premier of Lower Saxony, Gerhard Schröder, selected as Social Democrat to run against Kohl.

(Apr.) France ratifies treaty banning testing of nuclear weapons. French parliament votes 334 to 49 to join the single European currency.

(May) Official inauguration of the single European currency in the European Union.

(Sept.) Helmut Kohl ousted in general election; Social Democrats under Schröder seek coalition with Greens.

(Oct.) Renewed crisis for Romano Prodi after Communists withdraw from government. Prodi defeated by one vote in confidence motion over tough budget. Massimo D'Alema constructs new coalition.

1999

(Feb.) Schröder loses majority in Upper House after gains by Christian Democrats in Hessen.

(Mar.) Resignation of Oskar Lafontaine as Finance Minister (succeeded by Hans Eichel). Schröder succeeds Lafontaine as party chairman. Romano Prodi nominated to succeed Jacques Santer as EU Commission President.

(May) Carlo Azeglio Ciampi (Treasury Minister) elected President of Italy.

(Aug.) First hints of scandal involving Kohl and undisclosed financial donations to party.

(Oct.) Further electoral defeat for Social Democrats in Berlin elections (SDP take only 22.4%, former Communists secure 18%). Guterres leads Socialist Party to major victory in Portugal.

(Dec.) Election of Johannes Rau as President of Germany. Helmut Kohl faces increasing pressure over allegations that secret contributions had been made to the Christian Democrats.

2000

(Jan.) Death of Italian politician Bettino Craxi. Resignation of Helmut Kohl as honorary chairman of Christian Democrats.

(Mar.) José Maria Aznar wins overall majority in Spanish general election.

(Sept.) Referendum in France approves reduction in length of presidential term from seven to five years (70% majority on 30% turnout).

2001

(Jan.) Jorge Sampãio re-elected as President for second term in Portugal.

(June) Collapse of 'grand coalition' in Berlin which had ruled the city for a decade.

(Dec.) Resignation of Guterres as Prime Minister in Portugal. José Manuel Durâo Barroso becomes Prime Minister.

2002

(Feb.) Italian Senate votes by overwhelming majority to allow return of male heirs of country's royal family, the House of Savoy.

(Mar.) Massive demonstration (2 million march in Rome) against terrorism and anti-labour laws. Left loses Portuguese general election.

(Aug.) Spanish MPs vote to ban ETA's political wing.

(Sept.) Schröder narrowly retains power in closest-fought post-war German elections (helped by strong showing of Greens). Stoiber's Christian Democrats poll strongly, but weak performance by their Free Democrat allies.

2003

(July) Home rule referendum in Corsica.

(Dec.) Italy rocked by financial scandals in Parmalat company. Conviction of 15 members of '17 November' terrorist group in Greece., Arrest of leading ETA leaders, Gorka Palacios and Juan Luis Rubenach, 'decapitates' group's leadership.

2004

(Feb.) Resignation of Gerhard Schröder as chairman of SPD (he remains as German Chancellor).

(Mar.) Carnage in Madrid; 191 die and over 1,400 injured in al-Qaeda terrorist bombing of rail network. Surprise victory for Left follows in Spanish general election.

(Apr.) Largest expansion in NATO's history as seven former communist states join (including Baltic States, Bulgaria and Romania).

(May) European Union expansion brings in Baltic States and former members of communist Eastern bloc.

THE MOVEMENT FOR
EUROPEAN UNITY

1948

Organization for European Economic Co-operation (OEEC) set up to receive Marshall Aid from the United States, consisting of Austria, the Benelux countries (Belgium, The Netherlands and Luxembourg), Denmark, France, West Germany, Greece, Iceland, Ireland, Italy, Norway, Portugal, Spain, Sweden, Switzerland, Turkey and the UK.

1949

Council of Europe set up for 'political co-operation', consisting of the OEEC states except for Spain and Portugal. A Consultative Assembly is set up with Strasbourg as headquarters.

1950

At Strasbourg, Churchill advocates a single European army, but Macmillan rejects the idea of joining a coal and steel organization.

1951

Paris Treaty between the Benelux countries, France, Italy and West Germany. 'The Six' set up a 'common market' in coal and steel. A European Commission is set up as the supreme authority, a Council of Ministers, Court of Justice and an appointed Parliament – the prototype for the European Community.

1953

European Court of Human Rights set up in Strasbourg.

1954

Western European Union proposed by the British as a substitute for a single European army.

1955

Messina Conference of 'the Six' discusses a full customs union. Britain expresses preference for a larger free trade area of the OEEC countries.

1957

The Rome Treaties between 'the Six' set up the European Economic Community (EEC) and Euratom.

1959

European Free Trade Association (EFTA) set up as a counterweight to the EEC, comprising Austria, Denmark, Norway, Portugal, Sweden, Switzerland and the United Kingdom.

1961

Britain, Ireland and Denmark decide to apply for membership of the EEC; Norway in 1962.

1962

Common Agricultural Policy (CAP) agreed between EEC members to come into operation in 1964; a system of high guaranteed prices for European farmers paid for out of a common agricultural fund with protective tariffs against imports.

1963

De Gaulle announces veto on British application for membership. Irish, Danish and Norwegian applications suspended.

1967

Britain, Ireland, Denmark and Norway re-apply to the EEC, but still opposed by de Gaulle.

1970

Plans to enlarge the EEC and give it its own resources are agreed.

1973

Britain, Denmark and Ireland join the EEC but Norway declines to join after a referendum.

1974

Agreement that heads of government should meet three times a year under the title of the European Council.

1975

Britain confirms membership of the EEC by referendum. Greece applies for membership, as do Spain and Portugal. European Regional Development Fund set up.

1979

European Monetary System introduced with a common European Currency Unit (ECU) linking the exchange rates of individual countries. First direct elections held to the European Parliament.

1981

Greece becomes a member of the EEC; entry phased over five years.

1983

Agreement at Stuttgart Summit on principle of budgetary reform and reform of Common Agricultural Policy.

1984

Fontainebleau Summit agrees principles of budgetary discipline and British budget rebate.

1985

Spain and Portugal sign accession treaty to join the EEC from 1 January 1986. At summit meeting in Luxembourg, heads of state draw up Single European Act, defining 1992 as date for completion of frontierless internal market within the EEC with open frontiers, harmonization of regulations, and free movement of labour and capital. The Act also extended majority voting in the Council of Ministers.

1986

Single European Act signed by member states and ratified by their parliaments.

1988

Delors reforms of the European budget agreed, putting controls on farm spending and expanding structural funds (Feb.). Committee set up under Delors to prepare plans for European Monetary Union (EMU). Mrs Thatcher makes Bruges speech (Sept.) attacking attempts to create a European 'superstate'.

1989

Third direct elections to European Parliament (June). Madrid Summit (June) receives Delors Plan for three-stage plan for European Monetary Union. Agreement reached that first stage of EMU would begin on 1 July 1990 with all twelve members beginning to adhere to the European Monetary System (EMS).

1990

Britain joins EMS. Inter-government conference on EMU (Dec.) plans further development of EMU.

1991

Luxembourg plan for inter-government conference at Maastricht turned down (Oct.). Maastricht Summit gives Britain opt-out clauses over monetary union and Social Charter (Dec.).

1992

Danes reject Maastricht in referendum (June); Mitterrand announces French referendum for 20 September. Irish ratify Maastricht. Britain and Italy forced out of Exchange Rate Mechanism (ERM), following huge speculation. France, Belgium, United Kingdom, Spain, Germany and The Netherlands vote to ratify Maastricht. Norway applies for EC membership (Nov.).

1993

Irish punt devalued (Jan.); Spanish and Portuguese currencies follow. Single market comes into force (Jan.). Austria agrees to seek EC membership (Jan.). Danes finally approve Maastricht Treaty (May). ERM bands widened to 15 per cent, virtually destroying the existing system (Aug.) Maastricht Treaty on European Union takes effect (Nov.), European Community (EC) now becomes European Union (EU).

1994

EU agrees basis for discussing membership applications of Finland, Austria, Norway and Sweden (Feb.). United Kingdom opposes dilution of veto rules consequent on EU enlargement (Mar.). Hungary and Poland apply for EU membership (Apr.); European Parliament votes to approve accession treaties of Austria, Finland, Norway and Sweden (May). Jacques Santer of Luxembourg chosen to succeed

Jacques Delors as President of European Commission (July). Austrian, Finnish and Swedish referendums approve EU membership. Norway votes against.

1995

Schengen Group, seven out of 15 EU states, remove all border controls (July). Czech Republic, Latvia and Estonia apply for EU membership. EU Summit in Madrid confirms timetable for a single European Currency by 1999, to be named the 'euro'. Italy rejoins ERM (Nov.).

1996

British beef banned after UK government announces link between BSE ('mad cow' disease) and Creutzsfeld-Jakob disease in humans (Mar.). Plans for 'euro' currency and timetable for single currency confirmed at Dublin Summit (Dec.).

1997

John Major effectively rules out Britain joining single currency in 1999 (now 'extremely unlikely') (Jan.). Labour victory in British general election (May) followed by outline acceptance of 'Social Chapter'. Amsterdam Treaty signed (June) on European border controls. European Union accepts principle of negotiated entry for Cyprus, Slovenia, Estonia, Hungary, Poland and the Czech Republic.

1998

Start of entry negotiations for 11 former Communist bloc states (plus Cyprus) under British presidency (Mar.). Brussels summit gives formal go-ahead for monetary union for 11 states.

1999

Eleven countries of the European Union enter the third phase of EMU and adopt the euro (1 Jan.). Entry into force of Amsterdam Treaty (1 May). Fifth direct elections to European Parliament (8–13 June). Romano Prodi invested as President of European Commission (15 Sept.).

2000

Referendum in Denmark narrowly (53.2%) rejects adoption of euro (Sept.). Nice Summit agrees framework for enlargement in Treaty of Nice.

2001

Greece becomes 12th country to join up to Euro (1 Jan.). Ireland votes against enlargement in referendum. Referendum in Switzerland rejects talks with EU on membership (Mar.).

2002

Successful launch of euro in 12 participating countries signals final end for mark, franc, lira, etc. (1 Jan.). Second referendum in Republic of Ireland approves Treaty of Nice, paving way for expansion of EU (19 Oct.).

2003

Succession of countries vote yes in referenda to join EU, including Malta, Slovenia, Hungary, Slovakia and Baltic States (Mar.–Sept.). Historic reforms to CAP announced (26 June) ending previous 'blank cheque' culture of production. Former French President Valéry Giscard d'Estaing produces draft EU constitution. Brussels Summit (Dec.) rapidly collapses over dispute over national voting rights, especially those of Spain and Poland.

2004

Enlargement of NATO (largest in its history) to embrace Baltic States, Romania, Bulgaria, etc. (Apr.). Former Communist bloc nations join EU (1 May). Draft EU Constitution agreed at Brussels Summit (18 June). José Durão Barroso, Portuguese Prime Minister, chosen as next EU President. Prodi ends term as EU President (Oct.). Crisis over nomination of Rocco Buttiglione as EU commissioner (27 Oct.). Second Treaty of Rome signed (agreeing EU constitution) by 25 heads of government (29 Oct.). EU offers to start membership negotiations in October 2005 with Turkey (Dec.).

III
WAR, DIPLOMACY AND IMPERIALISM

PRINCIPAL EUROPEAN WARS AND CAMPAIGNS

FIRST RUSSO–TURKISH WAR, 1768–74

The Ottoman Empire declared war on 6 October 1768 after Russian troops burnt the Turkish town of Balta. By 1771 the Russians had occupied Moldavia, Wallachia and the Crimea, but the Pugachev Revolt at home forced them to end the war by the Treaty of Kutchuk-Kainardji in 1774, before the Ottoman Empire was completely defeated.

WAR OF AMERICAN INDEPENDENCE, 1775–83

Beginning as a struggle between Britain and the American rebels, the conflict increasingly involved European powers after Britain's unexpected defeat at Saratoga (1777). In 1778 France declared war on Britain, and Spain entered the war in 1779. Britain was further isolated by the Armed Neutrality of the North, formed by Russia, Sweden and Denmark in 1780, and by war with Holland, the same year. Military operations took place in India and the West Indies, and Spain besieged Gibraltar, but the decisive battle came in America in 1781, when the French and Americans beat the British at Yorktown. This forced Britain to admit defeat in the Treaty of Versailles of 1783.

THE 'POTATO WAR', 1778–79

Also known as the War of the Bavarian Succession, the war began after Frederick the Great of Prussia invaded Bohemia in order to forestall Austrian claims to Bavaria. The struggle was called the 'Potato War' because no battles occurred and the main military efforts were devoted to finding food supplies. In 1779 peace was made at Teschen, by which Austria made only small gains in Bavaria.

THE SECOND TURKISH WAR, 1787–92

The Ottoman Empire declared war on Russia in August 1787 but Austria joined the Russians in February 1788 and the Ottoman Empire soon faced major setbacks. In 1788 Austria overran Moldavia and Russia defeated the Ottoman Empire at sea, and in 1789 the scale of the Austro–Russian advance seemed to point to the collapse of the Ottoman Empire. The Russians, however, were diverted by war with Sweden, and Austria faced diplomatic pressure from Prussia and Britain to make peace. In 1791 Austria agreed to the Treaty of Sistova with the Ottoman Empire and Russia made peace at Jassy in 1792.

THE RUSSO–SWEDISH WAR, 1788–90

In June 1788 Gustavus III of Sweden took advantage of the Turkish War to declare war on Russia, but a mutiny in his army and a Danish invasion prevented the advances he had planned for 1788. Gustavus defeated the Danes and internal opposition, and in 1790 routed the Russian fleet at Svenskund, but he agreed to make peace with Russia soon afterwards on the basis of the prewar situation.

THE FRENCH REVOLUTIONARY WARS, 1792–99

Austria and Prussia went to war with the French revolutionaries in 1792, but, after initial advances into France, the Prussians were checked at Valmy on 20 September and the Austrians were defeated at Jemappes on 6 November. The French themselves made advances in the Low Countries, Germany and Italy and this, together with the execution of Louis XVI, led to the formation of the First Coalition, between Austria, Prussia, Britain, Spain and Holland in 1793. The coalition had some successes, notably the Austrian victory of Neerwinden in March and the British seizure of Toulon in August, but the French soon retrieved their losses, and the Coalition proved disunited. The French War Minister, Carnot, reformed the army, which defeated the Austrians at Wattignies (16 Oct. 1793), overran Holland and invaded Spain and Piedmont. In 1795 Prussia, Spain, Holland and other minor states made peace with France. In 1796–97 the defeat of Austria was completed, mainly thanks to a series of victories by Napoleon Bonaparte in Northern Italy, and the Franco–Austrian Treaty of Campo Formio was made. Only Britain remained to challenge the French. British landings on the continent, at Toulon and in the Low Countries, had been defeated, but at sea the British were supreme.

THE EGYPTIAN EXPEDITION, 1798–1801

The expedition was planned as an attempt to defeat Britain by threatening her possessions in the East, and was placed under Bonaparte's control. Although Bonaparte defeated the Mameluke rulers of Egypt in 1799 in the battle of the Pyramids (21 July), the British fleet under Nelson destroyed the French fleet in the battle of the Nile (2 Aug.) and cut Bonaparte's force off from France. An expedition to Syria in 1799 was halted at Acre and Bonaparte decided to return to France. The troops he left behind were forced to surrender to the British in August 1801.

THE NAPOLEONIC WARS, 1799–1815

The War of the Second Coalition, 1799–1802

By early 1799 British diplomacy had brought together the Second Coalition against France with Russia, Austria, Portugal and Naples. A series of allied victories in 1799 in Italy and Germany was soon reversed, however, and on 14 June 1800 Bonaparte, now First Consul of France, won a great victory over the Austrians at Marengo.

Russia left the Coalition in 1800, Austria made peace at Lunéville in 1801, and even the British decided to come to terms with France in 1802 at Amiens.

The War of the Third Coalition, 1803–07

In 1803 war again broke out between Britain and France and in 1804 a new anti-French Coalition was formed by Britain, Russia, Austria and Sweden. But while the British fleet was triumphant at Trafalgar (21 Oct. 1805), the Austrians and Russians were defeated by Bonaparte, who had crowned himself Emperor of France, at Austerlitz (2 Dec. 1805). Austria was forced to make peace, and when Prussia joined the Coalition in 1806 she in turn was defeated at Jena-Auerstadt (14 Oct.). Napoleon proved unable to defeat the Russians at Eylau, on 8 February 1807, but had greater success at Friedland on 14 June, after which Russia and Prussia made the Peace of Tilsit.

The Peninsular War, 1808–14

In 1808 Napoleon, who had conquered Portugal in 1807, tried to make his brother, Joseph, King of Spain, but the Spaniards resisted and were aided by the British. A British army landed in Lisbon in August and drove the French from Portugal. Although Sir John Moore's expedition into Spain was defeated by Napoleon, Wellington was able to resume the British advance in 1809. His victories at Talavera (1809), Salamanca (1812) and Vittoria (1813) eventually allowed the war to be carried into southern France in 1814. Throughout, the guerrilla war of the Spaniards sapped French morale and assisted Wellington's efforts.

The Austrian War, 1809

Austria was encouraged by the Peninsular War to open hostilities against France in April 1809, but in May Napoleon captured Vienna. The Austrians were able to defeat the French at Aspern (22 May) but Napoleon had his revenge at Wagram (6 July), after which peace was made.

The Russian Campaign, 1812

In June 1812 the peace between France and Russia, which had been established at Tilsit, finally broke down and Napoleon invaded Russia. He had early successes, capturing Smolensk (18 Aug.) and worsting the Russians at Borodino (7 Sept.) before taking Moscow (14 Sept.). But the army had already suffered heavy losses and the Russians refused to come to terms. In October Napoleon was forced to abandon Moscow, in the face of winter, and carry out a long retreat through the snow, constantly harassed by the Russians. In all, over 500,000 men had taken part in the invasion, but by the time they left Russia in December only several thousand remained in the army.

The War of Liberation, 1813–14

In March Prussia joined Russia in the war against France, and Sweden soon followed. In May Napoleon won two victories at Lutzen and Bautzen but in August Austria joined the Allies and, despite another French victory at Dresden, Napoleon was finally decisively defeated at Leipzig (16–19 Oct.). The war was carried into France, and despite gallant resistance by Napoleon Paris was taken on 31 March 1814. Napoleon was exiled to Elba.

The Hundred Days, 1815

In March 1815 Napoleon returned from Elba to Paris, regained power, and moved quickly to attack the British, Dutch and Prussian armies in Belgium. He defeated the Prussians at Ligny (16 June) but, on 18 June, was unable to overcome Wellington's Anglo–Dutch army at Waterloo. The Prussians joined the battle late in the day, and helped Wellington rout the French. Napoleon abdicated soon after.

THE THIRD RUSSO–TURKISH WAR, 1806–12

The Ottoman Empire declared war due to Russian claims on her territory, but again the Russians proved the dominant power. The imminent danger of war with France induced Russia to sign the Treaty of Bucharest in 1812 in which the Ottoman Empire lost Bessarabia.

THE SPANISH UPRISING, 1820–23

In early 1820 Spanish troops began to revolt in order to secure a liberal constitution and forced King Ferdinand VII to agree to their aims. By 1822 Spain was in a state of virtual civil war, however, and in 1823 a French army invaded and helped restore Ferdinand to full control.

THE GREEK REVOLT, 1821–29

In April 1821 the Greeks rose against Turkish rule and a bitter struggle began in which the Christian powers of Europe were sympathetic to Greek aims. In 1827 Britain, France and Russia agreed to use force against the Turks and on 20 October destroyed their fleet at Navarino. In April 1828 Russia went to war with the Ottoman Empire, and in 1829 the Treaty of Adrianople made Greece an autonomous state.

THE BELGIAN REVOLT, 1830–33

The Belgians rose against Dutch rule in August 1830, encouraged by the July Revolution in France. Britain, France and Prussia, who held a conference at London in November, favoured ending the Dutch–Belgian union of 1815 but the Dutch resisted this, and finally had to be coerced by the Great Powers to accept Belgian independence in 1833.

THE POLISH REVOLT, 1830–32

In November 1830, encouraged by the revolution in France, Polish nationalists seized Warsaw. But the Russians would not negotiate Polish independence and in September 1831 retook Warsaw. In 1832 Poland became a mere province of Russia and many Poles were sent to Siberia.

THE CARLIST WARS, 1834–39 AND 1872–76

The First Carlist War broke out in 1834 when regional (largely Basque) and Catholic groups supported the claims of Don Carlos to the throne of Spain, instead of his niece, Isabella. Isabella was supported by the army, as well as liberals and foreign powers (France and Britain), and the Carlists came to heel in 1839. They rose again in 1872, after a Republican government was established in Madrid, but they again had only local support. In 1874, with the monarchy restored, the Carlists were confined to the Basque territories and in 1876 Don Carlos fled into exile.

THE EGYPTIAN–TURKISH WAR, 1839–41

In April 1839 war broke out between Mehemet Ali, ruler of Egypt, and the Turks, to whom he was nominally subject. France showed sympathy for Ali but Britain, Russia, Austria and Prussia all acted to restore order in the area. In 1841 peace was made between the two sides and all the powers joined together in the 'Straits Convention' to settle their differences over the Ottoman Empire.

THE HUNGARIAN RISING, 1848–49

The Hungarians rose against Austrian control in March 1848, encouraged by revolution in France. The Austrians were able to recapture Budapest in January 1849, but Hungarian resistance continued, and it was only with Russian military assistance that the Austrians finally defeated the rebels in the battle of Vilagos on 13 August.

THE AUSTRO–SARDINIAN WAR, 1848–49

Encouraged by revolts elsewhere in Italy and Europe, the Sardinians declared war on Austria on 24 March 1848, but were defeated at Custozza in July and agreed to an armistice. In March 1849 Sardinia ended the armistice but was almost immediately defeated at Novara and forced to make peace.

THE FIRST SCHLESWIG WAR, 1848–50

In late March 1848 the provinces of Schleswig and Holstein rose against Danish rule. The Prussians went to the aid of their fellow Germans, and forced the Danes to accept a truce in August. War was revived for a short time in 1849 but peace was finally made the following year.

THE CRIMEAN WAR, 1853–56

In October 1853 the Ottoman Empire declared war on Russia, and the Turkish fleet was destroyed the following month at Sinope. Britain and France, fearing Russian success, joined the Ottoman Empire in March 1854 and launched an invasion in the Crimea in September. Bloody battles were fought at Alma, Balaclava and Inkerman before the Russian port of Sevastopol was taken in September 1855. Russia agreed to make peace at Paris in 1856.

THE FRANCO–AUSTRIAN WAR AND ITALIAN RISINGS, 1859–61

In 1858 Napoleon III of France agreed to help Sardinia make war on Austria. War was declared in April 1859 and the French proved victorious at Magenta and Solferino in June. But Napoleon, shocked by the bloodshed at these battles, agreed to make peace before Austria was completely defeated. Nonetheless the Sardinians were able to unite most of Italy into a new state by March 1861, aided by popular risings and the efforts of Garibaldi.

THE POLISH RISING, 1863–64

The Poles again rose against Russian rule in early 1863 but were unable to gain support from other powers, and by late 1864 the rising had been crushed.

THE SECOND SCHLESWIG WAR, 1864

In February 1864 Austria and Prussia went to war with Denmark over the future of Schleswig-Holstein, and by July had overrun strong Danish defensive fortifications and captured much of the Danish army. The Danes, who had rejected terms offered at a meeting in London in May–June, were now forced to accept peace at Vienna.

THE AUSTRO–PRUSSIAN WAR (SIX WEEKS WAR), 1866

In June 1866 Prussia declared war on Austria over the future of Schleswig-Holstein, and completely defeated their opponents at Sadowa-Königgrätz on 3 July. Austria managed to defeat Prussia's Italian allies at Custozza (24 June) but had to accept the end of its former domination of Italy and Germany in the Treaty of Prague in August.

THE FRANCO–PRUSSIAN WAR, 1870–71

On 19 July 1870 Napoleon III declared war on Prussia after a disagreement over the Spanish succession. As in the war against Austria, the Prussians completely outmanoeuvred their opponents, capturing most of the French army at Sedan (2 Sept.) and Metz (27 Oct.), and bringing the downfall of Napoleon. Paris itself fell in January 1871 and at Frankfurt, in May, the French accepted complete defeat.

THE RUSSO–TURKISH WAR, 1877–78

In 1875–76 revolts had broken out against Ottoman rule in Bosnia and Bulgaria, and the Turks responded ruthlessly. On 24 April 1877 the Russians declared war on the Ottoman Empire but their invasion stalled with the siege of Plevna, which did not fall until December. By the time the Turks made peace at San Stefano, in March 1878, the Great Powers were ready to oppose large-scale Russian gains and forced a new settlement on the Balkans at the Congress of Berlin in July.

THE SERBO–BULGARIAN WAR, 1885–86

In November 1885 Serbia declared war on Bulgaria but was soon defeated at Slivnitsa and peace was restored, under Austrian influence, on the basis of the prewar situation.

THE CRETAN RISING, 1896–98

In May 1896 the Cretans rose against Turkish rule, and gained support from Greece, which declared war on the Ottoman Empire in April 1897. Within a month the Greeks were defeated but the Great Powers intervened to ensure that Crete received autonomy in 1898.

THE RUSSO–JAPANESE WAR, 1904–05

The conflict began without declaration of war when Japan attacked the Russian fleet at Port Arthur (Feb.). Japanese forces eventually took Port Arthur, Korea and much of Manchuria. Russia was severely defeated at the battle of Mukden (21 Feb.–10 Mar. 1904). The Japanese scored a naval triumph at the battle of Tsushima (27 May 1905). After US mediation, peace was secured by the Treaty of Portsmouth (New Hampshire). Russian humiliation in the war was a major factor in provoking the 1905 revolution in Russia.

THE ITALO–TURKISH WAR, 1911–12

On 29 September 1911 Italy declared war on the Ottoman Empire, with the aim of seizing Cyrenaica and Tripoli (modern Libya) to which they had long advanced claims. By November they had defeated the Turks in North Africa and in May 1912 occupied the Dodecanese islands in the Aegean. Italian finances suffered severely in the war, but the Ottoman Empire recognized their gains by the Treaty of Ouchy in October.

THE BALKAN WARS, 1912–13

Encouraged by Italy's success the Balkan states of Serbia, Bulgaria, Greece and Montenegro went to war with the Ottoman Empire in October 1912 and soon overran most of the Ottoman Empire in Europe. The Ottoman Empire acknowledged her losses at London in May 1913 but in June war broke out between Bulgaria, who felt cheated by the peace, and her Serb and Greek allies, supported by the Ottoman Empire and Romania. The Bulgarians were defeated and forced to surrender territory.

THE FIRST WORLD WAR, 1914–18

On 28 July 1914 Austria–Hungary declared war on Serbia whom she blamed for the assassination of the Austrian heir to the throne a month earlier. Austria was supported by her ally Germany, but they were faced by the 'Entente' powers, Russia, France and Britain. In late 1914 the Germans failed to capture Paris, despite the boldness of their invasion plan (the Schlieffen plan), and the war settled into the deadlock of trench warfare. In 1915 the Entente tried to break the deadlock by expeditions to the Dardanelles and Salonika in south-east Europe, and by inducing Italy to attack Austria, but to no avail. In 1916 both sides launched grand offensives on the Western Front, the Germans against Verdun and the Allies on the Somme, but despite enormous casualties the deadlock continued. At sea the British and Germans fought the drawn battle of Jutland. In 1917 both sides were given hope – the Germans by the Russian Revolution (which eventually removed Russia from the war) and the Allies by the USA's entry into the war. The next year proved decisive. The Germans launched a last great offensive in spring 1918 but this was halted, and American support tipped the scales the Allied way. Germany agreed to an armistice in November. Her allies, Austria and the Ottoman Empire, had already given up the fight – the Austrians defeated at Vittorio Veneto in Italy and the Turks defeated by the British in Palestine and Mesopotamia.

THE RUSSIAN CIVIL WAR, 1917–20

In November 1917 the communists seized power in Russia but were opposed by the Tsarists and others. In 1918 the victorious Allied powers intervened to help the Tsarists, but the divisions between the 'White' generals, and the strong central position of the Bolsheviks, ensured that the intervention ended in failure. The Poles, who invaded Russia in April 1919, were able to make gains, following their unexpected victory over the Russians in 1920, and Estonia, Latvia and Lithuania gained their independence, but the communist government survived.

THE HUNGARIAN–ROMANIAN WAR, 1919

In 1919 a communist government under Béla Kun took power in Hungary. Resentful of the armistice terms proposed by the Allies after the war, the Hungarians invaded Slovakia and the Romanians, fearing that they too would be attacked, attacked Hungary to forestall any further communist advances. In August the Romanians captured Budapest and Béla Kun fled. The Romanians left in November. In 1920 Hungary's territorial losses were confirmed by the Treaty of the Trianon.

THE GREEK–TURKISH WAR, 1920–23

By the Treaty of Sèvres, 1920, the Allies handed territory in Asia Minor to Greek control, but the Turks refused to accept this change, and General Mustapha Kemal resisted the Greek occupation. In 1922 he drove the Greeks from their last stronghold at Smyrna, secured control of the area around Constantinople, and overthrew the Ottoman Sultan. In 1923 the Allies renegotiated the peace treaty with Turkey at Lausanne.

THE ITALO–ABYSSINIAN WAR, 1935–36

In October 1935 Mussolini invaded Abyssinia (Ethiopia) and caused an international outcry. An Anglo–French plan to partition Abyssinia between its ruler, Haile Selassie, and Italy failed, as did economic sanctions against Italy to force her to end her aggression. In May 1936 the Italian conquest was complete.

THE SPANISH CIVIL WAR, 1936–39

In July 1936 Spanish generals, led by Franco, rose against the Republican government and plunged Spain into civil war. Despite international declarations against foreign involvement, Italy, Germany and Portugal aided the generals and Russia and France helped the Republicans. In addition, International Brigades were formed by volunteers from many states to fight for the Republicans, and helped to defeat the Nationalists in the battle of Guadalajara, 1937. But by early 1939 the Nationalists held most of Spain. Madrid fell on 28 March.

THE SECOND WORLD WAR, 1939–45

Britain and France declared war on Germany on 3 September 1939, following Hitler's invasion of Poland. Poland soon fell and in 1940 Germany overran Denmark, Norway, the Low Countries and, finally, France. Italy joined the Germans, and for a year Britain and her Empire stood alone against the 'Axis' Powers. In 1941, however, the war was vastly extended, Japan joining the Axis and Russia, China and America joining Britain. The Japanese rapidly overran many of the European colonies in South-East Asia, but Hitler's invasion of Russia (June 1941) eventually proved a decisive mistake. In 1942 the Germans were defeated in North Africa and Russia, in 1943 the Allies invaded Italy, and in 1944 Britain and America opened the 'Second Front' in France. The Third Reich finally collapsed on 8 May 1945 and in August the Japanese were defeated by the use of atomic bombs.

THE RUSSO–FINNISH WAR (THE WINTER WAR), 1939–40

War broke out on 30 November over Russian border claims, but Finnish resistance along the Mannerheim Line ensured that Russia's victory was hard-fought. The war ended in March and peace was made at Moscow. In June 1941 the Finns joined the German invasion of Russia but were again defeated.

THE GREEK CIVIL WAR, 1944–49

The Greek Civil War developed out of the rivalry between communist and monarchist partisans for control of Greece as the Axis forces retreated at the end of the Second World War. British troops were sent to aid the pro-monarchist forces in 1944, while the Soviet Union took the side of the communist insurgents. After 1945 American aid enabled British troops to remain in Greece and assist the return of the monarchy. Communist resistance was seriously weakened by the break between Yugoslavia and Russia in 1948, resulting in the closure of much of Greece's northern border to infiltration and aid. The communists announced an end to open conflict in October 1949.

WARS OF DECOLONIZATION SINCE 1945

There have been numerous struggles linked to the process of decolonization since 1945. Two of the worst defeats were suffered by the French in the Indo-China War, 1946–54, and Algeria, 1956–62. The Dutch were forced to recognize Indonesian independence in 1949, the British were forced to abandon Palestine in 1948, and in 1956 the British and French were forced to give up an attempt to reassert control of the Suez Canal.

EAST EUROPEAN RISINGS, 1953–68

In 1944–48 Russia established domination of most of Eastern Europe through local communist parties. There were risings against Russian control, in East Germany (June 1953), Hungary (Oct. 1956) and Czechoslovakia (1968) but all were put down by Russian troops aided, in the case of Czechoslovakia, by other East European forces. See also Cold War, p. 337.

NORTHERN IRELAND 1969–98

As a result of a request by the government of Northern Ireland, facing severe rioting, British troops moved into Londonderry on 14 August 1969 and into Belfast on

15 August. The first British soldier was killed by a sniper in Belfast on 6 February 1971. Internment without trial was introduced on 9 August 1971; it was ended on 7 December 1975. Direct rule from London was imposed from 30 March 1972. At the peak in August 1972 there were 21,500 British soldiers in Northern Ireland. Subsequently, a policy of 'normalization' led to a reduction of the number of regular troops to under 10,000 by the mid-1980s, with increasing security work carried out by police and the part-time Ulster Defence Regiment. Over 3,160 persons had died in the conflict by the end of August 1994, when the IRA called a 'complete cessation' of military operations. The ceasefire was ended in February 1996. The Good–Friday Agreement signed in 1998 effectively ended the violence.

THE PARTITION OF CYPRUS, 1974

In July 1974 a coup in Cyprus brought to power a government favouring *'enosis'* (union) with Greece, but Turkey quickly responded by invading the island to safeguard the Turkish half of the population. An armistice was agreed on 16 August, which left Turkish rule over one-third of the island.

SOVIET INVASION OF AFGHANISTAN, 1979–89

The instability of the Soviet-backed regime and growing resistance to reforms led to a full-scale Soviet invasion of Afghanistan on 27 December 1979. A new government was installed under Babrak Karmal, but a considerable Soviet military presence had to be maintained in the country to combat the Mujaheddin guerrillas. Following Babrak Karmal's resignation on 4 May 1986, his successor, Major-General Najibullah, announced a six-months' cease-fire on 15 January 1987, but this was rejected by the Mujaheddin. Russian troops began to withdraw in 1988 and completed withdrawal in early 1989, having lost 15,000 dead.

THE SOVIET UNION: DISINTEGRATION AND ETHNIC CONFLICT, 1988–91

During the final days of the Soviet Union, ethnic clashes were already developing. Rioting between Armenians and Azerbaijanis, sparked by a dispute over control of the Nagorno-Karabakh region, began on 20 February 1988. In Uzbekistan, fighting between Uzbeks and Meskhetian Turks began on 4 June 1989. The armed forces also moved against nationalist movements in Georgia, Moldova, Azerbaijan and the Baltic Republics. After the collapse of the Soviet Union, serious conflicts developed in the following areas: Azerbaijan-Armenia; the Abkhazia region of Georgia; Moldova and Tajikistan. By far the most serious conflict within Russia was in Chechnya (see p. 214).

ROMANIAN REVOLUTION AND CIVIL WAR, 1989

On 16–17 December 1989 security forces fired on protesters in the Romanian city of Timisoara. On 18 December Romania closed its frontiers. On 20 December troops surrendered in Timisoara. Fighting spread to Bucharest and other major cities. The army switched sides, joining the popular uprising against the Ceausescu dictatorship and the hated security police (the *Securitate*). By 24 December all strategic points were controlled by the revolutionary National Salvation Front. Ceausescu and his wife were executed by firing squad on 25 December 1989.

YUGOSLAVIAN CIVIL WAR (SERBO–CROAT WAR), 1991–95

Declarations of independence by the former Yugoslav Republics of Slovenia and Croatia led to clashes on Slovenia's borders from July, followed by heavy fighting on Croatian territory between Croatian militia and Serbian irregulars (chetniks) backed by the Yugoslav Federal Army. Main centres of fighting were eastern and central Croatia and the Adriatic coast around Dubrovnik. Yugoslavia officially ceased to exist in January 1992 and Slovenia and Croatia were recognized as independent states. On 29 February 1992, Muslim leaders in Bosnia–Herzegovina declared independence. Bosnian Serbs and the Serbian leadership in Belgrade rejected this, and war began on 6 April with the opening of the siege of the capital, Sarajevo. Serbs were accused of 'ethnic cleansing' to secure territorial domination, and a UN trade embargo was imposed on Serbia on 31 May. Peace talks in Geneva, mediated by Lord Owen and Cyrus Vance, began on 26 August. On 16 November a UN naval blockade was mounted against Serbia and Montenegro. Fighting continued as a further peace conference was held in Geneva on 22–23 January 1993, with Serbs attacking Muslim enclaves at Srebenica and Goradze. Numerous peace talks collapsed. In 1995 Croatia launched major offensives and an uneasy peace accord was signed at Dayton (Ohio).

RUSSO–CHECHNYA WAR, 1994–CONTINUING

Russian troops were ordered into Chechnya in December 1994 to end the rebel republic's bid for independence. The fighting was the worst on Russian soil since the Second World War, with Grozny, the Chechnya capital, razed to the ground. On 31 August 1996 Russia and Chechnya signed a peace deal, freezing the issue of independence for five years, but effectively recognising the autonomy of Chechnya. In January 1997 the withdrawal of all Russian troops from Chechnya was completed. However, partly provoked by Chechen support for guerrillas in the adjacent Caucasus region of Dagestan, and partly because of terrorist bomb outrages in Russia itself, a renewed Russian offensive was launched against Chechnya in September 1999. Massive Russian aerial bombardment was followed by a major ground offensive against Grozny launched on 25 December 1999. The conflict continues.

THE BALKAN WAR, 1999

Conflict in Kosovo, until 1989 an autonomous province in 'rump' Yugoslavia mainly inhabited by Kosovar Albanians, gradually intensified as Serbian forces embarked on a policy of ethnic cleansing. Yugoslav President Slobodan Milosević ignored a series of NATO warnings during 1998. On 24 March 1999 NATO forces (including British aircraft) launched air strikes against Yugoslavia. Cruise missile attacks followed. Milosević intensified his ethnic cleansing policy, sending a human tide of refugees into Macedonia and Albania. NATO air strikes were marked by a series of calamitous errors (including the missile attack on the Chinese embassy in Belgrade on 8 May) and a serious worsening of relations with Russia. Eventually air power (backed by a threat of a land offensive) caused Milosević to sue for peace and a mainly NATO peacekeeping force (KFOR, with some Russian troops) was stationed in Kosovo.

KEY EUROPEAN TREATIES AND ALLIANCES

1763

Treaty of Paris, 10 February, between Britain, France and Spain. France ceded Canada, Grenada and Senegal to Britain. Spain ceded Florida to Britain. Treaty of Hubertusburg, 15 February, between Prussia, Austria and Saxony restored all conquests by the signatories.

1764

Treaty of alliance, 11 April, between Prussia and Russia agreed to make Stanislaw Poniatowski King of Poland.

1772

First Partition of Poland, 5 August, between Russia, Prussia and Austria. Each obtained parts of Poland.

1774

Treaty of Kutchuk-Kainardji, 21 July, ended war between Russia and the Ottoman Empire. Russia gained territory and rights of navigation in Turkish waters.

1778

Alliance between France and the United States, 6 February.

1779

Treaty of Teschen, 13 May, between Austria and Prussia regarding the future of Bavaria.

1780

Armed Neutrality of the North, August, formed by Russia, Sweden and Denmark, to safeguard shipping from British searches.

1783

Treaty of Versailles, 3 September, between Britain, United States, France and Spain, established American independence. France received Senegal, St Lucia and trading posts in India.

1784

Convention of Constantinople, 6 January. The Ottoman Empire recognized the Russian acquisition of the Crimea. Peace between Britain and Holland, 20 March.

1785

Treaty of Fontainebleau, 10 November, between Austria and Holland, regarding Dutch fortresses.

1788

Treaty of Uddevalla, 6 November. The Danes agreed to evacuate Sweden, which they had invaded.

1790

Convention of Reichenbach, 27 July, between Prussia and Austria regarding the Ottoman Empire and The Netherlands. Treaty of Varala, 15 August, ended war between Russia and Sweden.

1791

Treaty of Sistova, 4 August, ended war between Austria and the Ottoman Empire. Declaration of Pilnitz, 27 August, by Austria and Prussia promised intervention against the French revolutionaries if other powers agreed.

1792

Treaty of Jassy, 9 January, between Russia and the Ottoman Empire established the River Dneister as their mutual border. Treaty of Berlin, 7 February, between Austria and Prussia promised mutual support in war with France.

1793

Second Partition of Poland, 23 January, by Russia and Prussia. First Coalition against France formed by Britain, Austria, Prussia, Holland, Spain and Sardinia.

1795

Treaties of Basle between France and Prussia, 5 April, France and Holland, 16 May, and France and Spain, 22 July, effectively marked the defeat of the First Coalition. Third Partition of Poland, 24 October, by Russia, Prussia and Austria ended Polish independence.

1796

Armistice of Cherasco, 28 April, between France and Sardinia, made Sardinia neutral in the war against France.

1797

Treaty of Campo Formio, 17 October, established peace between France and Austria. Austria recognized French conquests.

1798

Formation of the Second Coalition against France by Britain, Russia, Austria, Portugal and Naples.

1800

Revival of the Armed Neutrality of the North, 15 December, by Russia, Sweden and Denmark.

1801

Treaty of Lunéville, 9 February, established peace between France and Austria.

1802

Treaty of Amiens, 25 March, established peace between Britain and France; Britain obtained Ceylon and Trinidad.

1804

Third Coalition against France by Britain, Russia, Austria and Sweden.

1805

Treaty of Schönbrunn, 15 December, between France and Prussia. Prussia obtained Hanover in return for territorial losses. Treaty of Pressburg, 26 December, established peace between Austria and France. Austria lost territory to French client states and agreed to pay a war indemnity of 40,000 francs.

1807

Treaty of Bartenstein, 26 April, between Russia and Prussia, promised to maintain the war against France. Treaty of Tilsit, 7 July, established peace between France and Russia, while (9 July) Prussia ceded all lands west of the Elbe to new Kingdom of Westphalia. Treaty of Fontainebleau, 27 October, between France and Spain, agreed to partition Portugal.

1808

Convention of Cintra, 30 August, allowed French troops to evacuate Portugal without harassment by the British. Conference of Erfurt, 12 October, reaffirmed co-operation between France and Russia.

1809

Sweden ceded Finland to Russia by the Treaty of Fredericksham, 17 September. Treaty of Vienna or Schönbrunn, 14 October, established peace between France and Austria. Austria ceded territory to France and her clients.

1812

Treaty of Abo, 9 April, established an alliance between Russia and Sweden. Treaty of Bucharest, 28 May, ended war between Russia and the Ottoman Empire, Russia annexing Bessarabia.

1813

Treaty of Kalisch, 27 February, established an alliance between Prussia and Russia against France. Treaty of Teplitz, 9 September, between Russia, Prussia and Austria agreed on their aims in war against France.

1814

Treaty of Kiel, 14 January, between Sweden and Denmark, exchanged Norway for Swedish Pomerania. Treaty of Chaumont, 1 March, between Britain, Russia, Prussia and Austria promised not to make a separate peace with Napoleon. Treaty of Fontainebleau, 6 April, gave Napoleon rule over Elba, and a pension, following his abdication. Treaty of Paris, 3 May, between France and the Allies reduced France to her 1792 borders and gave territorial concessions to the Allies. A comprehensive peace would be discussed in Vienna.

1815

Britain, Russia, Prussia and Austria formed a new alliance to defeat Napoleon. Act of the Congress of Vienna, 9 June, between Britain, Russia, Prussia, Austria, France, Sweden and Portugal established a comprehensive peace in Europe, including a complete reorganization of Germany. The Holy Alliance, 26 September, between Russia, Austria and Prussia declared the faith of their monarchs in Christian brotherhood. Second Treaty of Paris, 20 November, reduced France to her 1789 borders, forced her to pay an indemnity and provided for a five-year occupation. On the same day, Britain, Russia, Austria and Prussia agreed to hold regular meetings in future to discuss pressing problems.

1818

The Quadruple Alliance between Britain, Russia, Austria and Prussia was renewed on 15 November in secret, to safeguard against another possible revolution in France, and these powers declared their intention to maintain their close union.

1820

Troppau Protocol, 19 November, between Austria, Russia and Prussia promised united action if revolutionary changes threatened international order.

1826

Protocol of St Petersburg, 4 April, between Britain and Russia agreed that Greece should become an autonomous state.

1827

Treaty of London, 6 July, between Britain, Russia and France threatened to use force if the Ottoman Empire did not agree to the Protocol of St Petersburg.

1829

Treaty of Adrianople, 14 September, between Russia and the Ottoman Empire gave Russia navigation rights in the Straits and confirmed Greek independence. Russia occupied Moldavia and Wallachia.

1833

Treaty of Unkiar Skelessi, 8 July, formed a defensive alliance between Russia and the Ottoman Empire, but was practically meaningless. Treaty of Berlin, 15 October, between Austria, Russia and Prussia reaffirmed the Troppau Protocol of 1820.

1834

Quadruple Alliance, 22 April, between Britain, France, Spain and Portugal, to reestablish stability in the Iberian peninsula through liberal constitutions.

1839

Treaty of London, 19 May. The Great Powers guaranteed Belgian neutrality and independence.

1840

Quadruple Alliance, 15 July, between Britain, Russia, Austria and Prussia, agreed to protect the Turkish Sultan from being overthrown.

1841

The Straits Act, 13 July, between the Ottoman Empire, Britain, Russia, Austria, Prussia and France, closed the Dardanelles to all but Turkish warships.

1849

Treaty of Milan, 6 August, established peace between Austria and Sardinia.

1850

Treaty of Berlin, 2 July, established peace between Prussia and Denmark. Convention of Olmutz, 29 November, between Austria and Prussia regarding Schleswig-Holstein and Hesse-Cassel.

1852

Treaty of London, 8 May, between Britain, France, Russia, Austria, Prussia and Sweden guaranteed Danish integrity and decided the Danish succession.

1854

Treaty of alliance, 12 March, between Britain, France and the Ottoman Empire, made at Constantinople. Treaty of alliance, 2 December, between Britain, France and Austria, made at Vienna.

1855

Turin military convention, 26 January, between Britain, France and Sardinia, against Russia.

1856

Treaty of Paris, 30 March, between Britain, France, Russia, the Ottoman Empire, Sardinia, Austria and Prussia ended the Crimean War and neutralized the Black Sea. On 15 April Britain, France and Austria guaranteed Turkish integrity.

1858

Secret alliance between France and Sardinia made at Plombières, 20 July. Paris agreement, 19 August, between Britain, France, Russia, the Ottoman Empire, Sardinia, Austria and Prussia, united the provinces of Moldavia and Wallachia which later became Romania.

1859

Peace of Villafranca, 11 June, ended war between Austria and France. Sardinia to obtain Lombardy. Treaty of Zurich, 10 November, between Austria, France and Sardinia, confirmed the Peace of Villafranca.

1860

Treaty of Turin, 24 March, between France and Sardinia. French annexation of Nice and Savoy.

1864

Treaty of Vienna, 27 October, between Prussia, Austria and Denmark, ended war between them. The Danish King renounced claims to Schleswig and Holstein.

1865

Convention of Gastein, 14 August, between Prussia and Austria regarding the future of Schleswig and Holstein.

1866

Treaty of Prague, 23 August, established peace between Prussia and Austria. Prussia obtained territory and the leadership of the North German Confederation. Austria ceded Venetia to Italy.

1870

London agreements between Britain and Prussia, 9 August, and Britain and France, 11 August, confirmed Belgian neutrality.

1871

London Agreement, 13 March, between Britain, Russia, Germany, France, Austria–Hungary, the Ottoman Empire and Italy ended the neutralization of the Black Sea. Treaty of Frankfurt, 10 May, ended the Franco–Prussian War. France ceded Alsace–Lorraine to Germany, paid an indemnity and was subjected to occupation.

1872

The Emperors of Germany, Austria–Hungary and Russia meeting in Berlin, September, formed the Three Emperors' League (*Dreikaiserbund*), an informal alliance.

1877

Treaty of Reichstadt, 15 January, between Austria–Hungary and Russia, promised Austrian neutrality in war between Russia and the Ottoman Empire.

1878

Treaty of San Stefano, 3 March, ended war between Russia and the Ottoman Empire and created a large, new Bulgarian state. But this was superceded by the terms of the Congress of Berlin, 13 June, between Britain, Russia, Austria–Hungary, Germany, France, Italy and the Ottoman Empire which created a small, autonomous Bulgaria and semi-independent Eastern Roumelia. Britain obtained Cyprus; Austria–Hungary to administer Bosnia–Herzegovina.

1879

The Dual Alliance, 7 October, between Germany and Austria–Hungary, signed in Vienna. Mutual aid in the event of war with Russia; neutrality in the event of war with other powers.

1881

Formal agreements were made under the League of the Three Emperors, 18 June, between Germany, Austria–Hungary and Russia, including a commitment to consultation in the event of problems in the Balkans. Alliance between Austria–Hungary and Serbia, 28 June, made in Belgrade.

1882

Triple Alliance, 20 May, between Germany, Austria–Hungary and Italy formed in Vienna, extended the Dual Alliance of 1879. Renewed in 1887, 1891, 1902 and 1912. Alliance between Austria–Hungary and Romania, 30 October. Later extended to Germany and Italy. Renewed 1892, 1896, 1902 and 1913.

1884

The League of the Three Emperors was renewed in Berlin, 27 March.

1885

Act of the Conference of Berlin, 26 February, between Austria–Hungary, Belgium, Denmark, France, Germany, Holland, Italy, Portugal, Russia, Spain, Sweden and the Ottoman Empire settled claims with regard to colonization in Africa.

1886

Treaty of Bucharest, 3 March, ended war between Serbia and Bulgaria.

1887

Mediterranean Agreements, 24 March and 16 December, between Britain, Austria–Hungary and Italy, to preserve stability in the Balkans and Mediterranean, made in London. Lapsed in 1896. The Reinsurance Treaty, 18 June, between Germany and Russia, made in Berlin following the end of the League of the Three Emperors. Neutrality in war with another power. Lapsed in 1890.

1890

Berlin agreement, 1 July, between Britain and Germany on colonies.

1893

'Dual Entente', 27 December, formed between France and Russia in St Petersburg. Mutual aid in the event of war with Germany. Ratified in 1894.

1897

Vienna Agreement, 17 May, between Austria–Hungary and Russia on policy in the Balkans. Treaty of Constantinople, 4 December, established peace between the Ottoman Empire and Greece.

1900

Exchange of letters, 20 March, between Britain, France, Germany, Italy, Russia, the United States and Japan, accepted an open door for trade with China.

1902

Secret treaty between France and Italy, November. Italy to be neutral in any war which involved France.

1904

Treaty of Sofia, 31 March, established an alliance between Serbia and Bulgaria. The 'Entente Cordiale', 8 April, between Britain and France settled colonial disputes and promised friendship.

1906

Act of the Conference of Algeçiras, 7 April, between Austria–Hungary, Belgium, Britain, France, Germany, Holland, Italy, Morocco, Portugal, Russia, Spain, Sweden and the United States regarding the future of Morocco.

1907

'Triple Entente' of Britain, France and Russia came into being with an agreement between Britain and Russia, 31 August, in St Petersburg on areas of influence in Asia.

1911

Berlin Convention, 4 November, between France and Germany gave France predomi-nance in Morocco in return for German gains elsewhere in Africa.

1912

The 'Balkan League' of Bulgaria, Serbia, Greece and Montenegro was formed against the Ottoman Empire by a series of agree-ments, February–September. Treaty of Ouchy, 15 October, between Italy and the Ottoman Empire. The Ottoman Empire ceded Tripoli and Cyrenaica to Italy.

1913

Treaty of London, 13 May, established peace between the Ottoman Empire and the Balkan League. The Ottoman Empire in Europe reduced to the area around Con-stantinople; Albania established. Treaty of Bucharest, 10 August, established peace between Bulgaria, Serbia, Greece, Romania and Montenegro. Bulgaria reduced in size.

1914

London Agreement, 15 June, between Britain and Germany concerning the Baghdad Railway. London Declaration, 5 September, by Britain, France and Russia not to make a separate peace with the Central Powers.

1915

Treaty of London, 25 April, between Britain, France and Italy promised Italy territorial gains in return for entering the First World War.

1918

Treaty of Brest-Litovsk, 3 March, between Russia and the Central Powers. Russia ceded territory, and made Finland and the Ukraine independent. Later invalidated.

1919

Treaty of Versailles 28 June, between Germany and the Allies. See p. 130. Treaty of St Germain, 10 September, between Austria and the Allies. See p. 130. Treaty of Neuilly, 27 November, between Bulgaria and the Allies. See p. 131.

1920

Treaty of the Trianon, 4 June, between Hungary and the Allies. See p. 131. Treaty of Sèvres, 10 August, between the Ottoman Empire and the Allies. See p. 131.

1921

Alliance between France and Poland, 19 February. Treaty of Riga, 18 March, between Russia and Poland, ended war between them and defined their mutual border.

1922

Washington Naval Agreement, 6 February, between Britain, France, the United States, Japan, Italy and others restricted the size of navies. Treaty of Rapallo, 16 April, formed an alliance between Russia and Germany.

The 'Little Entente', 31 August, formed between Czechoslovakia, Yugoslavia and Romania under French auspices.

1923

Treaty of Lausanne, 24 July, between the Ottoman Empire and the Allies replaced the Treaty of Sèvres, Confined the Ottoman Empire to Asia Minor and the area around Constantinople.

1925

Locarno Pact between Britain, France, Germany, Italy and Belgium guaranteed the current West European borders.

1928

Kellogg–Briand Pact, 27 August, between Britain, France, the United States, Germany, Italy and Japan renounced war as a means to settle disputes. Later adhered to by other states.

1930

London Naval Agreement, 22 April, between Britain, France, the United States, Japan and Italy expanded the 1922 Washington agreements.

1934

Non-aggression pact, between Germany and Poland, 26 January.

1935

Franco–Italian agreement, 6 January, concerning colonies and Austria. Alliance between France and Russia, 2 May, providing for mutual aid against aggression. Anglo–German Naval Agreement, 18 June.

1936

Non-intervention agreement, 7 August, between Britain, France, Germany, Italy, Russia and others, regarding the Spanish Civil War. Anti-Comintern Pact, 25 November, between Germany and Japan.

1937

Italy joined the Anti-Comintern Pact, 6 November.

1938

Munich Agreement, 29 September, between Britain, France, Germany and Italy forced Czechoslovakia to cede territory to Germany, Hungary and Poland.

1939

France and Britain guaranteed Polish integrity, 31 March. 'Pact of Steel', 22 May, between Germany and Italy formalized the Rome–Berlin 'Axis'. German–Soviet Pact, 23 August, promised Russian neutrality in war involving Germany.

1940

Treaty of Moscow, 12 March, established peace between Russia and Finland. Tripartite Pact, 27 September, between Germany, Italy and Japan.

1942

Alliance between Britain and Russia, 26 May, promised mutual aid against German aggression. Twenty-year term, but abrogated by Russia in 1955.

1944

Alliance between France and Russia, 10 December, promised mutual aid against German aggression. Twenty-year term but abrogated by Russia in 1955.

1945

Yalta Agreement, 11 February, between Britain, Russia and the United States on the future of Germany, Europe and world security. United Nations Charter, 26 June, established new world security system, with Britain, Russia, France, the United States and China as leading powers. Potsdam Agreement, 2 August, between Britain, Russia and the United States expanded the Yalta Agreement.

1947

Peace treaties, 10 February, with Italy, Finland, Hungary, Bulgaria and Romania. Treaty of Dunkirk, 4 March, between Britain and France promised mutual aid against German aggression. Benelux customs union created, 14 March, between Belgium, Holland and Luxembourg.

1948

Brussels Treaty, 17 March, between Britain, France, Belgium, Holland and Luxembourg providing for mutual aid against aggression, economic and social co-operation. Organization for European Economic Co-operation (OEEC) formed by 16 West European nations, 16 April.

1949

North Atlantic Treaty, 4 April, between the United States, Canada, Britain, France, Belgium, Holland, Luxembourg, Norway, Denmark, Portugal and Iceland. Later joined by Greece, Turkey and West Germany. Mutual aid against aggression. Statute of the Council of Europe signed in London, 5 May, by ten West European states.

1952

Treaty signed in Paris between France, West Germany, Italy, Belgium, Holland and Luxembourg, 27 May, to create a European Defence Community and common army. Later rejected by France and common army failed to develop.

1954

London agreement, 3 October, to extend the Brussels Pact to West Germany and Italy, forming the West European Union.

1955

London and Paris agreements, 5 May, gave West Germany full sovereignty and brought her into the North Atlantic Treaty Organization. Warsaw Pact, 13 May, between Russia, East Germany, Poland, Czechoslovakia, Hungary, Bulgaria, Romania and Albania. Mutual assistance in the event of war. Austrian State Treaty, 15 May, between Britain, the United States, Russia and France established a neutral but sovereign Austria.

1957

Treaty of Rome, 22 March, between France, West Germany, Italy, Belgium, Holland and Luxembourg established the European Economic Community. Extended to Britain, Denmark and Eire, 1973.

1960

Stockholm Convention, 3 May, between Britain, Denmark, Norway, Portugal, Austria, Sweden and Switzerland established the European Free Trade Association. Later joined by Finland and Iceland. Britain and Denmark left in 1972 to join the EEC.

1961

Organization for Economic Co-operation and Development (OECD), 30 September, replaced the OEEC, and included the United States and Canada.

1963

Treaty of co-operation between France and West Germany, 22 January. Nuclear Test-Ban Treaty, 5 August, between Britain, the United States and Russia limited nuclear tests.

1966

France withdraws from military commitments to NATO.

1970

Treaty between West Germany and Russia, 12 August, renounced use of war. Treaty between West Germany and Poland, 18 November, renounced use of war and confirmed their present mutual border.

1972

Treaty of Accession signed, 27 January, bringing the United Kingdom, Ireland and Denmark into the EEC with effect from 1 January 1973.

1975

Act of the Helsinki Conference, 1 August, between 35 nations regarding European security, including a reaffirmation of human rights and proposals for economic collaboration between Eastern and Western 'blocs'.

1979

Greece signs Treaty of Accession to the EEC, 28 May, with effect from 1 January 1981.

1982

Spain joins NATO, 30 May; decision to remain part of NATO confirmed by referendum, 12 March 1984.

1985

Portugal and Spain sign Treaties of Accession to the EEC, 12 June, with effect from 1 January 1986. Anglo–Irish (Hillsborough) Agreement, 15 November, confirms that any change to the status of Northern Ireland must only be with the consent of the majority of its people, but gives the Irish Republic a consultative role in Northern Irish affairs through Intergovernmental Conferences.

1986

Single European Act signed, 1 February, between heads of EEC governments, coming into force on 1 July 1987 to create a single European market by 31 December 1992 and to promote greater harmonization of monetary and economic policy.

1987

Intermediate Nuclear Forces Treaty signed in Washington, 8 December, between United States and the Soviet Union. It provided for the withdrawal and destruction of all land-based nuclear missiles in Europe with ranges of between 500 and 5,500 km, including American Cruise and Pershing II missiles and Soviet SS–20s. Verification procedures provide for on-site inspection of compliance.

1988

Geneva Accord, 14 April, on removal of Soviet troops from Afghanistan by mid-February 1989.

1989

Agreement in principle between Pope John Paul II and President Gorbachev in Rome, 2 December, to re-establish diplomatic relations between the Vatican and the Soviet Union and for lifting of ban on the Catholic (Uniate) Church in the Ukraine dating from 1946.

1990

East and West Germany agree and adopt economic unification on the basis of West German currency. West German–Soviet Agreement, 16 July, that united Germany will have full sovereignty, including freedom to join NATO, and on Soviet withdrawal of 350,000 troops from East Germany within three to four years. Paris Agreement in 'Two Plus Four' talks, 17 July, guarantees existing Polish–German border to be secured in treaty after German unification to define German–Polish relations. London Declaration of NATO leaders accepts need to remodel NATO as a political rather than a military alliance and agrees to invite Warsaw Pact representatives and President Gorbachev to future meetings. Treaty concluding 'Two Plus Four' talks, 12 September, ends special Allied Powers over Germany and agrees to unification with full sovereignty of East and West Germany. Conference on Security and Co-operation in Europe (CSCE) signs agreement in Paris, 19 November, marking formal end of the Cold War. Signature of Conventional Forces in Europe (CFE) Treaty by 22 NATO and Warsaw Pact countries formalizing largest cuts in weapons and manpower since 1945.

1991

Massive reductions in armaments agreed between Presidents Bush and Gorbachev with signature of START Treaty. Signing of Treaty of Maastricht on European Union.

1992

Russian agreements with Baltic states on withdrawal of troops and with Ukraine on fleet.

1996

Hungary and Romania sign treaty to respect mutual borders and protect rights of Hungarian minority in Transylvania. Russian peace accord signed with Chechnya rebels (May). Agreement between Russia and China on troop reductions along their common frontier (December).

1997

Founding Act signed (agreement between Russia and NATO). Treaty of Amsterdam is signed (the successor to the Treaty of Maastricht). Only limited progress towards further European integration.

1998

Agreement on future EU defence policy concluded at St Malo between Britain and France (December).

1999

Anglo-Irish Treaty (December) to implement the Good Friday Agreement of 10 April 1998.

2002

Establishment of NATO–Russia Council (NRC) (May).

2004

Expansion of NATO to include Baltic States as well as Bulgaria and Romania. The largest expansion in the history of NATO (May).

EUROPE AND THE WIDER WORLD: IMPERIALISM AND DECOLONIZATION

1760

(Jan.) Battle of Windewash ends French power in India.
(Sept.) Montreal taken by British forces. Under secret agreement with East India Co., Mir Kasim becomes Nawab of Bengal.

1761

(Jan.) Shah Alam defeated by British at Patna. Pondicherry taken by Coote. Britain conquers Cuba and Antilles.

1762

Under secret treaty, France cedes Louisiana to Spain.

1763

(Feb.) Treaty of Paris: all French possessions in North America east of Mississippi, Grenada, St Vincent, Tobago, Windward Islands, Dominica and Senegal ceded to Britain, Britain returns Guadeloupe to France. Spain cedes Florida to Britain.

1764

(Oct.) British defeat Nawab of Oudh at Buxar

1765

(Mar.) Britain passes Stamp Act affecting thirteen colonies. Clive appointed Governor of Bengal. Privileges of the East India Co. are confirmed and increased by the Mogul.

1766

(Mar.) Britain passes Declaratory Act, affirming right to tax American colonies. First Mysore War breaks out. British occupy Turks and Caicos Islands and Falkland Islands.
(Nov.) Under treaty, Nizam Ali cedes Northern Circars to Britain.

1770

French East India Co. dissolved. Britain claims New South Wales.
(Mar.) Boston Massacre. Spanish expedition from Buenos Aires expels British from Falkland Islands.

1771

(Jan.) Spain surrenders Falkland Islands to Britain after threat of war.

1772

(Feb.) Boston Assembly threatens secession unless rights of American colonies are upheld.
(Apr.) Hastings becomes Governor of Bengal. Parliamentary enquiry into Clive's administration begins.

1773

Lord North's Regulating Act: British East India Co. to rule in India in name of Crown.
(Dec.) Boston Tea Party.

1774

(July) By Treaty of Kutchuk-Kainardji, Russia acquires mouth of Dneiper and Crimea from the Ottoman Empire.

(Sept.) Quebec Act makes Canada a Crown Colony and confirms rights of French Canadians. First Congress of Thirteen Colonies (except Georgia) meets at Philadelphia.

1775

(Apr.) Battles of Lexington and Concord (in Massachusetts).
(May) Second Congress meets.
(June) Washington is appointed American Commander-in-Chief. Austria acquires Delagoa Bay (Mozambique).

1776

(July) American colonies declare independence. Viceroyalty of River Plate formed (Argentina, Bolivia, Paraguay and Uruguay).

1777

Equatorial Guinea ceded by Portugal to Spain. France enters American War of Independence against Britain.
(Oct.) General Burgoyne surrenders at Saratoga.
(Nov.) Confederation Articles issued as first constitution of USA.

1778

Britain takes St Lucia.
(Feb.) France and America establish alliance.
(Sept.) Dominica seized by France. Annabon and Fernando Pó become Spanish possessions.

1779

First Maratha War begins. French cede Senegal and Gorée to Britain.

1780

Second Mysore War begins.

1781

Portugal acquires Delagoa Bay from Austria.
(Oct.) Cornwallis surrenders at Yorktown.

1782

(Feb.) Britain cedes Minorca.

1783

(Sept.) Treaty of Versailles: Britain recognizes American independence, recovers possessions in West Indies, and retains Gibraltar; France recovers stations in India, Senegal, St Lucia, Tobago and possessions in East Indies; Florida is restored to Spain. Russia annexes Georgia from the Ottoman Empire.

1784

(Aug.) Under India Act, political and commercial responsibilities of East India Co. are separated.

1785

(June) Rajah of Kedah (in Malaya) cedes Penang to Britain.

1786

Cornwallis is appointed Governor-General of India.

1787

France intervenes in Annam (Indo-China). Freetown, Sierra Leone, is founded as settlement for freed slaves.

1788

(Jan.) Convict settlement established at Port Jackson, Sydney.
(Feb.) Trial of Warren Hastings opens.

1789

(Dec.) Third Mysore War begins.

1790

(June) Maratha princes form alliance with Britain.
(July) Nizam of Hyderabad forms alliance with Britain.

(Oct.) Spain cedes British Columbia to Britain.

1791

(May) Under Canada Act, Canada becomes two provinces (Upper and Lower Canada) each having its own government subject to a joint Governor-General.

1792

(Jan.) Peace of Jassy between Russia and the Ottoman Empire: Russia acquires coast of Black Sea and Ochakov fortress; the Ottoman Empire recognizes Russia's annexation of Crimea.
(Feb.) Tipu Sahib, Sultan of Mysore, defeated at Seringapatam and cedes half his territory to the British. Sierra Leone Co. receives its Charter.

1793

British occupy French settlements in India.

1794

Slavery abolished in French colonies.
(Feb.) British capture Seychelles, Martinique and St Lucia.

1795

(Feb.) Dutch cede Ceylon to Britain.
(Apr.) Warren Hastings acquitted of accusation of financial misconduct.
(June) French retake St Lucia.
(Sept.) British occupy Cape of Good Hope. Spain cedes half of San Domingo to France.

1796

British take Demerara, Essequibo and Berbice (in Guiana).

1797

(Feb.) British seize Trinidad from Spain, and St Lucia.

1798

(Sept.) British take Honduras from Spain. Nizam accepts Treaty of Hyderabad with British.
(Nov.) British seize Minorca from Spain.

1798–1801

Egyptian expedition (see p. 204).

1800

(Sept.) British capture Malta from the French.
(Oct.) France buys Louisiana from Spain.

1801

(Mar.) British capture Danish and Swedish islands in West Indies.
(June) Portugal cedes part of Guiana to Spain.
(Sept.) Russia annexes Georgia.
(Oct.) France restores Egypt to the Ottoman Empire.

1802

(Dec.) East India Co. assumes control of Peshawar.

1803

(Apr.) France sells Louisiana to USA.
(June) British take Tobago.
(Aug.) Second Maratha War begins.
(Sept.) British seize Dutch Guiana.

1806

(Jan.) British reoccupy Cape of Good Hope.

1807

Britain abolishes slave trade. Heligoland seized by Britain from Denmark. Sierra Leone and The Gambia become Crown colonies.

1809

British take Martinique and Guadeloupe from France.

(Apr.) Treaty concluded between British and Sikhs.

(Sept.) Russia acquires Finland.

1810

Sukhumi (in Georgia) annexed by Russia from the Ottoman Empire.

(July) British occupy Mauritius.

1811

(Aug.) British occupy Java.

(Oct.) Paraguay renounces links with Spain and Argentina.

1812

(May) Treaty of Bucharest: Russia receives Bessarabia.

1813

Colombia declares itself independent of Spain.

(July) East India Co. loses its monopoly of Indian trade. Under terms of Peace of Gulistan, Russia receives Caucasus region from Persia.

1814

Following defeat of Napoleon, Britain acquires St Lucia, Malta, Mauritius, British Guiana, Seychelles, Windward Islands and Cape of Good Hope as recognized colonies. Uruguay declares itself independent of Spain.

1815

Britain establishes protectorate over Ionian Islands.

(Oct.) British occupy Ascension Island.

(Dec.) Brazil becomes an empire under John, Prince Regent of Portugal.

1816

Chile declares itself independent of Spain.

(Dec.) Java is restored to Dutch.

1817

(Dec.) Third Maratha War destroys Maratha power. Possessions in Guiana and Senegal restored to France.

1818

(Jan.) Rajputana States come under British protection.

1819

(Feb.) East India Co. founds Singapore.

(Dec.) Republic of Colombia established.

1820

(Oct.) Spain cedes Florida to USA.

1821

Amalgamation of North West Co. and Hudson's Bay Co. Royal African Co. dissolved and its possessions taken over by British Crown.

(July) Peru declares itself independent of Spain.

(Nov.) Panama declares itself independent of Spain and unites with Colombia.

1822

California becomes part of Republic of Mexico.

(Sept.) Brazil proclaims its independence of Portugal.

(Oct.) Dom Pedro proclaimed Emperor of Brazil.

1823

New South Wales becomes a Crown colony.

(Dec.) Promulgation of 'Monroe Doctrine'.

1824

(Feb.) First Burmese War breaks out.

1825

(Aug.) Portugal recognizes independence of Brazil. Bolivia and Uruguay declare themselves independent of Spain.

230

1826

Penang, Malacca and Singapore are joined to form Straits Settlements.

1827

Russia seizes Erivan from Persia. Spain leases Equatorial Guinea to Britain.
(Jan.) Peru withdraws from union with Colombia.

1828

(Feb.) By Peace of Turkmentchai, Russia acquires part of Armenia from the Ottoman Empire and Azerbaijan from Persia.

1829

(Sept.) Under Treaty of Adrianople, Russia receives land south of Caucasus from the Ottoman Empire.

1830

Edward Gibbon Wakefield founds the Colonization Society.
(June) French invade Algiers. East India Co. annexes Mysore and Cachar (in Assam).

1832

(Apr.) Britain proclaims sovereignty over Falkland Islands.

1833

East India Co. ceases trading. Slavery abolished in British Empire.

1834

Britain authorizes colonization of South Australia.

1835

Boers begin Great Trek from Cape Colony.

1837

(Jan.) Boer settlers found Natalia. Rebellion of Papineau and Mackenzie in Canada.

1838

Earl of Durham becomes Governor-General of Canada.
(Oct.) First Afghan War begins.
(Dec.) Boers defeat Zulus on Blood River, Natal.

1839

Britain annexes Aden. First 'Opium War' between Britain and China. Natal Republic established. Durham Report published.

1840

(Feb.) Treaty of Waitangi secures British sovereignty over New Zealand. Upper and Lower Canada reunited under a single administration. Transportation of convicts to New South Wales ends.

1841

British forces retreat from Kabul. Sultan of Brunei cedes Sarawak to Britain.

1842

(Jan.) British forces in Afghanistan suffer major defeat.
(Aug.) Treaty of Nanking ends war between Britain and China: Hong Kong is ceded to Britain and five treaty ports are opened to British trade. Ashburton Treaty defines Maine boundary between USA and Canada. British conquest of Assam and Burma begins. Tahiti becomes a French protectorate. New South Wales gains representative government.

1843

Maori Wars begin. British conquer Sind and annex Natal. France acquires Ivory Coast and Dahomey, and establishes protectorate over Mayotte (Comoro Islands).

1844

Spain re-acquires Fernando Pó.

1845

Anglo–French expedition against Madagascar.
(Dec.) First Sikh War begins.

1846

Sultan of Brunei cedes Labuan to Britain.
(June) Oregon Treaty defines boundary of
Canada at 49th Parallel.
(Dec.) British establish control over Punjab.

1847

Straits Settlements become a Crown colony.
Governor of Cape Colony becomes High
Commissioner of South Africa.
(Aug.) Liberia becomes independent.

1848

Orange Free State becomes a Crown colony.
(Mar.) Second Sikh War begins. Nova Scotia
becomes first British colony to attain responsible government.

1849

(Mar.) Britain annexes Punjab.
(May) Britain repeals Navigation Acts. Portugal
claims sovereignty over Macao. France founds
Libreville (Gabon) as settlement for freed
slaves.

1850

(Aug.) Britain buys Denmark's Gold Coast
possessions.

1851

Australian gold rush. Victoria becomes a
separate colony.
(Sept.) Cuban revolt suppressed by Spain.

1852

Second Burmese War: Burma becomes a
province of India.
(Jan.) Sand River Convention establishes
South African Republic. New Zealand gains
responsible government.

1853

Cape Colony gains representative government.
(Dec.) Britain annexes Nagpur (India). Russia
annexes Khiva (in Central Asia). France annexes
New Caledonia (in Pacific).

1854

(Feb.) Under Bloemfontein Convention, Orange
Free State gains self-rule.

1855

New South Wales, Victoria and Newfoundland
gain responsible government.

1856

(Feb.) Britain annexes Oudh.
(Mar.) At Paris Peace Congress, Russia cedes
Bessarabia.
(May) Natal becomes a separate colony. South
Australia and Tasmania gain responsible
government.
(Oct.) War between Britain and China renewed.

1857

Port of Dakar founded in Senegal (French
West Africa)
(Mar.) Indian Uprising (Mutiny) begins at
Meerut.
(Dec.) British and French forces take Canton.

1858

Britain, France and China conclude Treaty of
Tientsin, giving European traders access to
Chinese ports.
(Nov.) British Crown assumes direct control
of India, replacing rule of East India Co.
(Dec.) British Columbia becomes a Crown
colony. French begin to occupy Mekong Delta
area, Cochin China.

1859

Construction of Suez Canal begins. French
occupy Saigon. Timor divided between
Portuguese and Dutch. Sir George Grey,

Governor of Cape Colony, proposes South African federation.
(May) Queensland gains responsible government.

1860

Britain attains full free trade. Kowloon Peninsula ceded to Britain.
(Sept.) Anglo–French occupation of Peking.
(Apr.) Maori Wars resume. French occupy Gabon.

1861

(Mar.) Spain annexes San Domingo.
(Aug.) Britain annexes Lagos.
(Oct.) French expedition to Mexico.

1862

(Apr.) France annexes Cochin China and buys Obok (opposite Aden).

1863

(Aug.) France establishes protectorate over Cambodia.
(Nov.) Britain cedes Ionian Islands to Greece.

1864

(Apr.) Maximilian proclaimed Emperor of Mexico. Russia annexes Abkhazia (Central Asia).

1865

Morant rising in Jamaica suppressed.
(Sept.) Second Maori War ends.
(Oct.) Transportation of convicts to Australia abolished.

1866

French troops evacuate Mexico.

1867

(Mar.) USA buys Alaska from Russia.
(June) Emperor Maximilian executed in Mexico.

(July) British North America Act creates Dominion of Canada as self-governing federation. Russia establishes Governor Generalship of Turkestan. Straits Settlements become a Crown colony.

1868

(Jan.) British expedition against Ethiopia.
(Mar.) Britain claims Basutoland.
(May) Russia occupies Samarkand.

1869

(Mar.) Territorial rights of Hudson's Bay Co. transferred to Dominion of Canada. Rebellion of Louis Riel in Canada.
(Nov.) Suez Canal opens.

1870

Manitoba enters Dominion of Canada. Western Australia gains representative government.

1871

British Columbia joins Dominion of Canada. Basutoland united with Cape Colony.
(Oct.) Britain annexes diamond-producing area around Kimberley, Griqualand West.

1872

(Feb.) Netherlands sells Gold Coast trading stations to Britain.
(Oct.) Cape Colony gains responsible government.

1873

(Apr.) Beginning of British expedition against Ashanti in Gold Coast.
(June) Sultan of Zanzibar abolishes slave trade under British pressure.
(Aug.) Russia claims suzerainty over Khiva and Bokhara.

1874

(Mar.) Treaty of Fomena ends Ashanti War and promises Britain freedom of trade in Gold

Coast. France declares Annam a protectorate and secures trading rights in Southern China.
(Oct.) Britain annexes Fiji Islands.

1875

Lord Carnarvon reveals proposals for South African Confederation.
(Nov.) Britain buys majority holding in Suez Canal Co.

1876

Victoria created Empress of India.
(Apr.) Khedive of Egypt suspends payment on treasury bills.
(Sept.) Brussels Conference leads to formation of *Association Internationale Africaine* by Leopold II of the Belgians.

1877

(Apr.) Britain annexes Transvaal.

1878

(Mar.) Britain occupies Walvis Bay (South-West Africa).
(July) Britain occupies Cyprus following Treaty of Berlin. Russia acquires Bessarabia. Anglo–French Dual Control established in Egypt.
(Sept.) Second Afghan War begins.
(Nov.) Leopold II founds *Comité d'Etudes du Haut Congo* in order to finance occupation of Congo.

1879

(Jan.) Anglo–Zulu War begins. Treaty between Germany and Samoa initiates international rivalry in Pacific.
(Sept.) British Resident in Kabul murdered.
(Oct.) Britain invades Afghanistan.
(Dec.) Transvaal Republic proclaimed. Algeria enters semi-colonial relationship with France. Portuguese Guinea becomes a separate colony.

1880

(June) France annexes Tahiti.

(Sept.) Britain recognizes independence of Afghanistan.
(Oct.) Transvaal declares its independence. First Boer War begins.

1881

(Feb.) Boers defeat British at Majuba Hill.
(May) Tunisia becomes a French protectorate.
(Aug.) By Pretoria Convention, Britain recognizes independence of Transvaal.
(Sept.) Egyptian nationalist rising under Colonel Arabi. Mahdist rising in the Sudan. Sino–French War over future of Annam.
(Dec.) Stanley founds Leopoldville, Congo.

1882

Bahrain becomes a British protectorate.
(Apr.) French occupy Hanoi.
(July) British naval bombardment of Alexandria.
(Sept.) British defeat Egyptians at Tel-el-Kebir. Britain occupies Egypt and Sudan.
(Dec.) Italy occupies Assab, Eritrea.

1883

(May) Kruger becomes President of South African Republic.
(June) French commence invasion of Madagascar.
(Aug.) Treaty of Hué secures French control of Annam and Tonkin.
(Nov.) After military defeat, Britain decides to evacuate Sudan.

1884

(Jan.) Russia occupies Merv in Central Asia.
(Feb.) Under terms of London Convention, Britain recognizes Transvaal as South African Republic.
(Apr.–Aug.) Germany occupies South-West Africa, Togoland and Cameroons.
(July) Anglo–French treaty concerning Mekong Basin. Basutoland, Somali Coast, Nigeria and remainder of New Guinea become British protectorates.

(Oct.) Fall of Omdurman.

(Nov.) Britain annexes Walvis Bay.

1885

(Jan.) Death of General Gordon at Khartoum.

(Feb.) Congo Free State established under Leopold II. Italy occupies Massawa, Eritrea. Germany declares protectorates over Tanganyika and Zanzibar.

(Mar.) Russia occupies Penjdeh, on Afghan–Turkestan border. Northern Bechuanaland becomes a British protectorate.

(May) Germany annexes northern New Guinea and Bismarck Archipelago.

(June) Lower Niger area becomes a British protectorate. France establishes protectorate over Madagascar.

(Dec.) Indian National Congress founded.

1886

(Jan.) Britain annexes Upper Burma.

(June) France establishes colonies of Gabon and Congo.

(July) Royal Niger Co. receives charter.

(July–Nov.) Britain and Germany define their African and Pacific interests.

(Oct.) Socotra (Gulf of Aden) becomes a British protectorate. Gold discovered in Transvaal.

1887

British Somaliland declared a protectorate. Indo-Chinese Union established.

(June) Britain annexes Zululand.

(July) Anglo–Russian agreement over Afghanistan.

(Oct.) India absorbs Baluchistan,

(Nov.) Anglo–French condominium over New Hebrides agreed.

1888

(May) North Borneo, Brunei and Sarawak become a British protectorate. British East Africa Co. receives charter.

(Oct.) Matabele Chief Lobengula grants Rudd Concession. Pacific island of Nauru becomes a German protectorate.

1889

(Jan.) Ivory Coast becomes a French protectorate.

(May) Treaty of Ucciali between Italy and Ethiopia.

(June) Samoa becomes a British, German and US condominium.

(July) Brussels Act on slavery.

(Oct.) Rhodes's British South Africa Co. receives charter.

1890

Germany occupies Rwanda–Urundi.

(July) Britain cedes Heligoland to Germany in return for Zanzibar and Pemba. Rhodes becomes Prime Minister of Cape Colony.

(Aug.) Anglo–French agreement over Nigeria. Anglo–Portuguese agreement over Zambesi and Congo.

(Oct.) Western Australia attains responsible government.

(Dec.) Britain occupies Sikkim, Uganda and Mashonaland.

1891

(Mar.) Anglo–Italian agreement over Ethiopia.

(Apr.) Anglo–Portuguese treaty recognizes British protectorate in Nyasaland.

(May) Work begins on Trans-Siberian railway (completed 1904).

1892

Gold discovered in Western Australia.

(Oct.) Anglo–German agreement over Cameroons.

1893

(May) Natal gains responsible government.

(July) Matabele War leads to British occupation of Bulawayo.

(Oct.) Siam cedes left bank of Mekong to France.

(Nov.) Britain and Germany agree on their respective frontiers in West Africa.

Frontier between India and Afghanistan defined. Dahomey and Laos become French protectorates.

(Dec.) Anglo–French agreement over Siam.

1894

(Jan.) Britain occupies Matabeleland.

(Apr.) Uganda becomes a British protectorate.

(July) Italy begins expedition to occupy Ethiopia. Togoland becomes a German protectorate.

(Nov.) France begins final military conquest of Madagascar.

1895

British East African protectorate established.

(June) Joseph Chamberlain appointed British Colonial Secretary.

(Dec.) Jameson Raid into Transvaal fails.

1896

(Jan.) Rhodes resigns premiership of Cape Colony. William II sends 'Kruger Telegram'. Britain and France agree on their mutual interests in Siam. Second Ashanti War.

(Mar.) Italian forces defeated at Adowa, Ethiopia.

(June) Marchand begins mission from Gabon to Nile at Fashoda.

(Aug.) France annexes Madagascar. Rising in Philippines against Spanish rule.

(Sept.) France and Italy reach agreement over Tunis. Russia and China reach agreement over Manchuria.

(Oct.) By Treaty of Addis Ababa, Italy revokes protectorate over Ethiopia.

1897

Milner becomes High Commissioner of Cape Colony.

(Sept.) Britain and France agree over Tunis.

(Nov.) Germany occupies Kiao-Chow Bay (in Shantung Peninsula, China) as a naval base.

(Dec.) Russia occupies Port Arthur (China).

1898

(Mar.) Chinese treaty ports (Kiao-Chow, Port Arthur, Kwangchow, Wei-Hai-Wei) leased to Germany, Russia, France and Britain respectively.

(Apr.) USA declares war on Spain.

(June) Britain and France conclude Niger Convention.

(July) Marchand reaches Fashoda.

(Aug.) Anglo–German agreement over Portuguese African colonies.

(Sept.) Kitchener defeats Mahdist army at Omdurman and encounters Marchand at Fashoda, precipitating the Fashoda incident (see p. 342).

(Nov.) France evacuates Fashoda. Sudan declared an Anglo–Egyptian condominium.

(Dec.) Treaty of Paris: Spain cedes Cuba, Puerto Rico, Philippines and Guam to USA.

1899

(Mar.) Anglo–French agreement over Nile Valley.

(Aug.) Britain buys Niger Co.'s territories.

(Oct.) Second Boer War begins.

1900

(May) Britain annexes Tonga Islands and Orange Free State. Boxer rising in China.

(Sept.) Britain annexes Transvaal.

(Oct.) Russia completes occupation of Manchuria.

(Dec.) France and Italy secretly agree over respective claims to Morocco and Tripolitania.

1901

(Jan.) Commonwealth of Australia established. North West Frontier Province created in India as buffer with Afghanistan.

(June) Cook Islands annexed to New Zealand.

1902

(May) Peace of Vereeniging ends Boer War.

(Nov.) Franco–Italian agreement over Northern Africa.

1903

(July) Negotiations between Russia and Japan over Manchuria collapse.

1904

(Jan.) Herrero rising in South-West Africa.

(Feb.) Outbreak of Russo–Japanese War.

(Apr.) Anglo–French *entente* resolves outstanding colonial disputes.

(Sept.) Hottentot rising in South-West Africa.

(Oct.) Federation of French West Africa created. France and Spain reach agreement over Morocco.

1905

Partition of Bengal.

(Mar.) Moroccan Crisis.

(Sept.) Treaty of Portsmouth ends Russo–Japanese War: Russia cedes Port Arthur and Talienwan to Japan.

1906

(Jan.) Algeçiras Conference meets to discuss future of Morocco.

(July) Britain, France and Italy agree on independence of Ethiopia.

(Aug.) Anglo–Chinese Convention on Tibet.

(Dec.) All-India Muslim League formed. German Reichstag opposes funding colonial wars. Transvaal and Orange Free State given self-government.

1907

Australia and New Zealand achieve dominion status.

(Aug.) Anglo–Russian Convention on Persia, Afghanistan and Tibet.

1908

(June) Gabon, Congo and other territories federated as French Equatorial Africa.

(Aug.) Leopold II transfers sovereignty over Congo Free State to Belgium.

1909

(Feb.) Franco–German agreement over Morocco. 'Morley–Minto reforms' in India introduce participation of Indians in government.

1910

(July) Union of South Africa established, with dominion status. Russia and Japan reach agreement over Manchuria and Korea.

1911

(May) French occupation of Moroccan capital results in German gunboat *Panther* being sent to Agadir (July).

(Aug.) Italy declares war on the Ottoman Empire and seizes Tripoli.

(Nov.) France and Germany reach agreement on interests of France and Spain in Morocco.

1912

(Mar.) Under Treaty of Fez, Morocco becomes a French protectorate.

(Oct.) Italy receives Tripoli from the Ottoman Empire under Treaty of Ouchy.

(Nov.) Spain establishes a protectorate over her Moroccan territories.

1914

(Jan.) North and South Nigeria united under a single Governor-General.

(Aug.) Outbreak of First World War.

(Aug.–Sept.) Allied troops begin to occupy German colonies.

(Nov.) Britain annexes Cyprus.

(Dec.) Egypt declared a British protectorate.

1916

(Apr.) Easter Rising in Dublin.

1917

(Aug.) Montagu Declaration states Britain's eventual goal in India is self-government.

(Nov.) Balfour Declaration promises a national home in Palestine for the Jews.

1919

(Apr.) Massacre of Indians at Amritsar by British troops under Brigadier-General Dyer.
(June) Under Treaty of Versailles, Germany relinquishes all her colonial possessions. These are redistributed as mandates of the League of Nations among the Allies. Nationalist rising in Egypt.

1920

(Apr.) Transjordan becomes a British mandated territory.
(July) British East Africa is divided into colony of Kenya and protectorate of Uganda.
(Aug.) Gandhi begins non-co-operation campaign in India.

1921

(Jan.) New All-India parliament meets; India is given fiscal and tariff autonomy.
(Mar.) Britain accepts League of Nations mandate over Iraq.
(Dec.) Southern Ireland is granted dominion status as the Irish Free State. Washington agreement between USA, Britain, France and Japan over Pacific territories.

1922

(Feb.) Britain withdraws protectorate over Egypt.
(July) League of Nations Council confirms British and French mandates over Togo, Cameroons, Tanganyika and Palestine.
(Aug.) Arab Congress rejects Britain's Palestine mandate.

1923

(Aug.) Rwanda–Urundi becomes a Belgian mandated territory.
(Oct.) Southern Rhodesia becomes a self-governing colony.

1924

(Apr.) Protectorate of Northern Rhodesia established.

1925

(May) Cyprus becomes a British Crown colony.
(July) Insurrection against French rule begins in Syria.

1926

(Nov.) Imperial Conference declares that Britain and her dominions are autonomous and equal though 'freely associated as members of the British Commonwealth of Nations'. Communist rising begins in Java against Dutch rule.

1927

Simon Commission sent to investigate the effect of the Montagu–Chelmsford reforms of 1919.

1928

(Aug.) Italy and Ethiopia conclude treaty of friendship.

1930

(Mar.) Gandhi initiates civil disobedience campaign in India, Nehru declares Indian independence.
(Oct.) Britain evacuates base at Wei-Hai-Wei.
(Nov.) Round Table Conference on Indian self-government meets.

1931

(Mar.) 'Gandhi–Irwin Pact' ends civil disobedience in India.
(Dec.) Statute of Westminster defines status of dominions, and allows them to claim full sovereignty.

1932

(July) Imperial Economic Conference meets at Ottawa and introduces limited preferential tariffs within the British Empire.
(Oct.) Iraq becomes independent.

1934

(Apr.) Gandhi once more calls off civil disobedience.

(Dec.) Incident on border between Ethiopia and Italian Somaliland heightens tensions.

1935

(Aug.) Government of India Act gives India new constitution with provincial self-government and separates Burma and Aden from India.

(Oct.) Italy invades Ethiopia. League of Nations imposes sanctions against Italy.

1936

(May) Italian forces occupy Addis Ababa.

(July) League of Nations withdraws sanctions against Italy.

(Aug.) Anglo–Egyptian treaty re-defines Britain's rights in Egypt.

(Sept.) France agrees to grant Syria independence in 1939.

1937

(Nov.) Rising in Tunisia against French rule.

1940

(Aug.) Britain evacuates Somaliland following Italian invasion.

(Sept.) Italians invade Egypt. Japan invades Indo-China.

1941

(Jan.) British forces begin to occupy Italian East Africa.

(June) British and Free French occupy Syria.

(Dec.) Japan occupies Hong Kong and Siam.

1942

(Jan.) Japanese forces begin occupation of British, French, US and Dutch possessions in South-East Asia and Western Pacific.

(Feb.) Singapore surrenders to Japanese.

(Apr.) Indian nationalists reject offer of self-government made by Cripps.

1944

(Jan.) Free French hold Brazzaville Conference to discuss future of French possessions in Africa. Ho Chi Minh proclaims Vietnamese independence from France.

1946

(Mar.) Transjordan becomes independent (formerly a British mandate).

(Apr.) Malayan Union established.

(May) Sarawak is ceded to Britain.

(July) North Borneo becomes a British colony.

(Oct.) The constitution of the 'French Union' confirmed by referendum.

1947

(Mar.) Netherlands recognizes independence of Indonesia.

(June) Partition of India announced.

(Aug.) India and Pakistan become independent.

(Sept.) Britain announces withdrawal from Palestine.

1948

(Jan.) Burma becomes independent and leaves the Commonwealth.

(Feb.) Malayan Union becomes Federation of Malaya. Ceylon becomes independent.

(May) State of Israel established. Conflict with communist guerrillas in Malaya begins.

1949

(Apr.) Eire withdraws from Commonwealth.

(July) Laos becomes independent of France.

(Dec.) Netherlands grants formal independence to Indonesia.

1950

(Jan.) Dutch colonies in Latin America are promised autonomy.

1951

(Jan.) Gold Coast constitution becomes operative.

(Dec.) Libya becomes independent.

1952

Beginning of Mau Mau conflict in Kenya.
(Jan.) Nigerian constitution becomes operative.
(Sept.) Eritrea is united with Ethiopia.

1953

(Feb.) Anglo–Egyptian agreement on Sudan reached.
(Aug.) Southern Rhodesia, Nyasaland and Northern Rhodesia are united in the Federation of Rhodesia and Nyasaland.
(Nov.) Cambodia becomes independent of France.

1954

(May) French forces surrender to Vietminh at Dien Bien Phu, Vietnam.
(July) French Assembly approves Indo-China settlement.
(Nov.) National Liberation Front begins revolt in Algeria.

1955

(June) French agreement on Tunisian home rule.

1956

(Jan.) Sudan becomes independent (formerly under Anglo–Egyptian rule).
(Mar.) France recognizes independence of Morocco and Tunisia.
(Nov.) Suez Crisis: Britain and France intervene in war between Egypt and Israel. Mau Mau insurgency in Kenya suppressed.

1957

(Mar.) Gold Coast becomes independent as Ghana.
(Aug.) Federation of Malaya becomes independent.

1958

(Jan.) Federation of West Indies is established. French Guinea becomes independent.
(May) Revolt of French settlers and army in Algeria.

1960

(Jan.) Cameroun gains independence from France.
(Feb.) Harold Macmillan makes 'Wind of change' speech.
(Apr.) Togo becomes independent from France.
(June) Mali and Madagascar win independence from France.
(Aug.) Ivory Coast, Dahomey, Upper Volta, Niger, Chad, Gabon, (French) Congo, and Central African Republic gain independence from France. Cyprus becomes independent. British Somaliland gains independence and unites with Italian Somaliland to form the Somali Republic (Somalia).
(Oct.) Nigeria becomes independent.
(Nov.) Mauritania and Senegal win independence from France.

1961

(Mar.) South Africa leaves the Commonwealth.
(Apr.) Army revolt in Algeria collapses. Sierra Leone becomes independent.
(June) Northern Cameroons (British) unites with Nigeria.
(Oct.) Southern Cameroons (French) unites with Cameroun.
(Dec.) Tanganyika becomes independent.

1962

(Jan.) Western Samoa gains independence.
(Mar.) French and Algerians agree to ceasefire.
(July) Algeria becomes independent. Rwanda and Burundi become independent (formerly under Belgian rule).
(Aug.) Federation of West Indies dissolves when Jamaica and Trinidad and Tobago become independent.
(Oct.) Uganda becomes independent.

1963

(Sept.) Federation of Malaysia established, including Malaya, Singapore, Sarawak, and North Borneo.
(Dec.) Zanzibar and Kenya become independent. Federation of Rhodesia and Nyasaland is dissolved.

1964

(July) Nyasaland becomes independent as Malawi.

(Sept.) Malta becomes independent.

(Oct.) Northern Rhodesia becomes independent as Zambia.

1965

(Feb.) The Gambia becomes independent.

(July) The Maldive Islands gain independence.

(Nov.) Southern Rhodesia unilaterally declares its independence.

1966

(May) British Guiana becomes independent as Guyana.

(Sept.) Bechuanaland becomes independent as Botswana.

(Oct.) Basutoland becomes independent as Lesotho.

(Nov.) Barbados becomes independent.

(Dec.) Negotiations between Britain and Rhodesia aboard HMS *Tiger* collapse.

1967

(Nov.) Aden gains independence.

1968

(Jan.) Nauru becomes independent.

(Mar.) Mauritius becomes independent.

(Aug.) French military support given to Chad to combat rebels.

(Sept.) Swaziland becomes independent.

(Oct.) Spanish Equatorial Guinea becomes independent. Talks between Britain and Rhodesia aboard HMS *Fearless* reach stalemate.

1969

(Mar.) British police despatched to Anguilla. French troops called into Chad.

1970

(Mar.) Rhodesia declares itself a republic.

(June) Tonga becomes independent.

(Oct.) Fiji Islands become independent.

1971

(Aug.) Bahrain becomes independent.

(Sept.) Qatar becomes independent.

(Nov.) Oman becomes independent.

(Dec.) Britain leaves Gulf States.

1973

(July) Bahamas become independent.

1974

(Feb.) Grenada becomes independent.

(Sept.) Portuguese Guinea gains independence as Guinea–Bissau.

1975

(June) Mozambique gains independence from Portugal.

(July) Cape Verde Islands, São Tomé e Principe gain independence from Portugal. Comoro Islands declare themselves independent of France.

(Sept.) Papua New Guinea becomes independent.

(Nov.) Angola gains independence from Portugal. Surinam is granted independence by the Netherlands.

1976

(Feb.) Spain relinquishes all rights over Western Sahara.

(June) Seychelles becomes independent.

(July) Timor becomes a province of Indonesia.

1977

(June) French territory of the Afars and Issas becomes independent as Djibouti.

(Sept.) Anglo–American peace plan for Rhodesia receives support of 'front-line states' and provides for first elections on the basis of universal suffrage in April 1979, though still opposed by major guerrilla armies.

1978

(July) Solomon Islands become independent.

(Oct.) Ellice Islands gain independence as Tuvalu.

(Nov.) Dominica becomes independent.

1979

(Feb.) St Lucia gains independence. French paratroops sent to Chad (withdrawn in May).

(July) Kiribati becomes independent (formerly the Gilbert Islands).

(Oct.) St Vincent and the Grenadines gain independence.

(Dec.) Lancaster House agreement on future of Rhodesia. Ceasefire arranged and constitutional agreement reached. Commonwealth troops to supervise elections. Soviet troops invade Afghanistan. Widespread guerrilla resistance begins.

1980

(Feb.) Elections in Rhodesia result in sweeping victory for Mugabe's ZANU.

(Apr.) Rhodesia becomes independent republic of Zimbabwe.

(July) Vanuatu becomes independent (formerly known as New Hebrides).

1981

Belize becomes independent republic.

1982

(Apr.) Argentine troops invade Falkland Islands and South Georgia. Britain organizes task force to recapture islands.

(June) Argentine force in Falklands surrenders.

1983

(June) French troops sent to assist Chadian troops against rebel and Libyan forces.

1984

Brunei becomes independent.

(Sept.) Agreement with China, whereby Hong Kong reverts to Chinese sovereignty after 1 July 1997.

(Dec.) Band Aid pop stars led by Bob Geldof agree to hold concerts and promote charity record to raise aid for Ethiopian famine.

1985

(July) Live Aid concerts in London and Philadelphia raise £40 million for famine relief in Ethiopia.

1986

(Apr.) United Kingdom permits use of US bases in Britain for air strikes in Libya.

1987

Western powers, including United States, Britain, France and Italy, step up naval presence in the Persian Gulf and Straits of Hormuz after attacks on tankers by Iranian mines and gunboats. France sends 7,000 soldiers and riot police to quell unrest in New Caledonia prior to a referendum on independence.

1988

President Gorbachev agrees to begin the removal of Soviet troops from Afghanistan from May 1988, to be completed by February 1989.

1989

Last Soviet troops leave Afghanistan on 15 February.

1990

Britain, France and Italy send naval and air forces to Saudi Arabia and the Gulf to join US military deployment following Iraqi invasion of Kuwait. Other European states offer financial aid for relief of refugees and to compensate states implementing UN sanctions against Iraq.

1991

(Jan.) Allied forces launch air assault against Iraq and occupied Kuwait, Operation Desert Storm.

(Feb.) Allied land offensive opens in Gulf (24th) overwhelming Iraqi forces and forcing wholesale retreat from Kuwait (26th).

1994

(June) South Africa rejoins Commonwealth after historic multi-racial elections (1st).

1995

Mozambique (former Portuguese colony) and Cameroon join Commonwealth.

1997

(July) Return of Hong Kong to China (1st).

1999

Return of Portuguese enclave of Macao to China.

2002

(May) Final achievement of independence by East Timor.

2003

(Mar.) Allied forces attack Iraq to overthrow Saddam Hussein.

IV
SOCIAL AND ECONOMIC HISTORY

COMPARATIVE POPULATION OF MAJOR EUROPEAN COUNTRIES, 1750–2004*

(millions, rounded up to the nearest 100,000)

	c.1750	1800	1850	1900	1950	2004
Austria	—	14.0	17.5	26.2	6.9	8.1
Belarus	—	—	—	—	—	9.9
Belgium	—	3.1	4.3	6.7	8.5	10.3
Bosnia and Herzegovina	—	—	—	—	—	3.9
Bulgaria	—	—	—	3.8	7.0	7.9
Croatia	—	—	—	—	—	4.4
Czech Republic	—	—	—	—	—	10.2
Czechoslovakia	—	—	—	—	12.3	—
Denmark	—	0.9	1.4	2.5	4.3	5.4
Finland	0.4	0.8	1.6	2.7	4.0	5.2
France	21.0	27.4	35.8	38.5	42.8	59.4
Germany	18.0	23.0	33.4	56.4	69.1[1]	82.5
Great Britain	7.4	10.5	20.8	37.0	49.0	60.2
Greece	—	0.9	1.0	2.4	7.6	11.0
Hungary	3.5	5.0	13.2	19.3	9.2	10.2
Ireland	3.2	5.2	6.6	4.5	3.0	3.9
Italy	14.7	17.2	24.4	32.5	46.7	60.0
Latvia	—	—	—	—	—	2.3
Lithuania	—	—	—	—	—	3.5
Netherlands	1.6	2.1	3.1	5.1	9.6	16.1
Norway	0.6	0.9	1.4	2.2	3.3	4.5
Poland	—	9.0	—	25.1	25.0	38.6
Portugal	2.3	2.9	3.8	5.4	8.4	10.4
Romania	—	—	3.9	6.0	15.9	21.7
Russia	28.0	40.0	68.5	126.4	208.8[2]	143.7
Serbia and Montenegro	—	—	—	4.2[3]	—	10.7
Slovakia	—	—	—	—	—	5.4
Slovenia	—	—	—	—	—	1.9
Spain	8.2	10.5	15.5	18.6	28.0	41.0
Sweden	1.8	2.4	3.5	5.1	7.0	8.9
Switzerland	—	—	2.4	2.3	4.7	7.3
Ukraine	—	—	—	—	—	48.1
Yugoslavia	—	—	—	—	15.7	—

*Figures are given for the nearest year where not otherwise available.
[1]East and West Germany; unified Germany in 2004.
[2]USSR.
[3]Serbia only.
(*Sources*: B.R. Mitchell, *European Historical Statistics, 1750–1975* (2nd edn), Macmillan, 1980; C.M. Cipolla (ed.), *The Fontana Economic History of Europe*, vol. VI, Collins/Fontana, 1975; B. Turner (ed.), *The Statesman's Yearbook 2003–04*, Palgrave, 2003).
Readers should note that for more comprehensive figures the authoritative work is the third edition of B.R. Mitchell's *European Historical Statistics, 1750–1988* (Macmillan, 1992).

POPULATION OF MAJOR EUROPEAN CITIES

(thousands)

	1800	1850	1900	1950	2001*
Amsterdam	201	224	511	804	1,003
Athens	12	31	111	565	3,120
Barcelona	115	175	533	1,280	1,504
Belgrade	30	—	69	368	1,168
Berlin	172	419	1,889	3,337	3,393
Birmingham	71	233	523	1,113	1,010[1]
Brussels	66	251	599	956	959
Budapest	54	178	732	1,571	1,775
Cologne	50	97	373	595	963
Copenhagen	101	127	401	1,168[4]	1,082
Dresden	60	97	396	494	593
Edinburgh	83	194	394	467	453
Genoa	100	120	235	648	636
Glasgow	77	345	776	1,090	609[1]
Hamburg	130	132	706	1,606	1,702
Leipzig	30	63	456	618	494[1]
Lisbon	180	240	356	790	565[1]
Liverpool	80	376	704	789	457[1]
London	1,117	2,685	6,586	8,348	7,375[5]
Lyons	110	177	459	650	445[1]
Madrid	160	281	540	1,618	2,939
Manchester	75	303	645	703	439[1]
Marseilles	111	195	491	661	798
Milan	170	242	493	1,260	1,301
Moscow	250	365	989	5,046	8,546[4]
Munich	40	110	500	832	1,194
Naples	350	449	564	1,011	1,003
Palermo	140	150	228	491	684
Paris	547	1,053	2,714	2,850	2,125[1]
Prague	75	118	202	922	1,179
Rome	153	175	463	1,652	2,644
St Petersburg/Leningrad	220	485	1,267	3,321	4,628
Stockholm	76	93	301	744	755
Turin	78	135	336	711	904
Vienna	247	444	1,675	1,766	1,562[1]
Warsaw	60	114	423	279	1,610[2]

Note: As totals are based on varying definitions of the conurbations concerned, they are not exactly but only generally comparable between countries.

*Where no figure for 2001 is available, figure given to the nearest census.

[1]City area only.

[2]Metropolitan area.

[3]East and West Berlin totals combined.

[4]Conurbation totals.

[5]Based on a more restricted boundary of the area controlled by the Greater London Council after 1966.

(*Sources*: B.R. Mitchell, *European Historical Statistics, 1750–1975* (2nd edn), Macmillan, 1980; C.M. Cipolla (ed.), *The Fontana Economic History of Europe*, vol. IV, Collins/Fontana, 1975; A.F. Weber, *The Growth of Cities in the Nineteenth Century*, Macmillan, New York, 1899; B. Hunter (ed.), *The Statesman's Yearbook, 1996–97*, Macmillan, 1996; *Encyclopedia Britannica Almanac 2004* (Encyclopedia Britannica, 2003).

EMIGRATION FROM EUROPE, 1851–1960: SELECTED COUNTRIES

(in thousands)

	1851–60	1861–70	1871–80	1881–90	1891–1900	1901–10	1911–20	1921–30	1931–40	1941–50	1951–60
Austria-Hungary*	31	40	46	248	440	1,111	418	61	11	—	53
Belgium	1	2	2	21	16	30	21	33	20	29	109
Denmark	—	8	39	82	51	73	52	64	100	38	68
Finland	—	—	—	16	59	159	67	73	3	7	32
France	27	36	66	119	51	53	32	4	5	—	155
Germany[1]	671	779	626	1,342	527	274	91	564	121	618	872
Italy	5	27	168	992	1,580	3,615	2,194	1,370	235	467	858
Netherlands[2]	16	20	17	52	24	28	22	32	4[2]	75[2]	341[2]
Norway	36	98	85	187	95	191	62	87	6	10	25
Poland	—	—	—	—	—	—	—	634	164	—	—
Portugal	45	79	131	185	266	324	402	995	108	69	346
Russia	58	288	481	911	420	—	—	—	—	—	—
Spain	3	7	13	572	791	1,091	1,306	560	132	166	543
Sweden	17	122	103	327	205	324	86	107	8	23	43
UK and Ireland*	1,313	1,572	1,849	3,259	2,149	3,150	2,587	2,151	262	755	1,454

*Austria only after 1921.

[1]West Germany only after 1941.

[2]Excludes emigration to Dutch colonies.

[3]Excludes direct emigration from Irish ports.

(*Source:* B.R. Mitchell, *European Historical Statistics, 1750–1970,* Macmillan, 1975, p. 135).

OUTPUT OF GRAIN CROPS, 1800–1914: SELECTED COUNTRIES

(Annual averages in million quintals)

	1800–13	1835–44	1855–64	1885–94	1905–14
Austria	—	49.4	60.0	66.2	85.9
Hungary	—	51.0	68.1	102.6	131.7
France	94.5*	131.4	158.5	160.1	171.9
Germany	—	—	153.7	304.6	457.9
Italy	—	—	57.2	63.1	88.8
Russia	268.6	310.1	381.2	515.4	543.1
Sweden	5.0	8.4	14.7	21.7	26.1
UK	43.0	64.0†	68.0	56.9	51.7
Ireland	—	23.4†	16.7	11.2	11.3

*Average of 1803–12 only.
†Figures for 1845–54.
(*Source*: C.M. Cipolla (ed.), *The Fontana Economic History of Europe*, vol. IV. Collins/Fontana. 1975, p. 752).

OUTPUT OF WHEAT, 1913–2000: SELECTED COUNTRIES

(thousands of metric tons)

	1913	1924	1938	1950	1962	1972	1986	2000
Bulgaria	1,184	672	2,149	1,757	2,086	3,582	3,600[4]	3,800
France	8,690	7,650	9,800	7,700	14,050	17,850	27,504	37,554
Germany*	5,094	3,053	6,250	2,614	4,592	7,134	10,068	16,480
Greece	357[1]	210	980	850	1,722	1,768	2,131	2,086[5]
Hungary	4,119	1,403	2,688	2,040	1,973	4,095	4,800[4]	3,709
Italy	5,690	4,479	8,184	7,774	9,497	9,421	8,974	6,500
Poland	—	884	2,172	1,888	2,700	5,147	5,165[4]	8,193[5]
Romania	2,291	1,917	4,821	2,219	4,054	6,041	5,000[4]	7,000[5]
Spain	3,059	3,314	4,300	3,374	4,812	4,562	5,163	6,169[5]
USSR	28,000[2]	13,000	40,800	31,100	70,800	85,993	84,565	46,871[6]
UK	1,566	1,435	1,990	2,646	3,968	4,780	12,634	12,060
Yugoslavia	417[3]	1,662	3,030	1,833	3,514	4,844	5,519[4]	—

*West Germany after 1938; united Germany in 2000.
[1] 1914.
[2] Includes Baltic states.
[3] Serbia only.
[4] 1983.
[5] 1997.
[6] Russia only.

(*Sources:* B.R. Mitchell, *European Historical Statistics, 1750–1970*, Macmillan, 1975, pp. 249–75; J. Paxton (ed.), *The Statesman's Yearbook 1989–90*, Macmillan, 1989; B. Turner (ed.), *The Statesman's Yearbook 2000–01*, Macmillan, 2000.)

OUTPUT OF COAL AND LIGNITE, 1820–1939: SELECTED COUNTRIES

(Annual averages for quinquennia in million metric tons)

	Belgium	France	Germany	UK	Russia
1820–24	—	1	1	18	—
1825–29	—	2	2	22	—
1830–34	2	2	2	23	—
1835–39	3	3	3	28	—
1840–44	4	4	4	34	—
1845–49	5	4	6	47	—
1850–54	7	5	9	50	—
1855–59	9	8	15	68	—
1860–64	10	10	21	86	—
1865–69	11	13	31	105	1
1870–74	15	15	41	123	1
1875–79	15	17	50	136	2
1880–84	18	20	66	159	4
1885–89	18	22	78	168	5
1890–94	20	26	94	183	7
1895–99	22	31	120	205	11
1900–04	23	33	157	230	17
1905–09	25	36	201	260	24
1910–14	23	40	247	274	27
1915–19	15	24	244	247	28
1920–24	23	34	249	240	11
1925–29	26	52	316	227	31
1930–34	25	50	265	223	73
1935–39	29	47	351	233	133

(*Source*: C.M. Cipolla (ed.). *The Fontana Economic History of Europe*, vol. IV, 1975, p. 770).

OUTPUT OF COAL AND LIGNITE, 1950–2000: SELECTED COUNTRIES

(Annual totals in million metric tons)

	1952	1955	1960	1965	1970	1975	1987	2000
Austria	4	7	6	6	4	3	3*	1
Belgium	27	30	22	20	13	7	4	—
Bulgaria	6	9	16	25	29	24	34[†]	27
Czechoslovakia	45	61	85	101	107	107	123[†]	65**
France	53	57	58	54	41	27	16	3
West Germany	188	223	240	239	220	214	191	204[++]
East Germany	140	203	228	253	256	245	278*	—
Hungary	13	22	26	31	27	26	25*	13
Italy	2	2	2	1	2	2	2	—

(Continued)

(Continued)

	1952	1955	1960	1965	1970	1975	1987	2000
Netherlands	12	12	12	11	5	—	—	—
Poland	83	101	114	141	166	211	227[†]	164
Romania	4	6	8	12	19	29	49*	34
Russia	261	390	509	577	624	701	589[‡]	268
Spain	12	14	15	16	14	14	35	24
UK	220	225	197	191	153	124	102	31
Yugoslavia	13	15	23	30	26	23	47*	—

*1983. [†]1982. [‡]1986. **Czech Republic only. [++]United Germany.
(*Sources*: B.R. Mitchell, *European Historical Statistics, 1750–1970*, Macmillan, 1975, pp. 365–8; J. Paxton (ed.), *The Statesman's Yearbook 1989–90*. Macmillan, 1989; B. Turner (ed.), *The Statesman's Yearbook 2000–01*, Macmillan, 2000).

RAW COTTON CONSUMPTION, 1830–1970: SELECTED COUNTRIES

(thousands of metric tons)

	1830	1850	1880	1910	1930	1950	1970
Austria*	6	29	64	173	22	20	23
Hungary	—	—	—	—	15	30	67
Belgium	1	10	23	63	100	87	63
Czechoslovakia	—	—	—	—	113	60	108
Bulgaria	—	—	—	1	3	22[†]	72
Finland	—	—	3	7	7	11	16
France	34	59	89	158	361	252	244
Germany	8	26	137	383	346	189 (W)	255
						43[†] (E)	89
UK	24	267	617	740	577	461	176
Greece	—	—	—	—	—	21	46
Italy	—	—	—	175	205	203	221
Netherlands	—	—	14	20	52	61	62
Poland	—	—	—	—	61	87	141
Portugal	—	—	3	16	18	36	85
Romania	—	—	—	—	3	17	80
Russia	2	20	94	362	257	953	1,713
Spain	—	16	45	73	99	59	108
Sweden	—	2	9	21	23	28	15
Switzerland	—	—	22	24	31	30	41
Yugoslavia	—	—	—	—	88	35	91

*Figures for Austro–Hungarian Empire to 1910; 1830 and 1850 also include Lombardy and Venetia in Northern Italy.
[†]1951.
(*Source*: B.R. Mitchell, *European Historical Statistics, 1750–1970*, Macmillan, 1975, pp. 428–32).

OUTPUT OF STEEL, 1880–2000: SELECTED COUNTRIES

(Annual production in million metric tons)

	UK	France	Belgium	Germany		Italy	Russia*
1880	1.3	0.4	0.1	0.7		—	0.3
1890	3.6	0.7	0.2	2.2		0.1	0.4
1900	5.0	1.6	0.7	6.6		0.1	2.2
1910	6.5	3.4	1.9	13.7		0.7	3.5
1930	7.4	9.4	3.4	11.5		0.5	5.8
1940	13.4	4.4	1.9	19.0		1.0	18.0
				W	E		
1950	16.6	8.7	3.8	12.1	1.0	2.4	27.3
1960	24.7	17.3	7.1	34.1	3.8	8.2	65.3
1975	20.2	27.0	11.6	40.4	6.5	21.8	141.3
1986	14.8	17.7	9.7	37.1	7.2[†]	22.9	160.5
2000	17.3	18.2	12.1[‡]	40.8		25.8[‡]	59.2

*USSR for 1930–86.
[†]1983.
[‡]1997.
(*Sources*: B.R. Mitchell, *European Historical Statistics, 1750–1970*, Macmillan, 1975, pp. 399–402; B. Turner (ed.), *The Statesman's Yearbook, 2000–01*, Macmillan, 2000).

OUTPUT OF CRUDE OIL, 1900–2000: SELECTED COUNTRIES

(thousand metric tons)

	1900	1920	1930	1950	1960	1970	1987	2000
Austria	349	—	—	1,700	2,440	2,798	1,000	972
Germany*	50	35	174	1,119	5,560	7,536	3,727	2,850
Denmark	—	—	—	—	—	—	4,602	11,200
Netherlands	—	—	—	705	1,920	1,919	4,663	—
UK	—	—	—	40	90	84	119,244	128,200
France	—	55	76	128	2,260	2,308	3,236	2,800
Italy	2	5	8	8	1,990	1,408	3,908	5,900
Spain	—	—	—	—	—	156	1,639	554
Norway	—	—	—	—	—	—	56,000	156,200
Russia	10,684	3,851	18,451	37,878	147,859	352,667	625,000[1]	156,000
Romania	247	1,109	5,792	5,047	11,500	14,637	12,000[2]	6,700
Yugoslavia	—	—	—	110	1,040	2,854	4,000[2]	—
Hungary	2	—	—	512	1,215	1,937	2,000[2]	7,100
Poland	—	765	663	162	195	424	250[2]	2,100

*West Germany from 1950 to 1987. [1]Estimated output, 1986. [2]1984. [3]1993.
(*Sources*: B.R. Mitchell, *European Historical Statistics, 1750–1970*, Macmillan, 1975, p. 371; J. Paxton (ed.) *The Statesman's Yearbook 1989–90*, Macmillan, 1989; B. Turner (ed.), *The Statesman's Yearbook, 2000–01*, Macmillan, 2000).

MOTOR VEHICLES PRODUCED, 1910–2000: SELECTED COUNTRIES

(in thousands, commercial and private)

	1910	1925	1930	1938	1950	1965	1975	1985	2000
France	38	177	142	227	357	1,616	1,694	3,536	3,176
Germany	10	49	96	338	301 (W) 13 (E)	3,063 (W) 118 (E)	3,172 (W) NA	4,566 (W) 118[1] (E)	4,702[2]
Italy	—	49	47	71	129	1,186	1,459	1,842	1,063
Russia	—	—	4	231	259	814	763*	2,229	959
Spain	—	—	—	—	—	234	967	1,533	1,959
Sweden	—	—	2	7	17	207	NA	487	NA
UK	34	198	136	445	784	2,180	1,647	1,245	1,641

*Commercial vehicles only. [1]1983. [2]Unified Germany total.

(*Sources*: B.R. Mitchell, *European Historical Statistics, 1750–1970*, Macmillan, 1975, pp. 467–9; J. Paxton (ed.), *The Statesman's Yearbook 1989–90*, Macmillan, 1989; B. Turner (ed.), *The Statesman's Yearbook 2000–01*, Macmillan, 2000).

OUTPUT OF ELECTRICITY, 1920–2000: SELECTED COUNTRIES

(in million kWh)

	1920	1935	1955	1975	1987	2000
Austria	1.8	2.6	10.6	35.2	49.0	60.3
Belgium	1.2	4.3	10.9	39.0	60.0	83.2
Bulgaria	—	0.1	2.1	25.2	40.5[1]	40.9
Czechoslovakia	1.4	2.6	15.0	56.0	74.8[1]	73.5[7]
Denmark	0.3	0.9	3.9	17.4	27.5	35.8
Finland	—	2.1	6.8	25.1	50.9	67.3
France	5.8	17.5	49.6	180.0	360.7	544.0
Germany	15.0	35.7	78.9 (W)	301.8 (W)	392.7 (W)	529.1[5]
			28.7 (E)	84.5 (E)	104.9 (E)[2]	
Greece	0.1	0.4	1.4	8.9[3]	27.9	44.7
Hungary	—	0.9	5.4	20.5	25.8[2]	34.9
Ireland	—	0.2	1.6	7.3	12.2	19.8[6]
Italy	4.0	12.6	25.6	140.8	190.9	251.5[6]
Netherlands	0.7	2.8	11.2	54.3	66.1	89.6
Norway	5.3	7.8	22.6	76.7	103.3	111.6[6]
Poland	—	2.8	17.8	97.2	118.0[1]	142.6
Portugal	0.1	0.4	1.9	10.7	19.3	37.1
Romania	—	0.9	4.3	53.7	70.3[1]	57.4
Russia[4]	0.5	26.2	170.2	1,039.0	1,665.0	877.8
Spain	1.0	3.3	11.9	76.3	126.8	212.2
Sweden	2.6	6.9	24.7	80.6	142.3	144.9
Switzerland	2.8	5.7	15.5	42.9	58.2	63.4
UK	8.5	26.0	89.0	272.1	282.5	341.8
Yugoslavia	—	0.6	4.3	40.0	64.6[2]	—

[1]1982. [2]1983. [3]1970. [4]USSR apart from 1993. [5]Unified Germany. [6]1997. [7]Czech Rep. only.
(*Sources*: B.R. Mitchell, *European Historical Statistics, 1750–1970*, Macmillan, 1975, pp. 479–82; J. Paxton (ed.), *The Statesman's Yearbook 1989–90*, Macmillan, 1989; B. Turner (ed.), *The Statesman's Yearbook 2000–01*, Macmillan, 2000–01).

RAILWAY MILEAGE OPEN, 1840–1913: SELECTED COUNTRIES

(kilometres)

	1840	1860	1880	1900	1913*
Austria–Hungary	144	4,543	18,507	36,330	44,748
Belgium	334	1,729	4,112	4,562	4,676
France	410	9,167	23,089[†]	38,109[†]	40,770[†]
Germany	469	11,089	33,838[‡]	51,678[‡]	63,378[‡]
UK	2,411	16,798	28,846	36,004	38,114

(Continued)

(Continued)

	1840	1860	1880	1900	1913
Italy	20	2,404	9,290	16,429	18,873
Russia	—	1,626	22,865	53,234	70,156
Sweden	—	527	5,876	11,303	14,377
Spain	—	1,649	7,290	13,214	15,088
Switzerland	—	1,053	2,571	3,867	4,832

*1914 boundaries unless otherwise stated; countries with more than 4,000 km of track open in 1914.
†Excludes Alsace–Lorraine. ‡Includes Alsace–Lorraine.
(*Source*: B.R. Mitchell, *European Historical Statistics, 1750–1970*, Macmillan, 1975, pp. 581–4).

RAILWAY MILEAGE OPEN, 1920–2000: SELECTED COUNTRIES

(kilometres)

	1920	1950	1975	2000
Austria	6,639	6,734	5,858	5,643‡
Belgium	4,938	5,046	3,998	3,380‡
Bulgaria	2,205	3,967	4,045	6,518
Czechoslovakia	13,430	13,124	13,241	9,444**
Denmark	4,328	4,815	2,493	2,743
Finland	3,988	4,726	5,963	5,836‡
France	38,200	41,300	34,787	33,769†
Germany	57,545	36,924 (W) 12,895 (E)	32,072 (W) 14,298 (E)	46,300
Greece	2,396	2,553	2,572	2,299‡
Hungary	8,141	8,756	8,392	7,768
Ireland	5,542	2,440	1,361	1,945‡
Italy	20,385	21,550	20,176	19,527†
Netherlands	3,606	3,204	2,825	2,808†
Norway	3,286	4,469	4,241	4,021†
Poland	13,763	26,312*	23,773	22,981
Portugal	3,268	3,597	3,618	3,259†
Romania	4,968	10,853	10,403	11,365†
Russia++	71,600	116,900	138,300	87,000†
Spain	15,886	18,098	13,497	13,832
Sweden	14,869	16,516	12,065	10,961‡
Switzerland	5,078	5,152	NA	5,035†
UK	32,707	31,353	17,093	16,666†
Yugoslavia	9,321	11,541	10,068	—

*Figure reflects major boundary changes in 1945. †1997. ‡1989. **Czech Republic. ++USSR, 1920–75.
(*Source*: B.R. Mitchell, *European Historical Statistics, 1750–1970*, Macmillan, 1975, pp. 585–7;
B. Turner (ed.), *The Statesman's Yearbook 2000–01*, Macmillan, 2000).

MERCHANT SHIPS REGISTERED BY COUNTRY, 1840–2000

(thousand tons)

	1840	*1880*	*1910*	*1938*	*1960*	*1986*	*2000††*
Austria–Hungary*	199	262	414	—	—	—	—
Belgium	23	75	191	272	677	2,420	429
Denmark	69	250	522	1,233	2,389	4,651	5,559
Finland	—	272	411	644	801	2,360¶	1,616
France	663	920	1,452	1,664	4,809	5,422	1,564
Germany	352	1,104	2,890	2,482	4,724 (W) 197 (E)	5,565 (W) 1,224 (E)¶	6,002
Great Britain	2,768	6,575	11,556	10,702	11,988	11,567	10,100
Greece	111	361§	458	1,930	538	28,391	25,708
Ireland	—	—	—	115	76	149	193
Italy	NA	999	1,001	2,039	5,705	7,897	6,820
Netherlands	380†	328	534	2,242	4,661	4,324	2,795
Norway	205	1,520	1,526	2,782	11,402	9,295	18,886
Poland	—	—	—	102	578	3.005¶	3,370
Portugal	—	—	—	250	286	1,114	897
Russia**	—	468	723	1,273	3,429	24,961	13,755
Spain	245‡	560	775	214	1,754	5,422	637
Sweden	159	543	670	1,105	3,851	2,517	2,950
Yugoslavia	—	—	—	401	718	2,500¶	—

*To 1919. †1846. ‡1850. §1884. ¶1985. **USSR, 1938–86 ††as nearest date.
(*Sources*: B.R. Mitchell, *European Historical Statistics, 1750–1970*, Macmillan, 1975, pp. 613–31; J. Paxton (ed.), *The Statesman's Yearbook 1989–90*, Macmillan, 1989; B. Turner (ed.), *The Statesman's Yearbook 2000–01*, Macmillan, 2000).

VALUE OF EXTERNAL TRADE, 1815–1913: SELECTED COUNTRIES

	Germany (million marks)	*Austria–Hungary (million kronen)*	*France (million francs)*	*Russia (million roubles)*	*UK (million pounds)*
1815	—	—	791	341	140
1830	—	297	942	470	100
1850	—	554	1,859	192†	186
1870	5,741*	1,663	5,669	696†	547
1900	10,380	3,638	8,807	1,342	877
1913	20,848	6,177	15,301	2,894	1,404

*1880. †New roubles, *c.* 4 × old value.
(*Source*: B.R. Mitchell, *European Historical Statistics, 1750–1970*, Macmillan, 1975, pp. 487–97).

TOTAL VALUE OF EXTERNAL TRADE, 1913–2000: SELECTED COUNTRIES

	Germany (million marks)	France (million francs)	Russia (million roubles; million $ for 1993 and 2000)	Italy (million lira)	UK (million pounds)
1913	20,848	15,301	2,894	6,143	1,404
1925	27,713	99,850	1,020[4*]	44,370	2,248
1938	10,713	76,655	475[4*]	21,750	1,453
1955	50,089[1]	3,409,973	5,839[4*]	2,855[2]	6,854
1965	142,099[1]	100,661[3]	14,610[4*]	9,111[2]	10,652
1975	—	458,854[3]	50,699[4*]	47,846[2]	43,790
1985	—	1,495,001[3]	127,476[4*]	232,539[2]	163,168
1993	1,194,882	2,301,939[3]	61,104	499,269[2]	268,338
2000	2,231,651	3,460,700[3]	127,609	813,395	526,654

*New roubles. [1]West Germany. [2]Thousand million lira. [3]New francs. [4]USSR; Russia only after 1985.
(*Sources*: B.R. Mitchell, *European Historical Statistics, 1750–1970*, Macmillan, 1975, pp. 494–500; J. Paxton (ed.), *The Statesman's Yearbook 1989–90*, Macmillan, 1989; B. Turner (ed.), *The Statesman's Yearbook, 2000–01*, Macmillan, 2000.)

THE TELECOMMUNICATIONS REVOLUTION

1899

Marconi transmits by wireless across the English Channel. Magnetic recording of sound devised.

1900

Marconi transmits across the Atlantic.

1904

Fleming invents the electronic valve.

1907

First regular radio broadcasts begin in the US.

1910

Experimental radio broadcasts made by Lee de Forest from Paris.

1917

Lucien Lévy in France patents a tuning circuit making construction of radio sets much simpler.

1920

Marconi Wireless Telegraph Company begins broadcasting daily concerts from Chelmsford (23 Feb.). Recital by Dame Nellie Melba broadcast from Chelmsford to Europe (15 June).

1922

British Broadcasting Corporation set up for regular daily radio broadcasts.

1926

John Logie Baird demonstrates a working television system in London.

1928

Baird successfully transmits TV pictures from London to New York.

1929

Colour TV demonstrated in the US.

1931

Mechanical binary computer, the 'ZI', built by Konrad Zuse in Germany.

1933

Edwin Armstrong in the US patents FM (frequency modulation) radio system, permitting much higher-quality sound broadcasts. Discovery of radio emissions from stars by Karl Jansky in the US, developing the science of radio astronomy.

1933–34

First patents applied for a radio detection and ranging (radar) system in the US and France.

1935

A station in Berlin begins low-definition television broadcasting.

1936

First practical radar system developed by Watson-Watt in Britain for detection of enemy aircraft. BBC establishes first high-definition public service broadcasting service from Alexandra Palace in London using both Baird and American systems; Baird system eventually dropped.

1939

Binary calculator, the complex computer, using telephone relays developed in the US. Television transmissions abandoned in Britain and Germany for duration of war.

1940

Radar system in Britain plays a major defensive role in the Battle of Britain. Germany develops system of directional radio beams to direct bombers to targets in Britain. Similar systems and counter-measures produced by both sides during the ensuing bomber offensive on Germany.

1942–43

Development of airborne and shipborne radar during Second World War.

1943

Alan Turing develops Colossus computer to break German Enigma codes, using telephone relay and 1,500 valves, the world's first automatic digital computer.

1945

Whirlwind computer constructed.

1946

Television transmissions resumed in Britain. Turing presents UK's National Physical Laboratory (NPL) with design for stored-programme electronic digital computer, envisaging a plan for national computer development, but only pilot project is completed.

1947

Construction of UNIVAC computers for the US Census Bureau begins and is completed in 1951, eventually producing 48 UNIVAC I computers.

1948

First transistors produced. Konrad Zuse builds 'Z3' computer using electronic relays.

1949

Colour TV system produced in the US by RCA; first regular transmissions begin the following year.

1954

Britain opens up commercial TV channels. Pope opens Eurovision network in Rome.

1955

Computer firm IBM introduces magnetic disk storage for computers. Video tape recording developed. First mass transistorized radios produced by Sony Corporation.

1959

First patent for integrated circuit in the US. First transistorized portable TVs launched by Sony Corporation.

1962

First live TV transmitted from Europe to America by Telstar satellite.

1963

Philips introduces the first compact casette. First electronic calculators introduced. First mini-computer marketed in the United States.

1964

BASIC computer language developed.

1966

Colour TV transmissions begin in Europe.

1967

Texas Instruments begin work on pocket calculator.

1969

Advanced Research Projects Agency (ARPA) at the US Department of Defense conceives concept of a diffused network of computer sites to counter nuclear strikes, creating the Internet.

1971

First microprocessor (Intel 4004) introduced.

1975

First personal computers become commercially available.

1977

Apple and Commodore bring out microcomputers.

1978

IBM develops floppy disk.

1979

Sony Corporation introduce Sony Walkman casette player. First video recorders become available commercially.

1980

Sony and Philips introduce compact disk. Nintendo produces first hand-held game powered by microprocessor.

1989

World Wide Web developed. Nintendo Game Boy becomes world-wide success as hand-held games player.

1990

Sales of compact disks estimated to have outstripped world-wide those of vinyl records. Satellite broadcasting begins by Sky network.

1991

Permission granted to private companies to offer subscriptions giving access to the Internet.

1993

First 'virtual reality' videos launched.

1995

First internet 'cafés' set up in London. First 'laptop' computers become widely available.

1998

Digital TV broadcasting begins with terrestial and satellite TV services through most of Europe.

1999

Mobile phone sales take off in Europe with increasing minaturization of handsets.

2003

'Wireless' technology permits PCs and laptops to be used without cabling.

2004

An estimated 1 billion mobile phones are owned world-wide.

MAJOR EVENTS IN EUROPEAN RELIGIOUS HISTORY

1760
England
Wesley Methodist lay-preachers take out licences as dissenting teachers and administer the sacrament.

1762
France
Louis XV forbids Jesuits to teach and recruit new members, and orders the sale of their property.

1764
France
The Jesuit Order is suppressed in France. Pope Clement XIII issues a Bull defending the Order.

Bohemia
The Moravian Church is reformed by Spangenberg.

Portugal
Communication between Portugal and the Papacy is broken off as a result of the execution of Malagrida as a heretic. Beginning of Pombal's work to suppress the Jesuits.

1765
Papacy
Cult of the Sacred Heart sanctioned by the Pope.

1766
Spain
Secular education, supervision of monasteries and tax on church lands introduced by D'Aranda.

Russia
Religious toleration declared in Russia.

1767
Spain
Jesuits expelled from Spain, the Sicilies and Parma.

1769
Germany
List of anti-papal grievances, the 'Coblenz Articles', presented by the Archbishops of Mainz, Cologne and Trier to Maria Theresa.

Other
Spain, France and Naples demand the abolition of the Jesuit Order.

1773
Papacy
Jesuit Order suppressed.

1774
Poland
Jesuits expelled from Poland.

1776
Bavaria
Illuminati founded in Bavaria.

1778
Great Britain
Catholic Relief granted in Ireland and mainland Britain. Agitation in Scotland begun by Lord George Gordon and Protestant Association for repeal.

1780

England

Gordon riots in London with widespread attacks on Catholic (and other) property.

1781

Austria

Joseph II grants religious toleration to Protestants and members of the Greek Church. 700 monasteries dissolved; Papal Bulls restricted; funds for Rome stopped, and six new bishoprics created without papal approval.

1782

Austria

Pope visits Vienna to protest at Joseph's actions but to no effect.

1783

Germany

Eichhorn's *Introduction to the Old Testament* investigates its sources and contents and attributes parts to several different authors.

Austria

Joseph II makes marriage a civil contract and allows divorce. He proposes appointment of bishops without papal approval, suppresses diocesan seminaries and forms own schools for the education of clergy.

1784

Great Britain

Wesley ordains two Wesleyan 'superintendents' in America, effectively producing a major breach with the Anglican Church.

1787

Italy

Leopold II of Tuscany dismisses national synod in Florence for failing to agree with his church reforms and sets about them himself. King of the Two Sicilies refuses to pay annual tribute to the Pope.

England

Evangelical revival focuses around Beilby Porteus, appointed Bishop of London, the Countess of Huntingdon, William Wilberforce, Charles Simeon and Hannah More.

France

Edict of Versailles grants religious freedom and legal civil status to Protestants.

1789

France

Mirabeau carries a motion that the property of the Church belongs to the nation.

1790

France

Church property confiscated and monasteries abolished. The Civil Constitution of the Clergy reduces the number of bishops to one for each department; bishops to be chosen by the Parliamentary electors and instituted by the Metropolitan; the clergy chosen by the electors to communal offices. Papal confirmation dispensed with. All clergy to take the oath to the Civil Constitution. Protestants become eligible for office and receive back property confiscated by Louis XIV. Jews also received civil rights.

1791

General

Volney's *Ruins of Empires* compares the chief religions of the world to the disadvantage of Christianity.

1792

France

Clergy who refuse to take the oath to the Civil Constitution of the Clergy are given 14 days to leave after 10 Aug. The religious orders are dissolved and civil marriage and divorce are introduced.

Germany

Fichte's *Critique of all Revelation* rejects doctrinal Christianity.

1793

France

Convention abolishes Catholic faith and threatens recalcitrant clergy with death. Feast of Reason celebrated on 10 Nov. in Church of St Eustache.

1794

General

Paine's *Age of Reason* adopts Deistic position, attacking Christianity and the Old Testament.

France

Convention formally recognizes the existence of a Supreme Being and immortality (May). Robespierre presides over the Feast of the Supreme Being (June).

1795

Ireland

British government founds College of Maynooth in Ireland to train Catholic priests.

1797

England

Methodist New Connexion leaves the Wesleyans.

1801

France

Concordat with the Papacy. Catholicism is recognized as the religion of the nation; the State guarantees salaries and chooses bishops, subject to papal confirmation. The clergy are chosen by the bishops but confirmed by the State. Some bishops refuse to recognize the Concordat and form *La Petite Eglise*.

1802

France

Concordat promulgated, but with Organic Articles which have not been discussed by the Pope. Papal bulls and representatives not allowed into France without government permission, nor synods held. Chateaubriand's *Genius of Christianity* published. It asserts the irrational and aesthetic values of Christianity in opposition to the criticism of the philosophes.

1804

France

Napoleon tightens control over Church, restoring laws against perpetual vows.

1805

France

Napoleon brings Jews under State control.

1806

Papacy

Following a series of disputes with Napoleon, principally over the extension of the *Code Napoléon* to Italy and Napoleon's seizure of papal territory, the Pope refuses to expel French enemies from his territory, observe the continental system and appoint to the Venetian bishoprics under Napoleon's control.

England

Leaders of Evangelical movement form 'Clapham sect', named after John Venn, Rector of Clapham.

1808

Papacy

Rome occupied by French troops.

Spain

Napoleon abolishes the Inquisition and suppresses most of the monasteries.

Italy

Napoleon abolishes Italian Inquisition.

1809

Papacy

Rome formally added to French Empire (17 May); Pius VII excommunicates Napoleon (11 June); Pius arrested and imprisoned in Savona (6 July). The Pope refuses to institute French bishops. Napoleon calls an Ecclesiastical Commission for France to seek a solution to the deadlock, but it fails to offer a solution acceptable to Napoleon and is suppressed (Jan. 1810).

1810

France

Senate decrees that all future popes and all the clergy of the Empire must accept the Gallican articles of 1682.

Switzerland

Zinzendorf circle in Geneva form a Society of Friends and begin a Protestant revival.

1811

France

Napoleon calls a Council in Paris to sanction a scheme for the institution of bishops. Although securing papal approval, Napoleon dissolves the Council because of the restrictions he requests.

1813

France

Napoleon brings Pope to France and forces a new Concordat giving Napoleon the nomination of bishops in France and Italy and the Metropolitan the power to institute if the Pope had not done so within six months. The Pope, however, later repudiates the agreement.

1814

Spain and Italy

Spanish and Italian Inquisitions refounded. Index renewed.

Papacy

Jesuit Order and Index restored by the Pope.

1815

Germany

Wessenberg, Vicar-General of the diocese of Constance urges the Vienna Congress to found a German national Church under a German primate.

1817

Germany

Lutheran and Reformed Churches of Prussia unite in the Evangelical Union. The Union spreads to other German states.

France

Lamennais's *Essay on Indifference* attacks individualism and scepticism.

1818

Germany

Representatives of several German states meet at Frankfurt to revive the idea of a German national Church but frustrated by Niebuhr, the Prussian envoy at Rome.

1820

England

Plymouth Brethren founded by Darby, an Anglican ex-clergyman, on the basis of strict Calvinism. The headquarters of the Brethren eventually moves to Switzerland.

1821

Germany

Concordat concluded between Prussia and the Papacy.

1824

France

Lamennais visits Rome and on his return advocates the political supremacy of the Pope.

1828

Great Britain

Repeal of Test and Corporation Acts removes last civil disabilities on Protestant Dissenters.

1829

Great Britain

Catholic Emancipation Act makes Catholics eligible for almost all offices of state. No oath of supremacy required to sit in either House of Parliament.

1832

Papacy

Gregory XVI issues an Encyclical condemning freedom of conscience and of the press in reaction to the new Belgian Constitution.

1833

England

Keble's Assize Sermon on National Apostasy, denouncing the suppression of Irish bishoprics, seen as the beginning of the High Church Oxford Movement to revive Anglicanism.

1834

Portugal

Suppression of monasteries.

1835

Germany

Tübingen School of Theology founded by Professor Baur, dealing with theology from an historical and philosophical point of view.

1837

Germany

Dispute with the King of Prussia over mixed marriages leads to the imprisonment of the Archbishop of Cologne and several other bishops.

1838

France

Dominican Order revived in France.

1839

Russia

Catechism approved by the Russian Holy Synod and distributed to schools and churches.

Greece

Two million Uniate Christians incorporated within the Greek Church.

1841

England

Newman's Tract 90 draws hostile criticism from Anglicans for its Catholic tendency.

Italy

Don Bosco founds the Oratory of St Francis de Sales for work among boys.

1843

Scotland

'Disruption' in Presbyterian Church. 474 clergy leave the established Church over the issue of lay patronage.

1844

Germany

Short-lived German Catholic Church founded. The Pope condemns the rationalistic teaching of Hermes.

1845

England

Newman joins the Roman Church, with other leaders of the High Church movement.

Norway

Dissenter law permits freedom of religious expression. All except civil servants can leave the national Church and parents can exempt children from religious education in schools.

1846

England

Evangelical Alliance formed in England to oppose Romanism, Puseyism, and rationalism. It attracts support in America and on the Continent and holds conferences abroad.

Papacy

Election of Pius IX. Begins reform of Papal States, including an amnesty for 1,000 prisoners and reform of courts.

1847

Germany

Edict of Toleration in Prussia. Prussian government recognizes right of secession from state Church.

Papacy

Pope grants limited freedom of the press in Papal States and becomes focus of anti-Austrian feeling after protest to Austria over violation of the Papal States.

Scotland
United Presbyterian Church formed.

1848
Germany
Separation of Church and State decreed by Frankfurt Parliament (Mar.) Meeting of German Bishops at Wurzburg resolves to work for full independence from secular control of ecclesiastical legislation, administration, and control of education. These are incorporated in Concordats with several of the southern German States. 500 clergy meet at Wittenberg to celebrate success against revolution.

France
Falloux, Minister of Education, introduces a bill permitting Catholics to be educated at Catholic primary and secondary schools, but only obtain degrees at secular universities. The numbers receiving clerical education greatly increase.

Italy
Roman crowds demand lay ministers in Papal States. Papal armies cross into Austrian Italy. Pius IX states his unwillingness to declare war on Austrians and denies instigation of revolution. Effectively ended hopes of the Pope as champion of war against Austrian domination. Pope flees to Gaeta after demonstrations in Rome. Jesuits expelled from Kingdom of Sardinia and influence of clergy on education restricted.

Holland
Dutch Reformed Church disestablished.

1849
Papacy
Rome recaptured for the Pope. The Pope issues an encyclical to the Italian bishops condemning socialism and communism. He also issues an encyclical inviting views on the immaculate conception.

Denmark
By the constitution, the Evangelical Lutheran Church is supported by the State, parliament acting as legislative and money-voting authority, but full religious toleration also established.

1850
Germany
Prussian constitution provides that all religious associations should administer their affairs independently and remain in possession of their property and funds for religious, educational, and charity purposes. Communication with superiors and publication of ordinances largely unfettered. But nomination, election, and confirmation of ecclesiastical posts governed by the State.

Belgium
Pius IX protests against law making secondary education subject to State control. Bishops insist on there only being Catholic chaplains in State establishments.

England
Restoration of Catholic sees. Manning (later Cardinal) joins the Roman Church with other Anglicans.

Italy
Siccardi Laws suppress ecclesiastical immunities in Kingdom of Sardinia. Archbishops of Turin and Sardinia imprisoned.

1851
Germany
Prussian Evangelical Churches placed under control of a Church Council instead of the King.

Italy
Church's jurisdiction over heresy and sacrilege taken by civil power in Kingdom of Sardinia.

Spain
Concordat signed with the Papacy by which Catholicism is declared sole religion of the State. Church to supervise education and have sole jurisdiction over marriage disputes. Papacy guarantees the right of the crown to appoint bishops and recognizes loss of Church lands already secularized.

1852

Germany

The Eisenach biennial conference is instituted, made up of representatives of the Protestants of each State. Under its direction a revision of Luther's Bible is instituted.

Italy

Church property secularized and civil marriage introduced in Sardinia.

1853

Holland

Catholic hierarchy re-established in spite of protests.

Russia

Dispute over Holy Places. Tsar Nicholas I intervenes to 'protect' Christians in the Ottoman Empire and to confirm Russian rights over the Holy Places. Russia fails to obtain a treaty with the Ottoman Empire giving her protectorate over Christians in the Ottoman Empire through opposition of Great Britain.

1854

Germany

The New Lutherans attack pietism and individualism. Jewish seminary established at Breslau.

Papacy

The Immaculate Conception of the Virgin is declared an article of faith for Roman Catholics. The Curia is reformed and the Sacred College. Greater centralization of papal power.

Denmark

Kierkegaard–Martensen controversy on Christianity.

1855

Austria

Concordat with the Papacy. Austrian Catholic bishops empowered to issue ordinances without the approval of the civil power, set penalties and supervise education, marriage and the press. State control of the Church abolished.

Italy

A Monastic Law abolishes all religious orders in the Kingdom of Sardinia except those employed in preaching, education and the care of the sick.

Sweden

Obligatory communion for public office holders ended.

General

Spiritualist movement spreads from the USA to England and later to Europe.

1856

Sweden

Evangelical National Institute founded for lay work at home. Foreign missions and seamen's missions founded in 1861.

1858

France

First apparitions of the Virgin reported at Lourdes.

Russia

Metropolitan Philaret and other bishops oppose emancipation of serfs.

1859

Papacy

Pope refuses to renounce temporal power.

Great Britain

Darwin's *Origin of Species* provokes intense controversy about the literal accuracy of the Bible.

Sweden

Members of non-Lutheran faiths allowed to practise freely.

1860

Papacy

Encyclical *Nullis Certe* threatens to excommunicate all who attack papal domains. Papal army defeated by Austrians and Rome only saved by French troops.

1861
Italy
Prota-Giurleo, a Dominican, attempts to found a National Church, with radical changes in organization and liturgy. Monastic orders partially suppressed in Kingdom of Two Sicilies.

1863
France
Renan's *Vie de Jesus* (Life of Jesus), a strictly historical account of Christ's life, is published and arouses controversy.

Germany
Protestant Union founded, seeking federation into a National Church, greater power for the laity, and greater latitude in doctrinal matters.

Romania
Monasteries secularized and transferred to the State.

Russia
Concordat between Russia and Holy See repudiated by Tsar following the Russian repression of Polish rising.

1864
Poland
Catholic monasteries dissolved and control of Catholic affairs given to a Minister of Worship.

Papacy
Pope issues encyclical *Quanta Cura,* a syllabus of 80 errors, including Liberalism. Religious toleration, freedom of conscience and press, free discussion and secularist legislation are challenged.

Romania
Romanian Church proclaimed national and independent of the patriarchate of Constantinople.

Russia
Diplomatic relations between Russia and Holy See broken off.

1865
England
General Booth begins evangelical and rescue work in East London, leading to the formation of the Salvation Army.

1866
Papacy
Pope condemns attempts at Anglican–Catholic reunion.

Italy
Monasteries and congregations suppressed by law. Land held in mortmain sold by the State. Cathedral chapters and bishops forced to surrender their capital to the State. Seminarists made liable for military service and civil marriage made obligatory.

1867
Papacy
The Pope announces his intention to hold an Ecumenical Council. The doctrine of Papal Infallibility is widely canvassed.

1868
Ireland
Anglican Church in Ireland disestablished.

Austria
Civil marriage is restored and the schools are freed from clerical control. The Church can only open new ones. Jews granted full civil liberty and Jewish immigration increases substantially from neighbouring States. Pope condemns the new laws.

France
White Fathers founded by Lavigerie for missionary and educational work.

Spain
Following Liberal Revolution, the Cortes proclaims freedom of worship and teaching and introduces civil marriage. Religious houses suppressed and clergy deprived of salaries.

1869
Papacy
Vatican Council meets and begins discussion of Papal Infallibility.

Germany

Prince Hohenlohe, Minister President of Bavaria, invites powers to confer on the prospect of decree of Papal Infallibility. German bishops at Fulda produce a pastoral to allay fears of a new dogma.

1870

Papacy

Vatican Council declares papal *ex cathedra* definitions of faith and morals infallible by 533 votes to 2 (July). Rome falls to Piedmontese troops of Victor Emmanuel. Romans decide by plebiscite to become part of Italy. Decree of 9 October declares Rome and Roman provinces part of Kingdom of Italy. The Pope loses all temporal power.

Austria

Austrian government forbids promulgation of Council's decree and cancels Concordat with Papacy.

Germany

After first producing a memorial against the new dogma (Jan.), the German bishops accept the dogma of infallibility. Archbishop of Cologne orders theological professors of Bonn to accept the dogma on pain of being forbidden to lecture to Roman Catholic students or exercise their priestly function. Bavaria refuses to accept Papal Bull on Infallibility. Clergy and bishops accept and attempt to coerce opponents. Some German Catholics, now known as Old Catholics, prefer to secede from Rome rather than accept the decree. Several States give active support to the Old Catholic movement and its leaders Dr Dollinger and Dr Reinkens.

France

Communards enact separation of Church and State, the abolition of a budget for religious affairs, and execute 24 clergy, including the Archbishop of Paris.

Switzerland

Swiss Federal government breaks off relations with Papacy after disputes over mixed marriages, education, freedom of the press, and the doctrine of Infallibility.

Denmark

Sunday Schools introduced by Home Mission Movement (*Indre Misjon*).

1871

Germany

Catholic Centre Party founded to defend Catholic interests and wins 63 seats in Diet. Congress of Old Catholics held at Munich. Catholic members of the Prussian Landtag petition the Emperor to restore the temporal power of the Pope. He refuses to assist. When some Catholic bishops attempt to excommunicate those not accepting Infallibility the government declares them still Catholics with full civil rights. Political pronouncements from pulpit made a criminal offence and Roman Catholic Department of Spiritual Affairs abolished.

Italy

The Law of Guarantees declares the Pope's person inviolable, accords the honours of a sovereign prince, allows the possession of the Vatican and other palaces, and grants an annuity (rejected by the Pope). Church and State separated and Church property secularized, though religious orders once again allowed to own property. Restrictions on Church lifted.

Belgium

Prime Minister Frère-Orban obtains law creating free 'neutral' schools in which the Catholic faith may only be taught outside class hours. Catholic bishops protest and diplomatic relations with the Papacy ended. Private Catholic schools organized. *Congrès des Oeuvres Sociales* founded by Bishop of Liège.

1872

Germany

The Prussian government reduces 'clerical influence' in schools. The bishops protest and the Pope excommunicates the authors of the law. Bismarck banishes the Jesuits and forces clergy to swear allegiance before appointment.

1873

Germany

May Laws in Prussia give State control in the education of the clergy, jurisdiction over Church cases, excommunication, and the appointment and dismissal of ministers. Catholic bishops vote to oppose the laws and three are imprisoned and over 400 clergy dismissed.

Italy

1866 law extended to Rome. Proceeds of property of religious corporations divided between Holy See and charitable activities.

Sweden

By decree of toleration, Swedes allowed to leave Lutheran Church to join another Christian community.

1874

Great Britain

Gladstone declares acceptance of the papal decrees of 1870 inconsistent with civil allegiance.

Germany

Civil marriage made compulsory in Prussia and priests who refuse to accept the May Laws are threatened with banishment. Catholic Centre Party grows in strength at the General Election. German Old Catholics permit use of vernacular, allow marriage of priests, and abolish compulsory confession.

Austria

The May Laws replace Concordat of 1855. Powers of Church restricted. Bishops say they will only obey the laws in so far as in agreement with old Concordat.

Italy

Church declares it 'inexpedient' to vote in General Election, though many Catholics disobey.

Switzerland

Civil marriage made obligatory. No new monasteries to be founded, but religious freedom ensured.

1875

Germany

Pope declares recent anti-Catholic legislation in Germany invalid. The Prussian government refuses payment to clergy who will not obey; two-thirds of Prussian bishoprics and 1,400 curacies become vacant. Civil marriage made obligatory throughout the Empire. All religious orders suppressed in Prussia except those engaged in nursing.

Russia

Last Apostolic See of Roman Catholic Church suppressed.

Papacy

Pope institutes the cult of the Sacred Heart.

1876

Bulgaria

Massacre of thousands of Bulgarian Christians by the Turks provokes intense outrage in many parts of Europe.

Spain

Alfonso XII takes throne. Church property restored, Catholic schools reopened, diplomatic relations with Papacy restored. Catholicism once again official religion though recognized the existence of 'non-Catholic cults'. The State took responsibility for maintaining the Church. Civil marriage abolished and Protestant chapels closed.

1877

Germany

Eight Roman Catholic archbishops and bishops removed in Prussia, leaving only four.

Russia

Holy War against the Ottoman Empire to 'liberate Balkan Christians' and re-establish Constantinople as a great Christian centre.

1878

Germany

Roman Catholic seminaries closed.

Scotland

Catholic hierarchy restored in Scotland.

1879

Germany
Bismarck lessens persecution of Catholic Church after accession of Leo XIII.

France
Jules Ferry's education bill forbids members of unauthorized communities to teach.

General
Max Muller edits a translation of the sacred Books of the East.

1880

France
The Jesuit Order is dissolved, military chaplains are abolished, and candidates for the ministry are compelled to serve in the army for a year. State primary education made free and compulsory and religious teaching abolished.

Belgium
Diplomatic relations between the Papacy and Belgian government broken off over the School Law of 1879.

Germany
Bismarck relaxes application of the May Laws and reinstates clergy.

Russia
Constantine Petrovich Pobedonostsev becomes Procurator of the Holy Synod. An active promoter of Russian Orthodoxy, he sanctions the persecution or conversion of other religious groups.

1881

France
Ferry expels the unauthorized congregations.

Russia
Pobedonostsev begins a widespread persecution of the Jews following the assassination of Alexander II. Many Jews leave Russia for other parts of Europe and America. Pobedonostsev calls on Tsar Alexander III to reassert autocratic rule and opposes talks to improve the position of Catholics in Russia.

1882

Russia
Diplomatic relations between Russia and Holy See resumed. May Laws restrict Jews to the south-west of Russia; forbid Jews from becoming lawyers, owning land, holding administrative posts, appeal against court sentence or marry Christians without conversion. Jewish schools closed and Hebrew books banned.

1883

Russia
Pobedonostsev launches drive to establish parish schools throughout European Russia. Publishes Moscow Collection which sees religion as the foundation of a civilized life and threatened by modernism and democracy. He supports Leo Tolstoy's official removal from the Russian Orthodox Church for his support of student disorders. Act allows schismatics to hold religious services at home, to work, and hold internal passports, but not allowed to worship publicly, build new places of worship, nor proselytize.

Britain
Salvation Army founded.

1884

France
The Pope calls on the French bishops not to show hostility to the Republic.

Belgium
Catholic government elected. New education law makes many public schools Catholic and restores relations with Papacy. First worker priests among miners.

Russia
Lord Radstock and other Plymouth Brethren expelled from Russia. More parish schools established under direction of Holy Synod.

1885

Russia
Holy Synod forbids mixed marriages in largely Lutheran Baltic Provinces (Estonia and Latvia) unless children raised in Orthodox faith. Widespread protest.

1886

Portugal

Concordat with Vatican. Bishops to be nominated by the government, appointed by the Pope, and paid by the State. Parish clergy appointed by the state.

France

Teachers belonging to religious orders removed from State schools.

Germany

State examination and control of seminaries given up.

1887

Germany

Bismarck ends the *Kulturkampf.*

1888

Papacy

Papal encyclical *De libertate humana,* on human liberty.

1889

Italy

Penalties increased for clergy who use pulpit for political purposes.

1890

France

Pope Leo XIII's '*Ralliement*' policy encourages Catholics to accept the Republic through encyclical *Sapientiae christianae.* Right-wing and anti-Jewish Assumptionist Order dissolved.

Italy

Compulsory tithes abolished and Church charities taken over by State.

1891

France

Five French cardinals indict the government for its past anti-clerical legislation.

Papacy

Encyclical *Rerum novarum* condemns condition of workers, advocates just wage, right of association and right of peasants to land; missions encouraged and Vatican archives opened; but modernism and rationalism also condemned.

1892

France

Further papal encyclical declares that 'acceptance of the new regime is not only permitted but demanded'.

Germany

Revision of Luther's Bible completed.

Russia

Salaries of clergy increased and training streamlined, Anti-Jewish pogrom in Moscow forces thousands to flee.

1893

Romania

Priests become government officials and maintenance of Church and clergy becomes a charge on the general budget.

1894

France

Many Catholics support the prosecution of Dreyfus, intensifying anti-clerical feeling on the left.

Poland

Papal encyclical states that Polish Catholic clergy will no longer oppose Russia.

Russia

Pobedonostsev prevents appointment of papal nuncio to St Petersburg and frustrates Chúrch of England efforts to establish relations with the Orthodox Church. Protestant sects are persecuted.

Austria

Civil marriage made obligatory and declared sufficient without religious ceremony. Freedom of worship proclaimed.

Papacy

Discussion of reunion of Roman and Armenian Churches.

Belgium

Religious instruction made obligatory in all State schools.

1897

Jewry

First Zionist Congress held at Basle to promote resettlement of Palestine.

Austria

Los von Rom (Freedom from Rome) movement grows in Austria.

1898

Italy

Violence in Milan leads to suppression of 3,000 Catholic organizations.

1901

France

Law allows associations to be formed, but congregations have to be licensed.

1903

Denmark

Congregational councils of clergy and laity set up in each parish to manage church fabric and funds and elect clergy and bishops.

1904

France

Law suppressing teaching orders. Quarrel over choice of bishops between French government and Papacy.

1905

France

Separation of Church and State. Napoleon's concordat and organic articles repealed. Churches remained property of State but at the disposal of the ministers and orders.

Russia

Fr Gapon leads ill-fated 'Bloody Sunday' procession. Group of 32 formed by St Petersburg priests and petition for Church reform. Their leader Fr Petrov elected to the second Duma, but sentenced by the Synod to three months confinement and unfrocked. Group of 32 produce a declaration, approved by Metropolitan Antoni, calling for freedom

from State control, the restoration of the patriarchate abolished in 1700, and local religious councils. Religious tolerance law passed. Now legal to leave State Church. Evangelical sects form league of freedom whose platform includes schooling, equal rights for denominations, constitutional monarchy and equal suffrage. Nonetheless persecution of evangelicals, Old Believers, Jews and Roman Catholics (especially in Poland) continued. Pobedonostsev replaced by Lukyanov.

Italy

Bishops allowed to decide if Catholics of diocese can participate in political life.

1906

Papacy

Pius X refuses to recognize the separation of Church and State in France.

Netherlands

Catholic Social Weeks started.

Russia

Fr Gapon assassinated.

1907

Russia

Holy Synod declares it incompatible with priestly office to belong to parties opposed to the State and the Tsar.

Britain

Three Methodist churches unite as United Methodist Church.

1908

Portugal

New Portuguese republic expels religious congregations, parish administration is taken over by lay committees, and financed solely from contributions. Religious teaching in schools abolished and religious oaths for university and other courses.

Russia

Holy Synod tells bishops to encourage the participation of the Orthodox clergy in the right-wing League of the Russian People and other conservative societies. Russian Evangelical League founded, calling for moral regeneration to replace class struggle.

1909

Papacy

Pope condemns modernism in encyclical *Pascendi gregis.*

Spain

During '*Semana Trogica*' in Barcelona over 50 religious buildings destroyed by the populace during socialist uprising.

1910

General

World Missionary Conference in Edinburgh sees beginning of modern ecumenical movement.

Portugal

Prelates publish a pastoral censuring government. Minister of Justice orders its suspension. When defied, the Bishop of Oporto is deposed.

Russia

Protestant conferences to be vetted by Minister of Interior. They are not allowed to educate their children in their faith.

1911

Portugal

Law of separation. Church disestablished. Clergy forbidden to criticize the government or laws of the republic. Boards of laymen to take charge of Catholic worship. Ministers permitted to marry.

Russia

Rasputin, whose influence at court is very great, causes increasing embarrassment to ecclesiastical and political authorities and is forced to make pilgrimage to Holy Land, but returns and causes fresh scandals.

1912

Russia

40 conservative clergy elected to the fourth Duma.

1914

France

Clemenceau condemns Pope Benedict XV as 'the Bosche Pope'.

1916

Russia

Duma condemns Rasputin.

1917

Russia

Synod refuses to condemn February revolution. Provisional government puts church schools under Ministry of Education. All-Russian Council of the Church convened and rejects separation of Church and State. Patriarch Tikhon (elected Nov.) and council oppose Soviet revolution. Liberal clergy support it.

1918

Russia

Separation of Church and State (Jan.). Abolition of religious teaching and publications, censorship of sermons, and ban on church youth groups. Clergy deprived of vote, have to pay higher taxes, and children debarred from higher education. Churches may be used for secular purposes.

Portugal

Conservative regime of Sidonia Pais revokes anti-clerical measures and reopens diplomatic relations with the Papacy. Cult of Our Lady of Fatima becomes increasingly popular after three children claim to have seen the Virgin on a hillside in Estremadura.

1919

Italy

Catholic *Partito Popolare* formed (Jan.). Pope lifts ban on Catholic participation in political life and in following elections (Nov.) Catholics strongly represented.

Sweden

Religious instruction in schools made non-denominational.

Germany
United Evangelical Protestant National Church reorganized.

1920

France
Moves towards reconciliation with Papacy. Canonization of Joan of Arc.

Germany
Cardinal Pacelli, later Pius XII, becomes papal nuncio in Berlin.

1921

Russia
Anti-Soviet clergy call a *Sobor* (Church council) at Karlovtsy in Yugoslavia, endorsing anti-Bolshevik cause and calling for return of the monarchy.

1922

Russia
Trial and execution of Metropolitan Veniamin for resistance to seizure of church treasure decreed by State for famine relief in Volga region. Patriarch Tikhon put under house arrest.

1923

Russia
Reformist clergy of so-called 'Living Church' hold *Sobor*, strip Patriarch Tikhon of titles and clerical status, pass resolutions in favour of socialist reconstruction of society; also give more influence to clergy in church administration and make married priests eligible to become bishops. Produces split among faithful and eventually among the 'Living Church'. Patriarch Tikhon offers muted support for Soviet State and is released from house arrest.

1927

Russia
After period of uneasy compromise, Metropolitan Sergei proclaims full support for Soviet State. Beginnings of widespread

persecution of Islam and Islamic customs; mosques closed, mullahs displaced, veils banned, and Islamic courts and schools closed. Polygamy, bride-money and Ramadan stopped or discouraged.

General
World Conference on Faith and Order at Lausanne.

1928

General
Ecumenical Missionary Conference in Jerusalem stresses partnership of churches.

1929

Russia
Legislation on 'religious associations'. Religious activity only permitted to registered congregations each of which has to consist of at least 20 people over eighteen, who can hire church buildings and engage a priest. All outside religious activity prohibited. Evangelism banned.

Italy
Lateran treaties with Papacy recognizing the Vatican as a State and the Pontiff as its head. The Church assumes privileged status in Italy and formal reconciliation between the Papacy and Kingdom of Italy takes place.

Scotland
Presbyterian Churches of Scotland unite in the Church of Scotland.

General
World Conference of Lutherans at Copenhagen.

1931

Spain
Constitution of Republic separates Church and State; reduces clerical salaries; forbids Orders to teach and suppresses the Jesuits.

Papacy
Pius XI publishes encyclical *Quadragesimo Anno* on his ideas of the corporate state.

1932

Spain

Widespread attacks on Church property in Madrid, Barcelona and southern Spain. Over 55 churches or convents destroyed.

Germany

Protestant group founds pro-Nazi 'German Christians'.

1933

Papacy

Pope protests in encyclical *Dilectissima nobis* about anti-clerical measures in Spain.

Germany

Pope Pius XI publicly praises Hitler for his stand against communism and German bishops withdraw their opposition. Hitler and chairman of German Catholic Centre Party hold discussions and Centre Party supports Enabling Act (Mar.). Centre Party dissolves itself (July). Concordat signed between Nazi Germany and Holy See (July); ratified in September. Ludwig Müller of German Christians becomes Bishop of the Reich. Protestant Churches amalgamate as German Evangelical Church.

1934

Spain

Priests and religious in Oviedo murdered during Asturias rising.

Germany

The Protestant Barmen Synod accuses German Christians of departing from the Gospels and abandoning the legal basis of the Protestant Churches.

1935

Germany

Nuremberg Laws deprive Jews of citizen rights and forbid sexual relations and inter-marriage. Hitler sets up ministry of Church affairs.

Russia

Soviet Muslims prohibited from visiting Mecca.

Spain

Widespread attacks on Church property in the areas where anarchism and communism strong.

1936

Russia

Widespread purge of clergy and bishops. Of 163 bishops active in 1930 only 12 still at liberty in 1939.

Spain

Attacks on Church property following election of Popular Front; 160 churches or convents destroyed and 269 clergy killed. Renewed attacks and atrocities following the outbreak of war. 12 bishops and over 7,000 religious and clergy killed. Pius XI denounces 'the satanic enterprise' and blesses Franco's cause. Franco declares 'Spain shall be an empire turned towards God'.

1937

Germany

Protestant Church deprived of control of its finances. Protestant opposition forbidden. Pastor Niemöller and other Protestant pastors arrested and sent to concentration camps.

Papacy

Papal encyclical on atheistic communism.

1938

Spain

Diplomatic relations renewed between Papacy and Nationalists. The Pope calls for the re-establishment of a Catholic Spain.

Germany

Anti-Jewish pogrom on 9–10 November, the *Kristallnacht*, arouses protests from some Church groups.

1939

Papacy

Cardinal Pacelli becomes Pius XII.

1940

Great Britain

In letter to *The Times*, leading churchmen urge creation of a more egalitarian and just society as a postwar objective.

1941

Jewry

Germans begin extermination of Jews in occupied territories of Poland and Russia. By 1942 an estimated 1,400,000 Jews massacred by *Einsatzgruppen* murder squads. Beginning of construction of camps primarily for the systematic murder of Jews. Mass deportations of Jews from Germany to camps in the east begin.

Russia

Russian Orthodox Church pledges support for war with Germany.

Germany

Cardinal Galen of Munster condemns Nazi euthanasia programme.

1942

Jewry

Heydrich chairs 'Wannsee Conference' of Nazi officials in Berlin which adopts the 'final solution' of deportation and extermination of European Jewry. Extermination camps opened at Sobibor, Treblinka, Birkenau and elsewhere. Widespread deportations of French, Dutch, Polish and Slovak Jews to the camps for forced labour and gassing. Continued massacres of Russian, Baltic and Yugoslav Jews.

Great Britain

Archbishop William Temple's *Christianity and the Social Order* outlines advances in social welfare as necessary to a Christian society.

Papacy

Hitler closes diplomatic channels with the Vatican.

Holland

Dutch bishops issue a public protest against the deportation of Jews to Germany.

1943

Russia

Patriarchate and ecclesiastical administration re-established. Seminaries and theological academies opened, and churches permitted to reopen. Government appoints special Council for Church Affairs to supervise.

France

Archbishop Suchard of Paris founds worker-priest movement.

Jewry

Continuation of mass extermination programme by the Nazis. Belsen concentration camp opened. Destruction of Jewish Ghetto in Warsaw.

1945

Jewry

Mass extermination of European Jews continues until the last days of the war. Between 5 and 6 million Jews estimated to have been murdered or died of ill-treatment out of a European total of over 8.5 million in 1941.

1946

Russia

'Living Church' abolished.

General

Committee of World Council of Churches drafts plan for a reconstructed World International Assembly. International Christian Conference at Cambridge aims at closer relations between Protestant and Orthodox Churches.

1948

General

Representatives of 147 churches from 44 countries meet in Amsterdam to inaugurate World Council of Churches.

Jewry

End of British mandate in Palestine. Jews proclaim new State of Israel.

1950

Papacy

Papal decree *Humani Generis* against Existentialism and erroneous scientific theories. Pius XII pronounces dogma on bodily Assumption of the Virgin Mary.

1959

Papacy

Pope John XXIII announces the calling of the first Vatican Council since 1870. Vatican orders French worker-priest movement to discontinue.

1960

Great Britain

Archbishop of Canterbury visits Rome and meets the Pope. First to do so since the Reformation.

1961

Russia

Synod of bishops removes priests' function as legal administrator of parish and explicitly confines them to spiritual function. In next three years over half of existing parishes are disbanded, 10,000 churches and most monasteries closed. Closure of Jewish synagogues in Moscow.

Papacy

Papal encyclicals on Catholic social doctrine and for Christian reconciliation under Rome's Primacy.

General

Meeting of World Council of Churches at Delhi is joined by members of the Russian Orthodox Church and by Roman Catholic observers. The International Missionary Council is integrated with the World Council of Churches.

1962

Papacy

John XXIII insists on retention of Latin as the language of the Roman Catholic Church. Vatican Council opens with observer delegates from other Christian Churches.

1963

Great Britain

Anglican–Methodist 'Conversations' about unification.

Papacy

Vatican Council approves use of vernacular liturgies. Encyclical *Pacem in Terris* deals with peaceful settlement of disputes and with relations with non-Catholics and communists.

1964

Papacy

Paul VI makes pilgrimage to Holy Land.

1965

Papacy

Vatican Council promulgates documents exonerating the Jews from the death of Christ. The Catholic Church and the Eastern Orthodox Church agree to retract the excommunications put on each other in 1054. Worker-priests allowed to resume work.

1968

Papacy

Papal encyclical *Humanae Vitae* reaffirms Catholic doctrine of opposition to artificial birth control.

1970

Papacy

Pope reaffirms celibacy of clergy as a law of the Church.

1972

Great Britain

Presbyterian and Congregationalist Churches merge to form the United Reform Church.

1973

Papacy

Sacred Congregation for the Doctrine of the Faith reaffirms Papal Infallibility and the Church's unique claim to be the authentic Church of Christ.

1978
Papacy

Cardinal Karol Wojtyla of Cracow becomes first non-Italian Pope for 450 years as Pope John Paul II.

1979
Poland

Papal visit to Poland marks first visit of a Pope to a communist country since the Second World War.

Ireland

First papal visit to Ireland; Pope calls on young people to turn away from violence.

1980
Poland

Gdansk agreement with striking shipyard workers includes permission for religious broadcasts (Aug.); Roman Catholic hierarchy pledge their support for newly formed Solidarity organization (Oct.).

1981
Papacy

Pope John Paul II is seriously wounded by a Turkish gunman in Rome (13 May).

Yugoslavia

Appearence of the Virgin Mary (24 June) to six young people in Croatian village of Medjugorje.

Great Britain

Anglican General Synod votes overwhelmingly to admit women to Holy Orders as deacons.

Poland

Archbishop Glemp criticizes introduction of martial law (Dec.), but urges Poles to refrain from violence.

1982
Papacy

Pope attempts to mediate in dispute between Argentina and Great Britain after Argentina invades the Falkland Islands; first papal visit to Britain since 1531 is followed by papal visit to Argentina.

1983
Poland

Pope meets Lech Walesa during visit to Poland (June) and defends right to join free trade unions.

1984
Spain

Spanish socialist government introduces law requiring private schools in receipt of State funds to accept pupils without regard for religious views of the parents; mass demonstrations by Catholics who fear loss of control over church schools.

Poland

Pro-Solidarity priest Fr Jerzy Popieluszko kidnapped and killed by policemen. Major outcry leads to arrest, trial and imprisonment of the perpetrators.

1986
Ireland

Irish referendum votes against changes in the law on divorce following clerical opposition to the measure.

Papacy

First ever visit by a Pope to a Jewish Synagogue.

1987
USSR

President Gorbachev indicates a major relaxation towards the Russian Orthodox Church, the training of priests, and opening of places of worship.

1988
USSR

Russian Orthodox Church openly allowed to celebrate its millennium and three seminaries opened.

1989

USSR

Soviet Muslims demonstrate in Tashkent demanding the dismissal of the head of the 'spiritual directorate' of Central Asia and Kazakhstan and obtain his replacement by a religious leader; many mosques and religious training centres opened: new edition of the Koran prepared. President Gorbachev promises to allow Jewish 'refuseniks' the right to emigrate; confirmed in December at summit with President Bush in Malta. President Gorbachev meets the Pope in Rome and reaches agreement in principle on the opening of diplomatic relations with the Vatican and the ending of the ban on the Catholic Church (Uniate) of the Ukraine in force since 1946.

Great Britain

Salman Rushdie's novel, *The Satanic Verses*, is condemned by the Ayatollah Khomeini, whose *fatwa* pronounces a death sentence on the author; widespread protests in Britain by Muslims against the book and its author, who is forced to go into hiding.

1990

Papacy

Diplomatic relations re-established with many former East European communist states.

USSR

Catholics in Latvia and Lithuania in forefront of nationalist protests.

1991

Great Britain

Salman Rushdie apologizes for offence caused to Muslims and partial pardon offered by Iran.

1992

Russia

Kremlin cathedrals returned to Orthodox Church by State.

Great Britain

Vote for ordination of women in Anglican Church passed; many Anglicans defect to Rome.

1995

Ireland

Scandals over pay-offs of ex-mistresses of priests rock Catholic Church.

Scandinavia

Porvoo conference brings together Lutherans and Anglicans.

Papacy

Papal encyclical *Evangelium Vitae* (Gospel of Life) renews opposition to abortion, euthanasia and artificial contraception.

1996

Scotland

Desertion of Roman Catholic bishop to live with his mistress once again focuses attention on the celibacy issue.

England

Question of acceptance of homosexual clergy causes dissension in the Anglican Church.

1997

Bosnia

The Pope visits Bosnia, preaching religious and ethnic reconciliation.

Poland

Pope revisits Poland.

1998

Papacy

Pope issues conservative reassertion of Catholic doctrine, *Ad Tuendam Fidem* (On the Defence of Faith).

1999

Papacy

Pope makes first papal visit to Romania.

2000

Papacy

Pope issues historic apology for the sins of the church.

2002

Poland

Pope again goes to Poland revisiting scenes of his early life.

Papacy

Pope canonizes founder of Opus Dei, Mgr, Josémaria Escriva de Balaguer, who died in 1975.

Great Britain

Opening in London of largest Sikh temple outside India with room for 3,000 worshippers.

2003

France

Government insists on the removal of overt signs of religious affiliation in government premises, including schools, producing widespread protests from Muslim community.

England

Nomination of openly gay Canon Jeffrey John as Bishop of Reading splits Anglican church and threatens wider breach in the Anglican communion.

2004

France

French government insists ban on religious emblems must extend to Sikh turbans and other overt signs of religious affiliation such as large crucifixes.

Italy

Pope controversially canonizes Gianna Beretta Molla, heroine of the Italian anti-abortion movement, and the first mother to become a modern saint.

Spain

Clerical protests at law legalising same-sex marriages.

MAJOR LANDMARKS IN
WOMEN'S HISTORY

1869

Britain

Mill's *The Subjection of Women* pleads for women's political and social emancipation. Girton College, Cambridge, opened.

1870

Britain

Married Women's Property Act gives wives control over their earnings.

1873

General

Invention of typewriter opens up office employment to women.

1876

General

Deaths of two prominent Victorian female intellectuals, George Sand and Harriet Martineau.

1879

Norway

Henrik Ibsen's play *The Doll's House* protests against female subjection.

1881

Britain

High Schools instituted for women's secondary education in England.

1882

Britain

Married Women's Property Act gives married women the same legal status in regard to property as men.

1883

Germany

German SDP leader Auguste Babel publishes *Woman under Socialism.*

Britain

Repeal of Contagious Diseases Acts which made any women suspected of being a prostitute liable to compulsory medical examination.

1887

Germany

Fräulein Lange begins to work for opening of teaching profession to women.

1892

Finland

Establishment of the major feminist organization *Unioni.*

1893

General

Adoption of women's suffrage in New Zealand heightens question of female emancipation in Britain and Europe.

1896
Germany
Prussian universities admit women to lectures.

1899
General
International Women's Congress held in London.

1900
General
Women participate in Olympic Games for the first time.

Germany
German women petition the Reichstag to be allowed to sit state examinations and enter university.

1901
Norway
Women in Norway gain vote in local elections.

1902
Germany
Prussian government prohibits women from forming political associations.

1903
General
Marie Curie wins the Nobel Prize.

Britain
Women's Social and Political Union formed by Mrs Pankhurst to campaign for women's rights.

1905
General
Austrian Bertha von Suttner wins Nobel Peace Prize.

Britain
Suffragettes gaoled after demonstrations.

1906
General
Night shift work internationally forbidden for women.

Britain
British suffragettes go on hunger strike in prison.

1907
Austria
Women in Austria obtain equal employment rights in universities and hospitals.

1908
France
New divorce law grants automatic divorce after three years' legal separation.

Britain
London 'Women's Parliament' meets to discuss women's issues.

Denmark
Women taxpayers over 25 obtain the vote.

1909
Germany
Women admitted to German universities.

1910
Spain
Women admitted to Spanish universities.

1911
France
French Academy of Sciences refuses to admit Marie Curie.

Norway
Women admitted as MPs.

Portugal
Portuguese Constitutional Court acknowledges women's right to the vote.

Britain
Mass demonstration by 60,000 women in London demanding voting rights.

1912
Austria
First woman admitted to Austrian parliament.

Britain
Suffragettes launch militant campaign after women's suffrage bill defeated. Women on hunger strike are force-fed.

1913
Russia
Russian government bars women lawyers.

Britain
'Cat and Mouse Act' passed allowing release and rearrest of women on hunger strike. Suffragette Emily Davison kills herself by throwing herself under the King's horse at the Derby.

1914
Britain
Leading suffragettes declare support for the war.

1915
Netherlands
Dutch socialist feminist Aletta Jacobs calls International Women's Congress for Peace.

1916
Britain
Government figures reveal that over 2 million extra women have been recruited for war work since 1914 and announce recruitment of up to 400,000 women for a 'land army'.

Norway
Women win right to vote in national elections.

1917
Russia
Women's battalion formed by Provisional Government.

1918
Britain
Women over 30 given the vote and allowed to become MPs. *Married Love* by Marie Stopes calls for sexual fulfilment for women in marriage.

Soviet Union
Marriage Law Book of April 1918 institutes civil marriage and permits divorce; women given equal rights in relation to children.

1919
General
Women's International League for Peace and Freedom founded as international, non-violent disarmament organization.

Germany
Weimar constitution gives women the vote for the first time.

Britain
Nancy Astor becomes first woman MP to take her seat. Sex Disqualification Removal Act opens professions to women.

1920
Soviet Union
Soviet Union becomes the first country to allow women to obtain abortion on demand.

France
Pope canonizes Joan of Arc.

1921
Britain
First birth control clinic opened in Europe.

1922
General
Pius XI attacks new women's fashions as 'immodest'. First Congress of the International Federation of Feminine Athletes takes place in Geneva.

Hungary
New Hungarian constitution grants limited women's suffrage.

1923
France
First woman admitted to *Academic Française*.

Italy
Women given vote in Italian local elections.

1925
Greece
New Greek constitution provides for women to vote.

Italy
Launch of 'women into the home' campaign. Organisation set up to supervise children's and mother's welfare.

1926
Italy
Mussolini bars women from holding public office.

1927
Soviet Union
Marriage Law Book confirms right to divorce.

1929
General
World Congress on women's work meets in Berlin.

Britain
Women under 30 vote for the first time following act of 1928 admitting them to the franchise.

Italy
Law provides maternity leave and maternity grants for working mothers.

1930
General
Papal encyclical *Casti Connubi* urges women to return to home and family and find true equality as wives and mothers.

Britain
Women civil servants vote in favour of compulsory retirement of women at marriage in return for opening up more positions to women.

1931
Britain
First woman cabinet minister, Margaret Bondfield, appointed by the Labour Government.

1932
France
French government of Laval resigns after French Senate rejects votes for women.

1933
Germany
Nazis declare in favour of abolishing voting rights for women.

Italy
Extra allowances, loans, and prizes offered to large families.

1934

Poland

Poland extends conscription to women.

1936

Soviet Union

New family law attempts to strengthen families; divorce made more difficult and abortion banned.

1937

Italy

Fascists set up organisation for domestic women workers, enrolling 1.65 million by 1940.

1940

France

Vichy regime bans married women from public service occupations.

1941

Britain

Unmarried women between 20 and 30 conscripted for war work.

1944

Soviet Union

Monetary awards made to large families and single persons taxed.

1946

France

Constitution of Fourth Republic gives women the vote.

1948

Germany

Basic Law of the Federal Republic of Germany established on the basis of equal suffrage for men and women.

Italy

Italian Republic establishes full female suffrage.

1949

General

Simone de Beauvoir publishes *The Second Sex*.

1951–55

General

Research biologist Gregory Pincus develops oral contraceptive pill in the US.

1955

Soviet Union

Abortion again made legal.

1961

General

Contraceptive pill goes widely on sale in Western Europe.

1967

Britain

Abortion Act legalizes abortion.

1968

General

Papal encyclical *Humanae Vitae* reaffirms Catholic doctrine of opposition to artificial birth control.

Italy

Italian women demonstrate for women's rights and the legalization of abortion.

1969

Britain

Divorce law liberalized to allow 'no fault' divorce.

1970

General

Germaine Greer's *The Female Eunuch* popularizes feminist cause.

Britain

Equal Pay Act gives women equal pay for work of equal value.

Italy

Divorce law liberalized, giving women greater access to easy divorce.

1971

Switzerland

Women obtain the vote.

1972

General

International Women's Year.

Italy

Birth control legalized.

1975

Britain

Sex Discrimination Act forbids discrimination in employment, education, training, and the supply of goods and services.

France

Abortion legalized.

Italy

Major demonstrations by women for right to abortion.

1977

General

Northern Ireland peace women win Nobel Peace prize.

Italy

Abortion legalized.

1978

France

Monique Pelletier appointed France's first minister for women.

1979

Britain

Mrs Thatcher becomes first woman prime minister of Britain.

1980

Iceland

First woman becomes prime minister.

1981

Norway

First woman becomes prime minister.

1982

General

Women play leading role in opposition to siting of NATO Cruise missiles in Britain, the Netherlands and Germany.

1986

Austria

Austrian Green Party candidate, Frieda Meisser-Blau, campaigns unsuccessfully for the presidency.

Ireland

Irish referendum votes against change in divorce law.

1989

Denmark

Denmark becomes first European country to recognise same-sex, including lesbian, partnerships as having legal status for inheritance, tenancy and property rights.

1990

Ireland

Mary Robinson becomes first woman President of Ireland.

1990–91

General

Collapse of Eastern European regimes removes system of guaranteed employment, childcare and access to free healthcare for women.

1991

France

Edith Cresson becomes first woman prime minister.

1994

Britain

First women priests ordained in the Anglican communion.

1977

Britain

British Labour Party adopts 'women only' shortlists in some constituencies for the 1997 General Election, producing the largest ever number of women MPs.

2001

General

UN announces that for the first time over half of the people with HIV infection are women.

V
BIOGRAPHIES

A

ADENAUER, KONRAD (1876–1967) German statesman. Mayor of Cologne, 1917–33. Removed by Nazis. Prominent member of Catholic Centre Party in Weimar Republic. President of Prussian State Council, 1920–33. Twice imprisoned by Nazis. Founded Christian Democratic Union, 1945. Elected first chancellor of Federal Republic, 1949; re-elected 1953, 1957. Also foreign minister, 1951–55. Negotiated German entry into NATO, EEC. Established diplomatic relations with USSR, 1955. Resigned 1963.

ALEXANDER I (1777–1825) Tsar of Russia, 1801–25. Son of murdered Paul I. Entered War of Third Coalition against France, 1805. Obliged to conclude Treaty of Tilsit with Napoleon, 1807. Active in Fourth Coalition against France. Leading figure at Congress of Vienna, 1814–15. Secured creation of Polish Kingdom. Established 'Holy Alliance' with Prussia and Austria. Early promise of liberal rule gave way to reactionary policy, under influence of Metternich.

ALEXANDER II (1818–81) Tsar of Russia, 1855–81. 'The Liberator'. Son of Nicholas I. Succeeded to throne during Crimean War. Embarked on wide-ranging modernization of government. Most important reform was liberation of serfs, 1861. Innovations in legal code, 1862, and local government, education and army administration. Encouraged railway construction and banking. In foreign policy, concerned chiefly with expansion into Balkans, encouraging Pan-Slav movement. In Central Asia, Bokhara and Samarkand acquired, 1868. Russian troops reached Constantinople, 1878. Later in reign, more conservative in response to discontent in Poland, growth of revolutionary societies (e.g. Nihilists) and assassination attempts. Killed by bomb, 1881, before able to implement new constitution.

ALEXANDER III (1845–94) Tsar of Russia, 1881–94. Autocratic ruler, applying stern political repression. Pursued policy of 'Russification' of non-Russian nationalities within Empire, affected Jewish population in particular. Political opposition forced underground. First Marxist group formed in St Petersburg, 1883. In foreign policy, *Dreikaiserbund* lapsed following Bulgarian crisis, 1885–86. Secret alliance with France concluded 1894. In last years of reign, promoted development of Far Eastern territories, e.g. authorized building of Trans-Siberian railway.

ANDRÁSSY, COUNT GYULA (1823–90) Hungarian statesman. Radical nationalist and supporter of Kossuth, 1848–49, during struggle for Hungarian independence. Exiled until 1858. On return, supported moves towards *Ausgleich.* First prime minister of Hungary, 1867–71. Foreign minister of Austria–Hungary, 1871–79. Headed Austro–Hungarian delegation at Congress of Berlin, 1878, at which Austria–Hungary acquired control of Bosnia and Herzegovina. Sought to balance threat of Russian encroachment by allying with Germany.

AZAÑA, MANUEL (1881–1940) Spanish president. Founded Republican Party, 1924. Subsequently imprisoned. War minister, 1931. First prime minister of Second Republic, 1931–33, again 1936. Imprisoned for advocacy of Catalan self-rule, 1934. President, 1936–39. Fled to France, February 1939.

B

BABEUF, FRANÇOIS (1760–97) French journalist and early socialist. Emerged during Revolution as 'Gracchus Babeuf', publishing own newspaper, *Tribun du peuple*, advocating an egalitarian, communistic society. Formed

'Society of Equals', in Paris. Plotted armed rising to overthrow Directory, 1796. Arrested and executed. Influential on later French left-wing revolutionary thought.

BAKUNIN, MIKHAIL (1814–76) Russian anarchist. Resigned military commission over Russian treatment of Poles. Active in German revolutionary movement, 1848–49, also in Paris and Prague. Sentenced to death, transferred to Russian custody and exiled to Siberia, escaping 1861. Remaining years spent in Western Europe, funded by Herzen, encouraging anarchist revolution. Involved in risings in Lyons, 1870, and Spain, 1873. Opposed Marx and Engels in First International, 1869–72. Expelled at Hague Congress, 1872. Especially influential on Spanish and Italian anarcho-syndicalist thought.

BENEŠ, EDUARD (1884–1948) Czech statesman. Worked with Masaryk in Paris during First World War, seeking Czech independence. Principal Czech representative at Paris Peace Conference. Prime minister, 1921–22. Foreign minister, 1918–35. Active diplomat, chief proponent of Little Entente (Czechoslovakia, Romania and Yugoslavia, with French support). President of League of Nations Assembly, 1935. Succeeded Masaryk as president, 1935. Resigned, 1938, following Munich Agreement. President of Czech government-in-exile in London, 1941–45. Re-elected president, 1946. Resigned shortly after communist coup, 1948.

BERLUSCONI, SILVIO (1936–) Media tycoon and politician. Created his own party, *Forza Italia,* which gained support amid the break-up of the postwar Italian system in the 1990s. Formed his first government in 1994, but forced out of office in December as a result of accusations of corruption. Returned as leader of a coalition government in May 2001, supported by the right-wing Northern League and *Alleanza Nazionale,* pursuing pro-enterprise and anti-immigration policies. By May 2004 he had become Italy's longest-serving post-war prime minister.

BERNADOTTE, JEAN-BAPTISTE (1763–1844) Marshal of France, King of Sweden. Distinguished soldier, fought at Austerlitz and Wagram. Minister of War, 1799. Created Marshal, 1804. Created Duke of Ponte Corvo, 1806. Married into Bonaparte family. Governor of Hanseatic cities, 1807–09. Elected heir to Swedish throne, 1810. Ascended throne as Charles XIV, 1818. Encouraged pact with Britain and Russia against France. Received Norway in peace settlement. Liberal monarch, accepted principle of ministerial accountability to parliament, which also controlled finance.

BISMARCK, OTTO VON (1815–98) Prussian–German statesman, architect of German unification. Ultra-Royalist member of Prussian parliament, 1847. Hostile to liberal–national Revolution, 1848. Prussian member of German Diet at Frankfurt, 1851–59. Ambassador to St Petersburg, 1859. Ambassador to Paris, 1862. Recalled, 1862, to become Prussian chief minister. Dissolved parliament, undertook reorganization of army. Sought German unification under Prussian leadership, with exclusion of Austria. Engineered wars over Schleswig-Holstein, 1864, Seven Weeks' War with Austria, 1866, and Franco–Prussian War, 1870. Created Count, 1866. Chancellor of North German Confederation, 1867–71. Prince and Imperial Chancellor, 1871. Internal political struggles with Catholic Church, 1870s (*Kulturkampf*), and Socialists, 1880s. Introduced anti-Socialist legislation, universal suffrage, social insurance and protective tariffs. Foreign policy was geared to securing newly unified Germany. Devised system of alliances (*Dreikaiserbund*, Triple Alliance, Reinsurance Treaty), designed to preserve balance of power and isolate France. Presided at Congress of Berlin, 1878. After disagreements over policy with William II, resigned 1890.

BLAIR, ANTHONY (1953–) Prime Minister of Britain since 1997. Leader of the Labour Party from 1994, following sudden and unexpected death of John Smith. Pursued modernizing agenda under 'New Labour' banner, reforming party constitution and removing historic Clause IV commitment to nationalisation. Swept to huge victory in 1997 election, pledged to follow 'Third Way' of beneficial social improvements without major tax rises. Secured 'Good Friday Agreement' in Northern Ireland in 1998 and backed bombing of Serbia and intervention in the Balkans. Won a second landslide victory in June 2001, but his popularity was undermined by a perception of non-delivery of improvements in public services. A supporter of President's Bush's invasion of Afghanistan, his advocacy of war in Iraq in 2003 provoked huge opposition and continuing controversy about its justification and consequences.

BLANC, LOUIS (1811–82) French Socialist politician and writer. Chief work was *Organisation du Travail*, 1839, idealistic, stressing need for equality of wages. Critical of July Monarchy. Member of provisional government, 1848. Headed Luxembourg Commission on employment problems. Attacked for failure of 'National Workshops'. Accused of involvement in disorders, summer 1848. Elected to National Assembly, 1871. Elected to Chamber of Deputies, 1876, supporting left wing. Unpopular with French Marxists. Continued to advocate nationalization of property and establishment of worker co-operatives.

BLUM, LÉON (1872–1950) French Socialist statesman. Elected to Chamber of Deputies, 1919. By 1925, established as a leader of Socialist Party. First Socialist prime minister, 1936, leading 'Popular Front'. Introduced important reforms, including 40-hour working week. Formed second Popular Front, 1938. Imprisoned by Vichy regime, 1940. Accused of being responsible for French military weakness and tried, 1942. Interned in Germany during Second World War. Briefly prime minister of caretaker government, 1946.

BOULANGER, GENERAL GEORGES (1837–91) French soldier. Active in defence of Paris during Franco–Prussian War. As minister of war, 1886–87, replaced royalist army officers with republicans. Dismissed, 1888. Politically ambitious. Elected deputy, 1888, advocating nationalistic, expansionist policies. Sought limitations on constitution, won backing of militarists and royalists, and 'League of Patriots'. Suspected of planning coup, fled from France. Condemned in absence as a traitor. 'Boulangism' subsequently disintegrated. Death by suicide.

BRANDT, WILLY (1913–92) West German Social Democratic statesman. Active in opposition to Hitler. Member of Bundestag, 1949–57. President of Bundesrat, 1955–57. Mayor of West Berlin, 1957–66. Chairman of Social Democratic Party, 1964–89. Joined coalition with Christian Democrats under Chancellor Kiesinger, 1966. Chancellor in SPD – Free Democrat coalition, 1969. Awarded Nobel Peace Prize, 1971. Resigned following spy scandal, 1974, remaining Chairman of SPD until 1987. Consistent advocate of improved relations with Eastern Europe (*Ostpolitik*).

BREZHNEV, LEONID ILYICH (1906–82) Soviet politician. Communist Party official in Ukraine and Moldavia. Held military posts, 1933–34. Member of Praesidium of Supreme Soviet, 1952–57. President of Praesidium, 1960–64, succeeding Marshal Voroshilov. Succeeded Khrushchev as First Secretary of Central Committee, 1964. General Secretary of Central Committee, 1966. His period in power epitomized the ailing old-guard leadership of the Soviet Union.

BRIAND, ARISTIDE (1862–1932) French statesman. Allied with Socialists, 1894–1906. Elected deputy, 1902. Expelled by Socialists for accepting office as minister of public instruction and worship in Radical coalition, 1906–09. Drafted and implemented separation of Church and State. Prime minister 11 times between 1909 and 1929. Used force to end railway strike, 1910. Foreign minister, 1925–32. Major diplomatic role, worked for European unity. Sought *rapprochement* between France and Germany. Successes included Locarno Treaty, 1925, and Kellogg–Briand Pact, 1928. Awarded Nobel Peace Prize with Stresemann, 1926. Defeated in presidential elections, 1931.

C

CABALLERO, FRANCISCO LARGO (1869–1964) Spanish Socialist politician. Elected to parliament, 1918. Became leader of UGT, 1925. Minister of labour in several governments, 1931–33. Proponent of genuinely socialist policy, helping to provoke military reaction against government, 1936. Prime minister, 1936–37. During Civil War, failed to achieve cohesion among parties of the left. Went into exile in France, 1939. Interned by Germans, 1942–45. Minister of interior of Republican government-in-exile, 1946.

CALONNE, CHARLES ALEXANDRE DE (1734–1802) French statesman and financier. Appointed Comptroller-General of finance, 1783. Policy of heavy borrowing aggravated financial problems. Advised Louis XVI to summon Assembly of Notables, 1786, in order to achieve fairer distribution of taxes. Aroused aristocratic opposition by threatening privileged with taxation. Banished when Assembly requested explanation of national budgetary deficit. Served as finance minister in émigré government in London during Revolution.

CARNOT, LAZARE (1753–1823) French politician. Known as the 'organizer of victory' during French Revolutionary Wars. Entered Legislative Assembly, 1791. Endorsed execution of Louis XVI. Won victory at Wattignies. Member of Committee of Public Safety, 1793–94. Responsible for raising 14 Revolutionary armies. Sought to limit Robespierre's powers. Member of Directory. Imprisoned for opposition to Barras, 1797. Returned to power following Napoleon's coup of Brumaire. Minister of war, 1800–01. Partly responsible for French military success in Rhineland and Italy. Resigned in protest at Napoleon's imperial ambitions. Returned, 1814, to defend Antwerp. Minister of interior during 'Hundred Days'. Exiled by restored Louis XVIII.

CASTLEREAGH, VISCOUNT (1769–1822) ROBERT STEWART, 2ND MARQUESS OF LONDONDERRY British statesman. Chief Secretary for Ireland, 1798–1801. Secretary for war and colonies, 1805–06, 1807–09. Secured appointment of Wellington as commander in Portugal. Foreign secretary, 1812–22. Favoured union of Britain and Ireland. Resigned when George III vetoed Catholic Emancipation. Influential figure at Congress of Vienna, 1814–15. Advocate of balance of power in Europe. Disappointed with operation of 'Congress System'. Death by suicide.

CATHERINE II, THE GREAT (1729–96) German-born Empress of Russia, 1762–96. Married Peter, heir to Russian throne, 1745. Peter dethroned and murdered, Catherine made Empress. 'Enlightened Despot', favouring French philosophers, e.g. Voltaire. Few reforms actually introduced; abolished capital punishment (except for political crimes). During reign, number of serfs in Russia rose, as did economic burdens on peasantry. Turned to repression after Pugachev Revolt, 1773–75. Main development in reign was rapid territorial expansion: three Partitions of Poland, 1772, 1793 and 1795. Wars with the Ottoman Empire 1774 and 1792. War with Sweden, 1790. Annexed Crimea and Ukraine.

CAVOUR, COUNT CAMILLO BENSO DI (1810–61) Italian statesman. Architect of Italian unification. In newspaper, *Il Risorgimento*, called for republican system. Piedmontese minister of agriculture, marine and commerce, 1850. Succeeded D'Azeglio as prime minister of Piedmont, 1852. Strengthened constitutional government, reduced influence of Church and encouraged economic development. Brought Italian question before Congress of Paris, 1856.

Made pact with Napoleon III to expel Austrians from Italy (Plombières Agreement), 1858. Resigned when Napoleon failed to honour agreement. Returned, 1860; negotiated union of Parma, Modena, Tuscany and the Romagna with Piedmont–Sardinia. Encouraged Garibaldi's sweep through Sicily while occupying Papal States. First prime minister of unified Italian kingdom, 1861.

CEAUSESCU, NICOLAE (1918–89) Romanian dictator. Member of underground Communist Party, 1936. Party Secretariat member, 1954. Deputy leader, 1957–65. General secretary, 1965. Head of state, 1967. Combined independent foreign policy, notably criticism of the 1968 Warsaw Pact invasion of Czechoslovakia, with authoritarian regime, massive repression and personality cult. Repressed demonstrations prompted by economic crisis, 1967. Showed little sympathy for the Soviet line instituted by Gorbachev (q.v.). His corrupt regime and bankrupt economy provoked riots in 1989. Their savage repression led to the December 1989 'winter revolution'. Executed with his wife Elena by firing squad after secret trial, 25 December 1989.

CHAMBERLAIN, NEVILLE (1869–1940) British Conservative politician. Son of Joseph Chamberlain. Lord Mayor of Birmingham, 1915–16. Director General of National Service, 1916–17. Member of parliament, 1918–40. Postmaster General, 1922–23. Paymaster General, 1923. Minister of health, 1923, 1924–29. Chancellor of the exchequer, 1923–24, 1931–37. Prime minister, 1937–40. Resigned, 1940, becoming Lord President of the Council in wartime coalition, following rebellion by Conservative MPs in favour of Churchill. Much criticized for attempts to appease Germany and Italy, especially in Munich Agreement, 1938. Retired from politics, due to fatal illness, 1940.

CHARLES X (1757–1836) King of France, 1824–30. Brother of Louis XVIII. Lived in Britain during French Revolution. Returned to France to lead revolt in Vendée, 1795.

Appointed Lieutenant-General of France, 1814. After 1815, led reactionary 'Ultras' in struggle with Constitutionalists. Ascended throne, 1824. At first, promised loyalty to Constitution of 1814. Provoked opposition through his support of clerical party, favourable treatment of former émigrés and reactionary religious legislation. Appointed Prince de Polignac as head of government, 1829. Dissolved parliament, 1830. 'Five Ordinances', July 1830, limiting political and civil rights, led to revolution. Abdicated in favour of Comte de Chambord, but succeeded by his cousin, Louis Philippe.

CHIRAC, JACQUES (1932–) French Gaullist politician; elected to the National Assembly in 1967. Served as Prime Minister, 1974–76, 1986–88. Maintained power base as Mayor of Paris from 1977. Unsuccessful candidate in the 1981 and 1988 Presidential elections, he was elected in May 1995 and re-elected overwhelmingly in 2002 against the far-right candidate Le Pen on the second ballot.

CHURCHILL, SIR WINSTON (1874–1965) British statesman. Conservative MP, 1900–04. Became a Liberal in protest at Tariff Reform policies. Liberal MP, 1906–08, 1908–22. Constitutionalist, later Conservative MP, 1924–45. Conservative MP for Woodford, 1945–64. Under-secretary at Colonial Office, 1906–08. President of the Board of Trade, 1908–10. Home secretary, 1910–11. First Lord of the Admiralty, 1911–15. Chancellor of the Duchy of Lancaster, 1915. Minister of munitions, 1917–19. Secretary for war and air, 1919–21. Secretary for air and colonies, 1921. Colonial secretary, 1921–22. Chancellor of the exchequer, 1924–29. First Lord of the Admiralty, 1939–40. Prime minister and minister of defence, 1940–45. Leader of the Opposition, 1945–51. Prime minister, 1951–55. Minister of defence, 1951–52. Made Knight of the Order of the Garter, 1953. Resigned, 1955. Chequered career; during First World War involved in disputes over Admiralty policy and Gallipoli campaign. Opposed Conservative policies over India and rearmament during 1930s. Advocated prevention of German expansion. Wartime leadership earned him legendary status, though not returned to power in 1945. Negotiated wartime alliance with USA and USSR. After Second World War, favoured alliance with USA against USSR.

CIANO, COUNT GALEAZZO (1903–44) Italian politician. Son-in-law of Mussolini. Prominent Fascist minister of propaganda, 1935. Minister of foreign affairs, 1936–43. Negotiated 'Axis' agreements with Germany. Supported expansionist policy, e.g. annexation of Albania, 1939 and entry into Balkans, 1940–41. Began to oppose policy when its failure became clear after 1943, with defeats in North Africa. Appointed Ambassador to Vatican. Voted against Mussolini in Grand Council. Tried and executed by Fascists.

CLAUSEWITZ, KARL VON (1780–1831) German military strategist. His theory of war, outlined in *Vom Kriege,* dominated Prussian military thinking.

CLEMENCEAU, GEORGES (1841–1929) French Radical statesman. Mayor of Montmartre, 1870–71. Entered National Assembly, 1871. Elected deputy, 1876, becoming leader of extreme left, 1876–93. Founded radical newspaper, *La Justice,* 1880. Critical of government. Contributed to downfall of several ministries. Instrumental in securing resignation of President Grévy after honours scandal, 1887. Lost seat in Chamber, 1893. Returned after supporting Dreyfus. Senator, 1902–20. Minister of interior, 1906. Prime minister, 1906–09. Completed Church–State separation. Strike-breaking measures aroused Socialist opposition. Attacked military mismanagement during First World War. Appointed prime minister and minister of war, 1917–20. Semi-dictatorial rule. Secured appointment of Foch as Chief of Allied forces, March 1918. Presided at Paris Peace Conference, 1919, pressing for harsh penalties on Germany. Lost presidential election, 1920.

D

DANTON, GEORGES JACQUES (1759–94) French Revolutionary politician. Became an administrator of Paris, 1791. Founded Cordeliers Club with Marat and Desmoulins. Minister of justice, 1792. Voted for execution of Louis XVI, 1793. Original member of Committee of Public Safety. President of Jacobin Club, 1793. Achieved suppression of Girondins. Later sought conciliation, moving to right wing of Jacobins. Sought to moderate Revolutionary Tribunal. Opposed by Robespierre and the 'Mountain'. Arrested, 1794, and guillotined.

DE GAULLE, CHARLES (1890–1970) French soldier and statesman. Member of French military mission to Poland, 1919–20. Lectured at Staff College. Sought to modernize Army. Published *The Army of the Future*, 1932–34. Ideas subsequently employed by German Army. Briefly a member of Reynaud's government, 1940. Fled to Britain after fall of France. Became head of Committee of National Liberation ('Free French'), 1943. Claimed status of head of government. Led unsuccessful attempt to recapture Dakar. Entered Paris, August 1944. President of provisional government, 1945. Suspected of authoritarian ambitions. Resigned, 1946. Founded political party (Rally of the French People), retiring from its leadership, 1953. During Algerian Crisis, 1958, invited by President Coty to form temporary government with wide executive powers. Won overwhelming victory in referendum on new Constitution. Elected first president of Fifth Republic, 1959. Granted independence to former French colonies in Africa, 1959–60.

Granted Algeria independence, 1962. Developed independent nuclear deterrent. Encouraged closer ties with West Germany. Twice vetoed British entry to EEC, 1962–63, 1967. Re-elected on second ballot, 1965. Re-elected after May 1968 'Events', but resigned, 1969, following opposition to his plans to reform Constitution.

DELCASSÉ, THÉOPHILE (1852–1923) French politician. Elected deputy, 1889. Minister of colonies, 1893–95, favouring territorial expansion. Foreign minister, 1898–1905, 1914–15. Encouraged *Entente Cordiale* with Britain, 1904. Active in Moroccan Crisis, 1905. Forced to resign. Naval minister, 1911–13. Ambassador to St Petersburg. Involved in negotiations for treaty of London, 1915.

DELORS, JACQUES (1925–) French Socialist politician. Leading advocate of European federalism as embodied in the Delors Plan. President of the European Commission, 1985–95.

DE VALERA, EAMON (1882–1975) Irish states-man. Led group of Irish Volunteers in Easter Rising, 1916. Imprisoned, released 1917. Elected MP, 1917. Leader of Sinn Fein, 1917–26. Elected president of Dáil Eireann. Opposed 1921 treaty with Britain. Led extreme nationalists during Civil War, 1922–23. Leader of Fianna Fail, winning 1932 elections. Between 1932 and 1938 reduced links with Britain. After 1937, prime minister under revised constitution. Maintained Irish neutrality during Second World War. Lost power, 1948. Re-elected, 1951–54, 1957–59. President, 1959–73.

DISRAELI, BENJAMIN, 1ST EARL OF BEACONS-FIELD (1804–81) British Conservative poli-tician. Member of parliament, 1837–76. Opposed repeal of Corn Laws, 1846, heading Protectionist group until 1852. Leader of the Commons and chancellor of the exchequer, 1852, 1858–59, 1866–68. Prime minister, 1868, 1874–80. Lord Privy Seal, 1876–78.

Created Earl of Beaconsfield, 1876. Leader of Conservative Party until shortly before death. Introduced franchise reform, 1867, almost doubling electorate. Stressed Tory con-cern over social and imperial issues. Bought almost half share in Suez Canal Co., 1875. Created Queen Victoria Empress of India, 1876. Aimed to restrict Russian penetration of the Balkans. Attended Congress of Berlin, 1878, winning recognition of Britain's right to occupy Cyprus. Failed to resume office after election defeat, 1880.

DOLLFUSS, ENGELBERT (1892–1934) Austrian politician. Leader of Christian Socialist party. Chancellor, 1932–34. Opposed by Nazis and Socialists. Used political violence as pretext for dictatorial government. Sus-pended parliamentary rule, 1933. Provoked and suppressed Socialist revolt. Granted authority by parliament to implement new Fascist-style constitution. Murdered during attempted Nazi coup.

DREYFUS, ALFRED (1859–1935) French soldier. Artillery captain appointed to General Staff. Wrongly accused of espionage and impris-oned. Case revealed depth of anti-Semitism within French establishment (Dreyfus was himself Jewish), and provoked bitter division between 'Dreyfusards' (the left, intellectuals, anti-clericals) and 'anti-Dreyfusards' (espe-cially Army and Church). Retried and par-doned. Verdict finally overturned, 1906.

DUBČEK, ALEXANDER (1921–92) Czech politi-cian. First Secretary of the Czechoslovak Communist Party and key figure in the 'Prague Spring' (q.v.) reform movement, which culmi-nated in the Soviet invasion of Czechoslovakia in August 1968. Dismissed from his post, he was first president of the New Federal Assembly (Aug. 1968–Sept. 1969) then ambassador to Turkey (Dec. 1969–June 1970) before being expelled from the Communist Party. This attempt to build a national social-ism with a 'human face' posed a threat to Soviet control of Eastern Europe. By 1989, however, circumstances had changed. In

December 1989 Dubček was elected chairman (speaker) of the Czech parliament.

E

ENGELS, FRIEDRICH (1820–95) German political philosopher. Associate and colleague of Karl Marx. After 1842, lived mostly in Britain. Wrote *The Condition of the Working Classes in England,* 1844. Involved in revolutionary movement in Baden, 1844. With Marx, wrote *The Communist Manifesto,* 1848. Helped Marx financially. Final years engaged in preparing Marx's writings for publication, completing *Capital* in 1894.

ERHARD, LUDWIG (1897–1977) Architect of postwar West German 'economic miracle', finance minister, 1949–63 and subsequently chancellor, 1963–66. Resigned when his party refused to support his planned tax increases.

F

FERRY, JULES (1832–93) French politician. Critic of Second Empire. Elected to *Corps Législatif,* 1869. Opposed war with Prussia, 1870. Mayor of Paris, 1870–71. Prominent on Republican left. Minister of public instruction, 1879. Organized reformed, non-sectarian education system. Prime minister, 1880–81, 1883–85. Main interests were education and colonies. Responsible for colonial growth in North Africa and Indo-China. Assassinated by religious fanatic.

FOCH, FERDINAND (1851–1929) French soldier, Marshal of France. Served as military instructor, 1894–99. Director of *École de Guerre,* 1907–11. Wrote *Principles and Conduct of War,* 1899. Appointed Chief of Staff, 1917. Created Generalissimo of Allied forces from March 1918. Field marshal, 1919. Supervised implementation of military provisions of Treaty of Versailles.

FOUCHÉ, JOSEPH, DUKE OF OTRANTO (?1759–1820) French minister of police. Elected to National Convention, 1792. During Revolution, crushed rebellions in Vendée and Lyons. Endorsed execution of Louis XVI. Initially lent support to Robespierre, but came to oppose him over question of 'Cult of the Supreme Being'. Minister of police under Directory, 1799, and Napoleon, 1802, 1804–10. Maintained internal order by repressive means. Returned as minister of police, 1815. Under Louis XVIII held office briefly as ambassador to Dresden. Exiled as a regicide.

FRANCIS FERDINAND (1863–1914) Archduke of Austria. Nephew of Emperor Francis Joseph. Became heir to throne, 1896. Hoped to give autonomy to subject Slav peoples. Assassination by Bosnian Serb at Sarajevo, 28 June 1914, immediate cause of First World War.

FRANCIS JOSEPH (1830–1916) Emperor of Austria, 1848–1916. Succeeded during Revolution, King of Hungary from 1867. Quickly restored order after 1848 in Hungary and Lombardy. Abolished Constitution, 1851. Ruled personally until 1867. Favoured government by strong central bureaucracy. Hostile to party politics. Allied monarchy with Catholic Church. Accepted *Ausgleich,* 1867. Sought to maintain balance of power in Europe, but by annexing Bosnia–Herzegovina, 1908, provoked ill-feeling. Precipitated First World War by attacking Serbia, 1914.

FRANCO, FRANCISCO (1892–1975) Spanish soldier and military dictator. Held command of Foreign Legion in Morocco. Chief of Staff, 1935. Governor of Canaries, 1936. On outbreak of Civil War, integrated Foreign Legion and Moorish troops into rebel army.

Became leader of Nationalist forces, 1936. Defeated Republican government, 1939. Established corporatist, authoritarian state, acting as *'Caudillo'* ('Leader'), and permitting only one political party, the Falange. Maintained Spanish neutrality during Second World War. Presided over Spain's rapid postwar economic development. Faced growing problem of regional separatism in last years. Ensured his own succession by King Juan Carlos I.

FREDERICK II, THE GREAT (1712–86) King of Prussia, 1740–86. Son of Frederick William I. Laid claim to Silesia. Encouraged War of Austrian Succession, 1740–48. Made alliances with France and Bavaria. Won military victories at Mollwitz, 1741, and Chotusitz, 1742. Invaded Bohemia, 1744. Acquired Silesia by Peace of Dresden, 1745. Entered Seven Years' War, 1756–63, in alliance with Britain against Austria, France, Russia, Sweden and Saxony. Position of Prussia greatly strengthened after Peace of Hubertusburg, 1763. Took part in First Partition of Poland with Russia, 1772. Entered War of Bavarian Succession, 1778. Established *Fürstenbund*, 1785, in order to safeguard Imperial Constitution against Austria. Despite some reversals, a great military commander. Encouraged economic development. Began codification of Prussian law. Some liberalization, e.g. on laws of torture, religion and censorship. Chief interest was modernization of army.

G

GAMBETTA, LÉON MICHEL (1838–82) French politician. As a lawyer, defended critics of Second Empire. Elected deputy, 1869. One of group who declared the Republic, September 1870. Minister of the interior in government of National Defence. During siege of Paris, escaped to Tours, becoming nominal dictator for five months. Continued war against Germany even after fall of Paris. Re-elected, 1871. Not involved in crushing of Paris Commune. Emerged as leader of more radical Republicans, playing important part in downfall of President MacMahon, 1877. Became president of Chamber of Deputies, 1879. Formed government, 1881. Resigned when accused of having dictatorial ambitions, 1882.

GARIBALDI, GIUSEPPE (1807–82) Italian patriot. Involved in 'Young Italy' movement, 1834. Escaped to South America after sentenced to death for role in attempted seizure of Genoa. Fought against Austrians in Italy, 1848. Joined revolutionary government in Rome, 1849. Voted for a republic, repulsed French troops but forced to retreat by Austrians. Summoned by King Victor Emmanuel, 1859, and helped to liberate North Italy. Swept through Naples and Sicily, 1860, handing conquests over to Piedmont–Sardinia. Active in campaign against Austria in which Italy acquired Venice. Tried to seize Rome, 1867, but thwarted by French. Eventually secured Rome for Italy during Franco–Prussian War. Supported French Republican government after fall of Napoleon III.

GIOBERTI, VINCENZO (1801–51) Italian philosopher and politician. Ordained a priest, 1852. Held nationalist views. Saw Papacy as most appropriate vehicle for Italian independence and unity, as he argued in *Del primato morale e civile degli Italiani*, 1843, which influenced supporters of Pius IX. Briefly prime minister of Piedmont, 1848.

GIOLITTI, GIOVANNI (1842–1928) Italian statesman. Entered parliament as a liberal, 1882. Became minister of finance, 1889. Prime minister five times between 1892 and 1921. First ministry, 1892–93, was ended by 'Tanlongo Scandal', involving irregularities at Bank of Rome. Prime minister again, 1903–05, 1906–09. Sought reconciliation with Church. Fourth ministry, 1911–14, saw annexation of Tripoli, war with the Ottoman

Empire, acquisition of Libya, Rhodes and Dodecanese. Ministry fell after general strike in protest at heavy taxation. Fifth ministry, 1920, saw Italy convulsed by civil strife and disputes over Fiume. Resigned 1921. Had introduced universal suffrage, attempted to maintain Italian neutrality during First World War. Introduced wide-ranging social reforms after war. Critical of Mussolini after 1924.

GLADSTONE, WILLIAM EWART (1809–98) British Liberal politician. Entered parliament, 1832. Held several junior offices under Peel. President of the Board of Trade, 1843. Colonial secretary, 1845. Out of office following split over repeal of Corn Laws, 1846–52. Chancellor of the exchequer, 1852–55, 1858–66. Cut government expenditure and advocated free trade. Became leader of Liberal Party, 1866. Prime minister, 1868–74. Introduced national education system. Disestablished Church of Ireland, 1869. Introduced secret ballot in elections, army reforms under Cardwell. Second ministry, 1880–85, formed after success of 'Midlothian' election campaign. Widened franchise, 1884. Main preoccupation (as in last two administrations, 1885–86, 1892–94) was Home Rule for Ireland. Issue caused decisive breach in Liberal Party. Both Home Rule Bills, 1886 and 1893, were defeated. Retired, 1894.

GOEBBELS, JOSEPH (1897–1945) German Nazi propagandist. Early recruit to Nazi Party. Party chief in Berlin, 1926–30. Became Party's propaganda chief, 1929. Elected to Reichstag, 1930. Minister of propaganda, 1933–45. Held powerful position in Nazi leadership. Made skilful use of oratory, parades, demonstrations and radio. Attracted to 'radical' aspect of Nazi ideology. Death by suicide.

GOERING, HERMANN (1893–1946) German Nazi military and political leader. First World War ace pilot. Joined Nazi Party, 1922. Given command of Storm Troopers, 1923. Elected to Reichstag, 1928. President of Reichstag,

1932–33. Entered government, 1933, as Reich commissioner for air, minister president of Prussia and Prussian minister of the interior (hence controlled Prussian police). Created Gestapo, 1933. Head of Luftwaffe. Responsible for preparing Germany's war economy. Created general, 1933, field marshal, 1938 and Reich marshal, 1940. Became Hitler's deputy during Second World War. Influence declined after Battle of Britain, 1940. Disgraced after plotting to oust Hitler, 1945. Condemned to death at Nuremberg. Death by suicide.

GORBACHEV, MIKHAIL (1931–) Soviet statesman who succeeded Chernenko as general secretary of the Communist Party in 1985. His advent to power, after a succession of ailing old-guard leaders, marked a major departure in the Soviet leadership. Succeeded Gromyko as President, 1988. His reforming policies, especially *perestroika* and *glasnost*, were soon threatened by nationalism in such areas as Azerbaijan and the Baltic. His policy of non-interference was vital in the 1989 revolutions in Eastern Europe which overthrew the old communist regimes. He survived the August 1991 coup attempt, but his power base was fatally eroded as the old Soviet Union disintegrated. Resigned as President, 25 December 1991, after formation of Commonwealth of Independent States. Although Gorbachev has enjoyed popularity outside Russia, since 1991 his influence within Russia has been negligible.

GORCHAKOV, PRINCE ALEXANDER MICHAELE-VICH (1798–1883) Russian statesman. Ambassador to Vienna, 1854–56. Foreign minister, 1856–82. Chancellor, 1863. Secured Austrian neutrality during Franco–Prussian War, 1870. Co- operated with Prussia, winning release of Russia from provisions of treaty of Paris in 1870. Most powerful minister in Europe until advent of Bismarck.

GREY, 1ST VISCOUNT, SIR EDWARD GREY (1862–1933) Liberal MP for Berwick-on-Tweed, 1885–1916. Foreign secretary,

1905–16. His support of Britain's obligation to help Belgium in 1914 took Britain into the First World War. He believed in international arbitration, which was used successfully in the Balkan Wars. Later a champion of the League of Nations.

GROMYKO, ANDREI ANDREEVICH (1909–89) Soviet statesman. Attached to Soviet embassy in Washington, 1939. Ambassador in Washington, 1943. Attended Tehran, Yalta and Potsdam conferences. Elected deputy of Supreme Soviet, 1946. Became deputy foreign minister, and permanent delegate to United Nations Security Council, using veto frequently. Ambassador to Britain, 1952–53. Foreign minister, 1957–85. Signed nuclear test ban agreement, 1963. President, USSR, 1985–88.

GUIZOT, FRANÇOIS (1787–1874) French statesman. Professor of modern history at Sorbonne, 1812–22. Deprived of his posts because of his liberalism. Prevented from lecturing, 1825. Elected to Chamber of Deputies, 1830. Minister of the interior, minister of public instruction. Introduced system of primary education. Imposed restrictions on press freedom. Ambassador to London, 1840. Foreign minister, 1840–47. Prime minister, 1847–48. Resorted to repressive measures, contributing to fall of July Monarchy by refusal to make political concessions. Returned to Paris after 1848 Revolution, seeking to rally monarchists. Abortive coup attempt, 1851, led to his retirement from politics.

H

HAVEL, VÁCLAV (1936–) President of Czechoslovakia since unanimous election, 29 December 1989, until its demise on 31 December 1992. Subsequently, first President of the Czech Republic, 1993–2003. Former dissident and political prisoner. Born Prague. Playwright. Co-founder of Charter 77. Jailed for four months. Victim of smear campaign. Jailed again, 1979, for four and a half years for subversion. Co-founder of Civic Forum, November 1989. Reluctantly accepted popular draft as presidential candidate, December 1989. He presided over the 'Velvet Divorce' of the Czech and Slovak parts of Czechoslovakia, leading to the independence of the Czech Republic on 1 January 1993.

HEATH, SIR EDWARD (1916–) British Conservative politician. Entered parliament, 1950. Party whip, 1951–55. Chief whip, 1955–59. Minister of labour, 1959–60. Lord Privy Seal, 1960–63. Secretary for trade and industry, 1963–64. First leader of Conservative Party to be elected by ballot, 1965. Prime minister, 1970–74. Proponent of European integration. Achieved British entry into EEC, January 1973. Failed to solve problems of inflation and industrial relations. Improved British relations with China. Following electoral defeats of 1974, replaced as leader of Party by Margaret Thatcher, 1975. He has been a consistent critic of many aspects of Thatcherism.

HEGEL, GEORGE (1770–1831) German philosopher. Became professor of philosophy at Berlin, 1818. Described process of 'dialectic', i.e. interaction of two conflicting half-truths (thesis and antithesis), to produce synthesis. At first welcomed French Revolution and Napoleon. His ideas were interpreted as supporting an authoritarian state and being hostile to liberalism. Ideas on dialectic, in modified form, used by Marx. Writings include *The Philosophy of Right*, 1821, *The Science of Logic,* 1812–16.

HERZEN, ALEXANDER (1812–70) Russian political thinker. Civil servant, 1835–42; aroused suspicion of authorities because of his westernizing ideas. Went to Paris, 1847. Much influenced by experience of Revolution, 1848. Went to London, 1851. Stressed need for realism in revolutionary planning. Gave financial help to Bakunin and others.

HERZL, THEODOR (1860–1904) Zionist leader, born in Hungary. Influenced by the anti-Semitism of the Dreyfus Affair. In pamphlet, *Judenstaat*, 1896, proposed creation of a Jewish State. Called first Zionist Congress at Basel, 1897. First President of World Zionist Organization. Later years spent in unsuccessful negotiations with Kaiser, Sultan, Russian prime minister etc. with aim of securing land for new state.

HIMMLER, HEINRICH (1900–45) German Nazi leader and Chief of Police. Early member of Nazi Party. Involved in Munich Putsch, 1923. Head of *Schutzstaffel* (SS), 1929. Head of Gestapo, 1934, subsequently of all police forces, 1936. Head of Reich administration, 1939. Minister of the interior, 1943. Commander-in-Chief of Home Forces, 1944. Used elaborate system of terror, espionage, detention and murder to reinforce totalitarian state. Bore major responsibility for racial extermination policies. Made attempts to negotiate unconditional surrender before end of war. Tried at Nuremberg. Death by suicide.

HINDENBURG, PAUL VON (1847–1934) German soldier and president. Fought at Königgratz, 1866, and in Franco–Prussian War, 1870–71. Became general, 1903. Retired, 1911. Recalled to duty on outbreak of First World War. Victories won with Ludendorff at Tannenberg, 1914, and Masurian Lakes, 1915, made him a national hero. Became Chief of General Staff, 1916. Organized withdrawal from Western Front, 1918 (giving rise to myth of undefeated German Army). Advised Kaiser to abdicate and arranged Armistice. Retired, 1919. Elected president of Weimar Republic, 1925–34. Defeated Hitler in presidential election, 1932, but appointed him chancellor, January 1933.

HITLER, ADOLF (1889–1945) Dictator of Germany. Born in Austria. Served in Bavarian Army during First World War, becoming lance corporal, twice decorated with Iron Cross. Joined German Workers' Party in Munich, 1919, transforming it into National Socialist German Workers' Party (NSDAP/Nazi Party), based on extreme nationalism and anti-Semitism. Attempted putsch in Munich, 1923, which proved abortive, though making him a national figure. While in prison, wrote political testament, *Mein Kampf*. Began to reorganize Nazi Party, 1925, Established unrivalled position as leader of party. Created efficient propaganda machine and organized elite guard, *Schutzstaffel* (SS). Helped to power by Great Depression. Nazi Party won 107 seats in 1930 Reichstag elections, becoming second largest party. In elections, July 1932, won 230 seats (highest they ever achieved). Appointed Chancellor by Hindenburg, January 1933, though Nazis still a minority in Reichstag. Following Reichstag fire and Enabling Act, assumed dictatorial powers. Other political parties dissolved. Nazi Party purged of rivals by 1934. On death of Hindenburg, 1934, became president, uniting position with that of Chancellor or *Führer* ('Leader'). Internal opposition ruthlessly suppressed. Rearmament programme expanded, 1935, aiding economic recovery. Occupied Rhineland, 1936. Rome–Berlin 'Axis' negotiated, 1936. Annexed Austria, 1938 (*Anschluss*), Gained Sudetenland after Munich Agreement, 1938. Seized remainder of Czechoslovakia, 1939. After Non-Aggression Pact with USSR (Molotov–Ribbentrop Pact, August 1939), invaded Poland, 1 September 1939, precipitating Second World War. Achieved swift military successes through *Blitzkrieg* campaigns, but fatal error was in attacking Russia, June 1941. Faced combined opposition of USSR, USA and Britain. Survived assassination attempt, July 1944. Committed suicide during closing stage of war.

HONECKER, ERICH (1912–94) Head of state, German Democratic Republic (East Germany) 1976–89. Having held various offices in the East German Communist Party from 1958, he succeeded Ulbricht as first secretary in 1971, and in 1976 became chairman of the Council of State (head of state) and undisputed leader of East Germany. Ousted from power when communism collapsed in 1989. Faced numerous accusations of abuse of power. Given sanctuary in Soviet Union.

HORTHY DE NAGYBÁNYA, MIKLÓS (1886–1957) Hungarian admiral and Regent. Commander-in-Chief of Austro–Hungarian Navy, 1917. Minister of war in 'White' government, 1919. With Romanian help, crushed communist regime of Béla Kun, 1920. Chosen to be Regent, acting as head of state, on behalf of absent King Charles. Refused to give up office in favour of King Charles, 1921. Ruled virtually as a dictator. Formed alliance with Germany, 1941, but withdrew 1944. Imprisoned by Germans but freed by Allies. Retired to Portugal.

HUSAK, GUSTAV (1913–91) President of Czechoslovakia, 1975–89. Became first secretary of the Communist Party when Dubček (q.v.) was ousted from office in 1969, following Soviet invasion. Retained this position when he became president in 1975, thus strengthening his ascendancy in the leadership. Fell from power after the 'Velvet Revolution' of 1989. Expelled from the Communist Party, February 1990.

I

IZVOLSKI, ALEXANDER (1856–1919) Russian statesman. Entered diplomatic service, 1875. Held important post in Tokyo, 1899. Transferred to Copenhagen, 1903. Unexpectedly appointed foreign minister, 1905, holding post for five years. Worked for better relations with Britain and Japan. Successes marred by Bosnian Crisis, 1908–09. Aggrieved by Austria's seizure of Bosnia–Herzegovina

before Russia had secured 'compensation' through fresh solution to Straits Question. As ambassador in Paris, 1910–16, strengthened military alliance between Russia and French.

J

JARUZELSKI, GENERAL WOJCIECH (1923–) Polish soldier and politician. Long and distinguished army career. Became Chief of General Staff, 1965, minister of defence, 1968, and member of Politburo, 1971. Became prime minister after resignation of Pinkowski, 1981. Declared martial law in effort to tackle economic crisis and to counter growth of Solidarity (q.v.) movement. Solidarity banned and its leaders detained and tried. Lifted martial law, July 1983. Became president in 1989, but succeeded in 1990 by Lech Walesa (q.v.), elected by a nationwide vote.

JAURÈS, JEAN (1859–1914) French Socialist leader and writer. Elected deputy, 1885, again 1889, 1893. Founded Socialist newspaper, *L'Humanité*, 1904, giving support to Dreyfus. By 1905 had become leader of united Socialist Party. Never held office, in accordance with decision of Congress of Socialist International, 1905. Not a Marxist, but in French revolutionary tradition. Hoped to mobilize French and German workers to prevent outbreak of war. Assassinated by French nationalist fanatic.

JOSEPH II (1741–90) Holy Roman Emperor, 1765–90; Archduke of Austria, 1780–90. Succeeded his father, Francis I. Ruled Habsburg possessions jointly with his mother, Maria Theresa. Ruled alone after her death, 1780, as an enlightened monarch. Limited clerical influence, granted religious toleration, 1781. Abolished serfdom, extended education, reformed taxation. Established strong, centralized government. Aroused hostility, expressed in several revolts, 1788. Also, in 1788, waged unsuccessful war against the Ottoman Empire.

JUAN CARLOS I (1938–) King of Spain. Succeeded to the throne, 22 November 1975. Married Princess Sophia of Greece, 1962. After the long years of the Franco (q.v.) dictatorship, his accession marked the entry of Spain into a more modern, liberal era.

K

KAPP, WOLFGANG (1868–1922) German civil servant. Collaborated with group or ex-soldiers in attempt to overthrow Weimar Republic, 1920. Thwarted by general strike. Fled to Sweden. Returned to Germany, 1922. Died awaiting trial.

KÁDÁR, JÁNOS (1912–89) First secretary of the Hungarian Communist Party, 1956–65, and prime minister, 1956–58 and 1961–65. Minister of interior 1948–50; arrested and imprisoned, 1951–54. First secretary in 1956, Kádár initially favoured reform, but later supported Soviet intervention, which crushed the Hungarian rising. Remained prime minister until 1958 and first secretary thereafter. Greater freedom of expression was allowed from 1959 and when Kádár held the premiership for a second term, 1961–65, he took positive measures of reconciliation and cautious liberalization.

KÁROLYI, COUNT MIHÁLY (1875–1955) Hungarian statesman. Entered parliament, 1905. Politically liberal, became increasingly radical. Led Independent Party during First World War. Became prime minister, 1918 and sought armistice. Provisional president of Hungarian Republic, aimed to introduce reforms. Overthrown by communist coup,

1919 and went into exile. Returned, 1946, after downfall of Horthy. Served as a diplomat, 1946–49, before resuming exile.

KAUTSKY, KARL (1854–1938) German socialist of Czech descent. Colleague of Marx. Collaborated with Engels in London, 1881–82. Founded socialist newspaper, *Die Neue Zeit,* 1883. Criticized 'revisionism' of German Social Democrats. Disagreed with Lenin over interpretation of Marxism. Condemned Russian Revolution and refused to join German Communist Party. Remained a pacifist during First World War. Joined Austrian Social Democrats after war. Fled to Holland after *Anschluss.*

KEMAL ATATÜRK (MUSTAFA KEMAL) (1881–1938) Creator of modern Turkish nation. Joined Young Turk reform movement. Entered army, winning quick promotion. Fought Italians in Tripoli, 1911, and in Balkan Wars. Involved in Gallipoli campaign during First World War. Led national resistance after Greek invasion following the Ottoman Empire's defeat. Renounced loyalty to Sultan and formed provisional government in Ankara, 1920. Led Turks in War of Independence until 1922, expelling Greeks, deposing Sultan and establishing Republic. Became first president of Republic, 1923–38. Architect of modern, secularized state. Emancipated women. Sought to build strong nation from homelands of Anatolia and residue of European Turkey. Did not attempt to regain former Arab possessions. Territorial settlement with Greece achieved at Treaty of Lausanne, 1923.

KERENSKY, ALEXANDER (1881–1970) Russian politician. Entered Duma, 1912, as critic of Tsarist government. Led Social Revolutionary Party. Leading role in Revolution, March 1917. Became minister of justice, then minister of war. Prime minister of provisional government, July 1917. Continued war with Germany and attempted major offensive which reduced his popularity. Defeated Kornilov's military rising, September 1917.

Overthrown by Bolsheviks in November Revolution, 1917. Spent rest of life in exile in France, Australia and USA.

KEYNES, JOHN MAYNARD, 1ST BARON KEYNES (1883–1946) British economist. Worked at Treasury during First World War. Chief representative at negotiations prior to Treaty of Versailles. Criticized reparations plans in *The Economic Consequences of the Peace*, 1919. Made radical proposals for dealing with unemployment by provision of public works. Ideas influenced Liberal Party's election manifesto, 1929. Full proposals on economic controls in interests of maintaining full employment appeared in *The General Theory of Employment, Interest and Money*, 1936. Inspired 'Keynesian Revolution' during and after Second World War. Rejected classical belief in self-regulating economy. Argued need for government expenditure to be adjusted to control level of public demand. Advised chancellor of the exchequer during Second World War. Chief British delegate at Bretton Woods Conference, 1944. Involved in discussions leading to creation of International Monetary Fund and World Bank.

KHRUSHCHEV, NIKITA SERGEYEVICH (1894–1971) Soviet politician. Joined Communist Party, 1918. Fought in civil war. Member of Central Committee of Party, 1934. Full member of Politburo and of Praesidium of Supreme Soviet, 1939. Organized guerrilla warfare against Germans during Second World War. Premier of Ukraine, 1944–47. Undertook major restructuring of agriculture, 1949. Became First Secretary of All Union Party on death of Stalin, 1953. Denounced Stalinism, 1956. Relegated Molotov, Kaganovich and Malenkov (potential rivals), 1957. Succeeded Bulganin as prime minister, 1958–64. Official visits to USA, 1959, India and China, 1960. Deposed, 1964, following economic failures.

KOHL, HELMUT (1930–) Chancellor (prime minister) of the Federal Republic of Germany 1982–98; Christian Democrat minister–president, Rhineland Palatinate, 1969–76; leader of the opposition in the Bundestag, 1976–82. Presided over the reunification of Germany in 1990 and became first chancellor of a reunited Germany following victory in the December 1990 election. By November 1996 Kohl had become the longest-serving chancellor in German history (except for Bismarck). A strong advocate of European monetary union, the single currency and expansion of the European Union in the East. His later career was overshadowed by accusations of impropriety over party funds.

KOLCHAK, ALEXANDER VASILYEVICH (1874–1920) Russian sailor. After Russo–Japanese War, 1904–05, reorganized navy. Commanded Black Sea Fleet from 1916. After 1917 Revolution, led counter-revolutionary government in Siberia. Captured by Bolsheviks and executed.

KORNILOV, LAVR GEORGYEVICH (1870–1918) Russian soldier. Fought in Russo–Japanese War, 1904–05. Divisional commander in Galicia during First World War. Appointed Commander-in-Chief after Revolution, March 1917. Accused of planning military coup. Arrested, but managed to join anti-Bolshevik forces on Don. Killed in action.

KOSCIUSZKO, TADEUSZ ANDRZEJ (1746–1817) Polish patriot. Fought in American War of Independence. Returned to Poland, 1786. Led abortive rising against Tsar, 1794, following Second Partition of Poland, 1793. In France, rejected conciliatory moves by Napoleon. Present at Congress of Vienna, 1814. Failed to persuade Tsar of strength of Polish case.

KOSSUTH, LAJOS (LOUIS) (1802–94) Hungarian revolutionary and politician. Member of Hungarian Diet, 1825–27. As a journalist, wrote in support of Hungarian independence. Twice imprisoned. Insistence on Magyar supremacy within Hungary aroused suspicions of other nationalities. Returned to Diet, 1832–36, 1847–49. Speech in favour of independence, March 1848, signalled beginning of Revolution. Key role in enactment of 'March Laws', abolishing privileges of nobility and ending serfdom. Introduced responsible government. Served as minister of finance. Became provisional governor of Hungary, 1849, ruling in dictatorial style. Went into exile following Russian intervention in Hungary on behalf of Austria. Attempted to organize risings in Hungary against Austrian rule, 1859, 1861, 1866. Withdrew from politics following *Ausgleich*, 1867.

KRUGER, (STEPHANUS JOHANNES) PAULUS (1825–1904) Afrikaner politician. One of leaders of revolt against British, 1880, which restored independence of Transvaal. Elected president of Transvaal, 1883; re-elected 1888, 1893, 1898. Refused to grant political rights to incoming (non-Afrikaner) miners following discovery of gold on Rand. Resulting tensions contributed to Boer War, 1899–1902. Canvassed European support for Afrikaner cause, 1900.

KUN, BÉLA (1886–1937) Hungarian communist leader. Following capture by Russians during First World War, established brief Soviet Republic in Hungary, March–August 1919. Escaped to Vienna after counter-revolution, settled in USSR. Died in Stalinist purge.

L

LAFAYETTE, MARQUIS DE (1757–1834) French soldier and politician. Fought in American War of Independence, winning French support for America. Sat in Assembly of Notables, 1787. Elected to States-General, 1789, remaining when Third Estate decided to become National Assembly. Commander of National Guard. Politically moderate, earned hatred of Jacobins. Sought to restrain

popular violence and to protect Louis XVI. Obliged to relinquish post in Paris, becoming commander of army in the east. Military failure against Austrians, 1792, led to his impeachment by National Convention. Sought safety in Germany. Detained there until 1797. Entered Chamber of Deputies, 1818, becoming leader of left-wing opposition. Involved in 1830 Revolution, supporting Louis Philippe and commanding National Guard. Personified revolutionary ties between USA and France.

LAMARTINE, ALPHONSE MARIE LOUIS DE (1790–1869) French poet and politician. Held diplomatic posts in Italy until 1828. Politically a moderate royalist. Elected deputy, 1833. Declined position of foreign minister under Polignac, 1829. Criticized 1830 Revolution. After fall of July Monarchy, 1848, became foreign minister, but refused to grant aid to other revolutionary movements. Stood for election as president, but was defeated by Louis Napoleon. Subsequently retired from political life. Political and religious ideas expressed in writings such as *Harmonies poétiques et religieuses*, and *La Chute d'un Ange*.

LANDSBERGIS, VYTAUTAS (1932–) President of Lithuania, 1990–92, when his harsh nationalist position and failures of economic policy produced defeat. The symbol of modern Lithuanian nationalism.

LAVAL, PIERRE (1883–1945) French politician. Member of Chamber of Deputies, 1914–19, and from 1924 onwards. Originally a Socialist, became Independent after 1927, on elevation to Senate. Minister of public works, 1925. Minister of justice, 1926. Prime minister, 1931–32, 1935–36. Foreign minister, 1934–36. Negotiated Hoare–Laval Pact with Britain, 1935. Proponent of closer ties with Germany and Italy. After fall of France, 1940, played major role in creation of Pétain's Vichy regime. Prime minister, 1942–44. Collaborated with Germany, e.g. in supply of forced labour. Fled to Germany, then Spain, after liberation of France, Repatriated, tried and executed for treason.

LE PEN, JEAN-MARIE (1928–) French right-wing politician. Served in the Foreign Legion and youngest member of the National Assembly in 1956. From 1972 built up the *Front National* (FN) on an anti-immigrant platform, establishing a strong base in the area around Marseilles. Secured 35 seats in the 1986 elections and entered the presidential race in 1988, winning 14% of the vote, but eliminated on the first round. The Party lost all but one of its seats in June 1988 and illness and scandals reduced Le Pen's influence. In 2002, however, he secured second place in the first round of the presidential elections, but was heavily defeated by Chirac in the next round.

LENIN, VLADIMIR ILYICH, (V.I. ULYANOV) (1870–1924) Russian revolutionary leader and architect of Soviet State. After expulsion from Kazan University for political activity, absorbed writings of Marx. In St Petersburg, organized League for the Liberation of the Working Class. Exiled to Siberia, 1897. In London, 1903, when Russian Social Democratic Labour Party divided into Mensheviks and Bolsheviks. Led Bolshevik wing and published newspaper, *Iskra* ('The Spark'). Involved in abortive Russian Revolution, 1905. Controlled revolutionary movement from exile in Switzerland. Smuggled into Russia by Germans, 1917. Overthrew Kerensky's provisional government and became head of Council of People's Commissars. Ended war with Germany and concluded treaty of Brest-Litovsk, March 1918. Civil war with 'White' armies continued until 1921. As chairman of Communist Party, established virtual dictatorship and dissolved Constituent Assembly. Created Communist International, 1919, to encourage world revolution. Introduced New Economic Policy, 1921, in diversion from planned communist transformation of economy. Recognized dangers implicit in rise of Stalin. Important both as theoretical writer

on Marxism and as practical revolutionary organizer. Communist era in Soviet Union officially ended after 1991 coup attempt.

LITVINOV, MAXIM MAXIMOVICH (1876–1951) Soviet diplomat. Early recruit to Bolshevik Party. Diplomatic representative in Britain after November Revolution, 1917. Deported, 1918. Deputy foreign commissar, 1921–30, 1939–46. Foreign commissar, 1930–39. Sought to improve USSR's foreign relations. Took USSR into League of Nations, 1934. Advocate of collective security, supporting Franco–Russian Pact, 1935. Dismissed in favour of Molotov when Stalin required agreement with Hitler, 1939. Ambassador to Washington, 1941–42.

LLOYD GEORGE, DAVID, 1ST EARL LLOYD GEORGE OF DWYFOR (1863–1945) British Liberal statesman. Member of parliament, 1890–1945. President of the Board of Trade, 1905–08. Chancellor of the exchequer, 1908–15. Introduced controversial People's Budget, 1909, proposing increased taxation to fund social reform and naval rearmament. Budget rejected by House of Lords, causing constitutional crisis leading to Parliament Act, 1911. Minister of munitions, 1915–16. Secretary for war, 1916. Prime minister, 1916–22. Leader of the Liberal Party, 1926–31. Created Earl Lloyd George, 1945. Dynamic and efficient wartime leader. Attended Paris Peace Conference, 1919. Opposed calls at Versailles for draconian penalties on Germany. Faced economic problems at home in postwar period. Continuing violence in Ireland led to creation of Irish Free State, 1921, weakening Lloyd George's position, as did revelations of his sale of honours. Forced to resign, 1922, when Conservatives left coalition. Never held office again.

LOUIS XVI (1754–93) King of France, 1774–93. Grandson of Louis XV. In early years of reign, successive ministers (e.g. Turgot, Necker) attempted financial reforms, but nobility resisted proposals to include them in taxation net. Costly intervention in American

War of Independence spread constitutional theories in France. Summoned States-General, 1789, on advice of Necker (its first session since 1614). Third Estate's decision to meet separately as National Assembly constituted first act of French Revolution. With death of Mirabeau, 1791, Louis lost a valuable supporter. Sought refuge in Varennes, and appealed to fellow monarchs for help, while France was already at war with Prussia and Austria. Royal family subsequently imprisoned. Republican majority in Convention secured trial and execution of Louis, 1793.

LOUIS XVIII (1755–1824) King of France, 1814–24, but assumed royal title during Revolution in 1795. Younger brother of Louis XVI. Fled France during Revolution. Maintained links with groups of monarchist exiles. Returned to France on fall of Napoleon, 1814. Negotiated Charter (Constitution) with Talleyrand prior to return. Withdrew to Ghent during Napoleon's 'Hundred Days', resuming throne after battle of Waterloo. Sought national reconciliation by granting constitutional rule. Unable to prevent ascendancy of ultra-Royalists, e.g. in reactionary *Chambre Introuvable*. Former Republicans, Imperialists and Protestants suffered during 'White Terror'.

LOUIS PHILIPPE (1773–1850) King of the French, 1830–48. Son of Philippe Égalité. Duke of Orléans. Supported Revolution, later lived abroad. Permitted to return to France, 1817, though avoided political involvement. Appointed Lieutenant-General after 1830 Revolution. Chosen to replace Charles X as king. Initial popularity waned as government became increasingly reactionary, e.g. under Guizot, who limited press freedom and interfered with judicial process. Reign saw growth of middle-class prosperity and of republicanism. Toppled by 1848 Revolution. Settled in England. Known as the 'Citizen King'.

LUDENDORFF, ERICH (1865–1937) German soldier. Entered army, 1882. Major-General by 1914. Planned deployment of German armies at outbreak of First World War. With Hindenburg, won victory at Tannenberg, 1914. Transferred to Western Front, 1916. Shared increasing control of government with Hindenburg after 1916. Conceived spring offensive, 1918. Involved in abortive Kapp Putsch, 1920. Took part in Hitler's Munich Putsch, 1923. Founded extreme nationalist party, 1925. Unsuccessful candidate for Reich presidency, 1925.

LUXEMBURG, ROSA (1870–1919) Polish-born German revolutionary leader. Major theoretician of Marxism. Imprisoned for opposition to First World War, 1915–18. Founded German Communist Party in 1918 with Karl Liebknecht, based on earlier Spartacist group. Opposed the nationalism of existing Socialist groups, as shown by their participation in War. Critical of German Social Democrats in government. Sought to restrain more violent colleagues, but unable to prevent Spartacist uprising, January 1919. Brutally murdered by counter-revolutionary troops.

M

MACMAHON, PATRICE (1808–93) French soldier and president. Military career began under Charles X. Served in Algeria. Chief successes came under Second Empire. Fought in Crimean War. Created Marshal of France, 1859. Duke of Magenta, 1859–70. Governor-General of Algeria, 1864–70. Fought in Franco–Prussian War. Crushed Paris Commune, 1871. President of Third Republic, 1873–79. Politically a royalist. Sought to make full use of president's executive authority. Dismissed prime minister, 1877. Hoped to appoint Orléanist nominee, Duc de Broglie. Dissolved Chamber of Deputies, held elections, but did not secure royalist majority. Resigned, 1879.

MAHMUD II (1785–1839) Sultan of Turkey, 1808–39. Strong ruler, restored authority over Pashas, eliminated Janissaries from politics, 1826. Waged unsuccessful war against Russia, 1809–12. Implemented reforms in government, education and the army. Unable to maintain control of outlying territories, e.g. Serbia and Greece. Tried to crush Greek independence movement, 1821–29. Obliged to recognize Greek independence by treaty of Adrianople, 1829. Increasingly threatened by Mehemet Ali in Egypt, 1830s.

MANNERHEIM, BARON CARL GUSTAF EMIL (1867–1948) Finnish soldier and statesman. Served in Russian Imperial Army, 1889–1917. Became General during Russo–Japanese War, 1904–05. Commanded 'White' Guards, 1918, retaking Helsinki from communists. Regent of Finland, 1918–19. Head of state, 1919–20. Led Finnish armies against Russia. Gained independence of Finland from USSR. Created field marshal, 1933. President of Defence Council, 1931–39. Active in defence of Finland following Russian attack, 1939. Made pact with Germany against Russia, 1941. Marshal of Finland, 1942. President, 1944–46. Declared war on Germany, March 1945.

MARIA THERESA (1717–80) Archduchess of Austria, Queen of Hungary and Bohemia. Daughter of Charles VI. Succeeded to rule of Habsburg territories, 1740, as result of Pragmatic Sanction. Fought France, Spain and Prussia in War of Austrian Succession, 1740–48. Gained imperial title for her husband Francis, 1745. Ceded Silesia and Italian territories, 1748. Suffered humiliating losses while allied to France in Seven Years' War, 1756–63. Ruled jointly with her son, Joseph II, 1756–80. Took part in Partition of Poland, 1772. Introduced economic reforms which strengthened Austrian resources.

MARX, KARL (1818–83) German philosopher. Father of 'Scientific Socialism'. Editor of *Rheinische Zeitung,* 1842. Exile in Paris, 1843–45, and Brussels, 1845–48. Sympathized with early German socialists. Wrote *The Communist Manifesto,* 1848,

with Engels. Returned to Cologne during 1848 Revolution. Founded *Neue Rheinische Zeitung.* Expelled from Prussia, settled in London, 1849. European correspondent for *New York Tribune,* 1851–62. Developed philosophy of 'class struggle', described economic laws of capitalism. Derived ideas from dialectic of Hegel, and from materialism of Feuerbach. First volume of *Capital* published 1867. Helped establish International Workingmen's Association in London, 1864. Conflicts with Bakunin led to disintegration of Association, 1876.

MASARYK, TÓMAŠ (1850–1937) Czech philosopher and statesman. Became Professor of philosophy at Prague, 1882. Represented Young Czech Party in Austrian parliament, 1891–93. Led 'Czech Realists', 1907–14. Critical of Austrian policies. Became chairman of Czech National Council in London, 1914. Described views on nationality question in *The New Europe* (periodical), from 1916 onwards. Organized Czech Legion in Russia, 1917. Won support of President Wilson. Accepted by USA as head of an allied government, 1918. Returned to Czechoslovakia as president-elect, 1918. Re-elected twice. Resigned, 1935.

MATTEOTTI, GIACOMO (1885–1924) Italian Socialist politician. Elected deputy, 1919. Became general secretary of Socialist Party, 1924. Denounced Fascist violence in *The Fascisti Exposed.* Murdered by Fascists as a result. Death produced political crisis. Non-Fascist deputies blocked normal operation of parliament. Party meetings banned by Mussolini, censorship introduced. Incident cost Fascists foreign sympathy.

MAXIMILIAN (FERDINAND MAXIMILIAN JOSEPH) (1832–67) Archduke of Austria. Emperor of Mexico, 1864–67. Brother of Emperor Francis Joseph. Commanded Austrian Navy, 1854. Governor of Lombardy-Venetia, 1857–59. Unable to withstand Piedmontese– French attack on Lombardy, 1859. Became Emperor of Mexico as nominee of Napoleon III, 1863. Empire collapsed when

French withdrew military backing under US pressure. Captured by Liberals under Juárez and executed.

MAZZINI, GIUSEPPE (1805–72) Italian patriot. Member of *Carbonari*, 1830. Imprisoned and exiled to France. Founded 'Young Italy' revolutionary movement. Aimed to unify Italy under republican government. Proposed rising proved abortive, 1832. Movement became increasingly violent. Settled first in Marseilles, then London, 1837. Extended ideas by founding 'Young Europe' to foster concept of community of republican nations. Liberated Milan, 1848. Member of brief Roman Republican triumvirate, 1849. Lost prestige after fall of Rome, never returning to Italy. Prompted attempted risings in Mantua, 1852, Milan, 1853 and Genoa, 1857.

MEHEMET ALI (1769–1849) Ruler of Egypt. Led Albanian troops against France on behalf of the Ottoman Empire, 1799. Governor of Egypt, 1805. Granted supreme authority in Egypt by Sultan, 1811. Sponsored military and economic growth. Conquered Sudan, 1820–22. Founded Khartoum, 1823. Helped the Ottoman Empire during Greek War of Independence, 1823–28. Appointed governor of Crete. War against the Ottoman Empire, 1832–33, won him Syria and Adana. After second war, 1839–41, forced to give up earlier conquests by Great Powers, gaining status as hereditary ruler of Egypt in return.

METTERNICH, CLEMENS (1773–1859) Austrian statesman and diplomat. Created Prince, 1813. Represented Westphalia at Congress of Rastadt, 1797–99. Entered Austrian diplomatic service, holding posts in Dresden, 1801–03, Berlin, 1803–06, and Paris, 1806–09. Foreign minister, 1809–48. Chancellor, 1812–48. Led Austria into alliance with Russia against France, 1813. Presided at Congress of Vienna, 1814–15. Architect of 'Metternich System', i.e. balance of power in Europe in interests of general peace. Politically conservative, aiming at resisting liberal demands and maintaining stability. Led Austria to focus attention on territories in Italy rather than on interests in Germany. Obliged to resign during 1848 Revolution. Returned to Austria, 1849, but not to office.

MILOSEVIC, SLOBODAN (1941–) Serbian politician, former communist who manipulated nationalist forces to maintain his hold on power. President of Serbia from 1990, he played a key role in the wars against Croatia and Bosnia and was widely held responsible for policies of terror and 'ethnic cleansing'. Subject to UN economic sanctions from 1992 to 1995, he faced mass protests in 1996–97 for refusing to accept opposition victories in municipal elections and in Montenegro. Became President of the Federal Republic of Yugoslavia (Serbia and Montenegro) in July 1997. Following his involvement in the Kosovo crisis from 1997 and the bombing campaign against Serbia, he was removed from government and arraigned on war crime charges by international bodies. He was brought to trial in 2001 (the first head of state to be so charged).

MITTERRAND, FRANÇOIS MAURICE (1916–95) French politician. Socialist deputy, 1946. Ministerial office in 11 governments under the 4th Republic. Unsuccessful Left candidate against de Gaulle (q.v) in presidential election, 1965. Socialist Party secretary, 1971. Defeated in presidential election, 1974. Elected president, defeating Giscard d'Estaing 1981. Backed by a National Assembly Socialist majority, attempted radical economic policy, 1981–86. After 1986 Assembly elections, shared power with Gaullist majority led by Chirac and moderated policy. Re-elected president, 1988, defeating Chirac. Failed to win Socialist majority in ensuing Assembly elections. Longest-serving president of the Fifth Republic.

MOLOTOV, VYACHESLAV MIKHAILOVICH (1890–1986) Soviet politician. Emerged as prominent Bolshevik during November Revolution, 1917. Loyal colleague of Stalin,

1921 onwards. Member of Politburo, 1926–57. Helped implement Five-Year Plan, 1928. Premier, 1930–41. Foreign minister, 1939–49. Negotiated pact with Ribbentrop, August 1939. Deputy premier, 1941–57. Negotiated treaties with Eastern Bloc countries, 1945–49. Became member of ruling triumvirate following death of Stalin, 1953. Negotiated Austrian State Treaty, 1955. Minister of state control, 1956–57. Became foreign minister again, 1957. Influence declined with rise of Khrushchev. Ambassador to Mongolia, 1957–60. Retired, 1961–62.

MOLTKE, HELMUTH VON (1800–91) German soldier. Entered Prussian Army, 1822. Joined General Staff, 1832. Seconded as adviser to Turkish Army, 1835–39. Personal aide to Prince Henry, 1845–46, and to Frederick William, 1855–57. Appointed Chief of Prussian General Staff, 1857. Introduced major reorganization of army after 1858. Produced strategic planning which secured Prussian victories against Denmark, 1864, Austria, 1866, and France, 1870. Became Chief of Imperial General Staff, 1870. Created field-marshal, 1871.

MONNET, JEAN (1888–1979) French politician, economist and diplomat. Member of Inter-Allied Maritime Commission, 1915–17. First deputy Secretary-General of League of Nations, 1919–23. Chairman, Franco–British Economic Co-ordination Committee, 1939–40. Became minister of commerce, 1944. Fostered establishment of National Planning Council, becoming head of Council, 1945–47. Architect of European Community. Chairman, Action Committee for United States of Europe, 1955–75. Instrumental in foundation of European Coal and Steel Community. President of ECSC, 1952–55.

MONTGOMERY, 1ST VISCOUNT, SIR BERNARD LAW MONTGOMERY (1887–1976) British soldier. Lieutenant-Colonel and battalion commander by end of First World War. Evacuated from Dunkirk with 3rd Division under his command, 1940. By December 1941, head of South-Eastern Command as Lieutenant-General. Chosen to command 8th Army in North Africa, 1942. Halted Rommel's advance, defeating him at El Alamein. Led invasion of Sicily and Italy. Appointed land commander of Operation Overlord (Normandy landings), 1944. Uneasy relationship with American allies. Commander of occupation forces in Germany. After war, became Chief of Imperial General Staff. Deputy commander of NATO, 1951–58.

MURAT, JOACHIM (1767–1815) French soldier and King of Naples. French Cavalry Commander and colleague of Napoleon Bonaparte. Involved in suppression of Vendémiaire rising, 1795. Fought in first Italian campaign. Won military reputation during Egyptian expedition. Major role in Napoleon's Brumaire coup, 1799. Won victory at Marengo, 1800. Created Marshal, 1804. Crushed rising in Madrid, 1808. Created King of Naples as Joachim I Napoléon. Active in Russian campaign. Fought at Leipzig. Attempted to keep throne by negotiations with Allies, 1813–14. Sought to rally Italian aid for Napoleon without success, 1815. Led abortive rising in Calabria, 1815. Tried and executed.

MUSSOLINI, BENITO (1883–1945) Dictator of Italy. Originally a Socialist. Imprisoned for political activities, 1908. Editor of Socialist national newspaper, *Avanti*, 1912–14. Resigned from party having been criticized for supporting war with Austria. Founded newspaper, *Il Popolo d'Italia,* Milan, 1914. Organized groups (*fasci*) of workers to campaign for social improvements. Amalgamated into Fascist Party, 1919. Elected to Chamber of Deputies, 1921. During period of civil unrest, led 'March on Rome', 1922. Appointed prime minister by King Victor Emmanuel III, 1922. Headed Fascist–Nationalist coalition, as *Duce*. Acquired dictatorial powers, 1922. Dictatorship established, 1925. Single party, corporatist state instituted 1928–29. Large-scale public works introduced. Lateran Treaty settled Church–State relations, 1929. Expansionist foreign policy: Corfu incident, 1924; invasion of Abyssinia, 1935. Created 'Axis' with Hitler, 1936. Left League of Nations, 1937. Annexed Albania, 1939. Declared war on France and Britain, 1940. Invaded Greece, 1940. Military setbacks in East Africa and Libya. Heavily dependent on Germany by 1941. Forced to resign following coup by Victor Emmanuel III and Marshal Badoglio, 1943. Detained, but freed by Germans. Established Republican Fascist government in German-controlled North Italy. Captured and executed by Italian partisans, April 1945.

N

NAPOLEON I, BONAPARTE (1769–1821) Emperor of the French, 1804–15. Entered French army, 1785. Won recognition after campaigns in North Italy. Laid down peace terms to Austria at Campo Formio. Led unsuccessful expedition to Egypt. Overthrew Directory in 'Brumaire' coup, 1799. Created Consul for Life, 1802. Effective dictator of France, 1799–1814. During consulate, introduced legal reforms in *Code Napoléon,* and achieved Concordat with Church. After winning War of Second Coalition, crowned himself Emperor, 1804. Won victories at Austerlitz and Jena during War of Third Coalition, 1804–07. Obliged Russia to accept Peace of Tilsit, 1807. Power reduced after 1808 by failure of 'Continental System', and involvement in Peninsular War. Defeated Austrians at Wagram, 1809. Invaded Russia, 1812. Won victory at Borodino, but forced to retreat from Moscow. Defeated at Leipzig during War of Fourth Coalition. Abdicated, April 1814. Permitted by Allies to retain imperial title and sovereignty over Elba. Escaped from Elba, February 1815. During

'Hundred Days' resumed rule as Emperor. Finally defeated at Waterloo, June 1815, and exiled to St Helena.

NAPOLEON III (CHARLES LOUIS NAPOLEON BONAPARTE) (1808–73) Emperor of the French, 1852–70. Nephew of Napoleon I. Made two unsuccessful attempts to mount Bonapartist risings against July Monarchy, 1836, 1840. Imprisoned after second attempt, but escaped, 1845, settling in London. Exploited 'Napoleonic Legend'. Elected president of Second Republic, 1848. Undertook *coup d'état* in order to widen his authority. Established Second Empire, 1852. Entered Crimean War as ally of Britain, and ensured Peace Congress was held at Paris, 1856. Planned joint campaign to achieve Italian independence after meeting with Cavour at Plombières. Made peace with Austria, 1859, without consulting Piedmont. Founded Catholic Empire in Mexico, 1861. Secured Imperial title of Mexico for Archduke Maximilian of Austria, 1864. Diplomatically outflanked by Bismarck during Austro–Prussian War, 1866. Faced Franco–Prussian War, 1870, without allies. After defeat at Sedan, detained in Germany. Exiled in England, 1871–73.

NESSELRODE, COUNT KARL ROBERT (1780–1862) Russian statesman. Entered Russian Navy, 1797. Chief adviser to Tsar Alexander I in Paris, 1814. Prominent role in Congress of Vienna, 1815. Foreign minister, 1822–56. Chancellor, 1845–62. Pursued conservative policies. Sought to gain influence over the Ottoman Empire by conciliation. Engineered treaty of Unkiar Skelessi, 1833. Claimed Crimean War conflicted with his policy and advised suing for peace. Concluded Treaty of Paris, 1856. Saw dangers in exploiting Balkan nationalism and in Russian territorial growth in Asia. Resisted Polish national claims and helped Austria crush Hungarian Revolt, 1849.

NEY, MICHEL (1769–1815) French soldier. Organized Army of the Rhine, 1799. Fought at Hohenlinden, 1800. Created Marshal of France, 1804. Designated the 'Bravest of the Brave' after battle of Friedland. Created Prince of the Moscowa after Borodino, 1812. Given title Due d'Elchingen, 1808. Remained in army after Restoration of Louis XVIII. Reverted to support of Napoleon during 'Hundred Days'. Fought at Waterloo. Court-martialled by Chamber of Peers and executed.

NICHOLAS I (1796–1855) Tsar of Russia, 1825–55. Succeeded his brother, Alexander I. Repressed Decembrist plot. Pursued reactionary policies. Introduced codification of laws, 1833. Freed serfs on state lands, 1838. Strengthened autocratic government. Created secret police ('Third Section'), 1826. Through education minister, Uvarov, resisted development of higher education and schools. Crushed Polish Revolt, 1830–31. Helped Austria suppress Hungarian Revolt, 1849. Policy towards the Ottoman Empire alarmed Britain, resulting in war with the Ottoman Empire, 1853, and Crimean War, 1854–56.

NICHOLAS II (1868–1918) Tsar of Russia, 1894–1917. Son of Alexander III. Reluctant to introduce political reforms. Influential in achievement of International Peace Conference in The Hague, 1898. Encouraged building of Trans-Siberian railway. Forced by revolutionary mood of 1905 (stemming from industrial unrest, poor harvests and disastrous Russo–Japanese War) to summon elected Duma. Made gestures of reform under prime minister Stolypin. Fell under influence of Rasputin after 1906. Undertook Supreme Command of Russian Armies, 1915. Accused of maintaining communications with Germany during First World War. Abdicated after Revolution, March 1917. Murdered by local Bolsheviks at Ekaterinburg, 1918, together with family.

NIETZSCHE, FRIEDRICH WILHELM (1844–1900) German philosopher. Developed ideas of need for social elite of realists, led by a 'superman' unhindered by conventional morality. Later association of his writings with political developments (especially National Socialism and Fascism) has been questioned.

Essentially an individualist, suspicious of extreme nationalism. Writings edited posthumously by fanatically nationalistic sister. Insane in later life.

O'CONNELL, DANIEL (1775–1847) Irish nationalist; known as 'The Liberator'. Born in County Kerry, he founded the Catholic Association in 1823 as a mass movement to campaign for Catholic emancipation. Elected for County Clare in 1828, but as a Catholic not allowed to take his seat. His efforts helped to secure the passing of the Roman Catholic Relief Act, 1829. Subsequently, took seat as MP for County Clare, 1830, and for Waterford, 1832. Organized mass meetings in 1842 and 1843 to secure repeal of the 1800 Act of Union. His cancellation of the Clontarf meeting in October 1843 discredited him with many Irish extremists. He died at Genoa.

ORLANDO, VITTORIO EMMANUELE (1860–1952) Italian statesman. Professor of constitutional law at Palermo. Elected to parliament, 1897. Minister of justice, 1916. Prime minister, 1917–19, in aftermath of military defeat at Caporetto. President of Chamber of Deputies, 1919. Led Italian delegation at Paris Peace Conference, 1919–20. Disagreed with President Wilson over Italy's territorial aspirations. Influence declined thereafter. Resigned presidency of Chamber of Deputies in protest at Fascist electoral malpractice, 1925. President, Constituent Assembly, 1946–47.

ORSINI, FELICE (1819–58) Italian nationalist conspirator. Joined Mazzini's 'Young Italy' movement. After several plots against Papacy, attempted to assassinate Napoleon III and Empress Eugénie, believing Napoleon had betrayed Italy. After his execution, press published a letter in which he appealed to Napoleon to assist Italian cause. Ironically contributed to Napoleon's meeting with Cavour at Plombières.

P

PALMERSTON, 3RD VISCOUNT, HENRY JOHN TEMPLE (1784–1865) British statesman. Tory MP, 1807–31. Whig MP, 1831–65. Irish peer as Viscount Palmerston, 1802. Lord of the Admiralty, 1807–09. Secretary for war, 1809–28. Foreign secretary, 1830–34, 1835–41, 1846–51. Home secretary, 1852–55. Prime minister, 1855–58, 1859–65. As foreign secretary, supported British interests aggressively. Supported liberal causes abroad. Instrumental in securing Belgian independence, 1830–31. Formed Quadruple Alliance in defence of Spanish and Portuguese monarchs. Lent support to the Ottoman Empire against Egyptian and Russian threats. Declared war on China ('Opium War'), 1840. Conflict with Cabinet colleagues. Dismissed after recognizing Louis Napoleon's coup against Second Republic. As home secretary, encouraged prison and factory reforms. As prime minister, concluded Crimean War. Suppressed Indian Mutiny, 1857. Recognized new Kingdom of Italy. Achieved return of Ionian islands to Greece. During American Civil War, kept Britain neutral.

PAPANDREOU, ANDREAS (1919–96) Greek politician. One of the leading political figures of postwar Greece. Prime minister from 1981–89 and again 1993–96. His father, George Papandreou, was a centrist prime minister in 1964. Andreas Papandreou founded PASOK in 1974 after the collapse of the rule of the military junta. Although in the late 1980s his image became tarnished with political scandals (and revelations of his own private life), the 30 years during which he dominated Greek politics helped define modern democratic Greece as a part of the West.

PARNELL, CHARLES STEWART (1846–91) Irish nationalist leader. Son of Anglican gentry family, educated at Cambridge. Nationalist MP for County Meath, 1875–80, Cork 1880–91, leading Irish Nationalist Party in parliament from 1880. Led agitation for Home Rule, skilfully co-ordinating political bargaining at Westminster with more radical movements in Ireland. Career ruined when cited in O'Shea divorce case of 1890.

PASIC, NIKOLA (1845–1926) Serbian/Yugoslavian politician. One of founders of Radical Party, 1881. Became member of legislature, 1878. Exiled, 1883–89. Chief minister of Serbia, 1891–92. Ambassador to Russia, 1893–94. Exiled, 1899–1903. Helped engineer establishment of Karadjordjevic dynasty in Serbia, 1903. Chief minister, 1904–08. Minister of foreign affairs, 1904. Chief minister, 1910–18. Faced opposition from militant Serbian 'Black Hand' organization, which he suppressed in 1917. Led joint delegation of Serbs, Croats and Slovenes at Paris Peace Conference, 1919. Chief minister of Yugoslavia, 1921–26, giving priority to Serbian interests.

PAUL I (1754–1801) Tsar of Russia, 1796–1801. Succeeded his mother, Catherine the Great. Led Russia into War of Second Coalition, 1798–99. Switched to support of France, 1800. Introduced law of royal succession through male line. Liberalized laws on serfdom, 1797. Aroused opposition among nobility and army. Killed in palace coup, 1801.

PÉTAIN, HENRI PHILIPPE (1856–1951) French soldier and politician. Entered army, 1876. Lectured at *Ecole de Guerre,* 1906 onwards. Became colonel, 1912. Commanded an army corps, 1914. National renown followed defence of Verdun, 1916. Commander-in-Chief of French armies in the field, 1917. Created Marshal of France, 1918. Vice-president, Higher Council of War, 1920–30. Led joint French–Spanish campaign against insurgents in Morocco, 1925–26. Inspector-general of army, 1929. Became minister of war, 1934. Ambassador to Spain, 1939. Became prime minister, June 1940. Secured Armistice with Germany. Given powers by National Assembly to rule by authoritarian means, July 1940. Became head of state in unoccupied ('Vichy') France, 1942. Obliged to flee France with retreating Germans, 1944. Sentenced to death for treason, 1945, but sentence commuted to life imprisonment by de Gaulle.

PILSUDSKI, JOSEF (1867–1935) Polish soldier and statesman. Exiled to Siberia for political activities, 1887–92. Founded Polish Socialist Party, 1892. Became editor of Polish underground Socialist newspaper, *Robotnik.* Increasingly nationalist in outlook. Sought Japanese support for Polish rising during Russo–Japanese War, 1904. Recruited by Austria to lead Polish legion against Russia, 1914. Interned by Germans, 1917. On release, became commander of all Polish armies. Elected chief of state, 1918. Remained dictator until constitution established, 1922. Led Polish campaign against Bolsheviks, 1919–20. Created field-marshal, 1920, Commanded army until retirement, 1923. Executed military coup, 1926. Served as prime minister, 1926–28, 1930. Retained dictatorial powers until death, 1935. Unable to convince France of threat from Nazi Germany. Concluded Non-Aggression Pact with Germany, 1934.

PITT, WILLIAM, 'THE YOUNGER' (1759–1806) British politician. Son of Pitt 'The Elder'. MP, 1781–1806. Chancellor of the exchequer, 1782–83. Prime minister and chancellor of the exchequer, 1783–1801, 1804–06. Youngest ever prime minister. Undertook major administrative reforms in 1780s. Initially sympathetic to parliamentary reform. Led Britain in wars against Revolutionary France after 1793. Negotiated European coalitions against France, 1793, 1798, 1805. Took stern line with radical opposition at home. Secured bill for union of Great Britain and Ireland, 1800. Introduced income tax. Resigned, 1801, when George III vetoed Catholic Emancipation.

PIUS IX, POPE (1792–1878) Pontiff, 1846–78. Regarded as a progressive cardinal. Seen by Italian nationalists as the 'Liberal Pope' they had sought. Declared political amnesty, 1846. Refused to take part in war against Austria, thereby precipitating revolt in Rome, 1848. Obliged to flee Rome, but restored with French military backing, 1850, relying on this support until 1870. Following restoration, became reactionary in outlook. Failed to restore liberal constitution of 1848. Re-established Catholic hierarchy in Britain, 1850, and Holland, 1853. Established Concordats with Spain, 1851, and Austria, 1855. Stated doctrine of Immaculate Conception, 1854. Issued *Syllabus Errarum,* criticizing liberalism, 1864. Convoked First Vatican Council, 1869–70, which issued declaration of Papal Infallibility, provoking opposition, e.g. in Germany, leading to *'Kulturkampf'*. Rome occupied by Italian troops, 1870. Pius thereafter felt himself to be a prisoner.

PIUS XII (EUGENIO PACELLI) (1876–1958) Elected Pope 1939. Prior to this, he had been papal nuncio in Germany and papal secretary of state. Much controversy surrounds his conduct during Second World War, in particular his failure to condemn the Nazi regime.

POBEDONOSTSEV, KONSTANTIN PETROVICH (1827–1907) Professor of constitutional law, Moscow University, 1860–65. Tutor to both Alexander III and Nicholas II. Became member of Council of the Empire, 1872. Appointed Procurator of Holy Synod (i.e. lay administrator of Russian Orthodox Church), 1880. Used his influential position to resist parliamentary government, and to bolster *status quo.* Approved of oppression of non-Russian nationalities within Empire.

POINCARÉ, RAYMOND (1860–1934) French statesman. Elected deputy, 1887. Education minister, 1893–94. Finance minister, 1894–95. Senator and finance minister, 1906.

Became prime minister, 1912. Strengthened Dual Alliance with Russia. Supported *Entente* with Britain. President, 1913–20, influential on legislation. Prime minister, 1924–26, simultaneously foreign minister. Pursued nationalistic policy, disagreeing with Britain over reparations question. Authorized French occupation of Ruhr, 1923. Prime minister and finance minister of Government of National Union, 1926–29, imposing rigorous economies and achieving currency stabilization.

POMPIDOU, GEORGES (1911–74) French politician. Member of Resistance during Second World War. Aide to General de Gaulle, 1944–46. Member of Council of State, 1946–54. Deputy director-general of tourism, 1946–49. Director-general of Rothschild's (banking house), 1954–58. Chief of de Gaulle's personal staff 1958–59. Involved in drafting of Constitution of Fifth Republic. Negotiated ceasefire agreement with Algerian nationalists, 1961. Prime minister, 1962–68. President, 1969–74. Pursued policies similar to those of de Gaulle.

PRIMO DE RIVERA, MIGUEL (1870–1930) Spanish dictator, 1923–30. Entered Spanish army, 1888. Served in Morocco. Cuba and Philippines. Became major-general, 1910. Military governor of Cadiz, 1915–19, Valencia, 1919–22, Barcelona, 1922–23. Assumed power with support of King Alfonso XIII, 1923. Dissolved Spanish parliament, suspended trial by jury, imposed censorship of press. Political opponents imprisoned. Intended to establish Fascist regime. Faced growing opposition, e.g. over failure to implement agricultural reforms. Ended Moroccan War, 1927. Continued in office as prime minister, but obliged to resign when he lost support of army, 1930. Actions and policies contributed to collapse of monarchy.

PROUDHON, PIERRE JOSEPH (1809–65) Influential French socialist propagandist and theorist. His publications included *Qu'est-ce que la propriété* (1840) and the weighty *Système des contradictions economiques* (1846).

PUTIN, VLADIMIR (1952–) Russian President since January 2000. Former KGB officer, who entered politics with the collapse of the Soviet Union and became head of the Federal Security Service in 1998 and secretary to the presidential Security Council in 1999. Appointed premier by President Yeltsin in August 1999 and on Yeltsin's resignation at the end of the year succeeded him and was then confirmed as President in the March 2000 elections. Presided over attempts to conclude the Chechnya war and signed a major nuclear arms reduction treaty with President Bush in May 2002. Re-elected President in 2004 by a landslide.

QUISLING, VIDKUN (1887–1945) Norwegian soldier, politician and traitor. Military attaché in Petrograd, 1918–19, Helsinki, 1919–21. Minister of war, 1931–33. Expanded right-wing National Unity Party. Visited Germany, 1939. Advised Hitler on creation of sympathetic regime in Norway. Headed puppet regime following German occupation, 1940. Tried and executed, 1945.

RADETZKY, JOSEF (1766–1858) Austrian soldier. Fought Turks, 1788–89. Served in all major campaigns against France during Napoleonic Wars. Chief of Staff, 1809. Appointed Commander-in-Chief in Lombardy, 1831. Created field-marshal, 1836. After rising in Milan, obliged to retreat to 'Quadrilateral',

1848. Secured victory over Piedmontese at Custozza, 1848. Regained Venice, 1849. Continued as Governor-General in Lombardy–Venetia until 1857.

RANKE, LEOPOLD VON (1795–1886) German historian. Professor of history at Berlin, 1825–72. Established modern critical methods of historiography, stressing need for thorough examination of sources and objective analysis. Made use of documents previously unavailable. Wrote many major works, including *History of the Roman and German Peoples, 1494–1514,* 1824, and a history of the Papacy in the sixteenth and seventeenth centuries, 1834–37.

RASPUTIN, GREGORI (1869–1916) Russian mystic. Used hypnotic talents over ailing Tsarevich Alexei (1904–18) to gain influence at court. Interference in politics damaged position of monarchy and provoked opposition among court. Suspected of working on behalf of Germany during First World War. Murdered by aristocrats.

RATHENAU, WALTHER (1867–1922) German statesman. Director of giant AEG electrical combine. Made responsible for organizing war economy, 1916. Founded (liberal) Democratic Party, 1918. Became minister of reconstruction, 1921, and minister of foreign affairs, 1922. Represented Germany at Cannes Conference, 1922. Engineered reduction of Germany's reparations commitment for 1922. Played leading role in achieving Treaty of Rapallo with Russia, 1922. Assassinated by anti-Semitic nationalists.

RIBBENTROP, JOACHIM VON (1893–1946) German Nazi diplomat. Involved in negotiations between Hitler and German government. Helped organize Nazi government, 1933. Ambassador at large, 1935. Concluded Anglo–German Naval Treaty, 1935, and Anti-Comintern Pact, 1936. Ambassador in London, 1936–38. Foreign minister, 1938–45. Responsible for giving German foreign policy a distinctly 'Nazi' character. Negotiated Molotov–Ribbentrop Pact, 1939, and Pact with Italy and Japan, 1940. Tried as war criminal at Nuremberg. Hanged, 1946.

ROBESPIERRE, MAXIMILIEN DE (1758–94) French Revolutionary leader. Dubbed 'The Incorruptible'. Lawyer, 1781–89. Represented Third Estate of Artois in States-General, 1789. Emerged as radical in National Assembly, subsequently Constituent Assembly, 1789–91. Drew political inspiration from works of Rousseau. Believed himself to be embodiment of 'General Will'. Leader of radical Montagnard party. Elected to Committee of Public Safety, acquiring dominant position. Called for death of Louis XVI, 1793. Removed political opponents, e.g. Danton and Hébert, 1793–94. Created political dictatorship and attempted to transform society, involving 'Reign of Terror'. Provoked opposition among majority of National Convention. Deposed in 'Thermidorean Reaction', 1794, and executed.

ROMMEL, ERWIN (1891–1944) German soldier. Served on Romanian and Italian fronts during First World War. Lectured at War Academy. Joined Nazi Party, 1933. Commanded 7th Panzer Division, penetrated Ardennes, May 1940. Became commander of 'Afrika Corps', 1941, earning nickname 'The Desert Fox'. Defeated by campaigns of Alexander and Montgomery, 1942–43. Given task of strengthening defences in France, 1944. Active in resistance to Allied landings in Normandy, June 1944. Implicated in plot to assassinate Hitler. Apparently forced to commit suicide, October 1944.

ROUSSEAU, JEAN-JACQUES (1712–78) Swiss-born philosopher. Attracted interest through his writings which criticized existing social order. *Du Control social,* 1762, described his political views, *Emile*, 1762, his theories on education. *Du Control social* became extremely influential, especially during and after French Revolution. Saw society itself as source of contemporary ills. Claimed governments only derived their legitimacy from popular consent – 'the sovereignty of the people'.

S

SALAZAR, ANTONIO DE OLIVEIRA (1889–1970)
Portuguese dictator. Professor of economics
at Coimbra University, 1916. Minister of
finance, 1926, 1928–32. Prime minister,
1932–68. Also minister of war, 1936–44,
foreign minister, 1936–37. Principal architect
of authoritarian constitution introduced in
1933. Implemented Fascist-type government
on virtually dictatorial lines, stifling political
opposition. Restored public finances and
modernized transport system. Organized public
works schemes. Maintained Portuguese
neutrality during Second World War.

**SALISBURY, 3RD MARQUESS OF, ROBERT
ARTHUR TALBOT GASCOYNE-CECIL
(1830–1903)** Cecil was Conservative MP
for Stamford, 1853–68. In 1865 became
Viscount Cranbourne. Served as secretary for
India in 1866, resigning in protest at the 1867
Reform Bill. In 1868 succeeded as Marquess
of Salisbury. Returned as secretary for India,
1874–76, and as foreign secretary, 1878–80.
Leader of the opposition in the House of
Lords and joint leader of the Conservative
Party, 1881–85. In 1885 became prime minister and sole party leader. Acted as prime
minister and foreign secretary, 1886–92 and
1895–1900. Prime minister and Lord Privy
Seal, 1900–02. Salisbury was a remarkably
able diplomat, while in the domestic sphere
he had an incisive knowledge of the Conservative Party. As a Tory and a High Church
Anglican he was able to control an unruly
party, and by moderate social reform and
opposition to Home Rule succeeded in forg-
ing the Unionist alliance which dominated
British politics between 1886 and 1906.

**SCHARNHORST, GERHARD JOHANN VON
(1755–1813)** Prussian soldier. Served in
Hanoverian Army, 1793–95. Entered Prus-
sian army, 1801. Selected to train fresh armies.
Fought in campaigns, 1806–07. Head of Army
Reform Commission, 1807. Reorganized
Prussian army. Chief of Staff to Blücher.

SCHLIEFFEN, ALFRED, COUNT VON (1833–1913)
German soldier. Chief of German General
Staff, 1891–1905. Prepared strategic planning for war with France ('Schlieffen Plan').
In modified form, plan was used in German
attack on France, 1914. Believed rapid defeat
of France was essential to German success.
Plan provided for violation of neutrality
of Holland. Belgium and Luxembourg, by-
passing France's defences.

SCHWARZENBERG, PRINCE FELIX (1800–52)
Austrian statesman. Protégé of Metternich.
Engaged in diplomatic service in Italy.
Appointed adviser to Radetzky in Lombardy,
1848. Through influence of army, became
prime minister and foreign minister of Austria,
1848–52. Secured abdication of Emperor
Ferdinand and succession of Francis Joseph.
Took firm line with Hungarian rebels, 1849.
Temporary 'concessions' granted providing
for representative and responsible govern-
ment, 1849 (withdrawn, 1851). Created highly
centralized state administration. Achieved
Prussian recognition of Austrian primacy in
Germany, 1850.

SEECKT, HANS VON (1866–1936) German
soldier. Chief of Staff to Mockensen on
Eastern Front during First World War. Won
victory at Gorlice, 1915. Served in Balkans
and the Ottoman Empire. Appointed Head
of *Truppenamt*, 1919. Supervised Germany's
secret rearmament, 1919–26, especially
through co-operation with Russia. Head of
Reichswehr, 1920–26. Resigned in response
to President Hindenburg's hostility, 1926.
Member of Reichstag, 1930–32. Created
an army capable of rapid expansion after
1933.

SHEVARDNADZE, EDUARD (1928–) Soviet foreign minister from 1985 until his shock resignation in December 1990 over fears of
right-wing coup. As Gorbachev's key lieutenant, presided over the ending of the Cold
War and the freeing of the Eastern bloc from

Soviet control. Born in Georgia, he established his earlier reputation for rooting out corruption and nepotism in Georgia. His prophetic resignation increased very considerably the pressures on Gorbachev. Briefly reappointed foreign minister, November to December 1991. Subsequently became head of state in Georgia 1992, and first elected president, 1995. Deposed in a coup in 2004 (the 'Rose Revolution').

SIEYÈS, EMMANUEL JOSEPH ('ABBÉ SIEYÈS') (1748–1836) French Catholic priest and Revolutionary leader. Attracted interest of reformers by publishing *Essai sur les privileges* and *Qu'est-ce que le Tiers État?* Suggested Third Estate should meet as National Assembly, 1789. Involved in composing Constitution, 1791. Refused offer of Archbishopric of Paris, 1791. Member of Council of Five Hundred, 1795–99. Entered Directory, 1799. Supported Napoleon Bonaparte in Brumaire coup. Architect of Consulate system. Created Count and Senator under Empire. Lived in exile in Belgium, 1814–30. Returned to France under July Monarchy.

SMITH, ADAM (1723–90) Scottish economist. Professor of logic at Glasgow, 1751, and of moral philosophy, 1752. Friend of Hume. Greatest work, *An Enquiry into the Nature and Causes of the Wealth of Nations,* 1776. Criticized mercantilist economic thought. Proponent of free-market, *laissez-faire* system. Placed great stress on individual freedom. Devised theory of division of labour, money, prices, wages and distribution.

SOREL, GEORGES (1847–1922) French syndicalist philosopher. Studied Marxism after engineering career. Saw need for violent revolution under trade union control. Had little influence on French trade unions. Criticized both Socialist and Radical parties. Lent support to monarchist movement, 1909, and to Bolsheviks, 1917. Ideas on manipulating popular opinion impressed Hitler and Mussolini.

SPERANSKY, MICHAEL (1772–1839) Russian political reformer. Advised Alexander I on constitutional reforms. Instrumental in establishment of Council of State, 1810. Introduced state budgetary system. Earned hostility of reactionary elements by proposing creation of local and central representative bodies. Exiled, 1812. Returned to Russia under Nicholas I. Completed codification of Russian law, 1832.

STALIN, JOSEF VISARIONOVITCH (J.V. DJUGASHVILI) (1879–1953) Soviet leader. Expelled from seminary for political activities, 1899. Exiled to Siberia twice. Attended conferences of Russian Social Democrats in Stockholm, 1906, and London, 1907. Expert on racial minorities in Bolshevik Central Committee, 1912. Became editor of *Pravda,* 1917. Worked with Lenin in Petrograd during Revolution, 1917. Member of Revolutionary Military Council, 1920–23. People's Commissar for nationalities, 1921–23. General Secretary of Central Committee of Communist Party, 1922–53. During civil war, supervised defence of Petrograd. Co-operated with Kamenev and Zinoviev to exclude Trotsky from office, 1923. (Secured Trotsky's exile, 1929.) Gained control of Party at Fifteenth Congress, 1927. Embarked on policy of 'Socialism in One Country' through Five Year Plans, 1928. Achieved rapid economic development. Eliminated political opponents in series of 'show trials', 1936–38. Chairman of Council of Ministers, 1941–53. During Second World War, as commissar of defence and marshal of the Soviet Union, took over direction of war effort. Present at Tehran, Yalta and Potsdam conferences. Established firm control of Eastern European Communist 'satellites', with exception of Yugoslavia, during postwar period. 'Personality cult' of Stalin officially condemned by Khrushchev at Party Congress, 1956.

STAMBOLISKY, ALEXANDER (1879–1923) Bulgarian politician. Involved in peasant agitation, 1897. As member of Agrarian Union, won fame as popular orator, 1908–15.

Imprisoned for opposing entry into First World War. Instrumental in forcing King Ferdinand to abdicate, 1918. Proclaimed Republic, 1918. Prime minister, 1919–23. Wielded almost dictatorial power. Concluded Treaty of Neuilly, 1919. Introduced land reforms and revised taxation in favour of peasants. Deposed and murdered in coup, 1923, having sought to help Yugoslav government crush Macedonian revolutionaries.

STAMBULOV, STEFAN (1854–95) Bulgarian statesman. Active in revolutionary movement, 1875. Emerged as national leader following Bulgarian union with Eastern Roumelia, 1886. Appointed Regent, September 1886. Lent support to Prince Ferdinand of Saxe Coburg. Hoped to conciliate the Ottoman Empire. Dismissed by Ferdinand, 1894. Murdered, 1895.

STAVISKY, SERGE (d. 1934) Central figure in 'Stavisky Case', 1934. Russian–Jewish financier, living in France. Sold valueless bonds. Took own life before charges could be made. Revelations of his involvement in other questionable activities and protection by public figures caused outcry. Murder of member of Public Prosecutor's staff attributed to attempted cover-up. Case had political repercussions, providing ammunition for extremes of right and left against corruption in Third Republic. Rioting and general strike, February 1934, led to formation of broad coalition government.

STEIN, BARON HEINRICH FRIEDRICH KARL VOM UND ZUM (1757–1831) Prussian statesman. Entered Prussian Civil Service, 1780. Appointed chief minister, 1807. Implemented social transformation. Serfs freed, 1810. Land reforms introduced. Administrative changes at central and local levels. After flight from Prussia, 1808, entered service of Alexander I. Administrator of liberated German territories, 1813–14. Proposals for German unification vetoed by Metternich.

STOLYPIN, PETER (1862–1911) Russian statesman. Governor of Saratov Province. Subdued agrarian disturbances, 1905. Became minister of interior, 1906. Prime minister, 1906–11. Advocated moderate political reforms. Sought to create class of independent middle-sized farmers (*Kulaks*) as counterweight to liberals in Duma. Introduced property qualification for candidates for Duma. Took repressive line with rioters. Renewed anti-Semitic policies. Planned improvements in education, local government and system of social insurance. Assassinated, 1911.

STRESEMANN, GUSTAV (1878–1929) German statesman. Elected to Reichstag, 1907–12, 1914–29. Leader of National Liberals, 1917. Took nationalistic position during First World War, supporting High Command. Became more moderate after war. Founded People's Party (DVP), 1919. Advocated meeting Germany's commitments under Treaty of Versailles, thereby gaining confidence of Allies. Became chancellor during crisis year, 1923. Foreign minister, 1923–29. Restored Germany's diplomatic position. Concluded Locarno Pact, 1925. Achieved German entry into League of Nations, 1926. Secured reduction of reparations demands. Negotiated terms for Allied evacuation of Rhineland. Supported Dawes Plan, 1924, and Young Plan, 1929. Awarded Nobel Peace Prize, 1926.

STROSSMAYER, JOSEF (1815–1905) Croatian priest. Bishop of Djakovo, 1849–1905. Supporter of Yugoslav nationalism. Influential in curbing repressive policies of Hungarian authorities. Established South Slav Academy at Zagreb, 1867, and Zagreb University, 1874. As a 'Liberal Catholic', opposed doctrine of Papal Infallibility. In close contact with Gladstone. Fostered interest of western liberals in possibilities of union of southern Slavs.

SUVOROV, ALEXANDER (1729–1800) Russian soldier. Active in campaigns against Sweden, Prussia and the Ottoman Empire. Popular with Catherine the Great. Renowned for severity of his actions in Bessarabia, 1790, and against Polish rebels, 1795. Commanded Russian Army against French in North Italy. In joint effort with Austrians, expelled French armies from Milan and Turin, 1799. Recalled to St Petersburg having been obliged to retreat. Fell into disfavour.

T

TALLEYRAND, CHARLES MAURICE DE (1754–1838) French cleric and politician. Bishop of Autun, 1789. Supported Revolutionaries in States-General, though retained see until 1791. Suggested confiscation of Church property to increase government revenue. Excommunicated, 1791. Sent to London as envoy, 1792. Left France for USA after death of Louis XVI, not returning until establishment of Directory. Foreign minister, 1797–99. Supported Napoleon during Brumaire coup. Foreign minister, 1799–1807. Played major role in creation of Confederation of the Rhine. Created Prince of Benevento, 1806. Attended Erfurt Conference, 1808. Opportunistically established contact with Allies, 1814. Obtained Louis XVIII's agreement to issue constitution following Restoration. Represented France at Congress of Vienna, securing recognition of France as a Great Power. Drove diplomatic wedge between former Allies. Retired, 1815, but active in creation of July Monarchy, 1830. Ambassador to London, 1830–34. Eventually reconciled with Catholic Church.

THATCHER, MARGARET HILDA (*NÉE* ROBERTS) (1925–) Conservative MP for Finchley, 1959–92. Parliamentary secretary to the Ministry of Pensions and National Insurance 1961–64, and secretary of state for educa-tion and science 1970–74. In 1975 she was elected leader of the Conservative Party. Between 1975 and 1979 led the party away from the centrist policies of Heath (q.v.) and adopted a monetarist stance on economic problems and a tough line on law and order, defence and immigration. In May 1979 became Britain's first woman prime minister, following her election victory. In spite of considerable unpopularity and very high unemployment, Mrs Thatcher's conduct of the Falklands War and Labour's disarray led to a landslide victory at the polls in 1983. Second term marked by growing emphasis on liberalizing the economy, especially the privatization of major public concerns. In 1987 she achieved a record third term of office with a majority of over 100. Third term marked by economic problems, differences over Europe and major personality clashes over her style of government. She resigned in November 1990 after a leadership challenge undermined her position. After losing office she was a leading Eurosceptic and often critical of her successor, John Major. Created Baroness Thatcher of Kesteven, 1992.

THIERS, ADOLPHE (1797–1877) French politician and journalist. Among group which persuaded Louis Philippe to accept throne in 1830. Politically an Orléanist throughout career. Minister of interior, 1832, 1834–36. Suppressed rioting in Paris and Lyons. Prime minister and foreign minister, 1836, 1840. During 1848 Revolution, advised King to leave Paris, and reassert authority with provincial help. Detained during Louis Napoleon's coup, 1851. Re-elected Deputy, 1863. Prominent among liberal opposition. Elected 'Head of the Executive Power' of Third Republic, Bordeaux, 1871. Negotiated Peace Treaty with Bismarck following Franco–Prussian War. Raised loans to pay war indemnity. President of Third Republic, 1871–73.

TIRPITZ, ALFRED VON (1849–1930) German Grand Admiral. Entered Prussian Navy, 1865. Won support of Kaiser after stressing importance of battle fleet, 1891. Minister of marine, 1897–1916. Expanded High Seas Fleet. Proponent of unrestricted submarine warfare. Resigned when suggestions not acted upon.

TISZA, ISTVÁN (1861–1918) Son of Kálmán Tisza. Prime minister, 1904–05, 1913–17. Took strong line in quelling political disputes. Linked Hungary's policy closely with that of Austria during crisis, 1914. Engineered succession of Charles after abdication of Francis Joseph. Murdered during violence in Hungary in last stage of war.

TISZA, KÁLMÁN (1830–1902) Founded Hungarian Liberal Party, 1875. Prime minister, 1875–90. Implemented policy of 'magyarization' of subject national groups.

TITO, JOSIP BROZ (1892–1980) Yugoslav statesman. Member of Yugoslav Communist Party since early 1920s, becoming its secretary-general, 1937. Led Yugoslav partisan forces during Second World War. Became Marshal 1943. After war, secured independence from USSR, 1948. First president of Yugoslav Republic, 1953–80. Pursued independent foreign policy, encouraging co-operation among non-aligned nations.

TOCQUEVILLE, ALEXIS DE (1805–59) French politician and historian. Studied American penal system during 1820s. Published *Democracy in America*, 1835–40. Profoundly interested in question of liberal society. Elected deputy, 1839–48. Elected deputy to National Assembly after 1848 Revolution. Involved in formulation of Constitution of Second Republic. Became foreign minister, 1849. Disillusioned by Louis Napoleon's retreat from liberalism. Wrote *The Ancien Régime and the Revolution*, 1856, and *Recollections of 1848*, published posthumously.

TROTSKY, LEV DAVIDOVICH (L.D. BRONSTEIN) (1879–1940) Russian revolutionary of Ukrainian–Jewish descent. Exiled to Siberia, 1898. Joined Lenin in London, 1902. Became an independent socialist, 1902. Hoped to achieve reconciliation between Bolsheviks and Mensheviks. Returned to Russia, 1905, and organized first soviet in St Petersburg.

Exiled to Siberia again. Returned to St Petersburg from New York, May 1917. Chairman of Petrograd Soviet, November 1917. First commissar for foreign affairs. Delayed conclusion of Treaty of Brest-Litovsk, 1918. Commissar for war during civil war, creating Red Army. After death of Lenin, and disagreements with Stalin, excluded from office. Theory of 'Permanent Revolution' condemned by Communist Party. Lost influence over Party policy, 1925. Expelled from Communist Party, 1927. Deported, 1929. Wrote *History of the Revolution* while in France. Murdered by Stalinist agent in Mexico, 1940.

TUDJMAN, FRANCO (1922–2002) Architect of independent Croatia. Fought with Tito's partisans and became a Yugoslav general. Left the army in 1961 and became a Professor at Zagreb University, taking up the cause of Croatian nationalism. Twice imprisoned as a nationalist dissident during the Tito era. He seized the opportunity on the break-up of the former Yugoslavia to declare independence in 1990. He led his Croatian Democratic Union (HDZ) to landslide victory in the first free elections, becoming President. After military reverses in 1991, he built up a strong army, intervening in Bosnia in 1995 and seizing Krajina. Signed the Dayton Accords, dividing Bosnia, and later securing eastern Slavonia as Croat territory. Although criticized for his corrupt and dictatorial control of Croatia, he was re-elected President in June 1997, though already terminally ill.

TURGOT, ANNE-ROBERT-JACQUES (1727–81) French administrator and economist. *Intendant* of Limoges, 1761–74. Became minister of marine, 1774. Comptroller-General of finance, 1774–76. One of central figures of Physiocrat school of economics. Abolished *corvée* (forced labour on roads). Encouraged building of roads and bridges. Reformed interest rates and imposed taxes more equitably. Ended some feudal privileges. Tried to re-establish free trade in grain between provinces.

V

VENIZELOS, ELEUTHERIOS (1864–1936) Greek statesman. Involved in rising against the Ottoman Empire, 1896. President of Cretan Assembly. Declared union of Crete with Greece, 1905. Became prime minister of Greece, 1910. Introduced financial, military and constitutional reforms. Took Greece into Balkan War. Gained Macedonia from peace settlement. Attempted to enter First World War on Allied side, 1915. Removed from office by King Constantine. Formed rebel government in Crete, 1916, later moved to Salonika. Declared war on Germany and Bulgaria. Secured abdication of Constantine and became legitimate prime minister in Athens, 1917. Attended Paris Peace Conference. In seeking to gain Anatolia for Greece, provoked war with the Ottoman Empire which produced electoral defeat, 1920. Briefly in office, 1924. Prime minister, 1928–32, again, 1933. Supporters staged uprising, 1935, leading to short civil war. Fled to France.

VICTOR EMMANUEL II (1820–78) King of Piedmont–Sardinia, 1849–78; King of Italy, 1861–78. Son of Charles Albert of Savoy. Succeeded to throne when Charles Albert abdicated after Radetsky expelled Piedmontese from Lombardy. Supported moves for Italian unity. Remained a constitutional monarch, upholding liberal Piedmontese constitution, 1849.

VICTORIA, QUEEN (1819–1901) Queen of United Kingdom, 1837–1901; Empress of India, 1876–1901. Longest-reigning British monarch. Symbol of period of British expansion. Last reigning Hanoverian. Married her cousin, Albert, 1840. Reign saw limitations on power of monarchy in relation to ministers. Victoria long claimed special supervision of foreign affairs, leading to disputes with Palmerston and Lord John Russell. Lived in seclusion for ten years after death of Albert, 1861. Popularity demonstrated by Golden Jubilee, 1887, and Diamond Jubilee, 1897. Disliked Gladstone, favouring Disraeli. Related to most of European royal houses through marriages of her children.

VOLTAIRE (FRANÇOIS MARIE AROUET) (1694–1778) French philosopher. Imprisoned in Bastille, 1717–18, 1726. In *Lettres philosophiques*, 1734, contrasted French and English institutions. Lived briefly in Potsdam under patronage of Frederick II. Corresponded with Catherine the Great. Philosophical works include *Dictionnaire philosophique*, 1764. Criticized dogmatic religions, especially Catholicism. Consistent theme in his writings is a lack of respect for authority and institutions, therefore preparing intellectual climate for French Revolution. Campaigned on behalf of victims of religious and political persecution.

W

WALESA, LECH (1943–) Polish trade unionist. Former Gdansk shipyard worker. Emerged as leader of independent 'Solidarity' trade union. Solidarity comprised some 40 per cent of Polish workers by late 1980. Mounted outspoken opposition to economic and social policies of government. Detained following imposition of martial law, December 1981. Released 11 months later. During his detention, Solidarity was banned. Continued to hold prominent position. Granted audience with Pope John Paul II, 1983. Awarded Nobel Peace Prize, 1983. Guided Solidarity throughout 1980s, but declined to hold office when, in September 1989, Solidarity became part of Poland's first non-Communist government for 40 years. However, in 1990 elected by direct vote as president of Poland. He was defeated in the 1995 presidential elections by a former communist.

WEIZMANN, CHAIM (1874–1952) Zionist leader. Headed British Zionist movement before First World War. Advised Foreign Office during planning of Balfour Declaration, 1917. Head of World Zionist Movement after 1920. Became head of Jewish Agency for Palestine, 1929. Elected first president of Israel, 1948.

WELLINGTON, 1ST DUKE OF, ARTHUR WELLESLEY (1769–1852) British soldier and politician. Outstanding military leader during Napoleonic Wars. MP, 1790–95, 1806, 1807, 1807–09. Commanded British force in Portugal, 1808. Created Earl Wellington, then Marquess, 1812. Campaigns in Peninsular War culminated in invasion of southern France, 1813. Created Duke of Wellington, 1814. British ambassador to Paris, 1814. Chief secretary for Ireland, 1807–09. Won decisive victory over Napoleon at Waterloo, June 1815. Commander of British occupying forces in France, 1815–18. Helped ensure moderate treatment of France by Allies. Master-General of the Ordnance, 1819–27. Prime minister, 1828–30. Achieved Catholic Emancipation, 1829. Reluctant to introduce electoral reform, 1830, consequently lost office. Prime minister and secretary of state for all Departments, November–December, 1834. Foreign secretary, 1834–35. Minister without portfolio, 1841–46. Commander-in-Chief, 1842–52.

WILLIAM II (1859–1941) German Emperor, King of Prussia, 1888–1918. Son of Emperor Frederick III. Dismissed Bismarck from chancellorship, 1890. Implemented 'New Course' in policy, aiming to assert German claims to world leadership. Increasingly under control of German High Command. Obliged by them to abdicate following Germany's military defeat, 1918. Went into exile in Holland.

WITTE, SERGE (1849–1915) Russian statesman. Minister of communications during 1880s. Minister of finance, 1892–1903, with supervisory role over commerce, industry and labour relations. Principal achievement was construction of Trans-Siberian railway. Able to stimulate industry with loans from France. Dismissed as result of military opposition, 1903. Returned to office to negotiate peace at Portsmouth following Russo–Japanese War. Became prime minister after 1905 Revolution. Substantial loans from Britain and France allowed him to by-pass Duma. Dismissed after six-month term of office. Strong critic of First World War.

Y

YELTSIN, BORIS NIKOLAYEVICH (1931–) Russian politician. Former Communist Party leader in Sverdlovsk, 1975. Promoted by Mikhail Gorbachev to be Party leader in Moscow, 1985. At that time, seen as Gorbachev's chief radical ally. In 1987, after increasingly bitter disagreements with Gorbachev, forced to resign. In 1989, elected for Moscow constituency with 90% of the vote. In May 1990, elected President of the Russian Federation, the largest republic within the former Soviet Union. A popular politician with his calls for more radical reform, his defence of democracy during the August 1991 coup attempt made him the undisputed leader of the Russian Federation. Created the Commonwealth of Independent States and this brought to an end the Soviet Union, December 1991. Became President of Russia in direct elections that month. Although he successfully overcame the 1993 communist rising in Moscow, he faced grave economic problems, a resurgence of nationalism and the war in Chechnya. Re-elected 1996 despite serious health problems which necessitated heart surgery; his increasingly erratic policies witnessed the appointment of five premiers in 17 months. In August 1999 he appointed Putin, who succeeded him when Yeltsin finally resigned at the end of that year.

Z

ZHIVKOV, TODOR (1911–98) Bulgarian communist. As president of Bulgaria from 1954 to 1989, was Eastern Europe's longest-serving political leader. Resigned office as the revolutions in Eastern Europe spread to the streets of Sofia, the capital. He was jailed for embezzlement in September 1992. Released from house arrest in 1997.

ZIMMERMANN, ARTHUR (1864–1940) German foreign minister. Sent telegram to German diplomat in Mexico, 1917, proposing alliance between Germany and Mexico, on understanding that Mexico would invade USA if USA entered war against Germany. In return, Mexico would receive lost territory in Texas, Arizona and New Mexico. Telegram intercepted by Britain and contents revealed to Washington. Instrumental in winning approval of Congress for US entry into war, 1917.

ZINOVIEV, GREGORI (1883–1936) Russian Bolshevik leader. Returned to Russia from exile with Lenin, April 1917. Held prominent office in Third International, 1920–26. Alleged to have written to British communists calling on them to cultivate revolution ('Red Letter Scare', 1924). Disagreed with Stalin, 1926. Discredited as ally of Trotsky and deposed from Politburo. Tried and sentenced to imprisonment for treason, 1935. Executed after second trial, 1936.

VI
GLOSSARY OF TERMS

A

ACTION FRANÇAISE French right-wing political movement founded by Charles Maurras in 1899 based on a royalist, nationalist and anti-Semitic programme. Although nominally supporting the Roman Catholic Church, the movement's other policies led to a papal ban in 1926. During the Second World War, the movement actively supported the Vichy regime, which resulted in its being banned after the war.

AGADIR CRISIS Diplomatic and military crisis in 1911 caused by arrival of German warship *Panther* in Moroccan port of Agadir. Although supposedly sent to protect German residents, the main aim was to gain colonial concessions from the French elsewhere in Africa in exchange for recognition of the French interest in Morocco.

ANCIEN RÉGIME (Fr. lit. 'old order') Describes the structure of government and society prevailing in Europe prior to the French Revolution of 1789. Its chief characteristics were absolute or despotic monarchy, and the division of society into three 'orders': aristocracy, clergy and the Third Estate (i.e. the ordinary people) (*see* Tiers Etat).

ANGLO–FRENCH ENTENTE *See Entente Cordiale.*

ANSCHLUSS The idea of union between Austria and Germany, current after the collapse of the Habsburg Monarchy in 1918 and given further impetus after Hitler became German chancellor in 1933. The deliberate destabilization of the Austrian government by the Nazis in 1938 led to the resignation of Chancellor Schuschnigg and his replacement by Arthur Seyss-Inquart, a Nazi nominee who invited the Germans to occupy Austria. The union of Austria with Germany was proclaimed on 13 March 1938.

ANTI-CLERICALISM Term applied to the opposition to organized religion, and largely directed against the power of the Roman Catholic Church. Anti-clericalism was prevalent during the revolutionary period in France and throughout the nineteenth century. Also apparent in Spain, especially during the Second Republic, 1931–39, in Germany as a result of the *Kulturkampf* (q.v.) and sporadically in Italy.

ANTI-COMINTERN PACT The agreement between Germany and Japan signed on 25 November 1936 which stated both countries' hostility to international communism. The pact was also signed by Italy in 1937 and, in addition to being a commitment to oppose the Soviet Union, it recognized the Japanese regime which had ruled Manchuria since 1931.

ANTI-SEMITISM Term used to describe animosity towards the Jews, either on a religious or a racial basis. Originally coined by racial theorists of the later nineteenth century, anti-Semitism can take a number of different political, economic or racial forms. A number of political parties in Germany and Austria were based on anti-Semitism, and it also appears in France via *Action Française* (q.v.). Economic and political anti-Semitism was a feature of Tsarist Russia with frequent pogroms (q.v.) against Jewish communities, a form of activity which seems to have recurred in the Soviet Union in 1958–59 and 1962–63. Anti-Semitism was one of the central planks of Nazi ideology and the major theme in Hitler's thinking, in which the Jews epitomized all that was wrong with German society. The idea of making Germany 'Jew-free' was given practical form in anti-Semitic legislation and the 'final solution' (q.v.) put into operation during the Second World War.

APRIL REVOLUTION Bloodless military coup, led by junior officers who constituted the Armed Forces Movement, which took place in Portugal on 25 April 1974, overthrowing the Caetano dictatorship, and opening the way to democracy and to independence for Portugal's African colonies. The coup was also known as the Carnation Revolution.

331

APRIL THESES Programme for power announced by the Bolshevik leader Lenin on his return to Petrograd in April 1917. Lenin – in effect challenging the Provisional Government – called for an end to the World War, the handing of political and economic power to the Soviets, abolition of the police, bureaucracy and armed forces, and the confiscation of private land. The Social Democratic Party was to be renamed the Communist Party and the Socialist International reconstructed as the Third International. Despite significant internal party opposition, and criticism from the Moscow and Petrograd Soviets, the April Theses became Bolshevik policy.

ARMED NEUTRALITY Declaration of policy by a state in times of war or international crisis that, while not wishing to become involved, it will nevertheless defend its interests and territorial integrity from incursions by any belligerent power.

ARMENIAN MASSACRES The systematic destruction of the monophysite Christian Armenian people in the Ottoman Empire by Muslim Turks in 1894–95. This action signalled the end of British support for the Empire and was followed by the extermination or deportation of the entire Armenian people by the Turkish government in 1914 and 1915 in one of the worst acts of genocide of the twentieth century.

ARYANIZATION Nazi racial policy based on Hitler's view that 'A State which in the epoch of race poisoning, dedicates itself to the cherishing of its best elements, must some day be master of the world.' The Nuremburg Laws for the 'Protection of German Blood and German Honour', 15 September 1935, forbade marriage or sexual relations between Jews and non-Jews, punishable by imprisonment and later by death. Later regulations excluded Jews from the professions and the civil service.

ASSIGNATS (Fr.) Interest-bearing Treasury bonds introduced by the French Constitutional Assembly in December 1789 to facilitate the purchase of nationalized Church lands. In September 1790 they became paper currency, but over-issue as a means of financing the revolutionary wars led to depreciation and the inflationary crisis in 1793.

ATLANTIC CHARTER A statement of principles agreed by Churchill and Roosevelt on behalf of Britain and the United States in August 1941, on the conduct of international policy in the postwar world. These included no territorial or other expansion; no wish for territorial changes other than those agreed by the peoples concerned; respect for the rights of all peoples to choose their form of government; desire for general economic development and collaboration; the need to disarm aggressor nations and the wish to construct a general system of international security. Although mainly a propaganda exercise, the USA refused to acknowledge any future international obligations in spite of British pressure. The charter was endorsed by the Soviet Union and fourteen other states at war with the Axis (q.v.) powers in September 1941.

AUSGLEICH (Ger. 'compromise') Agreement reached between the Austrian government and moderate Hungarian politicians in 1867 which transformed the Austrian Empire into the Dual Monarchy of Austria–Hungary. The system remained in operation until 1918, despite tensions resulting from commercial union and the resentment of other nationalities within the Empire at the privileged position of the Hungarians.

AUSTRO–MARXISM Revisionist Marxist trend which emerged in Austria in 1907. Its main figures were Max Adler, Otto Bauer and Rudolf Hilferding. Adler emphasized Marxism's scientific rather than ethical basis, Bauer wrote on the national question and imperialism, and Hilferding provided an economic analysis of imperialism which strongly influenced Lenin.

AXIS A term first used by Mussolini on 1 November 1936 to describe Fascist Italy's relationship with Nazi Germany established by the October protocols of 1936. He referred to the Rome–Berlin Axis, a term which was reinforced by a formal treaty in May 1939, the Pact of Steel. In September 1940, Germany, Italy and Japan signed a tripartite agreement which led to the term 'Axis Powers' being used to describe all three, as well as their Eastern European allies.

B

BAADER–MEINHOF GROUP Urban guerrillas in West Germany who emerged from the radical student movement of 1968. Led by Andreas Baader and Ulrike Meinhof, they were responsible for six killings, 50 attempted killings, bombings of American military installations, etc. Their leaders, captured in June 1972, later committed suicide.

BALANCE OF POWER A theory of international relations which aimed to secure peace by preventing any one state or group of states from attaining political or military strength sufficient to threaten the independence and liberty of others. The policy was based on the maintenance of a counterforce equal to that of the potential adversaries, and was the central theme of British policy in Europe against the French, and from 1904 to 1914, the Germans. This was epitomized by the creation of the *Entente Cordiale* (q.v.) with France to counter the threat from Germany, and later the Triple Entente (q.v.) of Britain, France and Russia to balance the Triple Alliance (q.v.) of Germany, Austria–Hungary and Italy. In the interwar period, Britain again attempted to create a balance against French power by encouraging the rapid recovery of Germany. The policy was abandoned in the 1930s as Germany and Japan began to pursue more aggressive foreign policies which could not be countered by the

League of Nations' security system, nor by further alliances.

BASTILLE Royal fortress commanding the eastern side of Paris. A radical pamphlet campaign on the eve of the Revolution gave it exaggerated notoriety as a state prison. Its destruction on 14 July 1789 by the workers of the Faubourg St Antoine has been commemorated ever since as a symbol of the fall of royal despotism and the beginning of the French Revolution.

BEER HALL PUTSCH Hitler's attempt to seize Bavaria on 9/10 November 1923 as a preliminary to overthrowing the Weimar Republic. The coup, the headquarters of which were in a beer cellar, collapsed when police fired on 2,000 Nazis, killing 14. Hitler was sentenced to five years in prison.

BERLIN BLOCKADE With Berlin under four-power administration, the USSR, alleging the West had broken postwar agreements on German status, and hoping to force out the USA, Britain and France, imposed obstacles to road and river traffic entering the western sector of Berlin in June 1948. The West responded with a round-the-clock airlift of fuel and food to relieve the beleaguered city. The blockade ended in May 1949.

BERLIN WALL The East Berlin riots of 1953 and the continuing disparity in living standards encouraged a stream of refugees from East to West Berlin. The communist authorities responded on 13 August 1961 by blocking 68 of 80 border crossing points and constructing a wire and concrete barrier that was to become a permanent feature of the city. All this changed with the revolutions in Eastern Europe in 1989. Dismantling of the wall began, and in October 1990 Berlin became capital of a reunited Germany.

BLACK HAND Popular name of the Serbian secret society (*Ujedinjenje ili Smrt*) formed in Belgrade in May 1911. Led by Col. Dragutin Dimitrievič and consisting mainly of army officers, the society's main aim was the unifying of Serb minorities in Austria–Hungary and the Ottoman Empire with the independent state of Serbia. They were responsible for the training of Gavrilo Princip, who assassinated the Austrian Archduke Francis Ferdinand in Sarajevo on 28 June 1914. The society was in conflict with the Serbian government throughout the First World War, culminating in the arrest and execution of Dimitrievič with two others, and the banning of the organization. These sentences were later quashed by the supreme court of Serbia in 1953 when the country had been incorporated into Yugoslavia.

BLANK CHEQUE The verbal reply given on 5 July 1914 in response to a letter from Emperor Francis Joseph of Austria by Kaiser Wilhelm II to Count Hoyos, an Austrian Foreign Ministry official, guaranteeing German support if Austria attacked Serbia as punishment for the assassination of Archduke Franz Ferdinand in Sarajevo on 28 June 1914.

BLITZKRIEG (Ger. 'lightning war') A theory of warfare which involved a rapid attack on a very narrow front to create penetration in depth. The technique involved prior aerial bombing to reduce enemy resistance and then the deployment of highly mobile armoured columns. Used extensively by the German army in the Second World War and especially by General Guderian in the campaign against France in 1940. Also abbreviated to 'Blitz' in English to describe the heavy bombing and night attacks on British cities by the German air force during the Second World War.

BLOODY SUNDAY A term used to describe a number of events, as follows:

(1) In Britain, Sunday, 13 November 1887. A meeting held by the Social Democratic Federation in London to demand the release of the nationalist Irish MP William O'Brien was dispersed by police and Life Guards, resulting in the deaths of two people and injuries to over a hundred.

(2) In Britain, Sunday, 30 January 1972. Thirteen civilians were killed in Londonderry after a demonstration in favour of a united Ireland was broken up by British paratroopers.

(3) In Russia, Sunday, 22 January 1905. A procession of workers and their families led by Fr George Gapon was fired on by troops guarding the Winter Palace in St Petersburg. The procession had intended to present a petition to the Tsar calling for an eight-hour day, a constituent assembly and an amnesty for political prisoners. Over one hundred people were killed and several hundred wounded, an event which helped to spark off the 1905 Russian Revolution.

BOLSHEVIK (Russ. lit. 'member of the majority') A term applied to the radical faction of the Russian Social Democratic Party which split in 1903. Lenin led the Bolsheviks in opposition to the more moderate Mensheviks (q.v.). The Bolsheviks came to power in Russia after the October Revolution of 1917, and the name was retained by the Soviet Communist Party until 1952.

BOULANGIST A supporter of General George Boulanger (1837–91) who in 1888 began a campaign for the revision of the French Constitution and the establishment of a more authoritarian government. He fled France in April 1889 and was condemned *in absentia* for treason. The Boulangist movement did not survive his flight.

BOXERS The popular name for the Society of Harmonious Fists, a movement active in China at the turn of the twentieth century. Its main targets were European commercial interests in the Chinese Empire and, with the tacit approval of the government, it carried out a series of attacks against missionaries and the foreign-owned railways, culminating in the siege of the foreign legations in Peking (Beijing) in the summer of 1900. The siege was finally lifted by an international expeditionary force in August of that year.

BREZHNEV DOCTRINE The ideological basis of the Warsaw Pact (q.v.) invasion of Czechoslovakia in August 1968. Leonid Brezhnev, General Secretary of the Soviet Communist Party, pronounced a doctrine of 'limited sovereignty', denying East European states the right to diverge widely from the Soviet model, and asserting the legitimacy of intervention. *See* 'Prague Spring'.

BRISSOTINS The followers of Jacques-Pierre Brissot, the dominant group of left-wing deputies in the French Legislative Assembly and subsequently known as the Girondins. Fervent advocates of the Revolutionary Wars. By October 1793, most had been imprisoned and guillotined.

BRUMAIRE (Fr. lit. 'foggy month') Month in the French revolutionary calendar from 21 October to 20 November. Napoleon's *coup d'état* of 18 Brumaire (9 November 1799) replaced the Directory (q.v.) with government by the Consulate (q.v.).

BUNDESTAG Federal Diet of the German Confederation (1815–66). Now one of the two legislative chambers of the Federal Republic of Germany. Elected by direct universal suffrage for four years, it in turn elects the Chancellor who is head of the government.

C

CAHIERS DE DOLÉANCES Lists of grievances drawn up by each of three estates in towns, villages and guilds for presentation at the meeting of the French Estates-General in 1789.

CARBONARI (It. lit. 'charcoal burners') Italian secret society aiming to overthrow governments established by the Vienna settlement of 1815, and to establish national unity. Instigated unsuccessful revolts in Naples (1820)

and Piedmont (1821) as well as wider series of risings in 1831. Eventually absorbed into Mazzini's 'Young Italy' movement.

CARLISTS Supporters of Don Carlos (1788–1855) and his descendants in their claim to the Spanish throne following Ferdinand VII's ending of the Salic Law in Spain to allow the succession of Queen Isabella in 1833. The resultant Carlist civil war lasted from 1834 until 1837 but disorder lasted until the end of the reign in 1868. Open war was resumed in 1870 and unrest continued throughout the nineteenth century. The Carlist movement also became prominent in opposition to the Second Spanish Republic, 1931–36, and as supporters of the Nationalist cause in the Spanish Civil War 1936–39.

CAUDILLO, EL (Sp. lit. 'the leader') Title assumed by Francisco Franco in 1937 as head of the insurgent nationalist forces in the Spanish Civil War, and of the so-called Burgos government. His authority was reinforced in July 1947 with the declaration that he should remain 'Caudillo' or head of state for life, pending the restoration of the monarchy.

CENTRAL POWERS Initially members of the Triple Alliance created by Bismarck in 1882, namely Germany, Austria–Hungary and Italy. As Italy remained neutral in the First World War, the term was applied to Germany, Austria–Hungary, their ally the Ottoman Empire and later also Bulgaria.

CGT (*CONFÉDÉRATION GÉNÉRALE DU TRAVAIL*) The largest French trade union federation, formed in 1906 on a non-political syndicalist platform. A communist minority broke away in 1921, the two sections reuniting in 1935, since when the CGT has been communist-led.

CHAMBRE INTROUVABLE The name given by the French King Louis XVIII to the French Assembly convened in 1815. Of extreme Royalist sympathies, it consisted of 402 deputies, many young and inexperienced, and 176 nobles of the *ancien régime*.

They favoured reprisals against Bonaparte's followers and condoned the reactionary White Terror. Their extremism proved unpopular with the countries which had restored Louis to the monarchy and the Assembly dissolved in September 1816.

CHEKA (Russ.) Extraordinary commission, or secret political police force established by the Bolsheviks (q.v.) in post-revolutionary Russia to defend the regime against internal enemies.

CHERNOBYL A major disaster in a Soviet light-water nuclear reactor in the Ukraine in April 1986 sent a radioactive cloud spreading through Scandinavia and Europe, contaminating agricultural produce. Though immediate casualties were said to be low, it has now been revealed as a major environmental and health disaster. It led to a surge of support for 'green' parties in Western Europe.

CHETNIKS Originally Serbian guerrillas seeking liberation from the Ottoman Empire. Active against German supply lines in occupied Balkan states during the First World War. They also opposed German occupation in the Second World War and were aided by the British until 1944. Some commanders collaborated with the Germans and Italians against Tito's partisans. The term was in use again after 1991 to refer to Serbian irregulars fighting the Croats.

CHRISTIAN DEMOCRACY Anti-communist, moderate political movement formed in many European countries with the development of a mass electorate in the late nineteenth and twentieth centuries. Among the largest was the old Italian Christian Democrat Party founded in 1943 as the successor to the pre-Fascist Popular Party, formed in 1919, and until the early 1990s the major representative of Catholic, moderate opinion. The German National People's Party, formed in 1918, and the German Centre Party, formed in 1870, also represent this tradition, latterly taken up by Adenauer's Christian-Democratic Union, formed in 1945. Many other European countries have similar political parties.

CHRISTMAS REVOLUTION Term applied to the popular uprising in Romania in December 1989 against the Ceausescu dictatorship. Sometimes called the 'winter revolution'.

CITIZEN KING Louis Philippe (1773–1850), King of France, 1830–48. So called because he was an ostensibly constitutional monarch, sharing the political and social attitudes (and the sartorial style) of his middle-class supporters. He fled to England after the February 1848 revolution.

CITOYEN (Fr. lit. 'citizen') Used during the French Revolution to indicate loyalty to the Republic or revolutionary cause. Refusal to be called by the title 'citoyen' often resulted in arrest and execution.

CNT (*CONFEDERACIÓN NACIONAL DEL TRABAJO*) National Confederation of Labour. Anarcho-syndicalist union federation formed in Spain in October 1910, strongest in industrial Catalonia and rural Andalusia, with two million members by the mid-1930s. The CNT resisted Franco's rising in 1936, encouraging industrial and agricultural collectivization. Weakened by growing communist influence in the Republic and driven underground by Nationalist victory in 1939, it re-emerged in the 1980s.

CODE NAPOLÉON The French Civil Law code, enacted on 21 March 1804 and renamed in honour of the Emperor in 1807. The need for a uniform civil law stemmed from the chaotic system which had emerged in the eighteenth century with Roman law in the south and custom law in the north, a situation further complicated by local laws and innumerable exemptions. The Code contained 2,281 articles and remains the basis of French law. It has formed the basis for legal codes in other states.

COHABITATION Term used to describe the political situation in France following the 1986 parliamentary election. With two years remaining before the end of President François Mitterrand's term of office, the right won a majority of seats in parliament. The subsequent conservative government and socialist president went on to tolerate and work alongside each other. The term was revived following the left-wing victory in 1997 under Lionel Jospin (with Chirac a right-wing President).

COLD WAR Protracted state of tension between countries falling short of actual war. The term was first used in a US Congress debate on 12 March 1947 on the doctrine, expounded by Harry S. Truman (1894–1972), promising aid to 'free peoples who are resisting attempted subjugation by armed minorities or by outside pressures'. A direct product of the civil war in Greece (1946–49), the doctrine bore the wider implication that the USA would actively respond anywhere in the world to what it saw as direct encroachment by the USSR. The practical division of Europe occurred as a result of the Eastern European states' rejection of US Marshall Aid, often under pressure from the Soviet Union, and their subsequent membership of Comecon (q.v.). This division into two hostile camps was completed by the creation of NATO (1949–50) (q.v.) and the Warsaw Pact (1955) (q.v.). The Cold War between the Soviet Union and the USA continued into the 1970s before being superceded by a period of *détente*. The main crises within the Cold War period were the Russian invasion of Hungary in 1956; of Czechoslovakia in 1968; the Berlin Blockade of 1948 and the Cuban Missile Crisis of 1962. Western outrage at these supposed manifestations of Soviet expansion was tempered by the British and French involvement in Suez in 1956 and the US involvement in Vietnam during the 1960s and early 1970s. With the advent of Gorbachev in the USSR, and the fall of communist regimes in Eastern Europe after 1989, it was effectively over. It was formally ended by the signing of the Conference on Security and Co-operation in Europe (CSCE) (q.v.) on 19 November 1990 and reinforced by the signing of the Founding Act in 1997 (on NATO–Russian cooperation).

COLLABORATION The relationship between sections of the population and Second World War German occupation forces in Europe. Collaboration ranged from active political, administrative and economic support for puppet governments, through unavoidable co-operation, to reluctant acquiescence. *See* Quisling.

COLLECTIVIZATION The process of transferring land from private to state or collective ownership. Extensively operated in the Soviet Union during the early 1930s when peasants' individual holdings were combined to form agricultural collectives (*Kolkhoz*) or in some cases state-owned farms (*Sovkhoz*) which were run by state employees.

COMECON (COUNCIL FOR MUTUAL ECONOMIC ASSISTANCE) Organization established in Moscow in January 1949 to improve trade between the Soviet Union and other Eastern European states. Regarded by Stalin as an instrument to enforce an economic boycott on Yugoslavia, and also used as a Soviet response to growing Western European economic interdependence. With the revolutions in Eastern Europe in 1989, Comecon effectively ceased to exist as the former communist states made moves towards creating market economies. In 1991 it was formally dissolved.

COMINTERN Abbreviated title of the Third International established in March 1919 to promote revolutionary Marxism. By 1928 it had become a vehicle for Stalin's ideas. Finally dissolved in May 1943 as a goodwill gesture to the Soviet Union's western allies.

COMMONWEALTH OF INDEPENDENT STATES (CIS) A voluntary association of 11 (formerly 12) states formed when the Soviet Union disintegrated. It is little more than a forum to keep alive some vague form of co-operation after the demise of the old USSR.

COMMUNARD A member of the Paris Commune which was formed on 26 March 1871 after the withdrawal of troops from the city by the Thiers government in response to rioting.

MacMahon's forces eventually retook the city after bitter street fighting and the Commune was suppressed. The Commune was inspired by democratic and socialist ideas of the time, although the rioting which led to the government's withdrawal of troops had been against the peace settlement with Germany and the conservatism of the newly formed Third Republic.

CONCERT OF EUROPE The term used to describe the workings of the Congress system (q.v.) whereby treaties were made and guaranteed by the European Powers meeting together. The idea of the 'summit' meeting extended to the settlement of the Eastern Question (q.v.) and colonial disputes in the later nineteenth and early twentieth centuries.

CONCORDAT An agreement between the Pope, as head of the Roman Catholic Church, and the secular authorities of individual states on the rights, privileges and obligations of the Church within those states.

CONDUCATOR (Rom. 'leader') The title used by the Romanian dictator, Nicolae Ceausescu (q.v.).

CONFERENCE ON SECURITY AND CO-OPERATION IN EUROPE (CSCE) Major agreement of 19 November 1990, signed in Paris, which marked the formal end of the Cold War. Part of this agreement was the signing of the Conventional Forces in Europe (CFE) Treaty by 22 NATO and Warsaw Pact countries, formalizing the biggest cuts in weapons and manpower since the end of the Second World War.

CONGRESS SYSTEM A system of settling international disputes and maintaining peace in Europe through the use of regular diplomatic conferences. Initiated by the Congress of Vienna in 1815 between the victorious powers in the Napoleonic Wars (Britain, Russia, Austria and Prussia), further congresses were held at Aix-la-Chapelle (1818), Troppau (1820), Laibach (1821), Verona (1822) and St Petersburg (1825). System was weakened by British withdrawal before the 1825 congress when it was realized that the other powers were anxious to use the power of the congress to interfere in the affairs of other states and to prevent the spread of liberalism.

CONSULATE The system of government used in France from the overthrow of the Directory (q.v.) in November 1799 until Napoleon declared himself Emperor in 1804. The government consisted of three legislative chambers and an executive headed by three consuls. In practice, Napoleon as First Consul dominated the proceedings of the government throughout its life.

CONTINENTAL SYSTEM Policy of economic warfare conducted by Napoleon Bonaparte in an attempt to bring Britain to her knees during the Napoleonic Wars. The Berlin Decree of 21 November 1806 sought to close continental ports to British trade and the Milan Decree of December 1807 attempted to extend the policy to neutral ships trading with Britain. In 1807 the policy was extended to Russian ports after Tilsit, and then to the Iberian peninsula in 1808. The policy proved only partially effective through the British retaliatory Orders in Council, blockading French trade, the diversion of British trade elsewhere, widespread smuggling, and the non-compliance of many states.

CORFU DECLARATION The declaration agreed by Serbia, Croatia, Slovenia and Montenegro on 27 July 1917 to establish a unified state of Yugoslavia following the military defeat of the Austro–Hungarian Empire after the First World War.

CORTES Spanish parliament. Originally a medieval institution, the Cortes has served as a representative body during periods of democratic rule in the nineteenth and twentieth centuries. Suppressed in 1923 by the dictatorship of Primo de Rivera, it was restructured by the Second Republic as a democratically elected institution, only to be swept away by the Civil War (1936–39). Restored again in 1942 as a cypher for

Franco's dictatorship, the institution was again restructured in 1978 when the monarchy was restored and free elections took place to the Cortes General. This body has two houses.

COUNCIL COMMUNISM Influenced by workers' councils activity in the 1917–20 European revolutionary upheavals, Council Communism rejected Bolshevik (q.v.) party-led socialism. Marxist, but with strong anarchist undertones, it advocated economic and social organization based on a network of factory councils. Its leading theorist was a Dutch astronomer, Anton Pannekoek (1873–1960).

CULT OF PERSONALITY Political phenomenon whereby a leader, usually the head of state, is elevated above his colleagues to a position where he is seen as responsible for all the nation's or party's achievements but for none of its failures. Such elevation is achieved by a massive propaganda exercise, including posters and statues of the leader, the naming of towns after him, etc. Joseph Stalin (1879–1953) set the pattern as Soviet leader but others have followed, for example Hitler in Germany, Mao Tse-tung in China and Kim Il-sung in North Korea. Such cults appear to flourish only in totalitarian regimes.

D

DAUPHIN Eldest son and heir to the French King. The last Dauphin was prevented from succeeding to his father's throne (Louis XVI) by the French Revolution and the establishment of the Republic after 1789.

DECEMBRISTS Members of an abortive conspiracy of army officers in St Petersburg and of gentry in southern Russia who aimed to overthrow Tsarist autocracy and replace it with a more liberal regime at the death of Alexander I in December 1825. The rising was severely put down by the new Tsar Nicholas I. It is sometimes known as the first Russian Revolution.

DELORS PLAN Plan drawn up by the Delors Committee headed by the President of the Commission of the European Economic Community, Jacques Delors, set up in 1988. The Plan involved a series of measures to create greater monetary and political unity in the EEC. The first phase created the European Monetary System (EMS). Phase two would set up a European system of central banks which would gradually assume greater control over national monetary policy. Much of the plan was opposed by former British Prime Minister Margaret Thatcher (q.v.).

DEMOCRATIC CENTRALISM The principle of authority of the Soviet and other Communist parties, formulated by Lenin. Democratic centralism was fundamentally dictatorial and involved obedience by each section of the party to decisions reached by superior organs.

DESTALINIZATION The overthrowing of the 'cult of personality' that had surrounded Soviet dictator Stalin (q.v.). Stalin died in 1953, and the process began in 1956 at the 20th Party Congress in Russia. The attack on Stalin and his purges was led by Khrushchev (q.v.). The process included renaming Stalingrad (which became Volgograd). Under Gorbachev's *glasnost*, there were further revelations of the evils of the Stalin era. Stalin's body was removed from Lenin's mausoleum, statues were removed and place names changed. Even in Albania, the last outpost of Stalinism, the process was complete by 1991.

DICTATORSHIP OF THE PROLETARIAT Marxist description of working-class rule between the collapse of capitalism in revolution and the birth of a classless, communist society. Developed by Lenin after the 1917 Bolshevik seizure of power, dictatorship was exercised by a centralized party. The concept was abandoned by West European communist parties in the 1970s and was replaced in the 1977 Soviet Constitution by the 'state of the whole people'.

DIRECTORY The Directory was established in France after the fall of Robespierre in August 1794 and Thermidor (q.v.). As the executive power in France it consisted of five directors and a Council of 500, together with a Council of Ancients. The period of the Directory was characterized by a period of chaos in provincial administration, and defeat in the wars of the Second Coalition coupled with the revolt in the Vendée made the government unpopular. It was finally overthrown by Napoleon on 9 November 1799 and replaced by the Consulate (q.v.).

DREIKAISERBUND (Ger. 'League of the Three Emperors') An informal alliance created in 1872 between the states of Germany, Russia and Austria as a result of the meeting of their respective Emperors. The alliance was already a dead letter before the creation of the Triple Alliance (q.v.) in 1882.

DREYFUS AFFAIR Scandal in France between 1894 and 1899 involving Alfred Dreyfus (1859–1935), a Jewish army officer who was accused, tried and convicted of passing information to the Germans. Having been sentenced to life imprisonment on Devil's Island, he was found innocent and later exonerated by a second trial in 1899 which proved that many of the documents used to convict him had been forgeries. It became apparent that the authorities had used Dreyfus as a scapegoat to cover up the activities of a Major Esterhazy. During the time taken to convince the authorities of the need for a second trial, many accusations were made, including Zola's letter '*J'accuse*', that anti-Semitism of the authorities and the army had ensured Dreyfus's conviction and delayed his retrial. The 'Dreyfusard' and 'Anti-Dreyfusard' camps displayed many of the characteristic cleavages in the Third Republic.

DUAL ALLIANCE Also known as the Dual Entente. An alliance between Russia and France which lasted from 1893 until the Bolshevik Revolution of October 1917.

DUAL MONARCHY Name given to the Austro–Hungarian Empire and, by extension, to its system of government.

DUCE (It. lit. 'leader') Title assumed by Benito Mussolini (*see* p. 313).

DUMA Russian parliament established by the Tsar in 1905 in response to demands which emanated from the abortive revolution of 1905. Free elections to the first two Dumas led to radical demands and rapid dissolution by the government. The Third Duma, elected with much greater government interference, did produce some limited administrative and land reform instigated by premier Stolypin. In spite of government disapproval, the Duma remained a platform for protest and in November 1916 warned the government of impending revolution. As a result of its criticisms of the government, the Duma was suspended for much of the war period. Since the fall of the Soviet Union, the lower house of the Russian parliament has again been known as the Duma.

E

EASTERN QUESTION The title given to the various problems of international, and especially European, relations created by the gradual decline of the Ottoman Empire in the late nineteenth and early twentieth centuries. A number of European powers vied for territorial concessions. Austria–Hungary looked to expand into the Balkans, Russia to gain access to the Mediterranean Sea for her Black Sea fleet. Until 1897, the fear of the Russians led Britain to support the Ottoman Empire, but most of this support disappeared after the Armenian massacres (q.v.). Germany began to play an increasing role in Turkish affairs after a personal visit by the Kaiser in 1898 gave valuable commercial and railway concessions in exchange for a German military mission. The independence of the Balkan states further complicated the issue, especially when Serbia and Romania combined against the Ottoman Empire during the Balkan Wars of 1912. The Empire's alliance with Germany led to its destruction in 1918 and the creation of a Turkish national state.

EMANCIPATION Term used to denote the freeing of religious groups such as Jews or Roman Catholics from institutionalized legislative or judicial disadvantage. Both Catholic and Jewish emancipation were important issues in western European states during the eighteenth and nineteenth centuries.

ÉMIGRÉS (Fr. lit 'emigrants') Term used originally to describe opponents of the French Revolution who chose, or were forced, to leave the country. Many were members of the nobility and some were active in trying to promote a coalition of European sovereigns against the Revolutionary government. The Revolutionaries enacted various punitive decrees against émigrés. More recently, the term has been applied to many types of refugee who have fled from political, religious or racial persecution.

EMS TELEGRAM Telegram sent by the King of Prussia to Bismarck from the German spa town of Ems in July 1870, reporting on his conversations with the French ambassador over the Hohenzollern candidature to the Spanish throne. The telegram was doctored by Bismarck in such a way that it appeared that the French ambassador had been insulted and vice versa, and was thereby calculated to inflame French opinion when released to the press. Its publication duly excited French national pride and led to their declaration of war against Prussia on 19 July, four days after the telegram had been sent.

ENLIGHTENED DESPOTISM Used to describe a form of government prevalent in the eighteenth century in which absolute rulers acted for the general welfare of their subjects rather than for their own benefit under the influence of the Enlightenment. Characterized by an interest in administrative reform, the reduction of feudal privilege, including serfdom, religious toleration, and economic development, a number of rulers, notably Catherine the Great, Frederick the Great, Leopold II of Tuscany, and Joseph II, have usually been grouped under this term, although a number of others display certain of its features.

ENLIGHTENMENT A widespread movement in Europe in the seventeenth and eighteenth centuries based on the conviction that through reason, man could achieve true knowledge. The philosophical base of the movement was extended by other thinkers into the realms of political and economic theory (e.g. Rousseau, Voltaire).

ENTENTE CORDIALE (Fr. 'cordial agreement') Term first used in the 1840s to describe the special relationship between Britain and France. Revived in the Anglo–French Entente of 8 April 1904 and a similar agreement with Russia in August 1907. These three were known as the Entente Powers until 1917, the agreements being converted to military alliances in September 1911. The basis of the Anglo–French agreement had been the settlement of colonial differences and it survived the First World War, but was strained by the French occupation of the Ruhr in 1923 and the British attack on the French fleet in 1940. Attempts were made after the Second World War to revive the Entente by the Treaty of Dunkirk (1947).

ESTADO NOVO The 'new state' in Portugal. The Fascist regime established in 1926 and which was for long ruled after 1932 by António de Oliveira Salazar.

ETHNIC CLEANSING Euphemism which emerged in the breakup of the former Yugoslavia in 1992 to describe attempts to remove minority ethnic groups by persuading communities to flee through threats and near-genocidal violence. Most often used to describe Serb actions against the Muslim community in Bosnia.

F

FALANGE The only political party permitted in Franco's Spain. Founded by José Antonio Primo de Rivera in 1933 as a right-wing movement opposed to the Republic. José Antonio was assassinated in November 1936 in the early months of the Spanish Civil War. The movement survived his death to be used by Franco when the Grand Council of the Falange replaced the Cortes as the legislative body in Spain between June 1939 and July 1942.

FASCIST An Italian nationalist, totalitarian, anti-communist movement developed by Mussolini after 1919 which eventually became the only authorized political party in Italy in December 1925. The movement derived its name from the 'fasces' (bundle of sticks), the symbol of state power in ancient Rome. More generally applied to authoritarian and National Socialist movements in Europe and elsewhere (*e.g.* Salazar's Portugal, Franco's Spain, the Arrow Cross in Hungary).

FASHODA INCIDENT Crisis in Anglo–French relations as a result of rival claims to Sudan. A French detachment under Marchand had marched to the town of Fashoda on the Upper Nile from French West Africa, reaching it in July 1898, just before the arrival of General Kitchener, fresh from his defeat of the Mahdi's forces at Omdurman, with a large Anglo–Egyptian army. France's claim to the area by right of prior conquest was hotly disputed by Britain who wished to retain control of the Nile Valley. A 'war scare' was fanned in both countries by the popular press, but France's distraction by the Dreyfus affair (q.v.) and lack of support from Russia forced her to back down. Marchand withdrew from

Fashoda in November 1898 and France agreed in March 1899 to renounce all claims to the Nile Valley.

FINAL SOLUTION Translation of the German *'entlösung'* used to describe the destruction of European Jewry carried out by Nazi Germany in occupied countries between 1941 and 1945 (*see* p. 167–171).

FIRST INTERNATIONAL The first International Working-Men's Association (IWMA) was formed by Marx (q.v.) in London in 1864. It aimed to establish socialism by co-ordinating the efforts of the working class in different countries. Riddled with disputes between Marx and the anarchists under Bakunin (q.v.), it moved headquarters to New York and was finally dissolved in 1876.

FIVE YEAR PLAN System of economic planning first adopted in the Soviet Union between 1928 and 1933. The plan laid down short-term aims and targets for the development of heavy industry and the collectivization of agriculture. The second plan, 1933–37, aimed at increased production of consumer goods but the third, 1938–42, returned to the primacy of heavy industry, largely directed towards rearmament. The Five Year Plan was adopted as a method of planning by other socialist countries.

FOURTEEN POINTS A peace programme put forward by President Woodrow Wilson to the US Congress on 8 January 1918 and accepted as the basis for an armistice by Germany and Austria–Hungary. Later it was alleged that the Allied Powers had violated the principles embodied in the Fourteen Points, especially in relation to the prohibition of *Anschluss* (q.v.), the union of Germany with Austria. The original points were: the renunciation of secret diplomacy; freedom of the seas; the removal of economic barriers between states; arms reductions; impartial settlement of colonial disputes; evacuation of Russia by Germany and her allies; restoration of Belgium; German withdrawal from France and the return of

Alsace–Lorraine; readjustment of the Italian frontiers; autonomous development of nationalities in Austria–Hungary; evacuation of Romania, Serbia and Montenegro and guarantees of Serbian access to the sea; free passage through the Dardanelles and the self-determination of minorities in the Ottoman Empire; creation of an independent Poland with access to the sea; and the creation of a general association of states.

FREE FRENCH The *Forces Françaises Libres*, made up of French troops and naval units, who continued the fight against Nazi Germany after the fall of France in the summer of 1940. In opposition to the Vichy regime in France, Gen. de Gaulle established a 'Council for the Defence of the Empire', and later the *Comité National Français*. The Free French were active against Vichy forces in Syria and Miquelon and St Pierre in 1941. On 19 July 1942 the Free French were renamed the *Forces Françaises Combatantes*, Fighting French Forces (FFC). The FFC represented de Gaulle's main claim as the true representative of French liberation. As the allied forces liberated France in the summer of 1944, the FFC were able to provide the first allied troops to enter Paris after an uprising organized by the *Forces Françaises de L'Intérieur*.

FÜHRER (Ger. lit. 'leader') Title first coined in 1921 to describe Hitler as head of the Nazi Party. After his appointment as chancellor in 1933, the term was used more widely to describe him as 'führer' of Germany.

G

GASTARBEITER (Ger. 'guestworker') Overseas labour, predominantly Greek, Turkish and Moroccan, recruited to meet the needs of West German industry from the 1960s.

GAULEITER (Ger.) Regional chief of the NSDAP. The party had divided Germany into areas for the purposes of administration. Each '*Gau*' was the basis of the party in Germany and the *Gauleiter* retained their positions of power even after the Nazi takeover of Germany through their access to Hitler, and the parallel operation of party and state organizations at national and local level. The more prominent *Gauleiter* were able to impose their authority locally and during the war gained control over political and economic policy as well as labour allocation and civil defence.

GERMAN DEMOCRATIC REPUBLIC (GDR) The state formed in 1949 from the post-war Soviet zone of occupation in Germany. Popularly called East Germany. It united with the Federal Republic of Germany on 3 October 1990, following the collapse of communism.

GESTAPO (Ger. abbreviation of *Geheime Staatspolizei*) Originally the political police force of the Prussian State Police, the Gestapo was developed as an instrument of internal control in Germany during the Nazi period by Heinrich Himmler as head of the German police. The Gestapo was used extensively to control and suppress opposition to Nazi rule, both inside Germany and later also in occupied territories.

GIRONDINS Middle-class republican group in the French Legislative Assembly of 1791 and the Convention of 1792. Many of the group's members came from the Gironde region in south-west France. Led by Brissot, Roland, Petion and Vergniaud, they supported the French involvement in war but opposed the Jacobins as to its conduct. The Girondins were overthrown and their leaders executed in 1793.

GLASNOST The liberalizing 'openness' of the Soviet intellectual atmosphere encouraged by Mikhail Gorbachev, following his appointment as Communist Party Secretary in March 1985. *Glasnost* appeared to set few limits on the discussion of contemporary Soviet society and politics and of Soviet history, particularly the Stalin period. The fall of the Soviet Union in 1991 ended the old restrictions of the communist era.

GRAND COALITION (Ger. *grosse Koalition*) Term used in Central European politics to denote coalition of two major parties as opposed to a small coalition (*kleine Koalition*) of one major party and a minor party. Such a coalition, between the conservative CDU/CSU and the social democratic SPD governed West Germany from 1966 until 1969. A grand coalition of the conservative ÖVP and the social democratic SPÖ governed Austria from 1945 to 1966.

GREAT FEAR Name given to wave of peasant revolt, riot and chateau-burning which began in France towards the end of 1788 and gathered pace during 1789, especially after news of the fall of the Bastille (q.v.). The disturbances were fuelled by rumours of an aristocratic plot to starve the people and of bands of brigands pillaging the countryside, arising out of distress and confused reports coming from Paris.

GREAT PURGE *See* Yezhovshchina.

GREENS Originally and principally the West German ecology party, which first emerged as a political force in Bremen in 1979, when environmentalists and anti-nuclear groups won 5.9 per cent of votes for the *Land* (federal state) parliament. Greens have since been elected to other *Land* parliaments and to the Bundestag, and similar parties have had success in other West European countries. The British Ecology Party changed its name to the Greens in 1985 but has met with only limited support.

GRUNDGESETZ The postwar constitution (i.e. the Basic Law) of (originally) West Germany. It came into force in 1949.

GUILLOTINE Instrument of execution first used in revolutionary France. Named after physician Joseph Ignace Guillotine, an advocate of capital punishment. Victims were decapitated by a falling blade.

GULAG The forced labour camps of the former Soviet Union, established by Stalin in 1930. Their infamous record (of perhaps 8 million deaths) was immortalized by Solzhenitsyn in *The Gulag Archipelago* (1973–8).

H

HABSBURGS The house of Habsburg–Lorraine, an Austrian royal dynasty which ruled from 1282 to 1918. The family held the title of Holy Roman Emperor from 1438 to 1740 and from 1745 to 1806. The dissolution of the Empire meant that they adopted the title Emperor of Austria but their acquisition of territory had been based on a series of marriages in the fifteenth and early sixteenth centuries, culminating in the reign of the Emperor Charles V. After this, the Empire was divided between the Austrian and Spanish Habsburg families. The murder of the heir to the Austrian Habsburg throne in 1914, Francis Ferdinand, led to the outbreak of the First World War, and the last Emperor, Charles I, was forced to abdicate in 1918. Attempts to place his son Otto on the Austrian throne in the 1920s and 1930s were ended by the *Anschluss* (q.v.) with Germany in 1938.

HELSINKI AGREEMENT Product of the Helsinki Conference, 1975, between 35 nations concerning European security, proposals for economic collaboration between Eastern and Western blocs, and a reaffirmation of human rights. The last was consistently utilized to raise the cases of dissidents suffering ill-treatment in the Soviet Union.

HERRENVOLK (Ger. lit. 'master race') A doctrine expounded by the Nazis who used the supposed superiority of the 'aryan' race as a justification for German territorial expansion and the enslavement of 'inferior races'.

HISTORIC COMPROMISE Term used to describe the support given by the Italian Communist Party (PCI) to the governing Christian Democrats after 1976. The support marked the end of more than a generation of Communist exclusion from the governing coalitions of modern Italy and reflected the need to form a strong base with which to deal with growing problems of inflation and terrorism. From 1978 the Communists were virtually unofficial members of the government, largely through the mediation of Aldo Moro, the Christian Democrat prime minister. His death in spring 1978 at the hands of terrorists and that of the Communist leader Enrico Berlinguer in 1984 undermined a long-term arrangement.

HOHENZOLLERN German royal dynasty which provided the three German emperors, 1871–1918. Originally the Prussian royal house, the monarchy was finally brought to an end by the abdication of Kaiser William II in November 1918.

HOLOCAUST, THE Name given to the death of around 6 million Jews at the hands of the Nazis in the Second World War. *See* p. 167.

HOLY ALLIANCE Alliance agreed by Russia, Prussia and Austria in September 1815 and eventually by most of the rulers of Europe, at the instigation of Alexander I of Russia, promising to conduct their policies on Christian principles. Dismissed by many statesmen as an irrelevance, the alliance came to be used by the conservative powers as a justification for repressing liberal and national movements.

HUNDRED DAYS, THE Period of Napoleon's escape from Elba in February 1815 until his defeat at Waterloo (18 June 1815) and exile to St Helena. Technically, the hundred days cover the period from 20 March to 22 June 1815 when Napoleon again ruled as Emperor from Paris.

I

INTENDANTS The chief agents of Louis XVI's government who were centrally appointed to control the social and economic administration of the '*départements*'. They had considerable authority in the 'Pays d'Etat' but their power was checked by permanent officials and commissions of local estates. They disappeared with the end of royal authority.

INTERNATIONAL BRIGADES Volunteer brigades formed to support the Republican cause in Spain during the Spanish Civil War. Composed mainly of left-wing and communist sympathizers from all parts of Europe and the USA, the volunteers saw the fight against Franco's Nationalist insurgents as part of the wider struggle against European Fascism.

INTERNATIONALS *See under* First International; Second International etc.

IRON GUARD Romanian nationalist and fascist organization, founded in 1927 as the Legion of the Archangel Michael, becoming known as the Iron Guard in the early 1930s. Founded by Cornelieu Codreanu (1899–1938), it combined anti-Semitism, peasant populism, and Christian nationalism in support of right-wing policies. Implicated in the murder of the Liberal premier Ion Duca in 1933, the Legion was reformed as the All-for-the-Fatherland Party which obtained 16 per cent of the vote in the 1937 election. Suppressed by King Carol II's royal dictatorship in 1938, which murdered Codreanu and its leaders, surviving members led the rising which forced Carol's abdication in September 1940 and formed one of the groups supporting the dictatorship of Antonescu (1882–1946). An insurrection led by the Iron Guard, during which it carried out savage massacres of thousands of Jews and other enemies, was crushed with the aid of German troops in January 1941.

IRREDENTISTS Italian political party founded about 1878, committed to the incorporation of territories neighbouring the kingdom of Italy (*see* Italia Irredenta).

ITALIA IRREDENTA Term applied to the territories of Trentino, Istria and South Tyrol which were acquired by Italy after the Treaty of St Germain (1919). Sometimes regarded as the completion of the *Risorgimento* (q.v.), the term irredentism has been used to describe any movement committed to the restoration of territory formerly held.

J

JACOBINS Name originally derived from a political club in 1789, the Jacobins became the most radical French revolutionary group. They were particularly associated with Robespierre and dominated the Montagnards (q.v.) and the Committees of Public Safety and General Security which effectively governed France until the coup of 9 Thermidor 1795.

JACQUERIE French peasant rising of 1358 named after 'Jacques Bonhomme', the popular name for a French peasant. The rebels murdered all those who refused to support them and burned over 22 chateaux. Their suppression was followed by equally severe reprisals. Sometimes applied to peasant movements of the modern period.

JULY CONSPIRACY Otherwise known as the Hitler Bomb Plot, this was an attempt by disaffected sections of the German officer corps to assassinate Hitler and end Nazi rule in order that negotiations could take place with the Western Allies. The plot involved a bomb placed in Hitler's East Prussian headquarters by Col. von Stauffenberg on 20 July 1944 and was assumed to have succeeded by accomplices in Berlin, who thus committed themselves to a new government. Hitler's almost miraculous survival signalled the failure of the plotters and the attempt was used as an excuse by Hitler to purge the army and other high-ranking officials known to oppose the regime.

JULY MONARCHY Term used to describe the rule of Louis Philippe in France from his inauguration after the revolution of 1830 until his abdication on 24 February 1848. His attempts to create an Orléanist dynasty by naming his grandson as successor were ignored by the revolutionaries and a republic was established.

JUNKERS Prussian aristocrats whose power rested on their large estates, predominantly east of the River Elbe, and their accepted role as army officers and civil servants. Considered as the bastions against liberalism, they found it consistently harder to defend their agrarian interests from the industrialization of the German Empire.

K

KAISER (Ger. 'Caesar', i.e. Emperor) Title assumed by the Prussian King William I following the unification of Germany and the creation of the German Empire. William accepted the crown of a united Germany in December 1870.

KREMLIN (Russ. 'citadel') Refers to the citadel in Moscow occupied by the former Imperial Palace. The administrative headquarters of, and synonymous with, the government of the former USSR.

KRUGER TELEGRAM Telegram sent by Kaiser William II to Paul Kruger, President of the Transvaal, on 3 January 1896, congratulating him on the defeat of the Jameson Raid. As an attempt to assert German prestige in Africa, the telegram led to a worsening of Anglo–German relations.

KULAKS (Russ. 'tight-fisted person') Term used to describe Russian peasants who were able to become landowners as a result of the agrarian reforms of 1906 and were encouraged by Lenin's NEP (q.v.). Their resistance to collectivisation under the Five Year Plan (q.v.) led to Stalin's order for the liquidation of the kulak class. As a result, large numbers were deported to Siberia or executed in their villages. In August 1942, Stalin confessed to Churchill that the numbers killed amounted to some ten million people.

KULTURKAMPF (Ger. 'culture struggle') The term used to describe the period between 1873 and 1887 when Bismarck, as Chancellor of Germany, came into conflict with the Roman Catholic Church. Ostensibly the result of alarm at the Vatican decrees which implied that the Church rather than the State had prior claim on the citizen's obedience, the Falk Laws were designed to subordinate the Church to State control after May 1873. In addition, they allowed an attack on the anti-Prussian Catholic Centre Party and enabled the creation of a political alliance of diverse interests based on anti-Catholicism. This means of creating a political alliance was superceded by the attack on the socialists after 1878 and negotiations with Pope Leo XIII led to the restoration of Catholic rights by 1887.

L

LEAGUE OF NATIONS International organization set up as an integral part of the Versailles settlement in 1920 to preserve the peace and settle disputes by negotiation. Although the USA refused to participate, it comprised 53 members by 1923. Based in Geneva, the League relied upon non-military means to coerce states, such as 'sanctions' (q.v.), but found itself virtually powerless in the face of the Japanese invasion of Manchuria and the Italian invasion of Abyssinia. The League was discredited by 1939 and was dissolved in April 1946 with the formation of the United Nations. See pp. 133–134.

LEAGUE OF THE THREE EMPERORS See Dreikaiserbund.

LEBENSRAUM (Ger. lit 'living space') Slogan adopted by German nationalists and especially the Nazi Party in the 1920s and 1930s to justify the need for Germany to expand territorially in the East. The theory was based on the alleged overpopulation of Germany and the need for more territory to ensure their food supplies. Interpreted by some Germans as the desire for a return to the frontiers of 1914, the attack on the Soviet Union suggests that Hitler's interpretation of the concept was much wider.

LEVÉE EN MASSE (Fr.) French Committee of Public Safety's enactment of compulsory enlistment for military service in August 1793. It was applied to all men between the ages of 18 and 25. Its introduction established the principle of total mobilization of the country's resources for defence purposes.

LIBERUM VETO The right of the Polish nobility to dissent from or veto measures in the national assembly. Used as a means of obstruction, often against Poland's perceived national interests, the right was abolished by the Constitution of 1791.

LOI FALLOUX Law introduced by Frederic Alfred Pierre Falloux, minister of education and public worship in Louis Napoleon's first government (1848–49). Promulgated in 1850, the law greatly increased the power of the Roman Catholic Church in French education.

LOI LE CHAPELIER Law named after Jean le Chapelier, a French revolutionary leader. The law, introduced on 14 June 1791, prohibited the formation of employer or worker associations. In fact, the law only really operated against worker associations as employer meetings were impossible to monitor. The law survived the revolutionary period and was not repealed until 1884.

LOS VON ROM (Ger. 'away from Rome') Movement in German areas of the Austro–Hungarian Empire after 1897 which gave rise to Old Catholic (q.v.) groups in those areas. The main aim was to make those areas more acceptable as constituent parts of the German Empire if the Dual Monarchy collapsed.

M

MAGINOT LINE French defensive fortifications stretching from Longwy to the Swiss border. Named after French minister of defence, André Maginot, the line was constructed between 1929 and 1934 as a means of countering a German attack. Due to the Belgians' refusal to extend the line along their frontier with Germany, and French reluctance to appear to 'abandon' Belgium and build the line along the Franco–Belgian border to the sea, the defensive strategy relied on the Germans' inability to penetrate the Ardennes forest. This hope was seen as misguided when the Germans were able to turn the French flank by an advance through Belgium and the Maginot Line was still virtually intact when France surrendered on 22 July 1940.

MAGYAR Native name for Hungarians but also a class term meaning one who owned land and was exempt from land tax, attended county assemblies and took part in elections to the Diet. The Austrian Habsburgs attempted to Germanize the Magyars on their territories but Hungarian nationalism provided sufficient pressure to ensure the creation of the Dual Monarchy in 1867 and independence for the state of Hungary after 1918.

MANDATES Rights granted to certain states at the end of the First World War by the League of Nations to administer the colonies and dependencies of Germany and the Ottoman Empire. The Mandates came in three forms. Some territories were only under a limited term mandate while they prepared for independence; the British control over Iraq, Palestine and Transjordan, and the French control of Lebanon and Syria came into this category. Others were to be administered indefinitely because of their lack of development. These included all the German colonies in Africa except for South West Africa. The third category were also to be administered indefinitely but could be treated as part of the mandate powers' territory. South West Africa, (now known as Namibia), New Guinea and Samoa were included in these.

MAQUIS Name derived from Corsican resistance movements which liberated Corsica in 1943. Maquis groups in mainland France increased greatly in 1943 and 1944, and those in Brittany were particularly effective in hampering German movements prior to D-Day on 6 June 1944.

MARSEILLAISE Rouget de Lisle's marching song of the army of the Rhine, it was popularized by the *Fédérés* from Marseilles who arrived in Paris shortly after the publication of the Brunswick manifesto. The song was made the French national anthem after the Franco–Prussian War of 1870.

MARSHALL PLAN United States Plan for the economic reconstruction of Europe, named after secretary of state General George C. Marshall. The Organization for European Economic Co-operation was established to administer the aid in April 1948 but the Soviet rejection of the Plan meant that most of the monetary aid went to Western Europe. Between 1948 and 1952 the US provided some $ 17,000 million dollars which was a crucial element in European postwar recovery.

MAY EVENTS The events of May 1968 when French students, demonstrating against education cuts in Paris, precipitated a political crisis in France. Police brutality against the students triggered riots and increasingly radical demands. Over 10 million workers also came out on general strike. The strike and riots went on into June, but the government eventually defused the situation by promising educational reform, and wage increases to the workers.

MEDITERRANEAN AGREEMENTS Agreements between Britain, Austria–Hungary and Italy signed in March 1887. Essentially a mutual aid pact against a fourth power and mainly directed against Russia and France.

MENSHEVIKS (Russ. lit. 'member of the minority') Moderate faction in Russian Social Democratic Party after the split of 1903. Operated in opposition to the more radical Bolsheviks (q.v.). Formally suppressed in 1922.

MÉTAYAGE A system of share-cropping which operated in more than two-thirds of pre-revolutionary France, especially in wine-growing areas. The exploitative nature and harshness of the system were important peasant grievances.

MITTELEUROPA (Ger.) The idea of a German-speaking supranational state in Central Europe which was pioneered by Austrian Minister Schwarzenberg in 1848. The idea was later rejected by Bismarck when it was used to support German domination of south-eastern Europe and the Balkans. In spite of this, the idea was revived in 1915 with the publication of Friedrich Naumann's book *Mitteleuropa*.

MONTAGNARDS (Fr. lit. 'members of the mountain') Extremist political party in the French Legislative Assembly and National Convention during the Revolution. The name was derived from their placement on the highest part of the left side in the Legislative Assembly. They developed the idea of the expediency of the Revolutionary War. The two constituent groups were the Cordeliers and the Jacobins (q.v.). The power of the Montagnards came to an end with the fall of Robespierre on 9 Thermidor 1794.

MOROCCAN CRISIS A European crisis precipitated by German attempts to break up the Anglo–French Entente of 1904. William II's landing at Tangier and his expression of German support for Moroccan independence led to acrimonious relations between Germany and France and succeeded only in strengthening the bond between France and Britain. The Algeçiras Conference of Jan.–Apr. 1906 recognized French predominance in Morocco and represented a defeat for the German stand.

MOUNTAIN, THE *See* Montagnards.

N

NARODNIKI (Russ.) Members of a secret Russian revolutionary movement in 1873–74 and 1876. Its first supporters were university students who attempted to convert villagers to socialism. They were savagely suppressed by the government in 1877.

NATIONAL SCHISM Term for the bitter division between Constantine I, King of Greece, and his leading minister, Venizelos, over which side Greece should support in the First World War. Dismissed in October 1915 after a clear election victory in June, the pro-Entente Venizelos set up a rival government in Crete, later moved to Salonika. In June 1917, with British and French support, he engineered the abdication of Constantine in favour of his son Alexander. The death of Alexander in October 1920 and Venizelos's defeat in the elections of November allowed Constantine to return. He was forced into exile again following the disastrous defeats of the Greek armies in Anatolia in 1921–22, abdicating in September 1922.

NATO The North Atlantic Treaty Organization, created by the North Atlantic Treaty of 4 April 1949. The organization represented the first US commitment to European defence in peacetime. NATO came in response to Western fears about the power of the Soviet Union and the failure of the UN Security Council to operate in the face of the Soviet veto. The treaty states are obliged to take such action as they deem necessary to assist a fellow signatory subjected to aggression, although there is no obligation to fight. The treaty states are Belgium, Luxembourg, The Netherlands, Britain, the USA, Canada, Italy, Norway, Denmark, Iceland, and Portugal, who were original signatories, plus Greece and Turkey (1952) and West Germany (1955). France was also an original signatory but withdrew from the organization in 1966. With the collapse of communism in Eastern Europe in 1989, and with the Warsaw Pact effectively moribund, NATO was forced to adapt to the changed military balance in Central Europe. In 1997 NATO accepted Hungary, Poland and the Czech Republic as members, and a further major expansion in 2004 brought in the Baltic States and such east European countries as Romania and Bulgaria.

NAZI Popular contraction of 'National Socialist' and used to describe both the NSDAP as a party and its individual members. The party was ideologically attached to right-wing authoritarianism (*see* Italian Fascism) but also included strong anti-Semitism and a belief in the racial supremacy of the 'aryan' race. The party was led by Adolf Hitler from 1921 until his death in 1945. It was initially based in Munich and was given a setback by its involvement in the Beer Hall Putsch (q.v.) of November 1923. Nevertheless, the Nazis under Hitler's guidance underwent a resurgence in the late 1920s and achieved a major electoral breakthrough when they captured 107 seats in the Reichstag. Their electoral success continued into 1932 and in an attempt to provide some form of consensus government, Hitler was offered the Chancellorship in 1933. After the 'seizure of power', Nazi Party organizations such as the SS came to dominate many facets of life in Germany. The party organization collapsed at the end of the Second World War and was made illegal after the German surrender.

NEW ECONOMIC POLICY Often shortened to NEP, the New Economic Policy was introduced in Russia by Lenin at the tenth Party Congress in March 1921. Disturbances and food shortages had made it impossible to impose communism and some amelioration was introduced. Private commerce was permitted and state banks reintroduced. The incentives this provided helped to improve food production and created a more contented peasantry. The NEP was finally abandoned in January 1929 in favour of the Five Year Plan (q.v.) and the collectivization of agriculture.

'NEW IMPERIALISM' Term used to describe the more aggressive colonial policies of western European states in the later nineteenth century. This was epitomized by the 'scramble for Africa' in the 1880s which has been variously attributed to the need for secure markets for domestic manufactures, the need for investment opportunities, the need to assert international standing through the acquisition of colonies, or the need to introduce a foreign policy adventure as a unifying measure in domestic politics.

NEW NATIONALISM Term used in the 1990s to describe the revival of nationalism following the collapse of communism. 'New Nationalism' was a major force in the Baltic states, in former Yugoslavia (as in the breakaway of Slovenia and Croatia) and in such conflicts as the civil war in Bosnia.

NORTH GERMAN FEDERATION A union of north German states created by Bismarck after the Prussian defeat of Austria in 1866. The federation was an attempt to allay south German fears about Prussia's ambitions to create a unitary German state. The constitution did allow for the rights of individual states but was, in practice, dominated by Prussia. Four years later, it became the constitution of the German Empire, almost without amendment. The constitution was adopted by the North German Reichstag on 17 April 1867.

OSTPOLITIK Eastern policy developed in the German Federal Republic by Kurt Kiesinger to normalize relations with those communist countries, other than the Soviet Union, which recognized the German Democratic Republic. It led to the conclusion of peace treaties with the USSR and Poland (1972) and border agreements over traffic and communication between East and West Berlin.

O

OCTOBRIST A section of the Russian liberal constitutional movement. The movement had been divided by the October Manifesto of 1905 into Octobrists and Kadets. The former were right-wing and prepared to co-operate with the government in the Duma. The party was supported by the right-wing of the Zemstvo movement (q.v.) and business classes.

OCTROI Tax levied by French local authorities such as communes or municipalities during the *ancien régime* on certain categories of goods entering the area.

OGPU Soviet security police agency, established in 1922 as the GPU and retitled OGPU after the formation of the USSR in 1923. Founded to suppress counter-revolution and enemies of the system, it was used by the leadership to uncover political dissidents and, after 1928, in enforcing the collectivization of agriculture. After 1930 it monopolized police activities in the Soviet Union before being absorbed by the NKVD in 1934.

OLD CATHOLICS Name given to groups of western Christians who believe themselves to maintain the true doctrines and traditions of the undivided Church, but who separated from the see of Rome after the first Vatican Council of 1869–70.

P

PAMYAT A right-wing Russian nationalist movement which emerged in the late 1980s. It contained anti-Semitic and Fascist elements.

PANAMA SCANDAL A corruption scandal involving the French Chamber of Deputies which came to light in 1892. A lottery loan voted on behalf of the French Panama Canal Co. in 1888 was rumoured to have involved the 'support' of over 150 deputies. The resultant scandal, which emerged in 1892 after the company had folded, led to the resignation of the Loubet government and the imprisonment of a former government minister.

PAN-SLAVISM The name given to the various movements for closer union of peoples speaking Slavic languages in the nineteenth and early twentieth centuries.

PAPAL INFALLIBILITY Doctrine of the Roman Catholic Church proclaimed at the Vatican Council of 1870 which holds that papal pronouncements on matters of faith and morals are not open to question. The basis of the doctrine is that not all questions are answered by the Bible and that further guidance has to be provided in an authoritative way. It has also been argued that the extension of the Pope's spiritual power was in response to the loss of temporal power over the previous 500 years.

PAPAL STATES Central Italian territory under papal authority until 1870. The area was dominated by Napoleon's army in the 1790s and again in 1808–09. Revolts against clerical rule took place 1830–31 and in 1849. The States remained an obstacle to Italian unification until French troops were withdrawn from Rome in 1870.

PAYS D'ELECTION Central core of the French kingdom where the authority of the crown and its *intendants* (q.v.) tended to go unchallenged.

PAYS D'ETAT Areas originally annexed to France where the relationship to the French crown was on a contractual basis. Provincial assemblies or estates functioned effectively in Brittany and Languedoc where they had fiscal privileges and shared authority with the crown.

PEOPLE'S WILL *See* Narodniki.

PERESTROIKA From the Russian 'restructuring', an attempt led by Mikhail Gorbachev (Communist Party Secretary, 1985, President 1988) to regenerate the stagnant Soviet economy. It has become synonymous with his attempt to regenerate Russia by encouraging market forces, decentralizing industrial management, and democratizing the Party and government machinery.

PHILOSOPHES Leading French thinkers of the pre-Revolutionary period who included Montesquieu, Voltaire, Rousseau, Condorcet and Diderot. The main theme of their thinking was marked by faith in the power of human reason. They were critical of irrational privileges and many other aspects of the *ancien régime*. Conservatives alleged that the writings of the philosophes influenced the Revolution.

PHYSIOCRATS Coterie of philosophes (q.v.) concerned with economic problems. Quesnay and Mirabeau were among the most prominent. They held that agriculture was the true source of national wealth and advocated fiscal equality through a universal land tax and other economic reforms, including free trade.

PLAIN, THE Independent and moderate members of the French Convention. They were led by Danton who was the chief intermediary between the Paris Commune and the Convention. Its members conspired with the right to overthrow Robespierre.

POGROM (Russ. 'destruction') Used to describe the physical persecution of Jews in Tsarist Russia. This form of anti-Semitic violence was especially marked in the Ukraine and, in the 1880s and in 1905, the authorities unofficially encouraged these attacks to divert popular discontent.

POLISH CORRIDOR The Treaty of Versailles decided that the new Polish state should have direct access to the sea. In order to provide this a large area of West Prussia and Posen, containing many Germans, was assigned to Poland. The 'Corridor' also had the effect of cutting East Prussia off from the rest of Germany. Danzig (Gdansk), standing at the mouth of the Vistula and the natural artery of Polish trade, but a German city and formerly part of Germany, was placed under League of Nations' control, Poland remaining responsible for her foreign relations. The creation of the 'Corridor' was bitterly resented by German nationalists and Hitler's demands for the return of Danzig and parts of the 'Corridor' formed part of the crisis which brought about war in September 1939.

POPULAR FRONT Name used to describe the alliance of communists, socialists and liberal democrats which was designed to combat Fascism in Europe between 1935 and 1939. Alliances under this name gained power in Spain and in France under Léon Blum.

POUJADISM A right-wing political movement in France between 1954 and 1958 named after Pierre Poujade (1920–2003), a bookseller. The *Union de Défense des Commerçants et Artisans* was anti-socialist, anti-intellectual and anti-European. The return of de Gaulle led to its rapid decline.

'PRAGUE SPRING' Name given to the period of attempted liberalization in Czechoslovakia under Dubček as Secretary of the Communist Party in spring 1968. The attempt was brought to an end by the intervention of Warsaw Pact troops in August 1968 and Dubček's replacement by Husak.

PRAIRIAL (Fr.) A law forced through the Convention in France by Robespierre on 10 June 1794 which allowed the Tribunal to dispense with evidence for the defence. Thus trial became a question of immediate acquittal or death, a process which greatly increased the Terror. Robespierre was deposed by his opponents before he could bring them to trial.

PROVISIONAL GOVERNMENT The government of Russia between March and October 1917. Brought to power after the deposition of the monarchy, the provisional government was made up of members of the Duma (q.v.) but had to share power in Petrograd with the Workers' and Soldiers' Soviet. Rule ended by the Bolshevik Revolution and the creation of a Soviet government.

PURGES *See* Yezhovshchina.

PUTSCH (Ger.) A term used to describe a right-wing *coup d'état* in Germany. Most notable was the Kapp Putsch in 1920 when a journalist, Wolfgang Kapp, and a number of disaffected army officers attempted to overthrow the government in Berlin. The plot was foiled by the indifference of the regular army and the opposition of the trade unions. Also notorious was the ill-fated Beer Hall Putsch (q.v.), involving Hitler and General Ludendorff in Munich on 9 November 1923.

Q

QUADRILATERAL Four fortified towns in Northern Italy (Peschiera, Verona, Mantua and Legnano) which formed the strong point of the Austrian defence of Venetia in 1848, and in 1859 during the struggle for Italian unification.

QUAI D'ORSAY Embankment of the River Seine in Paris where the French Foreign Office is situated. Term synonymous with the conduct of French foreign affairs.

QUISLING Eponym for leader of an enemy-sponsored regime, deriving from Vidkun Quisling (1887–1945) (q.v.).

R

RALLIEMENT A policy which attempted to end the estrangement of French Catholics from the Republic. It was initiated by an encyclical of Pope Leo XIII in 1892, but most Catholics and Monarchists remained hostile to the Republic and the conservative-monarchist right-wing continued to have a disruptive influence on French politics.

REALPOLITIK Word coined by the liberal journalist and historian Rochau in 1859 and used to describe Bismarck's attitude to politics as a naked struggle for power, with ruthless pursuit of self-interest being the only possible policy for a great state.

REICH (Ger.) The term used to describe the German Empire. The First Reich was considered to have been the Holy Roman Empire and thus the unified Germany after 1870 was known as the Second or *Kaiserreich*. This enabled Hitler's ideas of an enlarged Germany to be known as the Third Reich, although this name was officially dropped in the 1930s.

REICHSBANNER An unarmed uniformed defence force attached to the German Social

Democratic Party, formed in February 1924, and which collapsed as Hitler consolidated power in 1933.

REICHSTAG The German parliament (building) in Berlin created by the Constitution of 1871. Representatives were elected by universal suffrage and represented a concession to democracy although the Reichstag could not initiate legislation and could only block certain measures. Moreover, government ministers were not appointed by, nor responsible to, the Reichstag. Nevertheless, it became the focal point of politics (if not decision-making) in the 1890s during the reign of William II. The building was destroyed by fire on 28 February 1933; its destruction was used by the Nazis for propaganda purposes against the left and to pass a number of restrictive decrees.

REINSURANCE TREATY Treaty signed between Germany and Russia on 18 June 1887 which gave the Russians guarantees of support for their policies in Bulgaria and the Bosphorus as well as a German agreement to stay neutral unless Austria–Hungary was attacked.

REPARATIONS Payments imposed on powers defeated in war to recompense the costs to the victors. Most commonly associated with the payments inflicted on Germany at the end of the First World War, although the actual amount was not fixed until April 1921 when the sum was set at £6,600 million plus interest. The Dawes and Young Plans later reduced the repayments until the effects of the Depression caused reparations payments to be abandoned after Lausanne in 1932. Apart from their international ramifications, reparations payments played an important part in the domestic politics of the Weimar Republic.

RESISTANCE The popular term for the opposition to the Nazi regime, both inside Germany and in the occupied countries, 1940–45. From January 1942, the Free French began to organize resistance groups and in May 1943, the Maquis (q.v.) liberated Corsica. By 1945 resistance groups were active throughout Europe but were often divided among themselves on ideological grounds, providing the basis for postwar political conflicts.

REVISIONIST Term applied by orthodox Marxists to one who attempts to reassess the basic tenets of revolutionary socialism. Originating in Germany in the 1890s and 1900s, its chief exponents were Edouard Bernstein and Karl Kautsky. Regarded as heresy in the Soviet Union, the Cuban, Chinese and Albanian Communists used the same term to describe the Moscow line.

RIGHT DEVIATIONISM A faction in the Soviet Communist Party in 1927–28 led by Bukharin, Rykov and Tomsky which, while accepting Stalin's proposals for industrialization, urged a gradual approach and rejected too forceful a move against the Kulaks (q.v.) and the New Economic Policy (q.v.). Effectively removed from influence in 1929, the three leading spokesmen were later killed in Stalin's purges.

RISORGIMENTO (It. 'resurrection') The movement for the unification of Italy in the nineteenth century, the name was first used by Cavour in 1847 although the origins of the movement date from the post-Napoleonic period. The success of the movement culminated in the proclamation of the Kingdom of Italy in March 1861 and the later acquisition of Venetia (1866) and Rome (1870).

ROMANOV The family name of the Russian royal house whose dynasty was ended by the deposition of Tsar Nicholas II in 1917 after the Russian Revolution.

RUKH The name of the nationalist movement in the Ukraine in the late 1980s which achieved independence on the collapse of the USSR.

S

SA Abbreviation of the German *Sturmabteilung* or Storm Battalion, sometimes known as 'Brownshirts' from their uniform. Groups of ex-soldiers organized in quasi-military formations from 1923 to support the Nazis. Under their leader, Röhm, the force grew rapidly to an estimated four and a half million men by June 1934, when both Hitler's and the army's fear of its power prompted Hitler's murder of Röhm and the leaders of the SA in the 'Night of the Long Knives' (30 June 1934). Although it remained in existence, the power of the SA as a political force was broken.

SAJUDIS The name of the nationalist movement in the Baltic Republic of Lithuania, led by Vytautas Landsbergis.

SALT Strategic Arms Limitation Talks between America and the Soviet Union beginning in November 1969 and ending in May 1972 with a treaty restricting anti-ballistic missile development. A second round opened in November 1974 but proved less successful. Renewed talks under Gorbachev led to an outline agreement in 1991.

SANCTIONS Term usually applied to economic boycott of one country by another. Sanctions were the chief weapon of the League of Nations (q.v.) on countries which were not thought to be fulfilling their international obligations. An economic boycott was imposed on Italy in October 1935, following the invasion of Abyssinia, but its terms were limited and largely ineffective. These were finally lifted in July 1936. Similar sanctions were imposed on Rhodesia in 1965 by Britain and the UN but proved ineffective. European nations imposed sanctions on Iraq following its invasion of Kuwait in August 1990. Sanctions were also imposed on Serbia during the Bosnia conflict (see p. 214).

SANSCULOTTES (Fr. lit. 'without breeches') A name used by Parisian militants to signify that they were manual workers wearing trousers, and not the knee-breeches of polite society. Between 1792 and 1794, the name referred to a specific group of political activists attempting to put pressure on the Convention through clubs and assemblies.

SCHLIEFFEN PLAN German military plan for offensive action named after Chief of German General Staff, Count Alfred von Schlieffen, and first produced in 1905. In spite of constant revision, the plan was the basis for the German attack in the west in August 1914. The basic features of the plan were based upon the premise that Germany would have to fight both France and Russia in any future war. The plan therefore provided for a swift 'knock-out' blow against France, while remaining on the defensive against Russia. Crucially, the plan involved an attack through the neutral countries of Holland, Belgium and Luxembourg to avoid the strong defences on the Franco–German border, aiming to encircle Paris and force French surrender. Although modified subsequently, the plan to invade France via Belgium was used in 1914, bringing Great Britain into the war.

SCHUMAN PLAN A key proposal of 9 May 1950 towards European co-operation. It was the step on the road to the creation of the European Economic Community, with the suggestion by French Foreign Minister Robert Schuman that French and German coal and steel production be co-ordinated under a higher authority. The European Coal and Steel Community was created when Italy, Belgium and the Netherlands widened the agreement in 1952.

SCRAMBLE FOR AFRICA Period of rapid colonization of Africa in the last quarter of the nineteenth century, especially in the period following the British occupation of Egypt in 1882. By 1914 only Liberia and Ethiopia (Abyssinia) remained as independent African states.

SCRAP OF PAPER German Chancellor Bethmann-Hollweg's description of the 1839 Treaty of London, a five-power guarantee of Belgian neutrality which Germany violated by invasion on 4 August 1914, provoking a British declaration of war. He told the British ambassador that 'just for a scrap of paper, Great Britain is going to make war on a kindred nation which desires nothing better than to be friends with her'.

SECOND EMPIRE Created in France on 2 December 1852 when Louis Napoleon, then President of the Second Republic (q.v.) held a plebiscite and was elected Emperor and assumed the title Napoleon III. The Empire came to an end with the German invasion of France and Napoleon III's capture at Sedan in 1870.

SECOND FRONT Following the German attack on the Soviet Union in June 1941, Stalin asked Britain to launch an invasion in Western Europe to ease the pressure on Russia. Churchill was reluctant to do so without long preparation, despite a vigorous 'Second Front Now' campaign in Britain in 1942. The Second Front – agreed at the Quebec Conference in August 1943 – opened with the Normandy landings on 6 June 1944.

SECOND INTERNATIONAL Formed in Paris in 1889 and based on membership of national parties and trade unions, the Second International was a loose federation which held periodic international congresses. It stood for parliamentary democracy and thus rejected anarchist ideas, but also reaffirmed the commitment to Marxist ideas of the class struggle. Thus there was no question of co-operation with non-socialist parties in power. A main aim was to try to avert war, but the International effectively ended in 1914 although attempts to revive it were made in 1919.

SECOND REICH The German Empire 1871–1918, also known as the *Kaiserreich*; the period after German unification when William I, King of Prussia was offered the throne of the Empire. The last Kaiser, William II, was forced to abdicate after the German army refused to support him at the end of the First World War.

SECOND REPUBLIC Republic set up in France after the 1848 Revolution. Under the presidency of Louis Napoleon (*see* Second Empire) the Republic had a legislative assembly with a monarchist majority. Unable to agree among themselves, the monarchists were able to obstruct the workings of the Republic and prevent the re-election of president and legislature in 1852. In order to protect his position, Louis Napoleon organized a *coup d'état* on 1–2 December and had himself elected Emperor as Napoleon III.

SECURITATE The Romanian secret police under the Ceausescu (q.v.) dictatorship. Their brutal suppression of disturbances in Timisoara in December 1989 sparked the Romanian revolution (see p. 213).

SICK MAN OF EUROPE Nicholas I of Russia's description in the 1850s of the Ottoman Empire, which he dismissed as 'a sick man dying'. His plans for its division in the event of a sudden collapse aroused British suspicions of Russian motives, setting the scene for the Crimean War in 1854.

SINN FEIN Gaelic for 'Ourselves alone'. Irish Nationalist Party founded in 1902 by Arthur Griffiths (1872–1922) and formed into the Sinn Fein League in 1907–08 when it absorbed other nationalist groups. The group rose to prominence in the 1913–14 Home Rule crisis when many Sinn Feiners joined the Irish Volunteers and many Dublin workers joined the organization. Sinn Fein members were involved in the Easter Rising in 1916. Sinn Fein continues to campaign for a United Ireland to include the 'six counties' of Ulster.

SITUATIONISM A left-wing 'critique of everyday life' made by the Situationist International, which was formed in 1957, collapsed in the early 1970s, and had an affinity with Council Communism (q.v.). Situationism advocated a revolutionary overthrow of capitalism based not on traditional political methods but on total rejection in every sphere of what it saw as consumer society's banality. Situationist slogans were prominent in the May events (the 1968 student revolt in France) (q.v.) and its rhetoric has widely influenced the European left.

SLAVOPHILES A small group of Russian intellectuals in the 1840s and 1850s. Deeply nationalistic, they rejected the Westernizers' belief that Russia must follow western paths of development. They aimed to introduce reforms to restore an idealized pre-Petrine (Peter the Great) form of society. They also believed that the Tsar's authority should be personal and patriarchal.

SOCIAL CHARTER The European Community (EC) Charter of Social Rights of Workers, setting out a pattern for a European labour law. Largely the work of Jacques Delors and his colleagues and opposed by right-wing Conservatives, especially in Britain, it guarantees such things as freedom of movement and equal treatment for workers throughout the Community, the right to strike, a guaranteed 'decent standard of living', freedom to join trade unions, the right to collective bargaining etc. Britain secured an 'opt-out' from this provision (now called the Social Chapter) at Maastricht, but the Labour Government elected in 1997 signalled its intention to join.

SOCIAL DEMOCRACY Non-doctrinaire, socialist or socialist-inclined political movement of the nineteenth and twentieth centuries, combining concern for greater equality with acceptance of a mixed economy and representing a non-communist left-wing tradition often drawing support from organized labour. Notable examples include the Social Democratic Party of Germany, founded in 1875, and the Swedish Social Democratic Labour Party, formed in 1880.

SOCIAL FASCIST Communist term of abuse towards Social Democratic and Labour Parties from 1928 to 1934, reflecting the Comintern view that moderate socialists who were rivals for working-class support were 'the left wing of Fascism'.

SOCIALISM IN ONE COUNTRY Doctrine expounded by Lenin in Russia after it became clear that the Revolution of 1917 was not going to affect the other states of Europe. The main task was to create a socialist society without help from outside, either political or economic.

SOCIALIST REALISM The approved method of art and literature in the Soviet Union under Stalin, enforced by the control of the cultural Unions over the origination, production, and publication of artistic work. Expulsion from the appropriate Union meant an end to publication/exhibition, and during the purges a large number of artists were sent to labour camps or killed. Following Stalin's death there was a thaw under Khrushchev (q.v.) and during his de-Stalinization campaign the high-water mark came with the publication of Alexander Solzhenitsyn's *A Day in the Life of Ivan Denisovich* in *Novy mir* in 1962.

SOLIDARITY Polish trade union and reform movement formed in the 1970s to demand liberalization of the Polish communist regime and the formation of free trade unions. Under its leader, Lech Walesa, the movement won important concessions from the government before the threat of Soviet invasion and the assumption of power by the Polish army led to the banning of the organization and the imprisonment of its leaders. It survived as a clandestine organization. The cause of Solidarity was vindicated with the collapse of communism in Poland. Despite divisions within the movement, its leader, Lech Walesa, was elected president of Poland in December 1990 (although he was defeated in 1995).

SONDERBUND A League formed by seven Catholic Swiss Cantons in December 1845 to protect their interests against Liberal attempts to strengthen the control of the Federal government. The Federal Diet condemned the League as a secessionist movement and a brief civil war in 1847 led to its dissolution.

'SPLENDID ISOLATION' Phrase used to describe Britain's diplomatic position in the latter part of the nineteenth century and, more generally, during the nineteenth century as a whole when Britain stood aside from entanglement in European alliances. The phrase was used in *The Times* in January 1896 and subsequently (9 November) by Lord Salisbury. The 'isolation' is customarily seen as being ended by the Anglo–Japanese treaty of 1902.

SS Abbreviation of German *Schutzstaffel* or Guard Detachment, Hitler's personal bodyguard of dedicated Nazis founded in 1923 as a rival to Röhm's SA (q.v.). Placed under the command of Heinrich Himmler in 1929, the SS carried out the liquidation of the SA leadership in June 1934 and in July became an independent organization with its own armed units. *SS-Verfugunstruppe* (Special Task Troops), organized as regular soldiers, were formed from 1935 and as the *Waffen-SS* comprised a group of elite regiments, separate from army control. Other sections of the SS provided concentration camp guards – the *SS-Totenkopfverbande* – and police squads in occupied territory.

STALINISM Stalin's revolution from above to build 'Socialism in One Country' forced agricultural collectivization (q.v.), laying the basis for rapid heavy industrial development. It was carried out in an atmosphere of intense nationalism and increasingly arbitrary rule exerted through a bureaucracy and was connected with Stalin's 'cult of personality' and the brutal political purges of the 1930s. Latterly, a general description of the regimes in the Soviet Union and its East European satellites during the communist era.

STASI The name of the security police under the former communist regime in East Germany. They were disbanded in the revolution of 1989.

STATE CAPITALISM Lenin's description of the compromise made with financial interests in 1918 to ensure Bolshevik survival, while simultaneously reinforcing central control over the economy. More recently, a pejorative description of Soviet socialism in which a privileged bureaucracy is said collectively to dominate economic life with the same relationship to the working class as employers under private capitalism.

STATES-GENERAL The national assembly in France where the three 'estates' were represented (nobility, clergy and commons). It met only rarely as the power of the monarchy increased, and not at all between 1614 and 1789. Louis XVI finally called the States-General to try to quieten the growing discontent in the country, but it declared itself a National Assembly, an act which marked the beginning of the French Revolution. The term is also used to describe the present Dutch parliament.

STRAITS QUESTION The issue of rights of passage through the Dardanelles and the Bosphorus which was disputed between the Great Powers and the Ottoman Empire at several points in the nineteenth and twentieth centuries. A series of conventions has laid down restrictions on the classes of warships permitted to use the waterway.

STRESA FRONT Name of agreements made at the Stresa Conference, 11–14 April 1935, attended by the leaders of Italy, Britain, and France. They agreed a common front against Hitler's intention to rearm and reform the *Luftwaffe*, condemning Germany's actions and supporting the Locarno Treaties. Britain's separate agreement with Germany on naval matters in June 1935, France's negotiations with Russia to form a pact in May, and Italy's invasion of Ethiopia in October undermined the Front's impact.

SUCCESSION STATES The states formed after the First World War from the territory of the former Austro–Hungarian Empire, or incorporating parts of it. These included Poland, Czechoslovakia, Yugoslavia, Romania, Hungary and Austria. The term can also be applied to the new countries which emerged from the breakup of Yugoslavia (Slovenia,

Croatia, Bosnia–Herzegovina) and the Soviet Union (Belarus, Ukraine, Moldova, etc.) in the 1990s.

SUDETENLAND German-speaking area of northern Bohemia assigned to Czechoslovakia in 1919. Claimed by Hitler for the Reich, the Sudetenland became the centre of an international crisis in 1938 over Germany's attempt to revise the Versailles Treaty by force. The threat of general European war was temporarily averted by the Munich Agreement in which Czechoslovakia was forced to cede the Sudetenland to Germany.

SWASTIKA Ancient religious symbol in the shape of a hooked cross. In European mythology it became linked with the revival of Germanic legends at the end of the nineteenth century. Adopted by a number of extreme right-wing groups in Germany after the First World War, including the Erhardt Brigade, a *Freikorps* unit active in the Kapp Putsch. It was also adopted by Hitler as the symbol of National Socialism and in September 1935 became Nazi Germany's national emblem.

SYNDICALISM Theory which advocates the ownership and organization of industry by workers and their organizations – usually trade unions. This is in contrast to the socialist theory of ownership by the state. Syndicalism is also associated with the belief in the power of trade unionism and the use of the general strike as a weapon to bring about major social and political change. Although often associated with anarchists, many of the syndicalists in the 1920s joined the communist or fascist parties.

SYNDICAT (Fr. 'trade union') The basic form of syndicalist activity.

T

TENNIS COURT OATH Oath taken by the deputies of the French National Assembly on 20 June 1789, binding them to work together for the creation of a French constitution.

TERROR, THE In April 1793 the National Convention delegated powers to a Committee of Public Safety in order to preserve the Republic in the face of its enemies, internal and external. Robespierre and the Jacobins established a virtual dictatorship, known as the 'Reign of Terror', especially after the Law of Prairial (q.v.) in June 1793. Leading opponents, such as Danton and Hébert, aristocrats, and suspected counter-revolutionaries were executed, usually by guillotine, both in Paris and the provinces. As many as 13,000 people are said to have died, the majority of humble background. The Terror came to an end with Robespierre's arrest and execution in Thermidor.

THERMIDOR (Fr.) The 'hot weather' month of the French Revolutionary Calendar, 19 July–17 Aug. The period of Jacobin dictatorship ended on 9 Thermidor (27 July) 1794 when the Convention secured the proscription of Robespierre.

THIRD ESTATE *See* Tiers Etat.

THIRD INTERNATIONAL Otherwise known as the Communist International or the Comintern. Founded by Lenin in March 1919 to unite revolutionary socialists. Finally disbanded by Stalin in May 1943 as a concession to his western allies.

THIRD REICH Term used to describe the Nazi dictatorship in Germany, 1933–45. Originally coined by the Nazis to describe the expanded Germany of their theories, it was dropped from official usage in the 1930s.

THIRD REPUBLIC The term used to describe the government of France from the Franco–Prussian War in 1871 to the fall of France in 1940 and the establishment of the Vichy regime (q.v.).

TIERS ETAT The Third Estate, denotes all social classes in pre-revolutionary France other than the aristocracy, high-ranking clergy and privileged magistracy. Thus it included the bourgeoisie and '*sansculottes*' (q.v.).

TITOISM Term for the political philosophy of Josip Tito (*q.v.*) in Yugoslavia. It was characterized by rejection of Stalinism, and also of nationalism, and an emphasis on economic progress. Above all it was designed to preserve the political stability of Yugoslavia.

TOTAL WAR Term of twentieth century origin meaning a war in which all of a nation's resources (economic, human, ideological, etc.) are mobilized in the effort to win. Applicable, for example, to the war efforts of Germany, the Soviet Union and Great Britain in the Second World War.

TOTALITARIANISM Term used to describe governments in which almost all power is concentrated in the political leadership. There is a one-party state. Almost all aspects of social, political and economic life are under the control of the state. The USSR under Stalin, Nazi Germany under Hitler and Italy under Mussolini are obvious examples in Europe.

TRICOLEUR Popular name for the French national flag since 17 July 1789, it was made up of the red and blue colours of the city of Paris and the white Bourbon emblem. It signifies the victory of the people of Paris on 14 July 1789.

TRIPARTISM Name given to the joint governments of Christian Democrats, Socialists, and the Communists formed in France and Italy in the immediate aftermath of the Second World War. Tripartism lasted in France until May 1947 when Communist ministers were dismissed, while in Italy a Christian Democrat government was formed in April 1947 without communist support. The end of tripartism reflected the hardening of the battle-lines of the Cold War after the temporary co-operation of former resistance partners.

TRIPLE ALLIANCE Alliance formed between Germany, Austria–Hungary and Italy in 1882.

TRIPLE ENTENTE Agreement between Britain, France and Russia to resolve their outstanding colonial differences; it became a military alliance in 1914. Sometimes referred to as the Quadruple Entente because of the agreements with Japan.

TWENTY-ONE CONDITIONS The terms left-wing parties seeking affiliation to the Comintern (q.v.) had to accept. They included organizing on the Russian party model and acknowledging ultimate Comintern authority; agitating for a dictatorship of the proletariat; creating an illegal organization for subversive work; rejecting syndicalism (q.v.) and reformism; conducting revolutionary propaganda in the armed forces; and supporting colonial liberation.

U

ULTRAMONTANISM Belief in the ultimate authority of the Catholic Church and that it supercedes loyalty to the State. Particularly evident in nineteenth-century France, it was encouraged by the Vatican decrees of 1870. It also contributed to the *Kulturkampf* (q.v.). Its long-term result was to free the Papacy from dependence on civil powers and give the Church new freedom of action.

UNION SACRÉE (Fr. 'Sacred Union') Government formed in France at the outbreak of the First World War which included, for the first time and as a symbol of national unity, two Socialists among its members.

UNITED FRONT A Communist Party tactic which attempted to build temporary alliances with other socialist and working-class parties, ostensibly to face a common enemy, for example Fascism. *See* Popular Front.

UNITED NATIONS, THE International peacekeeping organization set up in 1945 to replace the

League of Nations (q.v.). From the 50 states who signed the Charter of the UN in 1945, numbers had more than doubled by 1970 with the rise of independent ex-colonial states. All states have one vote in the General Assembly and its executive, the Security Council, can call on member states to supply armed forces. UN troops have been involved in peacekeeping duties in many parts of the world since 1945, notably in the Middle East, Africa and Cyprus. By 2004 there were 190 members.

VELVET DIVORCE The division on 1 January 1993 of Czechoslovakia into the separate states of the Czech Republic and Slovakia. So called because of the apparently amicable nature of the separation, but also an ironic reference to the 1989 Velvet Revolution (q.v.) which overthrew communist rule.

VELVET REVOLUTION Title given to the popular uprisings in Prague and other Czech cities in 1989 which overthrew the communist regime. The peaceful separation of Czechoslovakia into the Czech and Slovak. republic was known as the Velvet Divorce.

VICHY French provincial spa town where the interim autocratic French government was established between July 1940 and July 1944. The Vichy regime was anti-republican, and collaborated extensively with the Germans who occupied the areas it controlled in November 1942. After the liberation of France in 1944, Pétain and the Vichy ministers established a headquarters in Germany.

VULGAR MARXISM A rigid reading of Marx which overemphasizes the role of the economic factor to the exclusion of the complexities of human action and creativity, and which rests too mechanically on a belief in historic inevitability.

WAR COMMUNISM Bolshevik (q.v.) policy in 1918 to meet the pressures of civil war and economic collapse, including nationalization of larger enterprises and a state monopoly of exchange; the partial militarization of labour, and the forced requisition of agricultural produce. War Communism's unpopularity and failure led to the New Economic Policy (q.v.) in March 1921.

WAR CRIMINAL A concept first enunciated in the 'Hang the Kaiser' campaign at the end of the First World War. In the 1946 Nuremburg Trials, 177 Nazis were indicted as war criminals for genocide and planning aggressive war, new and controversial concepts in international law. Ten were sentenced to death. Some of those accused of crimes in the wars of the 1990s in Yugoslavia have been brought to trial at The Hague as war criminals.

WAR GUILT CLAUSE Article 231 of the Versailles Treaty, compelling Germany to accept responsibility for the First World War and its ensuing damage. Intended to provide a legal basis for reparations claims (q.v.) made by the victors, it encouraged a bitterness which added to the difficulties of the Weimar Republic (q.v.).

WARSAW PACT Military alliance of the USSR and Eastern European satellites formed when the Eastern European Mutual Assistance Treaty was signed in 1955 by the communist states in Europe (except Albania and Yugoslavia). The treaty made joint provision for mutual defence for 20 years and represented the communist, especially Russian, response to the formation of NATO (q.v.) in 1949 and the rearming of the Federal Republic of Germany. The Pact permitted the USSR to keep forces in the satellite states and had a united command structure, reinforced by regular exercises and manoeuvres. Following the collapse of communism in

Eastern Europe the Warsaw Pact ceased to exist as a military alliance.

WARSAW UPRISING As the Soviets approached Warsaw in 1944, the Polish Home Army rose up against the Germans on 1 August. The Red Army halted its advance, leaving the Poles to fight on alone. All appeals for help were ignored and reinforcements disarmed. The Poles could not resist unaided and surrendered 2 October 1944. Warsaw was liberated on 17 January 1945.

WEIMAR Town where the German National Constituent Assembly met in February 1919. It gave its name to the German Republic of 1918–33. The town was chosen to allay fears of the Allied Powers and the other German states about Prussian domination in Berlin, and also to escape from the associations attached to the former capital city. The economic problems which beset the Weimar Republic and the concomitant unemployment, facilitated the rise of Hitler, and in March 1933 he suspended the Weimar Constitution of July 1919 to make way for the Third Reich (q.v.).

WELFARE CAPITALISM Post-Second World War West European mixed economies in which free enterprise capitalism co-existed with a State commitment to low unemployment, extensive social security and the provision of health and other social services. Called into question by the ascendancy of right-wing Conservatism and the pressures of economic depression in the 1970s and 1980s.

WELTPOLITIK (Ger. lit. 'world politics') A new trend in German foreign policy at the end of the nineteenth century. The Kaiser William II determined to transform Germany into a first-rank global power. Ultra-nationalistic pressure combined with social and economic forces to support new interest in colonial expansion, the scramble for territory in China and Africa, and the establishment of a powerful navy.

WHITE RUSSIANS Term for Russians living on western border of Soviet Union, but used generally to describe counter-revolutionary forces

in the aftermath of the Bolshevik Revolution of 1917.

WINTER REVOLUTION *See* Christmas Revolution.

Y

YEZHOVSHCHINA (Russ.) A word used to describe the Stalinist purges of the 1920s and 1930s. The name derives from the head of the Soviet secret police, N.I. Yezhov.

YOUNG ITALY Italian nationalist movement founded in 1832 by Giuseppe Mazzini, its main aim being the establishment of a free, independent and republican Italian nation. Acted as a pressure group on Cavour in the 1850s which speeded the creation of an independent Italian state.

YOUNG TURKS Liberal reform movement among young army officers in the Ottoman Empire, active between 1903 and 1909. The rebellion of 1908 led to the creation of a 'Committee of Union and Progress', headed by Enver Bey, Ahmed Djemel and Mehmed Talaat. They persuaded the Sultan to re-establish constitutional rule and convene a parliament. Splits arose between the three leaders (who went on to achieve prominence in the Balkan Wars and through their encouragement of the German alliance), and other radicals. Their influence lasted throughout the First World War.

Z

ZEMSTVO Russian provincial or district council first established by Tsar Alexander II in

January 1864. The councils were dominated by the local gentry and were especially active in 1865–66 and 1917 in areas such as public health, agricultural development, road building, and primary education. In many areas the zemstvo became a genuine force for liberalism and a means of arousing political awareness at local level.

ZENTRUM The conservative Roman Catholic Centre Party in Germany from 1871 to 1933. Developed in response to Bismarck's anti-Catholic policies, it was influential in early twentieth-century coalitions and again in the Weimar Republic. Dissolved by the Nazis in July 1933.

ZIMMERMANN TELEGRAM Coded message of 19 January 1917 from the German foreign minister, Arthur Zimmermann, to the German minister in Mexico, urging the conclusion of a German–Mexican alliance in the event of a declaration of war on Germany by America when Germany resumed unrestricted submarine warfare against shipping on 1 February. Mexico would be offered the recapture of her 'lost territories' in New Mexico, Arizona and Texas. Intercepted by British Naval Intelligence, the telegram was released to the American press on 1 March, greatly inflaming feeling against Germany, and helping to precipitate the American declaration of war against Germany on 6 April 1917.

ZOLLVEREIN (Ger.) The customs union established within the Prussian state after 1815 which gradually came to include most of the German states by 1833. The abolition of customs and the development of free trade helped to encourage industrialization in the German states and to make Prussia, rather than Austria, the focus of German nationalism.

VII
TOPIC BIBLIOGRAPHY

TOPICS

LIST OF ABBREVIATIONS

A.H.R.	*American Historical Review*
C.E.H.	*Central European History*
C.H.J.	*Cambridge Historical Journal (later, Historical Journal)*
Ec.H.R.	*Economic History Review*
E.H.Q.	*European History Quarterly*
E.H.R.	*English Historical Review*
E.S.R.	*European Studies Review (later, European History Quarterly)*
F.H.S.	*French Historical Studies*
H.	*History*
H.J.	*Historical Journal*
H.T.	*History Today*
H.W.J.	*History Workshop Journal*
I.R.S.H.	*International Review of Social History*
J.C.E.A.	*Journal of Central European Affairs*
J.C.H.	*Journal of Contemporary History*
J.Ec.H.	*Journal of Economic History*
J.H.I.	*Journal of the History of Ideas*
J.M.H.	*Journal of Modern History*
P.P.	*Past and Present*
R.P.	*Review of Politics*
S.E.E.R.	*Slavonic and East European Review*
S.H.	*Slavic History*
S.R.	*Slavic Review*
T.R.H.S.	*Transactions of the Royal Historical Society*

INTRODUCTORY NOTE

This bibliography is arranged in rough chronological order and is intended to represent many of the major topics and themes in modern European history. The essay titles are intended to focus attention on some of the most commonly raised issues, but should not be regarded as exhausting the range of possibilities on each subject. The reading is deliberately greater than would be required for an average essay, but does reflect the wealth of bibliographical material now available for most of these topics and allows a degree of specialization on particular aspects of a subject. Similarly, the article literature mentioned, while not an exhaustive list, is intended as a guide to some of the most important material available in academic journals. A selection of source material is also provided for topics, where appropriate.

GENERAL TEXTS

Two important general histories are N. Davies, *Europe: A History* (1996) and J.M. Roberts, *Europe* (1996), both including this period as part of their general coverage. For the first part of this period see J. Black, *Eighteenth Century Europe* (1990) and E.N. Williams, *The Ancien Regime in Europe* (1970); also the latter part of W. Doyle, *The Old European Order, 1660–1800* (1978). International politics are examined in P.W. Schroeder, *The Transformation of European Politics, 1763–1848* (1994), and on more general themes J.M. Roberts, *Revolution and Improvement: The Western World, 1775–1847*; see too I. Collins, *The Age of Progress, 1789–1848* (1964). E.J. Hobsbawm's trilogy, *The Age of Revolution, 1789–1848* (1964). *The Age of Capital, 1848–1875* (1975), and *The Age of Empire, 1875–1914* (1987) is especially strong on economic and intellectual themes. For the nineteenth and twentieth centuries see P. Clavin and A. Briggs, *Modern Europe, 1789 – Present* (2003); an introduction to the revolutionary era is J. Sperber, *Revolutionary Europe, 1780–1850* (2000), while on the nineteenth century there are several treatments, including R. Gildea, *Barricades and Borders: Europe, 1800–1914* (2nd edn, 1996), M. Rapport, *Nineteenth Century Europe* (2004), M.S. Anderson, *The Ascendency of Europe, 1815–1914* (3rd edn, 2003), and D. Thompson, *Europe since Napoleon* (rev. edn, 1966). For the twentieth century see J. Joll, *Europe since 1870: An International History* (1973), M. Mazower, *Dark Continent* (1998), J.M. Roberts, *Europe, 1880–1945* (3rd edn, 2000), E.J. Hobsbawn, *The Age of Extremes: The Short Twentieth Century, 1914–1991* (1994), and H. James, *Europe Reborn: A History, 1914–2000* (2003).

There are several titles covering shorter periods such as O. Hufton, *Europe: Privilege and Protest, 1730–1789* (1980), G. Rudé, *Revolutionary Europe, 1789–1815* (1964), M.S. Anderson, *Europe in the Eighteenth Century* (3rd edn, 1987), F.L. Ford, *Europe, 1780–1830* (2nd edn, 1989), H. Hearder, *Europe in the Nineteenth Century* (2nd edn, 1988), J.A.S. Grenville, *Europe Reshaped, 1848–1878* (1976), N. Stone, *Europe Transformed, 1878–1919* (1983), and J.M. Roberts, *Europe, 1880–1945* (3rd edn, 2000). Also of general importance are D. McKay and

H. Scott. *The Rise of the Great Powers. 1648–1815* (1983), G. Best. *War and Society in Revolutionary Europe, 1770–1870* (1982) and A. Sked (ed.), *Europe's Balance of Power, 1815–48* (1979). The history of diplomacy receives treatment in M.S. Anderson, *The Rise of Modern Diplomacy, 1450–1919* (1993).

There is a large selection of general works or series on national history which can be consulted. For France, see A. Cobban, *A History of Modern France, 1715–1945* (3 vols, 1961–65), while more recent are R. Tombs, *France, 1814–1914* (1996), W.H.C. Smith, *Second Empire and Commune: France 1848–1871* (2nd edn, 1996), and R. Gildea, *France, 1870–1914* (2nd edn, 1996). Large-scale works by F. Furet, *Revolutionary France, 1770–1880* (1992) and M. Agulhon, *The French Republic, 1879–1992* (1993) are important modern accounts. The older J.P.T. Bury, *France 1815–1940* (1949) remains a useful single volume treatment. The three-volume Fontana History of Modern France is a more recent addition, comprising D.M.G. Sutherland, *France 1789–1815: Revolution and Counterrevolution* (1985), R. Magraw, *France 1815–1914: The Bourgeois Century* (1984), and D. Johnson, *France 1914–1983: The Twentieth Century* (1986). See, too, the volumes in the Cambridge History of Modern France: A. Jardin and A.-J. Tudesq, *Restoration and Reaction, 1815–1848* (1984); M. Agulhon, *The Republican Experiment, 1848–1852* (1983); A. Plessis, *The Rise and Fall of the Second Empire, 1852–1871* (1985); J.-M. Mayeur and M. Reberioux, *The Third Republic from its Origins to the Great War, 1871–1914* (1987); P. Bernard and H. Dubief, *The Decline of the Third Republic, 1914–1938* (1985); and J.-P. Azema, *From Munich to the Liberation, 1938–1944* (1985). For the twentieth century, J.F. McMillan, *Dreyfus to de Gaulle: Politics and Society in France, 1898–1968* (1985) and the more recent *Twentieth-Century France: Politics, Society and Culture, 1898–2003* (2004); also C. Sowerdine, *France since 1870: Culture, Politics, and Sociology* (2000). Directly concerned with social history are G. Dupeux, *French Society, 1789–1970* (1976), P. McPhee, *A Social History of France, 1789–1914* (2nd edn, 2003), C. Charle, *A Social History of France in the Nineteenth Century* (1994), A. Moulin, *Peasantry and Society in France since 1789* (1991), and the volumes by T. Zeldin, *France, 1848–1945* (1973–77).

On Spain see T. Lynch, *Bourbon Spain, 1700–1808* (1989), C. Esdaile, *Spain in the Liberal Age: From Constitution to Civil War* (2000), R. Carr, *Spain, 1808–1875* (rev. edn, 1980), F.J. Romero Salvado, *Twentieth-Century Spain: Politics and Society, 1898–1998* (1999), the older A.R. Oliveira, *Politics, Economics, and Men of Modern Spain, 1808–1946* (1946), and R. Altamara, *A History of Spanish Civilisation* (1930). For Italy, R. Albrecht-Carrié, *Italy from Napoleon to Mussolini* (1950) and D. Mack Smith, *Italy* (1959) remain useful. More recent are the two volumes in the Longman History of Italy, H. Hearder, *Italy in the Age of the Risorgimento, 1790–1870* (1983) and M. Clark, *Modern Italy, 1871–1982* (1984); also S. Woolf, *A History of Italy, 1700–1870* (1979).

For Germany, see J. Gagliardo, *Germany under the Old Regime, 1600–1790* (1991), J.J. Sheehan, *German History, 1770–1866* (1989), W. Carr, *A History of Germany, 1815–1945* (rev. edn, 1979), A. Ramm, *Germany, 1789–1919* (1967), and *Germany* (3 vols, 1959–69), G.A. Craig, *Germany, 1866–1945* (1978), D.G. Williamson,

Germany since 1815 (2004), V.R. Berghahn, *Modern Germany: Society, Economy and Politics in the Twentieth Century* (1982), and M. Fulbrook, *Twentieth Century Germany: Politics, Culture and Society, 1918–1990* (2001). For economic and social development see S. Ogilvie and R. Overy, *Germany: A New Social and Economic History, vol.3: Since 1800* (2003), and on a major theme S. Berger, *Inventing the Nation: Germany* (2004). A guide to the Low Countries is E. Kossmann, *The Low Countries, 1780–1940* (1976), while for Scandinavia, see B.J. Hovde, *The Scandinavian Countries, 1720–1865, vol. I* (1943), F.D. Scott, *Sweden: The Nation's History* (1977), T.K. Derry, *A History of Modern Norway, 1814–1972* (1973), and F. Singleton, *A Short History of Finland* (1989). See also D. Kirby, *The Baltic World, 1772–1993* (1995).

For Russia, M.T. Florinski, *Russia: A History and Interpretation* (2 vols, 1953–54) and B. Pares, *A History of Russia* (3rd edn, 1955) are old, but still useful. See also G.V. Vernadsky, *A History of Russia* (rev. edn, 1961). H. Seton-Watson, *Imperial Russia, 1801–1917* (1967) covers a major part of this period. B.H. Sumner, *A Survey of Russian History* (1944) is thematically arranged but covers a long sweep of Russian history, as does R. Pipes, *Russia under the Old Régime* (1974). In the Longman History of Russia, the relevant published volumes are P. Dukes, *The Making of Russian Absolutism, 1613–1801* (1982), D. Saunders, *Russia in the Age of Reaction and Reform, 1801–1881* (1992), H. Rogger, *Russia in the Age of Modernisation and Revolution, 1881–1917* (1983), and M.M. McCauley, *The Soviet Union, 1917–1991* (2nd edn, 1993). J.N. Westwood, *Endurance and Endeavour: Russian History, 1812–1992* (1973; 4th edn, 1993) covers the last two centuries, but see also on the twentieth century G. Hosking, *A History of the Soviet Union* (2nd edn, 1990), R. Service, *A History of Twentieth Century Russia* (1997), and R. Sakwa, *The Rise and Fall of the Soviet Union* (1999). A major theme is covered over a long period in J. Blum, *Lord and Peasant in Russia* (1961); see also J. Channon, *The Russian and Soviet Peasantry, 1880–1991* (1997).

For Poland see A.J. Prazmowska, *A History of Poland* (2004), the older H. Frankel, *Poland: The Struggle for Power, 1772–1939* (1946), P.S. Wandycz, *The Lands of Partitioned Poland, 1759–1918* (1974), and N. Davies, *God's Playground: A History of Poland* (1981). For the Habsburg lands, see C. Ingrao, *The Habsburg Monarchy, 1618–1815* (1994), R. Okey, *Eastern Europe, 1740–1985* (2nd edn, 1986), H. Seton-Watson, *The 'Sick Heart' of Modern Europe: The Problem of the Danubian Lands* (1975), A. Sked, *The Decline and Fall of The Habsburg Empire, 1815–1918* (1989), C.A. Macartney, *The Habsburg Empire, 1790–1918* (1968), A.J.P. Taylor, *The Habsburg Monarchy, 1815–1918* (2nd edn, 1949), R.A. Kann, *The Multi-National Empire: Nationalism and National Reform in the Habsburg Monarchy, 1848–1918* (2 vols, 1950), and the more recent, R. Okey, *The Habsburg Monarchy, c. 1765–1918* (2000). On Hungary see C.A. Macartney, *Hungary* (1934), J.K. Hoensch, *A History of Modern Hungary* (1988), and L. Kontler, *A History of Hungary* (2002).

European economic development is discussed in B.H. Slicher Van Bath, *The Agrarian History of Western Europe* (1983), A. Milward and S.B. Saul, *The Economic Development of Continental Europe, 1780–1870* (1973), C. Trebilcock,

The Industrialisation of the Continental Powers, 1780–1914 (1981), W.W. Rostow, *The Stages of Economic Growth* (1960), W.O. Henderson, *The Industrial Revolution on the Continent* (1961), H. Feis, *Europe the World's Banker* (1930), W. Ashworth, *A Short History of the International Economy since 1850* (1952), and F.B. Tipton and R. Aldrich, *An Economic and Social History of Europe, 1890 to the Present* (1989). See also the last four volumes of C.M. Cipolla (ed.), *The Fontana Economic History of Europe* (1973) which contain articles on individual countries and more general themes. Two important general studies are D. Landes, *The Unbound Prometheus: Technological Change and Industrial Development in Western Europe since 1750* (1972) and J. Goodman and K. Honeyman, *Gainful Pursuits: The Making of Industrial Europe, 1600–1914* (1988). Also of importance is R. Porter and M. Teich, *The Industrial Revolution in National Context* (1995), while much of the economic and social history of the earlier part of the period is traced in F. Braudel, *Capitalism and Material Life, 1500–1800* (1967), also available in a recent three-volume edition, *Civilisation and Capitalism, 15th–18th Century* (1985). Also useful is H. Kamen, *Social History of Europe, 1500–1800* (1984). For the later period, see D. Geary, *A Social History of Western Europe, 1848–1945* (1985), P.N. Stearns, *European Society in Upheaval* (1967) and G. Mosse, *The Culture of Western Europe: The Nineteenth and Twentieth Centuries* (1961).

For Europe's relationship with the wider world, consult the later sections of two excellent histories of the world; W.H. McNeill, *A World History* (1967) and J.M. Roberts, *The Hutchinson Pelican History of the World* (1976). The latter's *The Triumph of the West* (1985) elevates Europeanization into a major theme of world history. R. Davis, *The Rise of the Atlantic Economies* (1973) deals with the earlier phases of European involvement; C.A. Bayly, *The Birth of the Modern World, 1780–1914: Global Connections and Comparisons* (2004), D.K. Fieldhouse, *The Colonial Empires* (1966), and V. Kiernan, *European Empires from Conquest to Collapse, 1815–1960* (1982) present them in maturity and after. Europe's place in the twentieth-century world is covered by J.A.S. Grenville, *A History of the World: from the 20th to the 21st Century* (2004).

For reference purposes, there is a wealth of statistical information in B.R. Mitchell, *European Historical Statistics, 1750–1988* (3rd edn, 1992). See also P. Flora (ed.), *State, Economy and Society in Western Europe, 1815–1975* (2 vols, 1983–84). For detailed reference works on a wide variety of political topics, see J. Babuscio and R. Dunn, *European Political Facts, 1648–1789* (1984), C. Cook and J. Paxton, *European Political Facts, 1789–1848* (1980), C. Cook and J. Paxton, *European Political Facts, 1848–1918* (1978) and C. Cook and J. Paxton, *European Political Facts of the Twentieth Century* (2001). S.H. Steinberg, *Historical Tables (58 BC–AD 1978)* (10th edn., 1979) is an invaluable chronological reference work.

1. THE ANCIEN RÉGIME

The latter half of the eighteenth century is inevitably overshadowed by the events of the Revolutionary and Napoleonic era, but deserves study in its own right. The age of 'enlightenment' witnessed a ferment of social, economic and intellectual changes, but ones which still seemed, prior to 1789, to permit the old order to adapt and maintain itself. The degree to which 'enlightened despotism' can be regarded as a coherent and serious influence on the attitude and behaviour of rulers is one aspect of the period which has received attention; another is the relationship between monarchs and their nobility; while the wider intellectual critique of the old order and its allies, notably the Church, should also be considered.

Essay topics

- How much substance was there to the claim of some *ancien régime* rulers to be 'enlightened'?
- Where and why did European aristocracies find themselves in conflict with their rulers in the latter part of the eighteenth century?
- Why did the Church find itself the target of so much criticism in late eighteenth-century Europe?

Sources and documents

T.C.W. Blanning, *Joseph II and Enlightened Despotism* (1970) has documents, is readily accessible and ranges beyond Joseph II in its coverage. For the philosophes' critique of the *ancien régime* there is little substitute for reading some of the great classics of enlightenment literature, such as Jean-Jacques Rousseau, *Du contrat social* (1762, trans. as *The Social Contract*), C.L. Montesquieu, *De l'esprit des lois* (1748) and *Persian Letters* (1721), and Voltaire's *Candide* (1759) and *Philosophical Dictionary* (1764). There is a mine of information in J. Yolton, P. Rogers, R. Porter and B. Stafford (eds), *The Blackwell Companion to the Enlightenment* (1990).

Secondary works

There are excellent broad surveys in E.N. Williams, *The Ancien Regime in Europe* (1970), M.S. Anderson, *Europe in the Eighteenth Century* (4th edn, 2000), R.R. Palmer, *The Age of the Democratic Revolution, vol. I: The Challenge* (1959), and J. Black, *Eighteenth Century Europe, 1700–1789* (1990). See also the later sections of W. Doyle, *The Old European Order, 1660–1800* (1978), and A.F. Upton, *Europe, 1600–1789* (2001), which is particularly strong on northern Europe; H.M. Scott, *The Emergence of the Eastern Powers, 1756–1775* (2001) again concentrates on more neglected parts of Europe. T.C.W. Blanning (ed.), *The Eighteenth Century* (2001) has an excellent group of essays on major themes.

For the ideas behind the enlightenment, see A. Cobban, *In Search of Humanity: The Enlightenment in Modern History* (1960), N. Hampson, *The Enlightenment* (1968), and P. Gay, *The Enlightenment: An Interpretation* (1967) and *The Party of Humanity* (1964). Also useful is P. Hazard, *European Thought in the Eighteenth Century* (1963) and C. Becker, *The Heavenly City of the Eighteenth Century*

Philosophers (1932). R. Darnton, *George Washington's False Teeth* (2001) has some excellent essays on the environment in which enlightened ideas were formed and communicated. The rise of the 'public sphere' is discussed in H. Barker and S. Burrows (eds), *Press, Politics and the Public Sphere in Europe and North America, 1760–1820* (2000) and J. van Horn Melton, *The Rise of the Public in Enlightened Europe* (2001).

On enlightened despotism in general, see H.M. Scott (ed.), *Enlightened Absolutism* (1990), C.B.A. Behrens, *Society, Government and the Enlightenment* (1985), P.P. Bernard, *From the Enlightenment to the Police State* (1991), and T.C.W. Blanning, *Joseph II and Enlightened Despotism* (1970), wider than its title suggests, but see too the older F. Hartung. *Enlightened Despotism* (1957), J.G. Gagliardo, *Enlightened Despotism* (1968) and S. Andrews, *Enlightened Despotism* (1967). R. Porter and M. Teich, *The Enlightenment in National Context* (1981) is an excellent modern study. See also A.R. Myers, *Parliaments and Estates in Europe to 1789* (1975), F. Venturi, *Utopia and Reform in the Enlightenment* (1971), and H.M. Scott (ed.), *Enlightened Absolutism* (1990).

Individual rulers are examined in C.A. Macartney, *The Habsburg and Hohenzollern Dynasties* (1970), A.C. Johnson, *Frederick the Great and his Officials* (1976), D.B. Horn, *Frederick the Great* (1964), G. Ritter, *Frederick the Great* (1968), and W. Hubstsch, *Frederick the Great* (1975). On the general history of Germany and Frederick's part in it, see J. Gagliardo, *Germany under the Old Regime, 1600–1790* (1991), S.B. Fay and K. Epstein, *The Rise of Brandenburg–Prussia to 1786* (rev. edn, 1964), and F.L. Carsten, *The Origins of Prussia* (1954). On the role of the army, see G.A. Craig, *The Politics of the Prussian Army, 1640–1945* (1955) and C. Duffy, *The Army of Frederick the Great* (1974). For economic developments see W.O. Henderson, *The State and the Industrial Revolution in Prussia, 1740–1870* (1958) and his *Studies in the Economic Policy of Frederick the Great* (1963).

On Catherine and Russia, see M. Raeff, *Imperial Russia, 1682–1825* (1971), P. Dukes, *Catherine the Great and the Russian Nobility* (1967), and P. Dukes (ed.), *Russia under Catherine the Great* (1977–78). M. Raeff (ed.), *Catherine the Great* (1972) has views on Catherine. See too W.F. Reddaway (ed.), *Documents of Catherine the Great: The Correspondence with Voltaire and the Instruction of 1767 in the English Text of 1768* (1931) and I. de Madariaga, *Russia in the Age of Catherine the Great* (1981). On the Pugachev rising, see P. Avrich, *Russian Rebels* (1973), M. Raeff, 'Pugachev's rebellion', in R. Forster and J.P. Greene (eds), *Preconditions of Revolution in Early Modern Europe* (1970), and P. Longworth, 'The Pugachev Revolt: the last great Cossack peasant rising', in H. Landsberger (ed.), *Rural Protest: Peasant Movements and Social Change* (1974). For Russian expansion see G.S. Thompson, *Catherine the Great and the Expansion of Russia* (1947) and A.W. Fisher, *The Russian Annexation of the Crimea, 1772–1783* (1970).

For Joseph II, see T.C.W. Blanning, *Joseph II* (1994); also S.K. Padover, *The Revolutionary Emperor – Joseph II* (1967), and E. Wangermann, *The Austrian Achievement, 1700–1800* (1973) and *From Joseph II to the Jacobin Trials* (1959). The early part of C.A. Macartney, *Habsburg Empire, 1790–1918* (1968) and

H. Holborn, *History of Modern Germany, Vol. II* (1964) are useful; see too, H. Strakosch, *State Absolutism and the Rule of Law* (1967) and K. Roider, *Austria's Eastern Question, 1700–90* (1982).

On the other eighteenth-century states, see J. Lynch, *Bourbon Spain, 1700–1808* (1989), R. Herr, *Eighteenth-Century Revolution in Spain* (1958), and A. Hull, *Charles III and the Revival of Spain* (1980). Scandinavia is less well-served for the period after 1760 than earlier, but for Gustavus III, see I. Anderson, *A History of Sweden* (1956) and S. Oakley, *The Story of Sweden* (1966), ch. 13. The impact of enlightened ideas on Italy is discussed in F. Venturi (ed.), *Italy and the Enlightenment* (1972), while Britain's experience is traced in R. Pares, *Limited Monarchy in Great Britain* (Historical Association, 1957) and J. Brooke, *George III* (1973).

Specifically on the Churches, see G.R. Cragg, *The Church and the Age of Reason* (1960) and R.R. Palmer, *Catholics and Unbelievers in Eighteenth Century France* (rev. edn, 1961), F.E. Manuel, *The Eighteenth Century Confronts the Gods* (1959), and R. Wollheim (ed.), *Hume on Religion* (1963). Of importance too are J. Delumeau, *Catholicism between Luther and Voltaire* (1977), H. Kamen, *The Spanish Inquisition* (1965), and T. Tackett, *Priest and Parish in Eighteenth Century France* (1977).

Articles

A useful starting point on the literature on 'enlightened despotism' is H. Scott, 'Whatever happened to the Enlightened Despots?', *H.* (1983); see also B. Behrens, 'Enlightened despotism', *H.J.* (1975), G. Parry, 'Enlightened government and its critics in eighteenth century Germany', *H.J.* (1963), and M. Raeff, 'The well-ordered police state and the development of modernity in seventeenth and eighteenth century Europe', *A.H.R.* (1975). Useful too are V.G. Kiernan, 'Foreign mercenaries and absolute monarchy', *P.P.* (1957) and 'State and nation in Western Europe', *P.P.* (1965).

On individual countries see also W.L. Dorn, 'The Prussian bureaucracy in the eighteenth century', *Political Science Quarterly* (1931 and 1932), D.E.D. Beales, 'The false Joseph II', *H.J.* (1975), I. de Madariaga, 'Catherine II and the serfs', *S.R.* (1974), A.H. Kamen, 'The decline of Spain: a historical myth?', *P.P.* (1978), E.J. Hamilton, 'Money and economic recovery in Spain under the first Bourbons', *J.M.H.* (1943), W.J. Callahan, 'Crown, nobility and industry in eighteenth century Spain', *International Review of Social History* (1966), and L. Rodriguez, 'The Spanish riots of 1766', *P.P.* (1973).

For the influence of the enlightenment in general, see P. Gay, 'The Enlightenment in the history of political theory', *Political Science Quarterly* (1954), T. Besterman, 'Reason and progress', *Studies on Voltaire and the Eighteenth Century* (1963), and G. Iggers, 'The idea of progress: a critical reassessment', *A.H.R.* (1965).

2. THE COMING OF THE FRENCH REVOLUTION

A huge topic which draws upon a great variety of explanations as to why and how the Revolution occurred. These range from the fundamentally structural accounts which find the roots of the Revolution in economic, social and intellectual changes to the more contingent and 'accidental' views of the coming of the Revolution. The literature is still dominated by the historians who see long-term processes at work which culminated in the Revolution, although there have been distinguished attempts by scholars of all perspectives to free the period from too much intellectual abstraction and to engage in detailed discussion of the nature of the *ancien régime* in France.

Essay topics

- How intractable were the problems facing the French government in the twenty years prior to the French Revolution?
- Discuss the influence of the philosophes upon the outbreak of the French Revolution.
- Account for the calling of the Estates-General in 1789.

Sources and documents

J. Hardman, *The French Revolution: The Fall of the Ancien Regime to the Thermidorian Reaction, 1785–1795* (1981) is comprehensive, but see also R.C. Cobb, J. Hardman, and J.M. Roberts, *French Revolution Documents* (1966–73). A. Young, *Travels in France during the Years 1787, 1788, 1789* (ed. C. Maxwell, 1929) is a valuable eye-witness account of the pre-revolutionary regime.

Secondary works

Of the general studies, W. Doyle, *The Oxford History of the French Revolution* (1989) and A. Forrest, *The French Revolution* (1994) are good starting points. S. Schama, *Citizens* (1989) is a brilliant narrative. P. Campbell, *The Ancien Regime in France* (1988) puts the final collapse in context and his *The Origins of the French Revolution* (2004) examines its breakdown. Similarly, W. Doyle, *The Ancien Regime* (2001) and *The Origins of the French Revolution* (4th edn, 2003) look at the regime and its fall. F. Furet, *Interpreting the French Revolution* (1981) represents a less 'structural' view; see also J. Hardman, *French Politics, 1774–1789* (1994). J.M. Roberts, *The French Revolution* (1978), ch. 1 and J. Godechot, *France and the Atlantic Revolution of the Eighteenth Century* (1965) are also valuable on the combination of long-term and short-term processes at work. Detailed studies of the last years of the French monarchy are also part of the canvas of the standard accounts of the French Revolution by G. Lefebvre, *The French Revolution: from its Origins to 1793* (1962) and A. Soboul, *The French Revolution, 1787–99* (1974). M. Vovelle, *The Fall of the French Monarchy, 1787–1792* (1984) is a modern view of the collapse of the French government, for which see also J. Godechot, *The Taking of the Bastille* (1970) and G. Lefebvre, *The Great Fear of 1789* (1973). The historiographical issues were taken up in A. Cobban, *Historians and the Causes of the French Revolution* (Historical Association pamphlet, 1958).

For the general social and economic background to the French Revolution see G. Lefebvre, *The Coming of the French Revolution* (1939) and the collection in D. Johnson (ed.), *French Society and the Revolution* (1976); see too D. Andress, *The French Revolution and the People* (2004) and his *French Society in Revolution* (2000). For the countryside, see P.M. Jones, *The Peasantry in the French Revolution* (1988). Individual social groups are discussed in O.H. Hufton, *The Poor of Eighteenth Century France* (1974), F.L. Ford, *Robe and Sword: The Regrouping of the French Aristocracy after Louis XIV* (1953), R. Forster, *The Nobility of Toulouse in the Eighteenth Century: A Social and Economic Study* (1960), E. Barber, *The Bourgeoisie in Eighteenth Century France* (1955), and useful case studies in O.H. Hulton, *Bayeux in the Eighteenth Century* (1967), and 'Life and death among the very poor', in A. Cobban (ed.), *The Eighteenth Century* (1969), C. Jones, *Charity and Bienfaisance: The Treatment of the Poor in the Montpellier Region, 1740–1815* (1983), and J.K.J. Thompson, *Charmont-de-Lodeve, 1633–1789: Fluctuations in the Prosperity of a Cloth-Making Town* (1982). For population see L. Henry, 'The population of France in the eighteenth century', in D.V. Glass and D.E.C. Eversley (eds), *Population in History* (1965).

Serious discussion of the economic features of France under the *ancien régime* can be found in the early parts of R. Price, *The Economic Modernisation of France* (1975) and T. Kemp, *Economic Forces in French History* (1971). See also the selection of articles in R. Greenlaw (ed.), *The Economic Origins of the French Revolution: Poverty or Prosperity* (1958). There is an important comparative essay on British and French economic development by F. Crouzet. 'England and France in the eighteenth century: a comparative analysis of two economic growths', in R.M. Hartwell (ed.), *The Causes of the Industrial Revolution in England* (1967). The definitive study of French finances is J.F. Bosher, *French Finances, 1770–1795* (1970), and on the influence of Turgot on economic policy, see D. Dakin, *Turgot and the Ancien Regime in France* (1939). An important case study of the impasse faced by reformers of the fiscal system is J.F. Bosher, *The Single Duty Project: A Study of the Movement for a French Customs Union* (1946).

On the place of the Church, see J. McManners, *French Ecclesiastical Society under the Old Regime* (1961) and R.R. Palmer, *Catholics and Unbelievers in Eighteenth Century France* (1939). For the role of the philosophes in preparing the ground for the revolution, see N. Hampson, *The Enlightenment* (1968), W.F. Church (ed.), *The Influence of the Enlightenment on the French Revolution: Creative, Disastrous, or Non-existent* (1964), and A. Cobban, *Aspects of the French Revolution* (1968), ch. 1. On the activities of the parlements, see J.H. Shennan, *The Parlement of Paris* (1968).

Articles

For the continuing debate about the origins of the French Revolution and their interpretation, see G. Ellis, 'The "Marxist interpretation" of the French Revolution', *E.H.R*: (1978) and G.C. Cavanaugh, 'The present state of French revolutionary historiography: Alfred Cobban and beyond', *F.H.S.* (1972).

On the social and economic background, see C. Lucas, 'Nobles, bourgeois and the origins of the French Revolution', *P.P.* (1973), A. Davies, 'The origins of the French Peasant Revolution of 1789', *H.* (1964), N. Temple, 'The control and exploitation of French towns during the Ancien Regime', *H.* (1996), and R. Forster, 'The provincial noble: a reappraisal', *A.H.R.* (1962–63). Other aspects are discussed in A. Woyd Moote, 'The French Crown *versus* its judicial and financial officials', *J.M.H.* (1962), W. Doyle, 'The parlements of France and the breakdown of the Old Regime, 1770–1788', *French Historical Studies* (1970), and A. Cobban, 'The Parlements of France in the eighteenth century', *H.* (1950). On the influence of the philosophes, see H. Peyre, 'The influence of eighteenth century ideas on the French Revolution', *Journal of the History of Ideas* (1949) and R.S. Tate, 'Voltaire and the parlements', *Studies on Voltaire and the Eighteenth Century* (1972).

For the immediate events leading up to the revolution, see A. Goodwin, 'Calonne, the assembly of French notables of 1787 and the origins of the *Révolte nobiliairé*, *E.H.R.* (1946).

3. THE FRENCH REVOLUTION

There are many and varied interpretations of the French Revolution. Almost all, however, confront certain basic issues, such as why it proved impossible to create a stable constitutional monarchy after 1789, the nature and character of the Jacobin 'Terror', and the establishment of a more moderate government after the fall of Robespierre. As well as the continuing debate on the interpretation of the Revolution and its personalities, there has been a considerable widening of the literature to examine the social context of the Revolution with analyses of the 'crowd' and of social groups such as artisans and women. A good deal of research in recent years has been devoted to the French Revolution as experienced in the provinces. This provides some useful perspectives on the extent to which change or continuity were the most significant aspects of the French Revolution.

Essay topics

- Why was France unable to evolve a stable system of constitutional monarchy in the period 1789 to 1793?
- What was the significance of the Terror?
- To what extent should the French Revolution be seen as an essentially Parisian phenomenon?

Sources and documents

Several collections of documents are available: see J. Hardman, *The French Revolution: The Fall of the Ancien Regime to the Thermidorian Reaction, 1785–1795* (1981) and *The French Revolution Sourcebook* (1998); D.G. Wright, *Revolution and Terror in France, 1789–1795* (2nd edn, 1991); and R.C. Cobb, J. Hardman and J.M. Roberts, *French Revolution Documents* (1966–73).

Secondary works

For an overall interpretation see W. Doyle, *The Oxford History of the French Revolution* (1989) and the opening sections of D.M.G. Sutherland, *France, 1789–1815: Revolution and Counter-Revolution* (1985). S. Schama, *Citizens* (1989) is a brilliant narrative with a point of view of its own. Two older books available in modern editions are J.M. Thompson, *The French Revolution* (new edn, 1985) and A. Goodwin, *The French Revolution* (1953). N. Hampson, *Prelude to Terror: The Constituent Assembly and the Failure of Consensus, 1789–1791* (1988) deals with the critical period when constitutional monarchy hung in the balance. The social forces underpinning the Revolution are examined in N. Hampson, *A Social History of the French Revolution* (1963) and R. Cobb, *The Revolutionary Armies* (trans. edn, 1989). The Republican period is considered as a whole in M.J. Sydenham, *The First French Republic, 1792–1804* (1974). The view of the great Marxist scholar of the French Revolution is contained in G. Lefebvre, *The French Revolution: From Its Origins to 1793* (1962) and *The French Revolution: From 1793 to 1799* (1964); see also A. Soboul, *The French Revolution, 1787–1799* (1964). Recent additions in English translation of French interpretations are M. Vovelle, *The Fall of the French Monarchy, 1787–1792* (1984), M. Bouloiseau, *The Jacobin Republic, 1792–1794* (1983), and D. Woronoff, *The Thermidorean Regime and the Directory, 1794–1799* (1984). One of the most influential recent French interpretations is F. Furet, *Interpreting the French Revolution* (1981).

For a major attack on the Marxist interpretation of the French Revolution, see A. Cobban, *The Social Interpretation of the French Revolution* (1964); see also his *Aspects of the French Revolution* (1968), especially the essay 'Myth of the French Revolution'. A wide-ranging survey of the field is J.M. Roberts, *The French Revolution* (1978). See also G. Rudé, *Interpretations of the French Revolution* (1961) and J. McManners, 'The historiography of the French Revolution', in Vol. VIII of the *The New Cambridge Modern History* (1979).

The personalities involved in the Revolution can be examined through J. Hardman, *Louis XVI: The Silent King* (2000) and his *Robespierre* (1999); also R.R. Palmer, *Twelve Who Ruled* (1941), M.J. Sydenham, *The Girondins* (1961), and J.M. Thompson, *Leaders of the French Revolution* (1929). On Robespierre, see J.M. Thompson, *Robespierre* (1930), and N. Hampson, *The Life and Opinions of Maximilien Robespierre* (1974) and *Danton* (1988). On other figures, see L. Gottschalk's, *Jean Paul Marat: A Study in Radicalism* (1967), L. Gershoy, *Bertrand Barere, A Reluctant Terrorist* (1962), R.B. Rose, *Gracchus Babeuf* (1978), and L. Gottschalk and M. Maddox, *Lafayette in the French Revolution, through the October Days* (1969) and *Lafayette in the French Revolution, from the October Days through the Federation* (1973). See also N. Hampson, *Saint-Just* (1991), O.J.G. Welch, *Mirabeau* (1951), and J.H. Clapham, *The Abbé Sieyès* (1912).

On the role of Paris, see G. Rudé, *The Crowd in the French Revolution* (1959) and *Paris and London in the Eighteenth Century: Studies in Popular Protest* (1970). J. Godechot, *The Taking of the Bastille* (1970) also looks at Paris. A. Soboul, *The Parisian Sans-Culottes and the French Revolution, 1793–4* (1964) deals with

379

a significant group, as does G.A. Williams, *Artisans and Sans-culottes* (1968). The wider perspective is offered by R. Cobb, *Paris and the Provinces* (1975) and A. Forrest, *Paris, the Provinces and the French Revolution* (2004). For more detailed regional studies, see W. Scott, *Terror and Repression in Revolutionary Marseilles* (1973), C. Lucas, *The Structure of the Terror: The Example of Javogues and the Loire* (1973), C. Tilly, *The Vendée* (1964), A. Forrest, *Society and Politics in Revolutionary Bordeaux* (1975) and *The Revolution in Provincial France: Aquitaine, 1789–1799* (1996), and C. Lewis and C. Lucas, *Beyond the Terror: Essays on French Regional and Social History, 1794–1815* (1984).

On particular themes, see R. Cobb, *The Police and the People: French Popular Protest 1789–1820* (1970), J. McManners, *The French Revolution and the Church* (1969), and S.G. Harris, *The Assignats* (1930). On the 'Terror', see N. Hampson, *The Terror in the French Revolution* (Historical Association pamphlet, 1981), D. Greer, *The Incidence of the Terror during the French Revolution* (1935) and *The Incidence of the Emigration during the French Revolution* (1951). Opposition to the revolution is considered in C. Tilly, *The Vendée* (1964), D. Sutherland, *The Chouans* (1982), and G. Lewis, *The Second Vendée* (1978). For the transition to the later 1790s, see I. Woloch, *Jacobin Legacy* (1971), M. Łyons, *France under the Directory* (1975), and C.H. Church, 'In search of the Directory', in *French Government and Society* (1973).

For society at large during the revolutionary period, see D. Andress, *French Society in Revolution, 1789–1799* (2000) and *The French Revolution and the People* (2004). On foreign affairs, see T.C.W. Blanning, *The Origins of the French Revolutionary Wars* (1986).

Articles

For general interpretations, see N. Hampson, 'What difference did the French Revolution make?' *H.* (1989), G. Ellis, 'The "Marxist Interpretation" of the French Revolution', *E.H.R.* (1978), G.C. Cavanaugh, 'The present state of French revolutionary historiography: Alfred Cobban and beyond', *F.H.S* (1972), and C.B.A. Behrens, 'Professor Cobban and his critics', *H.J.* (1966). On the experience of the revolution, see R. Cobb, 'The revolutionary mentality in France, 1793–4', *H.* (1957) and J. Le Goff and D.M.G. Sutherland, 'The Revolution and the rural community in eighteenth-century Brittany', *P.P.* (1974); R.B. Rose, 'Tax revolt and popular organisation in Picardy, 1789–1791', *P.P.* (1969) and H. Mitchell, 'The Vendée and Counter-revolution: a review essay', *F.H.S.* (1968). Aspects of revolutionary rule are considered in A. Soboul, 'Some problems of the revolutionary state, 1789–1796', *P.P.* (1974), T.D. Padova, 'The Girondins and the question of revolutionary government', *F.H.S.* (1975), and S. Scott, 'The regeneration of the line army in the French Revolution', *J.M.H.* (1970). For the later period, see A. Goodwin, 'The French Executive Directory: a revaluation', *H.* (1937) and C. Lucas, 'The first Directory and the rule of law', *F.H.S.* (1977). Also useful are C.H. Church, 'The social basis of the French Central Bureaucracy under the Directory', *P.P.* (1967) and R. Forster, 'The survival of the nobility during the French Revolution', *P.P.* (1967).

4. NAPOLEON

As one of the most titanic figures of modern European history, Napoleon can be looked at in a number of ways. How he came to achieve such power and how he held on to it is one line of enquiry. Another is the extent to which he exemplified or consolidated the revolutionary ideals of the 1790s. Some have even seen him as the last of the 'enlightened despots'. Considerably more information is now available about the regional and social history of France throughout the Revolutionary and Napoleonic periods and permits closer assessment of the impact of Napoleon on France. The European dimension of the Napoleonic Empire is discussed in the next topic.

Essay topics

- What factors enabled Napoleon to become Emperor of France?
- Was Napoleon the last of the Enlightened Despots?
- Who lost and who gained from Napoleon's exercise of power in France?

Sources and documents

J.M. Thompson, *Napoleon's Letters* (1934) is an edited collection of his correspondence; see too C. Harold, *The Mind of Napoleon* (1959).

Secondary works

Many of the general histories of the French Revolution cited in the last topic carry their analyses up to and beyond the Napoleonic *coup d'état*. For a detailed assessment of both Napoleon and the Napoleonic era G. Ellis, *Napoleon* (1996) offers a modern interpretation, but see also M. Lyons, *Napoleon Bonaparte and the Legacy of the French Revolution* (1994), L. Bergeron, *France under Napoleon* (1981), and J. Tulard, *Napoleon: The Myth of the Saviour* (trans. edn, 1984). Among the older studies, G. Lefebvre, *Napoleon* (1935), F. Markham, *Napoleon I* (1954), and J.M. Thompson, *Napoleon Bonaparte: His Rise and Fall* (1952) remain valuable and there are serviceable biographies by V. Cronin, *Napoleon* (1971) and C. Barnett, *Napoleon Bonaparte* (1978).

On internal affairs, see C. Church, *Revolution and Red Tape: The French Ministerial Bureaucracy, 1770–1850* (1981), I. Collins, *Napoleon and his Parliaments* (1979), G. Lewis and C. Lucas (eds), *Beyond the Terror: Essays on French Regional and Social History, 1794–1815* (1984), R. Cobb, *The Police and the People: French Popular Protest, 1789–1820* (1970), and A. Forrest, *Conscripts and Deserters: The Army and French Society during the Revolution and Empire* (1989). For relations with the Church, see E.E.Y. Hales, *Revolution and the Papacy, 1769–1846* (1960) and *Napoleon and the Pope* (1972), as well as the older H.H. Welsh, *The Concordat of 1801* (1934). L. Bergeron, *France under Napoleon* (1972) is a good study of French national life under Napoleon; see also M. Guerrini, *Napoleon and*

Paris (1970). On the servants of the Napoleonic empire, see E.A. Whitcombe, *Napoleon's Diplomatic Service* (1979) and P. Young, *Napoleon's Marshals* (1972). On its leading personalities, see J. Orieux, *Talleyrand* (1974) and J.F. Bernard, *Talleyrand* (1977), H. Cole, *Fouché* (1971), and J.H. Clapham, *The Abbé Sieyès* (1912). The last phase of Napoleon's career is covered in B. Norman, *Napoleon and Talleyrand, the Last Two Weeks* (1971). See also N.I. Mackenzie. *The Escape from Elba* (1982).

Articles

R. Forster, 'The survival of the nobility during the French Revolution', *P.P.* (1967), L. Hunt, D. Lansky and P. Hanson, 'The failure of the liberal republic in France, 1795–1799; the road to Brumaire', *J.M.H.* (1979), J. Woloch, 'Napoleonic Conscription', *P.P.* (1986), and E. Whitcombe, 'Napoleon's Perfects', *A.H.R.* (1974).

5. THE REVOLUTIONARY AND NAPOLEONIC WARS

The French Revolution developed into a large-scale European conflict which lasted almost a quarter of a century. Early attempts by the established powers to subvert and crush the Revolution failed, while significant minorities in many European countries showed enthusiasm for the ideals of the French Revolution. French expansionism and the rise of Napoleon gradually alienated many who had once welcomed the Revolution and began to arouse strong patriotic and national feelings. The early years of the conflict are less well covered than the Napoleonic period. The nature and fate of Napoleon's bid for European mastery inevitably occupies a central place, but the effects of the struggle upon individual countries is a major aspect. Napoleon's military abilities and the changing nature of warfare are also important themes.

Essay topics

- Why were the major European powers unable to defeat revolutionary France during the decade after 1789?
- To what extent was Napoleon defeated by the same forces he claimed to represent?
- To what extent did the conduct of warfare change in the course of the Revolutionary and Napoleonic Wars?

Sources and documents

See C. Emsley, *The Longman Companion to Napoleonic Europe* (1993); also for reference purposes, A. Palmer, *An Encyclopaedia of Napoleon's Europe* (1984) is an extremely valuable guide to events and personalities; on military matters, see D. Chandler, *Dictionary of the Napoleonic Wars* (1979).

Secondary works

The general texts (see the introductory bibliography) provide the most accessible accounts of the general European situation in 1789 and the following decade. The elderly study by J.H. Clapham, *The Cause of the War of 1792* (Cambridge, 1899) has now been superseded by T.C.W. Blanning, *The Origins of the French Revolutionary Wars* (London, 1986), discussing both the causes and impact of the wars of the 1790s. On the survival of the Republic, see J.M. Roberts, *The French Revolution* (1978), ch. 3 for a recent overview; also H. Mitchell, *The Underground War against Revolutionary France* (1965) and W.R. Fryer, *Republic or Restoration in France, 1794–7* (1965). On the Revolutionary wars see T.C.W. Blanning, *The French Revolutionary Wars* (1996).

On the Napoleonic Empire there are a number of excellent studies, including S. Woolf, *Napoleon's Integration of Europe* (1991), G. Ellis, *The Napoleonic Empire* (1991), D.G. Wright, *Napoleon and Europe* (1984), and M. Broers, *Europe under Napoleon, 1799–1815* (1996). The older O. Connelly, *Napoleon's Satellite Kingdoms* (1965) and F.H.M. Markham, *Napoleon and the Awakening of Europe* (1954) are still valuable.

As far as individual countries are concerned, for Britain, see H.T. Dickinson, *British Radicalism and the French Revolution, 1789–1815* (1985), C. Emsley, *British Society and the French Wars, 1792–1815* (1979), A. Goodwin, *The Friends of Liberty* (1979), E.P. Thompson, *The Making of the English Working Class* (rev. edn, 1968), and G.A. Williams, *Artisans and Sans Culottes* (1968). The Irish connection with revolutionary France has received definitive treatment in M. Elliott, *Partners in Revolution: The United Irishmen and France* (1982).

For Germany: T.C.W. Blanning, *The French Revolution in Germany: Occupation and Resistance in the Rhineland, 1792–1802* (1983) is a major work dealing with some parts of Germany; see also O. Connelly, *Napoleon's Satellite Kingdoms* (1965) (on Westphalia). G.S. Ford, *Stein and the Era of Reform in Prussia, 1807–15* (1922) remains the authoritative account of Prussia, but see also M. Gray, *Prussia in Transition: Society and Politics under the Stein Ministry of 1808* (1986), W.M. Simon, *The Failure of the Prussian Reform Movement, 1807–19* (1955), and R.C. Raack, *The Fall of Stein* (1965). The relevant parts of G.A. Craig, *The Politics of the Prussian Army, 1648–1948* (1955) are a very succinct view of the military and political reforms brought about by defeat in 1806. Dealing with a longer period is B. Simms, *The Struggle for Mastery in Germany, 1799–1830* (1998).

For Austria–Hungary: the opening sections of C.A. Macartney, *Habsburg Empire, 1790–1918* (1969) are a good introduction, but see too the important E. Wangerman, *From Joseph II to the Jacobin Trials* (1959) and the latter section of his *The Austrian Achievement, 1700–1800* (1973), as well as the older W.C. Langsam, *Napoleonic Wars and German Nationalism in Austria* (1930). For Hungary: see C.A. Macartney, *Hungary* (1934) and B.M. Kiraly, *Hungary in the Late Eighteenth Century* (1969). See also E.M. Link, *The Emancipation of the Austrian Peasant, 1740–1798* (1949). On the Tyrolean revolt, see F. Eyck, *Loyal Rebels: Andreas Hofer and the Tyrolean Uprising of 1809* (1988).

For the Low Countries: S. Schama, *Patriots and Liberators: Revolution in The Netherlands, 1780–1830* (1977) is now the standard work, replacing the massive older P.J. Blok, *History of the People of the Netherlands* (1898–1912); see also E.H. Kossman, *The Low Countries, 1780–1940* (1978) and his 'The crisis of the Dutch State, 1780–1813: nationalism, federalism, uniystidm', in J.S. Bromley and E.H. Kossman (eds), *Britain and the Netherlands, IV* (1971). See also A.C. Carter, *Neutrality or Commitment: The Evolution of Dutch Foreign Policy* (1975).

For Italy: M. Broers, *The Napoleonic Empire in Italy* (2004) and H. Hearder, *Italy in the Age of Risorgimento, 1790–1870* (1983); also J. Rath, *The Fall of the Napoleonic Kingdom of Italy* (1941) and the old R.M. Johnston, *The Napoleonic Empire in Southern Italy and the Rise of Secret Societies* (1904). O. Connelly, *Napoleon's Satellite Kingdoms* (1965) is also relevant. H. Cole, *The Betrayers* (1972) has material on the end of the Kingdom of Naples, while E.E.Y. Hales, *Napoleon and the Pope* (1962) details the relationship of Napoleon with Pius VII.

For Spain: R. Herr, *The Eighteenth Century Revolution in Spain* (1958) provides a background to Spanish developments and for the later period of Napoleonic Spain, C.J. Esdaile, *The Peninsular War: A New History* (2003), his *Fighting Napoleon: Guerrillas, Bandits, and Adventurers in Spain, 1800–1814* (2004) and *The Spanish Army in the Napoleonic Wars* (1989). See also G.H. Lovett, *Napoleon and the Birth of Modern Spain* (1965) and O. Connelly, *Napoleon's Satellite Kingdoms* (1965).

For Russia: see the relevant chapters of B. Pares, *A History of Russia* (1955), the early section of H. Seton-Watson, *The Russian Empire, 1801–1917* (1967), and the later parts of M. Raeff, *Imperial Russia, 1682–1825* (1971). On Alexander I, see A. Palmer, *Alexander I, Tsar of War and Peace* (1974) and A. McConnell, *Alexander I* (1970). On diplomatic relations between France and Russia, see H.A. Ragsdale, *Detente in the Napoleonic Era: Bonaparte and the Russians* (1980). For Poland: see *The Cambridge History of Poland, 1697–1935* (1941), N. Davies, *God's Playground: A History of Poland, vol. 1* (1981), and B. Grochulska, 'The place of the Enlightenment in Polish social history', in J.K. Fedorowicz, *A Republic of Nobles: Studies in Polish History to 1864* (1982).

On Napoleon's continental system, see E.F. Heckcher, *The Continental System: An Economic Interpretation* (1922) and the important article by Crouzet listed below. G. Ellis, *Napoleon's Continental Blockade* (1981) is an important modern study focusing on the effects of the system on Alsace. The wider effects upon the continent are considered in W.O. Henderson, *The Industrialisation of Europe, 1780–1914* (1969), R.E. Cameron, *France and the Economic Development of Europe 1800–1914* (1961), and A.S. Milward and S.B. Saul, *The Economic Development of Continental Europe, vol. I* (1973). The effects of the system on Britain are discussed in Emsley, *British Society* (see above) and W.F. Galpin, *The Grain Supply of England during the Napoleonic Wars* (1925).

There is a vast literature on the military aspects of the Napoleonic period. Serious studies of the development of warfare are G. Best, *War and Society in Revolutionary Europe, 1770–1870* (1982), G. Rothenberg, *The Art of Warfare in the Age of Napoleon* (1977), and D. Chandler, *The Campaigns of Napoleon* (1966). See also

J. Marshall-Cornwall, *Napoleon as Military Commander* (1967) and H.C.B. Rogers, *Napoleon's Army* (1974). More recent is C.J. Esdaile, *The Wars of Napoleon* (1995).

The naval war against Napoleon by Britain is discussed comprehensively in G.J. Marcus, *A Naval History of England*, 2 (1971); see also the classic Admiral Mahan, *The Influence of Sea Power upon the French Revolution and Empire* (1882). Britain's vital role in maintaining the wars by financial aid is discussed in J.M. Sherwig, *Guineas and Gunpowder: British Foreign Aid in the Wars with France, 1793–1815* (1969) and K.F. Helleiner, *The Imperial Loans, A Study in Financial and Diplomatic History* (1969).

The overall Napoleonic legacy has been reassessed in P.G. Dwyer, *Napoleon and Europe* (2001), but see also J. Sperber, *Revolutionary Europe* (above).

Articles

R.R. Palmer, 'Much in little: the Dutch revolution of 1795', *J.M.H.* (1954) examines one particular context of revolutionary influence; for others, see P.F. Sugar, 'The influence of the Enlightenment and the French Revolution in eighteenth century Hungary', *J.C.E.A.* (1958) and P. Body, 'The Hungarian Jacobin conspiracy of 1794–5', *J.C.E.A.* (1962). On Russia, see H. Schmitt, '1812: Stein, Alexander I and the crusade against Napoleon', *J.M.H.* (1959), I. Colhris, 'Variations on the theme of Napoleon's Moscow campaign,' *H.* (1976), H.A. Ragsdale, 'A continental system in 1801: Paul I and Bonaparte', *J.M.H.* (1970), and on the continental system, F. Crouzet, 'Wars, blockades, and economic change in Europe, 1792–1815', *J.M.H.* (1964). On Spain, see C. Esdaile, 'The Spanish guerillas and the Peninsular war', *H.T.* (1988). On the naval war with Britain, see P. Mackesy, 'Problems of an amphibious power: Britain against France, 1793–1815', *Naval War College Review* (1978).

6. THE CONGRESS OF VIENNA AND THE CONGRESS SYSTEM

The peace settlement at the end of the Napoleonic Wars represents one of the major arbitrations of European affairs in the modern period. The aims and objectives of the peacemakers and how they were fulfilled is an important theme. Traditionally, the peacemakers are condemned for failing to give sufficient weight to the forces of nationalism and liberalism, which produced major revisions of the settlement in the course of the nineteenth century, while still in some respects remaining the frame-work of European international relations until the First World War.

Essay topics

- What was attempted and on what principles by the framers of the peace treaties of 1814 and 1815?
- 'The strange thing is, not that the Congress System was finally abandoned, but that it and its work lasted for so long.' Discuss.
- What were Metternich's objectives?

Sources and documents

See *Autobiography of Prince Metternich, 1815–1829, 5 vols*, ed. A. Napier (1880–81). On one particular development, see R. Clogg (ed.), *The Movement for Greek Independence, 1770–1821* (1976).

Secondary works

For a brief introduction see T. Chapman, *The Congress of Vienna: Origins, Processes and Results* (1998). P. Schroeder, *The Transformation of European Politics, 1763–1848* (1994) puts the Congress in context, but C.K. Webster, *The Congress of Vienna* (1934) and *The European Alliance, 1815–1825* (1929) remain valuable. M. Broers, *Europe after Napoleon* (1995) is a modern general survey, but see too H. Kissinger, *A World Restored: Metternich, Castlereagh and the Problem of Peace, 1815–22* (1957). For the workings of the Congress see H. Nicolson, *The Congress of Vienna* (1946); a longer-term perspective is offered by E.V. Gulick, *Europe's Classical Balance of Power* (1955), L.C.B. Seaman, *From Vienna to Versailles* (1955), H.G. Schenk, *The Aftermath of the Napoleonic Wars* (1947), and F.R. Bridge and R. Bullen, *The Great Powers and the European States System, 1815–1914* (1981).

For the personalities involved, see C.K. Webster, *The Foreign Policy of Castlereagh, 1815–22* (1925), G. Ferraro, *Talleyrand and the Congress of Vienna* (1941), G. Mann, *Secretary of Europe: The Life of Friedrich Gentz* (1946). On Metternich, see A. Herman, *Metternich* (1932), A. Cecil, *Metternich, 1773–1859* (1947), Constantin de Grunwald, *Metternich* (1953), A. Palmer, *Metternich* (1972), and the older, standard biography, H. von Srbik, *Metternich* (1921–26); and, on Alexander I, A. Palmer, *Alexander I* (1974) and J.M. Hartley, *Alexander I* (1994).

Detailed studies of individual crises can be found in R. Carr, *Spain, 1808–1939* (1975) for the Spanish Revolution of 1820–22, E.H. Kossmann, *The Low Countries, 1780–1940* (1978) for the Belgian crisis of 1830, and H. Hearder, *Italy in the Age of the Risorgimento, 1790–1870* (1983) for Italian revolts in the period.

For Germany, see B. Simms, *The Struggle for Mastery in Germany, 1779–1830* (1998) and A. Ludtke, *Police and State in Prussia, 1815–1850* (1989). On the Habsburg monarchy, D.E. Emerson, *Metternich and the Political Police: Security and Subversion in the Habsburg Monarchy, 1815–1830* (1968). Poland is discussed generally in A.J. Prazmowska, *A History of Poland* (2004). See also *The Cambridge History of Poland, 1697–1935* (1941), H. Frankel, *Poland, the Struggle for Power, 1772–1939* (1946), and O. Halecki, *The History of Poland* (1942). More recent are P.S. Wandyck, *The Lands of Partitioned Poland, 1795–1910* (1975), R.F. Leslie, *Polish Politics and the Revolution of November 1830* (1956), and N. Davies, *God's Playground, vol. 2* (1981). J.A. Betley, *Belgium and Poland in International Relations, 1830–1* (1960) links up the two crises of those years. Austro–German relations are discussed in P.J. Katzenstein, *Disjoined Partners: Austria and Germany since 1815* (1976). For Greece, see the old C.W. Crawley, *The Question of Greek*

Independence, 1821–33 (1930) and D. Dakin, *The Greek Struggle for Independence, 1821–33* (1973).

Articles

On Metternich, see R.W. Seton-Watson, 'Metternich and Internal Austrian policy', *S.R.* (1939), P. Viereck, 'New views on Metternich', *R.P.* (1951), and R.A. Kann, 'Metternich: a reappraisal of his impact on international relations', *J.M.H.* (1960).

On Poland, see R.F. Leslie, 'Politics and economics in Congress Poland, 1815–64', *P.P.* (1955). On the Balkans, G.H. Bolsover, 'Nicholas I and the partition of Turkey', *S.E.E.R.* (1948).

7. FRANCE, 1815–51

The Restored Monarchy in France proved a more successful regime in the short term than might have been expected. But the divisions which remained from the revolutionary era and were to develop during the post-1815 period produced an unstable and difficult political situation. The accession of Charles X and his more reactionary policies provoked the revolution of 1830. A change of dynasty led to another period of seeming calm, only to be shattered by the revolutions of 1848. The nature of France's 'instability' and the role of the various political groupings within it raise important questions, particularly as France can be regarded as being in the forefront of many political developments. The underlying conservatism of the middle classes and the peasantry serve as a contrast to the ferment of ideas and the critical role of Paris in revolutionary politics. For France in 1848, see the topic bibliography on the revolutions of 1848.

Essay topics

- Was the restoration of the Bourbon monarchy doomed to failure?
- Who benefited from the French Revolution of 1830?
- Has the instability of France between 1815 and 1848 been exaggerated?

Sources and documents

Reactionary thought can be sampled in the writings of de Maistre in J.S. McClelland (ed.), *The French Right: From de Maistre to Maurras* (1970). A. de Tocqueville, *Recollections* (London edn, 1970) presents a compelling view of France in 1848, and on the last phase of this period see also R. Price, *1848 in France* (1975).

Secondary works

A. Cobban, *A History of Modern France, vol. 2* (1962–65), should now be supplemented by R. Tombs, *France, 1814–1914* (1996), A. Jardin and A.J. Tudesq,

Restoration and Reaction, 1815–1848 (1984), W. Fortescue, *Revolution and Counter-Revolution in France, 1815–1852* (1988). G. de Bertier de Sauvigny, *The Bourbon Restoration* (1955), F.B. Artz, *France under the Bourbon Restoration* (1931), and M.R.D. Leys, *Between Two Empires* (1955) remain useful. P. Mansel, *Louis XVIII* (1988) deals with the monarch, while the royalist 'revenge' is treated in G. Lewis, *The Second Vendée* (1978) and B. Fitzpatrick, *Catholic Royalism in the Department of the Gard, 1814–1852* (1983). The July Monarchy is considered in H.A.C. Collingham, *The July Monarchy: A Political History, 1830–1848* (1988).

On the ferment of ideas in post-revolutionary France, see F. Furet and M. Ozouf (eds), *The French Revolution and the Creation of Modern Political Culture, vol. 3: The Transformation of Political Culture, 1789–1848* (1989), J. Godechot, *The Counter-Revolution* (1961), P. Viereck, *Conservatism Revisited* (1965), and P. Pilbeam, *Republicanism in Nineteenth Century France* (1995); see also the older R.H. Soltau, *French Political Thought in the Nineteenth Century* (1931), J.P. Mayer, *Political Thought in France from the Revolution to the Fourth Republic* (1949), and J. Plamenatz, *The Revolutionary Movement in France, 1815–1871* (1952). M. Agulhon, *The Republic in the Village* (1982), E. Berenson, *Populist Religion and Left-wing Politics in France, 1830–1852* (1984), and P.F. Corcoran, *Before Marx: Socialism and Communism in France, 1830–1848* (1983) examine the left. The rise of new ideas about women is traced in M. Cross and T. Gray, *The Feminism of Flora Tristan* (1992). For particular institutions see D. Porch, *Army and Revolution: France, 1815–48* (1974) and C.H. Church, *Revolution and Red Tape: The French Ministerial Bureaucracy, 1770–1850* (1983).

For the 1830 Revolution, see D. Pinkney, *The French Revolution of 1830* (1973), P. Pilbeam, *The 1830 Revolution in France* (1991), and J. Merriman (ed.), *The 1830 Revolution in France* (1975), while for wider protest movements see C. Tilly, L. Tilly and R. Tilly, *The Rebellious Century* (1975) and R.J. Bezucha, *The Lyons Uprising of 1834* (1974).

Economic changes are discussed in W.O. Henderson, *The Industrialisation of Europe, 1780–1914* (1969), R.C. Cameron, *France and the Economic Development of Europe* (1961), A.S. Milward and S.B. Saul, *The Economic Development of Continental Europe* (1973), and R. Price, *The Economic Development of France* (1975) and his *A Social History of Nineteenth Century France* (1987).

On 1848 in France, see the commentary in R. Price, cited above, and his *The Second French Republic* (1972); also P.N. Stearns, *The Revolutions of 1848* (1974).

Articles

On post-Restoration conditions, see G. Lewis, 'The white terror of 1815 in the Department of the Gard', *P.P.* (1973), D. Higgs, 'Politics and landownership among the French nobility after the Revolution', *E.S.R.* (1971), N.G. Hudson, 'The circulation of the Ultra-Royalist press under the French Restoration', *E.H.R.* (1974), and L. O'Boyle, 'The problem of an excess of educated men in Western Europe, 1800–1850', *J.M.H.* (1970). On the 1830 revolution, see R.D. Price, 'The French army and the Revolution of 1830', *E.S.R.* (1973), D.H. Pinkney, 'The crowd in the French Revolution of 1830', *A.H.R.* (1964), E.L. Newman, 'The blouse and the frock coat', *J.M.H.* (1974), and R.D. Price, 'Legitimist opposition to the Revolution of 1830 in the French provinces', *H.J.* (1974). For the fall of the Orléanist monarchy, see P.L.R. Higonnet and T.B. Higonnet, 'Class corruption and politics in the French Chamber of Deputies, 1846–48', *F.H.S.* (1967), G. Fasel, 'Urban workers in provincial France, February–June 1848', *I.R.S.H.* (1972), and 'The wrong revolution: French Republicanism in 1848', *F.H.S.* (1974).

8. RUSSIA, 1801–56

The French Revolution and the death of Catherine the Great marked a new era in Russian history. The troubled reign of Paul I was followed by the accession of Alexander I, a Tsar whose contradictions have fascinated historians. Ostensibly liberal, he led Russia through the Napoleonic conflict and earned her a major place as an arbiter of European politics. His increasing conservatism, however, combined with the rise of an intelligentsia and the continuing backwardness of Russian society, produced conflict. The 'Decembrist' Revolt of 1825 marked the beginning of a long campaign against autocracy by intellectuals and others. The reign of Nicholas I marked an attempt to entrench Russia's own distinctive conservatism against the intellectual and social currents which were at work in the rest of Europe. The exposure of Russia's weaknesses in the Crimean War and the death of Nicholas I set the scene for new developments under Alexander II.

Essay topics

- Why did Alexander I fail to liberalize Russia?
- What was the significance of the Decembrist revolt for the development of a revolutionary movement in Russia?
- Did Nicholas I bequeath more problems to Russia than he inherited?

Sources and documents

See A. Herzen, *My Past and Thoughts: The Memoirs of Alexander Herzen* (6 vols, 1924–28). In a great age of Russian literature, M. Lermentov, *A Hero of Our Times* (1840), N. Gogol's *The Government Inspector* (1836), and *Dead Souls* (1842) give something of the flavour of the period.

Secondary sources

Consult the older general histories by B. Pares, *A History of Russia* (3rd edn, 1955) and H. Seton-Watson, *The Russian Empire, 1801–1917* (1967). A more recent work is D. Saunders, *Russia in the Age of Reaction and Reform, 1801–1881* (1992).

For Alexander I, see A. Palmer, *Alexander I, Tsar of War and Peace* (1974), T.M. Hartley, *Alexander I* (1994), and A. McConnell, *Tsar Alexander I* (1970). M. Raeff,

M. Speransky: Statesman of Imperial Russia, 1722–1839 (1957) deals with one of the most important figures of the period, while S. Monas, *The Third Section: Police and Society in Russia under Alexander I* (1961) looks at the repressive side of the regime. See also M. Jenkins, *Arakcheev: Grand Vizier of the Russian Empire* (1969), J.S. Curtiss, *The Russian Army under Nicholas I, 1825–55* (1965), and J. Keep. *Soldiers of the Tsar: Army and Society in Russia, 1462–1874* (1989). For Nicholas I, see W. Bruce Lincoln, *Nicholas I* (1978).

On the serf question, see J. Blum, *Lord and Peasant in Imperial Russia* (1961) and G.T. Robinson, *Rural Russia under the Old Regime* (1932).

For the opposition to the autocracy, see A.G. Mazour, *The First Russian Revolution, 1825* (1937), M. Zetlin, *The Decembrists* (1958), and M. Raeff, *The Decembrist Movement* (1966). For a wider perspective, see F. Venturi, *Roots of Revolution* (1960), J. Walkin, *The Rise of Democracy in Pre-revolutionary Russia* (1963), and M. Raeff, *The Growth of the Russian Intelligentsia* (1966). E.H. Carr, *The Romantic Exiles* (new edn, 1949) describes various revolutionaries in exile. On individuals, see E.H. Carr, *Michael Bakunin* (1937) and E. Acton, *Alexander Herzen and the Role of the Intellectual Revolutionary* (1979).

Russia's involvement with other nationalities is discussed in P.S. Wandycz, *The Lands of Partitioned Poland, 1793–1910* (1974), E.C. Thadden, *Russia's Western Borderlands, 1710–1870* (1984), and there is useful material in R. Pearson, *National Minorities in Eastern Europe, 1848–1944* (1983). Foreign policy is examined in G.H. Bolsover, 'Aspects of Russian policy, 1815–1914', in R. Pares and A.J.P. Taylor (eds), *Essays Presented to Sir Lewis Namier* (1956).

Articles

G. Vernadsky, 'Alexander I's reforms', *R.P.* (1947), W.M. Pinter, 'The social characteristics of the early nineteenth century Russian bureaucracy', *S.R.* (1970), and R. Pipes, 'The Russian military colonies 1810–31', *J.M.H.* (1950).

9. LIBERALISM, NATIONALISM, SOCIALISM AND FEMINISM IN THE NINETEENTH CENTURY

Many of the political developments of the nineteenth century are only comprehensible in terms of the ferment of ideas released by the French Revolution and the Napoleonic struggle. Generally, these are best understood in terms of the three main themes of liberalism, nationalism, and socialism which were often simultaneously represented in some of the great upheavals of the period. The relative importance of the different forces and the way in which they interrelated and developed during the nineteenth century and into the twentieth century require examination. Liberalism and nationalism are not easy to define with precision, while socialist, including communist, ideas took many different forms. The feminist movement also developed in the revolutionary era and has attracted growing attention.

Essay topics

- Assess the strength of liberalism and nationalism in Europe by 1848.
- Had liberalism or nationalism proved the stronger force in Europe by 1900?
- To what extent did socialism represent a coherent body of principles and practice by 1900?
- How far had European feminism developed by 1914?

Sources and documents

The major texts of the principal intellectual figures should obviously play an important part. For liberalism, see. J. Stuart Mill, *On Liberty* (1859), A. de Tocqueville, *Democracy in America* (1835), F. Guizot, *On Democracy in France* (1849), and H.S. Reiss (ed.), *Political Thought of the German Romantics* (1955). Also useful are the readings in E.K. Bramsted and K.J. Melhuish (eds), *Western Liberalism: A History in Documents from Locke to Croce* (1978).

For different socialist movements, see R. Owen, *Report to the County of Lanark* (1817), K. Marx and F. Engels, *The Communist Manifesto* (1848), and P.A. Kropotkin, *Fields, Factories, Workshops* (1899).

For feminism, see bibliography in G. Fraisse and M. Perrot (eds), *Emerging Feminism from Revolution to World War* (1993), which contains a useful guide to sources.

Secondary works

Of the general works E.J. Hobsbawm, *The Age of Revolution, 1789–1848* (1962) gives considerable space to the intellectual movements. See also J. Bowle, *Politics and Opinion in the Nineteenth Century* (1954).

On liberalism, there is a useful short introduction in I. Collins, *Liberalism in Nineteenth Century Europe* (Historical Association pamphlet, 1971) and see her *Revolutionaries in Europe, 1815–48* (Historical Association pamphlet, 1974). The older H.J. Laski, *The Rise of European Liberalism* (2nd edn, 1947) and Guido de Ruggiero, *The History of European Liberalism* (trans., 1927) can now be supplemented by J.J. Sheehan, *German Liberalism in the Nineteenth Century* (1982), a useful case study. Particular studies of relevance are S. Holmes, *Benjamin Constant: The Making of Modern Liberalism* (1984), J. Plamenatz, *The Revolutionary Movement in France, 1813–71* (1952), M. Raeff, *The Rise of the Russian Intelligentsia* (1966), and Sir Lewis Namier, *1848: The Revolution of the Intellectuals* (1944).

On nationalism see E.J. Hobsbawm, *Nations and Nationalism since 1780* (1990), E. Gellner, *Nations and Nationalism* (1983), C.J. Hayes, *Nationalism* (1966), E. Kedourie, *Nationalism* (1960), and H. Kohn, *Nationalism: Its Meaning and History* (1971). Liberalism's relationship with nationalism is discussed in one context in R. Hinton Thomas, *Liberalism, Nationalism, and the German Intellectuals, 1822–47* (1952). On Eastern European nationalism, see P. Sugar and I. Lederer, *Nationalism in*

Eastern Europe (1969), R. Pearson, *National Minorities in Eastern Europe, 1848–1944* (1983), and R.F. Leslie, *Polish Politics and the Revolution of 1830* (1974). For a brilliant case study of the consolidation of national identity, see E. Weber, *Peasants into Frenchmen* (1976) and on Germany, see A. Green, *Fatherlands: State Building and Nationhood in Nineteenth Century Germany* (2001).

On the socialist movements in general, see D. Geary, *Labour and Socialist Movements before 1914* (1989), G.D.H. Cole, *A History of Socialist Thought* (1953–60), D. McClelland, *Marx* (1974), G. Woodcock, *Anarchism* (1963), and J. Joll, *The Anarchists* (1969). On labour movements, see H. Pelling, *A History of British Trade Unionism* (rev. edn, 1986), H. Grebing, *A History of the German Labour Movement* (1969), B. Pimlott and C. Cook (eds), *Trade Unions in British Politics: The First 250 Years* (2nd edn, 1991), J. Breuilly, *Labour and Liberalism in Nineteenth Century Europe* (1992), dealing with Britain and Germany, R. Hostetter, *The Italian Socialist Movement, vol. I, Origins* (1958), M. Bookchin, *The Spanish Anarchists* (1977), T. Kaplan, *Anarchists of Andalusia, 1868–1903* (1977), V.T. Lidtke, *The Outlawed Party: Social Democracy in Germany, 1878–1890* (1966) and *The Alternative Culture: Socialist Labour in Imperial Germany* (1990); see also W.L. Guttsman, *The German Social Democratic Party, 1875–1933* (1981). On France, see R. Magraw, *A History of the French Working Class* (1992).

On feminism, see J. Rendall, *The Origins of Modern Feminism: Women in Britain, France and the United States, 1780–1860* (1985), B.G. Smith, *Changing Lives: Women in European History since 1700* (1989), R.J. Evans, *The Feminists: Women's Emancipation Movements in Europe, America and Australasia, 1840–1920* (1977), and G. Duby and M. Perrot (eds), *A History of Women in the West, vol. IV: Emerging Feminism from the Revolution to The First World War* (1993). Covering a narrower period is R. Fuchs and V. E. Thompson, *Women in Nineteenth Century Europe* (2004). On women's role in the enlightenment, see B. Taylor, *Women, Gender and Enlightenment* (2004) and in the economy, see D. Siminton, *A History of European Women's Work: 1700 to the Present* (1998). On France, see S.K. Foley, *Women in France since 1804: Gender, Politics, and Cultural Change* (2004) and, for later, P. K. Bidelman, *Pariahs Stand Up! The Founding of the Liberal Feminist Movement in France, 1880–1914* (1982), Charles Sowerine, *Sisters or Citizens? Women and Socialism in France since 1876* (1982), P. Hilden, *Working Women and Socialist Politics in France, 1880–1914* (1986), S. Hause and A.R. Kenney, *Women's Suffrage and Social Politics in the French Third Republic* (1984), and two biographies of French suffrage campaigners, S. Hause, *Hubertine Auclert: The French Suffragette* (1987) and F. Gordon, *The Integral Feminist: Madeleine Pelletier, 1874–1939* (1990). For Germany, see U. Frevert, *Women in German History: From Bourgeois Emancipation to Sexual Liberation* (1989), A. Taylor Allen, *Feminism and Motherhood in Germany, 1800–1914* (1991), and J.H. Quataert, *Reluctant Feminists in German Social Democracy, 1885–1917* (1979). For Russia, see R. Stites, *The Women's Liberation Movement in Russia: Feminism, Nihilism and Bolshevism, 1860–1930* (1978), L. Edmondson, *Feminism in Russia, 1900–1917* (1984), R.L. Glickman, *Russian Factory Women:*

Workplace and Society, 1880–1914 (1984), and W. Wagner, 'The Trojan Mare: women's rights and civil rights in late Imperial Russia', in O. Crisp (ed.), *Civil Rights in Imperial Russia* (1989).

10. THE REVOLUTIONS OF 1848

1848 was a year of widespread protest, rebellion and revolution in Europe, probably more widespread than at any time in the modern period. The varying causes of these revolts – economic, social, political and intellectual – need to be considered. The causes and background to the unrest in the different parts of Europe form one major theme, as well as the actual course of events. The reasons why the revolts largely failed in the short term, and their contribution to later events, form another. The revolutions can be studied as a whole or through the experience of individual countries.

Essay topics

- Why was 1848 a year of revolutions in Europe?
- To what extent could the events of 1848 be described as a 'revolution of the intellectuals'?
- Did the revolutions of 1848 fail?

Sources and documents

On events in France over the period 1848–51, see R. Price (ed.), *1848 in France* (1975) for a wide selection of documents. Also invaluable is A. de Tocqueville's *Recollections* (trans. edn, 1970). For a short general collection, see P. Jones, *1848 Revolutions* (1982).

Secondary works

For the broad context of the revolutions of 1848 it is wise to consult the general texts cited in the introduction. See especially I. Collins, *The Age of Progress 1789–1870* (1964), E.J. Hobsbawm, *The Age of Revolution, 1789–1848* (1962), and J. Roberts, *Revolution and Improvement* (1976).

General histories of the revolts include P.N. Stearns, *The Revolutions of 1848* (1974), J. Sigmann, *1848, the Romantic and Democratic Revolutions in Europe* (1973), R. Price, *The Revolutions of 1848* (1989), J. Sperber, *The European Revolutions, 1848–1851* (1994), F. Fejto, *The Opening of an Era: 1848* (1948), P. Robertson, *Revolution of 1848: A Social History* (1952), A. Whitridge, *Men in Crisis: The Revolutions of 1848* (1949), and L.B. Namier, *1848: The Revolution of the Intellectuals* (1944).

On the background to the revolts, see I. Collins, *Revolutionaries in Europe, 1815–48* (Historical Association, 1974), C. Morazé, *The Triumph of the Middle Classes* (1968),

J. Plamenatz, *The Revolutionary Movement in France, 1815–71* (1952), R. Hinton Thomas, *Liberalism, Nationalism and the German Intellectuals, 1822–47* (1952), and E. Kamenka and F.B. Smith (eds), *Intellectuals and Revolution* (1979). C. Tilly, L. Tilly and R. Tilly, *The Rebellious Century, 1830–1930* (1975) is an attempt to trace the pattern of collective violence in France, Germany and Italy in this period.

For France, see the major national histories, notably R. Tombs, *France, 1814–1914* (1996), A. Jardin and A.-J. Tudesq, *Restoration and Reaction 1815–1848* (1984) and M. Agulhon, *The Republican Experiment* (1983). R. Price, *The Second French Republic: A Social History* (1972) and his collection, *Revolution and Reaction: 1848 and the Second French Republic* (1975) are helpful; see also P. Amann, *Revolution and Mass Democracy: The Paris Club Movement in 1848* (1975), J. Merriman, *The Agony of the Republic: The Repression of the Left in Revolutionary France, 1848–51* (1978), and G. Rudé, *The Crowd in History* (1964), ch. 11. For Germany, see R. Stademann, *Social and Political History of the German 1848 Revolution* (1975), L.B. Namier, T*he Revolution of the Intellectuals* (1944), J. Sperber, *Rhineland Radicals: The Democratic Movement and the Revolution of 1848–1849* (1991), W. Carr, *The Origins of the Wars of German Unification* (1991), L. Krieger (ed.), *The German Revolutions* (1967), E. Eyck, *The Frankfurt Parliament 1848–1849* (1968), W. Siemann, *The German Revolution of 1848–9* (trans. edn, 1998), and H.J. Hahn, *The 1848 Revolution in German-speaking Europe* (2001). See too P. Noyes, *Organisations and Revolt* (1966), H. Grebing, *History of the German Labour Movement* (1969), and J. Kucynski, *A Short History of Labour Conditions, 1800–1945* (1942–46). On Austria–Hungary, see R.A. Kann, *The Multi-National Empire: Nationalism and National Reform in the Habsburg Monarchy, 1848–1918* (1950), C.A. Macartney, *Hungary* (1934), J. Blum, *Noble Landowners and Agriculture in Austria, 1815–1848* (1948), R.J. Rath, *The Viennese Revolution of 1848* (1969), P.J. Katzenstein, *Disjoined Partners: Austria and Germany since 1815* (1976), A. Sked, *The Survival of the Habsburg Empire: Radetsky, the Imperial Army and the Class War, 1848* (1979), and I. Deak, *The Lawful Revolution: Kossuth and the Hungarian Revolution, 1848–49* (1979). On Italy, see D. Mack Smith, *The Making of Italy, 1796–1866* (1969) and H. Hearder, *Italy in the Age of the Risorgimento, 1790–1870* (1983). The older G.F.H. Berkeley and J. Berkeley, *Italy in the Making, 1846–1848* (1936) and *Italy in the Making, 1848* (1940) are still useful, but see also A. Sked, *The Survival of the Habsburg Empire* (above) and P. Ginsborg, *Daniele Manin and the Venetian Revolution of 1848–9* (1979).

For the survival of the European order after 1848, see W.E. Mosse, *Liberal Europe: The Age of Bourgeois Realism, 1848–75* (1974), E.J. Hobsbawm, *The Age of Capital, 1848–75* (1975), and J. Blum, *The End of the Old Order in Rural Europe* (1978).

Articles

For a review of recent writing, see D.J. Mattheisen, 'History as current events: recent works on the German Revolution of 1848', *A.H.R.* (1983). For central Europe, see

C.A. Macartney, '1848 in the Habsburg Monarchy', *E.S.R.* (1977) and R.J. Rath, 'Public opinion during the Viennese Revolution of 1848', *J.C.E.A.* (1948–49). On Italy, see P. Ginsborg, 'Peasants and revolutionaries in Venice and the Veneto, 1848', *H.J.* (1974), L. Jennings, 'Lamartine's Italian policy in 1848', *J.M.H.* (1970), R.J. Rath, 'The Carbonari: their origins, initiation rites and aims', *A.H.R.* (1964), and H. Hearder, 'The making of the Roman Republic, 1848–9', *H.* (1975). On Germany, see L. O'Boyle, 'The democratic left in Germany, 1848', *J.M.H.* (1961), E. Hahn, 'German parliamentary and national aims, 1848–9', *C.E.H.* (1980), and T. Hamerow, 'The German Artisan Movement', *J.C.E.A.* (1961). For other parts of Europe, see J. Krnjevic, 'The Croats in 1848', *S.E.E.R.* (1948) and C.E. Black, 'Poznan and Europe in 1848', *J.C.E.A.* (1948).

11. THE ECONOMIC DEVELOPMENT OF EUROPE, 1760–1914

As with the intellectual developments examined earlier, much of European history in this period can only be understood against the background of the development of agriculture, commerce and industry from the late eighteenth century. The reasons why some countries enjoyed economic advance while others stagnated is an important question, often focused around the issue of why other countries were not able to industrialize at the same time as Britain. Such questions imply a knowledge of how economic growth and industrialization occur, by no means a matter of agreement among economic historians (see Kemp, below). Some knowledge of the experience of Great Britain is inevitably useful in this context as the yardstick by which other economies are measured, though Britain's particular version of economic growth should not be allowed to dominate analysis of why, how, and in what forms, economic development occurred. The character of industrial development in continental Europe by 1914 and its social and political repercussions is another aspect to be explored.

Essay topics

- 'For most Europeans in the century after 1760 by far the most important economic developments lay in trade and agriculture.' Discuss.
- Why was Great Britain able to become the leading industrial power in Europe by 1850?
- Who had gained and who had lost by the industrial development of Europe by 1914?

Sources and documents

There are useful documents in S. Pollard and C. Holmes (eds), *Documents of European Economic History* (3 vols, 1968–73) and B. Supple, *The Experience of Economic Growth* (1963). Vital works for the spread of ideas about economic development are A. Smith, *The Wealth of Nations* (1776) and F. Engels, *The Condition of the English Working Class in 1844* (1892). Amidst a wealth of 'social' literature, see especially, E. Zola, *Germinal* (1885).

Secondary works

C.M. Cipolla (ed.), *The Fontana Economic History of Europe*, vols 3 and 4 (1973) offers a wide-ranging analysis of economic development both in individual countries and for European-wide themes. For the commercial development of the period, see R.C. Davies, *The Rise of the Atlantic Economies* (1973) and P. Curtin, *The Atlantic Slave Trade* (1969). For agriculture, see B.H. Slicher van Bath, *The Agrarian History of Western Europe* (1963) and M. Tracey, *Agriculture in Western Europe* (1964).

The industrialization of Europe is discussed in M. Teich and R. Porter (eds), *The Industrial Revolution in National Context* (1996), T. Kemp, *Industrialisation in Nineteenth-century Europe* (1969), but see also A. Milward and S.B. Saul, *The Economic Development of Continental Europe, 1780–1870* (1973), C. Trebilcock, *The Industrialisation of the Continental Powers, 1780–1914* (1981), H.J. Habakkuk and M. Postan (eds), *The Cambridge Economic History of Europe, The Industrial Revolution and After, Vol. VI, pt. II* (1965), W.O. Henderson, *The Industrial Revolution on the Continent* (1961), and J.H. Clapham, *The Economic Development of France and Germany* (4th edn, 1936). The financial aspects of the industrial revolution are also considered in W.O. Henderson, *Britain and Industrial Europe, 1750–1870* (2nd edn, 1966), H. Feis, *Europe the World's Banker* (1930), and W. Ashworth, *A Short History of the International Economy since 1850* (4th edn, 1987). A wide-ranging perspective is J. Goodman and K. Honeyman, *Gainful Pursuits: The Making of Industrial Europe, 1600–1914* (1988).

On individual countries, see for Great Britain as an introduction, R.M. Hartwell, *The Industrial Revolution in England* (Historical Association, rev. edn, 1966) and M.W. Flinn, *The Origins of the Industrial Revolution* (1966). The standard modern works are P. Mathias, *The First Industrial Nation, an Economic History of Britain, 1700–1914* (1969) and R. Floud and D. McClosky (eds), *The Economic History of Britain since 1700* (2 vols, 1981). The older treatments, P. Mantoux, *The Industrial Revolution in the Eighteenth Century* (1928) and T.S. Ashton, *The Industrial Revolution, 1760–1830* (1948) are also still valuable.

For France, see R. Price, *The Economic Modernisation of France* (1975) and J.H. Clapham (1936, above). The most useful comparison of France and England appears in P. Crouzet, 'England and France in the eighteenth century, a comparative analysis of two economic growths', in R.M. Hartwell (ed.), *The Causes of the Industrial Revolution in England* (1967). See also A.L. Dunham, *The Industrial Revolution in France, 1815–1848* (1955). For Germany, see Clapham (1936, above) and T.S. Hamerow, *Restoration, Revolution, Reaction* (1966).

For other countries, see M. Falkus, *The Industrialisation of Russia* (1972), J. Blum, *Lord and Peasant in Imperial Russia* (1961), G.T. Robinson, *Rural Russia under the Old Regime* (1932), and R. Pipes, *Russia under the Old Regime* (1974). For southern Europe, see S.B. Clough, *Economic History of Modern Italy* (1964),

J. Vicens Vives, *Economic History of Spain* (1969), A.R. Oliveira, *Politics, Economics and Men of Modern Spain, 1808–1946* (1946), and C. la Force, *The Development of the Spanish Textile Industry, 1750–1850* (1965).

The broader consequences of industrialization can be traced in E.J. Hobsbawm, *The Age of Revolution* (1962), C. Morazé, *The Triumph of the Middle Classes* (1966), and M.D. Biddiss, *The Age of the Masses* (1977). The survival of the old order is discussed in J. Blum, *The End of the Old Order in Rural Europe* (1978) and A. Mayer, *The Persistence of the Old Regime* (1981).

Urban and social consequences are discussed in A. Weber, *The Growth of Cities in the Nineteenth Century* (1899), H.J. Dyos and M. Wolff (eds), *The Victorian City: Images and Realities* (1973), A. Briggs, *Victorian Cities* (1965) and L. Chevalier, *Labouring Classes and Dangerous Classes in Paris during the first half of the Nineteenth Century* (1973). For urban protest, see C. Tilly, L. Tilly and R. Tilly, *The Rebellious Century, 1830–1930* (1975) and G. Rudé, *The Crowd in History* (1964).

Articles

On French industrial performance, see S.B. Clough, 'Retardative factors in French economic growth', *J.Ec.H.* (1949), R.C. Cameron, 'Economic growth and stagnation in France', *J.M.H.* (1958), and T. Kemp, 'Structural factors in the retardation of French economic growth', *Kylos* (1962). For Belgium, see S. Clark, 'Nobility, bourgeoisie and the industrial revolution in Belgium', *P.P.* (1984) and on Russia, A. Baykov, 'The economic development of Russia', *Ec.H.R.* (1954–55) and H.J. Ellison, 'Economic modernisation in Imperial Russia', *J.Ec.H.* (1965). For southern Europe, see S.B. Clough and C. Livi, 'Economic growth in Italy', *J.Ec.H.* (1956).

12. THE RISORGIMENTO AND ITALIAN UNIFICATION

The Italian struggle for independence from foreign control and for a united, liberal state was one of the major alterations to the settlement of Europe reached in 1815. Failed revolts, principally in 1820 and 1848, did eventually make way for the successful unification of Italy. The role of the leading personalities and of the differing ideologies at work in the movement have to be considered, as well as the reasons why unification actually occurred when previous attempts had failed. The place of the movement in contemporary European diplomacy must be considered, as well as the weaknesses which the new Italian State inherited.

Essay topics

- What was the Risorgimento?
- Why was Italian unification not achieved earlier?
- What weaknesses were inherited by united Italy?

Sources and documents

J. Mazzini, *Duties of Man* (1877) is an example of some of the forces at work in Italy during this period; see too the documents in D. Beales, *The Risorgimento and the Unification of Italy* (1982).

Secondary sources

There are introductions in M. Clark, *The Italian Risorgimento* (1998), D. Beales and E. Biagini, *The Risorgimento and the Unification of Italy* (2nd edn, 2002), S.J. Woolf, *The Italian Risorgimento* (1969), and A. Ramm, *The Risorgimento* (Historical Association pamphlet, 1972). The standard histories by D. Mack Smith, *Italy: A Modern History* (1959) and *The Making of Italy, 1796–1870* (1968) should be consulted; see too D. Mack Smith, 'Italy', in the *New Cambridge Modern History,* vol. X (1960) and R. Albrecht-Carrié, *Italy from Napoleon to Mussolini* (1950). A more recent addition is H. Hearder, *Italy in the Age of the Risorgimento, 1790–1870* (1983) and F. Coppa, *The Italian Wars of Independence* (1992). On the leading personalities, see D. Mack Smith, *Cavour and Garibaldi in 1860* (1954), *Garibaldi* (1957) and his *Victor Emmanuel, Cavour and the Risorgimento* (1971). Older, but still useful are A.J. Whyte, *The Early Life and Letters of Cavour, 1810–1848* (1925) and *The Political Life and Letters of Cavour, 1848–1861* (1930). G.M. Trevelyan's trilogy, *Garibaldi's Defence of the Roman Republic* (1908), *Garibaldi and the Thousand* (1909), and *Garibaldi and the Making of Italy* (1911) remain useful. There is a brief account of Cavour's career in H. Hearder, *Cavour* (Historical Association pamphlet, 1972). For Mazzini, see D. Mack Smith, *Mazzini* (1991), G.O. Griffith, *Mazzini, Prophet of Modern Europe* (1932), G. Salvemini, *Mazzini* (1985), and E.E.Y. Hales, *Mazzini and the Secret Societies* (1956). For the role of the Church, see E.E.Y. Hales, *Pio Nono* (1954) and A.C. Jemolo, *Church and State in Italy, 1850–1950* (1960). R. Grew, *A Sterner Plan for Italian Unity* (1963) examines the part played by the liberal pressure group, the National Society.

The economic context is examined in L. Cafagna, 'Italy, 1830–1914', in C.M. Cipolla (ed.), *The Fontana Economic History of Europe, vol. 4* (1973), S.B. Clough, *Economic History of Modern Italy* (1964), and the southern problem in G. Schacter, *The Italian South* (1965).

Articles

D. Mack Smith, 'Cavour's attitude to Garibaldi's expedition to Sicily', *C.H.J.* (1949), H.M. Smyth, 'The armistice of Novara: a legend of a liberal king', *J.M.H.* (1935), and R. Grew, 'How success spoiled the Risorgimento', *J.M.H.* (1962) are useful.

13. FRANCE, 1848–71

The events of 1848 provoked a period of governmental instability in France in which a second French Republic was founded only to fall with the *coup d'état* of Louis Napoleon. Napoleon III's 'Second Empire' represents an enigmatic era in which initial dictatorship and repression gradually gave way to a more liberal regime. Napoleon's achievements, such as the rebuilding of Paris, his genuinely philanthropic impulses, and the glittering façade of Parisian society in this period, were overshadowed by disasters abroad, as in Mexico, internal disagreement about the status and legitimacy of the regime, and humiliating defeat by Prussia. Whether Napoleon's regime could have transformed itself into a constitutional monarchy had the Franco–Prussian War not intervened and how far the Commune was a representative verdict on the epoch are frequent questions. In spite of a commonly perceived chronic political instability, French society and administration had many strengths, paving the way for the era of the Third Republic.

Essay topics

* Was the Second French Republic doomed to failure?
* Could the Liberal Empire have succeeded in uniting France under Napoleon III?

Sources and documents

For 1848 and its aftermath, see R. Price, *1848 in France* (1975). S. Osgood, *Napoleon III and the Second Empire* (1973) is also useful. For some contemporary comment, see W. Bagehot, 'Letters on the French coup d'état of 1851' and 'Caesarism as it existed in 1865', in *Collected Letters and Essays* (1871).

Secondary works

The standard histories such as R. Tombs, *France, 1814–1914* (1996), A. Cobban, *A History of Modern France, 1715–1945* (3 vols, 1961–65), and J.P.T. Bury, *France, 1815–1940* (1949) give good general coverage. R. Price, *The Second French Republic* (1972) and *The Second Empire: An Anatomy of Political Power* (2001) fully examine how Napoleon III came to power and exercised it, as do M. Agulhon, *The Republican Experiment, 1848–1852* (1983) and A. Plessis, *The Rise and Fall of the Second Empire, 1852–1871* (trans. edn, 1985); but see also J. Macmillan, *Napoleon III* (1991) and W.H.C. Smith, *Napoleon III* (1972). Also still valuable are J.M. Thompson, *Louis Napoleon and the Second Empire* (1954) and H.A.L. Fisher, *Bonapartism* (1908). T. Zeldin, *The Political System of Napoleon III* (1958) is an invaluable insight into political life under Louis Napoleon, while his *Emile Ollivier and the Liberal Empire* (1963) deals with the later part of his reign, T.A.B. Corley, *Democratic Despot* (1961) is a useful biography. On the political undercurrents in French society, see J. Plamenatz, *The Revolutionary Movement in France, 1815–1871* (1952), J.P. Mayer, *Political Thought in France from the Revolution to the Fourth Republic* (1949), and R.H. Soltau, *French Political Thought in the Nineteenth Century* (1931). On Napoleon's foreign policy, see A.J.P. Taylor, *The Struggle for Mastery in Europe, 1848–1918* (1954) and, more specifically, D. Dawson, *The Mexican Adventure* (1935).

For Paris under the Empire, see D.H. Pickney, *Napoleon III and the Rebuilding of Paris* (1958) and H. Sealman, *Paris Transformed* (1971). Much of the texture of

French society in the period is conveyed by T. Zeldin's multi-volumed work, *France, 1848–1945* (1973–78), while his *Conflicts in French Society* (1970) also contains important essays. M. Howard, *The Franco–Prussian War* (1961) examines the conduct of the war which ended the Second Empire.

Articles

T. Zeldin, 'The myth of Napoleon III', *H.T.* (1958).

14. EUROPEAN EXPANSION OVERSEAS

A huge topic, which can be broken down into three main phases. The early European empires of the late eighteenth and the first half of the nineteenth centuries were often the legacy of even earlier colonial conquest and have an important bearing upon the economic expansion of Europe. The reasons for the 'new imperialism' of the late nineteenth and early twentieth centuries, which saw a vast extension of European (and North American) influence over the rest of the world, are a source of major debate, especially the question of the extent to which European colonization was the result of political, economic or social pressures from within Europe. The process of decolonization and its repercussions for European States is now much more fully covered.

Essay topics

- 'Millstones around our necks.' To what extent did Europe's colonies bear out this description between 1760 and 1870?
- Why was there a 'scramble' for colonies by the European powers in the later part of the nineteenth century?
- Was imperialism the 'highest stage of capitalism'?
- Why did the European powers decolonize so rapidly after 1945?

Sources and documents

For the earliest phase see M. Chamberlain, *Longman Companion to the Formation of the European Empires, 1488–1920* (2000). M.M. Wright (ed.), *The New Imperialism* (1961) and P.W. Winks (ed.), *British Imperialism: Gold, God, Glory* (1966) look at the later period. J.A. Hobson, *Imperialism: A Study* (1902) and V.I. Lenin, *Imperialism, The Highest Stage of Capitalism* (1917) are two important texts, emphasizing the economic theory of imperialism. D.K. Fieldhouse, *The Theory of Capitalist Imperialism* (1967) has texts with introductions.

Secondary sources

For the earlier phase of empire, see R. Davies, *The Rise of the Atlantic Economies* (1973), P. Curtin, *The Atlantic Slave Trade* (1969), V.T. Harlow, *The Founding of the*

Second British Empire, 1763–93 (1952) and C.A. Bayly, *The Birth of the Modern World* (2004). For other countries, see H.I. Priestley, *France Overseas through the Ancien Regime* (1939) and *France Overseas, a Study of Modern Imperialism* (1966), W.A. Roberts, *The French in the West Indies* (1942), G.M. Wrong, *The Rise and Fall of New France* (1928), G.S. Graham, *Empire of the North Atlantic* (1950), H.H. Dodwell, *Dupleix and Clive* (1920), J.H. Parry, *Trade and Dominion* (1971), G. Williams, *The Expansion of Europe in the Eighteenth Century* (1966), J.H. Parry, *The Spanish Seaborne Empire* (2nd edn, 1967), and C.R. Boxer, *The Portuguese Seaborne Empire* (1969) and *The Dutch Seaborne Empire* (1965).

For the earliest 'independence' struggles, see I.R. Christie, *Crisis of Empire: Great Britain and the American Colonies, 1754–1783* (1966) as a brief introduction to Britain's American crisis. Spain's is discussed in W.S. Robertson, *Rise of the Latin American Republics* (1965), J.H. Lynch, *The Spanish American Revolution* (1973), T. Anna, *Spain and the Loss of America* (1983), and more generally in R. Carr, *Spain, 1808–1939* (1975) and A.R. Oliveira, *Politics, Economics and Men of Modern Spain, 1808–1946* (1946). The economic background is discussed in J.H. Imlah, *Economic Elements of the Pax Britannica* (1958) and the mid-Victorian view of Empire is discussed in C.A. Bodelsen, *Studies in Mid-Victorian Imperialism* (1924).

M.E. Chamberlain, *The New Imperialism* (Historical Association pamphlet, 1967) is a good survey; see too D.K. Fieldhouse, *Colonialism, 1870–1945* (1983), *The Colonial Empires* (2nd edn, 1982), and *Economics and Empire* (1978). Also valuable is A. Porter, *European Imperialism, 1860–1914* (1994) and D.R. Headrick, *The Tools of Empire: Technology and European Imperialism in the Nineteenth Century* (1981). E.J. Hobsbawm, *The Age of Capital* (1975) and *The Age of Empire* (1987) are two sophisticated analyses from a Marxist perspective; see also V.G. Kiernan, *European Empires from Conquest to Collapse, 1815–1960* (1982). B. Porter, *The Lion's Share: A Short History of British Imperialism, 1850–1970* (1975) provides a comprehensive account of the British imperial experience. See too R. Hyam, *Britain's Imperial Century, 1815–1914: A Study of Empire and Expansion* (1976) and J. Bowle, *The Imperial Achievement: The Rise and Transformation of the British Empire* (1977). J. Gallagher and R. Robinson, *Africa and the Victorians: The Official Mind of Imperialism* (1961) examines how European conquest actually occurred. For other countries, see H. Brunschwig, *French Colonialism, 1871–1914: Myths and Realities* (1966) and W.O. Henderson, *Studies in German Colonial History* (1962).

Particular areas are discussed in J.D. Hargreaves, *Prelude to the Partition of West Africa* (1963), W.D. McIntyre, *The Imperial Frontier in the Tropics, 1865–75* (1967), and W.P. Morrell, *The Great Powers in the Pacific* (Historical Association pamphlet, 1965).

The economics of imperialism are discussed in D.C.M. Platt, *Finance, Trade and Politics in British Foreign Policy, 1815–1914* (1968), H. Feis, *Europe, the World's Banker, 1870–1914* (1930), A.R. Hall (ed.), *The Export of Capital from Britain, 1870–1914* (1968), A.K. Cairncross, *Home and Foreign Investment, 1870–1913* (1953), and S.B. Saul, *Studies in British Overseas Trade, 1870–1914* (1960). B. Semmel, *Imperialism and Social Reform* (1960) examines the domestic aspects of imperialism.

The diplomatic repercussions of the late nineteenth-century expansion are discussed in W. Langer, *The Diplomacy of Imperialism, 1890–1902* (1935).

For the early twentieth century, see M. Beloff, *Imperial Sunset, Vol. 1: Britain's Liberal Empire, 1897–1921* (1969) and for the later period M.E. Chamberlain, *Decolonization: The Fall of the European Empires* (1985) and C. Cross, *The Fall of the British Empire* (1968). Other publications include R. Betts, *France and Decolonisation* (1982), D. Judd, *The Evolution of the Modern Commonwealth* (1982), N. Mansergh, *The Commonwealth Experience* (1982), and J. Darwin, *Britain and Decolonization: The Retreat from Empire in the Post-War World* (1987).

Articles

See J. Gallagher and R. Robinson, 'The imperialism of free trade', *Ec.H.R.* (1953), D.C. Platt, 'Economic factors in British policy during the "New Imperialism"', *H.* (1968), R. Koebner, 'The concept of economic imperialism', *Ec.H.R.* (1949), D.K. Fieldhouse, '"Imperialism": an historiographical revision', *Ec.H.R.* (1961), and E. Stokes, 'Great Britain and Africa: the myth of imperialism', *H.T.* (1960) and 'Late nineteenth century colonial expansion and the attack on the theory of economic imperialism', *H.J.* (1969). Global theories of 'core-periphery' relations are discussed in P.O'Brien, 'European economic development: the contribution of the periphery', *Ec.H.R.* (1982). German expansion is discussed in H. Pogge van Strandmann, 'Domestic origins of Germany's colonial expansion under Bismarck', *P.P.* (1969).

15. THE UNIFICATION OF GERMANY

The notion of a united Germany had received considerable stimulus during the Napoleonic Wars and the period after 1815 was marked by the growth of national sentiment. Although the revolutions of 1848 failed to bring about the liberal, united Germany dreamt of by some, they showed the crucial importance of Prussia to any future plan for German unification. The rise of Prussia to a position of dominance in Central Europe, both politically and economically, and its influence upon the timing and character of German unification is a major topic. Bismarck's role in the process and the details of the conflicts with the other European powers are covered in a wide variety of studies. The creation of the most powerful European State by 1871 in military terms should not be allowed to distract from the weaknesses which the newly unified Empire carried into the later nineteenth and early twentieth centuries.

Essay topics

- Why was the unification of Germany not achieved before 1871?
- How far did militarism triumph over liberalism in the creation of the German Empire?

Sources and documents

For 1848 in Germany see the short collection by P. Jones, *1848 Revolutions* (1982), while W.M. Simon, *Germany in the Age of Bismarck* (1968) covers the later Bismarckian period. A. Ramm, *The Foundation of the German Empire* (1971) is a collection of texts and summaries.

Secondary sources

For the general history of Germany in this period, see W. Carr, *A History of Germany, 1815–1945* (rev. edn, 1979), H. Holborn, *A History of Modern Germany, Vol. III* (1969), the latter part of J.J. Sheehan, *German History, 1770–1866* (1989) and the early part of G.A. Craig, *Germany, 1866–1945* (1978). M. Kitchen, *The Political Economy of Germany, 1815–1914* (1978) examines the economic and social background to German unification. M. Fulbrook and J. Breuilly, *German History since 1800* (1997) and J.Breuilly (ed.), *Nineteenth Century Germany* (2001) have useful summary essays on Bismarckian and Wilhelmine Germany, while R. McLean and S. Seligmann, *Germany from Reich to Republic, 1871–1918* (2000) and D.G. Williamson, *Bismarck and Germany, 1862–1890* (1997) are short overviews. V. Berghahn, *Imperial Germany* (1994) covers the period from 1871 to 1914.

The clearest introductions on German unification are W. Carr, *The Origins of the Wars of German Unification* (1991), D. Showalter, *The Wars of German Unification* (2004), and H. Schulze, *The Course of German Nationalism* (1991). Two significant studies of German nationalism are A. Green, *Fatherlands: State Building and Nationhood in Nineteenth Century Germany* (2001) and S. Berger, *Inventing the Nation: Germany* (2004). On Bismarck, see Williamson (above), K. Lerman, *Bismarck* (2004), and L. Gall, *Bismarck: The White Revolutionary* (1986), but B. Waller, *Bismarck* (1985) and W. Richter, *Bismarck* (1984) are also helpful. The internal structure of Prussian politics is examined in E.N. Anderson, *The Social and Political Conflict in Prussia, 1858–64* (1954), G.A. Craig, *The Politics of the Prussian Army* (1955), and K. Jarausch and L.E. Jones (eds), *In Search of a Liberal Germany* (1990). H.-U. Wehler, *The German Empire, 1871–1914* (1984) argues that Bismarck unified Germany 'from above' to frustrate liberalism, a view discussed in the opening chapter of R. Evans (ed.), *Society and Politics in Wilhelmine Germany* (1978) and criticized in G. Eley and D. Blackbourn, *The Peculiarities of German History: Bourgeois Society and Politics in Nineteenth-Century Germany* (1984). J. Sheehan, *German Liberalism in the Nineteenth Century* (1978) is a modern treatment of an important strand of German politics.

Detailed discussion of the diplomatic context of German unification can be found in A.J.P. Taylor's *The Struggle for Mastery in Europe, 1848–1918* (1954), and H. Kohn (ed.), *German History: Some New German Views* (1954) contains revaluations of Bismarck's policy and diplomacy in the period before 1870. Also of value are F. Darmstaedter, *Bismarck and the Creation of the Second Reich* (1948), H. Friedjung, *The Struggle for Supremacy in Germany, 1859–1866* (1935), and L.D. Steefel, *The Schleswig–Holstein Question* (1932).

For economic developments which assisted German unification, see W.O. Henderson, *The Zollverein* (1939), J.H. Clapham, *The Economic Development of France and Germany* (4th edn, 1936), W.O. Henderson, *The Industrialisation of Europe, 1780–1914* (1969), T. Kemp, *Industrialisation in Nineteenth-century Europe* (1969), C. Trebilcock, *The Industrialisation of the Continental Powers, 1780–1914* (1981), and A. Milward and S.B. Saul, *The Economic Development of Continental Europe, 1780–1870* (1973).

On military matters, see G. Best, *War and Society in Revolutionary Europe, 1770–1870* (1982), M. Howard, *The Franco–Prussian War* (1981), and on the wider influence of the army, G.A. Craig, *The Politics of the Prussian Army, 1648–1945* (1955).

16. GERMANY, 1871–1914

The declaration of the German Empire in Germany, 1871, brought on to the world stage a major new power with a large and growing population and a rapidly expanding industry. Following victories over Austria and France, her size and industrial development made her the most powerful State in continental Europe. Under Bismarck, Germany was given the formal apparatus of democratic institutions – the Reichstag, or parliament, and universal suffrage, but power remained substantially vested in the Kaiser, the Chancellor, and the military. Bismarck enforced strict controls on any groups, such as the Catholics and the Socialists, whom he saw as threatening the Empire, and used foreign diversions, such as colonial expansion, to distract attention from domestic conflicts. The nature of Bismarck's political system and its long-term effects on Germany, at a time when democratic and social developments throughout Europe were causing unrest, needs to be considered.

After Bismarck's removal by the new Kaiser, William II, in 1890, social conflicts came increasingly to the fore in which both liberals and a growing labour movement found themselves at odds with a government dominated by junkers, industrialists and the military. By 1914, Germany faced deep political divisions which were to surface after the declaration of war.

Essay topics

- In what ways were the interests of Germany served by Bismarck after 1871?
- How united and stable was Germany on the eve of war in 1914?

Sources and documents

L. Snyder, *Documents of German History* (1958) has material on this period, but more accessible is W.N. Medlicott and D. Coveney, *Bismarck and Europe* (1971). Heinrich Mann's novel, *Man of Straw* (1918, trans. 1947) is a liberal critique of Imperial Germany.

Secondary works

There are several works which place this period in the wider context of modern German history: W. Carr, *A History of Germany, 1815–1945* (rev. edn, 1979), A. Ramm, *Germany, 1789–1919* (1967), G.A. Craig, *Germany, 1866–1945* (1978), and J.C.G. Rohl, *From Bismarck to Hitler* (1970). Two collections, M. Fulbrook and J. Breuilly, *German History since 1800* (1997) and J. Breuilly (ed.), *Nineteenth Century Germany* (2001), have synoptic essays on Wilhelmine Germany; see also the introductory R. McLean and M.S. Seligmann, *Germany from Reich to Republic* (2000), the longer V. Berghahn, *Imperial Germany* (1994), and also J. Retallack, *Germany in the Age of Kaiser Wilhelm II* (1996). Other important recent works are G. Mommsen, *Imperial Germany, 1867–1918* (1995) and M. John, *The German Empire, 1867–1914* (1996). Of work which provides an analysis of German politics in terms of its social and economic structure, see M. Kitchen, *The Political Economy of Germany, 1815–1914* (1978), and on the Imperial period as a whole H.-U. Wehler, *The German Empire, 1871–1914* (trans. edn, 1984) and G. Eley and D. Blackbourn, *The Peculiarities of German History: Bourgeois Society and Politics in Nineteenth Century Germany* (1984). See also J. Sheehan (ed.), *Imperial Germany* (1976). Analyses of Bismarck's character and importance can be found in L. Gall, *Bismarck: The White Revolutionary* (2 vols, 1986), B. Waller, *Bismarck* (1985), as well as the older studies such as A.J.P. Taylor, *Bismarck* (1955), W. Richter, *Bismarck* (1964), W.N. Medlicott, *Bismarck and Modern Germany* (1965), and E. Eyck, *Bismarck and the German Empire* (1950). E. Eyck, *Bismarck after Fifty Years* (Historical Association, 1965) examines historians' changing views of Bismarck.

For the Wilhelmine era, see M. Balfour, *The Kaiser and His Times* (1964) and the essay collection by R. Evans (ed.), *Society and Politics in Wilhelmine Germany* (1978). Dealing with the immediate aftermath of Bismarck's resignation, see A.J. Nichols, *Germany without Bismarck* (1967) which ends in 1900. On the prewar decade, see V.R. Berghahn, *Germany and the Approach of War in 1914* (1973) and B. Heckart, *From Basserman to Bebel* (1974). On personalities, see J.C.G. Rohl and N. Sombart (eds), *Kaiser Wilhelm II: New Interpretations* (1982), T. Kohut, *William II and the Germans* (1991), and K. Jarausch, *The Enigmatic Chancellor: Bethmann-Hollweg and the Hubris of Imperial Germany* (1973).

On the role of the right, see G. Eley, *Reshaping the Right: Radical Nationalism and Political Change after Bismarck* (1980), and on the military, M. Kitchen, *The German Officer Corps: 1870–1914* (1968) and G.A. Craig, *The Politics of the Prussian Army, 1640–1945* (1945). On the left, see C.E. Shorske, *German Social Democracy, 1905–17* (1955) and P. Gay, *The Dilemma of Democratic Socialism* (1952). R. Evans (ed.), *The German Working Class, 1888–1933* (1982), D. Geary, *European Labour Protest, 1848–1939* (1981), and H. Grebing, *The German Labour Movement* (1969) all have useful material on this period; see also D. Crew, *Town in the Ruhr: A Social History of Bochum* (1979) for the relationship of social conditions and political allegiance. On industrial development, see the chapter in C.M. Cipolla (ed.), *The Fontana Economic History of Europe, vol. IV* (1973), G. Stolper, *German Economy,*

1870 to the Present (2nd edn, 1967), and W.O. Henderson, *The Industrialisation of Europe, 1780–1914* (1969). On social conditions, see A.V. Desai, *Real Wages in Germany, 1871–1913* (1968).

A good general survey of foreign policy throughout the period is I. Geiss, *German Foreign Policy, 1871–1914* (1976). Geiss's views are influenced by F. Fischer, *Germany's Aims in the First World War* (1967), a controversial critique of German foreign policy under the Kaiser, which Fischer followed up in *War of Illusion* (1972); see also A.J.P. Taylor, *The Struggle for Mastery in Europe, 1848–1914* (1954). J. Steinberg, *Yesterday's Deterrent: Tirpitz and the Birth of the German Battle Fleet* (1955) is important on the creation of a German navy to rival that of Britain. See also P.A. Kennedy, *The Rise of the Anglo–German Antagonism, 1860–1914* (1980).

Articles

On politics, see J.C. Rohl, 'The Politics of Bismarck's Fall', *H.J.* (1966) and H.J. Pogge von Strandmann, 'The domestic origins of Germany's colonial expansion', *P.P.* (1969). On the Centre Party, see D. Blackbourn, 'The political alignment of the Centre Party in Wilhelmine Germany: a study of the party's emergence in nineteenth-century Wurttemberg', *H.J.* (1975), and also his 'The *Mittelstand* in German society and politics, 1871–1914', *S.H.* (1977) and 'Peasants and politics in Germany, 1871–1914', *E.H.Q.* (1984). J.P. Nettl, 'The German Social Democratic Party 1890–1914 as a political model', *P.P.* (1965) and D. Geary, 'The German labour movement', *E.S.R.* (1976) are useful on the left.

17. FRANCE, 1871–1914

On the surface France in this period presented a picture of political instability. The Third Republic was only established by a one-vote majority in 1875 and was characterized by short-lived governments and a series of scandals. Beneath the surface, however, France possessed certain strengths. The bulk of the population were conservative-minded peasants; the existence of a meritocratic system ensured the loyalty of professional groups, such as lawyers and teachers; while the low rates of population growth and also industrialization were such as to make social problems less pressing than elsewhere in Europe. Even in the political sphere there were signs of stability: the monarchist right was discredited, pressures from the left were channelled into anti-clericalism and the same ministers kept returning to power. The Third Republic became the longest-lived post-revolutionary regime, and survived the First World War triumphant.

Essay topics

- 'The regime that divided Frenchmen least.' Discuss this view of the Third Republic.
- Assess the significance of the Dreyfus affair for French politics and society.

Sources and documents

A wonderful period for French literature and culture with Zola's *Germinal* (1885) and *La Débâcle* (1892) of most direct historical relevance. For the French right see the writings of Drumont and Barres in J.S. McClelland (ed.), *The French Right: From de Maistre to Maurras* (1970).

Secondary works

There are numerous general introductions to French history in this period: R. Tombs, *France, 1814–1914* (1996), R. Gildea, *France, 1870–1914* (2nd edn, 1996), D.W. Brogan, *The Development of Modern France, 1870–1940* (1940), J.P.T. Bury, *France, 1814–1940* (1949), A. Cobban, *A History of Modern France, vol. III* (1965), G. Wright, *France in Modern Times* (1960), J.-M. Mayeur and J. Reberioux, *The Third Republic, 1871–1914* (1984), R.D. Anderson, *France, 1870–1914* (1983), R. Magraw, *France 1815–1914* (1984), and J.F. McMillan, *Dreyfus to de Gaulle: Politics and Society in France, 1898–1969* (1985). T. Zeldin, *France, 1848–1945* (3 vols, 1973–8) provides a full discussion of social, intellectual and political life, while E. Weber, *Peasants into Frenchmen, 1870–1914* (1979) concentrates on social change.

On the beginning of the period A. Horne, *The Fall of Paris* (1983) includes a discussion of the Commune, while the same author's *The French Army in Politics* (1984) covers the army's role in both the Commune and the Dreyfus affair. On the Commune, see also E. Schulkind, *The Paris Commune of 1871* (Historical Association, 1971), F. Jellinek, *The Paris Commune of 1871* (1937 and 1971), R.L. Williams, *The French Revolution of 1870–1871* (1969), S. Edwards, *The Paris Commune, 1871* (1971) and R. Tombs, *The War against Paris, 1871* (1981).

The threat from authoritarianism is considered in F.H. Seager, *The Boulanger Affair* (1969), and its wider implications are examined in R. Tombs (ed.), *Nationhood and Nationalism in France from Boulangism to the Great War* (1991). For the Dreyfus affair, see D. Johnson, *France and the Dreyfus Affair* (1966) and R. Kedward, *The Dreyfus Affair* (1969). The position of the Jewish community is examined in M. Marrus, *The Politics of Assimilation: A Study of the French Jewish Community at the Time of the Dreyfus Affair* (1971). Important political leaders are discussed in H. Holdberg, *The Life of Jean Jaures* (1962) and J.P.T. Bury, *Gambetta and the Making of the Third Republic* (1973). On social reform, see J.F. Stone, *The Search for Social Peace: Reform Legislation in France, 1890–1914* (1985). On the left, see R. Magraw, *A History of the French Working Class, vol. II* (1992) and R. Stuart, *Marxism at Work: Class and French Socialism during the Third Republic* (1992). Rural movements are discussed in L. Frader, *Peasants and Protest: Agricultural Workers, Politics and the Unions in the Aude, 1850–1914* (1991). The elites are examined in C. Charle, *A Social History of Modern France in the Nineteenth Century* (1994).

French foreign policy is discussed in C. Andrew, *Théophile Delcassé and the Making of the Entente Cordiale* (1968) and J. Keiger, *France and the Origins of the First World War* (1983).

Articles

R. Tombs 'The Thiers government and the outbreak of civil war in France, 1871', *H.J.* (1980) emphasizes the existence of political moderation even in 1871; see also P.H. Hutton, 'Boulangism and the rise of mass politics', *J.C.H.* (1976). For social dissent, see J. Harvey Smith, 'Agricultural workers and the French wine-growers revolt of 1907', *P.P.* (1978).

18. AUSTRIA–HUNGARY, 1867–1918

Despite the triumph of the Habsburg Monarchy over the liberal and national movements of 1848, pressures on the Imperial position soon revived. By 1867 Austrian influence in both Italy and Germany had been removed and the Emperor Franz Josef was forced to agree to an *Ausgleich* (compromise) with the largest national grouping in his Empire, the Hungarians. From 1867 to 1918 Austria and Hungary had separate governments, though with a single army, foreign policy and ruler. The *Ausgleich* did not end the pressures from other nationalities for equality and independence, however. Within Austria, the Czechs especially wanted reform, while in Hungary the Yugoslav movement was strengthened by the existence of an independent Slav State, Serbia. Austria–Hungary was not without some strengths, including loyalty to the monarchy, a multinational army, and a reasonably stable economy. Vienna also happened to be among the foremost centres of cultural and intellectual life in pre-1914 Europe. Although widely thought of as the 'sick man of Europe', the real questions lie in whether the collapse of the Empire was inevitable or primarily the result of the strain of war.

Essay topics

- Which nationality represented the greatest threat to the unity of Austria–Hungary, 1867–1914?
- Was it war or more deep-seated causes which explained the breakup of the Habsburg Monarchy?

Sources and documents

R.W. Seton-Watson, *Racial Problems in Hungary* (1908) and H. Wickham Steed, *The Habsburg Monarchy* (1913) are 'on the eve' accounts. Consult a good historical atlas for the national and ethnic complexities of Central Europe.

Secondary works

The period is placed in context by A. Sked, *The Decline and Fall of the Habsburg Empire, 1815–1918* (1989) and C.A. Macartney, *The Habsburg Monarchy, 1790–1918* (1968). R. Kann, *The Multinational Empire: Nationalism and National Reform in the Habsburg Monarchy, 1848–1918* (1950) provides a full coverage, though A.J. May, *The Habsburg Monarchy, 1867–1914* (1951) is shorter. On internal politics, see W.A. Jenks, *Austria under the Iron Ring* (1965).

On the nationalist problem, see R. Pearson, *National Minorities in Eastern Europe, 1848–1944* (1983), R. Okey, *Eastern Europe 1740–1985* (2nd edn, 1986), and V. Dedijer, *The Road to Sarajevo* (1967). Also useful are C. Regal, *The Slovenes and Yugoslavia* (1977) and J.K. Hoensch, *A History of Modern Hungary* (1988). A.G. Whiteside, *The Socialism of Fools: Georg von Schonerer and Austrian Pan-Germanism* (1975), G.B. Cohen, *The Politics of Ethnic Survival: Germans in Prague, 1861–1914* (1981), and H.G. Skilling, *T.G. Masaryk: Against the Current, 1882–1914* (1994) are also good case studies.

For foreign policy, see F. Bridge, *From Sadowa to Sarajevo* (1972), M. Cornwall (ed.), *The Last Years of Austria–Hungary* (1990), and S. Williamson, *Austria–Hungary and the Origins of the First World War* (1991).

N. Stone, *The Eastern Front* (1975) is a brilliant discussion of the fighting which throws considerable light on the Austrian State at war. Z.A.B. Zeman, *The Break-up of the Habsburg Empire, 1914–18* (1961) discusses the war years and the end of the empire, as does O. Jaszi, *The Destruction of the Habsburg Monarchy* (1929) and A.J. May, *The Passing of the Habsburg Monarchy, 1914–18* (1966). A.J.P. Taylor, 'Allied war aims', in R. Pares and A.J.P. Taylor (eds), *Essays Presented to Sir Lewis Namier* (1956) provides a critical link between the outcome of the war and the nationality question. F.L. Carsten, *Revolution in Central Europe, 1918–19* (1972) deals with events in Austria itself at the end of the war.

Articles

See K.R. Stadler, 'The disintegration of the Austrian Empire', *J.C.H.* (1968), N. Stone, 'Hungary and World War I', *J.C.H.* (1966), J. Remak, 'The Healthy Invalid: how doomed was the Habsburg Empire?', *J.M.H.* (1969), and A. Sked, 'Historians, the nationality question and the downfall of the Habsburg Empire', *T.R.H.S.* (1981).

19. RUSSIA, 1856–1917

Russian history in this period is inevitably coloured by the Revolution which occurred in 1917 and the unrest which preceded it. Following defeat in the Crimean War and faced by peasant discontent and a disaffected intelligentsia, Tsar Alexander II emancipated the serfs in 1861 and carried out a series of major institutional reforms. His assassination in 1881 brought to a halt further attempts at liberalization and the autocratic political system was maintained by Alexander III and Nicholas II. Russia's huge area, her backwardness and varied national make-up continued to present serious problems and drove many opponents into exile or terrorism.

There was, however, considerable industrial development under Count Witte in the 1890s and effective land reform under Stolypin. In 1905, following defeat by Japan, the regime faced a major crisis with widespread unrest and the emergence of workers-soldiers 'soviets'. Short-lived hopes for reform were frustrated and there was a growing divergence between moderate reformers and a militant Bolshevik minority. Conservative forces remained strong, however, and on the eve of the Great War it was still possible that Russia might have evolved without revolutionary upheaval. The huge losses and strain of the conflict finally brought revolution.

Essay topics

- To what extent did the reforms of Alexander II mark a turning point in Russian history?
- Was Tsarist autocracy doomed in Russia by 1914?

Sources and documents

Memoirs of revolutionary leaders include J.D. Duff (ed.), *Memoirs of Alexander Herzen* (1923), M. Gorky, *Autobiography* (trns., 1953), and Prince Kropotkin, *Memoirs of a Revolutionist* (1899). L. Trotsky, *1905* (1971) describes the thwarted revolution of that year by a leading participant. Of Lenin's writings, *What Is To Be Done?* (1902) was the seminal document outlining Bolshevik strategy. A great age of Russian literature, much of it political in tone, is perhaps best represented by Ivan Turgenev's, *On the Eve* (1860) and *Fathers and Children* (1862) and Maxim Gorky's, *The Lower Depths* (1902). See also S. Harcave, *Memoirs of Count Witte* (1990).

Secondary works

M. Kochan and R. Abraham, *The Making of Modern Russia* (1983) and H. Seton-Watson, *The Russian Empire* (1967) are valuable for placing the period in the context of Russian history in general, as are J.N. Westwood, *Endurance and Endeavour: Russian History, 1812–1992* (4th edn, 1993) and L. Kochan, *Russia in Revolution, 1890–1918* (1966). Two important recent works are R. Pipes, *The Russian Revolution, 1899–1919* (1990) and O. Figes, *A People's Tragedy: The Russian Revolution, 1891–1924* (1996).

On Alexander II, W.E. Mosse, *Alexander II and the Modernisation of Russia* (1959) is still useful, while for Alexander III, see P. Zaionchkovsky, *The Russian Autocracy under Alexander III* (1976). For rural Russia, see J. Blum, *Lord and Peasant in Russia* (1965), G.T. Robinson, *Rural Russia under the Old Regime* (1949), and the modern treatment by J. Channon, *The Russian and Soviet Peasantry, 1880–1991* (1997), while W.S. Vucinich, *The Peasant in Nineteenth Century Russia* (1968) has some valuable material; see also F.W. Wicislo, *Reforming Rural Russia: State, Local Society and National Politics, 1855–1914* (1990). On Witte, see T.H. von Laue, *Sergei Witte and the Industrialisation of Russia* (1963). On the Dumas, G.A. Hosking, *The Russian Constitutional Experiment: Government and Duma,*

1907–1914 (1973) and R.B. Mckean, *The Russian Constitutional Monarchy, 1907–1917* (Historical Association pamphlet, 1977) are valuable.

On economic development in general, see M.E. Falkus, *The Industrialisation of Russia, 1700–1914* (1972), A. Nove, *An Economic History of the U.S.S.R.* (1969), and W.O. Henderson, *The Industrial Revolution on the Continent: Germany, France and Russia, 1800–1914* (1961).

K. Fitzlyon and T. Browning, *Before the Revolution* (1977) surveys Russia under Nicholas II, and on the 1905 revolution see A. Ascher, *The Russian Revolution of 1905* (2 vols, 1988–92) and H. Harcave, *First Blood: The Russian Revolution of 1905* (1965), while G. Katkov (ed.), *Russia Enters the Twentieth Century* (1972) has valuable essays.

Specific works dealing with the opposition to the old order are F. Venturi, *The Roots of Revolution: A History of the Populist and Socialist Movements in Nineteenth Century Russia* (1960), P. Avrich, *The Russian Anarchists* (1967), J.L.H. Keep, *The Rise of Social Democracy in Russia* (1963), and A.B. Ulam, *Lenin and the Bolsheviks* (1965). A.K. Wildman, *The Making of a Workers' Revolution* (1967), M. Perrie, *The Agrarian Policy of the Russian Socialist Revolutionary Party, 1905–1907* (1976), and C. Rice, *Russian Workers and the Socialist Revolutionary Party through the Revolutions of 1905–1907* (1988) also offer detailed analysis. For constitutional politics, see T. Emmons, *The Formation of Political Parties and the First National Elections in Russia* (1983), R.T. Manning, *Crisis of the Old Order: Gentry and Government, 1905–17* (1982), and R. Edelman, *Gentry Politics on the Eve of the Russian Revolution: The National Party, 1907–1917* (1980).

For foreign policy, see the collections by K. Wilson (ed.), *Decisions for War, 1914* (1995) and R.J.W. Evans and H. Pogge von Strandmann (eds), *The Coming of the First World War* (1988), which have essays on Russia's involvement in the First World War, and more specifically, D. Lieven, *Russia and the Origins of the First World War* (1983). On the effects of the war, see Pipes, *The Russian Revolution* and Figes, *A People's Tragedy* (see above), R. Pearson, *The Russian Moderates and the Crisis of Tsarism, 1914–17* (1978), N. Stone, *The Eastern Front, 1914–17* (1978), and J. Dunn, *Modern Revolutions* (1972), ch. 1.

Articles

On unrest, see M. Perrie, 'The Russian peasant movement, 1905–7', *P.P.* (1972) and L.H. Harrison, 'Problems of social stability in urban Russia', *S.R.* (1964 and 1965); also A.P. Mendel, 'Peasant and worker on the eve of the First World War', *S.R.* (1965). On other aspects see T.H. von Laue, 'The chances for liberal constitutionalism', *S.R.* (1965) and G.L. Yaney, 'The concept of the Stolypin land reform', *S.R.* (1964).

20. EUROPEAN DIPLOMACY, 1871–1914

The European diplomatic scene after the Franco–Prussian War was dominated by Bismarck's attempts to ensure the lasting security of the new German Empire. At first he tried to achieve this through the 'Dreikaiserbund', a conservative alliance with Austria–Hungary and Russia in the 1870s, but this was increasingly undermined by Austrian and Russian ambitions in the Balkans, where the decline of the Ottoman Empire created a power vacuum. In 1879 Bismarck decided to ally with Austria–Hungary alone in the Dual Alliance, while in 1894 Russia made an alliance with France. Tension between the two blocs grew, notably over the Bosnian Crisis in 1908, and Britain too became suspicious of German ambitions. In 1914 another crisis in the Balkans brought the two sides to war. Various interpretations of the origins of the war have been put forward; from early anti-Germanism, there was a swing towards blaming the alliance systems in general. More recently, Fischer has revived interest in Germany's responsibility for the war and the wider factors affecting Europeans' readiness to go to war have to be considered.

Essay topics

- How stable was the European diplomatic system created by Bismarck?
- Why did a crisis in the Balkans lead to a general European war in 1914?

Sources and documents

G. Martel, *The Origins of the First World War* (3rd edn, 2004) is a short collection. M. Hurst (ed.), *Key Treaties for the Great Powers, vol. II, 1870–1914* (1972) covers the whole period, though mere treaty texts are rather unexciting sources. To be preferred perhaps is I. Geiss, *July, 1914: Selected Documents* (1967) which concentrates on the prewar crisis.

Secondary sources

A.J.P. Taylor, *The Struggle for Mastery in Europe, 1848–1918* (1954) remains a remarkably thorough analysis of the diplomatic struggles, while R. Albrecht-Carrié, *A Diplomatic History of Europe from the Congress of Vienna* (1961) provides the wider background. Another well-established but essential account is W.L. Langer, *European Alliances and Alignments, 1871–90* (1956), which he followed with *The Diplomacy of Imperialism, 1890–1902* (1961). See also F.R. Bridge and R. Bullen, *The Great Powers and the European States System* (1980). On individual countries see C. Andrew, *Théophile Delcassé and the Making of the Entente Cordiale* (1968) and P.V. Rolo, *Entente Cordiale* (1969).

The origins of the First World War have attracted a vast literature. J. Joll, *The Origins of the First World War* (1985) is a recent modern overview. The decision by individual countries to go to war is examined in K. Wilson (ed.), *Decisions for War, 1914* (1995) and R.J.W. Evans and H. Pogge von Strandmann (eds), *The Coming of the First World War* (1988). H. Strachan, *The First World War, vol. 1: To Arms* (2001) is a massive new treatment; parts 1 and 2 represent a fresh appraisal of the war's origins and the relationship of the European war to the worldwide rivalries of the great powers.

See too A. Mombauer, *The Origins of the First World War: Controversies and Consensus* (2002), which sets out to examine the current historiography concerning the war's origins. B. Schmitt, *The Outbreak of War in 1914* (Historical Association pamphlet, 1964) analyses the role of the Alliance systems in the outbreak of war, which is more fully related in his study, *The Coming of the War* (2 vols, 1930). The great classic of the 'diplomatic' school of thinking is L. Albertini, *The Origins of the War of 1914* (3 vols, 1952–57). Shorter and more recent accounts are L.C.F. Turner, *The Origins of the First World War* (1970) and H.W. Koch, *The Origins of the First World War* (1984 edn). Also useful is the short account of the breakup of the nineteenth-century international system, R. Langhorne, *The Collapse of the Concert of Europe, 1890–1914* (1981), while M.S. Anderson, *The Eastern Question, 1774–1923* (1966) provides a wider perspective on that particular problem. Among the most important later interpretations has been F. Fischer, *Germany's War Aims in the First World War* (1967) which sees the war as a result of Germany's prewar expansionism. See also his *War of Illusion* (1972) and *From Kaiserreich to Third Reich* (1986). On Germany, see V. Berghahn, *Germany and the Approach of War in 1914* (1973), I. Geiss, *German Foreign Policy, 1871–1914* (1976), and G. Ritter, *The Schlieffen Plan* (1958). J.C.G. Rohl (ed.), *1914: Delusion or Design? The Testimony of Two German Diplomats* (1973) has important material on attitudes in German ruling circles. Austria–Hungary's role is considered in R. Bridge, *From Sadowa to Sarajevo* (1972) and A.S. Williamson, *Austria–Hungary and the Origins of the First World War* (1991); France in J. Keiger, *France and the Origins of the First World War* (1983); Russia in D. Lieven, *Russia and the Origins of the First World War* (1983); and Britain in Z.S. Steiner, *Britain and the Origins of the First World War* (1977). The specific rivalry of Britain and Germany is considered in the classic E.L. Woodward, *Great Britain and the German Navy* (1935), but is now updated on the naval side by A.J. Marder, *From the Dreadnought to Scapa Flow, vol. I: The Road to War, 1904–14* (1961) and on the political side by P. Kennedy, *The Rise of the Anglo–German Antagonism, 1860–1914* (1980). The arms build-up in general is considered in D. Stevenson, *Armaments and the Coming of War in Europe, 1904–1914* (1996). M. Howard discusses the 'climate' of 1914 in Evans and Pogge von Strandmann (eds), *The Coming of the First World War* (above), and Europe's readiness for war is considered in his 'Reflections on the Great War' in his *Studies in War and Peace* (1970). The commercially published course units of the Open University course on War, Peace and Social Change: Europe, 1900–1955, have in A. Marwick, B. Waites, C. Emsley and I. Donnachie, *Book I: Europe on the Eve of War* (1990), Unit 6, a useful step-by-step guide to the debates.

Articles

Two articles which take up the theme of the relationship between domestic and foreign policy are W.J. Mommsen, 'Domestic factors in German foreign policy before 1914', *C.E.H.* (1973), reprinted in J. Sheehan (ed.), *Imperial Germany* (1976), and M.R. Gordon, 'Domestic conflict and the origins of the First World War: the British and German cases', *J.M.H.* (1974). An appraisal of the Fischer thesis and its critics can be found in R.J. Evans, 'From Hitler to Bismarck: Third Reich to Kaiserreich in recent historiography', *H.J.* (1984).

21. THE FIRST WORLD WAR, 1914–18

When war broke out in August 1914 it was widely expected to be 'over by Christmas'. Instead, in the West at least, the situation soon became one of trench warfare and deadlock. Modern weapons, especially the machine gun, barbed wire and heavy artillery, ensured huge casualties, concentrated among men aged between about twenty and forty. Armies numbering millions of men were mobilized, while behind them 'home fronts' were established: economies were geared to war production, women went to work in factories, propaganda machines ensured loyalty to the war effort and hatred of the enemy. The strain on European society was enormous. Governments were changed in France and Britain, revolutions broke out in Russia and Germany, and the Austro–Hungarian and Ottoman Empires were finally shattered. The world would never be the same again.

Essay topics

- Why did the First World War not end until November 1918?
- Why did western democratic regimes tend to survive the war more successfully than the eastern autocracies?

Sources and documents

P. Vansittart, *Voices from the Great War* (1983) draws together eye-witness evidence on the war from all levels of society. Of the memoirs, see D. Lloyd George, *War Memoirs* (2 vols, 1928) and W.S. Churchill, *The World Crisis* (1928). Of the literature produced by the war, H. Barbusse's *Le Feu (Under Fire)* (1917), E. Junger, *The Storm of Steel* (1929), R. Graves, *Goodbye to All That* (1929), and E.M. Remarque, *All Quiet on the Western Front* (1929) are outstanding.

Secondary works

There are numerous general histories of the war but among the most approachable are A.J.P. Taylor, *The First World War: An Illustrated History* (1966), invaluable because of its illustrations, C. Falls, *The First World War* (1966) and B.H. Liddell-Hart, *History of the First World War* (1970). M. Ferro, *The Great War* (1963) is another short, readable introduction. See also J. Terraine, *The Western Front, 1914–18* (1964). For works which place the military aspects of the war in a broader context see K. Robbins, *The First World War* (Oxford, 1984), B. Bond, *War and Society in Europe, 1870–1970* (1984) and G. Hardach, *The First World War* (1977).

Of more recent accounts see J. Keegan, *The First World War* (1998) and H. Strachan's *Oxford Illustrated History of the First World War* (1998). N. Ferguson, *The Pity of War* (1998) offers a stimulating set of fresh perspectives. H. Herwig, *The First World War: Germany and Austria-Hungary* (1997), although concerned with only two of the combatants, is vitally concerned with the war's conduct and conclusion. I.F.W. Beckett, *The Great War, 1914–1918* (2001) is a recent account, but see also C. Nicolson, *The Longman Companion to the First World War* (2001).

The nature of the new warfare is discussed in J. Ellis, *Eye-Deep in Hell* (1976) and A.E. Ashworth, *The Trench Warfare* (1980), while A. Horne, *The Price of Glory: Verdun, 1916* (1964), L. Macdonald, *They Called it Passchendaele* (1983) and M. Middlebrook, *The First Day on the Somme* (1971) and *The Kaiser's Battle* (1983) (on Germany's 1918 offensive) give full treatment of individual battles.

The effect of the war on individual societies can be traced in J. Kocka, *Facing Total War: German Society, 1914–1918* (1985), A. Rosenberg, *Imperial Germany: the birth of the German Republic* (1931), A. Marwick, *The Deluge: British Society and the First World* War (1965), A.J. May, *The Passing of the Habsburg Monarchy* (2 vols, 1966), L. Kochan, *Russia in Revolution, 1890–1918* (1966), J.J. Becker, *The Great War and the French People* (1983), and N. Stone, *The Eastern Front* (1978). General coverage of such issues is provided by A. Marwick, *War and Social Change in the Twentieth Century* (1974) and J.M. Winter and R.M. Wall (eds), *The Upheaval of War: Family, Work, and Welfare in Europe, 1914–1918* (1981). The wider cultural impact of the war is discussed in P. Fussell, *The Great War and Modern Memory* (1975), J.M. Winter, *The Experience of World War I* (1988), M. Ceadel, *Pacifism in Britain, 1914–1945* (1980), S. Ward (ed.), *The War Generation* (1975), F. Field, *Three French Writers and the Great War* (1970), and H. Klein (ed.), *The First World War in Fiction* (1976).

The revolutionary effects of the war are discussed in C.L. Bertrand (ed.), *Revolutionary Situations in Europe, 1917–1922* (1977) and F.L. Carsten, *Revolution in Central Europe, 1918–1919* (1972). For Germany, see A.J. Ryder, *The German Revolution* (1966) and D. Geary, 'Radicalism and the worker: metalworkers and revolution, 1914–1923', in R.J. Evans (ed.), *Society and Politics in Wilhelmine Germany (*1978).

War aims and the failure of early peace attempts are discussed in F. Fischer, *Germany's War Aims in the First World War* (1987), V. Rothwell, *British War Aims and Peace Diplomacy* (1971), C. Andrew and A. Kanya-Forstner, *France Overseas* (1981), as well as A.J.P. Taylor, *The Struggle for Mastery in Europe, 1848–1918* (1954). See also M. Kitchen, *The Silent Dictatorship* (1976) on the growing role of the German General Staff.

Articles

The thesis that sections of the German lower middle classes were radicalized by the war is raised in J. Kocka, 'The First World War and the "Mittelstand": German artisans and white-collar workers', *J.C.H.* (1973), and for a review of these views, see

W.J. Mommsen, 'Society and war: two new analyses of the First World War', *J.M.H.* (1977). D. Geary, 'The German labour movement, 1848–1918', *E.S.R.* (1976) is also useful for German reactions.

22. THE RUSSIAN REVOLUTION AND LENIN, 1917–24

Under the pressures of war the Tsarist autocracy finally collapsed early in 1917 and power was given to a more democratic regime of elected representatives. The change of government unleashed forces that were difficult to control, however: soldiers deserted from the army, factory workers adopted militant political views, and the peasants began to seize land for themselves from the great estates. In the 'October Revolution' the communist 'Bolsheviks' seized power under Lenin, and established a radically reformist but authoritarian regime. They made peace with Germany, overcame their conservative opponents and defeated the attempts of the Western powers to overthrow them. Historians debate about the kind of regime Lenin might have created had he not become increasingly ill and died in 1924.

Essay topics

- Was the Bolshevik seizure of power in 1917 primarily the result of their own strengths and abilities?
- What were the main achievements and failings of Lenin in power, 1917–24?

Sources and documents

M. McCauley (ed.), *The Russian Revolution and the Soviet State, 1917–21* (1980) provides a full set of documents, while L. Trotsky, *The History of the Russian Revolution* (1977) is an account by a leading revolutionary. H. Shukman (ed.), *The Blackwell Encyclopedia of the Russian Revolution* (1988) is a mine of information with a good, short introduction on the historiography of the Revolution. There are memoirs by N. Sukhanov, *The Russian Revolution, 1917* (1955), J. Reed, *Ten Days that Shook the World* (1961) (the latter an American observer of the October Revolution), and A. Kerensky, *The Kerensky Memoirs* (1966). For this and the later period of Soviet history, see M. McCauley, *The Longman Companion to Russia since 1914* (2000).

Secondary works

The basic account of the events of 1917–24 can be traced in the excellent general histories by R. Service, *A History of Twentieth-Century Russia* (1997) and by G. Hosking, *A History of the Soviet Union* (1990); see also McCauley (as above).

There are good starting points in R. Pipes, *The Russian Revolution, 1899–1919* (1990), O. Figes, *A People's Tragedy: The Russian Revolution, 1891–1924* (1996), J.D. White, *The Russian Revolution, 1917–1921* (1994), and E. Acton, *Rethinking the Russian Revolution* (1990). Among the national histories which deal with the breakdown of the regime, see H. Seton-Watson, *The Russian Empire, 1801–1917* (1967), J.N. Westwood, *Endurance and Endeavour: Russian History, 1812–1971* (1973), and L. Kochan and P. Abraham, *The Making of Modern Russia* (1983). R.B. Mckean, *The Russian Constitutional Monarchy, 1907–1917* (Historical Association pamphlet, 1977) synthesises much recent research. There are also useful essays in R. Pipes (ed.), *Revolutionary Russia* (1968) and a useful, short interpretative essay in J. Dunn, *Modern Revolutions* (1972), ch. I.

E.H. Carr, *A History of Soviet Russia: The Bolshevik Revolution* (3 vols, 1966) provides the standard account of these years, although his *The Russian Revolution from Lenin to Stalin* (1980) is shorter. See also G. Hosking, *A History of the Soviet Union* (1990). Other accounts on aspects of this period are provided by G. Katkov, *Russia, 1917: The February Revolution* (1967), R. Pipes, *The Formation of the Soviet Union* (1954), and M. Ferro, *October 1917: A Social History of the Russian Revolution* (1980).

Several works approach the period from a biographical viewpoint, including B. Wolfe, *Three Who Made a Revolution* (1966), on Lenin, Trotsky and Stalin, D. Shub, *Lenin* (1966), C. Hill, *Lenin and the Russian Revolution* (1971), A.B. Ulam, *Lenin and the Bolsheviks* (1965), I. Deutscher, *Stalin* (1966), and I. Deutscher, *The Prophet Armed: Trotsky, 1879–1921* (1963). On the Marxist background to Bolshevik thinking, see E. Wilson, *To the Finland Station* (1947).

The civil war period and allied intervention are discussed in G. Swain, *The Origins of the Russian Civil War* (1995), J. Bradley, *Allied Intervention in Russia* (1968), R. Ullman, *Intervention and the War: Anglo–Soviet Relations, 1917–21* (1961), while R. Service, *The Bolshevik Party in Revolution, 1917–23* (1979) and T. Rigby, *Lenin's Government* (1979) look at Soviet institutions in this period.

A work looking beyond 1924, towards Stalinism, is S. Fitzpatrick, *The Russian Revolution, 1917–32* (1982). The long-term development of foreign policy is considered in A.B. Ulam, *Expansion and Coexistence, Soviet Foreign Policy, 1917–27* (1968).

23. ITALY FROM UNIFICATION TO MUSSOLINI, 1871–1943

The final unification of Italy in 1871 failed to fulfil the great hopes of the 'risorgimento' period. Deep economic and social divisions between north and south, the alienation of the Catholic Church from the new Italian monarchy, and the narrow electoral franchise, left a picture of division and weakness in the late nineteenth century. Around 1900 there was increasing violence in the countryside and factories. The 'Giolitti era' marked a return to relative calm but the strains of the First World War, and the effects of electoral reform, created the conditions for Mussolini's rise to power in the 1920s. His Fascist regime was characterized by authoritarian rule and bold foreign adventures, but it failed to tackle Italy's deeper social problems and brought defeat, and Mussolini's overthrow, in the Second World War. The weaknesses of Italian democracy and the nature of Mussolini's brand of Fascism are common areas of interest.

Essay topics

- Why was Mussolini able to overthrow Italian democracy?
- What were the main successes and failings of Mussolini in office, 1922–43?

Sources and documents

Ciano's Diaries, 1937–8 (1952) and *1939–43* (1947) cover the later Fascist period from within the government, while the views of opponents can be found in G. Salvemini, *The Fascist Dictatorship in Italy* (1928) and *Under the Axe of Fascism* (1936).

Secondary works

For general background to Italian history see D. Mack Smith, *Italy: A Modern History* (1959) and M. Clark, *Modern Italy, 1871–1982* (1984). Helpful short introductions to the Fascist era are M. Blinkhorn, *Mussolini and Fascist Italy* (1984) and J. Whittam, *Fascist Italy* (1996).

On the pre-Fascist period, C. Seton-Watson, *Italy from Liberalism to Fascism* (1967) is the standard work. Relations between Church and State are examined in A. Jemolo, *Church and State in Italy, 1850–1950* (1960) and R.A. Webster, *The Cross and the Fasces: Christian Democracy in Italy, 1860–1960* (1960). Popular disorder is considered in J.A. Davis, *Conflict and Control: Law and Order in Nineteenth Century Italy* (1988). For the continuation of unrest up to the Fascist era, see F.M. Snowden, *Violence and the Great Estates in the South of Italy: Apulia, 1900–1922* (1986), and on the role of the army, J. Gooch, *Army, State and Society in Italy, 1870–1915* (1989). R. Bosworth, *Italy and the Approach of the First World War* (1983) covers foreign policy. See also C. Tilly, L. Tilly, and R. Tilly, *The Rebellious Century, 1830–1930* (1975), ch. 3. For post-1918 events see P. Spriano, *The Occupation of the Factories* (trans. edn, 1975), M. Clark, *Antonio Gramsci and the Revolution that Failed* (1977), and G. Williams, *Proletarian Order* (1975). The best overall study of the Fascist takeover is A. Lyttleton, *The Seizure of Power, 1919–29* (1973), while the local dimension is considered in P. Corner, *Fascism in Ferrara* (1975) and F. Snowden, *The Fascist Revolution in Tuscany, 1919–1922* (1989). The position of the monarchy, crucial in 1922 and thereafter, has received admirable treatment in D. Mack Smith, *Italy and its Monarchy* (1990). General treatments of the period include A. Cassels, *Fascist Italy* (1985) and A. De Grand *Italian Fascism: Its Origins and Development* (1989); see also P. Morgan, *Italian Fascism, 1915–1945* (new edn, 2003). Intellectual aspects of Fascism are considered in A. Lyttleton, *Italian Fascism from Pareto to Gentile* (1973), J. Pollard, *The Fascist Experience in Italy* (1998), and, comparatively, in A.J. De Grand, *Fascist Italy and Nazi Germany: The 'Fascist' Style of Rule* (1995) and R. Griffin, *The Nature of Fascism* (1993). Particular aspects of fascist policy are considered in C. Duggan, *Fascism and the Mafia* (1989), V. de Grazia, *The Culture of Consent: Mass Organisation of Leisure in Fascist Italy* (1981), and R. Sarti, *Fascism and Industrial Leadership in Italy,1919–1940* (1971).

The general effects of the fascist regime on society can be traced in J. Dunnage, *Twentieth Century Italy: A Social History* (2003), ch 3. For working-class responses, see P. Corner on 'Italy', in S. Salter and J. Stevenson (eds), *The Working Class and Politics in Europe and America, 1929–1945* (1990), and for women under fascism see M. Durham, *Women and Fascism* (1998).

For biographies of Mussolini, see D. Mack Smith, *Mussolini* (1982), R. Bosworth, *Mussolini* (2002), and the older L. Fermi, *Mussolini* (1961). On foreign policy, see R. Mallett, *Mussolini and the Origins of the Second World War, 1933–1940* (2003) and D. Mack Smith, *Mussolini's Roman* Empire (1977); also E.M. Robertson, *Mussolini as Empire Builder* (1977), mainly on 1932–36. E. Wiskemann, *The Rome–Berlin Axis* (1949) and F.W. Deakin, *The Brutal Friendship* (1966) concentrate on the German alliance.

Articles

On the unrest of wartime, see G. Procacci, 'Popular protest and labour conflict in Italy, 1915–18', *S.H.* (1989). On Mussolini, see S. Woolf, 'Mussolini as revolutionary', *J.C.H.* (1966) and on the economy, A. Albertoz, 'The crisis of the corporative state', *J.C.H.* (1969) and R. Sarti, 'Mussolini and the Italian industrial leadership in the battle of the lira, 1925–27', *P.P.* (1970).

24. THE WEIMAR REPUBLIC, 1919–33

The Weimar Republic was established in the wake of military defeat in the First World War and the overthrow of the Kaiser, and soon faced even greater problems – the harsh peace of Versailles, enforced by the Allies, and the massive inflation of the early 1920s. It was in this difficult period that the Nazi Party, under Adolf Hitler, came into being and attempted to overthrow the government in the Munich Putsch of 1923. In the years after this the Republic staged something of a recovery, achieving economic growth, political stability and even, thanks to Stresemann, international standing. Historians argue whether, but for the effects of the 'slump' after 1929, and the bankruptcies and political extremism which it created, Weimar could have survived. The appeal of Nazism and the role of army, business and churches under Weimar have all received attention.

Essay topics

- Did the possession of 'the most democratic constitution in the world' tend to help or hinder the Weimar Republic in its search for political stability?
- Assess the contribution of Hitler to the Nazi rise to power.

Sources and documents

For excellent selections of documents on Weimar and the rise of Nazism, see J. Noakes and G. Pridham (eds), *Documents on Nazism, 1919–1945* (1974) and J. Noakes and

G. Pridham (eds), *Nazism, 1919–1945. Vol. I. The Rise to Power, 1919–1934* (1983). J. Hiden, *The Weimar Republic* (2nd edn, 1996) has useful material specifically on Weimar. Hitler's *Mein Kampf* (1925–26) is available in translation (ed. D.C. Watt, 1969); see also N.H. Baynes, *The Speeches of Adolf Hitler, April 1922–August 1939* (1942).

Secondary works

Introductions include D. Bookbinder, *Weimar Germany* (1996), C. Fischer, *The Rise of the Nazis* (2nd edn, 2002), J. Hiden, *The Weimar Republic* (2nd edn, 1996), and *Republican and Fascist Germany: Themes and Variations in the History of the Third Reich, 1918–1945* (1996). More substantial works are H. Heiber, *The Weimar Republic: Germany, 1918–1933* (1993) and E. Kolb, *The Weimar Republic* (1988). E. Eyck, *History of the Weimar Republic* (2 vols, 1962, 1963) is a full and useful study of the period. A.J. Nicholls, *Weimar and the Rise of Hitler* (4th edn, 2000) is shorter and more analytical. A more recent reinterpretation is A. McElligot, *Rethinking the Weimar Republic: Problems and Perspectives* (2004) and there is an important group of essays in R.J. Bessel and E.J. Feuchtwanger (eds), *Social Change and Political Development in the Weimar Republic* (1981). A series of essays which amount to a general history of the period can be found in M. Fulbrook, *Twentieth Century Germany: Politics, Culture and Society, 1918–1990* (2001), pt I, chs 1–4.

The revolution of 1918–19 and the birth of Weimar has received quite full treatment. A. Rosenberg, *Imperial Germany: The Birth of the German Republic* (1931) remains a useful, if old, account; A.J. Ryder, *The German Revolution* (1967) concentrates on the Socialists (see also the shorter account in his Historical Association pamphlet of the same title, published in 1959). F.L. Carsten, *Revolution in Central Europe, 1918–19* (1971) is excellent on the 'grass roots' establishment of workers' and soldiers' councils, and J.P. Nettl, *Rosa Luxemburg* (1969) provides a biography of a leading revolutionary. R. Cooper, *Failure of a Revolution: Germany in 1918–19* (1955) criticizes the Social Democrats, for whom see also R.N. Hunt, *German Social Democracy, 1918–1933* (1970) and W.L. Guttsman, *The German Social Democratic Party, 1875–1933* (1981).

Two important studies of inflation of the early 1920s and its impact are G.D. Feldman, *The Great Disorder: Politics, Economics and Society in the German Inflation, 1914–24* (1996) and N. Ferguson, *Paper and Iron: Hamburg Business and German Politics in the Era of Inflation, 1897–1927* (1995). Two of the leading politicians of the Weimar era are examined in H.A. Turner, *Stresemann and the Politics of the Weimar Republic* (1963), H.W. Gatzke, *Stresemann and the Rearmament of Germany* (1954), and A. Dorpalen, *Hindenburg and the Weimar Republic* (1964).

J.W. Wheeler-Bennett, *The Nemesis of Power: The German Army in Politics, 1918–45* (1980 edn) is critical of the military under Weimar. The same theme is covered by F.L. Carsten, *The Reichswehr and German Politics, 1918–33* (1966) and the older and more general, G. Craig, *The Politics of the Prussian Army, 1640–1945* (1955). The political rise of the Nazis at 'grass roots' level can be traced in

M. Kater, *The Nazi Party, 1919–45* (1984), W.S. Allen, *The Nazi Seizure of Power* (1966), and J. Noakes, *The Nazi Party in Lower Saxony* (1971). There is a useful set of essays in E. Matthias and A.J. Nicholls (eds), *German Democracy and the Triumph of Hitler* (1971) and P.D. Stachura (ed.), *The Nazi Machtergreifung* (1983). On Nazi support, see also T. Childers, *The Nazi Voter, The Social Foundations of Fascism in Germany 1919–1933* (1983). The effects of the Depression are recorded in K. Harclach, *The Political Economy of Germany in the Twentieth Century* (1980); also D. Geary, 'Unemployment and Working Class Solidarity, 1929–33', in R.J. Evans and D. Geary (eds), *The German Unemployed* (1987) and P.D. Stachura (ed.), *Unemployment and the Great Depression in Weimar Germany* (1986).

For the impact of the Nazis on Weimar, see C. Fischer, *The Rise of the Nazis* (2nd edn, 2002), R.J. Evans, *The Coming of the Third Reich* (2003), F. McDonough, *Hitler and the Rise of the Nazi Party* (2003), and Nicholls (above). On Hitler himself, the fullest treatment is now I. Kershaw, *Hitler, 1889–1936: Hubris* (1998), but see also his shorter *Hitler* (2000), the older A. Bullock, *Hitler, A Study in Tyranny* (1964) and W.A. Carr, *Hitler: A Study in Personality and Politics* (1978). The 'failure' of Weimar and the rise of the Nazis is considered in I. Kershaw (ed.), *Weimar: Why Did German Democracy Fail?* (1990).

Articles

On the role of the KPD in assisting the Nazis' rise, see C. Fischer, 'Class enemies or class brothers? Communist–Nazi relations in Germany, 1929–33' and D. Geary, 'Nazis and workers, a response to Conan Fischer's "Class enemies or class brothers"', *E.H.Q.* (1985). On the role of business in the rise of the Nazis, see H. Ashby Turner, 'Big business and the rise of Hitler', *A.H.R.* (1969), G.D. Fieldman, 'The social and economic policies of German big business, 1918–1929', *A.H.R.* (1969), and E. Nolte, 'Big business and German politics', *A.H.R.* (1969). More generally on Nazi support, see T. Childers, 'The social basis of the National Socialist vote', *J.C.H.* (1976), J. Noakes, 'Nazi voters', *H.T.* (1980), and K. O'Lessker, 'Who voted for Hitler: a new look at the class basis of Nazism', *American Journal of Sociology* (1969).

25. NAZI GERMANY, 1933–45

Having obtained power by what, on the surface, could be portrayed as 'constitutional' means, Hitler overthrew the Weimar Republic and enforced authoritarian government, with himself as Führer and the Nazi Party as the only legitimate political force. At first, despite rigged elections, the imprisonment of opponents, and the enforcement of strict controls on the people, he had successes, reducing unemployment and increasing Germany's international standing. But in 1939 his expansionist foreign policy brought conflict with Britain and France. Already Hitler had inspired anti-Semitic outrages, blaming the Jews for Germany's past misfortunes, and during the war the 'Final Solution', involving the slaughter of millions of Jews, was adopted.

Meanwhile, however, the strain of 'total war' proved too much for Germany. Hitler himself, increasingly deranged, committed suicide in the midst of defeat in 1945. Exactly how such a man could gain and wield such power has concerned historians ever since.

Essay topics

- Why did the German people not overthrow Hitler?
- What were the main facets of Nazi political ideology?

Sources and documents

J. Noakes and G. Pridham (eds), *Documents on Nazism, 1919–1945* (1974) presents a good selection of documents on the whole era, and on the Hitlerite period see their *Nazism, 1919–1945: Vol. II. State, Economy and Society, 1933–1939* (1984). Hitler's *Mein Kampf* (1925–26, ed. D.C. Watt, 1969) and Goebbel's *Diaries* (1948) provide a valuable insight into the Nazi mind. More accessible and compelling on the war period is A. Speer, *Inside the Third Reich* (1970), though it should be approached with care, while H. Rauschning, *Germany's Revolution of Destruction* (1939) is remarkably perceptive on the revolutionary strand in Hitler's make-up. D.G. Williamson, *The Third Reich* (1982) is a short modern selection of documents with introductory chapters. G. Bielenberg, *The Past is Myself* (1968) is a remarkable inside account of life in the Third Reich by a British woman. T. Kirk, *Longman Companion to Nazi Germany* (1995) has extensive factual and reference information, while M. Freeman, *Atlas of Nazi Germany* (1995) also has valuable material.

Secondary works

There is an enormous amount of work on Hitler and the Nazis. H.R. Trevor-Roper's introduction to *The Last Days of Hitler* (1978 edn) remains impressively perceptive. Of the biographies of Hitler, the standard work is now I. Kershaw's two-volume study, *Hitler, 1889–1936: Hubris* (1998) and *Hitler, 1937–1945: Nemesis* (2001). Among a number of other studies, A. Bullock, *Hitler* (1964) remains a readable but full account, J.C. Fest, *Hitler* (1974) and J. Toland, *Adolf Hitler* (1976) are long and detailed, while N. Stone, *Hitler* (1980) is short but stimulating. J.C. Fest, *The Face of the Third Reich* (1970) looks at Hitler's deputies, one of whom receives full coverage in E.K. Bramsted, *Goebbels and National Socialist Propaganda* (1965). Two interesting attempts at 'psychohistory' can be found in W. Langer, *The Mind of Adolf Hitler* (1972) and W. Carr, *Hitler: A Study in Personality and Politics* (1978).

Up-to-date and succinct accounts of the rise of the Nazis can be found in C. Fischer, *The Rise of the Nazis* (2nd edn, 2002), R.J. Evans, *The Coming of the Third Reich* (2003), F. McDonough, *Hitler and the Rise of the Nazi Party* (2003), S.J. Lee, *Hitler and Nazi Germany* (1998), D. Geary, *Hitler and Nazism* (2000), J. Stephenson in M. Fulbrook (ed.), *Twentieth Century Germany: Politics, Culture and Society, 1918–1990* (2001), which also contains excellent short accounts of the main features of the Nazi state, by I. Kershaw (the Nazi dictatorship), O. Bartov (on the Germans at war) and N. Stargardt (on the 'final solution').

The best single account is I. Kershaw, *The Nazi Dictatorship* (3rd edn, 1993), but see also M. Brozat, *The Hitler State* (1981), N. Frei, *National Socialist Rule in Germany: The Führer State* (1993), J. Dulffer, *Nazi Germany, 1933–1945* (1995), K. Bracher, *The German Dictatorship* (1973), and K. Hilderbrand, *The Third Reich* (1984). D. Orlow, *A History of the Nazi Party, 1933–45* (1973), D. Welch, *The Third Reich: Politics and Propaganda* (1994), G.C. Browder, *Hitler's Enforcers: The Gestapo and the SS Security Service in the Nazi Revolution* (1996), D.F. Crew, *Nazism and German Society, 1933–1945* (1994), R. Gruenberger, *A Social History of the Third Reich* (1974), and J.P. Stern, *The Führer and the People* (1975) cover various aspects of the Third Reich, while J. Hiden and J. Farquharson, *Explaining Hitler's Germany* (1983) looks at historical views of the Nazi regime. J. Noakes (ed.), *Government, Party and People in Nazi Germany* (1980) has several good essays and a detailed bibliography. On other aspects of German society, see A. Schweitzer, *Big Business in the Third Reich* (1964), D. Guerin, *Fascism and Big Business* (1979), R.J. O'Neill, *The German Army and the Nazi Party, 1933–1939* (1966), Z.A.B. Zeman, *Nazi Propaganda* (1964), E.K. Bramsted, *Goebbels and National Socialist Propaganda 1925–1945* (1965), J.S. Conway, *The Nazi Persecution of the Churches* (1968), and G. Lewy, *The Catholic Church and Nazi Germany* (1964). On women, see J. Stephenson, *Women in Nazi Germany* (2001) and J. Stibbe, *Women in the Third Reich* (2003). On the performance of the economy, see H. James, *The German Slump* (1988).

Hitler's opponents are considered in H. Graml (ed.), *The German Resistance to Hitler* (1970) and I. Kershaw, *Popular Opinion and Political Dissent in the Third Reich: Bavaria, 1933–1945* (1986). On the position of the working class, see S. Salter, 'Germany', in S. Salter and J. Stevenson (eds), *The Working Class and Politics in Europe and America, 1929–1945* (1989); also useful is D.J.K. Peukert, *Inside Nazi Germany: Conformity, Opposition and Racism in Everyday Life* (1987). Hitler's anti-Semitism is considered in Kershaw, *Nazi Dictatorship,* ch. 5 (see above) and H. Krausnick, 'The persecution of the Jews', in H. Krausnick and M. Brozat, *Anatomy of the SS State* (1968), but see also L. Dawidowicz, *The War against the Jews, 1933–45* (1975), D.J. Goldhagen, *Hitler's Willing Executioners* (1996) and K. Schleunes, *The Twisted Road to Auschwitz* (1970). More recent treatments include M. Burleigh and W. Wippermann, *The Racial State: Germany, 1933–45* (1991). J. Burrin, *Hitler and the Jews* (1994) and on the euthanasia programme, M. Burleigh, *Death and Deliverance: Euthanasia in Germany, c. 1900–1945* (1994).

Foreign policy is considered in G.I. Weinberg, *The Foreign Policy of Hitler's Germany: Diplomatic Revolution in Europe, 1933–1936* (1970) and *The Foreign Policy of Hitler's Germany: Starting World War II* (1980). K. Hildebrand, *The Foreign Policy of the Third Reich* (1973) stresses Hitler's pragmatism, while W. Carr, *Arms, Autarky and Aggression: A Study in German Foreign Policy, 1933–1939*

(1972) relates economic policy to foreign policy. Two important recent studies of the outbreak of war in 1939 are D. Cameron Watt, *How War Came* (1989), and R. Overy and A. Wheatcroft, *The Road to War* (1989); see also P.M. Bell, *The Origins of the Second World War in Europe* (2nd edn, 1997), R.J. Overy, *The Origins of the Second World War* (2nd edn, 1998), and C. Leitz on Germany in R. Boyce and J.A. Maiolo (eds.), *The Origins of World War Two* (2003).

On Hitler's economic policies, see W. Carr, *Arms, Autarky and Aggression,* B.A. Caroll, *Design for Total War: Arms and Economics in the Third Reich* (1968), and B.H. Klein, *Germany's Economic Preparations for War* (1959). T. Mason, 'The primacy of politics: politics and economics in National Socialist Germany', in S.J. Woolf (ed.), *The Nature of Fascism* (1968) discusses the Nazi attitude to economics, a view taken up by A. Milward in W. Laqueur (ed.), *Fascism: A Readers' Guide* (1979). For the German economy at war, see A. Milward, *The German Economy at War* (1965) and his wider *War, Economy and Society 1939–1945* (1977).

Articles

R. Bessel, 'Living with the Nazis: some recent writing on the social history of the Third Reich', *E.H.Q.* (1984) comments on German domestic reactions. See also T. Mason, 'Labour in the Third Reich', *P.P.* (1966), 'Women in Germany, 1925–40: family, welfare and work', *H.W.J.* (1974), and 'The workers' opposition in Nazi Germany', *H.W.J.* (1981), and L.D. Stokes, 'The German people and the destruction of the European Jews', *C.E.H.* (1973). Two articles linking domestic politics and foreign policy are R.J. Overy, 'Hitler's war and the German economy: a reinterpretation', *Ec.H.R.* (1982), and 'Germany, "Domestic Crisis" and war in 1939', *P.P.* (1987).

26. STALIN'S RUSSIA, 1923–53

In the aftermath of Lenin's death Joseph Stalin gradually asserted himself in power, defeating even the able Leon Trotsky. Stalin's concept of 'socialism in one country' by arguing that Russia could achieve communism herself, without the 'world revolution' predicted by other Marxists, gave Russia new faith in herself. After 1928 the 'Stalinization' programme was pursued to industrialize Russia, by strict control of agriculture and strong central direction, and a series of 'five-year plans'. This was accompanied in the 1930s by increasingly totalitarian methods and the elimination of all possible opposition to Stalin. Nevertheless in 1941–45 the communist regime survived Hitler's invasion intact and Stalin's control remained secure down to his death in 1953. His totalitarian legacy has troubled his successors, but he had seen Russia become the world's second greatest power.

Essay topics

- Was the 'Stalinization' programme justified?
- What factors helped Stalin to establish and maintain his personal authority in Russia?

Sources and documents

M. McCauley, *Stalin and Stalinism* (1983) has some useful documents, but see also C. Read, *The Stalin Years: A Reader* (2002) and the documents in M. Maudsley, *Stalin and Stalinism* (1990). M. Fainsod, *Smolensk under Soviet Rule* (1959) was for a long time a unique first-hand account from the otherwise closed Soviet archives of the realities of the collectivization process. On the purges, see the experiences of V. Serge, *Memoirs of a Revolutionary* (1963) and E. Ginsberg, *Into the Whirlwind* (1968). M. Djilas, *Conversations with Stalin* (1969) shows the later Stalin; see also N. Khrushchev, *Khrushchev Remembers* (1970) and A. Solzhenitsyn, *The Gulag Archipelago, 1918–56* (1974).

Secondary works

For introductions see R. Service, *A History of Twentieth Century Russia* (1997), M. Maudsley, *Stalin and Stalinism* (1990), and G. Hosking, *A History of the Soviet Union* (1985). Stalin's place as legatee of the Revolution, whether fulfilling or betraying it, is raised in A.B. Ulam, *The New Face of Soviet Totalitarianism* (1963) and S. Fitzpatrick, *The Russian Revolution* (1982); the classic 'betrayal' view is L. Trotsky, *The Revolution Betrayed* (1937). There are several good biographies, notably I. Deutscher, *Stalin* (1966), A.B. Ulam, *Stalin* (1973), and R.H. McNeal, *Stalin: Man and Ruler* (1988). Recent general treatments include G. Ward, *Stalin's Russia* (1993), M. McCauley, *Stalin and Stalinism* (2nd edn, 1995), and C. Gill, *The Origins of the Stalinist Political System* (1990). Also helpful are R. Tucker, *Stalin in Power: the Revolution from Above, 1928–1941* (1990), M. Lewin and I. Kershaw (eds), *Stalinism and Nazism: Dictatorships in Comparison* (1997), S. Fitzpatrick, *Stalinism: New Directions* (1999), and P. Boobbyer, *The Stalin Era* (2000).

For the background to collectivization and industrialization, see Hosking, *History of the Soviet Union* (above) and A. Nove, *An Economic History of the U.S.S.R.* (1972). For collectivization, see R.W. Davies, *The Socialist Offensive* (1976) and on industrialization his *The Industrialisation of the Soviet Union* (1980). The political dimension of modernization is considered by H. Kuromiya, *Stalin's Industrial Revolution: Politics and Workers, 1928–1932* (1988) and his essay on the USSR in S. Salter and J. Stevenson (eds), *The Working Class and Politics in Europe and North America, 1929–45* (1989). Soviet claims to have avoided the world depression are examined in R.W. Davies, 'The Ending of Mass Unemployment in the USSR', in D. Lane (ed.), *Labour and Employment in the U.S.S.R.* (1986). Factors assisting support for the Stalinist regime are considered in S. Fitzpatrick, *Education and Social Mobility in the U.S.S.R., 1921–1934* (1979). On the Terror, see R. Conquest, *The Great Terror* (1968; rev. edn 1990) and J. Arch Getty, *Origins of the Great Purges: The Soviet Communist Party Reconsidered, 1933–1938* (1985). R. Medvedev, *Let History Judge: The Origins and Consequences of Stalinism* (2nd edn, 1989) is a view from a leading Soviet historian, reflecting the post-Gorbachev openness about the Stalinist past. For the development of recent ideas about the Terror, see B. McLoughlin and K. Mcdermott, *Stalin's Terror: High Politics and Mass Repression in the Soviet Union* (2002). Two important 'inside' accounts of Stalin's circle and the mentality behind the Terror are D. Rayfield, *Stalin and his Hangmen* (2004) and S. Sebag-Montefiore, *Stalin: The Court of the Red Tsar* (2003).

For the Communist Party see L. Shapiro, *The Communist Party of the Soviet Union* (1970) and the early sections of his *The Government and Politics of the Soviet Union* (rev. edn, 1967). The new working-class 'vanguard' is considered in L. Viola, *The Sons of the Fatherland* (1987), while the military are examined in J. Erickson, *The Soviet High Command: A Military–Political History, 1918–1941* (1962) and R.R. Reese, *The Soviet Military Experience* (1999). The position of the peasantry is put in long-term perspective in J. Channon, *The Russian and Soviet Peasantry, 1880–1991* (1997), but see also S. Fitzpatrick, *Stalin's Peasants: Resistance and Survival in the Russian Village after Collectivisation* (1996) and L.Viola, *Peasant Rebels under Stalin* (1996).

For Russia at war, see A. Werth, *Russia at War* (1965), A. Dallin, *German Rule in Russia, 1941–5* (1957), J. Barber and M. Harrison (eds), *The Soviet Home Front, 1941–1945* (1991), K.C. Berkhoff, *Harvest of Despair: Life and Death in the Ukraine under Nazi Rule* (2004), and S.J. Main, *The USSR and the Defeat of Nazi Germany, 1941–45* (1997). Two detailed accounts of major episodes in the war are A. Beevor, *Stalingrad* (2002) and J. Barber and A. Dzeniskevich (eds), *Life and Death in Besieged Leningrad, 1941–1944* (2004), while G. Uehling, *Beyond Memory: The 1944 Deportation of the Crimean Tatars* (2004) deals with the fate of one group.

The development of Soviet foreign policy is discussed in G.F. Kennan, *Russia and the West under Lenin and Stalin* (1961), A.B Ulam, *Expansion and Co-existence* (1967), J. Haslam, *Soviet Foreign Policy, 1930–33* (1983) and *The Soviet Union and the Struggle for Collective Security* (1984), R.C. Raack, *Stalin's Drive to the West, 1938–1945* (1995), G. Mastny, *Soviet Insecurity and the Cold War* (1994), G. Roberts, *The Soviet Union and World Politics, 1945–1991* (1998), and S. Goncharov, J. Lewis and X. Litai, *Uncertain Partners: Stalin, Mao, and the Korean War* (1995).

Articles

On the Stalin era between the wars, see S. Cohen, 'Stalin's Revolution reconsidered', *S.R.* (1973), D.R. Brower, 'Collectivised agriculture in Smolensk: the Party, the peasantry and the crisis of 1932', *The Russian Review* (1977), S. Fitzpatrick, 'The Russian Revolution and social mobility', *Politics and Society* (1984), M. Lewin, 'Society and the Stalinist state in the period of the Five Year Plans', *S.H.* (1976); and M.R. Dohan, 'The Economic Origins of Soviet Autarky, 1927/8–1934', *S.R.* (1976).

27. EASTERN EUROPE AND THE BALKANS BETWEEN THE WARS, 1918–39

The break-up of Austria–Hungary after the First World War, together with the defeats of Russia, Germany and Turkey, allowed more of the various nationalities of

Eastern Europe and the Balkans to assert their independence. Many, impressed with the victory of the Western powers in 1918, established democratic regimes. Unfortunately, these states soon faced enormous problems. Political inexperience, limited industry, illiteracy and inflation all took their toll; certain nationalities (such as the Slovaks and Ukrainians) still sought independent rights, while the defeated powers, like Hungary, resented the victors, like Romania. In most states democracy simply collapsed from within and with the coming of the 'slump' Eastern Europe fell prey to foreign domination, largely by Germany. The Balkan states also fell prey to ethnic rivalry, authoritarian government and foreign interference, primarily from Italy. But in 1938 Hitler absorbed Austria and much of Czechoslovakia by the following year. In 1939 events in Eastern Europe, rather than the Balkans as in 1914, became the cause for war, though the Balkan states were soon involved.

Essay topics

- Why were the states of Eastern Europe generally unable to establish stable, democratic regimes between the wars?
- Why was Czechoslovakia unable to resist Hitler's annexationist pressures in 1938?
- How stable were the Balkans after 1918?
- Why did Eastern European affairs, not Balkan ones, cause war in 1939?

Sources and documents

Eastern Europe was the stamping ground for many intellectuals and historians who sought to identify and, if possible, solve the problems of Eastern Europe's kaleidoscope of cultures, nationalities and prejudices. Many of their contemporary writings are historical documents in themselves. See, for example, E. Wiskemann, *Czechs and Germans* (1938) and *The Europe I Saw* (1968), E. Beneš, *My War Memoirs* (1928), C.A. Macartney, *Hungary and her Successors* (1937), and R.W. Seton-Watson, *A History of the Czechs and Slovaks* (1943). Changing frontiers and much more can be traced in R.J. and B. Crampton, *Atlas of Eastern Europe in the Twentieth Century* (1977) and chronologies and a mass of data can be found in A. Webb, *Longman Companion to Central and Eastern Europe since 1919* (2002) and R. Frucht (ed.), *Eastern Europe in the Nineteenth and Twentieth Centuries: An Historic Encyclopedia* (2000).

Secondary works

An introduction to the Balkans can be found in D.P. Hupchick, *The Balkans From Constantinople to Communism* (2002). An up-to-date and more closely focused study of Eastern Europe can be found in R.J. Crampton, *Eastern Europe in the Twentieth Century – and After* (1997), but see also R. Okey, *Eastern Europe, 1740–1985* (2nd edn, 1986), H. Seton-Watson, *The 'Sick-Heart' of Modern Europe: The Problem of the Danubian Lands* (1975) and his older general work on the whole region, *Eastern Europe between the Wars* (1962) and J. Rothschild, *East Central Europe between the Two World Wars* (1974), while a wider perspective is given in A. Palmer, *The Lands Between: A History of East Central Europe since the Congress of Vienna* (1970). C.A. Macartney and A. Palmer, *Independent Eastern Europe* (1962) and H. and C. Seton-Watson, *The Making of New Europe* (1981) are also helpful.

A. Polonsky, *The Little Dictators* (1975), covers each East European state after 1918 in turn, and there are various individual works on East European states, such as A.J. Prazmowska, *A History of Poland* (2004), L. Kontler, *A History of Hungary* (2002), H. Hoensch, *A History of Modern Hungary* (1988), R. Clogg, *A Short History of Modern Greece* (1979), L. Benson, *Yugoslavia: A Concise History* (rev. edn, 2003), M. Macdermott, *A History of Bulgaria* (1962), S. Pollo and A. Puto, *The History of Albania* (1981), and S. Fischer-Galati, *Twentieth Century Rumania* (1970).

With regard to German expansionism in the 1930s and the countries from which it sought territory or even annexation, see A. Polonsky, *Politics in Independent Poland, 1921–39* (1972); on Austria's position, J. Gehl, *Austria, Germany and the Anschluss, 1931–9* (1963) and G. Brook-Shepherd, *Anschluss* (1963). On the more complex Czechoslovakian issue, see I. Lukes, *Czechoslovakia between Stalin and Hitler* (1996), J.V. Bruegel, *Czechoslovakia before Munich* (1973), E.M. Smelser, *The Sudeten Problem, 1933–8* (1975), and, for background, J. Korbel, *Twentieth Century Czechoslovakia* (1977).

28. THE SPANISH CIVIL WAR, 1936–39

In 1931 the Second Republic was established in Spain, following a period of right-wing dictatorship and inept monarchical rule. But it soon fell victim to the deep, historical divisions in Spanish politics, and in July 1936 an army uprising led by General Franco and General Mola began the Civil War. Internally, this represented a struggle between conservative groups, such as the army, Church, landowners and fascist elements, against republicans, socialists, communists and anarchists. However, the war soon gained a wider European significance, representing to many the struggle against fascism by democratic and left-wing ideologies. Foreign volunteers, as 'International Brigades', fought for the Republic and it received important assistance from the Soviet Union. Franco received support from Mussolini and Hitler, while the Western democracies pursued a controversial policy of 'non-intervention'. Franco gradually conquered most of Spain and achieved victory in 1939, establishing a personal dictatorship which was to last until the 1970s. The origins of the war and the relative significance of historic as opposed to short-term factors in its outbreak and character are major issues, particularly in regard to the conduct of the Popular Front government prior to the outbreak of the war. The extent to which the war was, in fact, one between fascism and democracy, as opposed to one drawing on primarily Spanish issues, is important, as is the role of foreign intervention and the influence of the war on international relations.

Essay topics

- To what extent was the Spanish Republic established in 1931 the author of its own downfall?
- How important to the outcome of the Spanish Civil War were the policies of the major European powers?
- Was the Spanish Civil War primarily a war of rival ideologies?

Sources and documents

R. Fraser, *Blood of Spain* (1979) has eye-witness accounts of the conflict, while George Orwell, *Homage to Catalonia* (1938) and J. Gurney, *Crusade in Spain* (1974) are two accounts from British volunteers who fought for the Republic. See, too, P. Toynbee, *The Distant Drum: Reflections on the Spanish Civil War* (1979). Two contemporary novels which breathe something of the atmosphere of the conflict are E. Hemingway, *For Whom the Bell Tolls* (1940) and A. Malraux, *Days of Hope* (1938). F. Borkenau, *The Spanish Cockpit* (1937) was an influential tract for the times.

Secondary works

R. Carr, *Spain, 1808–1939* (1966; rev. edn, *Spain, 1808–1975*, 1982) is an essential starting point, rooting the Civil War in Spanish development, as does his *The Spanish Tragedy* (1977). G. Brenan, *The Spanish Labyrinth* (1943) is widely recognized as a modern classic for its deep understanding of the Spanish context. P. Preston (ed.), *Revolution and War in Spain, 1931–1939* (1984) has an extremely useful historiographical essay by the editor. See also F.R. de Meneses, *Franco and the Spanish Civil War* (2001).

H. Thomas, *The Spanish Civil War* (rev. edn, 1977) remains a well-balanced narrative, but see also G. Jackson, *The Spanish Republic and the Civil* War (1965). For the experience of the Spanish Republic as a whole during the war, the most comprehensive treatment is now H. Graham, *The Spanish Republic at War* (2002). On the origins of the war, P. Preston, *The Coming of the Spanish Civil War* (2nd edn, 1994) gives emphasis to the land question, as does E.E. Malefakis, *Agrarian Reform and Peasant Revolution* (1970). R. Carr (ed.), *The Republic and the Civil War in Spain* (1971) is another useful collection of essays, as is M. Blinkhorn (ed.), *Spain in Conflict, 1931–1939: Democracy and Its Enemies* (1986).

On the right-wing forces, see P. Preston, *The Politics of Revenge: Fascism and the Military in 20th Century Spain* (1995), F. Lannon, *Privilege, Persecution and Prophecy: The Catholic Church in Spain, 1875–1975* (1987), M. Vincent, 'Spain', in T. Buchanan and M. Conway (eds), *Political Catholicism in Europe, 1918–1965* (1996), R. Robinson, *The Origins of Franco's Spain* (1970), S. Payne, *Falange* (1961), and the biographies of Franco by P. Preston, *Franco* (1993), B. Crozier, *Franco* (1967), and J. Trythall, *Franco* (1970). On the left, see S. Payne, *The Spanish*

Revolution (1970) and P. Broué and E. Témine, *The Revolution and the Civil War in Spain* (1972), the latter critical of the communists' role. Two books sympathetic to the anarchists are V. Richards, *Lessons of the Spanish Revolution* (1957) and M. Bookchin, *The Spanish Anarchists* (1977). The role of the communists is also considered in D.T. Cattell, *Communism and the Spanish Civil War* (1955) and B. Balloten, *The Grand Camouflage* (1961), reissued as *The Spanish Revolution: The Left and the Struggle for Power during the Civil War* (1979). A fascinating case study of a group which exemplifies the complexities of Spanish politics is M. Blinkhorn, *Carlism and Crisis in Spain 1931–1939* (1975); see also M. Blinkhorn, 'Spain', in S. Salter and J. Stevenson (eds), *The Working Class and Politics in Europe and North America, 1929–1945* (1990).

The international dimension has received reassessment recently in M. Alpert, *A New International History of the Spanish Civil War* (2nd edn, 2004), but see the older D. Puzzo, *Spain and the Great Powers, 1936–41* (1962). Individual themes are considered in V. Brome, *The International Brigades* (1965), J.F. Coverdale, *Italian Intervention in the Spanish Civil War* (1977), J. Edwards, *Britain and the Spanish Civil War* (1979), and E.H. Carr, *The Comintern and the Spanish Civil War* (1984). G. Weintraub, *The Last Great Cause* (1976) is an exposé of the war of propaganda carried out by both sides to enlist support. On the most famous episode – the bombing of Guernica – see G. Thomas and M. Wilts, *Guernica* (1975) and H.R. Southworth, *Guernica! Guernica! A Study of Journalism, Diplomacy, Propaganda and History* (1977).

29. FRANCE, 1918–44

Although the Third Republic emerged victorious from the First World War, the interwar period was one of increasing self-doubt and division for France. Unstable governments, industrial and demographic weaknesses, and economic problems (especially the 'slump') were compounded by increasing extremism on the left and right, with the emergence of the communist party and fascist groups. In the 1930s the Stavisky riots and failure of the 'Popular Front' government, alongside the growing Nazi menace, created grave disillusion. Even so, the Third Republic retained many of its prewar strengths, including social stability and widespread sympathy for the regime, and historians question whether the Republic would have collapsed but for the overwhelming military defeat at German hands in 1940. In 1940 Marshal Pétain made peace with Germany and established a collaborationist regime at Vichy. France did not recover her independence for four years.

Essay topics

- How close did France come to civil war in the interwar period?
- Why was France defeated in 1940?
- To what extent did the Vichy regime represent what most of the French wanted between 1940 and 1944?

Sources and documents

W. Fortescue, *The Third Republic in France, 1870–1940: Conflicts and Continuities* (2000); on the later period see also N. Atkin, *The French at War, 1934–1944* (2001). J.-P. Sartre's novel, *Iron in the Soul* (1949, trans. 1950) and M. Bloch, *Strange Defeat* (1940) represent different reactions to France's defeat. P. Laval, *The Unpublished Diary of Pierre Laval* (1948) and S.M. Osgood (ed.), *The Fall of France, 1940* (1965) are also helpful.

Secondary works

Several general texts can be consulted, including J.F. McMillan, *Dreyfus to de Gaulle: Politics and Society in France, 1898–1969* (1985) and his *Twentieth Century France: Politics and Society in France, 1898–2003* (2004), M. Larkin, *France since the Popular Front: Government and People, 1936–1986* (1988), R. Vinen, *France, 1934–70* (1996) and M. Agulhon, *The French Republic, 1879–1992* (1993), but more narrowly see also P. Bernard and H. Dubieff, *The Decline of the Third Republic, 1914–38* (1985) and W. Fortescue, *The Third Republic in France, 1870–1940* (2000).

The important Popular Front era is discussed in J. Jackson, *The Popular Front in France: Defending Democracy, 1934–1938* (1988) and its leading figure in J. Coulton, *Léon Blum* (1974). The most important party of the interwar years is examined in P. Larmour, *The French Radical Party in the 1930s* (1964), while there is a useful survey of the right in R. Austin, 'The Conservative right and the far right in France: the search for power, 1934–44', in M. Blinkhorn (ed.), *Fascists and Conservatives* (1990); see also W.D. Irvine, *French Conservatism in Crisis* (1979) and C.A. Micaval, *The French Right and Nazi Germany, 1933–9* (1972). For the left see the survey essay by R. McGraw, 'France', in S. Salter and J. Stevenson (eds), *The Working Class and Politics in Europe and North America, 1929–45* (1990), R. Tiersky, *The French Communist Party, 1920–1970* (1974), and E. Mortimer, *The Rise of the French Communist Party, 1920–1947* (1984). The role of the army is considered in A. Horne, *The French Army in Politics* (1984). On the important question of social reform see P.V. Dutton, *Origins of the French Welfare State: The Struggle for Social Reform in France, 1914–1947* (2002).

On the approach to war, see A. Adamthwaite, *France and the Coming of the Second World War* (1977) and also his *Grandeur and Misery: France's Bid for Power in Europe, 1918–1939* (1992). The military fall of France is discussed in A. Horne, *To Lose a Battle: France, 1940* (1979) and R. Collier, *1940: the World in Flames* (1980). J. Jackson's studies, *The Fall of France* (2003) and *France: The Dark Years, 1940–44* (2001), link the collapse of France with the complex politics of occupation and Vichy. The politicians involved in the collapse are considered in H.R. Lottman, *Pétain: Hero or Traitor?* (1985), R. Griffiths, *Marshal Pétain* (1970), S. Hoffman, 'The Vichy circle of French conservatives' in his *Decline or Renewal? France since the 1930s* (1974), G. Warner, *Pierre Laval and the Eclipse of France* (1968), and J. Lacouture, *De Gaulle: The Rebel: 1890–1944* (trans. edn, 1990). The Vichy regime is examined in R. Aron, *The Vichy Régime, 1940–4* (1958), R. Paxton, *Vichy France* (1972), and R. Kedward, *Occupied France: Collaboration and Resistance, 1940–44* (1985). R. Cobb, *French and Germans, Germans and French* (1983) and R. Kedward and R. Austin (eds), *Vichy France and the Resistance: Ideology and Culture* (1985) examine aspects of the interaction. The resistance is the subject of P. Burrin, *Occupied France: Collaboration and Resistance, 1940–44* (1996), R. Kedward, *Resistance in Vichy France* (1978), M. Dank, *The French against the French* (1978), and M.R.D. Foot, *Resistance* (1976). The specific issue of anti-Semitism is set out in P. Kingston, *Anti-Semitism in France during the 1930s* (1983) and R. Paxton and M. Marrus, *Vichy France and the Jews* (1981). On the Liberation, see H. Footit, *War and Liberation in France: Living with the Liberators* (2004).

Articles

For an overview, see K. Passmore, 'The French Third Republic: Stalemate Society or Cradle of Fascism?', *French History* (1993). For important, more specialised aspects, D.R. Watson, 'The politics of electoral reform in France during the Third Republic, 1900–40', *P.P.* (1966), A. Sauvy, 'The economic crisis of the 1930s in France', *J.C.H.* (1969), and D. Johnson, 'Léon Blum and the Popular Front', *H.* (1970) are all helpful. W.D. Irvine, 'French conservatives and the "New Right" during the 1930s', *F.H.S.* (1974) and K.-J. Muller, 'French fascism and modernization', *J.C.H.* (1976) are useful on the right.

30. INTERWAR DIPLOMACY, 1919–39

Despite the enormous casualties of the First World War, the peacemakers who gathered in Paris in 1919 failed to achieve a stable diplomatic framework in Europe. The Treaty of Versailles with Germany seemed vindictive in retrospect and many powers came away from Paris determined to alter the settlement. The new international peacekeeping body, the League of Nations, proved weak and in the 1920s even Britain and France fell out over the treatment of Germany and colonial problems. In the 1930s Hitler's Germany and Mussolini's Italy adopted expansionist policies, which the Western democracies at first tried to end by 'appeasement'. By September 1939, however, Hitler had already established domination over much of Eastern Europe, and his invasion of Poland finally led to a European war.

Essay topics

- To what extent should the Versailles Peace Conference be described as a failure?
- Was there any point before 1939 when Hitler could have been more effectively opposed?
- 'The Second World War was Hitler's war.' Discuss.

Sources and documents

A. Adamthwaite, *The Lost Peace* (1980) provides an invaluable documentary source on the whole period. J.M. Keynes's *The Economic Consequences of the Peace* (1919) represents one of the most influential critiques of the peace. See also H. Nicholson, *Peacemaking, 1919* (1933). For the later period, see on German foreign policy, N.H. Baynes, *The Speeches of Adolf Hitler, April 1922–August 1939* (1942), and on Italy, *Ciano's Diaries, 1937–8* (1952) and *1939–43* (1947). For Britain, see Lord Avon, *Facing the Dictators* (1962) and *The Reckoning* (1965), and W.S. Churchill, *The Second World War, vol. I, The Gathering Storm* (1949). For Russia, see I. Maisky, *Who Helped Hitler?* (1964).

Secondary works

Of the overall accounts of the interwar period, E.H. Carr, *The Twenty Years Crisis* (new edn., 1981) remains a challenging work, but see also H. Gatzke, *European Diplomacy between the Two World Wars* (1972) and R.A.C. Parker, *Europe, 1919–45* (1969). The impact of the Paris peace conferences and their immediate aftermath are discussed in A.J. Mayer, *The Policy and Diplomacy of Peacemaking: Containment and Counter-revolution at Versailles, 1918–19* (1968) and G. Schulz, *Revolution and Peace Treaties* (1972), while F.P. Walters, *A History of the League of Nations* (1960) remains the most thorough account of that body. The longer-term effects of Versailles are discussed in R. Henig, *Versailles and After, 1919–1933* (1995) and S. Marks, *The Illusion of Peace: International Relations in Europe, 1918–1933* (2nd edn, 2003); M. Kitchen, *Europe between the Wars* (1999) and R. Overy, *The Inter-War Crisis, 1919–1939* (1994) take the story through to the Second World War, the latter with some documents.

On the origins of the Second World War there are a number of introductions: see P.M.H. Bell, *The Origins of the Second World War in Europe* (2nd edn, 1997), R. Overy, *The Origins of the Second World War* (2nd edn, 1998), E.M. Robertson, *The Origins of the Second World War* (1976), and A. Adamthwaite, *The Making of the Second World War* (3rd edn, 1992). A.J.P. Taylor, *The Origins of the Second World War* (1961) is still exciting and very readable, though its arguments have been undermined. The definitive account of the European crisis in September 1939 is now D. Cameron Watt, *How War Came: The Immediate Origins of the Second World War, 1938–9* (1989); also valuable is R. Overy and A. Wheatcroft, *The Road to War* (1989) and V. Rothwell, *The Origins of the Second World War* (1995). A very useful collection of essays is G. Martel, *Origins of the Second World War* (2nd edn, 1999). A study which embraces the outbreak of war in both Europe and Asia is M. Lamb and N. Tarling, *From Versailles to Pearl Harbor: The Origins of the War in Europe and Asia* (2001).

On specific events and issues, N. Rostow, *Anglo-French Relations, 1934–6* (1984) analyses Western policies at a key period, while K. Robbins, *Munich* (1968) and T. Taylor, *Munich* (1979) look at the most criticized episode in 1930s diplomacy. S. Newman, *March 1939* (1976) concentrates on the British guarantee to Poland, which was so vital in the outbreak of war. On French policy, see especially A. Adamthwaite, *France and the Coming of the Second World War* (1977), and on Germany, G.L. Weinberg, *The Foreign Policy of Hitler's Germany* (1970) and W. Carr, *Arms, Autarky and Aggression* (1972). On British appeasement in general, see especially M. Gilbert, *The Roots of Appeasement* (1966), K. Middlemas, *Diplomacy of Illusion* (1972), and W.R. Rock, *British Appeasement in the 1930s* (1976). See also the essays by N. Medlicott and M. Howard in D. Dilks (ed.), *Retreat from Power: Studies of Britain's Foreign Policy of the Twentieth Century: Vol. 1, 1906–1939* (1981).

Articles

On the Versailles Treaty see W.A. McDougall, M. Trachtenberg, and C.S. Maier, *J.M.H.* (1979), Special issue on Versailles; A. Lentin, 'What Really Happened at Paris?', *Diplomacy and Statecraft* (1990); D. Stevenson, 'French War Aims and the American Challenge', *H.J.* (1979). On the reparations issue, see S. Marks, 'Reparations Reconsidered: A Reminder', *C.E.H.* (1969); D. Felix, 'Reparations Considered with a Vengeance', *C.E.H.* (1971); S. Marks, 'The Myths of Reparations', *C.E.H.* (1978); and M. Trachtenberg, 'Reparation at the Paris Peace Conference', *J.M.H.* (1979).

Among the numerous articles on the various crises of the 1930s, see especially R.A.C. Parker, 'Great Britain, France and the Ethiopian Crisis, 1935–6', *E.H.R.* (1974), C.A. Macdonald, 'Britain, France and the April Crisis of 1939', *E.S.R.* (1972), and M. Newman, 'The origins of Munich', *H.J.* (1978).

31. THE SECOND WORLD WAR, 1939–45

Although Hitler was able to overrun Poland, Norway, Denmark, the Low Countries and France in 1939–40, Britain survived and in 1941 was joined by Russia and America. In the air the Germans lost the 'Battle of Britain' and were soon faced with Anglo–American bombing of their own cities; at sea, the Allied use of radar helped defeat the U-boat menace; while on land the German army proved unable to break Russian resistance. Economic factors, notably American industrial production and manpower, began to tell in the Allies' favour, and from 1943 Hitler's defeat was clearly inevitable. The use of German technology to produce the snorkel, jet aircraft and rockets came too late to affect the outcome. Nonetheless, many would argue that it was Hitler's own ambition which ultimately proved his greatest enemy. The social and political repercussions of 'total war' with mass civilian involvement have also become important areas of discussion.

Essay topics

- To what extent did economic considerations dictate the course of the Second World War in Europe?

- How far did European experience of 'total war' affect its conduct and its outcome?
- Why were the campaigns of the Second World War more mobile than those of the First?

Sources and documents

S.P. Mackenzie, *The Second World War in Europe* (1999) has a short selection. H. Jacobsen and A. Smith (eds), *World War II* (1980) has documents on military policy and strategy, and there are numerous collections of memoirs. W.S. Churchill, *The Second World War* (6 vols, 1948–54) and C. de Gaulle, *War Memoirs* (3 vols, 1955–59) are perhaps the best from European statesmen and, from the generals, Lord Alanbrooke, *War Diaries 1939–1945* (2001) and Montgomery of Alamein, *Memoirs* (1958). A. Speer, *Inside the Third Reich* (1970) remains a telling account of the resilience of the German war machine. On the civilian side, see on Holland O. Frank, *The Diary of Anne Frank* (1947), on Britain R. Broad and S. Fleming (eds), *Nella Last's Diary* (1981), and on the concentration camps O. Lengyel, *Five Chimneys* (1959). Two English language accounts of life within Germany are C. Bielenberg, *The Past is Myself* (1968) and *The Berlin Diaries, 1940–1945, of Marie 'Missie' Vassiltchikov* (1985).

Secondary works

For general introductions see A.W. Purdue, *The Second World War* (1999) and R.A.C. Parker, *Struggle for Survival: The History of the Second World War* (1990), both more balanced than the older but still valuable studies by B. Liddell Hart, *The Second World War* (1990) and A.J.P. Taylor, *The Second World War: An Illustrated History* (1976). G. Weinberg, *A World at Arms: A Global History of World War II* (1994) and P. Calvorcoressi and G. Wint, *Total War* (1974) put the European conflict in the wider context. On the crucial issue of outcome, see R. Overy, *Why the Allies Won* (1994). For the impact of the war on the combatants, A. Marwick, *War and Social Change in the Twentieth Century* (1974) concentrates on the social effects. D. Irving, *Hitler's War* (1983) gives an account of the war from the German perspective, for which see also O. Bartov, 'From blitzkrieg to total war' in M. Fulbrook (ed.), *Twentieth Century Germany* (2001). On Russia, see A. Werth, *Russia at War* (1965), J.D. Barber and M. Harrison, *The Soviet Home Front, 1941–1945: A Social and Economic History of the USSR in World War II* (1991), and S. Bialer (ed.), *Stalin and his Generals* (1971). For Britain, see A. Calder, *The People's War* (1969). On the economic conduct of the war, see A.S. Milward, *War, Economy and Society, 1939–1945* (1977), also his *The German Economy at War* (1965) and R. Overy, *War and Economy in the Third Reich* (1995).

The opening phase of the war is covered by B. Collier, *1940: The World in Flames* (1980) and *1941: Armageddon* (1982). The controversy over the effectiveness and morality of the bombing offensive against Germany is considered in N. Frankland,

The Bombing Offensive against Germany (1965) and M. Hastings, *Bomber Command* (1979). For the German side of the air war, see D. Irving, *The Rise and Fall of the Luftwaffe* (1973). For the war at sea, see D. Macintyre, *The Battle of the Atlantic* (1961), J. Costello and T. Hughes, *The Battle of the Atlantic* (1977), and W. Frank, *The Sea Wolves* (1955). The decisive struggle on the Eastern Front is considered in A. Clark, *Barbarossa* (1965), and J. Erickson, *The Road to Stalingrad: Stalin's War with Germany* (1975) and *The Road to Berlin* (1983).

For the final phase of the war, see E. Belfield and H. Essame, *The Battle for Normandy* (1965), C. Duffy, *Red Storm on the Reich: The Soviet March on Germany, 1945* (2000), C. Ryan, *The Last Battle* (Berlin) (1974), and A. Beevor, *Berlin: The Downfall, 1945* (2002). Specifically on the new forms of mobile warfare pioneered in 'blitzkreig', see H. Guderian, *Panzer Leader* (1952) and F.W. von Mellenthin, *Panzer Battles* (1955). Technical developments affecting the conduct of the war are discussed in R.V. Jones, *Most Secret War* (1978) and B. Johnson, *The Secret War* (1978). Increasing attention has been given to the conduct of the war and its effects upon those engaged in it. O. Bartov, *The Eastern Front, 1941–45: German Troops and the Barbarisation of Warfare* (1986) and *Hitler's Army: Soldiers, Nazis and War in the Third Reich* (1991) is a brilliant analysis of the conduct of the war in the east, but see also C. Browning, *Ordinary Men; Reserve Police Battalion 101 and the Final Solution in Poland* (1992), T. Schulte, *The German Army and Nazi Policies in Occupied Russia* (1989) and, more generally, P. Addison and A. Calder (eds), *Time to Kill* (1995) on servicemen.

The fate of areas conquered by the Germans is considered in W. Warmbrunn, *The Dutch under German Occupation* (1963), G. Hirschfield, *Nazi Rule and Dutch Collaboration* (1988), A.K. Hoidal, *Quisling: A Study in Treason* (1989), A. Dallin, *German Rule in Russia, 1941–5* (1957), and on France see especially P. Burrin, *Occupied France: Collaboration and Resistance* (1996), H.R. Kedward and R. Austin (eds), *Vichy France and Resistance* (1985), J. Sweets, *Choices in Vichy France: the French under German Occupation* (1986), H.R. Kedward and N. Wood (eds), *The Liberation of France* (1995), and R.O. Paxton, *Vichy France* (1973), while the synthesis by N. Atkin, *The French at War, 1934–1944* (2001) links interwar conflicts with wartime ones. Other important countries are considered in A. Pramowska, *Civil War in Poland, 1942–1948* (2004), R. Clogg, *Greece, 1940–1949: Occupation, Resistance, Civil War* (2002), containing annotated documents, and O. Vehvilainen, *Finland in the Second World War: Between Germany and Russia* (2002). The various resistance movements are analysed in H. Michel, *The Shadow War: Resistance in Europe, 1939–45* (1972), S. Hayes and R. White (eds), *Resistance in Europe, 1939–1945* (1975), and M.R.D. Foot, *Resistance* (1976). On the fate of the Jews, see M. Marrus, *The Holocaust in History* (1989), L.S. Dawidowicz, *The War against the Jews* (1975), and C. Fleming, *Hitler and the Final Solution* (1984).

On diplomacy during the war, see H. Feis, *Churchill, Roosevelt, Stalin* (1957), W.H. McNeill, *America, Britain and Russia* (1953), and G. Kolko, *The Politics of War* (1968). D. Carlton, *Churchill and Stalin* (1999), examines a key 'big power' relationship and the Soviet view is discussed in V. Mastny, *Russia's Road to the Cold War* (1979) and R.C. Raack, *Stalin's Drive to the West, 1938–1945: The Origins of the Cold War* (1995). For the origins of the Cold War see J. Young, *The Cold War in Europe, 1945–91* (2nd edn, 1996).

32. THE HOLOCAUST

The fate of European Jewry at the hands of the Nazis has given rise to an enormous literature which seeks to understand the processes which led from the often prevalent anti-Semitism of many European states to the industrialized mass slaughter carried out by the Nazis from 1941. The question of whether there was a particular German trait of anti-Semitism and why the Nazis of all fascist movements took a particularly virulent policy against the Jews has attracted attention. In particular there is considerable debate about the intentions of the Nazis and whether the 'Final Solution' was Hitler's objective from the outset or the product of the particular circumstances in which the Nazis found themselves from 1941, when millions of European Jews were under their control as a result of the conquests in the East. The link of the destruction of the European Jews with the euthanasia policy and other aspects of racial purity, such as the killing of gypsies, homosexuals and the unfit, has come under scrutiny. The collusion of other groups in Nazi policy, both in the occupied territories in the East and in the governments of collaborationist and allied countries, has also been examined. Questions remain about whether more could have been done by the Allies, the occupied powers or by Jews themselves to resist Nazi policy. A trickle of Holocaust memoirs in the aftermath of the war has given way to a flood of material in recent years more fully documenting Nazi policies and their consequences.

Essay topics

- Why did the Nazis persecute the Jews?
- To what extent was the 'Final Solution' the outcome of the circumstances Nazi Germany faced in 1941 rather than the result of long-term policy?
- Why did the Allied governments not act more directly to interfere with the 'Final Solution'?

Sources and documents

Hitler's *Mein Kampf* (1925–26) is available edited by D.C. Watt (1969) and there is considerable factual material in M. Freeman, *Atlas of Nazi Germany* (new edn, 1995) and W. Laqueur (ed.), *The Holocaust Encyclopedia* (2001). Participant accounts include O. Frank, *The Diary of Anne Frank* (1947), Primo Levi, *If This is Man* (1979), O. Lengyel, *Five Chimneys* (1959), E. Kogon, *The Theory and Practice of Hell* (1950), H. Kruk, *The Last Days of the Jerusalem of Lithuania: Chronicles from the Vilna Ghetto and the Camps, 1939–1944* (ed. B. Harshav, 2002), and H. Fried, *The Road to Auschwitz: Fragments of a Life* (ed. M. Meyer, 1990). Recently available in English is V. Klemperer, *I Shall Bear Witness: Diaries, 1933–41* and *Till the Bitter End, 1942–45* (1998–9).

Secondary works

For general perspectives see M. Marrus, *The Holocaust in History* (1989), Y. Bauer, *Rethinking the Holocaust* (2002), C. Browning, *The Origins of the Final Solution* (2004), P. Burrin, *Hitler and the Jews: The Genesis of the Holocaust* (1994), and R. Hilberg, *The Destruction of the European Jews* (3 vols, 1985). Older accounts include L.S. Dawidowicz, *The War against the Jews* (1975), K. Schleunes, *The Twisted Road to Auschwitz* (1970), and G. Fleming, *Hitler and the Final Solution* (1984). The latter tend to follow the view that the Holocaust was the outcome of long-term policy, the so-called 'intentionalist' view, which is usefully discussed in I. Kershaw, *The Nazi Dictatorship* (1989), especially ch. 5; see also N. Stargardt, 'The Holocaust' in M. Fulbrook, *Twentieth Century Germany* (2001). Recent collections of essays which examine aspects of the debate over Nazi policy are O. Bartov (ed.), *The Holocaust: Origins, Implementation, Aftermath* (2000), D. Cesarani (ed.), *The Final Solution: Origins and Implementation* (1994), G. Hirschfield (ed.), *The Policies of Genocide: Jews and Soviet Prisoners of War in Nazi Germany* (1986), and W. Pehle (ed.), *November 1938: From Reichkristallnacht to Genocide* (1991).

On non-Jewish victims, see Hirschfield (above), G. Grau (ed.), *Hidden Holocaust? Gay and Lesbian Persecution in Germany, 1933–1945* (1995), G. Lewy, *The Nazi Persecution of the Gypsies* (2000), M. Burleigh, *Death and Deliverance: 'Euthanasia' in Germany, c. 1900–1945* (1994), B. Muller-Hill, *Murderous Science: Elimination by Scientific Selection of Jews, Gypsies and others, Germany, 1933–1945* (1988), and U. Herbert, *A History of Foreign Labour in Germany, 1880–1980* (1990).

On the complicity or conformity of Germans with the Holocaust, see the controversial view of D. Goldhagen, *Hitler's Willing Executioners: Ordinary Germans and the Holocaust* (1996), but see also C. Browning, *Ordinary Men: Reserve Police Battalion 101 and the Final Solution in Poland* (1992) and his *Nazi Policy, Jewish Workers, German Killers* (2000), S. Friedlander, *Nazi Germany and the Jews: The Years of Persecution, 1933–1939* (1997), M. Burleigh and W. Wippermann, *The Racial State: Germany, 1933–1945* (1991), T. Schulte, *The German Army and Nazi Policies in Occupied Russia* (1989), O. Bartov, *Hitler's Army: Soldiers, Nazis, and War in the Third Reich* (1991), and D. Peukert, *Inside Nazi Germany: Conformity, Opposition and Racism in Everyday Life* (1993). See also D. Bankier, *The Germans and the Final Solution: Public Opinion under Nazism* (1992) and U. Herbert, *Forced Foreign Labour in the Third Reich* (1997). The 'denial' of one leading Nazi is considered in G. Sereny, *Albert Speer: His Struggle with Truth* (1995).

The complicity of other states is considered in M. Marrus and R. Paxton, *Vichy France and the Jews* (1981) and G. Hirschfield and P. Marsh (eds), *Collaboration in France: Politics and Culture During the Occupation, 1940–44* (1989), P.F. Sugar (ed.), *Native Fascism in the Successor States, 1918–45* (1971), E. Mendelsohn, *The Jews of East Central Europe between the World Wars* (1987), M. Michaelis, *Mussolini and the Jews* (1978), J. Steinberg, *All or Nothing: the Axis and the Holocaust* (1990), and M. Dean, *Collaboration in the Holocaust: Crimes of the Local Police in Belorussia and Ukraine, 1941–44* (2000). On the failure of the

Allies to assist the Jews more decisively, see W.D. Rubinstein, *The Myth of Rescue* (1999).

Reactions to the Holocaust by its victims are considered in E. Cohen, *Human Behaviour in the Concentration Camp* (1998) and P. Levi, *The Drowned and the Saved* (1980). The wider question of how the Holocaust is perceived and commemorated is examined in J.E. Young, *Holocaust Remembrance: The Shapes of Memory* (1994) and his *The Texture of Memory: Holocaust Memorials and Meaning* (1993). See also Z. Amishai-Maisels, *Depiction and Interpretation: The Influence of the Holocaust on the Visual Arts* (1993), T. Cole, *Images of the Holocaust: The Myth of the Shoah Business* (1999), and Y. Eliach, 'Documenting the Landscape of Death: The Politics of Commemoration and Holocaust Studies' in Y. Bauer (ed.), *Remembering the Future, vol. III* (1989).

Moral dilemmas raised by the Holocaust and the development of the idea of genocide are considered in J. Glover, *Humanity: A Moral History of the Twentieth Century* (1999) and W.D. Rubinstein, *Genocide* (2003).

Articles

On the often considered crucial Wannsee Conference, see C. Gerlach, 'The Wannsee Conference, the Fate of the Jews and Hitler's decision in principle to exterminate all the Jews', *J.M.H.* (1998).

33. THE COLD WAR

Despite their wartime alliance, the Soviet Union and the Western powers, America and Britain, soon differed over the shape of the postwar world. The Russian takeover in Eastern Europe and enforcement of communist regimes, together with Soviet pressures in Germany and the Balkans, led to the Truman Doctrine in 1947, by which the Americans undertook to resist communist pressure. America and the West Europeans joined together in NATO in 1949, and the following years were characterized by deep-seated tension, known as the Cold War, with notable crises over the Korean War, the future of Berlin and Cuba.

Essay topics

- To what extent may Russia be blamed for beginning the Cold War?
- Why did the Cold War end?

Sources and documents

A readily accessible selection can be found in M. McCauley, *The Origins of the Cold War* (1983), but the early period is well covered from the documentary side by W. Lafeber, *The Origins of the Cold War* (1977) and M. Carlyle (ed.), *Documents on International Affairs, 1947–8* (1952) and *1949–50* (1953). There are numerous memoirs on the Cold War theme but among the best are H.S. Truman, *Year of Decisions, 1945* (1955) and *Years of Trial and Hope, 1946–53* (1956), and D. Acheson, *Present at the Creation* (1970). See also J. Young, *The Longman Companion to Cold War and Detente, 1941–91* (1993) for a compendium of factual material and full bibliography, and T.S. Arms, *Encyclopedia of the Cold War* (1994).

Secondary works

Good introductions to the present state of knowledge can be found in J.L. Gaddis, *We Now Know: Rethinking Cold War History* (1997) and J. Young, *The Cold War in Europe, 1945–91* (new edn, 1996). J. Isaacs and T. Downing, *Cold War* (1998) is a good popular account with documents and illustrations to accompany a television series. Other introductory accounts are D. Painter, *The Cold War: An International History* (1999), B. Lightbody, *The Cold War* (1996), D. Reynolds, *The Origins of the Cold War in Europe* (1994), W. Loth, *The Division of the World, 1941–55* (1988), T.G. Paterson, *Meeting the Communist Threat: Truman to Reagan* (1988), and D. Painter and M. Leffler, *The Origins of the Cold War: An International History* (1994). Soviet policy is now better understood through the partial opening of the Soviet archives; see especially R.C. Raack, *Stalin's Drive to the West, 1938–1945: The Origins of the Cold War* (1995) and V. Mastny, *The Cold War and Soviet Insecurity: The Stalin Years* (1996). The older studies by A.B. Ulam, *Expansion and Coexistence* (1968) and T.W. Wolfe, *Soviet Power and Europe, 1945–70* (1970) have to be seen in the light of more recent work. There are other general works, most being American: J.W. Spanier, *American Foreign Policy since the Second World War* (1980) is pro-American, S.E. Ambrose, *Rise to Globalism* (1983) and W. Lafeber, *America, Russia and the Cold War* (1982) are more questioning of US policy, while L.J. Halle, *The Cold War as History* (1967) is still a useful, balanced account on part of the period.

The early years of the Cold War have received most coverage. Again there are conservative accounts, such as G.F. Hudson, *The Hard and Bitter Peace* (1966) and H.L. Feis, *From Trust to Terror* (1970), criticisms of America in G. and J. Kolko, *The Limits of Power* (1972) and D. Yergin, *Shattered Peace* (1977). J.L. Gaddis, *The United States and the Origins of the Cold War* (1973) is good, and on the British, see V. Rothwell, *Britain and the Cold War, 1941–7* (1983) and A. Deighton (ed.), *Britain and the First Cold War* (1989). Coverage of the continental states is slight, but on France, see G. de Carmoy, *The Foreign Policies of France* (1970) and, on the early years, E. Furniss, *France, Troubled Ally* (1960).

Articles

Two useful articles are J.L. Gaddis, 'The emerging post-revisionist synthesis', *Diplomatic History* (1983) and D. Reynolds, 'The Big Three and the division of Europe 1945–8: an overview', *Diplomacy and Statecraft* (1990). R. Ovendale, 'Britain, the U.S.A. and the European Cold War, 1945–8', *H.* (1982) is a discussion of the major issues in the early postwar years, and G. Warner, 'The Truman Doctrine and the

Marshall Plan', *International Affairs* (1974) discusses what was perhaps the key year. Of vital importance to the framing of America's anti-communist policy was G.F. Kennan, 'The sources of Soviet conduct', *Foreign Affairs* (1947), while A. Schlesinger, 'Origins of the Cold War', *Foreign Affairs* (1967) gives an intelligent, short discussion.

34. WESTERN EUROPEAN DEMOCRACY SINCE 1945

Western Europe in the aftermath of the Second World War proved far more stable and wealthy than after the First. Despite the reconstruction problems left by war, economic recovery, helped by the American Marshall Aid programme, was quite rapid, while democracy was re-established in France, Germany, Italy and elsewhere. The NATO alliance and extension of European unity created a feeling of security and solidarity, which helped make the 1950s and 1960s decades of relative calm. There were problems, however. In France, political instability and the difficulties of decolonization brought the fall of the Fourth Republic in 1958. Italian political life was characterized by rapid government changes and extremist pressures, and in the 1970s, despite the restoration of democracy in Spain, Portugal and Greece, all Europe was faced with the problems of inflation and unemployment.

Essay topics

- Why did West Germany prove more politically stable than Italy as a postwar democracy?
- To what extent can de Gaulle's period in office after 1958 be seen as a turning point in French history?

Sources and documents

For a wide-ranging set of documents, see P. Lane, *Europe since 1945* (1985) and for factual material on specific parts of Europe, A. Webb, *The Longman Companion to Germany since 1945* (1998) and A. Webb, *The Longman Companion to Central and Eastern Europe since 1919* (2002).

Secondary works

For general coverage, see D. Urwin, *A Political History of Western Europe since 1945* (1997), the latter sections of H. James, *Europe Reborn: A History, 1914–2000* (2003), and J.R. Wegs, *Europe since 1945* (5th edn, 2004). Europe's place in the world order is considered in P. Calvocoressi, *World Politics since 1945* (1982). Other general studies of the immediate postwar era include W. Laqueur, *Europe since Hitler* (1970), M. Crouzet, *The European Renaissance since 1945* (1970), and R. Morgan, *West European Politics since 1945* (1972). Rather narrower in interest is F.R. Willis, *France, Germany and the New Europe, 1945–67* (1969), while F. Fry and G. Raymond, *The Other Western Europe* (1980) looks at the smaller democracies.

On economic reconstruction, see A.S. Milward, *The Reconstruction of Western Europe 1945–51* (1984), and M.J. Hogan, *The Marshall Plan* (1988).

On France in this period, see R. Gildea, *France since 1945* (1996), R. Vinen, *Bourgeois Politics in France, 1945–1951* (1995), and on the Fourth and Fifth Republics, see P.M. Williams, *Crisis and Compromise: Politics in the Fourth Republic* (1964 edn), P.M. Williams and M. Harrison, *Politics and Compromise: Politics and Society in de Gaulle's Republic* (1971). P. Thody, *The Fifth French Republic: Presidents, Politics and Personalities* (1998) and N. Atkin, *The Fifth French Republic* (2004) are more recent studies. See also J. Ardagh, *The New France* (1978) and M. Anderson, *Conservative Politics in France* (1974). See also the studies of de Gaulle by D. Cook, *Charles de Gaulle* (1984), S. Berstein, *The Republic of de Gaulle, 1958–69* (1993), H. Gough and J. Hone, *De Gaulle and 20th Century France* (1994). For Germany, see as introduction M. Fulbrook (ed.), *Twentieth Century Germany: Politics, Culture, and Society, 1918–1990* (2001), Pt.II, which has synoptic essays on both West and East Germany, and on unification, L. Kattenacker, *Germany since 1945* (1997), I. Derbyshire, *Politics in Germany from Division to Unification* (1991), D. Childs, *The Fall of the GDR: Germany's Road to Unity* (2001), C. Ross, *The East German Dictatorship: Problems and Perspectives of the GDR* (2002), and K.H. Jarausch, *The Rush to German Unity* (1994). More generally see P. O'Dochartaigh, *Germany since 1945* (2003), A.J. Nicholls, *The Bonn Republic: West German Democracy, 1945–91* (1997), P. Pulzer, *German Politics, 1945–1995* (1995), D.L. Bark and D.R. Gress, *A History of West Germany, 1945–90* (2nd edn, 1993), and K. Larres and P. Panayi (eds), *The Federal Republic of Germany since 1949* (1996). On personalities, see T. Prittie, *The Velvet Chancellors* (1979) and his *Adenauer* (1971); R. Irving, *Adenauer* (2002).

On Italy, see M. Clark, *Modern Italy, 1871–1982* (1984), P. Ginsborg, *A History of Contemporary Italy: Society and Politics, 1943–1988* (1990), and also his *Italy and its Discontents; Family, Civil Society, State, 1980–2001* (2001), S. Tarrow, *Democracy and Disorder: Protest and Politics in Italy, 1965–75* (1989), and in the short Oxford History series, see P. McCarthy, *Italy since 1945* (2000) with a current bibliography. See also J. Dunnage, *Twentieth Century Italy: A Social History* (2003) and the latter sections of N. Carter, *Modern Italy in Historical Perspective* (2004).

Among other countries, Spain provides an interesting barometer of the spread of democracy in Western Europe: see R. Carr, *A History of Spain, 1808–1980* (rev. edn, 1980), R. Carr and J.P. Fusi, *Spain: Dictatorship to Democracy* (1979), D. Gilmour, *The Transformation of Spain* (1985), and P. Preston, *The Triumph of Democracy in Spain* (1986). For Greece see D.H. Close, *Greece since 1945: Politics, Economy and Society* (2002).

35. DECOLONIZATION

Decolonization was one of the great transformations of the postwar world, with immense repercussions for both the new states that arose from the European empires and for the European powers themselves. Theories of imperialism and its causes are inevitably linked with those for its demise, with an early fashion for Marxist theories of neo-colonialism giving way to more complex interpretations of European withdrawal and the processes of state formation that followed. The period covered was very long, from before the Second World War to the 1970s (in the case of Portugal) and even later in the destruction of 'white only' and apartheid regimes in Africa. Decolonization also overlapped with the Cold War, making the struggles in South-East Asia and parts of Africa particularly protracted and bloody.

Essay topics

- Why did the European powers decolonize so rapidly after 1945?
- To what extent did the colonizing powers merely replace political control with economic ties when they gave independence?
- Why did the experience of decolonization prove so bitter and protracted for some countries but relatively painless for others?
- Examine the impact of decolonization on any one Western colonial power.

Sources and documents

See D.K. Fieldhouse, *The Theory of Capitalist Imperialism* (1967) with texts and introduction. For chronologies, facts and figures and extensive bibliography, see M. Chamberlain, *The Longman Companion to European Decolonisation in the Twentieth Century* (1998); see also R.B. Smith and J. Stockwell (eds), *British Policy and the Transfer of Power in Asia: Documentary Perspectives* (1988).

Secondary works

See M.E. Chamberlain, *Decolonisation* (2nd edn, 1990), R. Holland, *European Decolonization, 1918–1981: An Introductory Survey* (1985), H. Grimal, *Decolonisation: The British, French, Dutch and Belgian Empires, 1919–1963* (1980), and W. Mommsen and J. Osterhammel, *Imperialism and After: Continuities and Discontinuities* (1986). For Africa, see J.D. Hargreaves, *Decolonisation in Africa* (1988), P. Gifford and W.R. Louis (eds), *The Transfer of Power in Africa: Decolonisation, 1940–1960* (1982), and on the French experience in Africa, A. Horne, *A Savage War of Peace: Algeria, 1954–1962* (1977) and D.S. White, *Black Africa and De Gaulle: From the French Empire to Independence* (1979). Asian independence is considered in H. Gelber, *Nations out of Empires: European Nationalism and the Transformation of Asia* (2001) and R. Jeffrey, *Asia: the Winning of Independence* (1981). For south-east Asia, see J. Stockwell and N. Tarling (eds), *The Cambridge History of South East Asia, vol. 2* (1992), B.W. and L. Andaya, *A History of Malaysia* (2nd edn., 2001), A. Short, *The Communist Insurrection in Malaya, 1948–1960* (1975), H. Tinker, *Burma: the Struggle for Independence, 1944–48* (1983–4), A. Reid, *The Indonesian National Revolution, 1945–1950* (1974), A. Short, *The Origins of the Vietnam War* (1990), M. Shipway, *The Road to War: France and Vietnam, 1944–7* (1996),

F. Logevall, *The Origins of the Vietnam War* (2001), and S. Karnow, *Vietnam: a History* (1994).

Specifically on Britain, see J. Darwin, *The End of the British Empire* (1991) and *Britain and Decolonisation* (1988); also N. White, *Decolonisation: the British Experience since 1945* (1999) and D. Kennedy, *Britain and Empire, 1880–1945* (2002). For the French experience of decolonisation see R. F. Betts, *France and Decolonisation, 1900–1960* (1991) and A. Clayton, *The Wars of French Decolonisation* (1994). F. Feredi, *Colonial Wars and the Politics of Third World Nationalism* (1994) and J. P. D. Dubbabin, *International Relations since 1945, Vol. II: The Post-imperial Age* (1994) put decolonisation in international perspective. The domestic impact is considered in M. Kahler, *Decolonisation in Britain and France: The Domestic Consequences of International Relations* (1984).

36. THE MOVEMENT FOR EUROPEAN UNITY

One of the most remarkable occurrences in Western Europe in the aftermath of the Second World War was the move towards some form of European unity. This was first seen in the Organization for European Economic Co-operation (1948) and the Council of Europe (1949). More far-reaching pressures of a 'supranational' kind led to the Schuman Plan (1950) and eventually the European Economic Community or Common Market (1957). Orginally, these supranational bodies included only six states but after 1973 they were gradually extended. There were many strong reasons for such greater unity to come about, not least the experiences of war. Doubts about 'supranationalism' from both Britain (down to the present) and France's President de Gaulle (during the 1960s) were a challenge to the European movement. After the fall of the communist regimes of eastern Europe the challenge became increasingly that of enlargement and co-ordination of a continent-wide union of states.

Essay topics

- Account for the rise of the European unity movement in the postwar period.
- To what extent was the move towards greater European unity shaped by French policy, 1950–69?

Sources and documents

Two very useful 'inside' accounts of the European unity movement can be found in the *Memoirs* (1978) of Jean Monnet, the 'father of European unity', and P.-H. Spaak, *The Continuing Battle* (1971). Relevant documents can be found in R. Vaughan, *Post-war Integration in Europe* (1976), and, on Britain and the Community, in U. Kitzinger (ed.), *The Second Try: Labour and the E.E.C.* (1968). For a wide-ranging set of material on the European Union, see A. Blair, *The Longman Companion to the European Union since 1945* (1999).

Secondary works

There are general introductions in D.W. Urwin, *The Community of Europe: A History of European Integration since 1945* (1994), A. Blair, *The European Union since 1945* (2004), P. Thody, *An Historical Introduction to the European Union* (1997), M. Dedman, *The Origin and Development of the European Union, 1945–1995* (1996), and S. Henig, *The Uniting of Europe: From Discord to Concord* (1997). Also useful on the movement towards unity are M. Anderson, *States and Nationalism in Europe since 1945* (2000) and A. Milward, *The European Rescue of the Nation State* (1999). The fullest account of the early years of the unity movement can be found in W. Lipgens, *A History of European Integration, 1945–7* (1982), though this is very detailed. J.W. Young, *Britain, France and the Unity of Europe, 1945–51* (1984) is shorter and more analytical, while on the early 1950s, see E. Fursdon, *The European Defence Community* (1981), on the vain bid to create a 'European Army'. On the Common Market itself, see R. Pryce, *The Politics of the European Community* (1973) and A.M. Williams, *The European Community* (1994).

American relations with the European unity movement are discussed by M. Beloff, *The United States and the Unity of Europe* (1963) and R. Manderson-Jones, *Special Relationship* (1972), while British relations are discussed in M. Camps, *Britain and the European Community, 1955–63* (1964) and U. Kitzinger, *Diplomacy and Persuasion* (1974).

For the development of the European Community in the 1970s, see W. Feld, *The European Community in World Affairs* (1976), J. Fitzmaurice, *The European Parliament* (1978), and V. Herman and J. Lodge, *The European Parliament and the European Community* (1978).

37. EASTERN EUROPE SINCE 1945

Although Britain and France went to war to defend Eastern Europe in 1939, the end of the Second World War largely saw German domination of the area replaced by that of Russia. Between 1944 and 1948 communist parties established themselves in power, removed their democratic and rightist opponents and carried out Soviet-style reforms. But although these states became linked to the USSR through the Warsaw Pact and COMECON, it became apparent that Russian control in the Eastern bloc had limitations. Yugoslavia and Albania managed to escape the Soviet orbit, and although Moscow crushed opposition in East Germany, Hungary and Czechoslovakia, the communist states of the region managed to achieve differing degrees of independence prior to the collapse of communism in 1989. The break-up of the Eastern bloc and the collapse of the Soviet Union dramatically altered the political landscape in Central and Eastern Europe. The creation of new states and regimes involved considerable upheaval, including the violent overthrow of the Romanian dictator, Ceausescu, and the series of conflicts in the former Yugoslavia which saw the greatest bloodshed and atrocity in Europe since the Second World War.

Essay topics

- How important was the presence of the Red Army as a factor in creating communist states in Eastern Europe, 1944–48?
- Why did the Soviet Union intervene militarily in Hungary (1956) and Czechoslovakia (1968) but not in Yugoslavia (1948)?
- Account for the collapse of the communist regimes in Eastern Europe in 1989.
- Why did the Balkans become a site of major ethnic conflict from the 1980s?

Sources and documents

M. McCauley, *The Origins of the Cold War* (1983) has some relevance; see also V. Dedijer, *Tito Speaks* (1954) on Yugoslavia. T. Garton Ash, *We the People: The Revolution of 1989* (1990) and L. Jones, *States of Change* (1990) are two reports on the events of 1989. Russian views are collected in C. Cerf and M. Albee, *Voices of Glasnost* (1989), letters to the Soviet magazine *Ogonyok*; see also M. Gorbachev, *Perestroika* (1986) and G. Stokes, *From Stalinism to Pluralism: A Documentary History of Eastern Europe since 1945* (2nd edn, 1996). For factual information on Eastern Europe spanning the communist era to the present, see the excellent volume by A. Webb, *The Longman Companion to Central and Eastern Europe since 1919* (2002). On the Soviet Union before *glasnost*, see W. Thompson, *The Soviet Union under Brezhnev* (2003) and on the fall of the Soviet Union see D. Marples, *The Collapse of the Soviet Union* (2004) for short selections of documents with commentary.

Secondary works

There are introductions to Eastern European affairs in R.J. Crampton, *Eastern Europe in the Twentieth Century–and After* (1997), M. Pittaway, *Brief Histories: Eastern Europe, 1939–2000* (2002), G. Swain, *Eastern Europe since 1945* (3rd edn, 2003), and R. Bideleux and I. Jeffries, *A History of Eastern Europe: Crisis and Change* (1987). For the Balkans, see R.J. Crampton, *The Balkans since the Second World War* (2002).

The essential background can be found in J.L.H. Keep, *Last of the Empires: A History of the Soviet Union, 1945–1991* (1996) and P.G. Lewis, *Central Europe since 1945* (1994); also F. Fejto, *A History of the People's Democracies* (1971), R. Okey, *Eastern Europe, 1740–1985* (2nd edn, 1986), and H. Seton-Watson, *The East European Revolution* (1985). On the early background to postwar Eastern Europe, see M. McCauley (ed.), *Communist Power in Europe, 1944–49* (1977), and on the general decay of Soviet influence, see G. Ionescu, *The Break-up of the Soviet Empire in Eastern Europe* (1965), Z. Brezezinski, *The Soviet Bloc* (1974), L. Labedz (ed.), *Revisionism* (1962), and H. Seton-Watson, *Nationalism and Communism, Essays, 1946–63* (1964); the impact of Gorbachev is considered in K. Dawisha, *Eastern Europe, Gorbachev and Reform: The Great Challenge* (1988).

446

For individual countries, see M. Fulbrook, *Anatomy of a Dictatorship: Inside the GDR, 1949–1989* (1995), M. McCauley, *The German Democratic Republic* (1983), M. Fulbrook's collection *Twentieth Century Germany: Politics, Culture, and Society, 1918–1990* (2001), Pt.II, which has synoptic essays on both East Germany and unification, L. Kattenacker, *Germany since 1945* (1997), I. Derbyshire, *Politics in Germany from Division to Unification* (1991), D. Childs, *The Fall of the GDR: Germany's Road to Unity* (2001), and K.H. Jarausch, *The Rush to German Unity* (1994). C. Ross, *The East German Dictatorship: Problems and Perspectives of the GDR* (2002), J. Madarasz, *Conflict and Compromise in East Germany, 1971–1989* (2003), and P. O'Dochartaigh, *Germany since 1945* (2003) are further recent treatments.

There are also valuable studies available in D. Childs (ed.), *Honecker's Germany* (1985), and *The GDR, Moscow's German Ally* (1983), J.P. Nettl, *The Eastern Zone and Soviet Policy in Germany, 1945–50* (1951), and J. Stele, *Socialism with a German Face* (1977). On Yugoslavia, see D. Rusinow, *Yugoslav Experiment, 1948–1974* (1977), P. Auty, *Tito* (1974) and, more generally, F. Singleton, *Twentieth Century Yugoslavia* (1976). On Hungary, see G. Litvan, *The Hungarian Revolution of 1956* (1996), F. Vali, *Rift and Revolt in Hungary* (1961), and M. Molnar, *Budapest 1956: A History of the Hungarian Revolution* (1971). On Czechoslovakia, see V.V. Kusin, *Intellectual Origins of the Prague Spring* (1971), G. Golan, *Reform Rule in Czechoslovakia* (1973), and H.G. Skilling, *Czechoslovakia: The Interrupted Revolution* (1976). For Poland, see generally R.F. Leslie (ed.), *A History of Poland since 1863* (1983), N. Bethell, *Gomulka* (1969), N. Ascherson, *The Polish August* (1981), and T. Garton Ash, *Polish Revolution: Solidarity 1980–82* (1983). A. Prazmowska, *A History of Poland* (2004) brings the picture up to date.

The collapse of communism is discussed in R. Okey, *The Demise of Communist Eastern Europe, 1989 in Context* (2004), while on Yugoslavia see V. Meier, *Yugoslavia: A History of its Demise* (1999); see also G. Stokes, *The Walls Came Tumbling Down* (1993), A. Heller and F. Feher, *From Yalta to Glasnost: The Dismantling of Stalin's Empire* (1990), and D. Selbourne, *Death of the Dark Hero: Eastern Europe, 1987–9* (1990). G. Prins (ed.), *Spring in Winter: The 1989 Revolutions* (1990), M. Frankland, *The Patriot's Revolution: How Eastern Europe Won Its Freedom* (1990), and M. Glenny, *The Rebirth of History* (1990) are all freshly drawn views of the momentous events of 1989. An analysis of Russian developments can be found in H. Smith, *The New Russians* (1990), M. Galeotti, *The Age of Anxiety: Society and Politics in Soviet and post-Soviet Russia* (1995), and G. Smith (ed.), *Nationalities of the Former Soviet Union* (1995). See also P. Desai, *Perestroika in Perspective: The Design and Dilemmas of Soviet Reform* (1989), S. Kull, *Burying Lenin: The Revolution in Soviet Ideology and Foreign Policy* (1992), and R. Sakwa, *Gorbachev and his Reforms, 1985–1990* (1991).

First-hand information is available now in M. Gorbachev, *Memoirs* (1997) and slightly greater distance from the events has sustained more considered accounts, such as R.K. Daniels, *Russia's Transformation: Snapshots of a Crumbling System* (1998), M. Galeotti, *Gorbachev and his Revolution* (1997), and M. McCauley,

Gorbachev (1998). G.W. Breslauer, *Gorbachev and Yeltsin as Leaders* (2002), D. Marples, *The Collapse of the Soviet Union* (2004), and J. Smith, *The Fall of Soviet Communism, 1986–1991* (2004) span the transition from Soviet rule to break-up. The longer-term factors affecting the collapse of the Soviet regime are considered in G. Roberts, *The Soviet Union in World Politics* (1998), R. Sakwa, *Soviet Politics in Perspective* (1998), P. Hanson, *The Rise and Fall of the Soviet Economy, 1945–1991* (2002), and M. Beissinger, *National Mobilisation and the Collapse of the Soviet State* (2002).

MAPS

Map 1 Europe in the late eighteenth century

Map 2 Europe at the height of Napoleon's power

Map 3 Europe in 1815

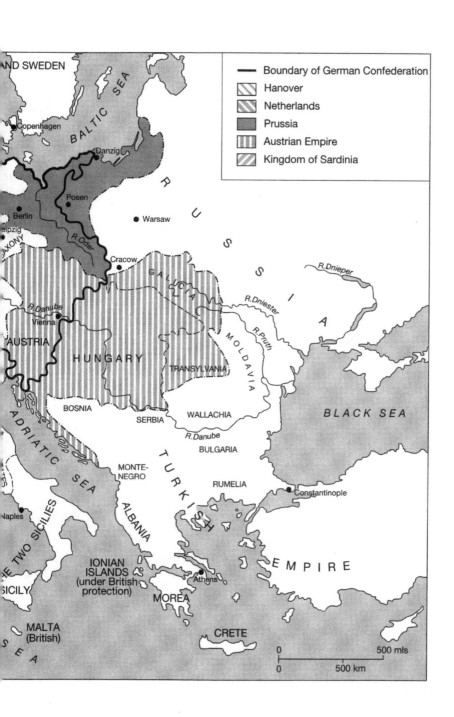

Legend

——	Boundary of German Confederation
Hanover
Netherlands
Prussia
Austrian Empire
Kingdom of Sardinia

AND SWEDEN

BALTIC SEA

Copenhagen

Danzig

R U S S I A

Posen

Berlin

eipzig

AXONY

R.Oder

Warsaw

Cracow

GALICIA

R.Dnieper

R.Danube

Vienna

R.Dniester

R.Pruth

AUSTRIA

HUNGARY

MOLDAVIA

TRANSYLVANIA

BLACK SEA

BOSNIA

WALLACHIA

ADRIATIC SEA

SERBIA

R.Danube

BULGARIA

MONTE-
NEGRO

TURKISH

RUMELIA

Constantinople

ES

Naples

ALBANIA

THE TWO SICILIES

SICILY

IONIAN
ISLANDS
(under British
protection)

Athens

E M P I R E

MOREA

MALTA
(British)

CRETE

S E A

0   500 mls

0   500 km

Map 4 Europe in 1871

SWEDEN AND NORWAY

Christiania

Stockholm

FINLAND

St. Petersburg

BALTIC SEA

MARK

Copenhagen

Danzig

RUSSIA

MANY

Berlin

Warsaw

POLAND

BOHEMIA

GALICIA

R.Dnieper

R.Dniester

Vienna

Budapest

AUSTRIA-HUNGARY

CRIMEA

R.Drave

R.Save

TRANSYLVANIA

ROMANIA

Belgrade

SERBIA

Bucharest

BLACK SEA

BOSNIA

TURKEY

R.Danube

ADRIATIC SEA

MONTE-NEGRO

Sofia

Bosphorus

ITALY

K   E   Y

Constantinople

Rome

ALBANIA

Dardanelles

SEA

GREECE

ASIA MINOR

Athens

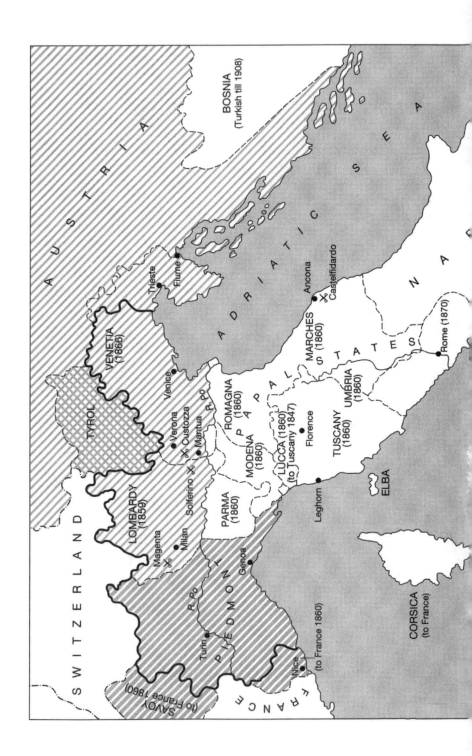

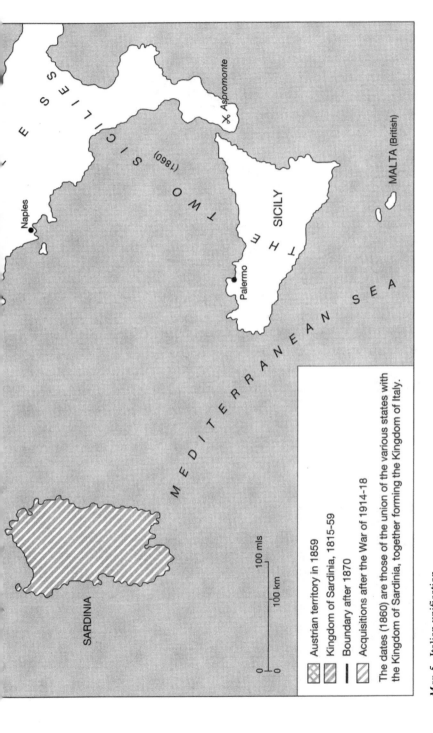

Map 5 Italian unification

459

Map 6 The Balkan peninsula, 1800–78

460

Map 7   The Balkan states in 1913

461

Map 8 European frontiers, 1919–37

Legend:

- **Lost by Germany 1919**
- **Saar: League of Nations control 1919–35**
- **Demilitarised Rhineland 1919–36**
- **Austria-Hungary until 1918**
- **Plebiscite Areas**
- **Former territory of Imperial Russia**

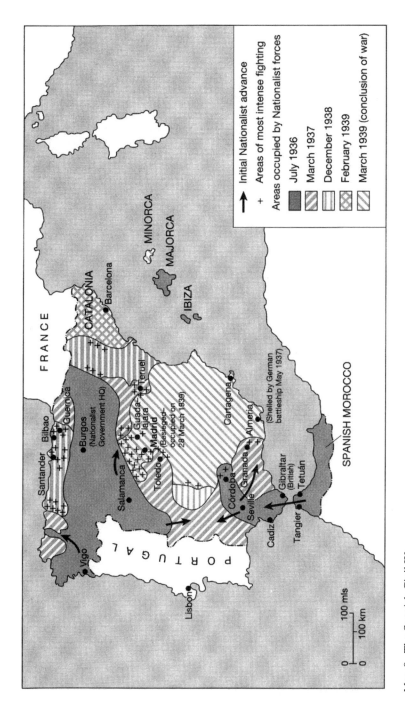

Map 9 The Spanish Civil War

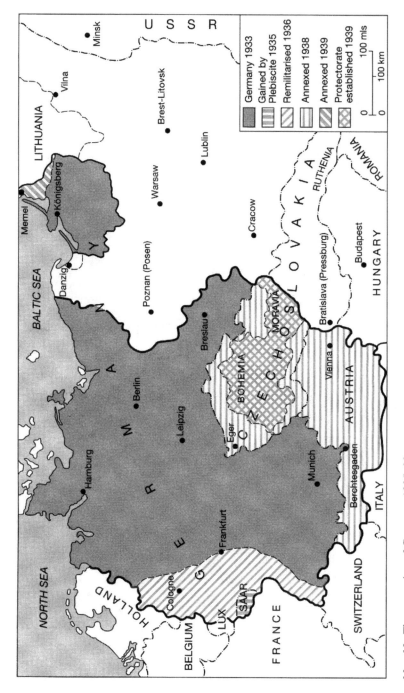

Map 10 The expansion of Germany, 1935–39

Legend:
- Germany 1933
- Gained by Plebiscite 1935
- Remilitarised 1936
- Annexed 1938
- Annexed 1939
- Protectorate established 1939

100 mls
100 km

Map 11 Europe in 1945

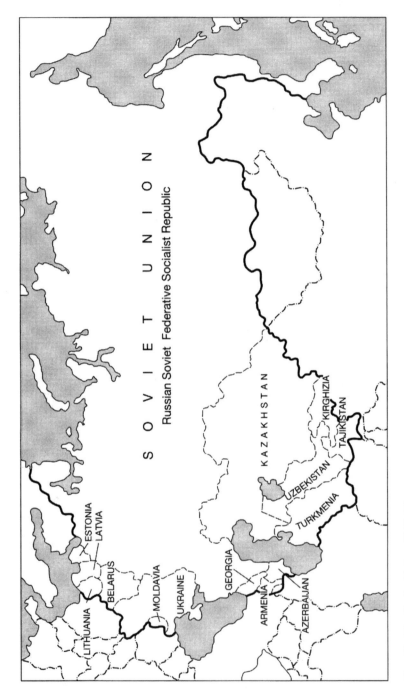

Map 12 The Soviet Union, 1945–90

Map 13 Eastern Europe since communism

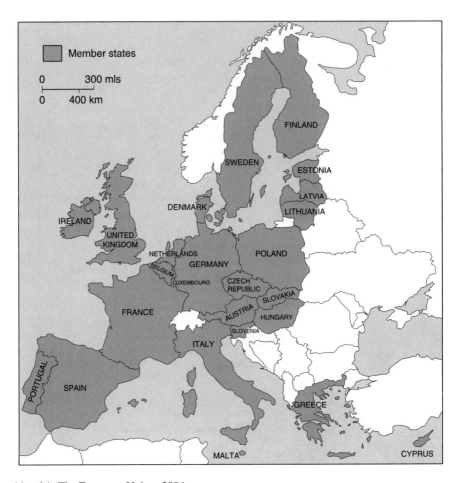

Map 14 The European Union, 2004

INDEX